The Writer's Presence
A Pool of Essays

The Writer's Presence

A Pool of Essays
Second Edition

EDITED BY

Donald McQuade
University of California, Berkeley

Robert Atwan

Bedford Books　Boston

For Bedford Books

President and Publisher: Charles H. Christensen
General Manager and Associate Publisher: Joan E. Feinberg
Managing Editor: Elizabeth M. Schaaf
Developmental Editor: Jane Betz
Production Editor: Julie Sullivan
Copyeditor: Susanna Brougham
Cover Design: Hannus Design Associates
Cover Illustration: Maureen Kehoe, Copyright 1996

Library of Congress Catalog Card Number: 96–86779

Manufactured in the United States of America.

1 0 9 8 7
f e d c

For information, write: Bedford Books, 75 Arlington Street, Boston, MA 02116
(617-426-7440)

ISBN: 0–312–13632–3

Acknowledgments

Maya Angelou. "What's Your Name, Girl?" From *I Know Why the Caged Bird Sings* by Maya Angelou. Copyright © 1969 by Maya Angelou. Reprinted by permission of Random House, Inc.

Russell Baker, "Gumption." Reprinted from *Growing Up* by Russell Baker. Copyright © 1982 by Russell Baker. Used with permission of Contemporary Books, Inc., Chicago.

James Baldwin, "Stranger in the Village." From *Notes of a Native Son* by James Baldwin. Copyright © 1955, renewed 1983 by James Baldwin. Reprinted by permission of Beacon Press, Boston.

Wendell Berry, "The Pleasures of Eating" from *What Are People For?* by Wendell Berry. Copyright © 1990 by Wendell Berry. Reprinted by permission of North Point Press, a division of Farrar, Straus & Giroux, Inc. Lines from "The Host" by William Carlos Williams from *The Collected Poems 1939–1962*, Volume II. Copyright 1948, 1962 by William Carlos Williams. Reprinted by permission of New Directions Publishing Corp.

Sven Birkerts, "Paging the Self: Privacies of Reading" from *The Gutenberg Elegies: The Fate of Reading in an Electronic Age* by Sven Birkerts. Copyright © 1994 by Sven Birkerts. Reprinted with permission of Faber and Faber, Inc.

Preface
for Instructors

We have designed *The Writer's Presence* with three goals in mind: to give students examples of writing with a strong writer's presence (or voice), to allow instructors maximum flexibility in assigning the essays and stories, and to support composition teachers and students as effectively as possible. We believe that the pieces we have chosen to reprint here, the way we have chosen to organize those pieces, and the materials we have prepared for the extensive instructor's manual make this a uniquely useful collection.

DIVERSE ESSAYS WITH
A STRONG WRITER'S PRESENCE

Each essay in the second edition of *The Writer's Presence* features the distinctive intellectual signature that marks all memorable prose: the presence of a lively individual mind attempting to explore one's self, shape information into meaning, or contend with issues through conversation or debate. Ranging widely across subjects, methods of development, and stylistic patterns, these essays illustrate the expectations as well as the uncertainties that surface when a writer attempts to create a memorable individual presence in prose.

We have built this second edition of *The Writer's Presence* around first-rate teaching material proven to work in the classroom and in writing. At the same time, we have increased the number of writers that instructors have reported that they especially enjoy teaching. These classroom favorites include essays by such well-known writers as Maya Angelou, Langston Hughes, George Orwell, Adrienne Rich, Alice Walker, and E. B. White. New to this edition are essays by such prominent writers as Russell Baker, Louise Erdrich, David Mamet, Toni Morrison, N. Scott Momaday, Leslie Marmon Silko, Gary Soto, Calvin Trillin, and John Edgar Wideman. In response to the suggestions of instructors who have worked with the first edition, we have added a sampling of short stories by Raymond Carver, Jamaica Kincaid, Joyce Carol Oates, and Amy Tan — to show writers working effectively within different genres.

FLEXIBLE ORGANIZATION

We have organized *The Writer's Presence* to showcase the balance of personal, expository, and argumentative writing without imposing an order or specifying an instructional context for working with individual selections. The selections are divided into the three most commonly taught essay types — personal, expository, and argumentative — but within these three sections we have simply arranged the writers in alphabetical order. The selections are numbered consecutively throughout the book, and these selection numbers appear in the running heads for easy retrieval. This organization makes the essays easy to retrieve, assign, and interpret in an unlimited number of ways and with different instructional emphases. To make it easier for you to explore different approaches, this second edition includes several alternate tables of contents at the back of the book. Embedded within the collection are a rhetorical reader, a thematic reader, a multicultural reader, an argument reader, a contemporary issues reader, and a short-essay reader.

HELPFUL AND UNOBTRUSIVE APPARATUS

We have kept the instructional apparatus to a minimum. In response to faculty and student suggestions, we have added brief biographical headnotes that also introduce students to each writer's compositional interests, practices, and goals. Following each essay are small clusters of questions that help guide students through a careful rereading of the essay. These questions draw attention to the specific ways in which a reader can be present in writing — either as an implied reader (the reader imagined by the writer) or as an actual reader.

RESOURCES FOR TEACHING
THE WRITER'S PRESENCE

Carefully managing the amount of instructional apparatus in *The Writer's Presence* does not weaken our commitment to provide you with a wealth of specific instructional activities. In 240 spiral-bound pages,

Resources for Teaching The Writer's Presence is the most extensive instructor's manual available for any composition reader.

This resource-full guide to *The Writer's Presence* opens with "Suggestions for Teaching," a specially annotated table of contents that explores each selection's teaching possibilities. These suggestions (which also appear as front matter in instructors' examination copies of *The Writer's Presence*) give a quick sense of each selection and explain why we chose each piece for this collection. In addition, *Resources for Teaching The Writer's Presence* includes the following four parts in each entry:

- "Approaching the Selection" provides a thorough overview of the pedagogical prospects of working with the essay in the classroom.
- "Additional Activities" offers imaginative classroom activities, including write-before-reading exercises, connections to other essays in the book, and collaborative projects.
- "Generating Writing" includes a range of writing exercises — from suggestions for informal writing to essay assignments and ideas for research papers.
- "The Reader's Presence" addresses the questions that follow each selection in the text, pointing to illuminating passages in the selection and anticipating possible responses from students.

ACKNOWLEDGMENTS

This revision of *The Writer's Presence* grew out of correspondence and conversation — on the phone, in person, in letters, and on the internet — with the many teachers and an appreciable number of students who have worked with *The Writer's Presence* in their writing classes. We continue to learn a great deal from these discussions, and we are grateful to the colleagues and friends who graciously have allowed us into their already crowded lives to seek advice and encouragement. From its inception, *The Writer's Presence* continues to be a truly collaborative enterprise.

Much in the manner of our plan to develop *The Writer's Presence*, this revision has emerged from spirited discussions with instructors who prefer to pick and choose — at their own discretion and with their own instructional purposes — from among a wide range of eminently readable and teachable essays. We are grateful to these colleagues across the country who took the time to tell us about what did — and did not — work well when they used the first edition: Lisa Altomari, Vermont Technical College; Maurice H. Barr, Spokane Community College; Todd W. Bersley, California State University—Northridge; Gerri Black, Stockton State College; Scott Brookman, Virginia Commonwealth University; Larry Brunt, Highline Community College; Irene Burgess, SUC Cortland; Dolores M. Burton, Boston University; Diane Challis, Virginia Commonwealth University; Jimmy Cheshire, Wright State University; Chet Childress, Virginia Commonwealth University; Alice Cleveland, College of Mareu; Michel S. Connell, University of Iowa; Chase Crossingham, University of South Carolina; Ruth Y. Davidson, Pennsylvania State University — Schuylkill Campus; Michael G. Davros, University of Illinois at Chicago; Peggy C. de Broux, Peninsula College; Jessica Deforest, Michigan State University; Mary Devaney, Rutgers University — Newark Campus; Debra DiPiazza, Bernard M. Baruch College (CUNY); Maria Rowena P. Dolorico, Bristol Community College; Alex Fagan, Virginia Commonwealth University; Grace Farrell, Butler University; Joan Gabriele, University of Colorado; Christie Anderson Garcia, Spokane Falls Community College; Jane Gatewood, Mary Washington College; Rae Greiner, Radford University; Brian Hale, University of South Carolina; Sarah Hanselman, Tufts University; Dave Hendrickson, Virginia Commonwealth University; Curtis W. Herr, Kutztown University; Professor Goldie Johnson, Winona State University; Nancy B. Johnson, Pace University; Ronald L. King, Virginia Commonwealth University; Harriet Malinowitz, Hunter College (CUNY); Barbara Mallonee, Loyola College; Denice Martone, New York University; Ilene Miele, Moorpark College; Andrew Mossin, Temple University; Cathryn A. Myers, Virginia Commonwealth University; Cheryl Pallant, Virginia Commonwealth University; Marty Patton, University of Missouri — Columbia; Gary D. Pratt, Brandeis University; Catherine S. Quick, University of Missouri — Columbia; Larry Rodgers, Kansas State University; Colleen Richmond, George Fox College; Lissa Schneider, University of Miami; Marilyn S. Scott, California State University — Hayward; Constance Fletcher Smith, Mary Washington College; Roger Sorkin, University of Massachusetts — Dartmouth; J. F. Stenerson, Pace University; Steven Strang, Massachusetts Institute of Technology; Pamela Topping, Long Island University — Southampton Campus; Mary Turnbull, University of Puget Sound; Donna M. Turner, University of North Dakota; Sandra Urban, Loyola University of Chicago; Jennifer Lynne Von Ammon, Florida State University; and Ed Wiltse, Tufts University.

We would especially like to acknowledge our colleagues in the Expository Writing Program at New York University — Alfred Guy, Lisa Altomari, Karen Boiko, Darlene Forrest, Mary Helen Kolisnyk, Jim Marcall, Denice Martone, and Will McCormack — for taking the time to talk with us and for sharing their ideas.

We would also like to express our appreciation to the professional staff at Bedford Books for their encouragement and for their innumerable contributions to this project. Once again, we drew frequently on the intelligence, imagination, good judgment, and patience of our editor, Jane Betz. Her understanding, advice, and support were indispensable in producing a book aimed at improving student reading and writing. We also appreciate the generous assistance of Pam Ozaroff. Julie Sullivan guided the project through the copy-editing and proofreading stages of the publication process with a remarkable combination of thorough professionalism and unfailing common sense and good cheer. John Amburg, assistant managing editor, coordinated the production process with admirable professionalism. We are also grateful to Dick Hannus and Maureen Kehoe for the attractive and inviting look of the book's cover.

As ever, Chuck Christensen, the publisher of Bedford Books, offered us spirited encouragement, first-rate and rigorous advice, as well as numerous suggestions for improving the project. He never hesitated to urge us to venture with an idea or to explore an instructional feature of the book if it might make our purposes clearer and more useful to teachers and students. And when our conversations veered occasionally toward uncertainty, we relied on the steady editorial presence of associate publisher Joan Feinberg, who invariably helped us convert pedagogical principle into sound instructional practice.

Alfred Guy of New York University, Jack Roberts of St. Thomas Aquinas College, and Alix Schwartz of the University of California–Berkeley contributed their intelligence, accomplishments as teachers, and, most importantly, their sense of pedagogical responsibility in helping us to develop *Resources for Teaching The Writer's Presence*. Their experience as dedicated and innovative teachers is everywhere evident in the comprehensive instructional guide that accompanies this book, and we are delighted that they participated in exploring the richness of the selections we have reprinted. We thank, too, Matthew Howard of *The Boston Review* and Sook Mee Hahn for their skills as researchers and for their expert assistance with manuscript preparation. We would also like to acknowledge Greg Mullins' skills as a researcher and interviewer and his accomplishments as a writer. His artful blendings of biographical sketches and quotations on writing are models of informative succinctness and invitations to further reading.

Finally, we hope that Helene, Gregory, and Emily Atwan, along with Susanne, Christine, and Marc McQuade, will once again share our satisfaction in seeing this project in print and our pleasure in continuing our productive collaboration.

Donald McQuade
Robert Atwan

Contents _____

matter how stringent the mashed-potatoes-and-lye formula of a man's 'process,' neither God nor woman nor Sammy Davis, Jr., could straighten the kitchen."

"When we read for joy — for beauty, for intelligence, for understanding — we must hear the words in order to read well. If we move our lips when we read silently, fine: It will slow us down and we will read better. Whether moving our lips or not, we must test literature's words in our mouths."

"Suddenly the whole room broke into a sea of shouting, as they saw me rise. Waves of rejoicing swept the place. Women leaped in the air. My aunt threw her arms around me. The minister took me by the hand and led me to the platform."

"Among the thousand white persons, I am a dark rock surged upon, and overswept, but through it all, I remain myself. When covered by the waters, I am; and the ebb but reveals me again."

"I didn't realize at the time that my flaws were imagined, not real. I felt compelled to measure up to a cultural ideal in a culture that had never asked me what my ideal was."

"We were raking the lawn, my sister and I. I was raking, and she was stuffing the leaves into a bag. I loathed the job, and my muscles and my mind rebelled, and I was viciously angry, and my sister said something, and I turned and threw the rake at her and it hit her in the face."

"Loneliness is an aspect of the land. All things in the plain are isolate; there is no confusion of objects in the eye, but one hill or one tree or one man. To look upon that landscape in the early morning, with the sun at your back, is to lose the sense of proportion. Your imagination comes to life, and this, you think, is where Creation was begun."

"When I pulled the trigger I did not hear the bang or feel the kick — one never does when a shot goes home — but I heard the devilish roar of glee that went up from the crowd."

someone who was so good I wondered what they would do to me. You see, I was turning out bad."

"She cast back a worried glance. To her, the youngish black man — a broad six feet two inches with a beard and billowing hair, both hands shoved into the pockets of a bulky military jacket — seemed menacingly close. After a few more quick glimpses, she picked up her pace and was soon running in earnest."

"Black though I may be, it is impossible for me to sit in my single-family house with two cars in the driveway and a swing set in the back yard and *not* see the role class has played in my life."

"Lately, I've been giving more thought to the kind of English my mother speaks. Like others, I have described it to people as 'broken' or 'fractured' English. But I wince when I say that. It has always bothered me that I can think of no way to describe it other than 'broken,' as if it were damaged and needed to be fixed, as if it lacked a certain wholeness and soundness."

"My mother believed you could be anything you wanted to be in America. You could open a restaurant. You could work for the government and get good retirement. You could buy a house with almost no money down. You could become rich. You could become instantly famous."

"As I now recall it, there was only one sensation in my head: pure elation mixed with amazement at such perfection. Swept off my feet, I floated from one side to the other, swiveling my brain, staring astounded at the beavers, then at the otters."

"Where the BB pellet struck there is a glob of whitish scar tissue, a hideous cataract, on my eye. Now when I stare at people — a favorite pastime, up to now — they will stare back. Not at the 'cute' little girl, but at her scar."

"Summertime, oh, summertime, pattern of life indelible, the fadeproof lake, the woods unshatterable, the pasture with the sweetfern and the juniper forever and ever, summer without end."

II. EXPOSITORY WRITING:
Shaping Information

Contents   xvii

the feminist revolution really is, and how tentatively it is embraced even by adults who fully expect their daughters to enter previously male-dominated professions and their sons to change diapers."

III. ARGUMENTATIVE WRITING:
Contending with Issues

The Writer's Presence
A Pool of Essays

Introduction for Students:
The Writer's Presence

Presence is a word — like *charisma* — that we reserve for people who create powerful and memorable impressions. Many public figures and political leaders are said to "have presence" (John F. Kennedy and Martin Luther King, Jr., were two superb examples) as well as many athletes, dancers, and musicians. In fact, the quality of presence is found abundantly in the performing arts; think of Michael Jackson or Madonna, two entertainers who have self-consciously fashioned — through style, costume, and gesture — an instantly recognizable public presence. Clearly, people with presence are able to command our attention. How do they do it?

Presence is far easier to identify than it is to define. We recognize it when we see it, but how do we capture it in words? Virtually everyone would agree, for example, that when Michael Jordan steps onto a basketball court, he displays an exceptional degree of presence; we acknowledge this whether or not we are basketball fans. But what is it about such individuals that commands our attention? How can we begin to understand this elusive characteristic known as presence?

On one level, *presence* simply means "being present." But the word is more complex than that; it suggests much more than the mere fact of being physically present. Most dictionaries define *presence* as an ability to project a sense of self-assurance, poise, ease, or dignity. We thus speak of someone's "stage presence" or "presence of mind." But the word is also used today to suggest an impressive personality, an individual who can make his or her presence felt. As every college student knows, to be present in a classroom is not the same thing as *having a presence* there. We may be present in body, but not in spirit. In that sense, presence is also a matter of individual energy and exertion, of putting something of ourselves into whatever it is we do.

Presence is especially important in writing, which is what this book is about. Just as we notice individual presence in sports, or music, or conversation, so too we discover it in good writing. If what we read seems dreary, dull, or dead, it's usually because the writer forgot to include an important ingredient: *personal presence*. That doesn't mean that your essays should be written *in* the first-person singular (this book contains many exceptional essays that aren't), but that your essays should be written *by* the first-person singular — by *you*. Interesting essays are produced by a real and distinct person, not an automaton following a set of mechanical rules and abstract principles.

PRESENCE IN WRITING

How can someone be present in writing? How can you project yourself into an essay so that it seems that you're personally there, even though all your reader sees are words on a piece of paper?

The Writer's Presence shows you how this is done. It shows how a wide variety of talented writers establish a distinct presence in many different kinds of writing and for many different purposes and audiences. Though the book offers numerous examples of how presence is compositionally established, there are several methods that nearly all experienced writers observe and that are worth pointing out at the start. Let's examine four of the chief ways a writer can be present in an essay.

1. Personal Experience. One of the most straightforward ways of making your presence felt in an essay is to include appropriate personal experiences. Of course, many assignments may call for a personal essay, and in those cases you will naturally be putting episodes from your own life at the center of your writing. But writers also find ways to build their personal experiences into essays that are basically informative or argumentative, essays on topics other than the self. They do this to show their close connection with a subject, to offer testimony, or to establish their personal authority on a subject. Many of the essays in this collection offer clear illustrations of how writers incorporate personal experience into an essay on a specific topic or issue.

Look, for example, at the essay by Amy Cunningham, "Why Women Smile" (p. 249). This essay is primarily an explanation of a cultural phenomenon — the way women are socially conditioned to maintain a smiling attitude. But note that Cunningham begins the essay not with a general observation but with a personal anecdote: "After smiling brilliantly for nearly four decades, I now find myself trying to quit." Though her essay is not "personal," her opening sentence, besides establishing her own connection with the topic, provides readers with a personal motive for her writing.

One of the first places to look for the writer's presence is in the motive, the purpose, for putting pen to paper. Virginia Woolf calls this a "fierce attachment to an idea." The extent of our success in making clear our motive for writing will largely depend on our interest both in our subject as well as in our idea about the subject. It will prove extremely difficult for any writer to establish a presence when he or she is either bored with — or simply uninterested in — the subject at hand. Investing in a clearly articulated purpose will yield an attractive return in reader attention.

2. Voice. Another way a writer makes his or her presence felt is through creating a distinctive and identifiable *voice.* All words are composed of sounds, and language itself is something nearly all of us originally learned through *hearing.* Any piece of writing can be read aloud, though many readers have developed such ingrained habits of silent reading that they no longer *hear* the writing. Good writers, however, want their words to be heard. They want their sentences to have rhythm, cadence, and balance. Experienced authors revise a great deal of their writing just to make sure the sentences *sound* right. They're writing for the reader's ear as well as the reader's mind.

In many respects, voice is the writer's "signature," what finally distinguishes the work of one writer from another. Consider how quickly we recognize voice. We only *hear* the opening lines of a humorous sketch on television, yet we instantly recognize the comedian. So, too, whenever we read a piece of writing, we ought to think of it as an experience similar to listening to someone speak aloud. Doing so adds drama to writing and reading. Here is what the poet Robert Frost had to say on the subject:

> Everything written is as good as it is dramatic. . . . A dramatic necessity goes deep into the nature of the sentence. Sentences are not different enough to hold the attention unless they are dramatic. No ingenuity of varying structure will do. All that can save them is the speaking tone of voice somehow entangled in the words and fastened to the page for the ear of the imagination. That is all that can save poetry from singing, all that can save prose from itself. (Preface to *A Way Out,* in *Selected Prose of Robert Frost,* 1)

Frost spent a good portion of his celebrated public life encouraging people to cultivate what he called "the hearing imagination."

A writer's voice is usually fairly consistent from essay to essay and can be detected quickly by an experienced reader who pays attention to "the hearing imagination." To be distinctive and effective, a writer's voice need not be strange, artificial, or self-consciously literary. Many essayists develop a casual, familiar, flexible tone of voice that allows them to range easily from the intimate to the intellectual. Sentence rhythm and word choice play a large part in determining a writer's tone of voice. Observe how Raymond Carver begins an essay about his father (p. 23):

> My dad's name was Clevie Raymond Carver. His family called him Raymond and friends called him C.R. I was named Raymond Clevie Carver, Jr. I hated the "Junior" part. When I was little my dad called me Frog, which was okay. . . .

Carver's voice here is casual and almost childlike, a quality he is striving for in an essay intended to be candid, intimate, and low-key. Throughout the essay, for example, he rarely uses the word *father* but always the more colloquial *dad.* If you read this passage aloud, you will get the feeling that someone is speaking directly to you.

A more specific dimension of voice is *tone,* which refers not only to the implied social relationship of the writer to the reader, but also to the manner the writer adopts in addressing the reader. When considering tone as a feature of the writer's presence, it is useful to remember that tone addresses the ways in which writers convey attitudes. In this respect, tone does not speak to the attitudes themselves but to the manner in which those attitudes are revealed. In either projecting or analyzing the writer's tone, writers and readers ought to consider its intensity, the force with which the writer's attitudes are expressed. The strength of the writer's tone depends on such factors as the seriousness of the situation, the nature and extent of the writer's involvement in the situation, and the control the writer exercises over expression. In practical terms, tone is usually a matter of diction and individual word choice.

3. *Point of View.* Another sure way to establish presence is in the point of view we adopt toward a subject. In this sense, point of view comprises the "whereness" of the writer's presence. Sometimes a point of view can be a literal reality, an actual place or situation in which we physically locate ourselves as writers. This occurs most frequently in autobiographical essays in which the writer is present both as the narrator and as a character. For example, in "A Clack of Tiny Sparks: Remembrances of a Gay Boyhood" (p. 46), Bernard Cooper is always meticulous about telling us his actual location at any given moment in his writing. The essay begins: "Theresa Sanchez sat behind me in ninth-grade algebra."

Note, too, how extremely important point of view is to another essayist in the volume, Brent Staples, in "Just Walk on By: A Black Man Ponders His Power to Alter Public Space" (p. 182). Here is how Staples opens his essay:

> My first victim was a woman — white, well dressed, probably in her early twenties. I came upon her late one evening on a deserted street in Hyde Park, a relatively affluent neighborhood in an otherwise mean, impoverished section of Chicago. As I swung onto the avenue behind her, there seemed to be a discreet, uninflammatory distance between us. Not so. She cast back a worried glance. To her, the youngish black man — a broad six feet two inches with a beard and billowing hair, both hands shoved into the pockets of a bulky military jacket — seemed menacingly close. After a few more quick glimpses, she picked up her pace and was soon running in earnest. Within seconds she disappeared into a cross street.

Point of view in this essay is crucial to Staples, since, in order to see why he frightens people, he needs to see himself in the stereotypical ways that others see him. Thus, by the middle of this opening paragraph (in the sentence beginning "To her"), he literally switches the point of view from his own perspective to that of the young and terrified white woman, describing his appearance as she would perceive it.

Point of view is not always a matter of a specific location or position. Writers are not always present in their essays as dramatic characters. In many reflective, informative, or argumentative essays, the point of view is determined more by a writer's intellectual attitude or opinions — an angle of vision — than by a precise physical perspective. As an example of how a writer establishes a personal perspective without introducing a first-person narrator or a characterized self, note the following passage from Stanley Crouch's essay "The Good News: The O. J. Simpson Verdict" (p. 461): "Those same people . . . turned in the other direction, dropped their pants, and contemptuously mooned the verdict." There is no first person singular here, nor a dramatically rendered self. Yet this passage conveys a very distinct point of view.

4. *Patterns.* A writer can also be present in an essay as a *writer* — that is, a person consciously crafting and shaping his or her work. This artistic presence is not always obvious. Yet when we begin to detect in our reading certain kinds of repeated elements — a metaphor or an image, a twist on an earlier episode, a conclusion that echoes the opening — we become aware that someone is deliberately shaping experience or ideas in a special manner. We often find this type of presence in imaginative literature — especially in novels and poems — as well as in essays that possess a distinct literary flavor.

As an example of creating a presence through patterns, look at the opening paragraph of E. B. White's now-classic essay, "Once More to the Lake" (p. 222).

> One summer, along about 1904, my father rented a camp on a lake in Maine and took us all there for the month of August. We all got ringworm from some kittens and had to rub Pond's Extract on our arms and legs night and morning, and my father rolled over in a canoe with all his clothes on; but outside of that the vacation was a success and from then on none of us ever thought there was any place in the world like that lake in Maine. We returned summer after summer — always on August 1st for one month. I have since become a salt-water man, but sometimes in summer there are days when the restlessness of the tides and the fearful cold of the sea water and the incessant wind that blows across the afternoon and into the evening make me wish for the placidity of a lake in the woods. A few weeks ago this feeling got so strong I bought myself a couple of bass hooks and a spinner and returned to the lake where we used to go, for a week's fishing and to revisit old haunts.

If in rereading this opening, you circle every use of the word *and,* you will clearly see a pattern of repetition. *And,* of course, is a very unobtrusive word, and you may not notice right off how White keeps it present throughout the passage. This repetition alone may strike you at first as of no special importance, but as you read through the essay and see how much of White's central theme depends on the idea of return and repetition, you will get a better sense of why the little word *and* — a word that subtly reinforces the idea of repetition itself — is so significant.

E. B. White is present in his essay in more obvious ways — he is both telling us the story and he appears in it as a character. But he is also present to us as a writer, someone consciously shaping the language and form of his essay. We are dealing here with three levels of presence (which might also be described as three levels of "I"). If this sounds confusing, just think of a movie in which a single person directs the film, writes the script, and plays a leading role. It's not that uncommon. If you watch the 1987 film *Hannah and Her Sisters*, for example, you can observe the three presences of Woody Allen. Allen is not only visibly present in the film as one of the chief characters, but we also can detect his creative and shaping presence as the author of the screenplay (for which he won an Oscar) and as the director. The audience can directly see him on the screen as an actor; but the audience can also infer his presence as a scriptwriter and especially as a director — presences that, though less directly observable, are still original and powerful.

THE ESSAYS IN THIS BOOK

The writer's presence, then, can be felt both directly and indirectly. In some of the essays in this book you will encounter the first-person point of view directly. These essays appear mostly in the opening part, "Personal Writing: Exploring Our Own Lives." In many of these essays, the writer will appear as both narrator and character, and the writer's presence will be quite observable.

But not all essays are about the self. In fact, autobiography and memoir occupy only a small part of the nonfiction writing that regularly appears in magazines and newspapers. Many essays are written on specific topics and deal with specific issues. Most of the essays appearing in America's dominant periodicals, for example, are intended to be either informative or persuasive; the author wants to convey information about a particular subject (a Civil War battle) or wants to express an opinion about a particular issue (how to deal with the homeless). The book's second and third chapters, "Expository Writing: Shaping Information" and "Argumentative Writing: Contending with Issues," contain a large number of selections that illustrate writing intended to inform, argue, and persuade.

You'll notice, however, a strong writer's presence in many of the informative and persuasive essays. This is deliberate. To write informatively or persuasively about subjects other than yourself doesn't mean that you have to disappear as a writer. Sometimes you will want to insert your own experiences and testimony into an argumentative essay; at other times you will want to assume a distinct viewpoint concerning a piece of information; and at still other times — though you may not introduce the first-person singular — you will make your presence strongly felt in your tone of voice or simply in the way you arrange your facts and juxtapose details. At the heart of the word *information* is *form*. Writers don't passively receive facts and information in a totally finished format; they need to shape their information, to give it form. This shaping or patterning is something the writer *contributes*. A large part of the instructional purpose of this collection is to encourage you to pay more attention to the different ways writers are present in their work.

THE READER'S PRESENCE

Because almost all writing (and *all* published writing) is intended to be read, we can't dismiss the importance of the reader. Just as we find different levels of a writer's presence in a given piece of writing, so too can we detect different ways in which a reader can be present.

An author writes a short essay offering an opinion about gun control. The author herself has been the victim of a shooting, and her piece, though it includes her personal experiences, is largely made up of a concrete plan to eliminate all guns — even hunting rifles — from American life. She would like lawmakers to adopt her plan. Yet, in writing her essay, she imagines a great deal of resistance to her argument. In other words, she imagines a reader who will most likely disagree with her and who needs to be won over. Let's imagine she gets her essay published in *Newsweek*.

Now imagine three people in a dentist's office who within the same afternoon pick up this issue of *Newsweek* and read the essay. One of them has also been victimized by guns (her son was accidentally wounded by a hunter), and she reads the essay with great sympathy and conviction. She understands perfectly what this woman has gone through and believes in her plan completely. The next reader, a man who has never once in his life committed a crime and has no tolerance for criminals, is outraged by the essay. He was practically brought up in the woods and loves to hunt. He could never adopt a gun control plan that would in effect criminalize hunting. He's ready to fire off a letter attacking this woman's plan. The third reader also enjoys hunting and has always felt that hunting rifles should be exempt from any government regulation of firearms. But he finds the woman's plan convincing and feasible. He spends the rest of the day trying to think of counterarguments.

Obviously, these are only three of many possibilities. But you should be able to see from this example the differences between the reader imagined by the writer and some actual readers. The one person who completely agreed with the writer was not the kind of reader the author had originally imagined or was trying to persuade; she was already persuaded. And though the other two readers were part of her intended audience, one of them could never be persuaded to her point of view, whereas the other one might.

The differences briefly outlined here are distinctions between what can be called implied readers and actual readers. The implied reader is the reader imagined by the writer for a particular piece of writing. In constructing arguments, for example, it is usually effective to imagine readers we are *trying* to win over to our views. Otherwise, we are simply asking people who already agree with us to agree with us — what's commonly known as "preaching to the converted."

In informative or critical essays, a writer also needs to be careful about the implied reader. For example, it's always important to ask how much your intended audience may already know about your subject. Here's a practical illustration. If you were asked to write a review of a recent film for your college newspaper, you would assume your readers had not yet seen it (or else you might annoy them by giving away some surprises). On the other hand, if you were asked to write a critical essay about the same movie for a film course, you could assume your readers had seen it. It's the same movie, and you have the same opinions about it, but your two essays had two different purposes, and in the process of writing them you imagined readers with two different levels of knowledge about the film.

Actual readers, of course, differ from implied readers in that they are real people who read the writing — not readers intended or imagined by the writer. As you read the essays in this collection, you should be aware of at least two readers — (1) the reader you think the writer imagines for the essay, and (2) the reader you are in actuality. Sometimes you will seem very close to the kind of reader the writer is imagining. In those cases, you might say that you "identify" with a particular writer, essay, or point of view. At other times, however, you will notice a great deal of distance between the reader the author imagines and you as an actual reader. For example, you may feel excluded by the author on the basis of race, gender, class, or expected education. Or you may feel you know more than the author does about a particular topic.

To help you get accustomed to your role as a reader, each selection in the book is followed by a set of questions, "The Reader's Presence." These questions are designed to orient you to the various levels of reading suggested by the selection. Some of the questions will ask you to identify the kind of reader you think the author imagines; other questions will prompt you to think about specific ways you may differ from the author's intended reader. In general, the questions are intended to make you more deeply aware of your *presence* as a reader.

In this brief introduction, we covered only two levels of readers (imagined and actual), but some literary essays demand more complex consideration. Whenever we think more than these two types of readers need to be identified in an essay, we will introduce this information in the questions.

We hope you will find *The Writer's Presence* a stimulating book to read and think about. To make our presence felt as writers is as much a matter of self-empowerment as it is of faith. It requires the confidence that we can affect others, or determine a course of action, or even surprise ourselves by new ideas or by acquiring new powers of articulation. Part of the enduring pleasure of writing is precisely that element of surprise, of originality — that lifelong pleasure of discovering new resources of language, finding new means of knowing ourselves, and inventing new ways to be present in the world.

Part I

Personal Writing: Exploring Our Own Lives

1

Maya Angelou

"What's Your Name, Girl?"

Maya Angelou (b. 1928) grew up in St. Louis, Missouri, and in Stamps, Arkansas, a victim of poverty, discrimination, and abuse. Angelou courageously confronts the pain and injustice of her childhood in I Know Why the Caged Bird Sings *(1969), from which the selection "What's Your Name, Girl?" is taken. James Baldwin praised this book as the mark of the "beginning of a new era in the minds and hearts of all black men and women." Angelou is currently Reynolds Professor of American Studies at Wake Forest University. In addition to the several volumes of her autobiography, she is the author of articles, short stories, and poetry. Her most recent publication is a book of poetry entitled* A Brave and Startling Truth *(1995).*

Angelou describes a typical day in her life as a writer in this way: "When I'm writing, everything shuts down. I get up about five. . . . I get in my car and drive off to a hotel room: I can't write in my house, I take a hotel room and ask them to take everything off the walls so there's me, the Bible, Roget's Thesaurus, and some good, dry sherry and I'm at work by 6:30. I write on the bed lying down — one elbow is darker than the other, really black from leaning on it — and I write in longhand on yellow pads. Once into it, all disbelief is suspended, it's beautiful. I hate to go, but I've set for myself 12:30 as the time to leave, because after that it's an indulgence, it becomes stuff I am going to edit out anyway. . . . After dinner I re-read what I have written . . . if April is the cruellest month, then 8:00 at night is the cruellest hour because that's when I start to edit and all that pretty stuff I've written gets axed out. So if I've written ten or twelve pages in six hours, it'll end up as three or four if I'm lucky."

Recently a white woman from Texas, who would quickly describe herself as a liberal, asked me about my hometown. When I told her that in Stamps[1] my grandmother had owned the only Negro general merchandise store since the turn of the century, she exclaimed, "Why, you were a debutante." Ridiculous and even ludicrous. But Negro girls in small Southern towns, whether poverty-stricken or just munching along on a

---

[1] *Stamps:* A town in southwestern Arkansas. — EDS.

few of life's necessities, were given as extensive and irrelevant prepara-
tions for adulthood as rich white girls shown in magazines. Admittedly
the training was not the same. While white girls learned to waltz and sit
gracefully with a teacup balanced on their knees, we were lagging behind,
learning the mid-Victorian values with very little money to indulge them.
(Come and see Edna Lomax spending the money she made picking cotton
on five balls of ecru tatting thread. Her fingers are bound to snag the
work and she'll have to repeat the stitches time and time again. But she
knows that when she buys the thread.)

Thesis

We were required to embroider and I had trunkfuls of colorful dish-
towels, pillowcases, runners, and handkerchiefs to my credit. I mastered
the art of crocheting and tatting, and there was a lifetime's supply of
dainty doilies that would never be used in sacheted dresser drawers. It
went without saying that all girls could iron and wash, but the finer
touches around the home, like setting a table with real silver, baking
roasts, and cooking vegetables without meat, had to be learned elsewhere. Usually at the source of those habits. During my tenth year, a
white woman's kitchen became my finishing school.

Mrs. Viola Cullinan was a plump woman who lived in a three-
bedroom house somewhere behind the post office. She was singularly unattractive until she smiled, and then the lines around her eyes and mouth
which made her look perpetually dirty disappeared, and her face looked
like the mask of an impish elf. She usually rested her smile until late afternoon when her women friends dropped in and Miss Glory, the cook,
served them cold drinks on the closed-in porch.

The exactness of her house was inhuman. This glass went here and
only here. That cup had its place and it was an act of impudent rebellion
to place it anywhere else. At twelve o'clock the table was set. At 12:15
Mrs. Cullinan sat down to dinner (whether her husband had arrived or
not). At 12:16 Miss Glory brought out the food.

It took me a week to learn the difference between a salad plate, a   5
bread plate, and a dessert plate.

Mrs. Cullinan kept up the tradition of her wealthy parents. She was
from Virginia. Miss Glory, who was a descendant of slaves that had
worked for the Cullinans, told me her history. She had married beneath
her (according to Miss Glory). Her husband's family hadn't had their
money very long and what they had "didn't 'mount to much."

As ugly as she was, I thought privately, she was lucky to get a husband
above or beneath her station. But Miss Glory wouldn't let me say a thing
against her mistress. She was very patient with me, however, over the
housework. She explained the dishware, silverware, and servants' bells.

The large round bowl in which soup was served wasn't a soup bowl,
it was a tureen. There were goblets, sherbet glasses, ice-cream glasses,
wine glasses, green glass coffee cups with matching saucers, and water
glasses. I had a glass to drink from, and it sat with Miss Glory's on a separate shelf from the others. Soup spoons, gravy boat, butter knives, salad

forks, and carving platter were additions to my vocabulary and in fact almost represented a new language. I was fascinated with the novelty, with the fluttering Mrs. Cullinan and her Alice-in-Wonderland house.

Her husband remains, in my memory, undefined. I lumped him with all the other white men that I had ever seen and tried not to see.

On our way home one evening, Miss Glory told me that Mrs. Cullinan couldn't have children. She said that she was too delicate-boned. It was hard to imagine bones at all under those layers of fat. Miss Glory went on to say that the doctor had taken out all her lady organs. I reasoned that a pig's organs included the lungs, heart, and liver, so if Mrs. Cullinan was walking around without these essentials, it explained why she drank alcohol out of unmarked bottles. She was keeping herself embalmed.

When I spoke to Bailey[2] about it, he agreed that I was right, but he also informed me that Mr. Cullinan had two daughters by a colored lady and that I knew them very well. He added that the girls were the spitting image of their father. I was unable to remember what he looked like, although I had just left him a few hours before, but I thought of the Coleman girls. They were very light-skinned and certainly didn't look very much like their mother (no one ever mentioned Mr. Coleman).

My pity for Mrs. Cullinan preceded me the next morning like the Cheshire cat's smile. Those girls, who could have been her daughters, were beautiful. They didn't have to straighten their hair. Even when they were caught in the rain, their braids still hung down straight like tamed snakes. Their mouths were pouty little cupid's bows. Mrs. Cullinan didn't know what she missed. Or maybe she did. Poor Mrs. Cullinan.

For weeks after, I arrived early, left late, and tried very hard to make up for her barrenness. If she had had her own children, she wouldn't have had to ask me to run a thousand errands from her back door to the back door of her friends. Poor old Mrs. Cullinan.

Then one evening Miss Glory told me to serve the ladies on the porch. After I set the tray down and turned toward the kitchen, one of the women asked, "What's your name, girl?" It was the speckled-face one. Mrs. Cullinan said, "She doesn't talk much. Her name's Margaret."

"Is she dumb?"

"No. As I understand it, she can talk when she wants to but she's usually quiet as a little mouse. Aren't you, Margaret?"

I smiled at her. Poor thing. No organs and couldn't even pronounce my name correctly.[3]

"She's a sweet little thing, though."

"Well, that may be, but the name's too long. I'd never bother myself. I'd call her Mary if I was you."

I fumed into the kitchen. That horrible woman would never have the chance to call me Mary because if I was starving I'd never work for her. I

10

15

20

---

[2]*Bailey:* Her brother. — EDS.
[3]Angelou's first name is actually Marguerite. — EDS.

decided I wouldn't pee on her if her heart was on fire. Giggles drifted in off the porch and into Miss Glory's pots. I wondered what they could be laughing about.

Whitefolks were so strange. Could they be talking about me? Everybody knew that they stuck together better than the Negroes did. It was possible that Mrs. Cullinan had friends in St. Louis who heard about a girl from Stamps being in court and wrote to tell her. Maybe she knew about Mr. Freeman.[4]

My lunch was in my mouth a second time and I went outside and relieved myself on the bed of four-o'clocks. Miss Glory thought I might be coming down with something and told me to go on home, that Momma would give me some herb tea, and she'd explain to her mistress.

I realized how foolish I was being before I reached the pond. Of course Mrs. Cullinan didn't know. Otherwise she wouldn't have given me the two nice dresses that Momma cut down, and she certainly wouldn't have called me a "sweet little thing." My stomach felt fine, and I didn't mention anything to Momma.

That evening I decided to write a poem on being white, fat, old, and without children. It was going to be a tragic ballad. I would have to watch her carefully to capture the essence of her loneliness and pain.

The very next day, she called me by the wrong name. Miss Glory and   25
I were washing up the lunch dishes when Mrs. Cullinan came to the doorway. "Mary?"

Miss Glory asked, "Who?"

Mrs. Cullinan, sagging a little, knew and I knew. "I want Mary to go down to Mrs. Randall's and take her some soup. She's not been feeling well for a few days."

Miss Glory's face was a wonder to see. "You mean Margaret, ma'am. Her name's Margaret."

"That's too long. She's Mary from now on. Heat that soup from last night and put it in the china tureen and, Mary, I want you to carry it carefully."

Every person I knew had a hellish horror of being "called out of his   30
name." It was a dangerous practice to call a Negro anything that could be loosely construed as insulting because of the centuries of their having been called niggers, jigs, dinges, blackbirds, crows, boots, and spooks.

Miss Glory had a fleeting second of feeling sorry for me. Then as she handed me the hot tureen she said, "Don't mind, don't pay that no mind. Sticks and stones may break your bones, but words . . . You know, I been working for her for twenty years."

She held the back door open for me. "Twenty years; I wasn't much older than you. My name used to be Hallelujah. That's what Ma named me, but my mistress give me 'Glory,' and it stuck. I likes it better too."

---

[4]*Mr. Freeman:* A friend of Angelou's mother; he was convicted of raping Angelou when she was a child. — EDS.

I was in the little path that ran behind the houses when Miss Glory shouted. "It's shorter too."

For a few seconds it was a tossup over whether I would laugh (imagine being named Hallelujah) or cry (imagine letting some white woman rename you for her convenience). My anger saved me from either outburst. I had to quit the job, but the problem was going to be how to do it. Momma wouldn't allow me to quit for just any reason.

"She's a peach. That woman is a real peach." Mrs. Randall's maid 35 was talking as she took the soup from me, and I wondered what her name used to be and what she answered to now.

For a week I looked into Mrs. Cullinan's face as she called me Mary. She ignored my coming late and leaving early. Miss Glory was a little annoyed because I had begun to leave egg yolk on the dishes and wasn't putting much heart in polishing the silver. I hoped that she would complain to our boss, but she didn't.

Then Bailey solved my dilemma. He had me describe the contents of the cupboard and the particular plates she liked best. Her favorite piece was a casserole shaped like a fish and the green glass coffee cups. I kept his instructions in mind, so on the next day when Miss Glory was hanging out clothes and I had again been told to serve the old biddies on the porch, I dropped the empty serving tray. When I heard Mrs. Cullinan scream, "Mary!" I picked up the casserole and two of the green glass cups in readiness. As she rounded the kitchen door I let them fall on the tiled floor.

I could never absolutely describe to Bailey what happened next, because each time I got to the part where she fell on the floor and screwed up her ugly face to cry, we burst out laughing. She actually wobbled around on the floor and picked up shards of the cups and cried, "Oh, Momma. Oh, dear Gawd. It's Momma's china from Virginia. Oh, Momma, I sorry."

Miss Glory came running in from the yard and the women from the porch crowded around. Miss Glory was almost as broken up as her mistress. "You mean to say she broke our Virginia dishes? What we gone do?"

Mrs. Cullinan cried louder. "That clumsy nigger. Clumsy little black 40 nigger."

Old speckled-face leaned down and asked, "Who did it, Viola? Was it Mary? Who did it?"

Everything was happening so fast I can't remember whether her action preceded her words, but I know that Mrs. Cullinan said, "Her name's Margaret, goddamn it, her name's Margaret!" And she threw a wedge of the broken plate at me. It could have been the hysteria which put her aim off, but the flying crockery caught Miss Glory right over her ear and she started screaming.

I left the front door wide open so all the neighbors could hear.

Mrs. Cullinan was right about one thing. My name wasn't Mary.

The Reader's Presence

1. At the center of this autobiographical episode is the importance of people's names in African American culture. Where does Angelou make this point clear? If she hadn't explained the problem of names directly, how might your interpretation of the episode be different? To what extent do the names of things also play an important role in the essay?
2. After rereading the essay, try to describe the emotional attitudes of the characters to one another. What, for example, is Marguerite's attitude toward Mrs. Cullinan? Do you feel pity or sympathy at any point for Mrs. Cullinan? How does Marguerite's attitude toward her fluctuate throughout the episode? With whom do you sympathize most in the final scene, and why? For which character do you have the least sympathy?
3. Consider Marguerite's final act very carefully. Why does she respond by deliberately destroying Mrs. Cullinan's china? What else could she have done? Why was that act especially appropriate? What does the china represent?

2

Russell Baker

Gumption

Since 1962, Russell Baker (b. 1925) has written the "Observer" column in the New York Times, *a column that is syndicated to over four hundred and fifty newspapers across the nation. Baker's articles on contemporary American politics, culture, and language are consistently funny and often sharply satiric. Collections of his articles have been published in several volumes, including* So This Is Depravity *(1980) and* There's a Country in My Cellar *(1990). He is also the author of fiction and children's literature. Recently, Baker has acted as the host for* Masterpiece Theater *on public television.*

Among other professional honors, he has twice been awarded the Pulitzer Prize, in 1979 for commentary and in 1983 for his autobiography, Growing Up *(1982), from which the selection "Gumption" is taken. Baker's second volume of memoirs,* The Good Times, *was published in 1989. Baker engaged in extensive research efforts in preparation for writing these memoirs. After all, he explains, "I was writing about a world that seemed to exist 200 years ago. I had one foot*

*back there in this primitive country life where the women did the laundry running
their knuckles on scrub boards and heated irons on coal stoves."*

I began working in journalism when I was eight years old. It was my
mother's idea. She wanted me to "make something" of myself and, after a
levelheaded appraisal of my strengths, decided I had better start young if I
was to have any chance of keeping up with the competition.

The flaw in my character which she had already spotted was the lack
of "gumption." My idea of a perfect afternoon was lying in front of the
radio rereading my favorite Big Little Book, *Dick Tracy Meets Stooge
Viller*. My mother despised inactivity. Seeing me having a good time in repose, she was powerless to hide her disgust. "You've got no more gumption than a bump on a log," she said. "Get out in the kitchen and help
Doris do those dirty dishes."

My sister Doris, though two years younger than I, had enough gumption for a dozen people. She positively enjoyed washing dishes, making
beds, and cleaning the house. When she was only seven she could carry a
piece of short-weighted cheese back to the A&P, threaten the manager
with legal action, and come back triumphantly with the full quarter-
pound we'd paid for and a few extra ounces thrown in for forgiveness.
Doris could have made something of herself if she hadn't been a girl. Because of this defect, however, the best she could hope for was a career as
a nurse or schoolteacher, the only work that capable females were considered up to in those days.

This must have saddened my mother, this twist of fate that had allocated all the gumption to the daughter and left her with a son who was
content with Dick Tracy and Stooge Viller. If disappointed, though, she
wasted no energy on self-pity. She would make me make something of
myself whether I wanted to or not. "The Lord helps those who help
themselves," she said. That was the way her mind worked.

She was realistic about the difficulty. Having sized up the material the   5
Lord had given her to mold, she didn't overestimate what she could do with
it. She didn't insist that I grow up to be president of the United States.

Fifty years ago parents still asked boys if they wanted to grow up to
be president, and asked it not jokingly but seriously. Many parents who
were hardly more than paupers still believed their sons could do it. Abraham Lincoln had done it. We were only sixty-five years from Lincoln.
Many a grandfather who walked among us could remember Lincoln's
time. Men of grandfatherly age were the worst for asking if you wanted
to grow up to be president. A surprising number of little boys said yes
and meant it.

I was asked many times myself. No, I would say, I didn't want to
grow up to be president. My mother was present during one of these in-
terrogations. An elderly uncle, having posed the usual question and exposed my lack of interest in the presidency, asked, "Well, what *do* you
want to be when you grow up?"

I loved to pick through trash piles and collect empty bottles, tin cans with pretty labels, and discarded magazines. The most desirable job on earth sprang instantly to mind. "I want to be a garbage man," I said.

My uncle smiled, but my mother had seen the first distressing evidence of a bump budding on a log. "Have a little gumption, Russell," she said. Her calling me Russell was a signal of unhappiness. When she approved of me I was always "Buddy."

When I turned eight years old she decided that the job of starting me   10
on the road toward making something of myself could no longer be safely delayed. "Buddy," she said one day, "I want you to come home right after school this afternoon. Somebody's coming and I want you to meet him."

When I burst in that afternoon she was in conference in the parlor with an executive of the Curtis Publishing Company. She introduced me. He bent low from the waist and shook my hand. Was it true as my mother had told him, he asked, that I longed for the opportunity to conquer the world of business?

My mother replied that I was blessed with a rare determination to make something of myself.

"That's right," I whispered.

"But have you got the grit, the character, the never-say-quit spirit it takes to succeed in business?"

My mother said I certainly did.   15

"That's right," I said.

He eyed me silently for a long pause, as though weighing whether I could be trusted to keep his confidence, then spoke man-to-man. Before taking a crucial step, he said, he wanted to advise me that working for the Curtis Publishing Company placed enormous responsibility on a young man. It was one of the great companies of America. Perhaps the greatest publishing house in the world. I had heard, no doubt, of the *Saturday Evening Post*?

Heard of it? My mother said that everyone in our house had heard of the *Saturday Post* and that I, in fact, read it with religious devotion.

Then doubtless, he said, we were also familiar with those two monthly pillars of the magazine world, the *Ladies Home Journal* and the *Country Gentleman.*

Indeed we were familiar with them, said my mother.   20

Representing the *Saturday Evening Post* was one of the weightiest honors that could be bestowed in the world of business, he said. He was personally proud of being a part of that great corporation.

My mother said he had every right to be.

Again he studied me as though debating whether I was worthy of a knighthood. Finally: "Are you trustworthy?"

My mother said I was the soul of honesty.

"That's right," I said.   25

The caller smiled for the first time. He told me I was a lucky young man. He admired my spunk. Too many young men thought life was all play. Those young men would not go far in this world. Only a young man willing to work and save and keep his face washed and his hair neatly combed could hope to come out on top in a world such as ours. Did I truly and sincerely believe that I was such a young man?

"He certainly does," said my mother.

"That's right," I said.

He said he had been so impressed by what he had seen of me that he was going to make me a representative of the Curtis Publishing Company. On the following Tuesday, he said, thirty freshly printed copies of the *Saturday Evening Post* would be delivered at our door. I would place these magazines, still damp with the ink of the presses, in a handsome canvas bag, sling it over my shoulder, and set forth through the streets to bring the best in journalism, fiction, and cartoons to the American public.

He had brought the canvas bag with him. He presented it with a reverence fit for a chasuble. He showed me how to drape the sling over my left shoulder and across the chest so that the pouch lay easily accessible to my right hand, allowing the best in journalism, fiction, and cartoons to be swiftly extracted and sold to a citizenry whose happiness and security depended upon us soldiers of the free press.   30

The following Tuesday I raced home from school, put the canvas bag over my shoulder, dumped the magazines in, and, tilting to the left to balance their weight on my right hip, embarked on the highway of journalism.

We lived in Belleville, New Jersey, a commuter town at the northern fringe of Newark. It was 1932, the bleakest year of the Depression. My father had died two years before, leaving us with a few pieces of Sears, Roebuck furniture and not much else, and my mother had taken Doris and me to live with one of her younger brothers. This was my Uncle Allen. Uncle Allen had made something of himself by 1932. As salesman for a soft-drink bottler in Newark, he had an income of $30 a week; wore pearl-gray spats, detachable collars, and a three-piece suit; was happily married; and took in threadbare relatives.

With my load of magazines I headed toward Belleville Avenue. That's where the people were. There were two filling stations at the intersection with Union Avenue, as well as an A&P, a fruit stand, a bakery, a barbershop, Zuccarelli's drugstore, and a diner shaped like a railroad car. For several hours I made myself highly visible, shifting position now and then from corner to corner, from shop window to shop window, to make sure everyone could see the heavy black lettering on the canvas bag that said THE SATURDAY EVENING POST. When the angle of the light indicated that it was suppertime, I walked back to the house.

"How many did you sell, Buddy?" my mother asked.

"None."   35

"Where did you go?"

"The corner of Belleville and Union Avenues."

"What did you do?"

"Stood on the corner waiting for somebody to buy a *Saturday Evening Post*."

"You just stood there?"   40

"Didn't sell a single one."

"For God's sake, Russell!"

Uncle Allen intervened. "I've been thinking about it for some time," he said, "and I've about decided to take the *Post* regularly. Put me down as a regular customer." And I handed him a magazine and he paid me a nickel. It was the first nickel I earned.

Afterwards my mother instructed me in salesmanship. I would have to ring doorbells, address adults with charming self-confidence, and break down resistance with a sales talk pointing out that no one, no matter how poor, could afford to be without the *Saturday Evening Post* in the home.

I told my mother I'd changed my mind about wanting to succeed in   45 the magazine business.

"If you think I'm going to raise a good-for-nothing," she replied, "you've got another think coming." She told me to hit the streets with the canvas bag and start ringing doorbells the instant school was out the next day. When I objected that I didn't feel any aptitude for salesmanship, she asked how I'd like to lend her my leather belt so she could whack some sense into me. I bowed to superior will and entered journalism with a heavy heart.

My mother and I had fought this battle almost as long as I could remember. It probably started even before memory began, when I was a country child in northern Virginia and my mother, dissatisfied with my father's plain workman's life, determined that I would not grow up like him and his people, with calluses on their hands, overalls on their backs, and fourth-grade educations in their heads. She had fancier ideas of life's possibilities. Introducing me to the *Saturday Evening Post*, she was trying to wean me as early as possible from my father's world where men left with their lunch pails at sunup, worked with their hands until the grime ate into the pores, and died with a few sticks of mail-order furniture as their legacy. In my mother's vision of the better life there were desks and white collars, well-pressed suits, evenings of reading and lively talk, and perhaps — if a man were very, very lucky and hit the jackpot, really made something important of himself — perhaps there might be a fantastic salary of $5,000 a year to support a big house and a Buick with a rumble seat and a vacation in Atlantic City.

And so I set forth with my sack of magazines. I was afraid of the dogs that snarled behind the doors of potential buyers. I was timid about ringing the doorbells of strangers, relieved when no one came to the door, and scared when someone did. Despite my mother's instructions, I could not deliver an engaging sales pitch. When a door opened I simply asked, "Want to buy a *Saturday Evening Post*?" In Belleville few persons did. It was a town of thirty thousand people, and most weeks I rang a fair majority of its doorbells. But I rarely sold my thirty copies. Some weeks I canvassed the entire town for six days and still had four or five unsold magazines on Monday evening; then I dreaded the coming of Tuesday morning, when a batch of thirty fresh *Saturday Evening Post*s was due at the front door.

"Better get out there and sell the rest of those magazines tonight," my mother would say.

I usually posted myself then at a busy intersection where a traffic light controlled commuter flow from Newark. When the light turned red I stood on the curb and shouted my sales pitch at the motorists. 50

"Want to buy a *Saturday Evening Post?*"

One rainy night when car windows were sealed against me I came back soaked and with not a single sale to report. My mother beckoned to Doris.

"Go back down there with Buddy and show him how to sell these magazines," she said.

Brimming with zest, Doris, who was then seven years old, returned with me to the corner. She took a magazine from the bag, and when the light turned red she strode to the nearest car and banged her small fist against the closed window. The driver, probably startled at what he took to be a midget assaulting his car, lowered the window to stare, and Doris thrust a *Saturday Evening Post* at him.

"You need this magazine," she piped, "and it only costs a nickel." 55

Her salesmanship was irresistible. Before the light changed half a dozen times she disposed of the entire batch. I didn't feel humiliated. To the contrary. I was so happy I decided to give her a treat. Leading her to the vegetable store on Belleville Avenue, I bought three apples, which cost a nickel, and gave her one.

"You shouldn't waste your money," she said.

"Eat your apple." I bit into mine.

"You shouldn't eat before supper," she said. "It'll spoil your appetite."

Back at the house that evening, she dutifully reported me for wasting 60 a nickel. Instead of a scolding, I was rewarded with a pat on the back for having the good sense to buy fruit instead of candy. My mother reached into her bottomless supply of maxims and told Doris, "An apple a day keeps the doctor away."

By the time I was ten I had learned all my mother's maxims by heart. Asking to stay up past normal bedtime, I knew the refusal would be explained with, "Early to bed and early to rise, makes a man healthy, wealthy, and wise." If I whimpered about having to get up early in the morning, I could depend on her to say, "The early bird gets the worm."

The one I most despised was, "If at first you don't succeed, try, try again." This was the battle cry with which she constantly sent me back into the hopeless struggle whenever I moaned that I had rung every doorbell in town and knew there wasn't a single potential buyer left in Belleville that week. After listening to my explanation, she handed me the canvas bag and said, "If at first you don't succeed . . ."

Three years in that job, which I would gladly have quit after the first day except for her insistence, produced at least one valuable result. My mother finally concluded that I would never make something of myself by pursuing a life in business and started considering careers that demanded less competitive zeal.

One evening when I was eleven I brought home a short "composition" on my summer vacation which the teacher had graded with an A. Reading it with her own schoolteacher's eye, my mother agreed that it was top-drawer seventh grade prose and complimented me. Nothing more was said about it immediately, but a new idea had taken life in her mind. Halfway through supper she suddenly interrupted the conversation.

"Buddy," she said, "maybe you could be a writer."   65

I clasped the idea to my heart. I had never met a writer, had shown no previous urge to write, and hadn't a notion how to become a writer, but I loved stories and thought that making up stories must surely be almost as much fun as reading them. Best of all, though, and what really gladdened my heart, was the ease of a writer's life. Writers did not have to trudge through the town peddling from canvas bags, defending themselves against angry dogs, being rejected by surly strangers. Writers did not have to ring doorbells. So far as I could make out, what writers did couldn't even be classified as work.

I was enchanted. Writers didn't have to have any gumption at all. I did not dare tell anybody for fear of being laughed at in the schoolyard, but secretly I decided that what I'd like to be when I grew up was a writer.

The Reader's Presence

1. Baker writes that his sister "could have made something of herself if she hadn't been a girl. Because of this defect, however, the best she could hope for was a career as a nurse or schoolteacher, the only work that capable females were considered up to in those days" (paragraph 3). How would you describe Baker's tone in this passage? Do you think he really believes his sister's gender is a "defect"?

2. Baker's autobiographical essay is sprinkled with maxims and clichés (for example, "an apple a day," "bump on a log"). Such language is usually considered a flaw in writing; how can you tell that Baker is using these phrases intentionally? What effect on the reader do you think they are intended to have?

3. What sort of word is *gumption*? What synonyms can you think of for the term? How does Baker convey what his mother meant by the word without resorting to definitions? Do you believe Baker when he says in the final paragraph that writers don't need any gumption at all?

3

Raymond Carver

My Father's Life

Son of a laborer and a homemaker in Clatskanie, Oregon, Raymond Carver (1938–1988) resembled the characters in the short stories for which he is widely acclaimed. Once a manual laborer, a gas station attendant, and a janitor himself, Carver acquired his vision of the working class and the desperate lives of ordinary folk through direct experience. The Pacific Northwest of Carver's writing is peopled with types such as "the waitress, the bus driver, the mechanic, the hotel keeper" — people Carver feels are "good people." First published in Esquire *in 1984, "My Father's Life," Carver's account of his father's hardships during the Great Depression, puts a biographical spin on these "good people." Carver's short story collections,* Will You Please Be Quiet, Please? *(1976),* Cathedral *(1984), and* Where I'm Calling From *(1988), were all nominated for the National Book Critics Circle Award. The latter two collections were also nominated for the Pulitzer Prize for fiction in 1985 and 1989, respectively. Carver's poetry is collected in* Where Water Comes Together with Other Water *(1985), recipient of the 1986 Los Angeles Times Book Prize;* Ultramarine *(1986); and* A New Path to the Waterfall *(1989).*

In his essay "On Writing," Carver states, "Writers don't need tricks or gimmicks or even necessarily to be the smartest fellows on the block. At the risk of appearing foolish, a writer sometimes needs to be able to just stand and gape at this or that thing — a sunset or an old shoe — in absolute and simple amazement."

My dad's name was Clevie Raymond Carver. His family called him Raymond and friends called him C. R. I was named Raymond Clevie Carver, Jr. I hated the "Junior" part. When I was little my dad called me Frog, which was okay. But later, like everybody else in the family, he began calling me Junior. He went on calling me this until I was thirteen or fourteen and announced that I wouldn't answer to that name any longer. So he began calling me Doc. From then until his death, on June 17, 1967, he called me Doc, or else Son.

When he died, my mother telephoned my wife with the news. I was away from my family at the time, between lives, trying to enroll in the

School of Library Science at the University of Iowa. When my wife answered the phone, my mother blurted out, "Raymond's dead!" For a moment, my wife thought my mother was telling her that I was dead. Then my mother made it clear *which* Raymond she was talking about and my wife said, "Thank God. I thought you meant *my* Raymond."

My dad walked, hitched rides, and rode in empty boxcars when he went from Arkansas to Washington State in 1934, looking for work. I don't know whether he was pursuing a dream when he went out to Washington. I doubt it. I don't think he dreamed much. I believe he was simply looking for steady work at decent pay. Steady work was meaningful work. He picked apples for a time and then landed a construction laborer's job on the Grand Coulee Dam. After he'd put aside a little money, he bought a car and drove back to Arkansas to help his folks, my grandparents, pack up for the move west. He said later that they were about to starve down there, and this wasn't meant as a figure of speech. It was during that short while in Arkansas, in a town called Leola, that my mother met my dad on the sidewalk as he came out of a tavern.

"He was drunk," she said. "I don't know why I let him talk to me. His eyes were glittery. I wish I'd had a crystal ball." They'd met once, a year or so before, at a dance. He'd had girlfriends before her, my mother told me. "Your dad always had a girlfriend, even after we married. He was my first and last. I never had another man. But I didn't miss anything."

They were married by a justice of the peace on the day they left for Washington, this big, tall country girl and a farmhand-turned-construction worker. My mother spent her wedding night with my dad and his folks, all of them camped beside the road in Arkansas.   5

In Omak, Washington, my dad and mother lived in a little place not much bigger than a cabin. My grandparents lived next door. My dad was still working on the dam, and later, with the huge turbines producing electricity and the water backed up for a hundred miles into Canada, he stood in the crowd and heard Franklin D. Roosevelt when he spoke at the construction site. "He never mentioned those guys who died building that dam," my dad said. Some of his friends had died there, men from Arkansas, Oklahoma, and Missouri.

He then took a job in a sawmill in Clatskanie, Oregon, a little town alongside the Columbia River. I was born there, and my mother has a picture of my dad standing in front of the gate to the mill, proudly holding me up to face the camera. My bonnet is on crooked and about to come untied. His hat is pushed back on his forehead, and he's wearing a big grin. Was he going in to work or just finishing his shift? It doesn't matter. In either case, he had a job and a family. These were his salad days.

In 1941 we moved to Yakima, Washington, where my dad went to work as a saw filer, a skilled trade he'd learned in Clatskanie. When war broke out, he was given a deferment because his work was considered necessary to the war effort. Finished lumber was in demand by the armed services, and he kept his saws so sharp they could shave the hair off your arm.

After my dad had moved us to Yakima, he moved his folks into the same neighborhood. By the mid-1940s the rest of my dad's family — his brother, his sister, and her husband, as well as uncles, cousins, nephews, and most of their extended family and friends — had come out from Arkansas. All because my dad came out first. The men went to work at Boise Cascade, where my dad worked, and the women packed apples in the canneries. And in just a little while, it seemed — according to my mother — everybody was better off than my dad. "Your dad couldn't keep money," my mother said. "Money burned a hole in his pocket. He was always doing for others."

The first house I clearly remember living in, at 1515 South Fifteenth   10
Street, in Yakima, had an outdoor toilet. On Halloween night, or just any night, for the hell of it, neighbor kids, kids in their early teens, would carry our toilet away and leave it next to the road. My dad would have to get somebody to help him bring it home. Or these kids would take the toilet and stand it in somebody else's backyard. Once they actually set it on fire. But ours wasn't the only house that had an outdoor toilet. When I was old enough to know what I was doing, I threw rocks at the other toilets when I'd see someone go inside. This was called bombing the toilets. After a while, though, everyone went to indoor plumbing until, suddenly, our toilet was the last outdoor one in the neighborhood. I remember the shame I felt when my third-grade teacher, Mr. Wise, drove me home from school one day. I asked him to stop at the house just before ours, claiming I lived there.

I can recall what happened one night when my dad came home late to find that my mother had locked all the doors on him from the inside. He was drunk, and we could feel the house shudder as he rattled the door. When he'd managed to force open a window, she hit him between the eyes with a colander and knocked him out. We could see him down there on the grass. For years afterward, I used to pick up this colander — it was as heavy as a rolling pin — and imagine what it would feel like to be hit in the head with something like that.

It was during this period that I remember my dad taking me into the bedroom, sitting me down on the bed, and telling me that I might have to go live with my Aunt LaVon for a while. I couldn't understand what I'd done that meant I'd have to go away from home to live. But this, too — whatever prompted it — must have blown over, more or less, anyway, because we stayed together, and I didn't have to go live with her or anyone else.

I remember my mother pouring his whiskey down the sink. Sometimes she'd pour it all out and sometimes, if she was afraid of getting caught, she'd only pour half of it out and then add water to the rest. I tasted some of his whiskey once myself. It was terrible stuff, and I don't see how anybody could drink it.

After a long time without one, we finally got a car, in 1949 or 1950, a 1938 Ford. But it threw a rod the first week we had it, and my dad had to have the motor rebuilt.

"We drove the oldest car in town," my mother said. "We could have   15
had a Cadillac for all he spent on car repairs." One time she found someone else's tube of lipstick on the floorboard, along with a lacy handkerchief. "See this?" she said to me. "Some floozy left this in the car."

Once I saw her take a pan of warm water into the bedroom where
my dad was sleeping. She took his hand from under the covers and held it
in the water. I stood in the doorway and watched. I wanted to know
what was going on. This would make him talk in his sleep, she told me.
There were things she needed to know, things she was sure he was keeping from her.

Every year or so, when I was little, we would take the North Coast
Limited across the Cascade Range from Yakima to Seattle and stay in the
Vance Hotel and eat, I remember, at a place called the Dinner Bell Cafe.
Once we went to Ivar's Acres of Clams and drank glasses of warm clam
broth.

In 1956, the year I was to graduate from high school, my dad quit his
job at the mill in Yakima and took a job in Chester, a little sawmill town
in northern California. The reasons given at the time for his taking the
job had to do with a higher hourly wage and the vague promise that he
might, in a few years' time, succeed to the job of head filer in this new
mill. But I think, in the main, that my dad had grown restless and simply
wanted to try his luck elsewhere. Things had gotten a little too predictable for him in Yakima. Also, the year before, there had been the
deaths, within six months of each other, of both his parents.

But just a few days after graduation, when my mother and I were
packed to move to Chester, my dad penciled a letter to say he'd been sick
for a while. He didn't want us to worry, he said, but he'd cut himself on a
saw. Maybe he'd got a tiny sliver of steel in his blood. Anyway, something had happened and he'd had to miss work, he said. In the same mail
was an unsigned postcard from somebody down there telling my mother
that my dad was about to die and that he was drinking "raw whiskey."

When we arrived in Chester, my dad was living in a trailer that be-   20
longed to the company. I didn't recognize him immediately. I guess for a
moment I didn't want to recognize him. He was skinny and pale and
looked bewildered. His pants wouldn't stay up. He didn't look like my
dad. My mother began to cry. My dad put his arm around her and patted
her shoulder vaguely, like he didn't know what this was all about, either.
The three of us took up life together in the trailer, and we looked after
him as best we could. But my dad was sick, and he couldn't get any better. I worked with him in the mill that summer and part of the fall. We'd
get up in the mornings and eat eggs and toast while we listened to the
radio, and then go out the door with our lunch pails. We'd pass through
the gate together at eight in the morning, and I wouldn't see him again
until quitting time. In November I went back to Yakima to be closer to
my girlfriend, the girl I'd made up my mind I was going to marry.

He worked at the mill in Chester until the following February, when he
collapsed on the job and was taken to the hospital. My mother asked if I

would come down there and help. I caught a bus from Yakima to Chester, intending to drive them back to Yakima. But now, in addition to being physically sick, my dad was in the midst of a nervous breakdown, though none of us knew to call it that at the time. During the entire trip back to Yakima, he didn't speak, not even when asked a direct question. ("How do you feel, Raymond?" "You okay, Dad?") He'd communicate, if he communicated at all, by moving his head or by turning his palms up as if to say he didn't know or care. The only time he said anything on the trip, and for nearly a month afterward, was when I was speeding down a gravel road in Oregon and the car muffler came loose. "You were going too fast," he said.

Back in Yakima a doctor saw to it that my dad went to a psychiatrist. My mother and dad had to go on relief, as it was called, and the county paid for the psychiatrist. The psychiatrist asked my dad, "Who is the President?" He'd had a question put to him that he could answer. "Ike," my dad said. Nevertheless, they put him on the fifth floor of Valley Memorial Hospital and began giving him electroshock treatment. I was married by then and about to start my own family. My dad was still locked up when my wife went into this same hospital, just one floor down, to have our first baby. After she had delivered, I went upstairs to give my dad the news. They let me in through a steel door and showed me where I could find him. He was sitting on a couch with a blanket over his lap. *Hey,* I thought. *What in hell is happening to my dad?* I sat down next to him and told him he was a grandfather. He waited a minute and then he said, "I feel like a grandfather." That's all he said. He didn't smile or move. He was in a big room with a lot of other people. Then I hugged him, and he began to cry.

Somehow he got out of there. But now came the years when he couldn't work and just sat around the house trying to figure what next and what he'd done wrong in his life that he'd wound up like this. My mother went from job to crummy job. Much later she referred to that time he was in the hospital, and those years just afterward, as "when Raymond was sick." The word *sick* was never the same for me again.

In 1964, through the help of a friend, he was lucky enough to be hired on at a mill in Klamath, California. He moved down there by himself to see if he could hack it. He lived not far from the mill, in a one-room cabin not much different from the place he and my mother had started out living in when they went west. He scrawled letters to my mother, and if I called she'd read them aloud to me over the phone. In the letters, he said it was touch and go. Every day that he went to work, he felt like it was the most important day of his life. But every day, he told her, made the next day that much easier. He said for her to tell me he said hello. If he couldn't sleep at night, he said, he thought about me and the good times we used to have. Finally, after a couple of months, he regained some of his confidence. He could do the work and didn't think he had to worry that he'd let anybody down ever again. When he was sure, he sent for my mother.

He'd been off from work for six years and had lost everything in that   25 time — home, car, furniture, and appliances, including the big freezer that had been my mother's pride and joy. He'd lost his good name too — Raymond Carver was someone who couldn't pay his bills — and his self-respect was gone. He'd even lost his virility. My mother told my wife, "All during that time Raymond was sick we slept together in the same bed, but we didn't have relations. He wanted to a few times, but nothing happened. I didn't miss it, but I think he wanted to, you know."

During those years I was trying to raise my own family and earn a living. But, one thing and another, we found ourselves having to move a lot. I couldn't keep track of what was going down in my dad's life. But I did have a chance one Christmas to tell him I wanted to be a writer. I might as well have told him I wanted to become a plastic surgeon. "What are you going to write about?" he wanted to know. Then, as if to help me out, he said, "Write about stuff you know about. Write about some of those fishing trips we took." I said I would, but I knew I wouldn't. "Send me what you write," he said. I said I'd do that, but then I didn't. I wasn't writing anything about fishing, and I didn't think he'd particularly care about, or even necessarily understand, what I was writing in those days. Besides, he wasn't a reader. Not the sort, anyway, I imagined I was writing for.

Then he died. I was a long way off, in Iowa City, with things still to say to him. I didn't have the chance to tell him goodbye, or that I thought he was doing great at his new job. That I was proud of him for making a comeback.

My mother said he came in from work that night and ate a big supper. Then he sat at the table by himself and finished what was left of a bottle of whiskey, a bottle she found hidden in the bottom of the garbage under some coffee grounds a day or so later. Then he got up and went to bed, where my mother joined him a little later. But in the night she had to get up and make a bed for herself on the couch. "He was snoring so loud I couldn't sleep," she said. The next morning when she looked in on him, he was on his back with his mouth open, his cheeks caved in. *Graylooking*, she said. She knew he was dead — she didn't need a doctor to tell her that. But she called one anyway, and then she called my wife.

Among the pictures my mother kept of my dad and herself during those early days in Washington was a photograph of him standing in front of a car, holding a beer and a stringer of fish. In the photograph he is wearing his hat back on his forehead and has this awkward grin on his face. I asked her for it and she gave it to me, along with some others. I put it up on my wall, and each time we moved, I took the picture along and put it up on another wall. I looked at it carefully from time to time, trying to figure out some things about my dad, and maybe myself in the process. But I couldn't. My dad just kept moving further and further away from me and back into time. Finally, in the course of another move, I lost the photograph. It was then that I tried to recall it, and at the same time make an attempt to say something about my dad, and how I thought that in some important ways we might be alike. I wrote the poem when I was living in an apartment house in an urban area south of San Francisco, at a time when I found myself, like my dad, having trouble with alcohol. The poem was a way of trying to connect up with him.

PHOTOGRAPH OF MY FATHER IN HIS TWENTY-SECOND YEAR

October. Here in this dank, unfamiliar kitchen
I study my father's embarrassed young man's face.
Sheepish grin, he holds in one hand a string
of spiny yellow perch, in the other
a bottle of Carlsberg beer.

In jeans and flannel shirt, he leans
against the front fender of a 1934 Ford.
He would like to pose brave and hearty for his posterity,
wear his old hat cocked over his ear.
All his life my father wanted to be bold.

But the eyes give him away, and the hands
that limply offer the string of dead perch
and the bottle of beer. Father, I love you,
yet how can I say thank you, I who can't hold my liquor either
and don't even know the places to fish.

The poem is true in its particulars, except that my dad died in June 30 and not October, as the first word of the poem says. I wanted a word with more than one syllable to it to make it linger a little. But more than that, I wanted a month appropriate to what I felt at the time I wrote the poem — a month of short days and failing light, smoke in the air, things perishing. June was summer nights and days, graduations, my wedding anniversary, the birthday of one of my children. June wasn't a month your father died in.

After the service at the funeral home, after we had moved outside, a woman I didn't know came over to me and said, "He's happier where he is now." I stared at this woman until she moved away. I still remember the little knob of a hat she was wearing. Then one of my dad's cousins — I didn't know the man's name — reached out and took my hand. "We all miss him," he said, and I knew he wasn't saying it just to be polite.

I began to weep for the first time since receiving the news. I hadn't been able to before. I hadn't had the time, for one thing. Now, suddenly, I couldn't stop. I held my wife and wept while she said and did what she could do to comfort me there in the middle of that summer afternoon.

I listened to people say consoling things to my mother, and I was glad that my dad's family had turned up, had come to where he was. I thought I'd remember everything that was said and done that day and maybe find a way to tell it sometime. But I didn't. I forgot it all, or nearly. What I do remember is that I heard our name used a lot that afternoon, my dad's name and mine. But I knew they were talking about my dad. *Raymond*, these people kept saying in their beautiful voices out of my childhood. *Raymond.*

The Reader's Presence

1. You may have noticed that Carver begins and ends his essay with a reference to his and his father's name. Of what importance is this information at the opening? What do we learn about his relationship with his father through their names? How do names matter in the final paragraph?
2. Though the essay is titled "My Father's Life," Carver throughout uses the word *dad*. Why do you think he chose to do this? What difference does it make? Why do you think Carver used *father* instead of *dad* in the poem he wrote years earlier?
3. Try rereading the essay with particular attention to the conversations between father and son. How many reported conversations can you find? What do the conversations sound like? Can you find any pattern to them? To what extent do these conversations help you understand Carver's relationship with his father?

4 _____

Raymond Carver

Bicycles, Muscles, Cigarettes

Raymond Carver (1938–1988) is best known for his tightly crafted, spare, and often grim short stories. In fact, his mastery of dialogue and his fine eye for detail have made his collections of short stories best-sellers in the United States and abroad. These collections include Where I'm Calling From *(1988), in which "Bicycles, Muscles, Cigarettes" can be found. In 1993 Robert Altman made the critically acclaimed film* Short Cuts *based on a number of Carver's short stories.*

Describing the process of writing fiction, Carver says, "I never start with an idea. I always see something. I start with an image, a cigarette being put out in a jar of mustard, for instance, or the remains, the wreckage, of a dinner left on the table. Pop cans in the fireplace, that sort of thing. And a feeling goes with that. And that feeling seems to transport me back to that particular time and place, and the ambience of time. But it is the image, and the emotion that goes with that image — that's what's important."

For more information on Raymond Carver, see page 23.

It had been two days since Evan Hamilton had stopped smoking, and it seemed to him everything he'd said and thought for two days somehow suggested cigarettes. He looked at his hands under the kitchen light. He sniffed his knuckles and fingers.

"I can smell it," he said.

"I know. It's as if it sweats out of you," Ann Hamilton said. "For three days after I stopped I could smell it on me. Even when I got out of the bath. It was disgusting." She was putting plates on the table for dinner. "I'm so sorry, dear. I know what you're going through. But, if it's any consolation, the second day is always the hardest. The third day is hard, too, of course, but from then on, if you can stay with it that long, you're over the hump. But I'm so happy you're serious about quitting, I can't tell you." She touched his arm. "Now if you'll just call Roger, we'll eat."

Hamilton opened the front door. It was already dark. It was early in November and the days were short and cool. An older boy he had never seen before was sitting on a small, well-equipped bicycle in the driveway. The boy leaned forward just off the seat, the toes of his shoes touching the pavement keeping him upright.

"You Mr. Hamilton?" the boy said. 5

"Yes, I am," Hamilton said. "What is it? Is it Roger?"

"I guess Roger is down at my house talking to my mother. Kip is there and this boy named Gary Berman. It is about my brother's bike. I don't know for sure," the boy said, twisting his handle grips, "but my mother asked me to come and get you. One of Roger's parents."

"But he's all right?" Hamilton said. "Yes, of course, I'll be right with you."

He went into the house to put his shoes on.

"Did you find him?" Ann Hamilton said. 10

"He's in some kind of jam," Hamilton answered. "Over a bicycle. Some boy — I didn't catch his name — is outside. He wants one of us to go back with him to his house."

"Is he all right?" Ann Hamilton said and took her apron off.

"Sure, he's all right." Hamilton looked at her and shook his head. "It sounds like it's just a childish argument, and the boy's mother is getting herself involved."

"Do you want me to go?" Ann Hamilton asked.

He thought for a minute. "Yes, I'd rather you went, but I'll go. Just 15 hold dinner until we're back. We shouldn't be long."

"I don't like his being out after dark," Ann Hamilton said, "I don't like it."

The boy was sitting on his bicycle and working the handbrake now.

"How far?" Hamilton said as they started down the sidewalk.

"Over in Arbuckle Court," the boy answered, and when Hamilton looked at him, the boy added, "Not far. About two blocks from here."

"What seems to be the trouble?" Hamilton asked. 20

"I don't know for sure. I don't understand all of it. He and Kip and this Gary Berman are supposed to have used my brother's bike while we were on vacation, and I guess they wrecked it. On purpose. But I don't know. Anyway, that's what they're talking about. My brother can't find his bike and they had it last, Kip and Roger. My mom is trying to find out where it's at."

"I know Kip," Hamilton said. "Who's this other boy?"

"Gary Berman. I guess he's new in the neighborhood. His dad is coming as soon as he gets home."

They turned a corner. The boy pushed himself along, keeping just slightly ahead. Hamilton saw an orchard, and they turned another corner onto a dead-end street. He hadn't known the existence of this street and was sure he would not recognize any of the people who lived here. He looked around him at the unfamiliar houses and was struck with the range of his son's personal life.

The boy turned into a driveway and got off the bicycle and leaned it   25
against the house. When the boy opened the front door, Hamilton followed him through the living room and into the kitchen, where he saw his son sitting on one side of a table along with Kip Hollister and another boy. Hamilton looked closely at Roger and then he turned to the stout, dark-haired woman at the head of the table.

"You're Roger's father?" the woman said to him.

"Yes, my name is Evan Hamilton. Good evening."

"I'm Mrs. Miller, Gilbert's mother," she said. "Sorry to ask you over here, but we have a problem."

Hamilton sat down in a chair at the other end of the table and looked around. A boy of nine or ten, the boy whose bicycle was missing, Hamilton supposed, sat next to the woman. Another boy, fourteen or so, sat on the draining board, legs dangling, and watched another boy who was talking on the telephone. Grinning slyly at something that had just been said to him over the line, the boy reached over to the sink with a cigarette. Hamilton heard the sound of the cigarette sputting out in a glass of water. The boy who had brought him leaned against the refrigerator and crossed his arms.

"Did you get one of Kip's parents?" the woman said to the boy.   30

"His sister said they were shopping. I went to Gary Berman's and his father will be here in a few minutes. I left the address."

"Mr. Hamilton," the woman said, "I'll tell you what happened. We were on vacation last month and Kip wanted to borrow Gilbert's bike so that Roger could help him with Kip's paper route. I guess Roger's bike had a flat tire or something. Well, as it turns out —"

"Gary was choking me, Dad," Roger said.

"What?" Hamilton said, looking at his son carefully.

"He was choking me. I got the marks." His son pulled down the col-   35
lar of his T-shirt to show his neck.

"They were out in the garage," the woman continued. "I didn't know what they were doing until Curt, my oldest, went out to see."

"He started it!" Gary Berman said to Hamilton. "He called me a jerk." Gary Berman looked toward the front door.

"I think my bike cost about sixty dollars, you guys," the boy named Gilbert said. "You can pay me for it."

"You keep out of this, Gilbert," the woman said to him.

Hamilton took a breath. "Go on," he said.   40

"Well, as it turns out, Kip and Roger used Gilbert's bike to help Kip deliver his papers, and then the two of them, and Gary too, they say, took turns rolling it."

"What do you mean 'rolling it'?" Hamilton said.

"Rolling it," the woman said. "Sending it down the street with a push and letting it fall over. Then, mind you — and they just admitted this a few minutes ago — Kip and Roger took it up to the school and threw it against a goalpost."

"Is that true, Roger?" Hamilton said, looking at his son again.   45

"Part of it's true, Dad," Roger said, looking down and rubbing his finger over the table. "But we only rolled it once. Kip did it, then Gary, and then I did it."

"Once is too much," Hamilton said. "Once is too many times, Roger. I'm surprised and disappointed in you. And you too, Kip," Hamilton said.

"But you see," the woman said, "someone's fibbing tonight or else not telling all he knows, for the fact is the bike's still missing."

The older boys in the kitchen laughed and kidded with the boy who still talked on the telephone.

"We don't know where the bike is, Mrs. Miller," the boy named Kip said. "We told you already. The last time we saw it was when me and Roger took it to my house after we had it at school. I mean, that was the next to the last time. The very last time was when I took it back here the next morning and parked it behind the house." He shook his head. "We don't know where it is," the boy said.

"Sixty dollars," the boy named Gilbert said to the boy named Kip.   50
"You can pay me off like five dollars a week."

"Gilbert, I'm warning you," the woman said. "You see, *they* claim," the woman went on, frowning now, "it disappeared from *here,* from behind the house. But how can we believe them when they haven't been all that truthful this evening?"

"We've told the truth," Roger said. "Everything."

Gilbert leaned back in his chair and shook his head at Hamilton's son.

The doorbell sounded and the boy on the draining board jumped down and went into the living room.

A stiff-shouldered man with a crew haircut and sharp gray eyes entered the kitchen without speaking. He glanced at the woman and moved over behind Gary Berman's chair.   55

"You must be Mr. Berman?" the woman said. "Happy to meet you. I'm Gilbert's mother, and this is Mr. Hamilton, Roger's father."

The man inclined his head at Hamilton but did not offer his hand.

"What's this all about?" Berman said to his son.

The boys at the table began to speak at once.

"Quiet down!" Berman said. "I'm talking to Gary. You'll get your   60
turn."

The boy began his account of the affair. His father listened closely,
now and then narrowing his eyes to study the other two boys.

When Gary Berman had finished, the woman said, "I'd like to get to
the bottom of this. I'm not accusing any one of them, you understand,
Mr. Hamilton, Mr. Berman — I'd just like to get to the bottom of this."
She looked steadily at Roger and Kip, who were shaking their heads at
Gary Berman.

"It's not true, Gary," Roger said.

"Dad, can I talk to you in private?" Gary Berman said.

"Let's go," the man said, and they walked into the living room.   65

Hamilton watched them go. He had the feeling he should stop them,
this secrecy. His palms were wet, and he reached to his shirt pocket for a
cigarette. Then, breathing deeply, he passed the back of his hand under
his nose and said, "Roger, do you know any more about this, other than
what you've already said? Do you know where Gilbert's bike is?"

"No, I don't," the boy said. "I swear it."

"When was the last time you saw the bicycle?" Hamilton said.

"When we brought it home from school and left it at Kip's house."

"Kip," Hamilton said, "do you know where Gilbert's bicycle is   70
now?"

"I swear I don't, either," the boy answered. "I brought it back the
next morning after we had it at school and I parked it behind the
garage."

"I thought you said you left it behind the *house,*" the woman said
quickly.

"I mean the house! That's what I meant," the boy said.

"Did you come back here some other day to ride it?" she asked, leaning forward.

"No, I didn't," Kip answered.   75

"Kip?" she said.

"I didn't! I don't know where it is!" the boy shouted.

The woman raised her shoulders and let them drop. "How do we
know who or what to believe?" she said to Hamilton. "All I know is,
Gilbert's missing a bicycle."

Gary Berman and his father returned to the kitchen.

"It was Roger's idea to roll it," Gary Berman said.   80

"It was yours!" Roger said, coming out of his chair. "You wanted to!
Then you wanted to take it to the orchard and strip it!"

"You shut up!" Berman said to Roger. "You can speak when spoken
to, young man, not before. Gary, I'll handle this — dragged out at night
because of a couple of roughnecks! Now if either of you," Berman said,

looking first at Kip and then Roger, "know where this kid's bicycle is, I'd advise you to start talking."

"I think you're getting out of line," Hamilton said.

"What?" Berman said, his forehead darkening. "And I think you'd do better to mind your own business."

"Let's go, Roger," Hamilton said, standing up. "Kip, you can come   85
now or stay." He turned to the woman. "I don't know what else we can do tonight. I intend to talk this over more with Roger, but if there is a question of restitution I feel since Roger did help manhandle the bike, he can pay a third if it comes to that."

"I don't know what to say," the woman replied, following Hamilton through the living room. "I'll talk to Gilbert's father — he's out of town now. We'll see. It's probably one of those things finally, but I'll talk to his father."

Hamilton moved to one side so that the boys could pass ahead of him onto the porch, and from behind him he heard Gary Berman say, "He called me a jerk, Dad."

"He did, did he?" Hamilton heard Berman say. "Well, he's the jerk. He looks like a jerk."

Hamilton turned and said, "I think you're seriously out of line here tonight, Mr. Berman. Why don't you get control of yourself?"

"And I told you I think you should keep out of it!" Berman said.   90

"You get home, Roger," Hamilton said, moistening his lips. "I mean it," he said, "get going!" Roger and Kip moved out to the sidewalk. Hamilton stood in the doorway and looked at Berman, who was crossing the living room with his son.

"Mr. Hamilton," the woman began nervously but did not finish.

"What do you want?" Berman said to him. "Watch out now, get out of my way!" Berman brushed Hamilton's shoulder and Hamilton stepped off the porch into some prickly cracking bushes. He couldn't believe it was happening. He moved out of the bushes and lunged at the man where he stood on the porch. They fell heavily onto the lawn. They rolled on the lawn, Hamilton wrestling Berman onto his back and coming down hard with his knees on the man's biceps. He had Berman by the collar now and began to pound his head against the lawn while the woman cried, "God almighty, someone stop them! For God's sake, someone call the police!"

Hamilton stopped.

Berman looked up at him and said, "Get off me."   95

"Are you all right?" the woman called to the men as they separated. "For God's sake," she said. She looked at the men, who stood a few feet apart, backs to each other, breathing hard. The older boys had crowded onto the porch to watch; now that it was over, they waited, watching the men, and they began feinting and punching each other on the arms and ribs.

"You boys get back in the house," the woman said. "I never thought I'd see," she said and put her hand on her breast.

Hamilton was sweating and his lungs burned when he tried to take a deep breath. There was a ball of something in his throat so that he couldn't swallow for a minute. He started walking, his son and the boy named Kip at his sides. He heard car doors slam, an engine start. Headlights swept over him as he walked.

Roger sobbed once, and Hamilton put his arm around the boy's shoulders.

"I better get home," Kip said and began to cry. "My dad'll be look-   100
ing for me," and the boy ran.

"I'm sorry," Hamilton said. "I'm sorry you had to see something like that," Hamilton said to his son.

They kept walking and when they reached their block, Hamilton took his arm away.

"What if he'd picked up a knife, Dad? Or a club?"

"He wouldn't have done anything like that," Hamilton said.

"But what if he had?" his son said.   105

"It's hard to say what people will do when they're angry," Hamilton said.

They started up the walk to their door. His heart moved when Hamilton saw the lighted windows.

"Let me feel your muscle," his son said.

"Not now," Hamilton said. "You better just go in now and have your dinner and hurry up to bed. Tell your mother I'm all right and I'm going to sit on the porch for a few minutes."

The boy rocked from one foot to the other and looked at his father,   110
and then he dashed into the house and began calling, "Mom! Mom!"

He sat on the porch and leaned against the garage wall and stretched his legs. The sweat had dried on his forehead. He felt clammy under his clothes.

He had once seen his father — a pale, slow-talking man with slumped shoulders — in something like this. It was a bad one, and both men had been hurt. It had happened in a café. The other man was a farmhand. Hamilton had loved his father and could recall many things about him. But now he recalled his father's one fistfight as if it were all there was to the man.

He was still sitting on the porch when his wife came out.

"Dear God," she said and took his head in her hands. "Come in and shower and then have something to eat and tell me about it. Everything is still warm. Roger has gone to bed."

But he heard his son calling him.   115

"He's still awake," she said.

"I'll be down in a minute," Hamilton said, "Then maybe we should have a drink."

She shook her head. "I really don't believe any of this yet."

He went into the boy's room and sat down at the foot of the bed.

"It's pretty late and you're still up, so I'll say good night," Hamilton   120
said.

"Good night," the boy said, hands behind his neck, elbows jutting.

He was in his pajamas and had a warm fresh smell about him that
Hamilton breathed deeply. He patted his son through the covers.

"You take it easy from now on. Stay away from that part of the
neighborhood, and don't let me ever hear of you damaging a bicycle or
any other personal property. Is that clear?" Hamilton said.

The boy nodded. He took his hands from behind his neck and began
picking at something on the bedspread.

"Okay, then," Hamilton said, "I'll say goodnight."   125

He moved to kiss his son, but the boy began talking.

"Dad, was Grandfather strong like you? When he was your age, I
mean, you know, and you —"

"And I was nine years old? Is that what you mean? Yes, I guess he
was," Hamilton said.

"Sometimes I can hardly remember him," the boy said. "I don't
want to forget him or anything, you know? You know what I mean,
Dad?"

When Hamilton did not answer at once, the boy went on. "When   130
you were young, was it like it is with you and me? Did you love him more
than me? Or just the same?" The boy said this abruptly. He moved his
feet under the covers and looked away. When Hamilton still did not answer, the boy said, "Did he smoke? I think I remember a pipe or something."

"He started smoking a pipe before he died, that's true," Hamilton
said. "He used to smoke cigarettes a long time ago and then he'd get depressed with something or other and quit, but later he'd change brands
and start in again. Let me show you something," Hamilton said. "Smell
the back of my hand."

The boy took the hand in his, sniffed it, and said, "I guess I don't
smell anything, Dad. What is it?"

Hamilton sniffed the hand and then the fingers. "Now I can't smell
anything either," he said. "It was there before, but now it's gone." Maybe
it was scared out of me, he thought. "I wanted to show you something.
All right, it's late now. You better go to sleep," Hamilton said.

The boy rolled onto his side and watched his father walk to the door
and watched him put his hand to the switch. And then the boy said,
"Dad? You'll think I'm pretty crazy, but I wish I'd known you when you
were little. I mean, about as old as I am now. I don't know how to say it,
but I'm lonesome about it. It's like — it's like I miss you already if I think
about it now. That's pretty crazy, isn't it? Anyway, please leave the door
open."

Hamilton left the door open, and then he thought better of it and   135
closed it halfway.

The Reader's Presence

1. Carver begins his story with Hamilton's attempt to quit smoking. How do cigarettes function in this story? Of what significance are they?

2. Consider the story's title carefully. Why do you think Carver chose this title? Do the three items have anything in common? What kinds of experiences do they each represent? Often titles point the reader in the direction of a story's central meaning. Does "Bicycles, Muscles, Cigarettes" do this? Why, or why not?

3. Like his autobiographical essay, "My Father's Life," Carver's "Bicycles, Muscles, Cigarettes" deals with the relationship between a father and son. Can you find any elements of Carver's own life in this story? Do you see any indications of Carver's having projected characteristics of his own father onto Evan Hamilton, or onto Hamilton's father?

5

Judith Ortiz Cofer

Silent Dancing

Born in Puerto Rico in 1952, Judith Ortiz Cofer moved to the United States in 1960. Her poetry has appeared in numerous literary magazines, and several collections of her poems have been published. Her first novel, The Line of the Sun *(1989), was nominated for the Pulitzer Prize. "Silent Dancing" is from Cofer's 1990 essay collection,* Silent Dancing: A Partial Remembrance of a Puerto Rican Childhood. *Her most recent books are* The Latin Deli: Prose and Poetry *(1993) and* An Island Like You: Stories of the Barrio *(1995).*

Reflecting on her life as a writer, Cofer has said, "The 'infinite variety' and power of language interest me. I never cease to experiment with it. As a native Puerto Rican, my first language was Spanish. It was a challenge, not only to learn English, but to master it enough to teach it and — the ultimate goal — to write poetry in it." Cofer is currently associate professor of English at the University of Georgia.

We have a home movie of this party. Several times my mother and I have watched it together, and I have asked questions about the silent revelers coming in and out of focus. It is grainy and of short duration, but it's a great visual aid to my memory of life at that time. And it is in color—-the only complete scene in color I can recall from those years.

We lived in Puerto Rico until my brother was born in 1954. Soon after, because of economic pressures of our growing family, my father joined the United States Navy. He was assigned to duty on a ship in Brooklyn Yard — a place of cement and steel that was to be his home base in the States until his retirement more than twenty years later. He left the Island first, alone, going to New York City and tracking down his uncle who lived with his family across the Hudson River in Paterson, New Jersey. There my father found a tiny apartment in a huge tenement that had once housed Jewish families but was just being taken over and transformed by Puerto Ricans, overflowing from New York City. In 1955 he sent for us. My mother was only twenty years old, I was not quite three, and my brother was a toddler when we arrived at *El Building*, as the place had been christened by its newest residents.

My memories of life in Paterson during those first few years are all in shades of gray. Maybe I was too young to absorb vivid colors and details, or to discriminate between the slate blue of the winter sky and the darker hues of the snow-bearing clouds, but that single color washes over the whole period. The building we lived in was gray, as were the streets, filled with slush the first few months of my life there. The coat my father had bought for me was similar in color and too big; it sat heavily on my thin frame.

I do remember the way the heater pipes banged and rattled, startling all of us out of sleep until we got so used to the sound that we automatically shut it out or raised our voices above the racket. The hiss from the valve punctuated my sleep (which has always been fitful) like a nonhuman presence in the room — a dragon sleeping at the entrance of my childhood. But the pipes were also a connection to all the other lives being lived around us. Having come from a house designed for a single family back in Puerto Rico — my mother's extended-family home — it was curious to know that strangers lived under our floor and above our heads, and that the heater pipe went through everyone's apartments. (My first spanking in Paterson came as a result of playing tunes on the pipes in my room to see if there would be an answer.) My mother was as new to this concept of beehive life as I was, but she had been given strict orders by my father to keep the doors locked, the noise down, ourselves to ourselves.

It seems that Father had learned some painful lessons about prejudice   5 while searching for an apartment in Paterson. Not until years later did I hear how much resistance he had encountered with landlords who were panicking at the influx of Latinos into a neighborhood that had been Jewish for a couple of generations. It made no difference that it was the American phenomenon of ethnic turnover which was changing the urban core of Paterson, and that the human flood could not be held back with an accusing finger.

"You Cuban?" one man had asked my father, pointing at his name tag on the Navy uniform — even though my father had the fair skin and

light-brown hair of his northern Spanish background, and the name Ortiz
is as common in Puerto Rico as Johnson is in the United States.

"No," my father had answered, looking past the finger into his adversary's angry eyes. "I'm Puerto Rican."

"Same shit." And the door closed.

My father could have passed as European, but we couldn't. My
brother and I both have our mother's black hair and olive skin, and so we
lived in El Building and visited our great-uncle and his fair children on the
next block. It was their private joke that they were the German branch of
the family. Not many years later that area too would be mainly Puerto
Rican. It was as if the heart of the city map were being gradually colored
brown — *café con leche*[1] brown. Our color.

The movie opens with a sweep of the living room. It is "typical" im-   10
*migrant Puerto Rican decor for the time: The sofa and chairs are square
and hard-looking, upholstered in bright colors (blue and yellow in this instance), and covered with the transparent plastic that furniture salesmen
then were so adept at convincing women to buy. The linoleum on the
floor is light blue; if it had been subjected to spike heels (as it was in most
places), there were dime-sized indentations all over it that cannot be seen
in this movie. The room is full of people dressed up: dark suits for the
men, red dresses for the women. When I have asked my mother why most
of the women are in red that night, she has shrugged, "I don't remember.
Just a coincidence." She doesn't have my obsession for assigning symbol-
ism to everything.*

*The three women in red sitting on the couch are my mother, my eigh-
teen-year-old cousin, and her brother's girlfriend. The novia is just up
from the Island, which is apparent in her body language. She sits up formally, her dress pulled over her knees. She is a pretty girl, but her posture
makes her look insecure, lost in her full-skirted dress, which she has carefully tucked around her to make room for my gorgeous cousin, her future
sister-in-law. My cousin has grown up in Paterson and is in her last year
of high school. She doesn't have a trace of what Puerto Ricans call* la
mancha *(literally, the stain: the mark of the new immigrant — something
about the posture, the voice, or the humble demeanor that makes it obvious to everyone the person has just arrived on the mainland). My cousin
is wearing a tight, sequined, cocktail dress. Her brown hair has been
lightened with peroxide around the bangs, and she is holding a cigarette
expertly between her fingers, bringing it up to her mouth in a sensuous
arc of her arm as she talks animatedly. My mother, who has come up to
sit between the two women, both only a few years younger then herself, is
somewhere between the poles they represent in our culture.*

[1]*café con leche:* Coffee with cream. In Puerto Rico it is sometimes prepared with
boiled milk. — COFER'S NOTE.

It became my father's obsession to get out of the barrio, and thus we were never permitted to form bonds with the place or with the people who lived there. Yet El Building was a comfort to my mother, who never got over yearning for *la isla*. She felt surrounded by her language: The walls were thin, and voices speaking and arguing in Spanish could be heard all day. *Salsas* blasted out of radios, turned on early in the morning and left on for company. Women seemed to cook rice and beans perpetually — the strong aroma of boiling red kidney beans permeated the hallways.

Though Father preferred that we do our grocery shopping at the supermarket when he came home on weekend leaves, my mother insisted that she could cook only with products whose labels she could read. Consequently, during the week I accompanied her and my little brother to *La Bodega* — a hole-in-the-wall grocery store across the street from El Building. There we squeezed down three narrow aisles jammed with various products. Goya's and Libby's — those were the trademarks that were trusted by *her mamá*, so my mother bought many cans of Goya beans, soups, and condiments, as well as little cans of Libby's fruit juices for us. And she also bought Colgate toothpaste and Palmolive soap. (The final *e* is pronounced in both these products in Spanish, so for many years I believed that they were manufactured on the Island. I remember my surprise at first hearing a commercial on television in which Colgate rhymed with "ate.") We always lingered at La Bodega, for it was there that Mother breathed best, taking in the familiar aromas of the foods she knew from Mamá's kitchen. It was also there that she got to speak to the other women of El Building without violating outright Father's dictates against fraternizing with our neighbors.

Yet Father did his best to make our "assimilation" painless. I can still see him carrying a real Christmas tree up several flights of stairs to our apartment, leaving a trail of aromatic pine. He carried it formally, as if it were a flag in a parade. We were the only ones in El Building that I knew of who got presents on both Christmas day AND *dia de Reyes,* the day when the Three Kings brought gifts to Christ and to Hispanic children.

Our supreme luxury in El Building was having our own television set.   15 It must have been a result of Father's guilt feelings over the isolation he had imposed on us, but we were among the first in the barrio to have one. My brother quickly became an avid watcher of Captain Kangaroo and Jungle Jim, while I loved all the series showing families. By the time I started first grade, I could have drawn a map of Middle America as exemplified by the lives of characters in "Father Knows Best," "The Donna Reed Show," "Leave It to Beaver," "My Three Sons," and (my favorite) "Bachelor Father," where John Forsythe treated his adopted teenage daughter like a princess because he was rich and had a Chinese houseboy to do everything for him. In truth, compared to our neighbors in El Building, *we* were rich. My father's Navy check provided us with financial security and a standard of life that the factory workers envied. The only thing his money could not buy us was a place to live away from the barrio — his greatest wish, Mother's greatest fear.

In the home movie the men are shown next, sitting around a card table set up in one corner of the living room, playing dominoes. The clack of the ivory pieces was a familiar sound. I heard it in many houses on the Island and in many apartments in Paterson. In "Leave It to Beaver," the Cleavers played bridge in every other episode; in my childhood, the men started every social occasion with a hotly debated round of dominoes. The women would sit around and watch, but they never participated in the games.

Here and there you can see a small child. Children were always brought to parties and, whenever they got sleepy, were put to bed in the host's bedroom. Babysitting was a concept unrecognized by the Puerto Rican women I knew: A responsible mother did not leave her children with any stranger. And in a culture where children are not considered intrusive, there was no need to leave the children at home. We went where our mother went.

Of my preschool years I have only impressions: the sharp bite of the wind in December as we walked with our parents toward the brightly lit stores downtown; how I felt like a stuffed doll in my heavy coat, boots, and mittens; how good it was to walk into the five-and-dime and sit at the counter drinking hot chocolate. On Saturdays our whole family would walk downtown to shop at the big department stores on Broadway. Mother bought all our clothes at Penney's and Sears, and she liked to buy her dresses at the women's specialty shops like Lerner's and Diana's. At some point we'd go into Woolworth's and sit at the soda fountain to eat.

We never ran into other Latinos at these stores or when eating out, and it became clear to me only years later that the women from El Building shopped mainly in other places — stores owned by other Puerto Ricans or by Jewish merchants who had philosophically accepted our presence in the city and decided to make us their good customers, if not real neighbors and friends. These establishments were located not downtown but in the blocks around our street, and they were referred to generically as *La Tienda, El Bazar, La Bodega, La Botánica*. Everyone knew what was meant. These were the stores where your face did not turn a clerk to stone, where your money was as green as anyone else's.

One New Year's Eve we were dressed up like child models in the   20
Sears catalogue: my brother in a miniature man's suit and bow tie, and I in black patent-leather shoes and a frilly dress with several layers of crinoline underneath. My mother wore a bright red dress that night, I remember, and spike heels; her long black hair hung to her waist. Father, who usually wore his Navy uniform during his short visits home, had put on a dark civilian suit for the occasion: We had been invited to his uncle's

house for a big celebration. Everyone was excited because my mother's brother Hernan — a bachelor who could indulge himself with luxuries — had bought a home movie camera, which he would be trying out that night.

Even the home movie cannot fill in the sensory details such a gathering left imprinted in a child's brain. The thick sweetness of women's perfumes mixing with the ever-present smells of food cooking in the kitchen: meat and plantain *pasteles,* as well as the ubiquitous rice dish made special with pigeon peas — *gandules* — and seasoned with precious *sofrito*[2] sent up from the Island by somebody's mother or smuggled in by a recent traveler. *Sofrito* was one of the items that women hoarded, since it was hardly ever in stock at La Bodega. It was the flavor of Puerto Rico.

The men drank Palo Viejo rum, and some of the younger ones got weepy. The first time I saw a grown man cry was at a New Year's Eve party: He had been reminded of his mother by the smells in the kitchen. But what I remember most were the boiled *pasteles* — plantain or yucca rectangles stuffed with corned beef or other meats, olives, and many other savory ingredients, all wrapped in banana leaves. Everybody had to fish one out with a fork. There was always a "trick" pastel — one without stuffing — and whoever got that one was the "New Year's Fool."

There was also the music. Long-playing albums were treated like precious china in these homes. Mexican recordings were popular, but the songs that brought tears to my mother's eyes were sung by the melancholy Daniel Santos, whose life as a drug addict was the stuff of legend. Felipe Rodríguez was a particular favorite of couples, since he sang about faithless women and brokenhearted men. There is a snatch of one lyric that has stuck in my mind like a needle on a worn groove: *De piedra ha de ser mi cama, de piedra la cabezera . . . la mujer que a mi me quiera . . . ha de quererme de veras. Ay, Ay, Ay, corazón, porque no amas.*[3] . . . I must have heard it a thousand times since the idea of a bed made of stone, and its connection to love, first troubled me with its disturbing images.

The five-minute home movie ends with people dancing in a circle — the creative filmmaker must have set it up, so that all of them could file past him. It is both comical and sad to watch silent dancing. Since there is no justification for the absurd movements that music provides for some of us, people appear frantic, their faces embarrassingly intense. It's as if you were watching sex. Yet for years I've had dreams in the form of this home movie. In a recurring scene, familiar faces push themselves forward

[2]*sofrito:* A cooked condiment. A sauce composed of a mixture of fatback, ham, tomatoes, and many island spices and herbs. It is added to many typical Puerto Rican dishes for a distinctive flavor. — COFER'S NOTE.

[3]*De piedra ha de ser . . . amas:* Lyrics from a popular romantic ballad (called a *bolero* in Puerto Rico). Freely translated: "My bed will be made of stone, of stone also my headrest (or pillow), the woman who (dares to) loves me, will have to love me for real. Ay, Ay, Ay, my heart, why can't you (let me) love. . . ." — COFER'S NOTE.

into my mind's eyes, plastering their features into distorted close-ups. And I'm asking them: "Who is *she*? Who is the old woman I don't recognize? Is she an aunt? Somebody's wife? Tell me who she is."

"See the beauty mark on her cheek as big as a hill on the lunar landscape of her face — well, that runs in the family. The women on your father's side of the family wrinkle early; it's the price they pay for that fair skin. The young girl with the green stain on her wedding dress is *La Novia* — just up from the Island. See, she lowers her eyes when she approaches the camera, as she's supposed to. Decent girls never look at you directly in the face. *Humilde*, humble, a girl should express humility in all her actions. She will make a good wife for your cousin. He should consider himself lucky to have met her only weeks after she arrived here. If he marries her quickly, she will make him a good Puerto Rican–style wife; but if he waits too long, she will be corrupted by the city — just like your cousin there."

"She means me. I do what I want. This is not some primitive island I live on. Do they expect me to wear a black mantilla on my head and go to mass every day? Not me. I'm an American woman, and I will do as I please. I can type faster than anyone in my senior class at Central High, and I'm going to be a secretary to a lawyer when I graduate. I can pass for an American girl anywhere — I've tried it. At least for Italian, anyway — I never speak Spanish in public. I hate these parties, but I wanted the dress. I look better than any of these *humildes* here. *My* life is going to be different. I have an American boyfriend. He is older and has a car. My parents don't know it, but I sneak out of the house late at night sometimes to be with him. If I marry him, even my name will be American. I hate rice and beans — that's what makes these women fat."

"Your *prima*[4] is pregnant by that man she's been sneaking around with. Would I lie to you? I'm your *Tía Política*,[5] your great-uncle's common-law wife — the one he abandoned on the Island to go marry your cousin's mother. *I* was not invited to this party, of course, but I came anyway. I came to tell you that story about your cousin that you've always wanted to hear. Do you remember the comment your mother made to a neighbor that has always haunted you? The only thing you heard was your cousin's name, and then you saw your mother pick up your doll from the couch and say: 'It was as big as this doll when they flushed it down the toilet.' This image has bothered you for years, hasn't it? You had nightmares about babies being flushed down the toilet, and you wondered why anyone would do such a horrible thing. You didn't dare ask your mother about it. She would only tell you that you had not heard her right, and yell at you for listening to adult conversations. But later, when you were old enough to know about abortions, you suspected.

"I am here to tell you that you were right. Your cousin was growing an *Americanito* in her belly when this movie was made. Soon after she put something long and pointy into her pretty self, thinking maybe she could get rid of the problem before breakfast and still make it to her first class at the

---

[4]*prima:* Female cousin. — COFER'S NOTE.
[5]*Tía Política:* Aunt by marriage. — COFER'S NOTE.

high school. Well, *Niña*,[6] her screams could be heard downtown. Your aunt, her mamá, who had been a midwife on the Island, managed to pull the little thing out. Yes, they probably flushed it down the toilet. What else could they do with it — give it a Christian burial in a little white casket with blue bows and ribbons? Nobody wanted that baby — least of all the father, a teacher at her school with a house in West Paterson that he was filling with real children, and a wife who was a natural blonde.

"Girl, the scandal sent your uncle back to the bottle. And guess where your cousin ended up? Irony of ironies. She was sent to a village in Puerto Rico to live with a relative on her mother's side: a place so far away from civilization that you have to ride a mule to reach it. A real change in scenery. She found a man there — women like that cannot live without male company — but believe me, the men in Puerto Rico know how a put a saddle on a woman like her. *La Gringa*,[7] they call her. Ha, ha, ha. *La Gringa* is what she always wanted to be. . . ."

The old woman's mouth becomes a cavernous black hole I fall into. And as I fall, I can feel the reverberations of her laughter. I hear the echoes of her last mocking words: *La Gringa, La Gringa!* And the conga line keeps moving silently past me. There is no music in my dream for the dancers.

When Odysseus visits Hades to see the spirit of his mother, he makes   25
an offering of sacrificial blood, but since all the souls crave an audience with the living, he has to listen to many of them before he can ask questions. I, too, have to hear the dead and the forgotten speak in my dream. Those who are still part of my life remain silent, going around and around in their dance. The others keep pressing their faces forward to say things about the past.

My father's uncle is last in line. He is dying of alcoholism, shrunken and shriveled like a monkey, his face a mass of wrinkles and broken arteries. As he comes closer I realize that in his features I can see my whole family. If you were to stretch that rubbery flesh, you could find my father's face, and deep within *that* face — my own. I don't want to look into those eyes ringed in purple. In a few years he will retreat into silence, and take a long, long time to die. *Move back, Tio,* I tell him. *I don't want to hear what you have to say. Give the dancers room to move. Soon it will be midnight. Who is the New Year's Fool this time?*

The Reader's Presence

1. "Silent Dancing" explores the personal, familial, and communal transformations that resulted from moving in the 1950s to Paterson, New Jersey — to "a huge tenement that had once housed

---

[6]*Niña:* Girl. — COFER'S NOTE.
[7]*La Gringa:* Derogatory epithet used here to ridicule a Puerto Rican girl who wants to look like a blonde North American. — COFER'S NOTE.

Jewish families," and to a new community that emerged from the sprawling barrio that Puerto Ricans "overflowing from New York City" called home. Reread the essay carefully, and summarize the transformations that occurred in the life of the narrator, her family, and their larger Puerto Rican community.

2. Judith Ortiz Cofer uses an account of a home movie to create a structure for her essay. Comment on the specific advantages and disadvantages of this strategy. How, for example, does the home movie serve as "a great visual aid" to recounting life in the barrio of Paterson, New Jersey? What effect does the fact that the home movie is in color have on what she notices? on how she writes?

3. Because Cofer's essay is built around the occasion of watching a home movie, the narrator assumes the position of an observer of the scenes and people she describes. What specific strategies as a writer does Cofer use to establish a presence for herself in this narrative and descriptive account of growing up?

6

Bernard Cooper

A Clack of Tiny Sparks: Remembrances of a Gay Boyhood

Born (1951), raised, and still residing in Los Angeles, Bernard Cooper received his B.F.A. and M.F.A. from the California Institute of the Arts. He has taught at the Otis/Parsons Institute of Art and Design and Southern California Institute of Architecture, Los Angeles. His collection of essays, Maps to Anywhere *(1990), covers a wide range of topics as varying as the aging of his father, the extinction of the dinosaur, and the future of American life and culture. Cooper contributes to various periodicals such as* Harper's, *where "A Clack of Tiny Sparks: Remembrances of a Gay Boyhood" first appeared in January 1991. His most recent book is* Truth Serum: Memoirs *(1996).*

Commenting on his 1993 novel, A Year of Rhymes, *Cooper notes, "One of the reasons why there is so much detail in my work is that I'm a person that essentially shies away from abstractions, from Large Issues and Big Ideas. The world only seems real and vivid and meaningful to me in the smaller details, what's heard and felt and smelled and tasted."*

Theresa Sanchez sat behind me in ninth-grade algebra. When Mr. Hubbley faced the blackboard, I'd turn around to see what she was read-

ing; each week a new book was wedged inside her copy of *Today's Equations.* The deception worked; from Mr. Hubbley's point of view, Theresa
was engrossed in the value of *X,* but I knew otherwise. One week she pe-
rused *The Wisdom of the Orient,* and I could tell from Theresa's contemplative expression that the book contained exotic thoughts, guidelines
handed down from high. Another week it was a paperback novel whose
title, *Let Me Live My Life,* appeared in bold print atop every page, and
whose cover, a gauzy photograph of a woman biting a strand of pearls,
head thrown back in an attitude of ecstasy, confirmed my suspicion that
Theresa Sanchez was mature beyond her years. She was the tallest girl in
school. Her bouffant hairdo, streaked with blond, was higher than the
flaccid bouffants of other girls. Her smooth skin, plucked eyebrows, and
painted fingernails suggested hours of pampering, a worldly and sensual
vanity that placed her within the domain of adults. Smiling dimly, steeped
in daydreams, Theresa moved through the crowded halls with a languid,
self-satisfied indifference to those around her. "You are merely children,"
her posture seemed to say. "I can't be bothered." The week Theresa hid
101 Ways to Cook Hamburger behind her algebra book, I could stand it
no longer and, after the bell rang, ventured a question.
    "Because I'm having a dinner party," said Theresa. "Just a couple of
intimate friends."
    No fourteen-year-old I knew had ever given a dinner party, let alone
used the word "intimate" in conversation. "Don't you have a mother?" I
asked.
    Theresa sighed a weary sigh, suffered my strange inquiry. "Don't be so
naive," she said. "Everyone has a mother." She waved her hand to indicate
the brick school buildings outside the window. "A higher education should
have taught you that." Theresa draped an angora sweater over her shoulders, scooped her books from the graffiti-covered desk, and just as she was
about to walk away, she turned and asked me, "Are you a fag?"
    There wasn't the slightest hint of rancor or condescension in her   5
voice. The tone was direct, casual. Still I was stunned, giving a sidelong
glance to make sure no one had heard. "No," I said. Blurted really, with
too much defensiveness, too much transparent fear in my response. Oc-
taves lower than usual, I tried a "Why?"
    Theresa shrugged. "Oh, I don't know. I have lots of friends who are
fags. You remind me of them." Seeing me bristle, Theresa added, "It was
just a guess." I watched her erect, angora back as she sauntered out the
classroom door.
    She had made an incisive and timely guess. Only days before, I'd in-
vited Grady Rogers to my house after school to go swimming. The instant
Grady shot from the pool, shaking water from his orange hair, freckled
shoulders shining, my attraction to members of my own sex became a
matter I could no longer suppress or rationalize. Sturdy and boisterous
and gap-toothed, Grady was an inveterate backslapper, a formidable arm
wrestler, a wizard at basketball. Grady was a boy at home in his body.

My body was a marvel I hadn't gotten used to; my arms and legs would sometimes act of their own accord, knocking over a glass at dinner or flinching at an oncoming pitch. I was never singled out as a sissy, but I could have been just as easily as Bobby Keagan, a gentle, intelligent, and introverted boy reviled by my classmates. And although I had always been aware of a tacit rapport with Bobby, a suspicion that I might find with him a rich friendship, I stayed away. Instead, I emulated Grady in the belief that being seen with him, being like him, would somehow vanquish my self-doubt, would make me normal by association.

Apart from his athletic prowess, Grady had been gifted with all the trappings of what I imagined to be a charmed life: a fastidious, aproned mother who radiated calm, maternal concern; a ruddy, stoic father with a knack for home repairs. Even the Rogerses' small suburban house in Hollywood, with its spindly Colonial furniture and chintz curtains, was a testament to normalcy.

Grady and his family bore little resemblance to my clan of Eastern   10
European Jews, a dark and vociferous people who ate with abandon — matzo and halvah and gefilte fish; foods the goyim couldn't pronounce — who cajoled one another during endless games of canasta, making the simplest remark about the weather into a lengthy philosophical discourse on the sun and the seasons and the passage of time. My mother was a chain-smoker, a dervish in a frowsy housedress. She showed her love in the most peculiar and obsessive ways, like spending hours extracting every seed from a watermelon before she served it in perfectly bite-sized, geometric pieces. Preoccupied and perpetually frantic, my mother succumbed to bouts of absentmindedness so profound she'd forget what she was saying midsentence, smile and blush and walk away. A divorce attorney, my father wore roomy, iridescent suits, and the intricacies, the deceits inherent in his profession, had the effect of making him forever tense and vigilant. He was "all wound up," as my mother put it. But when he relaxed, his laughter was explosive, his disposition prankish: "Walk this way," a waitress would say, leading us to our table, and my father would mimic the way she walked, arms akimbo, hips liquid, while my mother and I were wracked with laughter. Buoyant or brooding, my parents' moods were unpredictable, and in a household fraught with extravagant emotion it was odd and awful to keep my longing secret.

One day I made the mistake of asking my mother what a "fag" was. I knew exactly what Theresa had meant but hoped against hope it was not what I thought; maybe "fag" was some French word, a harmless term like "naive." My mother turned from the stove, flew at me, and grabbed me by the shoulders. "Did someone call you that?" she cried.

"Not me," I said. "Bobby Keagan."

"Oh," she said, loosening her grip. She was visibly relieved. And didn't answer. The answer was unthinkable.

For weeks after, I shook with the reverberations from that afternoon in the kitchen with my mother, pained by the memory of her shocked expression and, most of all, her silence. My longing was wrong in the eyes of my mother, whose hazel eyes were the eyes of the world, and if that longing continued unchecked, the unwieldy shape of my fate would be cast, and I'd be subjected to a lifetime of scorn.

During the remainder of the semester, I became the scientist of my own desire, plotting ways to change my yearning for boys into a yearning for girls. I had enough evidence to believe that any habit, regardless of how compulsive, how deeply ingrained, could be broken once and for all: The plastic cigarette my mother purchased at the Thrifty pharmacy — one end was red to approximate an ember, the other tan like a filtered tip — was designed to wean her from the real thing. To change a behavior required self-analysis, cold resolve, and the substitution of one thing for another: plastic, say, for tobacco. Could I also find a substitute for Grady? What I needed to do, I figured, was kiss a girl and learn to like it.

This conclusion was affirmed one Sunday morning when my father, seeing me wrinkle my nose at the pink slabs of lox he layered on a bagel, tried to convince me of its salty appeal. "You should try some," he said. "You don't know what you're missing."

"It's loaded with protein," added my mother, slapping a platter of sliced onions onto the dinette table. She hovered above us, cinching her housedress, eyes wet from onion fumes, the mock cigarette dangling from her lips.

My father sat there chomping with gusto, emitting a couple of hearty grunts to dramatize his satisfaction. And still I was not convinced. After a loud and labored swallow, he told me I may not be fond of lox today, but sooner or later I'd learn to like it. One's tastes, he assured me, are destined to change.

"Live," shouted my mother over the rumble of the Mixmaster. "Expand your horizons. Try new things." And the room grew fragrant with the batter of a spice cake.

The opportunity to put their advice into practice, and try out my plan to adapt to girls, came the following week when Debbie Coburn, a member of Mr. Hubbley's algebra class, invited me to a party. She cornered me in the hall, furtive as a spy, telling me her parents would be gone for the evening and slipping into my palm a wrinkled sheet of notebook paper. On it were her address and telephone number, the lavender ink in a tidy cursive. "Wear cologne," she advised, wary eyes darting back and forth. "It's a make-out party. Anything can happen."

The Santa Ana wind blew relentlessly the night of Debbie's party, careening down the slopes of the Hollywood hills, shaking the road signs and stoplights in its path. As I walked down Beachwood Avenue, trees thrashed, surrendered their leaves, and carob pods bombarded the pavement. The sky was a deep but luminous blue, the air hot, abrasive, electric. I had to squint in order to check the number of the Coburns' apartment, a three-story building with glitter embedded in its stucco walls. Above the honeycombed balconies was a sign that read BEACHWOOD TERRACE in lavender script resembling Debbie's.

From down the hall, I could hear the plaintive strains of Little Anthony's "I Think I'm Going Out of My Head." Debbie answered the door bedecked in an Empire dress, the bodice blue and orange polka dots, the rest a sheath of black and white stripes. "Op art," proclaimed Debbie. She turned in a circle, then proudly announced that she'd rolled her hair in orange juice cans. She patted the huge unmoving curls and dragged me inside. Reflections from the swimming pool in the courtyard, its surface ruffled by wind, shuddered over the ceiling and walls. A dozen of my classmates were seated on the sofa or huddled together in corners, their whispers full of excited imminence, their bodies barely discernible in the dim light. Drapes flanking the sliding glass doors bowed out with every gust of wind, and it seemed that the room might lurch from its foundations and sail with its cargo of silhouettes into the hot October night.

Grady was the last to arrive. He tossed a six-pack of beer into Debbie's arms, barreled toward me, and slapped my back. His hair was slicked back with Vitalis, lacquered furrows left by the comb. The wind hadn't shifted a single hair. "Ya ready?" he asked, flashing the gap between his front teeth and leering into the darkened room. "You bet," I lied.

Once the beers had been passed around, Debbie provoked everyone's attention by flicking on the overhead light. "Okay," she called. "Find a partner." This was the blunt command of a hostess determined to have her guests aroused in an orderly fashion. Everyone blinked, shuffled about, and grabbed a member of the opposite sex. Sheila Garabedian landed beside me — entirely at random, though I wanted to believe she was driven by passion — her timid smile giving way to plain fear as the light went out. Nothing for a moment but the heave of the wind and the distant banter of dogs. I caught a whiff of Sheila's perfume, tangy and sweet as Hawaiian Punch. I probed her face with my own, grazing the small scallop of an ear, a velvety temple, and though Sheila's trembling made me want to stop, I persisted with my mission until I found her lips, tightly sealed as a private letter. I held my mouth over hers and gathered her shoulders closer, resigned to the possibility that, no matter how long we stood there, Sheila would be too scared to kiss me back. Still, she exhaled through her nose, and I listened to the squeak of every breath as though it were a sigh of inordinate pleasure. Diving within myself, I monitored my heartbeat and respiration, trying to will stimulation into being, and all the while an image intruded, an image of Grady erupting from our pool, rivulets of water sliding down his chest. "Change," shouted Debbie, switching on the light. Sheila thanked me, pulled away, and continued her routine of gracious terror with every boy throughout the evening. It didn't matter whom I held — Margaret Sims, Betty Vernon, Elizabeth Lee — my experiment was a failure; I continued to picture Grady's wet chest, and Debbie would bellow "change" with such fervor, it could have been my own voice, my own incessant reprimand.

Our hostess commandeered the light switch for nearly half an hour.   25
Whenever the light came on, I watched Grady pivot his head toward the

newest prospect, his eyebrows arched in expectation, his neck blooming with hickeys, his hair, at last, in disarray. All that shuffling across the carpet charged everyone's arms and lips with static, and eventually, between low moans and soft osculations, I could hear the clack of tiny sparks and see them flare here and there in the dark like meager, short-lived stars.

I saw Theresa, sultry and aloof as ever, read three more books — *North American Reptiles, Bonjour Tristesse,* and *MGM: A Pictorial History* — before she vanished early in December. Rumors of her fate abounded. Debbie Coburn swore that Theresa had been "knocked up" by an older man, a traffic cop, she thought, or a grocer. Nearly quivering with relish, Debbie told me and Grady about the home for unwed mothers in the San Fernando Valley, a compound teeming with pregnant girls who had nothing to do but touch their stomachs and contemplate their mistake. Even Bobby Keagan, who took Theresa's place behind me in algebra, had a theory regarding her disappearance colored by his own wish for escape; he imagined that Theresa, disillusioned with society, booked passage to a tropical island, there to live out the rest of her days without restrictions or ridicule. "No wonder she flunked out of school," I overheard Mr. Hubbley tell a fellow teacher one afternoon. "Her head was always in a book."

Along with Theresa went my secret, or at least the dread that she might divulge it, and I felt, for a while, exempt from suspicion. I was, however, to run across Theresa one last time. It happened during a period of torrential rain that, according to reports on the six o'clock news, washed houses from the hillsides and flooded the downtown streets. The halls of Joseph Le Conte Junior High were festooned with Christmas decorations: crepe-paper garlands, wreaths studded with plastic berries, and one requisite Star of David twirling above the attendance desk. In Arts and Crafts, our teacher, Gerald (he was the only teacher who allowed us — *required* us — to call him by his first name), handed out blocks of balsa wood and instructed us to carve them into bugs. We would paint eyes and antennae with tempera and hang them on a Christmas tree he'd made the previous night. "Voilà," he crooned, unveiling his creation from a burlap sack. Before us sat a tortured scrub, a wardrobe-worth of wire hangers that were bent like branches and soldered together. Gerald credited his inspiration to a Charles Addams cartoon he's seen in which Morticia, grimly preparing for the holidays, hangs vampire bats on a withered pine. "All that red and green," said Gerald. "So predictable. So *boring.*"

As I chiseled a beetle and listened to rain pummel the earth, Gerald handed me an envelope and asked me to take it to Mr. Kendrick, the drama teacher. I would have thought nothing of his request if I hadn't seen Theresa on my way down the hall. She was cleaning out her locker, blithely dropping the sum of its contents — pens and textbooks and mimeographs — into a trash can. "Have a nice life," she sang as I passed. I mustered the courage to ask her what had happened. We stood alone in the silent hall, the reflections of wreaths and garlands submerged in brown linoleum.

"I transferred to another school. They don't have grades or bells, and you get to study whatever you want." Theresa was quick to sense my incredulity. "Honest," she said. "The school is progressive." She gazed into a glass cabinet that held the trophies of track meets and intramural spelling bees. "God," she sighed, "this place is so . . . barbaric." I was still trying to decide whether or not to believe her story when she asked me where I was headed. "Dear," she said, her exclamation pooling in the silence, "that's no ordinary note, if you catch my drift." The envelope was blank and white; I looked up at Theresa, baffled. "Don't be so naive," she muttered, tossing an empty bottle of nail polish into the trash can. It struck bottom with a resolute thud. "Well," she said, closing her locker and breathing deeply, "bon voyage." Theresa swept through the double doors and in seconds her figure was obscured by rain.

As I walked toward Mr. Kendrick's room, I could feel Theresa's insinuation burrow in. I stood for a moment and watched Mr. Kendrick through the pane in the door. He paced intently in front of the class, handsome in his shirt and tie, reading from a thick book. Chalked on the blackboard behind him was THE ODYSSEY BY HOMER. I have no recollection of how Mr. Kendrick reacted to the note, whether he accepted it with pleasure or embarrassment, slipped it into his desk drawer or the pocket of his shirt. I have scavenged that day in retrospect, trying to see Mr. Kendrick's expression, wondering if he acknowledged me in any way as his liaison. All I recall is the sight of his mime through a pane of glass, a lone man mouthing an epic, his gestures ardent in empty air.

Had I delivered a declaration of love? I was haunted by the need to know. In fantasy, a kettle shot steam, the glue released its grip, and I read the letter with impunity. But how would such a letter begin? Did the common endearments apply? This was a message between two men, a message for which I had no precedent, and when I tried to envision the contents, apart from a hasty, impassioned scrawl, my imagination faltered.

Once or twice I witnessed Gerald and Mr. Kendrick walk together into the faculty lounge or say hello at the water fountain, but there was nothing especially clandestine or flirtatious in their manner. Besides, no matter how acute my scrutiny, I wasn't sure, short of a kiss, exactly what to look for — what semaphore of gesture, what encoded word. I suspected there were signs, covert signs that would give them away, just as I'd unwittingly given myself away to Theresa.

In the school library, a *Webster's* unabridged dictionary lay on a wooden podium, and I padded toward it with apprehension; along with clues to the bond between my teachers, I risked discovering information that might incriminate me as well. I had decided to consult the dictionary during lunch period, when most of the students would be on the playground. I clutched my notebook, moving in such a way as to appear both studious and nonchalant, actually believing that, unless I took precau-

tions, someone would see me and guess what I was up to. The closer I
came to the podium, the more obvious, I thought, was my endeavor; I felt
like the model of The Visible Man in our science class, my heart's undula-
tions, my overwrought nerves legible through transparent skin. A couple
of kids riffled through the card catalogue. The librarian, a skinny woman
whose perpetual whisper and rubber-soled shoes caused her to drift
through the room like a phantom, didn't seem to register my presence.
Though I'd looked up dozens of words before, the pages felt strange beneath my fingers. *Homer* was the first word I saw. *Hominid. Homoge-
nize.* I feigned interest and skirted other words before I found the word I
was after. Under the heading HO•MO•SEX•U•AL was the terse definition:
*adj. Pertaining to, characteristic of, or exhibiting homosexuality. — n. A
homosexual person.* I read the definition again and again, hoping the
words would yield more than they could. I shut the dictionary, swallowed
hard, and, none the wiser, hurried away.

As for Gerald and Mr. Kendrick, I never discovered evidence to prove
or dispute Theresa's claim. By the following summer, however, I had
overheard from my peers a confounding amount about homosexuals:
They wore green on Thursday, couldn't whistle, hypnotized boys with a
piercing glance. To this lore, Grady added a surefire test to ferret them
out.

"A test?" I said.   35

"You ask a guy to look at his fingernails, and if he looks at them like
this" — Grady closed his fingers into a fist and examined his nails with
manly detachment — "then he's okay. But if he does this" — he held out
his hands at arm's length, splayed his fingers, and coyly cocked his head
— "you'd better watch out." Once he'd completed his demonstration,
Grady peeled off his shirt and plunged into our pool. I dove in after. It
was early June, the sky immense, glassy, placid. My father was cooking
spareribs on the barbecue, an artist with a basting brush. His apron bore
the caricature of a frazzled French chef. Mother curled on a chaise
lounge, plumes of smoke wafting from her nostrils. In a stupor of contentment she took another drag, closed her eyes, and arched her face toward the sun.

Grady dog-paddled through the deep end, spouting a fountain of
chlorinated water. Despite shame and confusion, my longing for him had-
n't diminished; it continued to thrive without air and light, like a luminous fish in the dregs of the sea. In the name of play, I swam up behind
him, encircled his shoulders, astonished by his taut flesh. The two of us
flailed, pretended to drown. Beneath the heavy press of water, Grady's
orange hair wavered, a flame that couldn't be doused.

I've lived with a man for seven years. Some nights, when I'm half-
asleep and the room is suffused with blue light, I reach out to touch the
expanse of his back, and it seems as if my fingers sink into his skin, and I
feel the pleasure a diver feels the instant he enters a body of water.

I have few regrets. But one is that I hadn't said to Theresa, "Of course I'm a fag." Maybe I'd have met her friends. Or become friends with her. Imagine the meals we might have concocted: hamburger Stroganoff, Swedish meatballs in a sweet translucent sauce, steaming slabs of Salisbury steak.

The Reader's Presence

1. Cooper's essay begins and ends with references to a sophisticated classmate, Theresa Sanchez. Of what importance is she to the essay? Why does Cooper like her? What information does she provide the reader?
2. Cooper's first stirrings of attraction for his friend Grady occur in a swimming pool. What importance does swimming play in Cooper's essay? How does it provide him with a cluster of images for sexual experience?
3. Why does Cooper attend the "make-out party"? What does he hope will happen? Why do you think he ends his description of the party with the observation of the "clack of tiny sparks"? Why do you think he used that image for his title?

7

Joan Didion

On Keeping a Notebook

The author of novels, short stories, and essays, Joan Didion (b. 1934) began her career in 1956 as a staff writer at Vogue *magazine in New York. In 1963 she published her first novel,* Run River, *and the following year returned to her native California. Didion's essays have appeared in periodicals ranging from* Mademoiselle *to the* National Review. *Her essay "On Keeping a Notebook" can be found in her collection of essays,* Slouching Towards Bethlehem *(1968). Didion's other nonfiction publications include* The White Album *(1979),* Salvador *(1983),* Miami *(1987), and* After Henry *(1992).*

Didion has defined a writer as "a person whose most absorbed and passionate hours are spent arranging words on pieces of paper. I write entirely to find out what's on my mind, what I'm thinking, what I'm looking at, what I'm seeing and what it means, what I want and what I'm afraid of." She has also said that "all writing is an attempt to find out what matters, to find the pattern in disorder, to find the grammar in the shimmer. Actually I don't know whether you find the grammar in the shimmer or you impose a grammar on the shimmer, but I am quite specific about the grammar — I mean it literally. The scene that you see in your mind finds its own structure; the structure dictates the arrangement of the words. . . . All the writer has to do really is to find the words." However, she warns, "You have to be alone to do this."

"'That woman Estelle,'" the note reads, "'is partly the reason why George Sharp and I are separated today.' *Dirty crepe-de-Chine wrapper, hotel bar, Wilmington RR, 9:45 a.m. August Monday morning."*

Since the note is in my notebook, it presumably has some meaning to me. I study it for a long while. At first I have only the most general notion of what I was doing on an August Monday morning in the bar of the hotel across from the Pennsylvania Railroad station in Wilmington, Delaware (waiting for a train? missing one? 1960? 1961? why Wilmington?), but I do remember being there. The woman in the dirty crepe-de-Chine wrapper had come down from her room for a beer, and the bartender had heard before the reason why George Sharp and she were separated today. "Sure," he said, and went on mopping the floor. "You told me." At the other end of the bar is a girl. She is talking, pointedly, not to the man beside her but to a cat lying in the triangle of sunlight cast through the open door. She is wearing a plaid silk dress from Peck & Peck, and the hem is coming down.

Here is what it is: The girl has been on the Eastern Shore, and now she is going back to the city, leaving the man beside her, and all she can see ahead are the viscous summer sidewalks and the 3 A.M. long-distance calls that will make her lie awake and then sleep drugged through all the steaming mornings left in August (1960? 1961?). Because she must go directly from the train to lunch in New York, she wishes that she had a safety pin for the hem of the plaid silk dress, and she also wishes that she could forget about the hem and the lunch and stay in the cool bar that smells of disinfectant and malt and make friends with the woman in the crepe-de-Chine wrapper. She is afflicted by a little self-pity, and she wants to compare Estelles. That is what that was all about.

Why did I write it down? In order to remember, of course, but exactly what was it I wanted to remember? How much of it actually happened? Did any of it? Why do I keep a notebook at all? It is easy to deceive oneself on all those scores. The impulse to write things down is a peculiarly compulsive one, inexplicable to those who do not share it, useful only accidentally, only secondarily, in the way that any compulsion tries to justify itself. I suppose that it begins or does not begin in the cradle. Although I have felt compelled to write things down since I was five years old, I doubt that my daughter ever will, for she is a singularly blessed and accepting child, delighted with life exactly as life presents itself to her, unafraid to go to sleep and unafraid to wake up. Keepers of private notebooks are a different breed altogether, lonely and resistant re-arrangers of things, anxious malcontents, children afflicted apparently at birth with some presentiment of loss.

My first notebook was a Big Five tablet, given to me by my mother   5
with the sensible suggestion that I stop whining and learn to amuse my-self by writing down my thoughts. She returned the tablet to me a few years ago; the first entry is an account of a woman who believed herself to be freezing to death in the Arctic night, only to find, when day broke, that she had stumbled onto the Sahara Desert, where she would die of the heat before lunch. I have no idea what turn of a five-year-old's mind could have prompted so insistently "ironic" and exotic a story, but it does reveal a certain predilection for the extreme which has dogged me into adult life; perhaps if I were analytically inclined I would find it a truer story than any I might have told about Donald Johnson's birthday party or the day my cousin Brenda put Kitty Litter in the aquarium.

So the point of my keeping a notebook has never been, nor is it now, to have an accurate factual record of what I have been doing or thinking. That would be a different impulse entirely, an instinct for reality which I sometimes envy but do not possess. At no point have I ever been able suc-cessfully to keep a diary; my approach to daily life ranges from the grossly negligent to the merely absent, and on those few occasions when I have tried dutifully to record a day's events, boredom has so overcome me that the results are mysterious at best. What is this business about "shopping, typing piece, dinner with E, depressed"? Shopping for what? Typing what piece? Who is E? Was this "E" depressed, or was I de-pressed? Who cares?

In fact I have abandoned altogether that kind of pointless entry; in-stead I tell what some would call lies. "That's simply not true," the mem-bers of my family frequently tell me when they come up against my mem-ory of a shared event. "The party was *not* for you, the spider was *not* a black widow, *it wasn't that way at all.*" Very likely they are right, for not only have I always had trouble distinguishing between what happened and what merely might have happened, but I remain unconvinced that the distinction, for my purposes, matters. The cracked crab that I recall hav-ing for lunch the day my father came home from Detroit in 1945 must certainly be embroidery, worked into the day's pattern to lend verisimili-tude; I was ten years old and would not now remember the cracked crab. The day's events did not turn on cracked crab. And yet it is precisely that fictitious crab that makes me see the afternoon all over again, a home movie run all too often, the father bearing gifts, the child weeping, an ex-ercise in family love and guilt. Or that is what it was to me. Similarly, perhaps it never did snow that August in Vermont; perhaps there never were flurries in the night wind, and maybe no one else felt the ground hardening and summer already dead even as we pretended to bask in it, but that was how it felt to me, and it might as well have snowed, could have snowed, did snow.

How it felt to me: that is getting closer to the truth about a notebook. I sometimes delude myself about why I keep a notebook, imagine that some thrifty virtue derives from preserving everything observed. See enough and write it down, I tell myself, and then some morning when the world seems drained of wonder, some day when I am only going through the motions of doing what I am supposed to do, which is write — on that bankrupt morning I will simply open my notebook and there it will all be, a forgotten account with accumulated interest, paid passage back to the world out there: dialogue overheard in hotels and elevators and at the hatcheck counter in Pavillon (one middle-aged man shows his hat check to another and says, "That's my old football number"); impressions of Bettina Aptheker and Benjamin Sonnenberg and Teddy ("Mr. Acapulco") Stauffer; careful *aperçus*[1] about tennis bums and failed fashion models and Greek shipping heiresses, one of whom taught me a significant lesson (a lesson I could have learned from F. Scott Fitzgerald, but perhaps we all must meet the very rich for ourselves) by asking, when I arrived to interview her in her orchid-filled sitting room on the second day of a paralyzing New York blizzard, whether it was snowing outside.

I imagine, in other words, that the notebook is about other people. But of course it is not. I have no real business with what one stranger said to another at the hatcheck counter in Pavillon; in fact I suspect that the line "That's my old football number" touched not my own imagination at all, but merely some memory of something once read, probably "The Eighty-Yard Run."[2] Nor is my concern with a woman in a dirty crepe-de-Chine wrapper in a Wilmington bar. My stake is always, of course, in the unmentioned girl in the plaid silk dress. *Remember what it was to be me*: that is always the point.

It is a difficult point to admit. We are brought up in the ethic that   10 others, any others, all others, are by definition more interesting than ourselves; taught to be diffident, just this side of self-effacing. ("You're the least important person in the room and don't forget it," Jessica Mitford's[3] governess would hiss in her ear on the advent of any social occasion; I copied that into my notebook because it is only recently that I have been able to enter a room without hearing some such phrase in my inner ear.) Only the very young and the very old may recount their dreams at breakfast, dwell upon self, interrupt with memories of beach picnics and favorite Liberty lawn dresses and the rainbow trout in a creek near Colorado Springs. The rest of us are expected, rightly, to affect absorption in other people's favorite dresses, other people's trout.

And so we do. But our notebooks give us away, for however dutifully we record what we see around us, the common denominator of all we see is always, transparently, shamelessly, the implacable "I." We are not talk-

[1]*aperç65*

ing here about the kind of notebook that is patently for public consumption, a structural conceit for binding together a series of graceful *pensées;*[4] we are talking about something private, about bits of the mind's string too short to use, an indiscriminate and erratic assemblage with meaning only for its maker.

And sometimes even the maker has difficulty with the meaning. There does not seem to be, for example, any point in my knowing for the rest of my life that, during 1964, 720 tons of soot fell on every square mile of New York City, yet there it is in my notebook, labeled "FACT." Nor do I really need to remember that Ambrose Bierce liked to spell Leland Stanford's[5] name "£eland $tanford" or that "smart women almost always wear black in Cuba," a fashion hint without much potential for practical application. And does not the relevance of these notes seem marginal at best?:

> In the basement museum of the Inyo County Courthouse in Independence, California, sign pinned to a mandarin coat: "This MANDARIN COAT was often worn by Mrs. Minnie S. Brooks when giving lectures on her TEAPOT COLLECTION."

> Redhead getting out of car in front of Beverly Wilshire Hotel, chinchilla stole, Vuitton bags with tags reading:
> MRS. LOU FOX
> HOTEL SAHARA
> VEGAS

Well, perhaps not entirely marginal. As a matter of fact, Mrs. Minnie S. Brooks and her MANDARIN COAT pull me back into my own childhood, for although I never knew Mrs. Brooks and did not visit Inyo County until I was thirty, I grew up in just such a world, in houses cluttered with Indian relics and bits of gold ore and ambergris and the souvenirs my Aunt Mercy Farnsworth brought back from the Orient. It is a long way from that world to Mrs. Lou Fox's world, where we all live now, and is it not just as well to remember that? Might not Mrs. Minnie S. Brooks help me to remember what I am? Might not Mrs. Lou Fox help me to remember what I am not?

But sometimes the point is harder to discern. What exactly did I have in mind when I noted down that it cost the father of someone I know $650 a month to light the place on the Hudson in which he lived before the Crash? What use was I planning to make of this line by Jimmy Hoffa[6]: "I may have my faults, but being wrong ain't one of them"? And

---

[4]*pensées:* Thoughts or reflections (French). — EDS.
[5]*Bierce . . . Stanford's:* Ambrose Bierce (1842–1914?), American journalist and short story writer known for his savage wit; Leland Stanford (1824–1893), wealthy railroad builder who was a governor of California and the founder of Stanford University. — EDS.
[6]*Jimmy Hoffa* (1913–1975?): Controversial leader of the Teamsters Union who disappeared in the mid-seventies. — EDS.

although I think it interesting to know where the girls who travel with the Syndicate have their hair done when they find themselves on the West Coast, will I ever make suitable use of it? Might I not be better off just passing it on to John O'Hara?[7] What is a recipe for sauerkraut doing in my notebook? What kind of magpie keeps this notebook? "*He was born the night the* Titanic *went down.*" That seems a nice enough line, and I even recall who said it, but is it not really a better line in life than it could ever be in fiction?

But of course that is exactly it: not that I should ever use the line, but   15
that I should remember the woman who said it and the afternoon I heard it. We were on her terrace by the sea, and we were finishing the wine left from lunch, trying to get what sun there was, a California winter sun. The woman whose husband was born the night the *Titanic* went down wanted to rent her house, wanted to go back to her children in Paris. I remember wishing that I could afford the house, which cost $1,000 a month. "Someday you will," she said lazily. "Someday it all comes." There in the sun on her terrace it seemed easy to believe in someday, but later I had a low-grade afternoon hangover and ran over a black snake on the way to the supermarket and was flooded with inexplicable fear when I heard the checkout clerk explaining to the man ahead of me why she was finally divorcing her husband. "He left me no choice," she said over and over as she punched the register. "He has a little seven-month-old baby by her, he left me no choice." I would like to believe that my dread then was for the human condition, but of course it was for me, because I wanted a baby and did not then have one and because I wanted to own the house that cost $1,000 a month to rent and because I had a hangover.

It all comes back. Perhaps it is difficult to see the value in having one's self back in that kind of mood, but I do see it; I think we are well advised to keep on nodding terms with the people we used to be whether we find them attractive company or not. Otherwise they turn up unannounced and surprise us, come hammering on the mind's door at 4 A.M. of a bad night and demand to know who deserted them, who betrayed them, who is going to make amends. We forget all too soon the things we thought we could never forget. We forget the loves and the betrayals alike, forget what we whispered and what we screamed, forget who we were. I have already lost touch with a couple of people I used to be; one of them, a seventeen-year-old, presents little threat, although it would be of some interest to me to know again what it feels like to sit on a river levee drinking vodka-and-orange-juice and listening to Les Paul and Mary Ford[8] and their echoes sing "How High the Moon" on the car radio. (You see I still have the scenes, but I no longer perceive myself

---

[7]*John O'Hara* (1905–1970): American novelist who wrote several books about gangsters. — EDS.

[8]*Les Paul and Mary Ford:* Husband-and-wife musical team of the forties and fifties who had many hit records. — EDS.

among those present, no longer could even improvise the dialogue.) The other one, a twenty-three-year-old, bothers me more. She was always a good deal of trouble, and I suspect she will reappear when I least want to see her, skirts too long, shy to the point of aggravation, always the injured party, full of recriminations and little hurts and stories I do not want to hear again, at once saddening me and angering me with her vulnerability and ignorance, an apparition all the more insistent for being so long banished.

It is a good idea, then, to keep in touch, and I suppose that keeping in touch is what notebooks are all about. And we are all on our own when it comes to keeping those lines open to ourselves: your notebook will never help me, nor mine you. "*So what's new in the whiskey business?*" What could that possibly mean to you? To me it means a blonde in a Pucci bathing suit sitting with a couple of fat men by the pool at the Beverly Hills Hotel. Another man approaches, and they all regard one another in silence for a while. "So what's new in the whiskey business?" one of the fat men finally says by way of welcome, and the blonde stands up, arches one foot and dips it in the pool, looking all the while at the cabaña where Baby Pignatari is talking on the telephone. That is all there is to that, except that several years later I saw the blonde coming out of Saks Fifth Avenue in New York with her California complexion and a voluminous mink coat. In the harsh wind that day she looked old and irrevocably tired to me, and even the skins in the mink coat were not worked the way they were doing them that year, not the way she would have wanted them done, and there is the point of the story. For a while after that I did not like to look in the mirror, and my eyes would skim the newspapers and pick out only the deaths, the cancer victims, the premature coronaries, the suicides, and I stopped riding the Lexington Avenue IRT because I noticed for the first time that all the strangers I had seen for years — the man with the seeing-eye dog, the spinster who read the classified pages every day, the fat girl who always got off with me at Grand Central — looked older than they once had.

It all comes back. Even that recipe for sauerkraut: even that brings it back. I was on Fire Island when I first made that sauerkraut, and it was raining, and we drank a lot of bourbon and ate the sauerkraut and went to bed at ten, and I listened to the rain and the Atlantic and felt safe. I made the sauerkraut again last night and it did not make me feel any safer, but that is, as they say, another story.

The Reader's Presence

1. Notice that Didion begins her essay not with a general comment about notebooks but with an actual notebook entry. What does the entry sound like at first? What effect do you think Didion wants it to have on you as a reader?

2. Consider the comparison Didion makes in paragraph 6 between a notebook and a diary. How do they differ? Why is she fond of one and not the other? How does her example of a diary entry support her distinction?

3. Didion's notebook entries were never intended to have an audience. How is that apparent from the entries themselves? In what sense is Didion now the audience for her own writing? Where do you fit in as a reader? How has she now created a public audience for her private writing?

8

Frederick Douglass

Learning to Read and Write

Born into slavery, Frederick Douglass (1817?–1895) was taken from his mother as an infant and denied any knowledge of his father's identity. He escaped to the north at the age of twenty-one and created a new identity for himself as a free man. He educated himself and went on to become one of the most eloquent orators and persuasive writers of the nineteenth century. He was a national leader in the abolition movement and, among other activities, founded and edited the North Star *and* Douglass' Monthly. *His public service included appointments as United States marshal and consul general to the Republic of Haiti. His most lasting literary accomplishment was his memoirs, which he revised several times before they were published as the* Life and Times of Frederick Douglass *(1881 and 1892). "Learning to Read and Write" is taken from these memoirs.*

Douglass overcame his initial reluctance to write his memoirs because, as he put it, "not only is slavery on trial, but unfortunately, the enslaved people are also on trial. It is alleged that they are, naturally, inferior; that they are so low in the scale of humanity, and so utterly stupid, that they are unconscious of their wrongs, and do not apprehend their rights." Therefore, wishing to put his talents to work "to the benefit of my afflicted people," Douglass agreed to write the story of his life.

I lived in Master Hugh's family about seven years. During this time, I succeeded in learning to read and write. In accomplishing this, I was compelled to resort to various stratagems. I had no regular teacher. My mistress, who had kindly commenced to instruct me, had, in compliance with the advice and direction of her husband, not only ceased to instruct, but had set her face against my being instructed by anyone else. It is due, however, to my mistress to say of her, that she did not adopt this course of treatment immediately. She at first lacked the depravity indispensable to shutting me up in mental darkness. It was at least necessary for her to have some training in the exercise of irresponsible power, to make her equal to the task of treating me as though I were a brute.

My mistress was, as I have said, a kind and tender-hearted woman; and in the simplicity of her soul she commenced, when I first went to live with her, to treat me as she supposed one human being ought to treat another. In entering upon the duties of a slaveholder, she did not seem to perceive that I sustained to her the relation of a mere chattel, and that for her to treat me as a human being was not only wrong, but dangerously so. Slavery proved as injurious to her as it did to me. When I went there, she was a pious, warm, and tender-hearted woman. There was no sorrow or suffering for which she had not a tear. She had bread for the hungry, clothes for the naked, and comfort for every mourner that came within her reach. Slavery soon proved its ability to divest her of these heavenly qualities. Under its influence, the tender heart became stone, and the lamb-like disposition gave way to one of tiger-like fierceness. The first step in her downward course was in her ceasing to instruct me. She now commenced to practice her husband's precepts. She finally became even more violent in her opposition than her husband himself. She was not satisfied with simply doing as well as he had commanded; she seemed anxious to do better. Nothing seemed to make her more angry than to see me with a newspaper. She seemed to think that here lay the danger. I have had her rush at me with a face made all up of fury, and snatch from me a newspaper, in a manner that fully revealed her apprehension. She was an apt woman; and a little experience soon demonstrated, to her satisfaction, that education and slavery were incompatible with each other.

From this time I was most narrowly watched. If I was in a separate room any considerable length of time, I was sure to be suspected of having a book, and was at once called to give an account of myself. All this, however, was too late. The first step had been taken. Mistress, in teaching me the alphabet, had given me the *inch*, and no precaution could prevent me from taking the *ell*.

The plan which I adopted, and the one by which I was most successful, was that of making friends of all the little white boys whom I met in the street. As many of these as I could, I converted into teachers. With their kindly aid, obtained at different times and in different places, I finally succeeded in learning to read. When I was sent to errands, I always took my book with me, and by going one part of my errand quickly, I found time to get a lesson before my return. I used also to carry bread with me, enough of which was always in the house, and to which I was always welcome; for I was much better off in this regard than many of the poor white children in our neighborhood. This bread I used to bestow upon the hungry little urchins, who, in return, would give me that more valuable bread of knowledge. I am strongly tempted to give the names of two or three of those little boys, as a testimonial of the gratitude and affection I bear them; but prudence forbids — not that it would injure me, but it might embarrass them; for it is almost an unpardonable offense to teach slaves to read in this (Christian) country. It is enough to say of the dear little fellows, that they lived on Philpot Street, very near Durgin and Bailey's ship-yard. I used to talk this matter of slavery over with them. I would sometimes say to them, I wished I could be as free as they would be when they got to be men. "You will be free as soon as you are twenty-one, *but I am a slave for life!* Have not I as good a right to be free as you have?" These words used to trouble them; they would express for me the liveliest sympathy, and console me with the hope that something would occur by which I might be free.

I was now about twelve-years-old, and the thought of being *a slave for life* began to bear heavily upon my heart. Just about this time, I got hold of a book entitled "The Columbian Orator." Every opportunity I got, I used to read this book. Among much of other interesting matter, I found in it a dialogue between a master and his slave. The slave was represented as having run away from his master three times. The dialogue represented the conversation which took place between them, when the slave was retaken the third time. In this dialogue, the whole argument in behalf of slavery was brought forward by the master, all of which was disposed of by the slave. The slave was made to say some very smart as well as impressive things in reply to his master — things which had the desired though unexpected effect; for the conversation resulted in the voluntary emancipation of the slave on the part of the master.

In the same book, I met with one of Sheridan's[1] mighty speeches on and in behalf of Catholic emancipation. These were choice documents to me. I read them over and over again with unabated interest. They gave tongue to interesting thoughts of my own soul, which had frequently flashed through my mind, and died away for want of utterance. The moral which I gained from the dialogue was the power of truth over the conscience of even a slaveholder. What I got from Sheridan was a bold denunciation of slavery, and a powerful vindication of human rights. The reading of these documents enabled me to utter my thoughts, and to meet the arguments brought forward to sustain slavery; but while they relieved me of one difficulty, they brought on another even more painful than the one of which I was relieved. The more I read, the more I was led to abhor and detest my enslavers. I could regard them in no other light than a band of successful robbers, who had left their homes, and gone to Africa, and stolen us from our homes, and in a strange land reduced us to slavery. I loathed them as being the meanest as well as the most wicked of men. As I read and contemplated the subject, behold! that very discontentment

[1]*Sheridan's:* Richard Brinsley Butler Sheridan (1751–1816), Irish dramatist and orator. — EDS.

Knowledge is power!

which Master Hugh had predicted would follow my learning to read had already come, to torment and sting my soul to unutterable anguish. As I writhed under it, I would at times feel that learning to read had been a curse rather than a blessing. It had given me a view of my wretched condition, without the remedy. It opened my eyes to the horrible pit, but to no ladder upon which to get out. In moments of agony, I envied my fellow-slaves for their stupidity. I have often wished myself a beast. I preferred the condition of the meanest reptile to my own. Anything, no matter what, to get rid of thinking! It was this everlasting thinking of my condition that tormented me. There was no getting rid of it. It was pressed upon me by every object within sight or hearing, animate or inanimate. The silver trump of freedom had roused my soul to eternal wakefulness. Freedom now appeared, to disappear no more forever. It was heard in every sound, and seen in every thing. It was ever present to torment me with a sense of my wretched condition. I saw nothing without seeing it, I heard nothing without hearing it, and felt nothing without feeling it. It looked from every star, it smiled in every calm, breathed in every wind, and moved in every storm.

I often found myself regretting my own existence, and wishing myself dead; and but for the hope of being free, I have no doubt but that I should have killed myself, or done something for which I should have been killed. While in this state of mind, I was eager to hear anyone speak of slavery. I was a ready listener. Every little while, I could hear something about the abolitionists. It was some time before I found what the word meant. It was always used in such connections as to make it an interesting word to me. If a slave ran away and succeeded in getting clear, or if a slave killed his master, set fire to a barn, or did anything very wrong in the mind of a slaveholder, it was spoken of as the fruit of *abolition*. Hearing the word in this connection very often, I set about learning what it meant. The dictionary afforded me little or no help. I found it was "the act of abolishing"; but then I did not know what was to be abolished. Here I was perplexed. I did not dare to ask anyone about its meaning, for I was satisfied that it was something they wanted me to know very little about. After a patient waiting, I got one of our city papers, containing an account of the number of petitions from the North, praying for the abolition of slavery in the District of Columbia, and of the slave trade between the States. From this time I understood the words *abolition* and *abolitionist,* and always drew near when that word was spoken, expecting to hear something of importance to myself and fellow-slaves. The light broke in upon me by degrees. I went one day down on the wharf of Mr. Waters; and seeing two Irishmen unloading a scow of stone, I went, unasked, and helped them. When we had finished, one of them came to me and asked me if I were a slave. I told him I was. He asked, "Are ye a slave for life?" I told him that I was. The good Irishman seemed to be deeply affected by the statement. He said to the other that it was a pity so fine a little fellow as myself should be a slave for life. He said it was a shame to hold me. They both advised me to run away to the North; that I should find friends there, and that I should be free. I pretended not to be interested in what they said, and treated them as if I did not understand them; for I feared they might be treacherous. White men have been known to encourage slaves to escape, and then, to get the reward, catch them and return them to their masters. I was afraid that these seemingly good men might use me so; but I nevertheless remembered their advice, and from that time I resolved to run away. I looked forward to a time at which it would be safe for me to escape. I was too young to think of doing so immediately; besides, I wished to learn how to write, as I might have occasion to write my own pass. I consoled myself with the hope that I should one day find a good chance. Meanwhile, I would learn to write.

The idea as to how I might learn to write was suggested to me by being in Durgin and Bailey's ship-yard, and frequently seeing the ship carpenters, after hewing, and getting a piece of timber ready for use, write on the timber the name of that part of the ship for which it was intended. When a piece of timber was intended for the larboard side, it would be marked thus — "L." When a piece was for the starboard side, it would be marked thus — "S." A piece for the larboard side forward, would be marked thus — "L.F." When a piece was for starboard side forward, it would be marked thus — "S.F." For larboard aft, it would be marked thus — "L.A." For starboard aft, it would be marked thus — "S.A." I soon learned the names of these letters, and for what they were intended when placed upon a piece of timber in the shipyard. I immediately commenced copying them, and in a short time was able to make the four letters named. After that, when I met with any boy who I knew could write, I would tell him I could write as well as he. The next word would be, "I don't believe you. Let me see you try it." I would then make the letters which I had been so fortunate as to learn, and ask him to beat that. In this way I got a good many lessons in writing, which it is quite possible I should never have gotten in any other way. During this time, my copy-book was the board fence, brick wall, and pavement; my pen and ink was a lump of chalk. With these, I learned mainly how to write. I then commenced and continued copying the Italics in *Webster's Spelling Book*, until I could make them all without looking on the book. By this time, my little Master Thomas had gone to school, and learned how to write, and had written over a number of copy-books. These had been brought home, and shown to some of our near neighbors, and then laid aside. My mistress used to go to class meeting at the Wilk Street meeting-house every Monday afternoon, and leave me to take care of the house. When left thus, I used to spend the time in writing in the spaces left in master Thomas's copy-book, copying what he had written. I continued to do this until I could write a hand very similar to that of Master Thomas. Thus, after a long, tedious effort for years, I finally succeeded in learning how to write.

The Reader's Presence

1. What sort of audience does Douglass anticipate for his reminis-
    cence? How much does he assume his readers know about the
    conditions of slavery?
2. What kind of book seems to interest Douglass the most? What
    lessons does he learn from his reading? Why does he say that
    learning to read was more of a curse than a blessing? In general,
    what are his motives for wanting to read and write?
3. Notice that Douglass learns to read *before* he learns to write. Is
    that the way you learned? What other ways are possible? What
    method seems best to you? While rereading the essay, try making
    a chart of Douglass's educational progress. Having already
    learned to read, why does he need the letters used by ship carpen-
    ters in order to learn how to write?

9

Stephen Dunn

Locker Room Talk

*Stephen Dunn was born in 1939 in New York City. His poetry, published in
several collections over the course of the past twenty years, has been consistently
praised for the clarity of its language and vision. Dunn writes about the pleasures
and pressures of everyday life with sensitivity and optimism. His most recent
books are* Walking Light: Essays and Memoirs *(1992), and* New and Selected
Poems *(1994). In the early 1960s Dunn was a semiprofessional basketball player;
since 1974 he has been the poet-in-residence at Stockton State College in New Jersey. He has also taught poetry at Columbia University.*

*In his essay "Poetry and Manners," Dunn writes, "I of course don't believe
in democracy when it comes to poetry. Poets try to exercise a sweet tyranny over
their words. That their words often seem willful is one of the difficulties and, I
should add, pleasures of composition."*

Having been athletic most of my life, I've spent a fair amount of time
in locker rooms and have overheard my share of "locker room talk." For
reasons I couldn't understand for many years, I rarely participated in it
and certainly never felt smug or superior about my lack of participation.
In fact, I felt quite the opposite; I thought something was wrong with me.

As a teenager and well into my twenties I'd hear someone recount his latest real or wishful conquest, there'd be a kind of general congratulatory laughter, tacit envy, but what I remember feeling most was wonderment and then embarrassment.

There was of course little or no public information about sex when I was growing up in the forties and fifties. The first time I heard someone talk about having sex was in the school yard (the locker room without walls) when I was twelve or thirteen. Frankie Salvo, a big boy of sixteen. Frankie made it sound dirty, something great you do with a bad girl. It was my first real experience with pornography and it was thrilling, a little terrifying too. My mind conjured its pictures. Wonderment. Not wonderful.

Some years later, after experience, wonderment gave way to embarrassment. I wasn't sure for whom I was embarrassed, the girl spoken about, the story teller, or myself. Nevertheless, I understood the need to tell. I, too, wanted to tell my good friend, Alan, but for some reason I never told him very much. In retrospect, it was my first test with what Robert Frost calls knowing "the delicacy of when to stop short," a delicacy I took no pride in. I felt excessively private, cut off.

I began thinking about all of this recently because in the locker room at college a young man was telling his friend — loud enough for all of us to hear — what he did to this particular young woman the night before, and what she did to him. It was clear how important it was for him to impress his friends, far more important than the intimacy itself, as if the sexual act weren't complete until he had completed it among other men.

This time I knew something about the nature of my embarrassment. 5 It wasn't just that he had cheapened himself in the telling, but like all things which embarrass us it had struck some part of me that was complicitous, to a degree guilty, the kind of guilt you feel every time there's a discrepancy between what you know you're supposed to feel (correct feelings) and what in fact you've thought of, if not done. But more than that, I was embarrassed by the young man's assumption — culturally correct for the most part — that we other men in the locker room were his natural audience. There were five or six of us, and we certainly didn't boo or hiss. Those of us who were silent (all of us except his friend) had given our quiet sanctions.

What did it all mean? That men, more often than not, in a very fundamental way prefer other men? Or was it all about power, an old story, success with women as a kind of badge, an accoutrement of power? Was the young man saying to the rest of us, "I'm powerful"? I thought so for a while, but then I thought that he seemed to be saying something different. He was saying out loud to himself and to the rest of us that he hadn't succumbed to the greatest loss of power, yielding to the attractiveness and power of women, which could mean admitting he felt something or, at the furthest extreme, had fallen in love.

From Samson, to the knight in Keat's poem "La Belle Dame Sans Merci," to countless examples in world literature, the warning is clear:

women take away your power. To fall in love with one is to be distracted from the world of accomplishment and acquisitiveness. But to have sex and then to talk about it publicly is a kind of final protection, the ultimate prophylactic against the dangers of feeling.

"Love means always having to say you're sorry," a friend once said to me. The joke had its truth, and it implied — among other things — a mature love, a presumption of mutual respect and equality. On some level the young man in the locker room sensed and feared such a relationship. He had ventured into the dark and strange world of women and had come out unscathed, literally untouched. He was back with us, in the locker room which was the country he understood and lived in, with immunity. He thought we'd be happy for him.

The Reader's Presence

1. Some would argue that listening to sexist or racist language without objecting to it amounts to complicity or approval. Do you think that "locker room talk" is sexist or offensive? Do you feel Dunn is condoning sexist speech? Explain your position.

2. Dunn repeatedly says that he feels embarrassed by locker room talk. Does he express this embarrassment to the other men in the locker room? How would you describe his attitude toward the young man who is reporting his sexual experiences?

3. Dunn describes the act of talking about sex to other men as "a kind of final protection, the ultimate prophylactic against the dangers of feeling" (paragraph 7). What metaphor is Dunn suggesting here? Do you find the metaphor appropriate or inappropriate?

10 _____

Nora Ephron

A Few Words about Breasts

Nora Ephron (b. 1941) started her writing career as a reporter for the New York Post, *and since then has written for numerous magazines, including* New York, McCall's, *and* Cosmopolitan. *Ephron has published four collections of essays on popular culture, including* Crazy Salad (1975), *from which the essay "A Few Words about Breasts" is taken. She also wrote the screenplays* Silkwood *(with Alice Arden),* When Harry Met Sally, *and* Sleepless in Seattle. *In 1992 she directed her first movie,* This is My Life, *written with her sister Delia Ephron. Her most recent books are* Heartburn *(1983), and* Nora Ephron Collected *(1991).*

Ephron relies heavily on events from her own life to inspire her writing. She told an interviewer, "I've always written about my life. That's how I grew up. 'Take notes. Everything is copy.' All that stuff my mother said to us." As you read the essay that follows, notice the way that Ephron draws on her personal experience.

I have to begin with a few words about androgyny. In grammar school, in the fifth and sixth grades, we were all tyrannized by a rigid set of rules that supposedly determined whether we were boys or girls. The episode in *Huckleberry Finn* where Huck is disguised as a girl and gives himself away by the way he threads a needle and catches a ball — that kind of thing. We learned that the way you sat, crossed your legs, held a cigarette, and looked at your nails — the way you did these things instinctively was absolute proof of your sex. Now obviously most children did not take this literally, but I did. I thought that just one slip, just one incorrect cross of my legs or flick of an imaginary cigarette ash would turn me from whatever I was into the other thing; that would be all it took, really. Even though I was outwardly a girl and had many of the trappings generally associated with girldom — a girl's name, for example, and dresses, my own telephone, an autograph book — I spent the early years of my adolescence absolutely certain that I might at any point gum it up. I did not feel at all like a girl. I was boyish. I was athletic, ambitious, outspoken, competitive, noisy, rambunctious. I had scabs on my knees and my socks slid into my loafers and I could throw a football. I wanted desperately not to be that way, not to be a mixture of both things, but instead just one, a girl, a definite indisputable girl. As soft and as pink as a nursery. And nothing would do that for me, I felt, but breasts.

I was about six months younger than everyone else in my class, and so for about six months after it began, for six months after my friends had begun to develop (that was the word we used, develop), I was not particularly worried. I would sit in the bathtub and look down at my breasts and know that any day now, any second now, they would start growing like everyone else's. They didn't. "I want to buy a bra," I said to my mother one night. "What for?" she said. My mother was really hateful about bras, and by the time my third sister had gotten to the point where she was ready to want one, my mother had worked the whole business into a comedy routine. "Why not use a Band-Aid instead?" she would say. It was a source of great pride to my mother that she had never even had to wear a brassiere until she had her fourth child, and then only because her gynecologist made her. It was incomprehensible to me that anyone could ever be proud of something like that. It was the 1950s, for God's sake. Jane Russell. Cashmere sweaters. Couldn't my mother see that? "*I am too old to wear an undershirt.*" Screaming. Weeping. Shouting. "Then don't wear an undershirt," said my mother. "But I want to buy a bra." "What for?"

I suppose that for most girls, breasts, brassieres, that entire thing, has more trauma, more to do with the coming of adolescence, with becoming a woman, than anything else. Certainly more than getting your period, although that, too, was traumatic, symbolic. But you could see breasts; they were there; they were visible. Whereas a girl could claim to have her period for months before she actually got it and nobody would ever know the difference. Which is exactly what I did. All you had to do was make a great fuss over having enough nickels for the Kotex machine and walk around clutching your stomach and moaning for three to five days a month about The Curse and you could convince anybody. There is a school of thought somewhere in the women's lib/women's mag/gynecology establishment that claims that menstrual cramps are purely psychological, and I lean toward it. Not that I didn't have them finally. Agonizing cramps, heating-pad cramps, go-down-to-the-school-nurse-and-lie-on-the-cot cramps. But unlike any pain I had ever suffered, I adored the pain of cramps, welcomed it, wallowed in it, bragged about it. "I can't go. I have cramps." "I can't do that. I have cramps." And most of all, gigglingly, blushingly: "I can't swim. I have cramps." Nobody ever used the hard-core word. Menstruation. God, what an awful word. Never that. "I have cramps."

The morning I first got my period, I went into my mother's bedroom to tell her. And my mother, my utterly-hateful-about-bras mother, burst into tears. It was really a lovely moment, and I remember it so clearly not just because it was one of the two times I ever saw my mother cry on my account (the other was when I was caught being a six-year-old kleptomaniac), but also because the incident did not mean to me what it meant to her. Her little girl, her firstborn, had finally become a woman. That was what she was crying about. My reaction to the event, however, was that I might well be a woman in some scientific, textbook sense (and could at least stop faking every month and stop wasting all those nickels). But in another sense — in a visible sense — I was as androgynous and as liable to tip over into boyhood as ever.

I started with a 28 AA bra. I don't think they made them any smaller   5
in those days, although I gather that now you can buy bras for five-year-olds that don't have any cups whatsoever in them; trainer bras they are called. My first brassiere came from Robinson's Department Store in Beverly Hills. I went there alone, shaking, positive they would look me over and smile and tell me to come back next year. An actual fitter took me into the dressing room and stood over me while I took off my blouse and tried the first one on. The little puffs stood out on my chest. "Lean over," said the fitter. (To this day, I am not sure what fitters in bra departments do except to tell you to lean over.) I leaned over, with the fleeting hope

that my breasts would miraculously fall out of my body and into the puffs. Nothing.

"Don't worry about it," said my friend Libby some months later, when things had not improved. "You'll get them after you're married."

"What are you talking about?" I said.

"When you get married," Libby explained, "your husband will touch your breasts and rub them and kiss them and they'll grow."

That was the killer. Necking I could deal with. Intercourse I could deal with. But it had never crossed by mind that a man was going to touch my breasts, that breasts had something to do with all that, petting, my God, they never mentioned petting in my little sex manual about the fertilization of the ovum. I became dizzy. For I knew instantly — as naïve as I had been only a moment before — that only part of what she was saying was true: the touching, rubbing, kissing part, not the growing part. And I knew that no one would ever want to marry me. I had no breasts. I would never have breasts.

My best friend in school was Diana Raskob. She lived a block from me in a house full of wonders. English muffins, for instance. The Raskobs were the first people in Beverly Hills to have English muffins for breakfast. They also had an apricot tree in the back, and a badminton court, and a subscription to *Seventeen* magazine, and hundreds of games, like Sorry and Parcheesi and Treasure Hunt and Anagrams. Diana and I spent three or four afternoons a week in their den reading and playing and eating. Diana's mother's kitchen was full of the most colossal assortment of junk food I have ever been exposed to. My house was full of apples and peaches and milk and homemade chocolate-chip cookies — which were nice, and good for you, but-not-right-before-dinner-or-you'll-spoil-your-appetite. Diana's house had nothing in it that was good for you, and what's more, you could stuff it in right up until dinner and nobody cared. Bar-B-Q potato chips (they were the first in them, too), giant bottles of ginger ale, fresh popcorn with melted butter, hot fudge sauce on Baskin-Robbins jamoca ice cream, powdered-sugar doughnuts from Van de Kamp's. Diana and I had been best friends since we were seven; we were about equally popular in school (which is to say, not particularly), we had about the same success with boys (extremely intermittent), and we looked much the same. Dark. Tall. Gangly.

It is September, just before school begins. I am eleven years old, about to enter the seventh grade, and Diana and I have not seen each other all summer. I have been to camp and she has been somewhere like Banff with her parents. We are meeting, as we often do, on the street midway between our two houses, and we will walk back to Diana's and eat junk and talk about what has happened to each of us that summer. I am walking down Walden Drive in my jeans and my father's shirt hanging out and my old red loafers with the socks falling into them and coming toward me is . . . I take a deep breath . . . a young woman. Diana. Her hair is curled and she has a waist and hips and a bust and she is wearing a straight skirt, an article of clothing I have been repeatedly told I will be unable to wear until I have the hips to hold it up. My jaw drops, and suddenly I am crying, crying hysterically, can't catch my breath sobbing. My best friend has betrayed me. She has gone ahead without me and done it. She has shaped up.

Here are some things I did to help:
Bought a Mark Eden Bust Developer.
Slept on my back for four years.
Splashed cold water on them every night because some French actress   15 said in *Life* magazine that that was what *she* did for her perfect bustline.

Ultimately, I resigned myself to a bad toss and began to wear padded bras. I think about them now, think about all those years in high school that I went around in them, my three padded bras, every single one of them with different-sized breasts. Each time I changed bras I changed sizes: one week nice perky but not too obtrusive breasts, the next medium-sized slightly pointy ones, the next week knockers, true knockers; all the time, whatever size I was, carrying around this rubberized appendage on my chest that occasionally crashed into a wall and was poked inward and had to be poked outward — I think about all that and wonder how anyone kept a straight face through it. My parents, who normally had no restraints about needling me — why did they say nothing as they watched my chest go up and down? My friends, who would periodically inspect my breasts for signs of growth and reassure me — why didn't they at least counsel consistency?

And the bathing suits. I die when I think about the bathing suits. That was the era when you could lay an uninhabited bathing suit on the beach and someone would make a pass at it. I would put one on, an absurd swimsuit with its enormous bust built into it, the bones from the suit stabbing me in the rib cage and leaving little red welts on my body, and there I would be, my chest plunging straight downward absolutely vertically from my collarbone to the top of my suit and then suddenly, wham, out came all that padding and material and wiring absolutely horizontally.

Buster Klepper was the first boy who ever touched them. He was my boyfriend my senior year of high school. There is a picture of him in my high-school yearbook that makes him look quite attractive in a Jewish, horn-rimmed-glasses sort of way, but the picture does not show the pimples, which were air-brushed out, or the dumbness. Well, that isn't really fair. He wasn't dumb. He just wasn't terribly bright. His mother refused to accept it, refused to accept the relentlessly average report cards, refused to deal with her son's inevitable destiny in some junior college or other. "He was tested," she would say to me, apropos of nothing, "and it came out a hundred and forty-five. That's near-genius." Had the word "underachiever" been coined, she probably would have lobbed that one at me, too. Anyway, Buster was really very sweet — which is, I know, damning with faint praise, but there it is. I was the editor of the front page of the high-school newspaper and he was editor of the back page; we had to work together, side by side, in the print shop, and that was how it started. On our first date, we went to see *April Love,* starring Pat Boone. Then we started going together. Buster had a green coupe, a 1950 Ford with an engine he had hand-chromed until it shone, dazzled, reflected the image of anyone who looked into it, anyone usually being Buster polishing it or the gas-station attendants he constantly asked to check the oil in order for them to be overwhelmed by the sparkle on the valves. The car also had a boot stretched over the back seat for reasons I never understood; hanging from the rearview mirror, as was the custom, was a pair of angora dice. A previous girlfriend named Solange, who was famous throughout Beverly Hills High School for having no pigment in her right eyebrow, had knitted them for him. Buster and I would ride around town, the two of us seated to the left of the steering wheel. I would shift gears. It was nice.

There was necking. Terrific necking. First in the car, overlooking Los Angeles from what is now the Trousdale Estates. Then on the bed of his parents' cabana at Ocean House. Incredibly wonderful, frustrating necking, I loved it, really, but no further than necking, please don't, please, because there I was absolutely terrified of the general implications of going-a-step-further with a near-dummy and also terrified of his finding out there was next to nothing there (which he knew, of course; he wasn't that dumb).

I broke up with him at one point. I think we were apart for about   20
two weeks. At the end of that time, I drove down to see a friend at a boarding school in Palos Verdes Estates and a disc jockey played "April Love" on the radio four times during the trip. I took it as a sign. I drove straight back to Griffith Park to a golf tournament Buster was playing in (he was the sixth-seeded teenage golf player in southern California) and presented myself back to him on the green of the eighteenth hole. It was all very dramatic. That night we went to a drive-in and I let him get his hand under my protuberances and onto my breasts. He really didn't seem to mind at all.

"Do you want to marry my son?" the woman asked me.

"Yes," I said.

I was nineteen years old, a virgin, going with this woman's son, this big strange woman who was married to a Lutheran minister in New Hampshire and pretended she was gentile and had this son, by her first husband, this total fool of a son who ran the hero-sandwich concession at Harvard Business School and whom for one moment one December in New Hampshire I said — as much out of politeness as anything else — that I wanted to marry.

"Fine," she said. "Now, here's what you do. Always make sure you're on top of him so you won't seem so small. My bust is very large, you see, so I always lie on my back to make it look smaller, but you'll have to be on top most of the time."

I nodded. "Thank you," I said.

"I have a book for you to read," she went on. "Take it with you when you leave. Keep it." She went to the bookshelf, found it, and gave it to me. It was a book on frigidity.

"Thank you," I said.

That is a true story. Everything in this article is a true story, but I feel I have to point out that that story in particular is true. It happened on December 30, 1960. I think about it often. When it first happened, I naturally assumed that the woman's son, my boyfriend, was responsible. I invented a scenario where he had had a little heart-to-heart with his mother and had confessed that his only objection to me was that my breasts were small; his mother then took it upon herself to help out. Now I think I was wrong about the incident. The mother was acting on her own, I think: That was her way of being cruel and competitive under the guise of being helpful and maternal. You have small breasts, she was saying; therefore you will never make him as happy as I have. Or you have small breasts; therefore you will doubtless have sexual problems. Or you have small breasts; therefore you are less woman than I am. She was, as it happens, only the first of what seems to me to be a never-ending string of women who have made competitive remarks to me about breast size. "I would love to wear a dress like that," my friend Emily says to me, "but my bust is too big." Like that. Why do women say these things to me? Do I attract these remarks the way other women attract married men or alcoholics or homosexuals? This summer, for example. I am at a party in East Hampton and I am introduced to a woman from Washington. She is a minor celebrity, very pretty and Southern and blond and outspoken, and I am flattered because she has read something I have written. We are talking animatedly, we have been talking no more than five minutes, when a man comes up to join us. "Look at the two of us," the woman says to the man, indicating me and her. "The two of us together couldn't fill an A cup." Why does she say that? It isn't even true, dammit, so why? Is she even more addled than I am on this subject? Does she honestly believe there is something wrong with her size breasts, which, it seems to me, now that I look hard at them, are just right? Do I unconsciously bring out competitiveness in women? In that form? What did I do to deserve it?

As for men.

There were men who minded and let me know that they minded. There were men who did not mind. In any case, *I* always minded.

And even now, now that I have been countlessly reassured that my figure is a good one, now that I am grown-up enough to understand that most of my feelings have very little to do with the reality of my shape, I am nonetheless obsessed by breasts. I cannot help it. I grew up in the terrible fifties — with rigid stereotypical sex roles, the insistence that men be men and dress like men and women be women and dress like women, the intolerance of androgyny — and I cannot shake it, cannot shake my feelings of inadequacy. Well, that time is gone, right? All those exaggerated examples of breast worship are gone, right? Those women were freaks, right? I know all that. And yet here I am, stuck with the psychological remains of it all, stuck with my own peculiar version of breast worship. You probably think I am crazy to go on like this: Here I have set out to write a confession that is meant to hit you with the shock of recognition, and instead you are sitting there thinking I am thoroughly warped. Well, what can I tell you? If I had had them, I would have been a completely different person. I honestly believe that.

After I went into therapy, a process that made it possible for me to tell total strangers at cocktail parties that breasts were the hang-up of my life, I was often told that I was insane to have been bothered by my condition. I was also frequently told, by close friends, that I was extremely boring on the subject. And my girlfriends, the ones with nice big breasts, would go on endlessly about how their lives had been far more miserable than mine. Their bra straps were snapped in class. They couldn't sleep on their stomachs. They were stared at whenever the word "mountain" cropped up in geography. And *Evangeline,* good God what they went through every time someone had to stand up and recite the Prologue to Longfellow's *Evangeline:* ". . . stand like druids of eld . . . / With beards that rest on their bosoms." It was much worse for them, they tell me. They had a terrible time of it, they assure me. I don't know how lucky I was, they say.

I have thought about their remarks, tried to put myself in their place, considered their point of view. I think they are full of shit.

The Reader's Presence

1. How does Ephron make small breasts a matter of identity as well as appearance? Do you agree with her? Do you think her reasons for this are well founded? Are they based only on her personal experience?
2. "That is a true story. Everything in this article is a true story, . . ." Ephron maintains in paragraph 21. Why does she feel she must say this? What attitude does she anticipate in her reader? Why might she think her readers would doubt her story? Do you?
3. In paragraph 24, Ephron addresses her readers directly: "You probably think I am crazy to go on like this: Here I have set out to write a confession that is meant to hit you with the shock of recognition, and instead you are sitting there thinking I am thoroughly warped." What are her assumptions about her readers at this point? What does she seem worried about? What is your response as a reader? How closely do you fit into the role she is assigning for her readers?

11

Louise Erdrich

Skunk Dreams

Poet, novelist, and short story writer Louise Erdrich (b. 1954) was raised near the Turtle Mountain Chippewa Reservation in North Dakota. Her mother was a Chippewa, and her German-born father taught on the reservation. She met her husband and literary collaborator, Michael Dorris, while studying at Dartmouth College. Her first novel, Love Medicine *(1984), won the National Book Critics Circle Award and the American Academy and Institute of Arts and Letters award for the best first work of fiction. Her other novels are* The Beet Queen *(1986),* Tracks *(1988),* The Bingo Palace *(1994), and* The Crown of Columbus *(1991), which she co-authored with Dorris. Her poetry is collected in* Jacklight *(1984) and* Baptism of Desire *(1989). "Skunk Dreams" appears in her recent essay collection,* The Blue Jay's Dance *(1995). Edrich's most recent novel is* Tales of Burning Love *(1996).*

Erdrich got a very early start as a writer; she recalls the encouragement of her parents during her childhood: "My father used to give me a nickel for every story I wrote, and my mother wove strips of construction paper together and stapled them into book covers. So at an early age, I felt myself to be a published author earning substantial royalties."

When I was fourteen, I slept alone on a north Dakota football field under cold stars on an early September night. Fall progresses swiftly in the Red River Valley, and I happened to hit a night when frost formed in the grass. A skunk trailed a plume of steam across the forty-yard line near moonrise. I tucked the top of my sleeping bag over my head and was just dozing off when the skunk walked onto me with simple authority.

Its ripe odor must have dissipated in the heavy summer grass and ditch weeds, because it didn't smell all that bad, or perhaps it was just that I took shallow breaths in numb surprise. I felt him, her, whatever, pause on the side of my hip and turn around twice before evidently deciding I was a good place to sleep. At the back of my knees, on the quilting of my sleeping bag, it trod out a spot for itself and then, with a serene little groan, curled up and lay perfectly still. That made two of us. I was wildly awake, trying to forget the sharpness and number of skunk teeth, trying not to think of the high percentage of skunks with rabies, or the reason that on camping trips my father always kept a hatchet under his pillow.

Inside the bag, I felt as if I might smother. Carefully, making only the slightest of rustles, I drew the bag away from my face and took a deep breath of the night air, enriched with skunk, but clear and watery and cold. It wasn't so bad, and the skunk didn't stir at all, so I watched the moon — caught that night in an envelope of silk, a mist — pass over my sleeping field of teenage guts and glory. The grass harbored a sere dust both old and fresh. I smelled the heat of spent growth beneath the rank tone of my bag-mate — the stiff fragrance of damp earth and the thick pungency of newly manured fields a mile or two away — along with my sleeping bag's smell, slightly mildewed, forever smoky. The skunk settled even closer and began to breath rapidly; its feet jerked a little like a dog's. I sank against the earth, and fell asleep too.

Of what easily tipped cans, what molten sludge, what dogs in yards on chains, what leftover macaroni casseroles, what cellar holes, crawl spaces, burrows taken from meek woodchucks, of what miracles of garbage did my skunk dream? Or did it, since we can't be sure, dream the plot of *Moby-Dick,* how to properly age Parmesan, or how to restore the brick-walled tumble-down creamery that was its home? We don't know about the dreams of any other biota, and even much about our own. If dreams are an actual dimension, as some assert, then the usual rules of life by which we abide do not apply. In that place, skunks may certainly dream themselves into the vests of stockbrokers. Perhaps that night the skunk and I dreamed each other's thoughts or are still dreaming them. To paraphrase the problem of the Taoist philosopher Chuang Tzu, I may be a woman who has dreamed herself a skunk, or a skunk still dreaming that she is a woman.

In a book called *Death and Consciousness,* David H. Lund — who   5 wants very much to believe in life after death — describes human dream life as a possible model for a disembodied existence.

"Many of one's dreams," he says, "are such that they involve the activities of an apparently embodied person whom one takes to be oneself as long as one dreams. . . . Whatever is the source of the imagery . . . apparently has the capacity to bring about the images of a hu-man body and to impart the feeling that the body is mine. It is, of course, just an image body, but it serves as a perfectly good body for the dream experience. I regard it as mine, I act on the dream environment by means of it, and it constitutes the center of the perpetual world of my dream."

Over the years I have acquired and reshuffled my beliefs and doubts about whether we live on after death — in any shape or form, that is, besides the molecular level at which I am to be absorbed by the taproots of cemetery elms or pines and the tangled mats of fearfully poisoned, too green lawn grass. I want something of the self on whom I have worked so hard to survive the loss of the body (which, incidentally, the self has done a fairly decent job of looking after, excepting spells of too much cabernet and a few idiotic years of rolling my own cigarettes out of Virginia Blond tobacco.) I am put out with the marvelous discoveries of the intricate bio-chemical configuration of our brains, though I realize that the processes themselves are quite miraculous. I understand that I should be self-proud, content to gee-whiz at the fact that I am the world's only mechanism that can admire itself. I should be grateful that life is here today, though gone tomorrow, but I can't help it. I want more.

Skunks don't mind each other's vile perfume. Obviously, they find each other more than tolerable. And even I, who have been in the presence of a direct skunk hit, wouldn't classify their weapon as mere smell. It is more on the order of a reality-enhancing experience. It's not so pleasant as standing in a grove of old-growth cedars, or on a lyrical moonshed plain, or watching trout rise to the shadow of your hand on the placid surface of Alpine lake. When the skunk lets go, you're surrounded by skunk presence: inhabited, owned, involved with something that you can only describe as powerfully *there*.

I woke at dawn, stunned into that sprayed sense of being. The dog that had approached me was rolling in the grass, half addled, sprayed too. My skunk was gone. I abandoned my sleeping bag and started home. Up Eighth Street, past the tiny blue and pink houses, past my grade school, past all the addresses where I baby-sat, I walked in my own strange wind. The streets were wide and empty; I met no one — not a dog, not a squirrel, not even an early robin. Perhaps they had all scattered before me, blocks away. I had gone out to sleep on the football field because I was afflicted with a sadness I had to dramatize. Mood swings had begun, hormones, feverish and raw. They were nothing to me now. My emotions had seemed vast, dark, and sickeningly private. But they were minor, mere wisps, compared to skunk.

A SHORT PERSONAL DREAM HISTORY.
THE FENCE.

I have found that my best dreams come to me in cheap motels. One 10 such dream about an especially haunting place occurred in a rattling room in Valley City, North Dakota. There, in the home of the Winter Show, in the old Rudolph Hotel, I was to spend a week-long residency as a poet-in-the-schools. I was supporting myself, at the time, by teaching poetry to children, convicts, rehabilitation patients, high school hoods, and recovering alcoholics. What a marvelous job it was, and what opportunities I had to dream, since I paid my own lodging and lived low, sometimes taking rooms for less than ten dollars a night in motels that had already been closed by local health departments.

The images that assailed me in Valley City came about because the bedspread was so thin and worn — a mere brown tissuey curtain — that I had to sleep beneath my faux-fur Salvation Army coat, wearing all of my clothing, even a scarf. Cold often brings on the most spectacular of dreams, as though the brain has been incited to fevered activity. On that particular frigid night, the cold somehow seemed to snap boundaries, shift my time continuum, and perhaps even allow me to visit my own life in a future moment. After waking once, transferring the contents of my entire suitcase onto my person, and shivering to sleep again, I dreamed of a vast, dark, fenced place. The fencing was chain-link in places, chicken wire, sagging X wire, barbed wire on top, jerry-built with tipped-out poles and uncertain corners nailed to log posts and growing trees. And yet, it was quite impermeable and solid, as time-tested, broken-looking things so often are.

Behind it, trees ran for miles — large trees, grown trees, big pines the likes of which do not exist on the Great Plains. In my dream I walked up to the fence, looked within, and saw tawny, humpbacked elk move among the great trunks and slashing green arms. Suave, imponderable, magnificently dumb, they lurched and floated through the dim-complexioned air. One turned, however, before they all vanished, and from either side of that flimsy-looking barrier there passed between us a look, a communion, a long measureless regard that left me, on waking, with a sensation of penetrating sorrow.

THE WOMAN PINE. THE DREAM FENCE.

I don't think about my dream for many years, until after I move to New Hampshire. I have become civilized and sedentary since the days when I slept with skunks, and I've turned inward. Unused to walking in the woods, at first I do not even realize that trees drop branches — often large ones — or that there is any possible danger in going out on windy days, drawn by the natural drama. There is a white pine I love, a tree of the size foresters call overgrown, a waste, a thing made of long-since harvestable material. The tree is so big that three people can barely reach around it. Standing at the bottom, craning back, fingers clenched in grooves of bark, I hold on as the crown of the tree roars and beats the air a hundred feet above. The movement is frantic, the soft-needled branches long and supple, I think of a woman tossing, anchored in passion: calm one instant, full-throated the next, hair vast and dark, shedding the piercing, fresh oil of broken needles. I go to visit her often, and walk onward, farther, though it is not so far at all, and then one day I reach the fence.

Chain-link in places, chicken wire, sagging X wire, barbed wire on top, jerry-built with tipped-out poles and uncertain corners nailed to log posts and growing trees, still it seems impermeable and solid. Behind it, there are trees for miles: large trees, grown trees, big pines. I walk up to the fence, look within, and can see elk moving. Suave, imponderable, magnificently dumb, they lurch and float through the dim air.

I am on the edge of a game park, a rich man's huge wilderness, prob- 15 ably the largest parcel of protected land in western New Hampshire, certainly the largest privately owned piece I know about. At forty square miles — more than 25,000 acres — it is bigger than my mother's home reservation. And it has the oddest fence around it that I've ever seen, the longest and the tackiest. Though partially electrified, the side closest to our house is so piddling that an elk could easily toss it apart. Certainly a half-ton wild boar, the condensed and living version of a tank, could stroll right through. But then animals, much like most humans, don't charge through fences unless they have sound reasons. As I soon find out, because I naturally grow fascinated with the place, there are many more animals trying to get into the park than out, and they couldn't care less about ending up in a hunter's stew pot.

These are not wild animals, the elk — since they are grained at feeding stations, how can they be? They are not domesticated either, however, for beyond the no-hunt boundaries they flee and vanish. They are game. Since there is no sport in shooting feedlot steers, these animals — still harboring wild traits and therefore more challenging to kill — are maintained to provide blood pleasure for the members of the Blue Mountain Forest Association.

As I walk away from the fence that day, I am of two minds about the place — and I am still. Shooting animals inside fences, no matter how big the area they have to hide in, seems abominable and silly. And yet, I am glad for that wilderness. Though secretly managed and off limits to me, it is the source of flocks of evening grosbeaks and pine siskins, of wild turkeys, ravens, pileated woodpeckers, and grouse, vireo, of Eastern coyotes, oxygen-rich air, foxes, goldfinches, skunks, and bears that tunnel in and out.

I dreamed of this place in Valley City, or it dreamed me. There is an affinity here, beyond any explanation I can offer, so I don't try. I continue to visit the tracts of big trees, and on deep nights — windy nights, especially when it storms — I like to fall asleep imagining details. I see the great crowns touching, hearing the raving sound of wind and thriving, knocking cries as the blackest of ravens fling themselves across acres upon indifferent acres of tossing, old-growth pine. I fall asleep picturing how, below that dark air, taproots thrust into a deeper blankness, drinking the powerful rain.

Or is it so only in my dreams? The park, known locally as Corbin's Park, after its founder Austin Corbin, is knit together of land and farmsteads he bought in the late nineteenth century from 275 individuals. Among the first animals released there, before the place became a hunting club, were thirty buffalo, remnants of the vast western herds. Their presence piqued the interest of Ernest Harold Bayne, a conservation-minded local journalist, who attempted to break a pair of buffalo calves to the yoke. He exhibited them at county fairs and even knit mittens out of buffalo wool, hoping to persuade the skeptical of their usefulness. His work inspired sympathy, if not a trend for buffalo yarn, and collective zeal for the salvation of the buffalo grew so that by 1915 the American Bison Society, of which Bayne was secretary, had helped form government reserves that eventually more than doubled the herd that remained.

The buffalo dream seems to have been the park's most noble hour.   20
Since that time it has been the haunt of wealthy hunting enthusiasts. The owner of Ruger Arms currently inhabits the stunning, butter yellow original Corbin mansion and would like to buy the whole park for his exclusive use, or so local gossip has it.

OBSTACLES AND DESIRE

For some months I walk the boundary admiring the tangled landscape, at least all that I, or baby and I, can see. She comes with me most days in her blue backpack with the aluminum frame. The walking lulls her. I feel her head settle on my back, her weight go from lively to inert. After my first apprehension and discovery, I ignore the fence. I walk along it as if it simply does not exist, as if I really am part of that place just beyond my reach. The British psychotherapist Adam Phillips has examined obstacles from several different angles, attempting to define their emotional use. "It is impossible to imagine desire without obstacles," he writes, "and wherever we find something to be an obstacle we are at the same time desiring something. It is part of the fascination of the Oedipus story in particular, and perhaps narrative in general, that we and the heroes and heroines of our fiction never know whether obstacles create desire or desire creates obstacles." He goes on to characterize the unconscious, our dream world, as a place without obstacles: "A good question to ask of a dream is: What are the obstacles that have been removed to make this extraordinary scene possible?"

My current dream, however, is about obstacles still in place. The fence is the main component, the defining characteristic of the forbidden territory that I watch but cannot enter or experience. The obstacles that we overcome define us. We are composed of hurdles we set up to pace our headlong needs, to control our desires, or against which to measure our growth. "Without obstacles," Phillips writes, "the notion of development is inconceivable. There would be nothing to master."

Walking along the boundary of the park no longer satisfies me. The preciousness and deceptive stability of that fence begins to rankle. Longing fills me. I want to brush against the old pine bark and pass beyond the ridge, to see specifically what is there: what blue mountain, what empty views, what lavender hillside, what old cellar holes, what unlikely animals. I am filled with poacher's lust, except I want only to smell the air.

The linked web restraining me begins to grate, and I start to look for weak spots, holes, places where the rough wire sags. From the moment I begin to see the fence as permeable, it is no longer a fence. I return time after time — partly to see if I can spot anyone on the other side, partly because I know I must trespass.

Then, one clear morning, while Michael is taking care of our baby, I walk alone. I travel along the fence until I come to a place that looks shaky — and is. I go through. There are no trails that I can see, and I know I need to stay away from any perimeter roads or snowmobile paths, as well as from the feeding stations where the animals congregate. I want to see the animals, but only from a distance. Of course, as I walk on, leaving a trail easily backtracked, I encounter no animals at all. Still, the terrain is beautiful, the columns of pine tall, virgin, and second growth, the patches of oak and elderly maple from an occasional farmstead knotted and patient. I am satisfied and I decide to turn back and head toward the fence again. Skirting a low, boggy area that teems with wild turkey tracks, heading toward the edge of a deadfall of trashed branches and brush, I stare too hard into the sun, and stumble.

In a half crouch, I look straight into the face of a boar, massive as a   25
boulder. Corn-fed, razor-tusked, alert, sensitive ears pricked, it edges slightly backward into the convening shadows. Two ice picks of light gleam from its shrouded, tiny eyes, impossible to read. Beyond the rock of its shoulder, I see more: a sow and three well-grown cinnamon brown farrows crossing a small field lit by dazzling sun. The young skitter along, lumps of muscled fat on tiny hooves. They remind me of snowsuited toddlers on new skates. When they are out of sight the boar melts through the brush after them, leaving not a snapped twig or crushed leaf in his wake.

I almost don't breathe in the silence, letting the fact of that presence settle before I retrace my own tracks.

Next time, I go to the game park via front gates, driven by a friend down the avenues of tough old trees. I see herds of wild pigs and elk meandering past the residence of the gamekeeper. A no-hunting zone exists around the house, where the animals are almost tame. But I've been told by privileged hunters that just beyond that invisible boundary they vanish, becoming suddenly and preternaturally elusive.

So what is wild? What is wilderness? What are dreams but an internal wilderness and what is desire but a wilderness of the soul?

There is something in me that resists the notion of fair use of this land if the only alternative is to have it cut up, sold off in lots, condominiumized. I like to have it *there*. Yet the dumb fervor of the place depresses me — the wilderness locked up and managed but not for its sake, the animals imported and cultivated to give pleasure through their deaths. All animals, that is, except for skunks.

Not worth hunting, inedible except to old trappers like my uncle Ben   30
Gourneau, who boiled his skunk with onions and three changes of water,
skunks pass in and out of Corbin's Park without hindrance, without concern. They live off the corn in the feeding cribs (or the mice it draws), off
the garbage of my rural neighbors, off bugs and frogs and grubs. They
nudge their way onto our back porch for cat food, and even when disturbed they do not, ever, hurry. It's easy to get near a skunk, even to capture one. When skunks become a nuisance, people either shoot them or
catch them in crates, cardboard boxes, Havahart traps, plastic garbage
barrels.

Natives of the upper Connecticut River Valley have neatly solved the
problem of what to do with such catches. They hoist their trapped
mustelid into the back of a pickup truck and cart the animal across the
river to the neighboring state — New Hampshire to Vermont, Vermont
to New Hampshire — before releasing it. The skunk population is estimated as about even on both sides.

If I were an animal, I'd choose to be a skunk: live fearlessly, eat anything, gestate my young in just two months, and fall into a state of
dreaming torpor when the cold bit hard. Wherever I went, I'd leave my
sloppy tracks. I wouldn't walk so much as putter, destinationless, in a
serene belligerence — past hunters, past death overhead, past death all
around.

The Reader's Presence

1. Although Erdrich bases most of her observations on personal experience, she also quotes two authors on the subject of dreams.
   What effect does Erdrich's citation of external sources have? Does
   it make you trust her authority more or less?
2. Erdrich describes a dream she had about a fence during one freezing night in a North Dakota motel. Several pages later she repeats
   the same passage, this time as a description of an actual place in
   New Hampshire. What do you think Erdrich is saying about the
   connection between dreams and reality?
3. One of the key images in the essay is that of a "boundary." Why
   is this image important to Erdrich? In what ways are boundaries
   related to the processes of her thinking and writing?

12

Henry Louis Gates Jr.

In the Kitchen

The critic, educator, writer, and activist Henry Louis Gates Jr. (b. 1950) is perhaps the most recent in a long line of African American intellectuals who are also public figures. In 1979 he became the first African American to earn a Ph.D. from Cambridge University in its eight-hundred-year history. He has been the recipient of countless honors, including a Carnegie Foundation Fellowship, a Mellon Fellowship, and a MacArthur "genius" grant for his work in literary theory. Gates is currently the W. E. B. Du Bois Professor of the Humanities at Harvard University, where he also chairs the department of Afro-American Studies. He has been at the forefront of the movement to expand the literary canon that is studied in American schools to include the works of non-European authors. He is also known for his work as a "literary archaeologist," uncovering literally thousands of previously unknown stories, poems, and reviews written by African American authors between 1829 and 1940, and making those texts available to modern readers. Much of his writing, in particular for publications such as the New York Times, Newsweek, *and* Sports Illustrated, *is accessible to general audiences. His testimony on behalf of the rap group 2 Live Crew helped earn them an acquittal in their trial for obscenity, because he was able to bring his understanding of the history of black culture — specifically the language game known as "signifying" — to bear on their contemporary lyrics.*

Gates's publications include Figures in Black: Words, Signs, and the "Racial" Self *(1987),* The Signifying Monkey: A Theory of African-American Literary Criticism *(1988),* Loose Canons: Notes on the Culture Wars *(1992), and* Colored People: A Memoir *(1994), from which "In the Kitchen" is taken. About this book, Gates says, "I'm trying to recollect a lost era, what I can call a sepia time, a whole world that simply no longer exists." His most recent book, written with Cornel West, is* The Future of the Race *(1996).*

We always had a gas stove in the kitchen, though electric cooking became fashionable in Piedmont, like using Crest toothpaste rather than Colgate, or watching Huntley and Brinkley rather than Walter Cronkite. But for us it was gas, Colgate, and good ole Walter Cronkite, come what may. We used gas partly out of loyalty to Big Mom, Mama's mama, because she was mostly blind and still loved to cook, and she could feel her way better with gas than with electric.

But the most important thing about our gas-equipped kitchen was that Mama used to do hair there. She had a "hot comb" — a fine-tooth iron instrument with a long wooden handle — and a pair of iron curlers that opened and closed like scissors: Mama would put them into the gas fire until they glowed. You could smell those prongs heating up.

I liked what that smell meant for the shape of my day. There was an intimate warmth in the women's tones as they talked with my mama while she did their hair. I knew what the women had been through to get their hair ready to be "done," because I would watch Mama do it herself. How that scorched kink could be transformed though grease and fire into a magnificent head of wavy hair was a miracle to me. Still is.

Mama would wash her hair over the sink, a towel wrapped round her shoulders, wearing just her half-slip and her white bra. (We had no shower until we moved down Rat Tail Road into Doc Wolverton's house, in 1954.) After she had dried it, she would grease her scalp thoroughly with blue Bergamot hair grease, which came in a short, fat jar with a picture of a beautiful colored lady on it. It's important to grease your scalp real good, my mama would explain, to keep from burning yourself.

Of course, her hair would return to its natural kink almost as soon as   5
the hot water and shampoo hit it. To me, it was another miracle how hair so "straight" would so quickly become kinky again once it even approached some water.

My mama had only a "few" clients whose heads she "did" — and did, I think, because she enjoyed it, rather than for the few dollars it brought in. They would sit on one of our red plastic kitchen chairs, the kind with the shiny metal legs, and brace themselves for the process. Mama would stroke that red-hot iron, which by this time had been in the gas fire for a half hour or more, slowly but firmly through their hair, from scalp to strand's end. It made a scorching, crinkly sound, the hot iron did, as it burned its way though the damp kink, leaving in its wake the straightest of hair strands, each of them standing up long and tall but drooping at the end, like the top of a heavy willow tree. Slowly, steadily, with deftness and grace, Mama's hands would transform a round mound of Odetta kink[1] into a darkened swamp of everglades. The Bergamot made the hair shiny; the heat of the hot iron gave it a brownish-red cast. Once all the hair was as straight as God allows kink to get, Mama would take the well-heated curling iron and twirl the straightened strands into more or less loosely wrapped curls. She claimed that she owed her strength and skill as a hairdresser to her wrists, and her little finger would poke out the way it did when she sipped tea. Mama was a southpaw, who wrote upside down and backwards to produce the cleanest, roundest letters you've ever seen.

[1] *Odetta kink:* A reference to Odetta Holmes Felious Gorden, a popular African American folk singer of the 1960s who helped popularize the hairstyle known as the "afro." —EDS.

The "kitchen" she would all but remove from sight with a pair of shears bought for this purpose. Now, the *kitchen* was the room in which we were sitting, the room where Mama did hair and washed clothes, and where each of us bathed in a galvanized tub. But the word has another meaning, and the "kitchen" I'm speaking of now is the very kinky bit of hair at the back of the head, where our neck meets the shirt collar. If there ever was one part of our African past that resisted assimilation, it was the kitchen. No matter how hot the iron, no matter how powerful the chemical, no matter how stringent the mashed-potatoes-and-lye formula of a man's "process," neither God nor woman nor Sammy Davis, Jr., could straighten the kitchen. The kitchen was permanent, irredeemable, invincible kink. Unassimilably African. No matter what you did, no matter how hard you tried, nothing could dekink a person's kitchen. So you trimmed it off as best you could.

When hair had begun to "turn," as they'd say, or return to its natural kinky glory, it was the kitchen that turned first. When the kitchen started creeping up the back of the neck, it was time to get your hair done again. The kitchen around the back, and nappy edges at the temples.

Sometimes, after dark, Mr. Charlie Carroll would come to have his hair done. Mr. Charlie Carroll was very light-complected and had a ruddy nose, the kind of nose that made me think of Edmund Gwenn playing Kris Kringle in *Miracle on 34th Street*. At the beginning, they did it after Rocky and I had gone to sleep. It was only later that we found out he had come to our house so Mama could iron his hair — not with a comb and curling iron but with our very own Proctor-Silex steam iron. For some reason, Mr. Charlie would conceal his Frederick Douglass mane[2] under a big white Stetson hat, which I never saw him take off. Except when he came to our house, late at night, to have his hair pressed.

(Later, Daddy would tell us about Mr. Charlie's most prized piece of knowledge, which the man would confide only after his hair had been pressed, as a token of intimacy. "Not many people know this," he'd say in a tone of circumspection, "but George Washington was Abraham Lincoln's daddy." Nodding solemnly, he'd add the clincher: "A white man told me." Though he was in dead earnest, this became a humorous refrain around the house — "a white man told me" — used to punctuate especially preposterous assertions.)

My mother furtively examined my daughters' kitchens whenever we went home for a visit in the early eighties. It became a game between us. I had told her not to do it, because I didn't like the politics it suggested of "good" and "bad" hair. "Good" hair was straight. "Bad" hair was kinky. Even in the late sixties, at the height of Black Power, most people could not bring themselves to say "bad" for "good" and "good" for

[2]*Frederick Douglass mane:* Frederick Douglass (1817?–1895), an escaped slave who became a prominent African American writer, abolitionist, and orator. His photographs reveal an impressive head of hair. — EDS.

"bad." They still said that hair like white hair was "good," even if they encapsulated it in a disclaimer like "what we used to call 'good.'"

Maggie would be seated in her high chair, throwing food this way and that, and Mama would be cooing about how cute it all was, remembering how I used to do the same thing, and wondering whether Maggie's flinging her food with her left hand meant that she was going to be a southpaw too. When my daughter was just about covered with Franco-American SpaghettiOs, Mama would seize the opportunity and wipe her clean, dipping her head, tilted to one side, down under the back of Maggie's neck. Sometimes, if she could get away with it, she'd even rub a curl between her fingers, just to make sure that her bifocals had not deceived her. Then she'd sigh with satisfaction and relief, thankful that her prayers had been answered. No kink . . . yet. "Mama!" I'd shout, pretending to be angry. (Every once in a while, if no one was looking, I'd peek too.)

I say "yet" because most black babies are born with soft, silken hair. Then, sooner or later, it begins to "turn," as inevitably as do the seasons or the leaves turn on a tree. And if it's meant to turn, it *turns,* no matter how hard you try to stop it. People once thought baby oil would stop it. They were wrong.

Everybody I knew as a child wanted to have good hair. You could be as ugly as homemade sin dipped in misery and still be thought attractive if you had good hair. Jesus Moss was what the girls at Camp Lee, Virginia, had called Daddy's hair during World War II. I know he played that thick head of hair for all it was worth, too. Still would, if he could.

My own hair was "not a bad grade," as barbers would tell me when   15 they cut my head for the first time. It's like a doctor reporting the overall results of the first full physical that he had given you. "You're in good shape" or "Blood pressure's kind of high; better cut down on salt."

I spent much of my childhood and adolescence messing with my hair. I definitely wanted straight hair. Like Pop's.

When I was about three, I tried to stick a wad of Bazooka bubble gum to that straight hair of his. I suppose what fixed that memory for me is the spanking I got for doing so: he turned me upside down, holding me by the feet, the better to paddle my behind. Little *nigger,* he shouted, walloping away. I started to laugh about it two days later, when my behind stopped hurting.

When black people say "straight," of course, they don't usually mean "straight" literally, like, say, the hair of Peggy Lipton (the white girl on *The Mod Squad*) or Mary of Peter, Paul and Mary fame; black people call that "stringy" hair. No, "straight" just means not kinky, no matter what contours the curl might take. Because Daddy had straight hair, I would have done *anything* to have straight hair — and I used to try everything to make it straight, short of getting a process, which only riffraff were dumb enough to do.

Of the wide variety of techniques and methods I came to master in the great and challenging follicle prestidigitation, almost all had two things in common: a heavy, oil-based grease and evenly applied pressure. It's no accident that many of the biggest black companies in the fifties and sixties made hair products. Indeed, we do have a vast array of hair grease. And I have tried it all, in search of that certain silky touch, one that leaves neither the hand nor the pillow sullied by grease.

I always wondered what Frederick Douglass put on *his* hair, or Phillis   20
Wheatley.[3] Or why Wheatley has that rag on her head in the little engraving in the frontispiece of her book. One thing is for sure: you can bet that when Wheatley went to England to see the Countess of Huntington, she did not stop by the Queen's Coiffeur on the way. So many black people still get their hair straightened that it's a wonder we don't have a national holiday for Madame C. J. Walker, who invented the process for straightening kinky hair, rather than for Dr. King. Jheri-curled or "relaxed" — it's still fried hair.

I used all the greases, from sea-blue Bergamot, to creamy vanilla Duke (in its orange-and-white jar), to the godfather of grease, the formidable Murray's. Now, Murray's was some *serious* grease. Whereas Bergamot was like oily Jell-O and Duke was viscous and sickly sweet, Murray's was light brown and *hard*. Hard as lard and twice as greasy, Daddy used to say whenever the subject of Murray's came up. Murray's came in an orange can with a screw-on top. It was so hard that some people would put a match to the can, just to soften it and make it more manageable. In the late sixties, when Afros came into style, I'd use Afro-Sheen. From Murray's to Duke to Afro-Sheen: that was my progression in black consciousness.

We started putting hot towels or washrags over our greased-down Murray's-coated heads, in order to melt the wax into the scalp and follicles. Unfortunately, the wax had a curious habit of running down your neck, ears, and forehead. Not to mention your pillowcase.

Another problem was that if you put two palmfuls of Murray's on your head, your hair turned white. Duke did the same thing. It was a challenge: if you got rid of the white stuff, you had a magnificent head of wavy hair. Murray's turned kink into waves. Lots of waves. Frozen waves. A hurricane couldn't have blown those waves around.

That was the beauty of it. Murray's was so hard that it froze your hair into the wavy style you brushed it into. It looked really good if you wore a part. A lot of guys had parts *cut* into their hair by a barber, with clippers or a straight-edge razor. Especially if you had kinky hair — in which case you'd generally wear a short razor cut, or what we called a Quo Vadis.

Being obsessed with our hair, we tried to be as innovative as possible.   25
Everyone knew about using a stocking cap, because your father or your uncle or the older guys wore them whenever something really big was

---

[3]*Phillis Wheatley* (1753?–1784): An African-born slave who became America's first major black poet. — EDS.

about to happen, secular or sacred, a funeral or a dance, a wedding or a trip in which you confronted official white people, or when you were trying to look really sharp. When it was time to be clean, you wore a stocking cap. If the event was really a big one, you made a new cap for the occasion.

A stocking cap was made by asking your mother for one of her hose, cutting it with a pair of scissors about six inches or so from the open end, where the elastic goes to the top of the thigh. Then you'd knot the cut end, and behold — a conical-shaped hat or cap, with an elastic band that you pulled down low on your forehead and down around your neck in the back. A good stocking cap, to work well, had to fit tight and snug, like a press. And it had to fit that tightly because it *was* a press: it pressed your hair with the force of the hose's elastic. If you greased your hair down real good and left the stocking cap on long enough — *voilà*: you got a head of pressed-against-the-scalp waves. If you used Murray's, and if you wore a stocking cap to sleep, you got a *whole lot* of waves. (You also got a ring around your forehead when you woke up, but eventually that disappeared.)

And then you could enjoy your concrete 'do. Swore we were bad, too, with all that grease and those flat heads. My brother and I would brush it out a bit in the morning so it would look — ahem — "natural."

Grown men still wear stocking caps, especially older men, who generally keep their caps in their top drawer, along with their cuff links and their see-through silk socks, their Maverick tie, their silk handkerchief, and whatever else they prize most.

A Murrayed-down stocking cap was the respectable version of the process, which, by contrast, was most definitely not a cool thing to have, at least if you weren't an entertainer by trade.

Zeke and Keith and Poochie and a few other stars of the basketball   30
team all used to get a process once or twice a year. It was expensive, and to get one you had to go to Pittsburgh or D.C. or Uniontown, someplace where there were enough colored people to support a business. They'd disappear, then reappear a day or two later, strutting like peacocks, their hair burned slightly red from the chemical lye base. They'd also wear "rags" or cloths or handkerchiefs around it when they slept or played basketball. Do-rags, they were called. But the result was *straight* hair with a hint of wave. No curl. Do-it-yourselfers took their chances at home with a concoction of mashed potatoes and lye.

The most famous process, outside of what Malcolm X describes in his *Autobiography* and maybe that of Sammy Davis, Jr., was Nat King Cole's. Nat King Cole had patent-leather hair.

"That man's got the finest process money can buy." That's what Daddy said the night Cole's TV show aired on NBC, November 5, 1956. I remember the date because everyone came to our house to watch it and to celebrate one of Daddy's buddies' birthdays. Yeah, Uncle Joe chimed in, they can do shit to his hair that the average Negro can't even *think* about — secret shit.

Nat King Cole was *clean*. I've had an ongoing argument with a Nigerian friend about Nat King Cole for twenty years now. Not whether or not he could sing; any fool knows that he could sing. But whether or not he was a handkerchief-head for wearing that patent-leather process.

Sammy Davis's process I detested. It didn't look good on him. Worse still, he liked to have a fried strand dangling down the middle of his forehead, shaking it out from the crown when he sang. But Nat King Cole's hair was a thing unto itself, a beautifully sculpted work of art that he and he alone should have had the right to wear.

The only difference between a process and a stocking cap, really, was   35 taste; yet Nat King Cole — unlike, say, Michael Jackson — looked *good* in his process. His head looked like Rudolph Valentino's in the twenties, and some say it was Valentino that the process imitated. But Nat King Cole wore a process because it suited his face, his demeanor, his name, his style. He was as clean as he wanted to be.

I had forgotten all about Nat King Cole and that patent-leather look until the day in 1971 when I was sitting in an Arab restaurant on the island of Zanzibar, surrounded by men in fezzes and white caftans, trying to learn how to eat curried goat and rice with the fingers of my right hand, feeling two million miles from home, when all of a sudden the old transistor radio sitting on top of a china cupboard stopped blaring out its Swahili music to play "Fly Me to the Moon" by Nat King Cole. The restaurant's din was not affected at all, not even by half a decibel. But in my mind's eye, I saw it: the King's sleek black magnificent tiara. I managed, barely, to blink back the tears.

The Reader's Presence

1. At what point in the essay do you, as a reader, begin to become aware of the social or political significance of the hair-straightening process? At what point in his own development does Gates begin to ascribe a political significance to hair? How would you describe his attitude toward the "kitchen"? toward "the process"? toward the prominent black Americans whom he names in the essay?

2. Reread the essay carefully, and mark any references to nature, including the word *natural* and any metaphors drawn from nature. What conclusions might you draw from their use and placement in the essay? How do they help complicate the meaning of the hairstyle choices available to the characters?

3. How would you characterize the author's voice in this essay? Which words and phrases hark back to the language of his home

and family? How does Gates integrate these words and phrases into the text? What difference, if any, does it make to you as a reader when he puts certain words, such as *kitchen* or *good,* in quotation marks, as opposed to the passages in which phrases (such as "ugly as homemade sin dipped in misery" [paragraph 14]) are not set off in the text in this way?

13

Donald Hall

On Moving One's Lips, While Reading

Donald Hall (b. 1928) is a poet who has also found success as an essayist. His writing appears regularly in the Atlantic, *the* New Yorker, Yankee, Esquire, Playboy, *and* Sports Illustrated, *and he has published several collections of essays. His tenth book of poetry,* The One Day *(1988), won a National Book Critics Circle Award; since that time he has also published* Old and New Poems *(1990),* The Museum of Clear Ideas *(1993), and* The Old Life *(1996). His recent essay collections include* Death to the Death of Poetry: Essays, Reviews, Notes, Interviews *(1994) and* Principal Products of Portugal *(1995), in which "On Moving One's Lips, While Reading" appears.*

In 1975, Hall settled on a farm in New Hampshire, and the rural environment in which he lives strongly influences his writing. Hall finds his greatest happiness in his work: "In this house and on this land I lose the hour — inhabiting contentment — in my lucky double absorption with work and with land. At the desk, writing and trying to write, I do not know who I am; I do not even know that I will die. The whole of me enters the hand that holds the pen that digs at word-weeds, trying to set the garden straight."

Miss Stephanie Ford stepped to the blackboard. My first-grade teacher was angular, elderly, and black-haired. (Once I heard a grown-up say, "She must *do* something to her hair," which bewildered me.) The day before, Miss Ford had announced, "Tomorrow, we will begin to learn to read." The whole school year, we had prepared for this day. It was a moment, I told myself at the age of six, that I would remember forever. My house was a temple of reading. Every night after supper, when my parents finished the afternoon newspaper, and my father the work he brought home from the office, they concealed their faces behind books. Reading was what grown-ups did; now I, eager to overcome the obstacle of childhood, would join the reading world.

Miss Ford drew a series of sharp lines, making large printed letters, which we had learned as the alphabet, stringing together T, H, A, and T — white on black. She stood back and raised her long wooden pointer. "That," she said in her stiff clear voice, "is 'that.'" If her enunciation was stiff, it was not cold, because she moved her lips in an exaggerated fashion — she opened her mouth wide; her tongue curled and snapped — so that we might understand or imitate the oral formation of sounds. This angular, elderly, black-haired person taught us to read by acts of mouth and body.

We had studied the alphabet for weeks, late in 1934, by chanting it aloud in unison and copying it in pencil on large yellowish lined sheets of paper. All through grammar school, much of our learning was memorization and repetition by rote, "two plus two is four," whatever the subject: state capitals, the presidents with their years of office. Eight years later, when we started Latin in high school, we singsonged "amo, amas, amat" for Mr. Brown who always wore brown. Meanwhile we repeated multiplication tables, the dates of battles, poems, the principal products of Portugal, and the Gettysburg Address.

We did not speak pieces competitively as our parents and grandparents had done; entertainment by movies and radio had replaced recitation of poems and oratory. A pity. Loss of recitation helped to detach words from the sounds they make, which is the castration of reading. This loss took the name of educational reform, which attacked not speaking pieces but the memorization required for speaking pieces. Beginning in the late 1920s, spreading over years into the educational trenches, American Educators crusaded against memorization. Doubtless the crusade was in general good. There are better ways to learn history, social studies, and geography. Reasoning by rule is more useful for mathematics than memorizing tables for consultation. (As for balancing a checkbook, our calculators will do that for us.) Learning French or Spanish by talking it, or reading real examples of its literature, will bring us inside the syntax of a culture better than the rote imprint of conjugations.

But when they discarded recitation of dates and declensions, educa-   5
tors threw out as well the practice of reciting and performing literary work, and with it the habit of understanding literature by hearing it, by absorbing the noises it makes. In my [essay on] "Casey at the Bat," I praised the old culture that centered on the written word performed aloud for edification and entertainment. Before the automobile took farmers to the movies, before the radio's chatter ended the millennia of silences, our entertainment was local; piano solo, drama group, chorus, barbershop quartet — and recitation or performance of the written word.

When we looked at print a hundred years ago (or fifty, or whenever), we imbibed it as *sound* (with or without committing it to memory) at school or church, in nursery or living room. People performed literary art, or popular entertainment, even while doing other tasks. Memorization let the woodworker recite the "Raven" or "The Heathen Chinee" while turning a lathe, and the mother chant "Baa, baa black sheep" for her baby while her hands assembled a pie. On Sunday the preacher read from the book, prophet and gospel; on worknights after milking, an elocutionary cousin performed chapters from Scott and Dickens. At school we recited gems of political oratory and stanzas from the poets.

In a few blessed backwaters, school children still do prize speaking once a year. My town of Danbury, New Hampshire, is a surviving culture of the nineteenth century, like those Greek colonies in the Italian hills, founded four centuries before Christ, that still spoke Athenian Greek after World War II. Prize Speaking Night at Danbury School is a measure of what we were, a memory alive reconstituting the old world. I recommend it.

Technology exists to make memory unnecessary; we invented the alphabet so that we needed no longer to memorize Homer. But the alphabet was a device for the preservation of noise not of information. For a long time the written poem was a mnemonic device for the poem itself — and the spoken poem was the poem. It was more than a thousand years before humans invented silent reading. Literature was something heard not seen. Almost until Gutenberg, literary performance (and perception) was sound not sight, mouth and ear not eye and mind. When silent reading became common, roughly during the Renaissance, literature flourished — but:

This silent reading remained a noisy matter.

Until recently, when we have read silently we have heard every word.   10 Spending our childhoods listening to people read aloud or recite, ourselves reciting and performing in school and for the fun of it, we could not read in silence without inwardly hearing the words read. Even people too shy to read aloud heard print make noises in their heads.

Even now, if we read literature properly, we hear the words on the page — in our own minds. Hearing the words, we make constant unconscious decisions about tone, feeling and import; we remain alert to the gestures of words. Hearing the words, we cannot skim; passivity is impossible. By imagining how the words would sound if spoken aloud, we understand their tone. If we see on the page the sentence "Mr. Rumble nodded his head," our inward voicing requires us to understand whether Mr. Rumble disapproved, or was outraged, or merely passed on information ("No, it's not raining").

If we do not hear the words inside our heads, we are reading passively. Speed reading is sloppy reading, an abomination, and turns the reader into a slack-jawed receiver of surfaces, of mere information. We hear about Mr. Rumble's head gesture but we pass over its implication. When we allow words to be abstracted to the page or screen, detached from the body and the sensations of the human, we abandon the site of feelings. Do Mr. Rumble's palms sweat? Does he feel an erection starting? Does his toe hurt? Mr. Rumble looks bland and speaks without affect, like a voice generated by a computer. Who knows what Mr. Rumble is thinking?

Of course sometimes we need only information. By necessity all of us must learn a selective difference in modes of reading. We must read quickly in order to process newspapers, manuals of instruction, and business journals — or we would go crazy; it would take us a month to read the Sunday *Times* hearing every word. We would lose our minds if we listened with an inner ear to the instructions that come with 1040A.

On the other hand, when we read for joy — for beauty, for intelligence, for understanding — we must hear the words in order to read well. If we move our lips when we read silently, fine; it will slow us down, and we will read better. Whether moving our lips or not, we must test literature's words in our mouths. When I read good poems, in perfect silence, after twenty minutes my throat muscles feel tired.

Most people have become passive readers, and passive reading is diminished literacy. Television takes most of the blame, but there were earlier reasons: The motor car invented shopping and the movie, for Americans who lived outside cities; there was also radio, wonderful radio: We stopped singing for each other and let Rudy Vallee take over. We listened no more to public recitations of "Little Orphant Annie" because radio soap operas were available every day. We didn't need "The Owl and the Pussycat" because we had Fibber McGee and Molly.   15

But . . . when the automobile replaces walking, we need to take up jogging. We can learn to read again, and maybe to move our lips, by becoming conscious of the sound of words. The recent habit of taped books certainly helps. Commuting, we hear words acted, language made human by empathetic mouths, lips, and tongues. (It helps if the book is literature and entire.) Hearing books helps restore blood and flesh to the language, bringing sound back to literary experience.

But, listening to tapes, we are only receptors: Actors are active for us; other voices, other minds make decisions of tone. Better is reading aloud ourselves, preferably as a regular part of the day, and such reading aloud is not only for parents entertaining children. My wife and I have read a hundred books aloud, thirty minutes a day of *Huckleberry Finn, Madame Bovary,* the *New Testament,* Fitzgerald's *Odyssey,* and enormous quantities of Henry James. It's our local perversity, perhaps, but we find late James superb on the tongue. I've read every syllable of *The Ambassadors* aloud twice. I've read aloud *Portrait of a Lady,* wonderful late stories like "The Beast in the Jungle," *The Golden Bowl,* and *Wings of the Dove.* Maybe they read aloud so well because James dictated them.

The voice that reads late James aloud may not be monotone. To read parenthesis within parenthesis, the reader must drop pitches and build them up again, and a sentence by Henry James becomes an exercise for voice-athletes to train by, pitches and pauses in particular. Representing James by your mouth, lips, tongue, contracted throat, and vocal cords, you accomplish literary analysis by means of your vocal equipment. Your larynx could write a doctoral thesis on the Jamesian parenthesis.

This reading aloud, and this association of words with sounds, started for me when I was small: my mother reading aloud from *Silver Pennies;* my grandfather reciting "Casey" and a thousand other funny, sentimental, and melodramatic poems. I was lucky to be born while traces of the old culture survived. It survived also in Miss Stephanie Ford with her exaggerated mouthing of T-H-A-T. We learned to read by moving our lips — and tongue and larynx — and "that was that" for literacy and ultimately literature. If reading, and the love of literature, continues, we need again to connect words with the noises they make in our mouths.

The Reader's Presence

1. What, according to Donald Hall, are the reasons that reading has become a silent activity, decoupled from sound? What are the detrimental consequences of this? Considering that most of us cannot move to a "blessed backwater" (paragraph 7) such as Danbury, New Hampshire, what might we do to recapture some of the advantages of a bygone way of reading? Alternatively, if you think Hall shows signs of unwarranted nostalgia, make a case for the advantages of silent reading *without* moving one's lips.

2. In the first paragraph, Hall writes, "It was a moment, I told myself at the age of six, that I would remember forever." This is a remarkable instance of the author's looking backward at himself looking forward: an instance of a memory being caught in the making. Discuss the various roles played by memory in this essay. Are Hall's memories of his childhood perfectly consistent, or is he, according to paragraph 1, "remembering" a time before his own childhood when he reminisces about the woodworker reciting "The Raven" and the mother chanting to her baby (paragraph 6)? How, according to Hall, do technology and memory work against each other? What does he mean when he says, "For a long time the written poem was a mnemonic device for the poem itself — and the spoken poem was the poem" (paragraph 9)?

3. In Hall's account, reading is ideally a very muscular activity. Look at all the passages in which he mentions specific body parts or draws analogies to activities such as hard physical labor and exercise. What is the effect of this emphasis on the body in describing an activity that is largely considered to be mental? How does Hall, from his title onward, work against the expectations of his reader?

14

Langston Hughes

Salvation

One of the leading figures of the Harlem Renaissance, Langston Hughes (1902–1967) was a prolific writer. He started his career as a poet, but also wrote fiction, autobiography, biography, history, plays, and worked at various times as a journalist. One of his most famous poems, "The Negro Speaks of Rivers," was written while he was a high school student. Although Langston Hughes traveled widely, most of his writings are concerned with the lives of urban working-class African Americans.

Hughes used the rhythms of blues and jazz to bring to his writing a distinctive expression of black culture and experience. His work continues to be popular today, especially collections of short stories such as The Ways of White Folks *(1934), volumes of poetry such as* Montage of a Dream Deferred *(1951), and his series of vignettes on the character Jesse B. Simple, collected and published from 1950 to 1965. Hughes published two volumes of autobiography; "Salvation" is taken from the first of these,* The Big Sea *(1940).*

Throughout his work, Hughes refused to idealize his subject. "Certainly," he said, "I personally knew very few people anywhere who were wholly beautiful and wholly good. Besides I felt that the masses of our people had as much in their lives to put into books as did those more fortunate ones who had been born with some means and the ability to work up to a master's degree at a Northern college." Expressing the writer's truism about writing about what one knows best, he continued, "Anyway, I didn't know the upper-class Negroes well enough to write much about them. I only knew the people I had grown up with, and they weren't the people whose shoes were always shined, who had been to Harvard, or who had heard of Bach. But they seemed to me good people too."

I was saved from sin when I was going on thirteen. But not really saved. It happened like this. There was a big revival at my Auntie Reed's church. Every night for weeks there had been much preaching, singing, praying, and shouting, and some very hardened sinners had been brought to Christ, and the membership of the church had grown by leaps and bounds. Then just before the revival ended, they held a special meeting for children, "to bring the young lambs to the fold." My aunt spoke of it for days ahead. That night I was escorted to the front row and placed on the mourners' bench with all the other young sinners, who had not yet been brought to Jesus.

My aunt told me that when you were saved you saw a light, and something happened to you inside! And Jesus came into your life! And God was with you from then on! She said you could see and hear and feel Jesus in your soul. I believed her. I had heard a great many old people say the same thing and it seemed to me they ought to know. So I sat there calmly in the hot, crowded church, waiting for Jesus to come to me.

The preacher preached a wonderful rhythmical sermon, all moans and shouts and lonely cries and dire pictures of hell, and then he sang a song about the ninety and nine safe in the fold, but one little lamb was left out in the cold. Then he said: "Won't you come? Won't you come to Jesus? Young lambs, won't you come?" And he held out his arms to all us young sinners there on the mourners' bench. And the little girls cried. And some of them jumped up and went to Jesus right away. But most of us just sat there.

A great many old people came and knelt around us and prayed, old women with jet-black faces and braided hair, old men with work-gnarled hands. And the church sang a song about the lower lights are burning, some poor sinner to be saved. And the whole building rocked with prayer and song.

Still I kept waiting to *see* Jesus. *In a literal sense* .   5

Finally all the young people had gone to the altar and were saved, but one boy and me. He was a rounder's son named Westley. Westley and I were surrounded by sisters and deacons praying. It was very hot in the church, and getting late now. Finally Westley said to me in a whisper: "God damn! I'm tired o' sitting here. Let's get up and be saved." So he got up and was saved.

Then I was left all alone on the mourners' bench. My aunt came and knelt at my knees and cried, while prayers and song swirled all around me in the little church. The whole congregation prayed for me alone, in a mighty wail of moans and voices. And I kept waiting serenely for Jesus, waiting, waiting — but he didn't come. I wanted to see him, but nothing happened to me. Nothing! I wanted something to happen to me, but nothing happened.

I heard the songs and the minister saying: "Why don't you come? My dear child, why don't you come to Jesus? Jesus is waiting for you. He wants you. Why don't you come? Sister Reed, what is this child's name?"

"Langston," my aunt sobbed.

"Langston, why don't you come? Why don't you come and be saved?   10
Oh, Lamb of God! Why don't you come?"

Now it was really getting late. I began to be ashamed of myself, holding everything up so long. I began to wonder what God thought about Westley, who certainly hadn't seen Jesus either, but who was now sitting proudly on the platform, swinging his knickerbockered legs and grinning down at me, surrounded by deacons and old women on their knees pray-ing. God had not struck Westley dead for taking his name in vain or for lying in the temple. So I decided that maybe to save further trouble, I'd better lie, too, and say that Jesus had come, and get up and be saved.

So I got up.

Suddenly the whole room broke into a sea of shouting, as they saw me rise. Waves of rejoicing swept the place. Women leaped in the air. My aunt threw her arms around me. The minister took me by the hand and led me to the platform.

When things quieted down, in a hushed silence, punctuated by a few ecstatic "Amens," all the new young lambs were blessed in the name of God. Then joyous singing filled the room.

That night, for the first time in my life but one — for I was a big boy   15
twelve years old — I cried. I cried, in bed alone, and couldn't stop. I buried my head under the quilts, but my aunt heard me. She woke up and told my uncle I was crying because the Holy Ghost had come into my life, and because I had seen Jesus. But I was really crying because I couldn't bear to tell her that I had lied, that I had deceived everybody in the church, that I hadn't seen Jesus, and that now I didn't believe there was a Jesus anymore, since he didn't come to help me.

The Reader's Presence

1. Pay close attention to Hughes's two opening sentences. How would you describe their tone? How do they suggest the underly-ing pattern of the essay? How do they introduce the idea of decep-tion right from the start? Who is being deceived in the essay? Is it the congregation? God? Hughes's aunt? the reader?

2. Consider the character of Westley. Why is he important to Hughes's narrative? What would happen to the essay if Westley were not introduced and described?

3. In many ways this is an essay about belief. What is it that Hughes has been asked to believe? What does he expect to see? Reread the essay and consider the word *come*. Hughes waits for Jesus to come to him. Yet the preacher invites the children to come to Jesus. How does an awareness of this difference affect your read-ing of the essay?

15

Zora Neale Hurston

How It Feels to Be Colored Me

Born in Eatonville, Florida, in a year that she never remembered the same way twice, Zora Neale Hurston (1901?–1960) entered Howard University in 1923. In 1926 she won a scholarship to Barnard College, where she was the first black woman to be admitted. There Hurston developed an interest in anthropology, which was cultivated by Columbia University's distinguished anthropologist, Frank Boas. From 1928 to 1931 she collected voodoo folklore in the South and published her findings in Mules and Men *(1935). Two successive Guggenheim Fellowships allowed her to do field work in the Caribbean, resulting in another anthropological study,* Tell My Horse *(1938). She also collected folklore about Florida for the Works Progress Administration and published the two novels for which she is justly famous,* Jonah's Gourd Vine *(1934), and* Their Eyes Were Watching God *(1937).*

Langston Hughes said that "she was always getting scholarships and things from wealthy white people." But when the economy collapsed and brought the famous Harlem Renaissance down with it, Hurston's patrons all but disappeared. She managed to publish two more books, Moses, Man of the Mountain *(1939) and* Seraph on the Suwanee *(1948), and her autobiography,* Dust Tracks on a Road *(1942), before her reputation suffered a serious decline during the 1950s. After working as a librarian, part-time teacher, and maid near the end of her life, Hurston died in a county welfare home in Florida in virtual obscurity. The rediscovery of her work is largely attributed to Alice Walker, who edited a collection of Hurston's writings,* I Love Myself When I'm Laughing *(1975). "How It Feels to Be Colored Me" originally appeared in* The World Tomorrow *in 1928.*

Hurston said, "I regret all my books. It is one of the tragedies of life that one cannot have all the wisdom one is ever to possess in the beginning. Perhaps, it is just as well to be rash and foolish for a while. If writers were too wise, perhaps no books would be written at all. It might be better to ask yourself 'Why?' afterwards than before. Anyway, the force from somewhere in Space which commands you to write in the first place, gives you no choice. You take up the pen when you are told, and write what is commanded. There is no agony like bearing an untold story inside you."

I am colored but I offer nothing in the way of extenuating circumstances except the fact that I am the only Negro in the United States whose grandfather on the mother's side was *not* an Indian chief.

I remember the very day that I became colored. Up to my thirteenth year I lived in the little Negro town of Eatonville, Florida. It is exclusively a colored town. The only white people I knew passed through the town going to or coming from Orlando. The native whites rode dusty horses, the Northern tourists chugged down the sandy village road in automobiles. The town knew the Southerners and never stopped cane chewing[1] when they passed. But the Northerners were something else again. They were peered at cautiously from behind curtains by the timid. The more venturesome would come out on the porch to watch them go past and got just as much pleasure out of the tourists as the tourists got out of the village.

The front porch might seem a daring place for the rest of the town, but it was a gallery seat for me. My favorite place was atop the gate-post. Proscenium box for a born first-nighter. Not only did I enjoy the show, but I didn't mind the actors knowing that I liked it. I usually spoke to them in passing. I'd wave at them and when they returned my salute, I would say something like this: "Howdy-do-well-I-thank-you-where-you-goin'?" Usually automobile or the horse paused at this, and after a queer exchange of compliments, I would probably "go a piece of the way" with them, as we say in farthest Florida. If one of my family happened to come to the front in time to see me, of course negotiations would be rudely broken off. But even so, it is clear that I was the first "welcome-to-our-state" Floridian, and I hope the Miami Chamber of Commerce will please take notice.

During this period, white people differed from colored to me only in that they rode through town and never lived there. They liked to hear me "speak pieces" and sing and wanted to see me dance the parse-me-la,[2] and gave me generously of their small silver for doing these things, which seemed strange to me for I wanted to do them so much that I needed bribing to stop. Only they didn't know it. The colored people gave no dimes. They deplored any joyful tendencies in me, but I was their Zora nevertheless. I belonged to them, to the nearby hotels, to the county — everybody's Zora.

But changes came in the family when I was thirteen, and I was sent to school in Jacksonville. I left Eatonville, the town of the oleanders, as Zora. When I disembarked from the river-boat at Jacksonville, she was no more. It seemed that I had suffered a sea change. I was not Zora of Orange County any more, I was now a little colored girl. I found it out in certain ways. In my heart as well as in the mirror, I became a fast brown — warranted not to rub nor run.

But I am not tragically colored. There is no great sorrow dammed up in my soul, nor lurking behind my eyes. I do not mind at all. I do not belong to the sobbing school of Negrohood who hold that nature somehow has given them a lowdown dirty deal and whose feelings are all hurt about it. Even in

[1]*cane chewing:* Chewing on sugar cane. — EDS.
[2]*parse-me-la:* Probably an old dance song. — EDS.

the helter-skelter skirmish that is my life, I have seen that the world is to the strong regardless of a little pigmentation more or less. No, I do not weep at the world — I am too busy sharpening my oyster knife.

Someone is always at my elbow reminding me that I am the grand-daughter of slaves. It fails to register depression with me. Slavery is sixty years in the past. The operation was successful and the patient is doing well, thank you. The terrible struggle that made me an American out of a potential slave said "On the line!" The Reconstruction[3] said "Get set!"; and the generation before said "Go!" I am off to a flying start and I must not halt in the stretch to look behind and weep. Slavery is the price I paid for civilization, and the choice was not with me. It is a bully adventure and worth all that I have paid through my ancestors for it. No one on earth ever had a greater chance for glory. The world to be won and noth-ing to be lost. It is thrilling to think — to know that for any act of mine, I shall get twice as much praise or twice as much blame. It is quite exciting to hold the center of the national stage, with the spectators not knowing whether to laugh or to weep.

The position of my white neighbor is much more difficult. No brown specter pulls up a chair beside me when I sit down to eat. No dark ghost thrusts its leg against mine in bed. The game of keeping what one has is never so exciting as the game of getting.

I do not always feel colored. Even now I often achieve the uncon-scious Zora of Eatonville before the Hegira.[4] I feel most colored when I am thrown against a sharp white background.

For instance at Barnard. "Beside the waters of the Hudson" I feel my race. Among the thousand white persons, I am a dark rock surged upon, and overswept, but through it all, I remain myself. When covered by the waters, I am; and the ebb but reveals me again.

10

Sometimes it is the other way around. A white person is set down in our midst, but the contrast is just as sharp for me. For instance, when I sit in the drafty basement that is The New World Cabaret with a white person, my color comes. We enter chatting about any little nothing that we have in common and are seated by the jazz waiters. In the abrupt way that jazz or-chestras have, this one plunges into a number. It loses no time in circumlo-cutions, but gets right down to business. It constricts the thorax and splits the heart with its tempo and narcotic harmonies. This orchestra grows ram-bunctious, rears on its hind legs and attacks the tonal veil with primitive fury, rending it, clawing it until it breaks through to the jungle beyond. I follow those heathen — follow them exultingly. I dance wildly inside my-self; I yell within, I whoop; I shake my assegai[5] above my head, I hurl it true

[3]*Reconstruction:* The period of rebuilding and reorganizing immediately following the Civil War. — EDS.

[4]*Hegira:* A journey to safety. Historically it refers to Mohammed's flight from Mecca in A.D. 622. — EDS.

[5]*assegai:* A hunting spear. — EDS.

to the mark *yeeeeoowww!* I am in the jungle and living in the jungle way. My face is painted red and yellow and my body is painted blue. My pulse is throbbing like a war drum. I want to slaughter something — give pain, give death to what, I do not know. But the piece ends. The men of the orchestra wipe their lips and rest their fingers. I creep back slowly to the veneer we call civilization with the last tone and find the white friend sitting motionless in his seat, smoking calmly.

"Good music they have here," he remarks, drumming the table with his fingertips.

Music. The great blobs of purple and red emotion have not touched him. He has only heard what I felt. He is far away and I see him but dimly across the ocean and the continent that have fallen between us. He is so pale with his whiteness then and I am *so* colored.

At certain times I have no race, I am *me*. When I set my hat at a certain angle and saunter down Seventh Avenue, Harlem City, feeling as snooty as the lions in front of the Forty-Second Street Library, for instance. So far as my feelings are concerned, Peggy Hopkins Joyce[6] on the Boule Mich[7] with her gorgeous raiment, stately carriage, knees knocking together in a most aristocratic manner, has nothing on me. The cosmic Zora emerges. I belong to no race nor time. I am the eternal feminine with its string of beads.

I have no separate feeling about being an American citizen and colored. I am merely a fragment of the Great Soul that surges within the boundaries. My country, right or wrong.

Sometimes, I feel discriminated against, but it does not make me angry. It merely astonishes me. How *can* any deny themselves the pleasure of my company? It's beyond me.

But in the main, I feel like a brown bag of miscellany propped against a wall. Against a wall in company with other bags, white, red, and yellow. Pour out the contents, and there is discovered a jumble of small things priceless and worthless. A first-water diamond, an empty spool, bits of broken glass, lengths of string, a key to a door long since crumbled away, a rusty knife-blade, old shoes saved for a road that never was and never will be, a nail bent under the weight of things too heavy for any nail, a dried flower or two still a little fragrant. In your hand is the brown bag. On the ground before you is the jumble it held — so much like the jumble in the bags, could they be emptied, that all might be dumped in a single heap and the bags refilled without altering the content of any greatly. A bit of colored glass more or less would not matter. Perhaps that is how the Great Stuffer of Bags filled them in the first place — who knows?

---

[6]***Peggy Hopkins Joyce:*** A fashionable American who was a celebrity in the 1920s. — EDS.

[7]***Boule Mich:*** The Boulevard Saint-Michel in Paris. — EDS.

The Reader's Presence

1. Hurston's essay is divided into four sections. Do you find this division significant? What relationships can you detect among the separate parts?

2. How much does being "colored" inform Hurston's identity? Does it seem to matter throughout the essay? At what points does color seem deeply important to Hurston? When does it seem less important? What do you think the reasons are for these differences?

3. Consider Hurston's startling image in the final paragraph: "But in the main, I feel like a brown bag of miscellany propped against a wall." Try rereading the essay with this image in mind. In what ways does it help you understand Hurston's sense of personal identity? In what ways can it be said to describe the form and style of the essay itself?

16

Edward Iwata

Race without Face

Edward Iwata (b. 1957) is a business writer for the San Francisco Examiner. *He has worked as a freelance journalist, writing extensively about the media, literature, racial issues, Asian-American culture, and the Pacific Rim for the* Los Angeles Times, Editor & Publisher *magazine,* Newsweek Japan, San Francisco Focus *(where "Race without Face" appeared in 1991), and other publications. He and his wife are former residential educators at Stanford University's Okada House, a residence hall and community center for students interested in Asian American, Asian, and cross-cultural topics.*

Asked for his reflections on the essay that is reprinted here, Iwata said, "Personal essays are the first draft of one's history. And that unique and spirited history is always changing, always evolving. If you can craft your vision with a bit of skill and precision, you're a lucky dude. Keep at it. Go for it."

I would soon discover I was different from white people.

A cosmetic surgeon was about to cut into my face that gray winter morning. Hot lights glared as I lay on the operating table. Surgical tools clattered in containers, sharp metal against metal. I felt like a lamb awaiting a shearing of its wool.

Shivering from the air-conditioned chill, I wondered if I'd made a mistake. Had my hatred of Oriental facial features, fanned by my desire to do well in a white world, blinded me so easily?

An instant before the anesthetic numbed my brain cells, I felt the urge to cry out. I imagined ripping off my gown and sprinting to freedom. But at that point, even wetting my cracked lips was hard to do.

"I trust you implicitly," I said, as a supplicant might beseech a priest.   5

Oddly, I imagined seeing, as if peering through a bloody gauze, the contours of two faces rushing toward me. One face was twisted into sadness. The other glowed with a look akin to pride. One white, one yellow; one white, one yellow. I did not know which was which.

A month earlier in her Beverly Hills medical office, the surgeon said she planned to taper the thick, round tip of my nose. She also wanted to build up my flat bridge with strips of cartilage.

"Oriental noses have no definition," she said, waving a clipboard like an inspector on an auto assembly line.

While she was at it, she suggested, why not work on the eyes, also? They looked dark and tired, even though I was twenty years old then. A simple slash along my eyelids would remove the fat cells that kept my eyes from springing into full, double-lidded glory.

Why not? I had thought. Didn't I want to distance myself from the   10
faceless, Asian masses? I hated the pale image in the mirror. I hated the slurs hurled at me that I couldn't shut out. I hated being a gook, a Nip.

It's a taboo subject, but true: Many people of color have, at some point in their youths, imagined themselves as Caucasian, the Nordic or Western European ideal. Hop Sing meets Rock Hudson. Michael Jackson magically transformed into Robert Redford.

For myself, an eye and nose job — or *blepharoplasty* and *rhinoplasty* in surgeons' tongue — would bring me the gift of acceptance. The flick of a scalpel would buy me respect.

To make the decision easier, a close friend loaned me $1500. I didn't tell my parents or anyone else about it.

The surgery was quick and painless. My friend drove me at dawn to the medical clinic. At 7 A.M. sharp, the surgeon, a brusque Hispanic woman, swept into the office and rushed passed us.

The next time I saw her, she was peering down at me and penciling   15
lines on my face to guide her scalpel. A surgeon's mask and cap hid her own face; I saw only a large pair of eyes plotting the attack on my epidermis and cartilage. While I shivered, a nurse and an anesthesiologist laughed and gossiped.

"You have beautiful eyelashes, Edward," the surgeon said. It seemed like an odd thing to notice at that moment.

I tumbled into darkness. My last memory was a deep desire to yell or strike out, to stab the surgeon and her conspirators with their knives.

The surgeon went for my eyes first. Gently, she cut and scooped out the fat cells that lined my upper eyelid. That created a small furrow, which popped open my eyes a bit and created double-lids, every Asian model's dream.

Ignoring the blood, she then slit the upper inside of my nostril. Like a shortorder cook trimming a steak, she carved the cartilage and snipped off bits of bone and tissue. Soon she was done. After a coffee break or lunch, she would move on to the next patient.

Later that day, I was wheeled out of a bright recovery room. My head and limbs felt dull and heavy, as if buried in mud. A draft swept up my surgical gown and chilled my legs. Although my face was bound in bandages, I felt naked. Without warning, a sharp sense of loss engulfed me, a child away from home who is not sure why he aches so.

"Eddie, what did you do?" asked my mother when I next saw her. Then, her voice shaking, "Why did you do this? Were you ashamed of yourself?" As if struck by a lance, my legs weakened, my body cleaved. I was lost, flailing away in shadows, but I shrugged off her question and said something lame. I didn't sense at the time that whatever had compelled me to scar my face could also drive me further from home.

One week passed before I was brave enough to take my first look in the mirror. I stood in the bathroom, staring at my reflection until my feet got sore.

Stitch marks scarred my face like tracks on a drug addict's arm. My haggard eyes were rounder; my nose smaller and pudgy. In the glare of the bathroom light, my skin seemed pale and washed out, a claylike shade of light brown. I looked like a medical illustration from a century ago, when doctors would have measured my facial angle and cranium size for racial intelligence.

I wanted to claw my new face.

The image I pictured in the mirror was an idealized Anglo man, an abstraction. I didn't realize at the time that my flaws were imagined, not real. I felt compelled to measure up to a cultural ideal in a culture that had never asked me what my ideal was.

Indeed, to many Anglos, the males of our culture are a mystery. Most whites know us only through the neutered images: Japanese salarymen. Sumo wrestlers. Sushi chefs. We're judged by our slant of eye and color of skin. We're seen only as eunuchs, as timid dentists and engineers. Books and movies portray us as ugly and demonic. We're truly a race of Invisible Men.

Clearly, Asian-American men have been psychologically castrated in this country. Our history is one of emasculation and accommodation. Japanese-Americans, for the most part, filed quietly into the internment camps. Proud Cantonese immigrants were trapped in their Chinatown ghettoes and bachelor societies by poverty and discrimination.

In the corporate arena, Asian-American men find their cultural values and strengths overshadowed by ego-driven, back-slapping, hypercompetitive whites. And, while socially we may be more "acceptable" than blacks and Hispanics, we are not acceptable enough to run legislatures, schools, corporations. Our women may be marriage material for whites, but our men are still seen as gooks. On the street, we're cursed or spat upon — even killed — because of our looks.

It cannot be denied, either, that we're regarded as kowtowing wimps not only by whites, but by a lot of Asian-American women — even those with racial and ethnic pride. Privately, they confess they see a lack of strong Asian-American men who fit an ideal of manhood: virile and sensitive, intelligent and intuitive, articulate and confident.

Of course, we must share part of the blame. Many of us grow up   30
swallowing the stereotypes, accepting the role white society imposes on us. And aside from a handful of us in politics, law, the media, education, and the arts, the rest of us are too reserved and opinionless in the white world.

Simone de Beauvoir wrote that a woman "insinuates herself into a world that has doomed her to passivity." The same could have been said of too many Asian-American men, including myself.

I recall an episode four years ago when a former boss and I lunched at a Thai restaurant. I thought I deserved a promotion — new status, new duties, a bigger paycheck — real fast. He disagreed. Between bites of curry chicken, I was startled to hear this executive label me in words used for "docile" Asian men and "uppity" blacks.

"You're a quiet, reserved kind of guy," he said, waving his hands in the air. A few bites later, he veered the other way and portrayed me as a "cocky, arrogant young reporter . . . with a chip on your shoulder."

I was confused. Was I an obedient employee, or a hard-charging militant? And how could I be both? I ate my rice and said little. My face flushed with anger. Later that day, I left work early, fantasizing about a bloody, *ninja*-style revenge.

Why didn't I fight back? Instead of sitting silently, why didn't I chal-   35
lenge his superficial view of me?

Part of it was cultural. Our Eastern values are living, breathing elements in our lives, not topics we study in Zen Buddhism class. Regardless of how assimilated we may be, these values rise to claim our attention at unpredictable moments. So while I fancied myself a strong-minded journalist, I still felt shackled by cultural bonds, afraid of arguing back. It was the whole *deference* thing, this Asian habit of respecting authority to a fault.

I yearned for my boss' acceptance. I was blinded by my desire to fit in as a man, a journalist, a corporate player. In Japan, this could be called *ittaikan*, a longing for oneness with a person or a group. Readers of the Japanese psychiatrist Takeo Doi might think of it as *amae*, a passive dependency on another's love or kindness.

And so, by others and by ourselves, we're rendered impotent. I wasn't a limp lover. But outside my home or bedroom, I often felt powerless — desexed like a baby chick. It was as if I didn't exist. Employers didn't acknowledge my work. Professors in college rebuffed my remarks in the classroom. *Maître d*'s ignored my presence in restaurants. I felt voiceless, faceless.

A friend of mine, a San Francisco lawyer in her thirties, was thrilled to meet a liberal Japanese man from Tokyo after years of dating Asian-Americans. Several of her boyfriends had been bright and sensitive, but they lacked what she called "male energy" — a strength of purpose and destiny, a vision of one's goals in life.

"It's almost a *samurai* spirit that Asian-American men somehow lost 40 in white society, as if they'd been neutered," she said. "Even though I'm a career woman, sometimes I want a man to take the lead, while I play the mothering role. . . . Reconnecting with a strong, decisive Asian male has been an eye-opener."

My friend's opinion is not unusual. Unfortunately some Asian-American men, scared of the nerd label, charge blindly in the opposite direction, aping Western notions of kick-ass masculinity: Rambo. Mike Tyson. Michael Milken. They become obsessed with the art of war, obsessed with competition. It's yet another stereotype, and equally damaging.

One example, a hot item in our community, is an all-male calendar, featuring pin-ups of Asian-American hunks. While the men photographed are all respected, the beefcake images they project are caricatures of the white physical ideal: the well-oiled, muscular body, the chiseled face, the hint of male power and violence. They're like minorities in beauty pageants who look more like the blond Miss America prototype than their own race.

"How warped that sense of manhood and beauty is," observes King-Kok Cheung, a literary scholar at UCLA. "In some ways, our internal oppression as Asians is greater than white oppression. We need to understand that anyone who is comfortable with himself is attractive."

Probably the biggest blow to my young psyche occurred at my predominantly white high school. My advanced English class boasted students who were versed in Petrarchan sonnets before I had learned to read baseball box scores. Even so, as a teenager I saw myself as a maverick writer in the manner of Jack Kerouac or Jack London. Mrs. Worthy, our strict teacher, showed me otherwise.

"Mr. Iwata, I'd like you to work on 'A Book Is Like a Frigate' by 45 Emily Dickinson," she said, assigning homework. "That shouldn't be too difficult to handle, even for you."

I still get chills when I recall my classmates shifting in their seats, their blue and green eyes staring at me. To Mrs. Worthy, I was the slow, quiet Asian boy who sat by the window, waiting for the school bus to dump me back in the inner-city.

Outside the classroom, media images confused me even more. Nowhere — from racist children's books to great literature to movies with evil Jap soldiers — did I see my true reflection in the larger world.

Unlike students today, I had no Asian or Asian-American heroes, no cultural icons, to lead the way.

In sociological jargon, I was an Assimilationist, a Marginal Man, a Stranger. Like many Asian-Americans, I craved admiration and acceptance, mostly from whites. I worshipped Anglo models of success, the middle-class ethos carried to extremes.

But contrary to our shining image as model minorities, I learned I had *not* arrived. All the hard work and schooling and cosmetic surgery in the world couldn't change the way I looked, or the way I was perceived. I could not erase my skin color, no matter how hard I tried. My status in the white professional world was illusory; it did not transcend the harsh realities of race and class.

In my search for acceptance, I modeled myself after whites, especially   50
in college — in speech and diction, style and dress, body language and eye contact. I thought I was a failure when no white coeds danced with me at a frat party. At beer busts, I avoided Asian-American women because they looked like the girls in my old neighborhood, with their moon faces and *daikon* (white radish) legs.

Before that, I used to hang with Hispanic buddies from East L.A. I was a *vato*, an *esé*, a buddha brother. And before that, I played basketball and dodged gangs in Crenshaw, a black and Asian neighborhood in Los Angeles. I wasn't cool, but I could fake it. When black classmates called me "nigger" or "homes" (short for "homeboy"), I smiled inside. Another mask.

At the same time, I fought the tug of family and culture. Seeking a place beyond my ken, I left Crenshaw to live on campus as a college freshman. I saw my new world as a stage ripe for rebellion.

My courses — journalism, literature, history — disappointed my parents. They hoped I would study medicine or business, like all good Japanese-American kids.

I was studying, all right: the science of interviewing accident victims for newspaper stories. Themes of Dionysian abandon, from Blake to Lord Byron. My literary hero was James Joyce, whose modernist art promised to transport me to Arabys unknown. I had not yet begun to study myself.

My bid for a cultural identity, a sense of manhood, quickened as my   55
mother and father retired, and as Dad's health worsened. Clearly, a strong impulse pushed me to step up and fill their vacuum, to carry on a family legacy in some way.

My parents, Phillip and Midori, and sixteen relatives spent the years during World War II at Manzanar, the internment camp eight miles from the town of Independence in the Mojave Desert. When I was a kid, Mom never talked about Manzanar. Instead, she wove harmless tales for my brother, my sister, and me. The stories protected us from the truth.

Dad, a strong silent type, claimed he never cared about the political quest for redress — the twenty thousand dollars due each Japanese-American interned during the war. Interviewing him for the first story I did on Manzanar was not easy. "You don't have to write about this, do you?" he asked. Speaking to him the next time was even harder. "I told you I'm not a good person to interview," he snapped. "Talk to Mom again."

His reticence was understandable. Conservative Japanese-Americans hide their private faces in public. *Nomen no yo,* their ancestors said. *The face is like a Noh mask.* My mother and father calmly accepted their fates.

Like many Japanese-Americans, my parents veiled the past and white-washed their memories. They believed the government line that Uncle Sam sent them to the concentration camps for their own good, for their safety. The camps also gave them postwar opportunities by spreading them across the great land, they were told.

In truth, the internment was a horror for families, a civil rights disaster, the death of the old Japanese-American culture. For the men, the sense of powerlessness must have been devastating.   60

In my parents' desire to hide the past, I sensed a reflection of my own self-hate. Like most *sansei* (third generation), I ignored or never sought out the tragic facts of that era. As a student, I never read about the camps. As a young journalist, I picked up shards of history, but never the whole dark tale.

But after much cajoling, I persuaded my folks to join me on a pilgrimage to Manzanar in 1988. Only tumbleweeds, stone ruins, and barbed wire remained at the windy, desolate site. Nonetheless, the pilgrimage was a glimpse into a forgotten world, a gateway to the past. The ghosts were powerful. But I found no neat, easy answers.

There was no stopping now. The next spring, we flew to Japan. While trade wars dominated the news in Tokyo, my parents and I journeyed into the rural heart of our ancestral homeland.

For the first time, we met the Iwata and Kunitomi clans, who still live on the rice farms in Wakayama and Okayama that our families have owned since the eighteenth century. Among other revelations, I learned that the head of the Iwata family, my father's cousin, shared my Japanese name, Masao ("righteous boy").

Seated on a *tatami* floor at the Iwata homestead, we enjoyed *sukiyaki*   65 and country-style vegetables we hadn't eaten since my grandmothers died several years ago. The *gohan* (steamed rice) was the lightest and sweetest we had ever tasted. Masao smiled broadly as he served the hot food, its steam rising toward the small family altar in the corner of the dining room.

At one point, I noticed Masao staring at Dad. His steady gaze was rude by Japanese standards. But apparently struck by the family resemblance, Masao couldn't avert his eyes from Dad's face. With their wavy hair and thick eyebrows, their dark skin and rakish grins, they could have been brothers.

I'm not a misty-eyed romantic longing for an ancestral past. Peering for gods in mountain shrines and temple ruins is not my idea of good journalism. Still, this was my flesh and blood seated in an old farmhouse on that warm spring night. I thought of a line from *No-No Boy,* a novel of WWII by John Okada: "If he was to find his way back to that point of wholeness and belonging, he must do so in the place where he had begun to lose it." Here was my point of origin, where my family began. As we scooped bowlfuls of rice into our hungry selves, a light rain wet the furrows of black soil in the field outside.

For me, Japan brought to the surface cultural conflicts and competing values. Even though I was as American as teriyaki chicken, the old Buddhist and Confucian values reached me in Southern California. *Giri* (obligation). *Omoiyari* (empathy). *Oyakoko* (filial piety). The Japanese, in fact, have a phrase unique to them: *"Jibun ga nai,"* or "to have no self." They rarely use the first-person pronoun when they speak. Loyal *samurai* who followed their feudal barons to the grave had little over some Japanese-American kids.

Those values gave me strength — and also confused the hell out of me. The issue of personal independence and family ties was the most painful. How was I to pursue my goals, forge an identity, yet honor my parents without question? And if I chose filial piety, how was I to keep the bond strong without sacrificing my hard-won, American-style autonomy?

A Zen *koan*[1] asks, "What was your face like before you were born?"   70 I cannot know for sure how deeply the culture of my ancestors touches me, but I know I will never again see myself as a scarred, hollow man lost in the shadows, beating back death.

Japan freed my spirit and gave rise to an atavistic pride I had never known. The past, I realized, could be cradled like an heirloom found in an old trunk in the attic. I was a player in a family history that spanned the reigns of emperors, from feudal Japan to the modern Heisei Era, Year One — the year of my first visit to Japan. And my story would add a few scenes to that unfolding narrative.

After Manzanar and Japan, I began to see my surgery in a new slant of light. Like the victims of internment, I started coming to terms with my real and emotional scars.

Obviously, the surgery had been a rebellion against my "Japaneseness" and the traditional values of my parents. It was psychic surgery, an act of mutilation, a symbolic suicide. It was my self-hatred finding a stage.

Like many Asian Americans, I'm searching for a new cultural character   75 and destiny.

Certainly, we need to change many of our past goals. While much is known of our drive toward the American dream, little is written of our worship of materialism, our narcissism, our obsession with showing that we've *arrived.* We're brilliant students of what historian Richard Hofstadter called "status politics," the effort to enhance one's social standing.

---

[1]*koan:* A paradoxical question used for Zen Buddhist meditation. — EDS.

Somewhere between Asia and an "A+" in Achievement, we lost our way. The trappings of style and success — a fancy degree, a prestigious job, a Mercedes in every garage — have become more important than the accomplishments. Instead, the images we impress upon white society and other Asian-Americans are paramount. We have become the "racial bourgeoisie," a term coined by legal scholar Mari Matsuda. The hard work may bring "success," but this kind of success will not set us free.

The numbers reflect the reality. They tell a sad story, especially in education, supposedly our stronghold. Asian-Americans held 3.1 percent of administrative and management jobs in California colleges and universities, according to an analysis of 1980 census data by Amado Cabezas and Gary Kawaguchi of UC Berkeley's Ethnic Studies Department. Even more startling were the income figures. Asian-American faculty and staff were paid salaries *40 to 70 percent* of the mean annual income of white men. And this is only in one field.

A century ago, sugar plantation owners in Hawaii counted Asian laborers as part of their business supplies. Today, we're still regarded similarly: as bodies to fill affirmative-action goals, as background in movies. Even worse, we gladly accept what society imposes on us, so anxious are we to measure up to its standards of "success."

There is so much cultural brainwashing to undo, and so much to learn about our place in this country.

Many of us will not tolerate the status quo anymore. The *Miss Saigon*   80 controversy reflects our rising anger. It's *our* March on Washington, *our* Stonewall gay riot, *our* Jackson, Mississippi. In other recent shows of strength, we've rallied around the racial killings of Asian-Americans. Our congressional and community leaders won redress payments for the internment of Japanese-Americans. And more Asian-Americans are filling seats in public office.

But where do we go next? And how do we define our community, if at all?

Clearly, we need new visions, new models. Elaine Kim, a UC Berkeley dean and ethnic studies scholar, says our community defies easy branding. The boundaries of Asian America are changing, fusing, changing again. "We're much more than white versus nonwhite, suburbanites versus urban people of color, East versus West, tradition versus modernity," she argues. "We're creating our culture every day."

Slowly and surely, a strong Asian-American culture is coming of age. It's a bold culture, unashamed and true to itself. It's a culture with a common destiny, *a community of the mind and soul*. And it's taking many forms — in plays and films, in literature and journalism, in history and the social sciences, in professional groups and political caucuses. We can certainly start by realizing we don't need to parrot anyone else's notions of success and beauty. "We're not slaves to culture, but agents of culture, agents of change," says King-Kok Cheung. Instead of conforming to prefabricated images and stereotypes, we must define our own successes, our own personalities, our own images.

We must not vanish completely into the suburbs, nor must we isolate ourselves in our close-knit but ethnocentric Asian communities. Instead, we must find a new common ethos, a new aesthetic, a new psychology.

This new Asian America must transcend, yet embrace, our differ-   85
ences. It must value collective ethnic pride, yet respect individualism. It must honor equality of race and gender, and bury our hypocritical racism, sexism, and homophobia. And it must not hide behind moral self-righteousness or ideological rigidity, which poisons the radical left and fundamentalist right.

Our artists and scholars and educators, for the most part, create positive images, but we need many more; we cannot wait for Hollywood. Role models in all fields are important. Parents must teach their kids inner strength, not outer conformity. We must build more bridges with whites and others in a meaningful sense, not merely for show.

And as for Asian-American manhood? For Buddha's sake, let's use our imagination. The Lone Ranger and Bruce Lee are dead. We don't need to out-gun or measure up to anyone. We can return to the original meaning of compete, which comes from the Latin word *competere*, "to come together." Manhood now is a destructive, stereotyped, behavioral trap. Asian-Americans must recast our concept of masculinity, sculpting it into a larger definition of humanity.

For our role models, we can look to the past. The Japanese *bushido* ethic, the *samurai* spiritual and martial philosophy, is one. The scholarly Sage-King and Superior Man of Confucian thought is another, as is the Greek concept of *areté* — virtue in thought and action. All prized a male beauty and an ethos of strength and serenity, action and calmness, *yin* and *yang*.

To be sure, more Asian-American men are refusing to lock themselves into narrow roles and models. Rick Yuen, for example, a dean at Stanford, often finds himself caring for his two children and deferring to his wife, SF Community College board member Mabel Teng, on many family and career decisions. "I start with the basic assumption that we're men and women of equal standing," he says simply.

In the literary arts, playwrights David Henry Hwang and Philip   90
Gotanda and poet David Mura explore themes of ethnic manhood and sexuality. In the social arena, gay Asians are starting to emerge, attacking the layer upon layer of racism and homophobia they face in the straight and gay worlds.

On a recent trip to Los Angeles, I stumbled across an irresistible metaphor for our culture. A journalist friend, Brenda Sunoo of the *Korea Times,* had invited me to join her family at a concert of young Asian-American musicians, all amateurs.

The concert was a romp in culture-bending and blending. There were Korean rappers. A Japanese folksinger. A Filipino multimedia artist.

When the rap dancers blew a tricky move and fell to the ground, drawing laughs, they hid their faces in their hands in embarrassment. Another singer, his set delayed by technical problems, repeatedly thanked the audience for its patience.

The performers seemed much like Asian America: shy but daring; apologetic but confident; imitative yet novel. "There's no blueprint for us," said Brenda. "Our history is being written now. Our individual choices will make us unique."

We've barely started to explore the beauty of our culture. With a little luck, the new Asian America will be a choral celebration, not an aria sung to an elite few. This will keep us from fading into white society as admired but bleached Americans.

We're trying to change the cultural paradigm, image by image. We   95
have to. For it is how we see each other that will ultimately transform the world. How we see each other, and how we see ourselves.

So where does this all lead me? Do I feel more whole in my newfound identity? Have I tossed the masks slapped on me by society, my family, myself? Do I know why I cut off my nose to spite my race?

Yes, to all of the above. Now I see my image and others in a less harsh light. I know one's slant of eye and color of skin are bogus issues. For beyond acculturation, beyond racial identity, is the larger question of *kokoro* — Japanese for heart and soul. Make no mistake: I've learned I *am* different from white people. Not better, not worse, but distinct. The faces rushing toward me in my pre-surgical daze were neither white nor yellow. They were mine.

The Reader's Presence

1. What does Iwata believe are the common assumptions whites make about Asian men? Does he imply that you (the reader) personally make these assumptions? Did you see yourself as inside or outside of his intended audience?

2. What image of himself does Iwata create for his readers? What does he say to establish his presence in the essay as an independent, tough-minded thinker? Why do you think he wants to project that image of himself?

3. Iwata discusses the importance of "cultural brainwashing" on his decision. Who is responsible for that brainwashing? Why was he unable at first to resist it? Do you or do you not believe his surgery has transformed him intellectually? *Why? How?*

17

David Mamet

The Rake: A Few Scenes from My Childhood

David Mamet (b. 1947) is a playwright, screenwriter, and director whose work is appreciated for the attention he pays to language as it is spoken by ordinary people in the contemporary world. His Pulitzer Prize–winning play, Glengarry Glen Ross, *explores the psychology of ambition, competition, failure, and despair among a group of Chicago real estate agents who are driven to sell worthless property to unsuspecting customers.*

Mamet has said that "playwriting is simply showing how words influence actions and vise versa. All my plays attempt to bring out the poetry in the plain, everyday language people use. That's the only way to put art back in the theater." Mamet's sensitivity to working-class language and experience is due in part to his own work experience in factories, at a real estate agency, and as a window washer, office cleaner, and taxi driver. More recently, he has taught theater at several leading universities and has published two collections of essays; his most recent collection of plays, Cryptogram, *was published in 1995. "The Rake: A Few Scenes from My Childhood" appeared in* Harper's *in 1992.*

There was the incident of the rake and there was the incident of the school play, and it seems to me that they both took place at the round kitchen table.

The table was not in the kitchen proper but in an area called "the nook," which held its claim to that small measure of charm by dint of a waist-high wall separating it from an adjacent area known as the living room.

All family meals were eaten in the nook. There was a dining room to the right, but, as in most rooms of that name at the time and in those surroundings, it was never used.

The round table was of wrought iron and topped with glass; it was noteworthy for that glass, for it was more than once and rather more than several times, I am inclined to think, that my stepfather would grow so angry as to bring some object down on the glass top, shattering it, thus giving us to know how we had forced him out of control.

114

And it seems that most times when he would shatter the table, as   5
often as that might have been, he would cut some portion of himself on
the glass, or that he or his wife, our mother, would cut their hands on
picking up the glass afterward, and that we children were to understand,
and did understand, that these wounds were our fault.

So the table was associated in our minds with the notion of blood.

The house was in a brand-new housing development in the southern
suburbs. The new community was built upon, and now bordered, the remains of what had once been a cornfield. When our new family moved
in, there were but a few homes in the development completed, and a few
more under construction. Most streets were mud, and boasted a house
here or there, and many empty lots marked out by white stakes.

The house we lived in was the development's Model Home. The first
time we had seen it, it had signs plastered on the front and throughout
the interior telling of the various conveniences it contained. And it had a
lawn, and was one of the only homes in the new community that did.

My stepfather was fond of the lawn, and he detailed me and my sister
to care for it, and one fall afternoon we found ourselves assigned to rake
the leaves.

Why this chore should have been so hated I cannot say, except that   10
we children, and I especially, felt ourselves less than full members of this
new, cobbled-together family, and disliked being assigned to the beautifi-
cation of a home that we found unbeautiful in all respects, and for which
we had neither natural affection nor a sense of proprietary interest.

We went to the new high school. We walked the mile down the open
two-lane road on one side of which was the just-begun suburban community and on the other side of which was the cornfield.

The school was as new as the community, and still under construction for the first three years of its occupancy. One of its innovations was
the notion that honesty would be engendered by the absence of security,
and so the lockers were designed and built both without locks and without the possibility of attaching locks. And there was the corresponding
rash of thievery and many lectures about the same from the school administration, but it was difficult to point with pride to any scholastic or
community tradition supporting the suggestion that we, the students,
pull together in this new, utopian way. We were, in school, in an un-
completed building in the midst of a mud field in the midst of a cornfield. Our various sports teams were called The Spartans; and I played
on those teams, which were of a wretchedness consistent with their novelty.

Meanwhile my sister interested herself in the drama society. The year
after I had left the school she obtained the lead in the school play. It
called for acting and singing, both of which she had talent for, and it
looked to be a signal triumph for her in her otherwise unremarkable and
unenjoyed school career.

On the night of the play's opening, she sat down to dinner with our mother and our stepfather. It may be that they ate a trifle early to allow her to get to the school to enjoy the excitement of opening night. But however it was, my sister had no appetite, and she nibbled a bit at her food, and then she got up from the table to carry her plate back to scrape it in the sink, when my mother suggested that she sit down, as she had not finished her food. My sister said she really had no appetite, but my mother insisted that, as the meal had been prepared, it would be good form to sit and eat it.

My sister sat down with the plate and pecked at her food and she   15 tried to eat a bit, and told my mother that, no, really, she possessed no appetite whatever, and that was due, no doubt, not to the food, but to her nervousness and excitement at the prospect of opening night.

My mother, again, said that, as the food had been cooked, it had to be eaten, and my sister tried and said that she could not; at which my mother nodded. She then got up from the table and went to the telephone and looked the number up and called the school and got the drama teacher and identified herself and told him that her daughter wouldn't be coming to school that night, that, no, she was not ill, but that she would not be coming in. Yes, yes, she said, she knew her daughter had the lead in the play, and, yes, she was aware that many children and teachers had worked hard for it, et cetera, and so my sister did not play the lead in her school play. But I was long gone, out of the house by that time, and well out of it. I heard that story, and others like, at the distance of twenty-five years.

In the model house our rooms were separated from their room, the master bedroom, by a bathroom and a study. On some weekends I would go alone to visit my father in the city and my sister would stay and sometimes grow frightened or lonely in her part of the house. And once, in the period when my grandfather, then in his sixties, was living with us, she became alarmed at a noise she had heard in the night; or perhaps she just became lonely, and she went out of her room and down the hall, calling for my mother, or my stepfather, or my grandfather, but the house was dark, and no one answered.

And, as she went farther down the hall, toward the living room, she heard voices, and she turned the corner, and saw a light coming from under the closed door in the master bedroom, and heard my stepfather crying, and the sound of my mother weeping. So my sister went up to the door, and she heard my stepfather talking to my grandfather and saying, "Jack. Say the words. Just say the words . . ." And my grandfather in his Eastern European accent, saying with obvious pain and difficulty, "No. No. I can't. Why are you making me do this? Why?" And the sound of my mother crying convulsively.

My sister opened the door, and she saw my grandfather sitting on the bed, and my stepfather standing by the closet and gesturing. On the floor of the closet she saw my mother, curled in a fetal position, moaning and crying and hugging herself. My stepfather was saying, "Say the words. Just say the words." And my grandfather was breathing fast and repeating, "I can't. She knows how I feel about her. I can't." And my stepfather said, "Say the words, Jack. Please. Just say you love her." At which my mother would moan louder. And my grandfather said, "I can't."

My sister pushed the door open farther and said — I don't know   20
what she said, but she asked, I'm sure, for some reassurance, or some explanation, and my stepfather turned around and saw her and picked up a hairbrush from a dresser that he passed as he walked toward her, and he hit her in the face and slammed the door on her. And she continued to hear "Jack, say the words."

She told me that on weekends when I was gone my stepfather ended every Sunday evening by hitting or beating her for some reason or other. He would come home from depositing his own kids back at their mother's house after their weekend visitation, and would settle down tired and angry, and, as a regular matter on those evenings, would find out some intolerable behavior on my sister's part and slap or hit or beat her.

Years later, at my mother's funeral, my sister spoke to our aunt, my mother's sister, who gave a footnote to this behavior. She said when they were young, my mother and my aunt, they and their parents lived in a small flat on the West Side. My grandfather was a salesman on the road from dawn on Monday until Friday night. Their family had a fiction, and that fiction, that article of faith, was that my mother was a naughty child. And each Friday, when he came home, his first question as he climbed the stairs was, "What has she done this week . . . ?" At which my grandmother would tell him the terrible things that my mother had done, after which she, my mother, was beaten.

This was general knowledge in my family. The footnote concerned my grandfather's behavior later in the night. My aunt had a room of her own, and it adjoined her parents' room. And she related that each Friday, when the house had gone to bed, she, through the thin wall, heard my grandfather pleading for sex. "Cookie, please." And my grandmother responding, "No, Jack." "Cookie, please." "No, Jack." "Cookie, please."

And once, my grandfather came home and asked, "What has she done this week?" and I do not know, but I imagine that the response was not completed, and perhaps hardly begun; in any case, he reached and grabbed my mother by the back of the neck and hurled her down the stairs.

And once, in our house in the suburbs there had been an outburst by   25
my stepfather directed at my sister. And she had, somehow, prevailed. It was, I think, that he had the facts of the case wrong, and had accused her of the commission of something for which she had demonstrably had no opportunity, and she pointed this out to him with what I can imagine, given the circumstances, was an understandable, and, given my prejudice, a com-

mendable degree of freedom. Thinking the incident closed she went back to her room to study, and, a few moments later, saw him throw open her door, bat the book out of her hands, and pick her up and throw her against the far wall, where she struck the back of her neck on the shelf.

She was told, the next morning, that her pain, real or pretended, held no weight, and that she would have to go to school. She protested that she could not walk, or, if at all, only with the greatest of difficulty and in great pain; but she was dressed and did walk to school, where she fainted, and was brought home. For years she suffered various headaches; an X ray taken twenty years later for an unrelated problem revealed that when he threw her against the shelf he had cracked her vertebrae.

When we left the house we left in good spirits. When we went out to dinner, it was an adventure, which was strange to me, looking back, because many of these dinners ended with my sister or myself being banished, sullen or in tears, from the restaurant, and told to wait in the car, as we were in disgrace.

These were the excursions that had ended, due to her or my intolerable arrogance, as it was explained to us.

The happy trips were celebrated and capped with a joke. Here is the joke: My stepfather, my mother, my sister, and I would exit the restaurant, my stepfather and mother would walk to the car, telling us that they would pick us up. We children would stand by the restaurant entrance. They would drive up in the car, open the passenger door, and wait until my sister and I had started to get in. They would then drive away.

They would drive ten or fifteen feet, and open the door again, and we   30
would walk up again, and they would drive away again. They sometimes would drive around the block. But they would always come back, and by that time the four of us would be laughing in camaraderie and appreciation of what, I believe, was our only family joke.

We were raking the lawn, my sister and I. I was raking, and she was stuffing the leaves into a bag. I loathed the job, and my muscles and my mind rebelled, and I was viciously angry, and my sister said something, and I turned and threw the rake at her and hit her in the face.

The rake was split bamboo and metal, and a piece of metal caught her lip and cut her badly.

We were both terrified, and I was sick with guilt, and we ran into the house, my sister holding her hand to her mouth, and her mouth and her hand and the front of her dress covered in blood.

We ran into the kitchen where my mother was cooking dinner, and my mother asked what happened.

Neither of us, myself out of guilt, of course, and my sister out of a de-   35
sire to avert the terrible punishment she knew I would receive, neither of us would say what occurred.

My mother pressed us, and neither of us would answer. She said that until one or the other answered, we would not go to the hospital; and so the family sat down to dinner where my sister clutched a napkin to her face and the blood soaked the napkin and ran down onto her food, which she had to eat; and I also ate my food and we cleared the table and went to the hospital.

I remember the walks home from school in the frigid winter, along the cornfield that was, for all its proximity to the city, part of the prairie. The winters were viciously cold. From the remove of years, I can see how the area might and may have been beautiful. One could have walked in the stubble of the cornfields, or hunted birds, or enjoyed any of a number of pleasures naturally occurring.

The Reader's Presence

1. Mamet relates that he and his sister hated doing chores, in part because they "had neither natural affection nor a sense of proprietary interest" (paragraph 10) toward their house. How does Mamet's choice of words and details in the essay's opening paragraphs echo this? Why does he emphasize that his was a "Model Home"?

2. Near the end of the essay, Mamet recalls a "joke" that his family shared. How does he present the joke to the reader? Do you think Mamet wants the reader to think the joke is funny? Would the joke seem different if Mamet had told it at the beginning of the essay?

3. Why do you think that the incident of the rake plays such a significant role in the essay? Mamet introduces the rake in his opening sentence but does not describe the incident itself until near the end. Why? Do you think the rake has a symbolic value? If so, what does it represent?

18

N. Scott Momaday
The Way to Rainy Mountain

N. Scott Momaday (b. 1934) was born on a Kiowa Indian reservation in Ok-
lahoma and grew up surrounded by the cultural traditions of his people. Since
1982, he has been professor of English at the University of Arizona. His first
novel, House Made of Dawn *(1968), won a Pulitzer Prize. The author of poetry*
and autobiography, Momaday has edited a collection of Kiowa oral literature.
His most recent publications include Ancestral Voice: Conversations with N.
Scott Momaday *(1989),* The Ancient Child *(1989),* In the Presence of the Sun:
Stories and Poems *(1991), and* Circle of Wonder: A Native American Christmas
Story *(1994). "The Way to Rainy Mountain" appears as the introduction to the*
book of that name, published in 1969.

Momaday thinks of himself as a storyteller. When asked to compare his writ-
ten voice with his speaking voice, he replied, "My physical voice is something that
bears on my writing in an important way. I listen to what I write. I work with it
until it is what I want it to be in my hearing. I think that the voice of my writing
is very much like the voice of my speaking. And I think in both cases it's distinc-
tive. At least, I mean for it to be. I think that most good writers have individual
voices, and that the best writers are those whose voices are most distinctive —
most recognizably individual."

A single knoll rises out of the plain in Oklahoma, north and west of
the Wichita Range. For my people, the Kiowas, it is an old landmark, and
they gave it the name Rainy Mountain. The hardest winter in the world is
there. Winter brings blizzards, hot tornadic winds arise in the spring, and
in summer the prairie is an anvil's edge. The grass turns brittle and
brown, and it cracks beneath your feet. There are green belts along the
rivers and creeks, linear groves of hickory and pecan, willow and witch
hazel. At a distance in July or August, the steaming foliage seems almost
to writhe in fire. Great green and yellow grasshoppers are everywhere in
the tall grass, popping up like corn to sting the flesh, and tortoises crawl
about on the red earth, going nowhere in the plenty of time. Loneliness is
an aspect of the land. All things in the plain are isolate; there is no confusion of objects in the eye, but *one* hill or *one* tree or *one* man. To look

upon that landscape in the early morning, with the sun at your back, is to lose the sense of proportion. Your imagination comes to life, and this, you think, is where Creation was begun.

I returned to Rainy Mountain in July. My grandmother had died in the spring, and I wanted to be at her grave. She had lived to be very old and at last infirm. Her only living daughter was with her when she died, and I was told that in death her face was that of a child.

I like to think of her as a child. When she was born, the Kiowas were living the last great moment of their history. For more than a hundred years they had controlled the open range from the Smoky Hill River to the Red, from the headwaters of the Canadian to the fork of the Arkansas and Cimarron. In alliance with the Comanches, they had ruled the whole of the southern Plains. War was their sacred business, and they were among the finest horsemen the world has ever known. But warfare for the Kiowas was pre-eminently a matter of disposition rather than of survival, and they never understood the grim, unrelenting advance of the U.S. Cavalry. When at last, divided and ill-provisioned, they were driven onto the Staked Plains in the cold rains of autumn, they fell into panic. In Palo Duro Canyon they abandoned their crucial stores to pillage and had nothing then but their lives. In order to save themselves, they surrendered to the soldiers of Fort Sill and were imprisoned in the old stone corral that now stands as a military museum. My grandmother was spared the humiliation of those high gray walls by eight or ten years, but she must have known from birth the affliction of defeat, the dark brooding of old warriors.

Her name was Aho, and she belonged to the last culture to evolve in North America. Her forebears came down from the high country in western Montana nearly three centuries ago. They were a mountain people, a mysterious tribe of hunters whose language has never been positively classified in any major group. In the late seventeenth century they began a long migration to the south and east. It was a journey toward the dawn, and it led to a golden age. Along the way the Kiowas were befriended by the Crows, who gave them the culture and religion of the Plains. They acquired horses, and their ancient nomadic spirit was suddenly free of the ground. They acquired Tai-me, the sacred Sun Dance doll, from that moment the object and symbol of their worship, and so shared in the divinity of the sun. Not least, they acquired the sense of destiny, therefore courage and pride. When they entered upon the southern Plains they had been transformed. No longer were they slaves to the simple necessity of survival; they were a lordly and dangerous society of fighters and thieves, hunters and priests of the sun. According to their origin myth, they entered the world through a hollow log. From one point of view, their migration was the fruit of an old prophecy, for indeed they emerged from a sunless world.

Although my grandmother lived out her long life in the shadow of Rainy Mountain, the immense landscape of the continental interior lay

5

like memory in her blood. She could tell of the Crows, whom she had never seen, and of the Black Hills, where she had never been. I wanted to see in reality what she had seen more perfectly in the mind's eye, and traveled fifteen hundred miles to begin my pilgrimage.

Yellowstone, it seemed to me, was the top of the world, a region of deep lakes and dark timber, canyons and waterfalls. But, beautiful as it is, one might have the sense of confinement there. The skyline in all directions is close at hand, the high wall of the woods and deep cleavages of shade. There is a perfect freedom in the mountains, but it belongs to the eagle and the elk, the badger and the bear. The Kiowas reckoned their stature by the distance they could see, and they were bent and blind in the wilderness.

Descending eastward, the highland meadows are a stairway to the plain. In July the inland slope of the Rockies is luxuriant with flax and buckwheat, stonecrop and larkspur. The earth unfolds and the limit of the land recedes. Clusters of trees, and animals grazing far in the distance, cause the vision to reach away and wonder to build upon the mind. The sun follows a longer course in the day, and the sky is immense beyond all comparison. The great billowing clouds that sail upon it are shadows that move upon the grain like water, dividing light. Farther down, in the land of the Crows and Blackfeet, the plain is yellow. Sweet clover takes hold of the hills and bends upon itself to cover and seal the soil. There the Kiowas paused on their way; they had come to the place where they must change their lives. The sun is at home on the plains. Precisely there does it have the certain character of a god. When the Kiowas came to the land of the Crows, they could see the dark lees of the hills at dawn across the Bighorn River, the profusion of light on the grain shelves, the oldest deity ranging after the solstices. Not yet would they veer southward to the caldron of the land that lay below; they must wean their blood from the northern winter and hold the mountains a while longer in their view. They bore Tai-me in procession to the east.

A dark mist lay over the Black Hills, and the land was like iron. At the top of the ridge I caught sight of Devil's Tower upthrust against the gray sky as if in the birth of time the core of the earth had broken through its crust and the motion of the world was begun. There are things in nature that engender an awful quiet in the heart of man; Devil's Tower is one of them. Two centuries ago, because they could not do otherwise, the Kiowas made a legend at the base of the rock. My grandmother said:

> Eight children were there at play, seven sisters and their brother. Suddenly the boy was struck dumb; he trembled and began to run upon his hands and feet. His fingers became claws, and his body was covered with fur. Directly there was a bear where the boy had been. The sisters were terrified; they ran, and the bear ran after them. They came to the stump of a great tree, and the tree spoke to them. It bade them climb upon it, and as they did so it began to rise into the air. The bear came to kill them, but they were just be-

yond its reach. It reared against the tree and scored the bark all around with its claws. The seven sisters were borne into the sky, and they became the stars of the Big Dipper.

From that moment, and so long as the legend lives, the Kiowas have kinsmen in the night sky. Whatever they were in the mountains, they could be no more. However tenuous their well-being, however much they had suffered and would suffer again, they had found a way out of the wilderness.

My grandmother had a reverence for the sun, a holy regard that now is all but gone out of mankind. There was a wariness in her, and an ancient awe. She was a Christian in her later years, but she had come a long way about, and she never forgot her birthright. As a child she had been to the Sun Dances; she had taken part in those annual rites, and by them she had learned the restoration of her people in the presence of Tai-me. She was about seven when the last Kiowa Sun Dance was held in 1887 in the Washita River above Rainy Mountain Creek. The buffalo were gone. In order to consummate the ancient sacrifice — to impale the head of a buffalo bull upon the medicine tree — a delegation of old men journeyed into Texas, there to beg and barter for an animal from the Goodnight herd. She was ten when the Kiowas came together for the last time as a living Sun Dance culture. They could find no buffalo; they had to hang an old hide from the sacred tree. Before the dance could begin, a company of soldiers rode out from Fort Sill under orders to disperse the tribe. Forbidden without cause the essential act of their faith, having seen the wild herds slaughtered and left to rot upon the ground, the Kiowas backed away forever from the medicine tree. That was July 20, 1890, at the great bend of the Washita. My grandmother was there. Without bitterness, and for as long as she lived, she bore a vision of deicide.

Now that I can have her only in memory, I see my grandmother in   10
the several postures that were peculiar to her: standing at the wood stove on a winter morning and turning meat in a great iron skillet; sitting at the south window, bent above her beadwork, and afterwards, when her vision failed, looking down for a long time into the fold of her hands; going out upon a cane, very slowly as she did when the weight of age came upon her; praying. I remember her most often at prayer. She made long, rambling prayers out of suffering and hope, having seen many things. I was never sure that I had the right to hear, so exclusive were they of all mere custom and company. The last time I saw her she prayed standing by the side of her bed at night, naked to the waist, the light of a kerosene lamp moving upon her dark skin. Her long, black hair, always drawn and braided in the day, lay upon her shoulders and against her breasts like a shawl. I do not speak Kiowa, and I never understood her prayers, but there was something inherently sad in the sound, some merest hesitation upon the syllables of sorrow. She began in a high and descending pitch, exhausting her breath to silence; then again and again — and always the same intensity of effort, of something that is, and is not, like urgency in

the human voice. Transported so in the dancing light among the shadows of her room, she seemed beyond the reach of time. But that was illusion; I think I knew then that I should not see her again.

Houses are like sentinels in the plain, old keepers of the weather watch. There, in a very little while, wood takes on the appearance of great age. All colors wear soon away in the wind and rain, and then the wood is burned gray and the grain appears and the nails turn red with rust. The window-panes are black and opaque; you imagine there is nothing within, and indeed there are many ghosts, bones given up to the land. They stand here and there against the sky, and you approach them for a longer time than you expect. They belong in the distance; it is their domain.

Once there was a lot of sound in my grandmother's house, a lot of coming and going, feasting and talk. The summers there were full of excitement and reunion. The Kiowas are a summer people; they abide the cold and keep to themselves, but when the season turns and the land becomes warm and vital they cannot hold still; an old love of going returns upon them. The aged visitors who came to my grandmother's house when I was a child were made of lean and leather, and they bore themselves upright. They wore great black hats and bright ample shirts that shook in the wind. They rubbed fat upon their hair and wound their braids with strips of colored cloth. Some of them painted their faces and carried the scars of old and cherished enmities. They were an old council of war-lords, come to remind and be reminded of who they were. Their wives and daughters served them well. The women might indulge themselves; gossip was at once the mark and compensation of their servitude. They made loud and elaborate talk among themselves, full of jest and gesture, fright and false alarm. They went abroad in fringed and flowered shawls, bright beadwork and German silver. They were at home in the kitchen, and they prepared meals that were banquets.

There were frequent prayer meetings, and great nocturnal feasts. When I was a child I played with my cousins outside, where the lamplight fell upon the ground and the singing of the old people rose up around us and carried away into the darkness. There were a lot of good things to eat, a lot of laughter and surprise. And afterwards, when the quiet returned, I lay down with my grandmother and could hear the frogs away by the river and feel the motion of the air.

Now there is a funeral silence in the rooms, the endless wake of some final word. The walls have closed in upon my grandmother's house. When I returned to it in mourning, I saw for the first time in my life how small it was. It was late at night, and there was a white moon, nearly full. I sat for a long time on the stone steps by the kitchen door. From there I could see out across the land; I could see the long row of trees by the creek, the low light upon the rolling plains, and the stars of the big dipper. Once I looked at the moon and caught sight of a strange thing. A cricket had perched upon the handrail, only a few inches away from me. My line of vision was such that the creature filled the moon like a fossil. It had gone there, I thought, to live and die, for there, of all places, was its small definition made whole and eternal. A warm wind rose up and purled like the longing within me.

The next morning I awoke at dawn and went out on the dirt road to Rainy Mountain. It was already hot, and the grasshoppers began to fill the air. Still, it was early in the morning, and the birds sang out of the shadows. The long yellow grass on the mountain shone in the bright light, and a scissortail hied above the land. There, where it ought to be, at the end of a long and legendary way, was my grandmother's grave. Here and there on the dark stones were ancestral names. Looking back once, I saw the mountain and came away.

The Reader's Presence

1. In the interview quoted in the introductory note to this selection, Momaday talks about capturing his speaking voice in his writing. What are some of the phrases and passages that make you hear his distinctive voice as you read? Point to — and analyze — specific words and phrases to discuss how the effect of each is created.

2. Momaday tells several stories in this selection, including the history of the Kiowa people, the story of his grandmother's life and death, the story of his homecoming, and the legend of Devil's Tower. How does each story overlap and intertwine with the others? What forces compel the telling or creation of each story? What needs do the stories satisfy? Look, for example, at the legend related in paragraph 8. The Kiowas made this legend "because they could not do otherwise." Why could they have not done otherwise? What does the legend explain for them? How does this embedded legend enhance and complicate the other stories Momaday tells here?

3. From the beginning of this essay, Momaday sets his remarks very firmly in space and then in time. Discuss the importance of physical space in this essay. Why does Momaday take the journey to Rainy Mountain, and the fifteen-hundred-mile "pilgrimage" (paragraph 5)? Why does he say that his grandmother's vision of this landscape is more perfect than his, even though she has never actually seen the landscape he travels? Consider the many remarks about perspective, and change of perspective, that he includes, as well as remarks on proportion. What significance does he attach to these remarks? Where, literally and figuratively, does his grandmother's grave lie? More generally, consider the temporal journeys that run parallel to the spatial journeys: the Kiowas' "journey toward the dawn [that] led to a golden age" (paragraph 4) and Momaday's own journeys that he relates in the essay. How would you characterize the sense of space and time and the relation between the two that are conveyed in this essay?

19

George Orwell

Shooting an Elephant

George Orwell (1903–1950) was born Eric Arthur Blair in Bengal, India, the son of a colonial administrator. He was sent to England for his education and attended Eton on a scholarship, but rather than go on to university in 1922 he returned to the East and served with the Indian Imperial Police in Burma. Orwell hated his work and the colonial system; published posthumously, the essay "Shooting an Elephant" was based on his experience in Burma and is found in Shooting an Elephant and Other Essays *(1950). In 1927 Orwell returned to England and began a career as a professional writer. He served briefly in the Spanish Civil War until he was wounded and then settled in Hertfordshire. Best remembered for his novels* Animal Farm *(1945) and* Nineteen Eighty-Four *(1949), Orwell also wrote articles, essays, and reviews, usually with a political point in mind. In 1969 Irving Howe honored Orwell as "the best English essayist since Hazlitt, perhaps since Dr. Johnson. He was the greatest moral force in English letters during the last several decades: craggy, fiercely polemical, sometimes mistaken, but an utterly free man."*

In his 1946 essay "Why I Write," Orwell said that from a very early age "I knew that when I grew up I should be a writer." At first he saw writing as a remedy for loneliness, but as he grew up his reasons for writing expanded: "Looking back through my work, I see it is invariably when I lacked a political *purpose that I wrote lifeless books." In his mature work, he relied on simple, clear prose to express his political and social convictions: "Good prose," he once wrote, "is like a windowpane."*

In Moulmein, in Lower Burma, I was hated by large numbers of people — the only time in my life that I have been important enough for this to happen to me. I was subdivisional police officer of the town, and in an aimless, petty kind of way anti-European feeling was very bitter. No one had the guts to raise a riot, but if a European woman went through the bazaars alone somebody would probably spit betel juice over her dress. As a police officer I was an obvious target and was baited whenever it seemed safe to do so. When a nimble Burman tripped me up on the football field and the referee (another Burman) looked the other way, the

126

crowd yelled with hideous laughter. This happened more than once. In the end the sneering yellow faces of young men that met me everywhere, the insults hooted after me when I was at a safe distance, got badly on my nerves. The young Buddhist priests were the worst of all. There were several thousands of them in the town and none of them seemed to have anything to do except stand on street corners and jeer at Europeans.

All this was perplexing and upsetting. For at that time I had already made up my mind that imperialism was an evil thing and the sooner I chucked up my job and got out of it the better. Theoretically — and secretly, of course — I was all for the Burmese and all against the oppressors, the British. As for the job I was doing, I hated it more bitterly than I can perhaps make clear. In a job like that you see the dirty work of Empire at close quarters. The wretched prisoners huddling in the stinking cages of the lockups, the grey, cowed faces of the long-term convicts, the scarred buttocks of the men who had been flogged with bamboos — all these oppressed me with an intolerable sense of guilt. But I could get nothing into perspective. I was young and ill-educated and I had had to think out my problems in the utter silence that is imposed on every Englishman in the East. I did not even know that the British Empire is dying, still less did I know that it is a great deal better than the younger empires that are going to supplant it. All I knew was that I was stuck between my hatred of the empire I served and my rage against the evil-spirited little beasts who tried to make my job impossible. With one part of my mind I thought of the British Raj[1] as an unbreakable tyranny, as something clamped down, in *saecula saeculorum*,[2] upon the will of prostrate peoples; with another part I thought that the greatest joy in the world would be to drive a bayonet into a Buddhist priest's guts. Feelings like these are the normal by-products of imperialism; ask any Anglo-Indian official, if you can catch him off duty.

One day something happened which in a roundabout way was enlightening. It was a tiny incident in itself, but it gave me a better glimpse than I had had before of the real nature of imperialism — the real motives for which despotic governments act. Early one morning the subinspector at a police station the other end of town rang me up on the phone and said that an elephant was ravaging the bazaar. Would I please come and do something about it? I did not know what I could do, but I wanted to see what was happening and I got on to a pony and started out. I took my rifle, an old .44 Winchester and much too small to kill an elephant, but I thought the noise might be useful *in terrorem*.[3] Various Burmans stopped me on the way and told me about the elephant's doings. It was not, of course, a wild elephant, but a tame one which had gone "must."[4] It had

[1] *Raj:* The British administration. — EDS.
[2] *saecula saeculorum:* Forever and ever (Latin). — EDS.
[3] *in terrorem:* As a warning (Latin). — EDS.
[4] *"must":* Sexual arousal. — EDS.

been chained up, as tame elephants always are when their attack of "must" is due, but on the previous night it had broken its chain and escaped. Its mahout,[5] the only person who could manage it when it was in that state, had set out in pursuit, but had taken the wrong direction and was now twelve hours' journey away, and in the morning the elephant had suddenly reappeared in the town. The Burmese population had no weapons and were quite helpless against it. It had already destroyed somebody's bamboo hut, killed a cow, and raided some fruit stalls and devoured the stock; also it had met the municipal rubbish van and, when the driver jumped out and took to his heels, had turned the van over and inflicted violences upon it.

The Burmese subinspector and some Indian constables were waiting for me in the quarter where the elephant had been seen. It was a very poor quarter, a labyrinth of squalid bamboo huts, thatched with palm-leaf, winding all over a steep hillside. I remember that it was a cloudy, stuffy morning at the beginning of the rains. We began questioning the people as to where the elephant had gone and, as usual, failed to get any definite information. That is invariably the case in the East; a story always sounds clear enough at a distance, but the nearer you get to the scene of events the vaguer it becomes. Some of the people said that the elephant had gone in one direction, some said that he had gone in another, some professed not even to have heard of any elephant. I had almost made up my mind that the whole story was a pack of lies, when we heard yells a little distance away. There was a loud, scandalized cry of "Go away, child! Go away this instant!" and an old woman with a switch in her hand came round the corner of a hut, violently shooing away a crowd of naked children. Some more women followed, clicking their tongues and exclaiming; evidently there was something that the children ought not to have seen. I rounded the hut and saw a man's dead body sprawling in the mud. He was an Indian, a black Dravidian[6] coolie, almost naked, and he could not have been dead many minutes. The people said that the elephant had come suddenly upon him round the corner of the hut, caught him with its trunk, put its foot on his back, and ground him into the earth. This was the rainy season and the ground was soft, and his face had scored a trench a foot deep and a couple of yards long. He was lying on his belly with arms crucified and head sharply twisted to one side. His face was coated with mud, the eyes wide open, the teeth bared and grinning with an expression of unendurable agony. (Never tell me, by the way, that the dead look peaceful. Most of the corpses I have seen looked devilish.) The friction of the great beast's foot had stripped the skin from his back as neatly as one skins a rabbit. As soon as I saw the dead man I sent an orderly to a friend's house nearby to borrow an

---

[5] *mahout:* Keeper (Hindi). — EDS.
[6] *Dravidian:* A populous Indian group. — EDS.

elephant rifle. I had already sent back the pony, not wanting it to go mad with fright and throw me if it smelled the elephant.

The orderly came back in a few minutes with a rifle and five car- 5 tridges, and meanwhile some Burmans had arrived and told us that the elephant was in the paddy fields below, only a few hundred yards away. As I started forward practically the whole population of the quarter flocked out of the houses and followed me. They had seen the rifle and were all shouting excitedly that I was going to shoot the elephant. They had not shown much interest in the elephant when he was merely ravaging their homes, but it was different now that he was going to be shot. It was a bit of fun to them, as it would be to an English crowd; besides they wanted the meat. It made me vaguely uneasy. I had no intention of shooting the elephant — I had merely sent for the rifle to defend myself if necessary — and it is always unnerving to have a crowd following you. I marched down the hill, looking and feeling a fool, with the rifle over my shoulder and an ever-growing army of people jostling at my heels. At the bottom, when you got away from the huts, there was a metalled road and beyond that a miry waste of paddy fields a thousand yards across, not yet ploughed but soggy from the first rains and dotted with coarse grass. The elephant was standing eight yards from the road, his left side towards us. He took not the slightest notice of the crowd's approach. He was tearing up bunches of grass, beating them against his knees to clean them and stuffing them into his mouth.

I had halted on the road. As soon as I saw the elephant I knew with perfect certainty that I ought not to shoot him. It is a serious matter to shoot a working elephant — it is comparable to destroying a huge and costly piece of machinery — and obviously one ought not to do it if it can possibly be avoided. And at that distance, peacefully eating, the elephant looked no more dangerous than a cow. I thought then and I think now that his attack of "must" was already passing off; in which case he would merely wander harmlessly about until the mahout came back and caught him. Moreover, I did not in the least want to shoot him. I decided that I would watch him for a little while to make sure that he did not turn savage again, and then go home.

But at that moment, I glanced round at the crowd that had followed me. It was an immense crowd, two thousand at the least and growing every minute. It blocked the road for a long distance on either side. I looked at the sea of yellow faces above the garish clothes — faces all happy and excited over this bit of fun, all certain that the elephant was going to be shot. They were watching me as they would watch a conjuror about to perform a trick. They did not like me, but with the magical rifle in my hands I was momentarily worth watching. And suddenly I realized that I should have to shoot the elephant after all: The people expected it of me and I had got to do it; I could feel their two thousand wills pressing me forward, irresistibly. And it was at this moment, as I stood there with the rifle in my hands, that I first grasped the hollowness, the futility of the white man's dominion in the

East. Here was I, the white man with his gun, standing in front of the un-armed native crowd — seemingly the leading actor of the piece; but in real-ity I was only an absurd puppet pushed to and fro by the will of those yel-low faces behind. I perceived in this moment that when the white man turns tyrant it is his own freedom that he destroys. He becomes a sort of hollow, posing dummy, the conventionalized figure of a sahib. For it is the condi-tion of his rule that he shall spend his life in trying to impress the "natives," and so in every crisis he has got to do what the "natives" expect of him. He wears a mask, and his face grows to fit it. I had got to shoot the elephant. I had committed myself to doing it when I sent for the rifle. A sahib has got to act like a sahib; he has got to appear resolute, to know his own mind and do definite things. To come all that way, rifle in hand, with two thousand people marching at my heels, and then to trail feebly away, having done nothing — no, that was impossible. The crowd would laugh at me. And my whole life, every white man's life in the East, was one long struggle not to be laughed at.

But I did not want to shoot the elephant. I watched him beating his bunch of grass against his knees, with that preoccupied grandmotherly air that elephants have. It seemed to me that it would be murder to shoot him. At that age I was not squeamish about killing animals, but I had never shot an elephant and never wanted to. (Somehow it always seems worse to kill a *large* animal.) Besides, there was the beast's owner to be considered. Alive, the elephant was worth at least a hundred pounds; dead, he would only be worth the value of his tusks, five pounds, possibly. But I had got to act quickly. I turned to some experienced-looking Burmans who had been there when we arrived, and asked them how the elephant had been behav-ing. They all said the same thing: He took no notice of you if you left him alone, but he might charge if you went too close to him.

It was perfectly clear to me what I ought to do. I ought to walk up to within, say, twenty-five yards of the elephant and test his behavior. If he charged, I could shoot; if he took no notice of me, it would be safe to leave him until the mahout came back. But also I knew that I was going to do no such thing. I was a poor shot with a rifle and the ground was soft mud into which one would sink at every step. If the elephant charged and I missed him, I should have about as much chance as a toad under a steamroller. But even then I was not thinking particularly of my own skin, only of the watchful yellow faces behind. For at that moment, with the crowd watching me, I was not afraid in the ordinary sense, as I would have been if I had been alone. A white man mustn't be frightened in front of "natives"; and so, in general, he isn't frightened. The sole thought in my mind was that if anything went wrong those two thousand Burmans would see me pursued, caught, trampled on, and reduced to a grinning corpse like that Indian up the hill. And if that happened it was quite probable that some of them would laugh. That would never do. There was only one alternative. I shoved the cartridges into the magazine and lay down on the road to get a better aim.

The crowd grew very still, and a deep, low, happy sigh, as of people   10
who see the theatre curtain go up at last, breathed from innumerable
throats. They were going to have their bit of fun after all. The rifle was a
beautiful German thing with cross-hair sights. I did not then know that in
shooting an elephant one would shoot to cut an imaginary bar running
from ear-hole to ear-hole. I ought, therefore, as the elephant was sideways on, to have aimed straight at his ear-hole; actually I aimed several
inches in front of this, thinking the brain would be further forward.

When I pulled the trigger I did not hear the bang or feel the kick —
one never does when a shot goes home — but I heard the devilish roar of
glee that went up from the crowd. In that instant, in too short a time, one
would have thought, even for the bullet to get there, a mysterious, terrible
change had come over the elephant. He neither stirred nor fell, but every
line of his body had altered. He looked suddenly stricken, shrunken, immensely old, as though the frightful impact of the bullet had paralyzed
him without knocking him down. At last, after what seemed a long time
— it might have been five seconds, I dare say — he sagged flabbily to his
knees. His mouth slobbered. An enormous senility seemed to have settled
upon him. One could have imagined him thousands of years old. I fired
again into the same spot. At the second shot he did not collapse but
climbed with desperate slowness to his feet and stood weakly upright,
with legs sagging and head drooping. I fired a third time. That was the
shot that did for him. You could see the agony of it jolt his whole body
and knock the last remnant of strength from his legs. But in falling he
seemed for a moment to rise, for as his hind legs collapsed beneath him he
seemed to tower upward like a huge rock toppling, his trunk reaching
skywards like a tree. He trumpeted, for the first and only time. And then
down he came, his belly towards me, with a crash that seemed to shake
the ground even where I lay.

I got up. The Burmans were already racing past me across the mud. It
was obvious that the elephant would never rise again, but he was not
dead. He was breathing very rhythmically with long rattling gasps, his
great mound of a side painfully rising and falling. His mouth was wide
open. I could see far down into caverns of pale pink throat. I waited a
long time for him to die, but his breathing did not weaken. Finally, I fired
my two remaining shots into the spot where I thought his heart must be.
The thick blood welled out of him like red velvet, but still he did not die.
His body did not even jerk when the shots hit him, the tortured breathing
continued without a pause. He was dying, very slowly and in great agony,
but in some world remote from me where not even a bullet could damage
him further. I felt I had got to put an end to that dreadful noise. It seemed
dreadful to see the great beast lying there, powerless to move and yet
powerless to die, and not even to be able to finish him. I sent back for my
small rifle and poured shot after shot into his heart, and down his throat.
They seemed to make no impression. The tortured gasps continued as
steadily as the ticking of a clock.

In the end I could not stand it any longer and went away. I heard later that it took him half an hour to die. Burmans were bringing dahs[7] and baskets even before I left, and I was told they had stripped his body almost to the bones by the afternoon.

Afterwards, of course, there were endless discussions about the shooting of the elephant. The owner was furious, but he was only an Indian and could do nothing. Besides, legally I had done the right thing, for a mad elephant has to be killed, like a mad dog, if its owner fails to control it. Among the Europeans opinion was divided. The older men said I was right, the younger men said it was a damn shame to shoot an elephant for killing a coolie, because the elephant was worth more than any damn Coringhee coolie. And afterwards I was very glad that the coolie had been killed; it put me legally in the right and it gave me sufficient pretext for shooting the elephant. I often wondered whether any of the others grasped that I had done it solely to avoid looking a fool.

The Reader's Presence

1. Discuss Orwell's dilemma. How would you react in his situation? Is he recommending that readers see his behavior as a model of what to do in such a conflict?

2. Do you find Orwell's final sentence believable? Do you think that Orwell shot the elephant solely to avoid looking like a fool? In what sense would he have looked like a fool if he refused to kill the creature? Why do you think he makes this claim, and how does it affect your reading of the entire essay?

3. Some literary critics doubt that Orwell really did shoot an elephant in Burma. No external historical documentation has ever been found to corroborate Orwell's account. Yet what *internal* elements in the essay — what details or features — help persuade you that the episode is fact and not fiction? In other words, what makes you think that you are reading an essay and not a short story?

[7]*dahs:* Large knives. — EDS.

20

Noel Perrin

The Androgynous Man

Noel Perrin (b. 1927) is professor of English at Dartmouth College and fre-
quently publishes essays and reviews in national magazines and newspapers. An
overview of his essays can be found in A Noel Perrin Sampler *(1991). Perrin lives*
in the Vermont countryside and has published numerous essays about his experi-
ences as a part-time farmer there; those essays are collected in a series that begins
with First Person Rural *(1978), proceeds through* Second Person Rural *(1980)*
and Third Person Rural *(1983), and concludes with* Last Person Rural *(1991).*
The unaffected yet lively quality of his writing led one reviewer to say that Perrin
"is to farming what that eloquent physician, Lewis Thomas, is to medicine."
"The Androgynous Man" was published in the New York Times *in 1984.*

The summer I was 16, I took a train from New York to Steamboat
Springs, Colo., where I was going to be assistant horse wrangler at a
camp. The trip took three days, and since I was much too shy to talk to
strangers, I had quite a lot of time for reading. I read all of "Gone With
the Wind." I read all the interesting articles in a couple of magazines I
had, and then I went back and read all the dull stuff. I also took all the
quizzes, a thing of which magazines were even fuller then than now.

The one that held my undivided attention was called "How Mascu-
line/Feminine Are You?" It consisted of a large number of inkblots. The
reader was supposed to decide which of the four objects each blot most
resembled. The choices might be a cloud, a steam engine, a caterpillar and
a sofa.

When I finished the test, I was shocked to find that I was barely masculine at all. On a scale of 1 to 10, I was about a 1.2. Me, the horse wrangler? (And not just wrangler, either. That summer, I had to skin a couple
of horses that died — the camp owner wanted the hides.)

The results of the test were so terrifying to me that for the first time
in my life I did a piece of original analysis. Having unlimited time on the
train, I looked at the "masculine" answers over and over, trying to find
what is was that distinguished real men from people like me — and eventually I discovered two very simple patterns. It was "masculine" to think

the blots looked like man-made objects, and "feminine" to think they looked like natural objects. It was masculine to think they looked like things capable of causing harm, and feminine to think of innocent things.

Even at 16, I had the sense to see that the compilers of the test were   5
using rather limited criteria — maleness and femaleness are both more complicated than *that* — and I breathed a huge sigh of relief. I wasn't necessarily a wimp, after all.

That the test did reveal something other than the superficiality of its makers I realized only many years later. What it revealed was that there is a large class of men and women both, to which I belong, who are essentially androgynous. That doesn't mean we're gay, or low in the appropriate hormones, or uncomfortable performing the jobs traditionally assigned our sexes. (A few years after that summer, I was leading troops in combat and, unfashionable as it now is to admit this, having a very good time. War is exciting. What a pity the 20th century went and spoiled it with high-tech weapons.)

What it does mean to be spiritually androgynous is a kind of freedom. Men who are all-male, or he-man, or 100 percent red-blooded Americans, have a little biological set that causes them to be attracted to physical power, and probably also to dominance. Maybe even to watching football. I don't say this to criticize them. Completely masculine men are quite often wonderful people: good husbands, good (though sometimes overwhelming) fathers, good members of society. Furthermore, they are often so un-self-consciously at ease in the world that other men seek to imitate them. They just aren't as free as us androgynes. They pretty nearly have to be what they are; we have a range of choices open.

The sad part is that many of us never discover that. Men who are not 100 percent red-blooded Americans — say, those who are only 75 percent red-blooded — often fail to notice their freedom. They are too busy trying to copy the he-men ever to realize that men, like women, come in a wide variety of acceptable types. Why this frantic imitation? My answer is mere speculation, but not casual. I have speculated on this for a long time.

Partly they're just envious of the he-man's unconscious ease. Mostly they're terrified of finding that there may be something wrong with them deep down, some weakness at the heart. To avoid discovering that, they spend their lives acting out the role that the he-man naturally lives. Sad.

One thing that men owe to the women's movement is that this kind   10
of failure is less common than it used to be. In releasing themselves from the single ideal of the dependent woman, women have more or less incidentally released a lot of men from the single ideal of the dominant male. The one mistake the feminists have made, I think, is in supposing that *all* men need this release, or that the world would be a better place if all men achieved it. It wouldn't. It would just be duller.

So far I have been pretty vague about just what the freedom of an androgynous man is. Obviously it varies with the case. In the case I know best, my own, I can be quite specific. It has freed me most as a parent. I am, among other things, a fairly good natural mother. I like the nurturing role. It makes me feel good to see a child eat — and it turns me to mush to see a 4-year-old holding a glass with both small hands, in order to drink. I even enjoyed sewing patches on the knees of my daughter Amy's Dr. Dentons when she was at the crawling stage. All that pleasure I would have lost if I had made myself stick to the notion of the paternal role that I started with.

Or take a smaller and rather ridiculous example. I feel free to kiss cats. Until recently it never occurred to me that I would want to, though my daughters have been doing it all their lives. But my elder daughter is now 22, and in London. Of course, I get to look after her cat while she is gone. He's a big, handsome farm cat named Petrushka, very unsentimental, though used from kittenhood to being kissed on the top of the head by Elizabeth. I've gotten very fond of him (he's the adventurous kind of cat who likes to climb hills with you), and one night I simply felt like kissing him on the top of the head, and did. Why did no one tell me sooner how silky cat fur is?

Then there's my relation to cars. I am completely unembarrassed by my inability to diagnose even minor problems in whatever object I happen to be driving, and don't have to make some insider's remark to mechanics to try to establish that I, too, am a "Man With His Machine."

The same ease extends to household maintenance. I do it, of course. Service people are expensive. But for the last decade my house has functioned better than it used to because I've had the aid of a volume called "Home Repairs Any Woman Can Do," which is pitched just right for people at my technical level. As a youth, I'd as soon have touched such a book as I would have become a transvestite. Even though common sense says there is really nothing sexual whatsoever about fixing sinks.

Or take public emotion. All my life I have easily been moved by certain kinds of voices. The actress Siobhan McKenna's, to take a notable case. Give her an emotional scene in a play, and within 10 words my eyes are full of tears. In boyhood, my great dread was that someone might notice. I struggled manfully, you might say, to suppress this weakness. Now, of course, I don't see it as a weakness at all, but as a kind of fulfillment. I even suspect that the true he-men feel the same way, or one kind of them does, at least, and it's only the poor imitators who have to struggle to repress themselves.

Let me come back to the inkblots, with their assumption that masculine equates with machinery and science, and feminine with art and nature. I have no idea whether the right pronoun for God is He, She or It. But this I'm pretty sure of. If God could somehow be induced to take that test, God would not come out macho, and not feminismo, either, but right in the middle. Fellow androgynes, it's a nice thought.

The Reader's Presence

1. What are some of the gender stereotypes that Perrin challenges, directly or indirectly, in this essay? Why do you suppose the makers of the inkblot test had such a superficial idea of gender? What gender-specific language does Perrin himself use in the course of this essay? How would you gauge the degree of irony with which Perrin employs these words and phrases?

2. What is Perrin's attitude toward the true "he-man"? How might he characterize such a person, and the value he brings to the spectrum of human behavior? How does he feel about the imitators of he-men, those who are only "75 percent red-blooded" (paragraph 8)? And what, according to Perrin, are the advantages of androgyny? Can you think of other advantages that he doesn't enumerate? Although Perrin spends very little time discussing women in this essay, what attitudes toward androgynous women might you infer from what he has written? What might be some advantages of being an androgynous woman?

3. Perrin spends much of this essay explicitly or implicitly demonstrating what he calls his feminine side. But he also includes evidence of his stereotypical masculine traits and activities, such as his prowess over large animals and death (as a horse wrangler and in combat). What possible impressions on the part of the reader is he careful to ward off in this essay on the topic of his own androgyny?

21

Adrienne Rich

Split at the Root: An Essay on Jewish Identity

Adrienne Rich (b. 1929) has published numerous volumes of poetry and her work has appeared in several anthologies. She received her first award for poetry, a Yale Series of Younger Poets Award, while a student at Radcliffe College in 1951. Since then Rich has received many other professional honors, including a National Institute of Art and Letters Award (1961), a National Book Award (1974), a Fund for Human Dignity Award from the National Gay Task Force (1981), and the Lenore Marshall Nation Poetry Prize for her 1991 book, An Atlas of the Difficult World. *Adrienne Rich's poetics are informed by her political work against the oppression of women and against homophobia.*

Besides poetry, Rich has published three prose collections, including Blood, Bread and Poetry: Selected Prose *(1986), from which "Split at the Root" is excerpted, and* What Is Found There: Notebooks on Poetry and Politics *(1993). She has taught at many colleges and universities and since 1986 has been professor of English and feminist studies at Stanford University.*

Rich has written about a pivotal moment in her life as a writer: "To write directly and overtly as a woman, out of a woman's body and experience, to take women's existence seriously as theme and source for art, was something I had been hungering to do, needing to do, all my writing life. It placed me nakedly face to face with both terror and anger; it did indeed imply the breakdown of the world as I had always known it, the end of safety, to paraphrase Baldwin. . . . But it released tremendous energy in me, as in many other women, to have that way of writing affirmed and validated in a growing political community. I felt for the first time the closing of the gap between poet and woman."

For about fifteen minutes I have been sitting chin in hand in front of the typewriter, staring out at the snow. Trying to be honest with myself, trying to figure out why writing this seems to be so dangerous an act, filled with fear and shame, and why it seems so necessary. It comes to me that in order to write this I have to be willing to do two things: I have to claim my father, for I have my Jewishness from him and not from my gentile mother, and I have to break his silence, his taboos; in order to claim him I have in a sense to expose him.

And there is, of course, the third thing: I have to face the sources and the flickering presence of my own ambivalence as a Jew; the daily, mundane anti-Semitisms of my entire life.

These are stories I have never tried to tell before. Why now? Why, I asked myself sometime last year, does this question of Jewish identity float so impalpably, so ungraspably around me, a cloud I can't quite see the outlines of, which feels to me to be without definition?

And yet I've been on the track of this longer than I think.

In a long poem written in 1960, when I was thirty-one years old, I described myself as "Split at the root, neither Gentile nor Jew, / Yankee nor Rebel."[1] I was still trying to have it both ways: to be neither/nor, trying to live (with my Jewish husband and three children more Jewish in ancestry than I) in the predominantly gentile Yankee academic world of Cambridge, Massachusetts.

But this begins, for me, in Baltimore, where I was born in my father's workplace, a hospital in the black ghetto, whose lobby contained an immense white marble statue of Christ.

My father was then a young teacher and researcher in the department of pathology at the Johns Hopkins Medical School, one of the very few

5

---

[1]Adrienne Rich, "Readings of History," in *Snapshots of a Daughter-in-Law* (New York: W. W. Norton, 1967), pp. 36–40. — RICH'S NOTE.

Jews to attend or teach at that institution. He was from Birmingham, Alabama; his father, Samuel, was Ashkenazic,[2] an immigrant from Austria-Hungary and his mother, Hattie Rice, a Sephardic[3] Jew from Vicksburg, Mississippi. My grandfather had had a shoe store in Birmingham, which did well enough to allow him to retire comfortably and to leave my grandmother income on his death. The only souvenirs of my grandfather, Samuel Rich, were his ivory flute, which lay on our living-room mantel and was not to be played with; his thin gold pocket watch, which my father wore; and his Hebrew prayer book, which I discovered among my father's books in the course of reading my way through his library. In this prayer book there was a newspaper clipping about my grandparents' wedding, which took place in a synagogue.

My father, Arnold, was sent in adolescence to a military school in the North Carolina mountains, a place for training white southern Christian gentlemen. I suspect that there were few, if any, other Jewish boys at Colonel Bingham's, or at "Mr. Jefferson's university" in Charlottesville, where he studied as an undergraduate. With whatever conscious forethought, Samuel and Hattie sent their son into the dominant southern WASP culture to become an "exception," to enter the professional class. Never, in describing these experiences, did he speak of having suffered — from loneliness, cultural alienation, or outsiderhood. Never did I hear him use the word *anti-Semitism*.

It was only in college, when I read a poem by Karl Shapiro beginning "To hate the Negro and avoid the Jew / is the curriculum," that it flashed on me that there was an untold side to my father's story of his student years. He looked recognizably Jewish, was short and slender in build with dark wiry hair and deep-set eyes, high forehead, and curved nose.

My mother is a gentile. In Jewish law I cannot count myself a Jew. If   10
it is true that "we think back through our mothers if we are women" (Virginia Woolf) — and I myself have affirmed this — then even according to lesbian theory, I cannot (or need not?) count myself a Jew.

The white southern Protestant woman, the gentile, has always been there for me to peel back into. That's a whole piece of history in itself, for my gentile grandmother and my mother were also frustrated artists and intellectuals, a lost writer and a lost composer between them. Readers and annotators of books, note takers, my mother a good pianist still, in her eighties. But there was also the obsession with ancestry, with "background," the southern talk of family, not as people you would necessarily know and depend on, but as heritage, the guarantee of "good breeding." There was the <u>inveterate</u> romantic heterosexual fantasy, the mother

[2]*Ashkenazic:* Descendants of the Jews, generally Yiddish-speaking, who settled in middle and northern Europe. — EDS.
[3]*Sephardic:* Descendants of the Jews who settled for the most part in Spain, Portugal, and northern Africa. — EDS.

telling the daughter how to attract men (my mother often used the word "fascinate"); the assumption that relations between the sexes could only be romantic, that it was in the woman's interest to cultivate "mystery," conceal her actual feelings. Survival tactics of a kind, I think today, knowing what I know about the white woman's sexual role in the southern racist scenario. Heterosexuality as protection, but also drawing white women deeper into collusion with white men.

It would be easy to push away and deny the gentile in me — that white southern woman, that social christian. At different times in my life I have wanted to push away one or the other burden of inheritance, to say merely *I am a woman; I am a lesbian*. If I call myself a Jewish lesbian, do I thereby try to shed some of my southern gentile white woman's culpability? If I call myself only through my mother, is it because I pass more easily through a world where being a lesbian often seems like outsiderhood enough?

According to Nazi logic, my two Jewish grandparents would have made me a *Mischling, first-degree* — nonexempt from the Final Solution.[4]

The social world in which I grew up was christian virtually without needing to say so — christian imagery, music, language, symbols, assumptions everywhere. It was also a genteel, white, middle-class world in which "common" was a term of deep opprobrium. "Common" white people might speak of "niggers"; *we* were taught never to use that word — *we* said "Negroes" (even as we accepted segregation, the eating taboo, the assumption that black people were simply of a separate species). Our language was more polite, distinguishing us from the "rednecks" or the lynch-mob mentality. But so charged with negative meaning was even the word "Negro" that as children we were taught never to use it in front of black people. We were taught that any mention of skin color in the presence of colored people was treacherous, forbidden ground. In a parallel way, the word *Jew* was not used by polite gentiles. I sometimes heard my best friend's father, a Presbyterian minister, allude to "the Hebrew people" or "people of the Jewish faith." The world of acceptable folk was white, gentile (christian, really), and had "ideals" (which colored people, white "common" people, were not supposed to have). "Ideals" and "manners" included not hurting someone's feelings by calling her or him a Negro or a Jew — naming the hated identity. This is the mental framework of the 1930s and 1940s in which I was raised.

(Writing this, I feel dimly like the betrayer: of my father, who did not   15
speak the word; of my mother, who must have trained me in the messages; of my caste and class; of my whiteness itself.)

---

[4]*Final Solution:* The Nazi plan to exterminate the Jews. — EDS.

Two memories: I am in a play reading at school of *The Merchant of Venice.* Whatever Jewish law says, I am quite sure I was *seen* as Jewish (with a reassuringly gentile mother) in that double vision that bigotry allows. I am the only Jewish girl in the class, and I am playing Portia. As always, I read my part aloud for my father the night before, and he tells me to convey, with my voice, more scorn and contempt with the word *Jew:* "Therefore, Jew . . . " I have to say the word out, and say it loudly. I was encouraged to pretend to be a non-Jewish child acting a non-Jewish character who has to speak the word *Jew* emphatically. Such a child would not have had trouble with the part. But *I* must have had trouble with the part, if only because the word itself was really taboo. I can see that there was a kind of terrible, bitter bravado about my father's way of handling this. And who would not dissociate from Shylock in order to identify with Portia? As a Jewish child who was also a female, I loved Portia — and, like every other Shakespearean heroine, she proved a treacherous role model.

A year or so later I am in another play, *The School for Scandal,* in which a notorious spendthrift is described as having "many excellent friends . . . among the Jews." In neither case was anything explained, either to me or to the class at large, about this scorn for Jews and the disgust surrounding Jews and money. Money, when Jews wanted it, had it, or lent it to others, seemed to take on a peculiar nastiness; Jews and money had some peculiar and unspeakable relation.

At the same school — in which we had Episcopalian hymns and prayers, and read aloud through the Bible morning after morning — I gained the impression that Jews were in the Bible and mentioned in English literature, that they had been persecuted centuries ago by the wicked Inquisition, but that they seemed not to exist in everyday life. These were the 1940s, and we were told a great deal about the Battle of Britain, the noble French Resistance fighters, the brave, starving Dutch — but I did not learn of the resistance of the Warsaw ghetto until I left home.

I was sent to the Episcopal church, baptized and confirmed, and attended it for about five years, though without belief. That religion seemed to have little to do with belief or commitment; it was liturgy that mattered, not spiritual passion. Neither of my parents ever entered that church, and my father would not enter *any* church for any reason — wedding or funeral. Nor did I enter a synagogue until I left Baltimore. When I came home from church, for a while, my father insisted on reading aloud to me from Thomas Paine's *The Age of Reason* — a diatribe against institutional religion. Thus, he explained, I would have a balanced view of these things, a choice. He — they — did not give me the choice to be a Jew. My mother explained to me when I was filling out forms for college that if any question was asked about "religion," I should put down "Episcopalian" rather than "none" — to seem to have no religion was, she implied, dangerous.

But it was white social christianity, rather than any particular christian sect, that the world was founded on. The very word *Christian* was   20 used as a synonym for virtuous, just, peace-loving, generous, etc., etc.[5] The norm was christian: "Religion: none" was indeed not acceptable. Anti-Semitism was so intrinsic as not to have a name. I don't recall exactly being taught that the Jews killed Jesus — "Christ killer" seems too strong a term for the bland Episcopal vocabulary — but certainly we got the impression that the Jews had been caught out in a terrible mistake, failing to recognize the true Messiah, and were thereby less advanced in moral and spiritual sensibility. The Jews had actually allowed *money-lenders in the Temple* (again, the unexplained obsession with Jews and money). They were of the past, archaic, primitive, as older (and darker) cultures are supposed to be primitive; christianity was lightness, fairness, peace on earth, and combined the feminine appeal of "The meek shall inherit the earth" with the masculine stride of "Onward, Christian Soldiers."

Sometime in 1946, while still in high school, I read in the newspaper that a theater in Baltimore was showing films of the Allied liberation of the Nazi concentration camps. Alone, I went downtown after school one afternoon and watched the stark, blurry, but unmistakable newsreels. When I try to go back and touch the pulse of that girl of sixteen, growing up in many ways so precocious and so ignorant, I am overwhelmed by a memory of despair, a sense of inevitability more enveloping than any I had ever known. Anne Frank's diary and many other personal narratives of the Holocaust were still unknown or unwritten. But it came to me that every one of those piles of corpses, mountains of shoes and clothing had contained, simply, individuals, who had believed, as I now believed of myself, that they were intended to live out a life of some kind of meaning, that the world possessed some kind of sense and order; yet *this* had happened to them. And I, who believed my life was intended to be so interesting and meaningful, was connected to those dead by something — not just mortality but a taboo name, a hated identity. Or was I — did I really have to be? Writing this now, I feel belated rage that I was so impoverished by the family and social worlds I lived in, that I had to try to figure out by myself what this did indeed mean for me. That I had never been taught about resistance, only about passing. That I had no language for anti-Semitism itself.

When I went home and told my parents where I had been, they were not pleased. I felt accused of being morbidly curious, not healthy, sniffing around death for the thrill of it. And since, at sixteen, I was often not sure of the sources of my feelings or of my motives for doing what I did, I probably accused myself as well. One thing was clear: There was nobody in my world with whom I could discuss those films. Probably at the same

[5]In a similar way the phrase *That's white of you* implied that you were behaving with the superior decency and morality expected of white but not of black people. — RICH'S NOTE.

time, I was reading accounts of the camps in magazines and newspapers; what I remember were the films and having questions that I could not even phrase, such as *Are those men and women "them" or "us"?*

To be able to ask even the child's astonished question *Why do they hate us so?* means knowing how to say "we." The guilt of not knowing, the guilt of perhaps having betrayed my parents or even those victims, those survivors, through mere curiosity — these also froze in me for years the impulse to find out more about the Holocaust.

1947: I left Baltimore to go to college in Cambridge, Massachusetts, left (I thought) the backward, enervating South for the intellectual, vital North. New England also had for me some vibration of higher moral rectitude, of moral passion even, with its seventeenth-century Puritan self-scrutiny, its nineteenth-century literary "flowering," its abolitionist righteousness, Colonel Shaw and his black Civil War regiment depicted in granite on Boston Common. At the same time, I found myself, at Radcliffe, among Jewish women. I used to sit for hours over coffee with what I thought of as the "real" Jewish students, who told me about middle-class Jewish culture in America. I described my background — for the first time to strangers — and they took me on, some with amusement at my illiteracy, some arguing that I could never marry into a strict Jewish family, some convinced I didn't "look Jewish," others that I did. I learned the names of holidays and foods, which surnames are Jewish and which are "changed names"; about girls who had had their noses "fixed," their hair straightened. For these young Jewish women, students in the late 1940s, it was acceptable, perhaps even necessary, to strive to look as gentile as possible; but they stuck proudly to being Jewish, expected to marry a Jew, have children, keep the holidays, carry on the culture.

I felt I was testing a forbidden current, that there was danger in these revelations. I bought a reproduction of a Chagall portrait of a rabbi in striped prayer shawl and hung it on the wall of my room. I was admittedly young and trying to educate myself, but I was also doing something that *is* dangerous: I was flirting with identity.   25

One day that year I was in a small shop where I had bought a dress with a too-long skirt. The shop employed a seamstress who did alterations, and she came in to pin up the skirt on me. I am sure that she was a recent immigrant, a survivor. I remember a short, dark woman wearing heavy glasses, with an accent so foreign I could not understand her words. Something about her presence was very powerful and disturbing to me. After marking and pinning up the skirt, she sat back on her knees, looked up at me, and asked in a hurried whisper: "You Jewish?" Eighteen years of training in assimilation sprang into the reflex by which I shook my head, rejecting her, and muttered, "No."

What was I actually saying "no" to? She was poor, older, struggling with a foreign tongue, anxious; she had escaped the death that had been intended for her, but I had no imagination of her possible courage and foresight, her resistance — I did not see in her a heroine who had perhaps saved many lives, including her own. I saw the frightened immigrant, the seamstress hemming the skirts of college girls, the wandering Jew. But I was an American college girl having her skirt hemmed. And I was frightened myself, I think, because she had recognized me ("It takes one to know one," my friend Edie at Radcliffe had said) even if I refused to recognize myself or her, even if her recognition was sharpened by loneliness or the need to feel safe with me.

But why should she have felt safe with me? I myself was living with a false sense of safety.

There are betrayals in my life that I have known at the very moment were betrayals: this was one of them. There are other betrayals committed so repeatedly, so mundanely, that they leave no memory trace behind, only a growing residue of misery, of dull, accreted self-hatred. Often these take the form not of words but of silence. Silence before the joke at which everyone is laughing: the anti-woman joke, the racist joke, the anti-Semitic joke. Silence and then amnesia. Blocking it out when the oppressor's language starts coming from the lips of one we admire, whose courage and eloquence have touched us: *She didn't really mean that; he didn't really say that.* But the accretions build up out of sight, like scale inside a kettle.

1948: I come home from my freshman year at college, flaming with new insights, new information. I am the daughter who has gone out into the world, to the pinnacle of intellectual prestige, Harvard, fulfilling my father's hopes for me, but also exposed to dangerous influences. I have already been reproved for attending a rally for Henry Wallace[6] and the Progressive party. I challenge my father: "Why haven't you told me that I am Jewish? Why do you never talk about being a Jew?" He answers measuredly, "You know that I have never denied that I am a Jew. But it's not important to me. I am a scientist, a deist. I have no use for organized religion. I choose to live in a world of many kinds of people. There are Jews I admire and others whom I despise. I am a person, not simply a Jew." The words are as I remember them, not perhaps exactly as spoken. But that was the message. And it contained enough truth — as all denial drugs itself on partial truth — so that it remained for the time being unanswerable, leaving me high and dry, split at the root, gasping for clarity, for air.

At that time Arnold Rich was living in suspension, waiting to be appointed to the professorship of pathology at Johns Hopkins. The appointment was delayed for years, no Jew ever having held a professional chair in that medical school. And he wanted it badly. It must have been a very bitter time for him, since he had believed so greatly in the redeeming

---

[6]*Henry Wallace* (1888–1965): American journalist, agriculturist, and politician, as well as the 1948 Progressive party's candidate for the presidency. — EDS.

30

power of excellence, of being the most brilliant, inspired man for the job. With enough excellence, you could presumably make it stop mattering that you were Jewish; you could become the *only* Jew in the gentile world, a Jew so "civilized," so far from "common," so attractively combining southern gentility with European cultural values that no one would ever confuse you with the raw, "pushy" Jews of New York, the "loud, hysterical" refugees from eastern Europe, the "overdressed" Jews of the urban South.

We — my sister, mother, and I — were constantly urged to speak quietly in public, to dress without ostentation, to repress all vividness or spontaneity, to assimilate with a world which might see us as too flamboyant. I suppose that my mother, pure gentile though she was, could be seen as acting "common" or "Jewish" if she laughed too loudly or spoke aggressively. My father's mother, who lived with us half the year, was a model of circumspect behavior, dressed in dark blue or lavender, retiring in company, ladylike to an extreme, wearing no jewelry except a good gold chain, a narrow brooch, or a string of pearls. A few times, within the family, I saw her anger flare, felt the passion she was repressing. But when Arnold took us out to a restaurant or on a trip, the Rich women were always tuned down to some WASP level my father believed, surely, would protect us all — maybe also make us unrecognizable to the "real Jews" who wanted to seize us, drag us back to the *shtetl,* the ghetto, in its many manifestations.

For, yes, that *was* a message — that some Jews would be after you, once they "knew," to rejoin them, to re-enter a world that was messy, noisy, unpredictable, maybe poor — "even though," as my mother once wrote me, criticizing my largely Jewish choice of friends in college, "some of them will be the most brilliant, fascinating people you'll ever meet." I wonder if that isn't one message of assimilation — of America — that the unlucky or the unachieving want to pull you backward, that to identify with them is to court downward mobility, lose the precious chance of passing, of token existence. There was always within this sense of Jewish identity a strong class discrimination. Jews might be "fascinating" as individuals but came with huge unruly families who "poured chicken soup over everyone's head" (in the phrase of a white southern male poet). Anti-Semitism could thus be justified by the bad behavior of certain Jews; and if you did not effectively deny family and community, there would always be a remote cousin claiming kinship with you who was the "wrong kind" of Jew.

I have always believed his attitude toward other Jews depended on who they were. . . . It was my impression that Jews of this background looked down on Eastern European Jews, including Polish Jews and Russian Jews, who generally were not as well educated. This from a letter written to me recently by a gentile who had worked in my father's department, whom I had asked about anti-Semitism there and in particular regarding my father. This informant also wrote me that it was hard to perceive anti-Semitism in Baltimore because the racism made so much more intense an impression: *I would almost have to think that blacks went to a different heaven than the whites, because the bodies were kept in a separate morgue, and some white persons did not even want blood transfusions from black donors.* My father's mind was predictably racist and misogynist; yet as a medical student he noted in his journal that southern male chivalry stopped at the point of any white man in a streetcar giving his seat to an old, weary black woman standing in the aisle. Was this a Jewish insight — an outsider's insight, even though the outsider was striving to be on the inside?

Because what isn't named is often more permeating than what is, I believe that my father's Jewishness profoundly shaped my own identity and our family existence. They were shaped both by external anti-Semitism and my father's self-hatred, and by his Jewish pride. What Arnold did, I think, was call his Jewish pride something else: achievement, aspiration, genius, idealism. Whatever was unacceptable got left back under the rubric of Jewishness or the "wrong kind" of Jews — uneducated, aggressive, loud. The message I got was that we were really superior: Nobody else's father had collected so many books, had traveled so far, knew so many languages. Baltimore was a musical city, but for the most part, in the families of my school friends, culture was for women. My father was an amateur musician, read poetry, adored encyclopedic knowledge. He prowled and pounced over my school papers, insisting I use "grown-up" sources; he criticized my poems for faulty technique and gave me books on rhyme and meter and form. His investment in my intellect and talent was egotistical, tyrannical, opinionated, and terribly wearing. He taught me, nevertheless, to believe in hard work, to mistrust easy inspiration, to write and rewrite; to feel that I *was* a person of the book, even though a woman; to take ideas seriously. He made me feel, at a very young age, the power of language and that I could share it.

The Riches were proud, but we also had to be very careful. Our behavior had to be more impeccable than other people's. Strangers were not to be trusted, nor even friends; family issues must never go beyond the family; the world was full of potential slanderers, betrayers, *people who could not understand.* Even within the family, I realize that I never in my whole life knew what my father was really feeling. Yet he spoke — monologued — with driving intensity. You could grow up in such a house mesmerized by the local electricity, the crucial meanings assumed by the merest things. This used to seem to me a sign that we were all living on some high emotional plane. It was a difficult force field for a favored daughter to disengage from.

Easy to call that intensity Jewish; and I have no doubt that passion is one of the qualities required for survival over generations of persecution. But what happens when passion is rent from its original base, when the white gentile world is softly saying "Be more like us and you can be almost one of us"? What happens when survival seems to mean closing off one emotional artery after another? His forebears in Europe had been forbidden to travel or expelled from one country after another, had special taxes levied on them if they left the city walls, had been forced to wear special clothes and badges, restricted to the poorest neighborhoods. He had wanted to be a "free spirit," to travel widely, among "all kinds of people." Yet in his prime of life he lived in an increasingly withdrawn world, in his house up on a hill in a neighborhood where Jews were not supposed to be able to buy property, depending almost exclusively on interactions with his wife and daughters to provide emotional connectedness. In his home, he created a private defense system so elaborate that even as he was dying, my mother felt unable to talk freely with his colleagues or others who might have helped her. Of course, she acquiesced in this.

The loneliness of the "only," the token, often doesn't feel like loneliness but like a kind of dead echo chamber. Certain things that ought to don't resonate. Somewhere Beverly Smith writes of women of color "inspiring the behavior" in each other. When there's nobody to "inspire the behavior," act out of the culture, there is an atrophy, a dwindling, which is partly invisible.

Sometimes I feel I have seen too long from too many disconnected angles: white, Jewish, anti-Semite, racist, anti-racist, once-married, lesbian, middle-class, feminist, exmatriate southerner, *split at the root* — that I will never bring them whole. I would have liked, in this essay, to bring together the meanings of anti-Semitism and racism as I have experienced them and as I believe they intersect in the world beyond my life. But I'm not able to do this yet. I feel the tension as I think, make notes: *If you really look at the one reality, the other will waver and disperse.* Trying in one week to read Angela Davis and Lucy Davidowicz,[7] trying to hold throughout to a feminist, a lesbian, perspective — what does this mean? Nothing has trained me for this. And sometimes I feel inadequate to make any statement as a Jew; I feel the history of denial within me like an injury, a scar. For assimilation has affected *my* perceptions; those early lapses in meaning, those blanks, are with me still. My ignorance can be dangerous to me and to others.

Yet we can't wait for the undamaged to make our connections for us;   40 we can't wait to speak until we are perfectly clear and righteous. There is no purity and, in our lifetimes, no end to this process.

This essay, then, has no conclusions: It is another beginning for me. Not just a way of saying, in 1982 Right Wing America, *I, too, will wear the yellow star.* It's a moving into accountability, enlarging the range of accountability. I know that in the rest of my life, the next half century or so, every aspect of my identity will have to be engaged. The middle-class

---

[7]Angela Y. Davis, *Women, Race and Class* (New York: Random House, 1981); Lucy S. Davidowicz, *The War against the Jews 1933–1945* (New York: Bantam, 1979). — RICH'S NOTE.

white girl taught to trade obedience for privilege. The Jewish lesbian raised to be a heterosexual gentile. The woman who first heard oppression named and analyzed in the black Civil Rights struggle. The woman with three sons, the feminist who hates male violence. The woman limping with a cane, the woman who has stopped bleeding are also accountable. The poet who knows that beautiful language can lie, that the oppressor's language sometimes sounds beautiful. The woman trying, as part of her resistance, to clean up her act.

The Reader's Presence

1. Why does Rich feel she needs to "claim" her father in order to come to terms with her identity? What does she mean by "claim"? How do we make such claims? Why is her father so closely tied to her sense of identity?

2. Rich doesn't begin with a statement about her personal history but with a reference to her act of writing at the moment. What is the effect of beginning this way? How does writing figure throughout the essay? What connection can you see between writing and identity?

3. In rereading Rich's essay, pay close attention to her use of time. Try to construct a chronology for the essay. How does she organize that chronology in the essay itself? Can you think of some explanations for why Rich does not proceed in an orderly and straightforward manner? Can you discover any patterns in the procedure she chose to follow?

22

Alberto Alvaro Ríos

Green Cards

Alberto Alvaro Ríos (b. 1952) is a first-generation American; his father was born in Mexico, and his mother in England. His writing reflects this double heritage and the experience of living in the borderlands between languages and cultures. Ríos was raised and educated in Arizona, where he now teaches in the English department at Arizona State University. He has received, among other honors, a fellowship from the National Endowment for the Arts. He has published several collections of poetry, including Whispering to Fool the Wind *(1982) and* The Warrington Poems *(1989), and fiction, including* The Iguana Killer: Twelve Stories of the Heart *(1984) and* Pig Cookies and Other Stories *(1995). "Green Cards" appeared in* Indiana Review *in 1995.*

Reflecting on his relationship to language, writing, and translation, Ríos talks "about the duality of language using the metaphor of binoculars, how by using two lenses one might see something better, closer, with more detail. The apparatus, the binoculars, are of course physically clumsy — as is the learning of two languages . . . but once put to the eyes a new world in that moment opens up to us. And it's not a new world at all — it's the same world, but simply better seen, and therefore better understood."

All colors exist to satisfy the longing for blue.

There's a folk saying in Spanish, *el que quira azul que le cueste.* One must pay for what one wants; it's a variation of the older Spanish proverb, "Take what you want and pay for it, says God." But the phrase means, more literally, *he who wants blue, let it cost him.*

A green card is what you get if you are a citizen of another country but you find yourself in, or cross over to, the United States. The card is a first step toward applying for citizenship. My wife, who was born in Mexico, had one. My mother, who was born in England, had one. My father, who was born in Mexico, didn't have one. But that's another story, involving some curious papers and shady explanations. My mother-in-law, after more than forty years here, still has one. She's never been quite sure what to do next. But she's learned well that you don't raise your hand to ask the Immigration Service anything. They notice you then. Everybody knows that.

They notice you, and then they do something. And they're everywhere, maybe. So you don't speak loudly, you don't ask questions, you don't make trouble. Run away when you have to. Don't sign anything. Get a job only where everybody else is getting one, where it's safe.

There were all kinds of stories. The one my mother-in-law lived with the longest was how, her sister in Guaymas told her, they had heard that when you become a citizen of the United States, you have to spit on the flag of Mexico. And they would all shake their heads in a *no*.

My mother, when she became a citizen, recalls a curious moment.   5
After the ceremony, the high-school band came in to the courtroom and, because she was special — which is to say, in this border town with Mexico, she was not Mexican — they played the British national anthem. Someone thought it was a good idea. At that moment, though, she says she felt a little funny. She never forgot.

None of this is easy, and nobody knows what will happen when you come, and everybody is not treated the same. And things do happen. I think, finally, they were right.

Crossing over from Mexico, for example, was more than just being there and then being here. It was a change in how one walked, and a change in color. Over there, the ground moved one way, coiled and trailed and offered itself. Here was not there, and the coiling and trailing and offering were to the left and to the right, but never the same. To this, the legs and the body had to adjust. It was not the same ground.

And in Mexico, the color was green. Here, it is blue. And that Latin-American green is not the green of here, in the way that this blue is not the same blue in Mexico. The eyes, like the legs, have to learn over.

It is more than the music and the food and the clothing. It is the walk, and the color. And smell — not of food, but of things. And if one walked this other walk, and smells were new so the nose had to accommodate itself, one then began to look different. The body and the mirror made their changes.

I remember something from the middle of all this, from the middle of   10
color and the middle of the century. During the '50s, I remember driving through town and seeing pickup trucks full of men dressed in white. They were *braceros,* the workers imported specifically from Mexico for a brief time, sometimes only a day, just to work. After work, either at the end of the day or the end of the growing season, they had to go back to Mexico. What that meant was taking the pickup truck to the border and dropping them all off.

Arizona was the last state to hold out against minimum wage, championing the *laissez-faire* system of government oversight: in this case, let the growers pay what the workers will accept and don't get in the way. And these workers worked for almost nothing. It seemed, for a while, like a good idea to the growers and to the government, whose program this was.

As a kid, I remember only all these men dressed in white. It was a color that meant they didn't belong anywhere.

Crossing over from Mexico to the United States is not a small thing, but not large either. This is an incorrect vocabulary. To cross over was big, but that part was easy. The big is like that. It was the small that was difficult.

To cross the border was made up of these smaller things, then. It was lived as these more difficult-to-explain changes in color, more like that, more something of the body than one might suspect. It was the different way of walking because the ground was new, in all things. A different way of walking or a different way of hiding. More surprise, or more dullness, dullness or quiet. Something.

It is a movement from green, but who would know it? How to ex-   15
plain it? This is what I've heard all my life. It is a movement like the planet's, a movement that is there absolute, but who can feel it? A movement from green, from green to what is next.

For my family, crossing over was crossing over from green, not from Mexico. Green from before, but sorted out, from all the moments of green in a life, sorted and lifted out and then assembled together, into a big green, into green only. Fresh from the inhuman jungles of Chiapas and farther still, somewhere middle on the Western-hemisphere map, into the green day, into the green night, into the in-between — the light and the dark greens, the green that is brown and the green that is white — but green, and inside green, green incarnate, from the back and from the front, from the shoulders and the feet, green from yesterday and green from before yesterday, all of it ocean-like, all of it water, all of it moving as claws and tendrils and tongues, as eyes, as webs, and as base and rough flight, so that to navigate upon it one needed to ride above it to move through it, and even then to be careful and to look around. One needed to paddle and to chart, the paddle as a half-weapon and a half-tool, remembering never to dangle foolishly — for the one moment green takes — an arm into it.

From green utterly and in whispers, green eyes and green tongue, green taste and green sound; green from tea, but then from coffee; from bitter, but then from sweet; green from garden, and a little then from bean and root and tuber, but then from sky and from air, and from light.

But at light, and in dream, sound and strong, four-square and, yet, in that moment of pellucid strength, in that moment also inexplicably tinged with rue, there it is that green wavers and is for a moment inconstant, is for a moment green that is hollowed, or absent; is, for a moment, blue. There is the pivotal point, the narrows in this repeating hourglass of colors, in this life. There for a second, but there absolutely: green shifts to blue, and it is done.

It is Blue. Only and just blue. It is the log sawed and in its moment of breaking. It is the yawn pushed fully and then fully engaged. It is a blue. Blue and not green. Only blue. Only blue and the memory of green. Not a desire yet — green is too close — but a memory.

So much was the green.

On the far other side of green was a yellow, somewhere out there, somewhere only in imagination perhaps, yellow and red and some other colors on the other side of memory. Yellow, then the green, but now blue. It was the end at last, or the beginning. It was not the middle. But it was the discovery of the middle.

In this way, the green stayed, the way the Virgin Mary was painted, and in the shades of the hillside houses. It stayed in the Chinese teas, in the *yerba buena*,[1] how that green was a cure for things, and in the afternoons, in talk. Green stayed, and had a place in my family, but always as a memory. It stayed as a sadness for something.

It stayed as what used to be.

The Reader's Presence

1. How does Ríos use color as a metaphor in this essay? In what ways does he suggest that the border between Mexico and the United States is like the border between blue and green? What do you think Ríos is saying in general about boundaries and divisions?

2. Ríos begins his essay with a Spanish phrase that he translates in several different ways. How does this opening amplify the essay's central themes? What difference would it make if Ríos were to give the phrase only in its English version?

3. How does Ríos's account of the immigrant experience compare to the images we often see of immigrants in the media? Do you think he is pro- or anti-immigration? Do you think that Ríos's use of literary and poetic language diminishes the political elements of the essay, or enhances them?

---

[1]*yerba buena:* A mint tea. — EDS.

23

Judy Ruiz

Oranges and Sweet Sister Boy

Judy Ruiz (b. 1944) earned an M.F.A. in poetry from the University of Arkansas in 1988 and has taught writing at Southwest Missouri State University in Springfield, Missouri. Her poems have been widely published in various literary journals and have been collected in her book, Talking Razzmatazz *(1991). "Oranges and Sweet Sister Boy," which originally appeared in* Iowa Woman *in 1988, was selected for* The Best American Essays 1989.

I am sleeping, hard, when the telephone rings. It's my brother, and he's calling to say that he is now my sister. I feel something fry a little, deep behind my eyes. Knowing how sometimes dreams get mixed up with not-dreams, I decide to do a reality test at once. "Let me get a cigarette," I say, knowing that if I reach for a Marlboro and it turns into a trombone or a snake or anything else on the way to my lips that I'm still out in the large world of dreams.

The cigarette stays a cigarette. I light it. I ask my brother to run that stuff by me again.

It is the Texas Zephyr[1] at midnight — the woman in a white suit, the man in a blue uniform; she carries flowers — I know they are flowers. The petals spill and spill into the aisle, and a child goes past this couple who have just come from their own wedding — goes past them and past them, going always to the toilet but really just going past them; and the child could be a horse or she could be the police and they'd not notice her any more than they do, which is not at all — the man's hands high up on the woman's legs, her skirt up, her stockings and garters, the petals and finally all the flowers spilling out into the aisle and his mouth open on her. My mother. My father. I am conceived near Dallas in the dark while a child passes, a young girl who knows and doesn't know, who witnesses, in glimpses, the creation of the universe, who feels an odd hurt as her own mother, fat and empty, snores with

---

[1]*Texas Zephyr:* A passenger train. — EDS.

her mouth open, her false teeth slipping down, snores and snores just two seats behind the Creators.

News can make a person stupid. It can make you think you can do something. So I ask The Blade question, thinking that if he hasn't had the operation yet that I can fly to him, rent a cabin out on Puget Sound. That we can talk. That I can get him to touch base with reality.

"Begin with an orange," I would tell him. "Because oranges are mildly intrusive by nature, put the orange somewhere so that it will not bother you — in the cupboard, in a drawer, even a pocket or a handbag will do. The orange, being a patient fruit, will wait for you much longer than say a banana or a peach."

I would hold an orange out to him. I would say, "This is the one that will save your life." And I would tell him about the woman I saw in a bus station who bit right into her orange like it was an apple. She was wild looking, as if she'd been outside for too long in a wind that blew the same way all the time. One of the dregs of humanity, our mother would have called her, the same mother who never brought fruit into the house except in cans. My children used to ask me to "start" their oranges for them. That meant to make a hole in the orange so they could peel the rind away, and their small hands weren't equipped with fingernails that were long enough or strong enough to do the job. Sometimes they would suck the juice out of the hole my thumbnail had made, leaving the orange flat and sad.

> The earrings are as big as dessert plates, filigree gold-plated with thin dangles hanging down that touch her bare shoulders. She stands in front of the Alamo while a bald man takes her picture. The sun is absorbed by the earrings so quickly that by the time she feels the heat, it is too late. The hanging dangles make small blisters on her shoulders, as if a centipede had traveled there. She takes the famous river walk in spiked heels, rides in a boat, eats some Italian noodles, returns to the motel room, soaks her feet, and applies small band-aids to her toes. She is briefly concerned about the gun on the nightstand. The toilet flushes. She pretends to be sleeping. The gun is just large and heavy. A .45? A .357 magnum? She's never been good with names. She hopes he doesn't try to. Or that if he does, that it's not loaded. But he'll say it's loaded just for fun. Or he'll pull the trigger and the bullet will lodge in her medulla oblongata, ripping through her womb first, taking everything else vital on the way.

In the magazine articles, you don't see this: "Well, yes. The testicles have to come out. And yes. The penis is cut off." What you get is tonsils. So-and-so has had a "sex change" operation. A sex change operation. How precious. How benign. Doctor, just what do you people do with those penises?

News can make a person a little crazy also. News like, "We regret to inform you that you have failed your sanity hearing."

The bracelet on my wrist bears the necessary information about me, but there is one small error. The receptionist typing the information asked me my religious preference. I said, "None." She typed, "Neon."

Pearl doesn't have any teeth and her tongue looks weird. She says "Pumpkin pie." That's all she says. Sometimes she runs her hands over my bed sheets and says pumpkin pie. Sometimes I am under the sheets. Marsha got stabbed in the chest, but she tells everyone she fell on a knife. Elizabeth — she's the one who thinks her shoe is a baby — hit me in the back with a tray right after one of the cooks gave me extra toast. There's a note on the bulletin board about a class for the nurses: "How Putting A Towel On Someone's Face Makes Them Stop Banging Their Spoon/OR Reduction of Disruptive Mealtime Behavior By Facial Screening — 7 P.M. — Conference Room." Another note announces the topic for remotivation class: "COWS." All the paranoid schizophrenics will be there.

Here, in the place for the permanently bewildered, I fit right in. Not because I stood at the window that first night and listened to the trains. Not because I imagined those trains were bracelets, the jewelry of earth. Not even because I imagined that one of those bracelets was on my own arm and was the Texas Zephyr where a young couple made love and conceived me. I am eighteen and beautiful and committed to the state hospital by a district court judge for a period of one day to life. Because I am a paranoid schizophrenic.

I will learn about cows.

So I'm being very quiet in the back of the classroom, and I'm peeling an orange. It's the smell that makes the others begin to turn around, that mildly intrusive nature. The course is called "Women and Modern Literature," and the diaries of Virginia Woolf are up for discussion except nobody has anything to say. I, of course, am making a mess with the orange; and I'm wanting to say that my brother is now my sister.

Later, with my hands still orangey, I wander in to leave something on   10
a desk in a professor's office, and he's reading so I'm being very quiet, and then he says, sort of out of nowhere, "Emily Dickinson up there in her room making poems while her brother was making love to her best friend right downstairs on the dining room table. A regular thing. Think of it. And Walt Whitman out sniffing around the boys. Our two great American poets." And I want to grab this professor's arm and say, "Listen. My brother called me and now he's my sister, and I'm having trouble making sense out of my life right now, so would you mind not telling me any more stuff about sex." And I want my knuckles to turn white while the pressure of my fingers leaves imprints right through his jacket, little indentations he can interpret as urgent. But I don't say anything. And I don't grab his arm. I go read a magazine. I find this:

"I've never found an explanation for why the human race has so many languages. When the brain became a language brain, it obviously needed to develop an intense degree of plasticity. Such plasticity allows languages to be logical, coherent systems and yet be extremely variable. The same brain that thinks in words and symbols is also a brain that has to be freed up with regard to sexual turn-on and partnering. God knows why sex attitudes have not been subject to the corresponding degrees of modification and variety as language. I suspect there's a close parallel between the two. The brain doesn't seem incredibly efficient with regard to sex."

John Money said that. The same John Money who, with surgeon Howard W. Jones, performed the first sex change operation in the United States in 1965 at Johns Hopkins University and Hospital in Baltimore.

Money also tells about the *hijra* of India who disgrace their families because they are too effeminate: "The ultimate stage of the *hijra* is to get up the courage to go through the amputation of penis and testicles. They had no anesthetic." Money also answers anyone who might think that "heartless members of the medical profession are forcing these poor darlings to go and get themselves cut up and mutilated," or who think the medical profession should leave them alone. "You'd have lots of patients willing to get a gun and blow off their own genitals if you don't do it. I've had several who got knives and cut themselves trying to get rid of their sex organs. That's their obsession!"

Perhaps better than all else, I understand obsession. It is of the mind. And it is language-bound. Sex is of the body. It has no words. I am stunned to learn that someone with an obsession of the mind can have parts of the body surgically removed. This is my brother I speak of. This is not some lunatic named Carl who becomes Carlene. This is my brother.

So while we're out in that cabin on Puget Sound, I'll tell him about LuAnn. She is the sort of woman who orders the in-season fruit and a little cottage cheese. I am the sort of woman who orders a double cheeseburger and fries. LuAnn and I are sitting in her car. She has a huge orange, and she peels it so the peel falls off in one neat strip. I have a sack of oranges, the small ones. The peel of my orange comes off in hunks about the size of a baby's nail. "Oh, you bought the *juice* oranges," LuAnn says to me. Her emphasis on the word "juice" makes me want to die or something. I lack the courage to admit my ignorance, so I smile and breathe "yes," as if I know some secret, when I'm wanting to scream at her about how my mother didn't teach me about fruit and my own blood pounds in my head wanting out, out.

> There is a pattern to this thought as there is a pattern for a jumpsuit. Sew the sleeve to the leg, sew the leg to the collar. Put the garment on. Sew the mouth shut. This is how I tell about being quiet because I am bad, and because I cannot stand it when he beats me or my brother.

"The first time I got caught in your clothes was when I was four years old and you were over at Sarah what's-her-name's babysitting. Dad beat me so hard I thought I was going to die. I really thought I was going to die. That was the day I made up my mind I would *never* get caught again. And I never got caught again." My brother goes on to say he continued to go through my things until I was hospitalized. A mystery is solved.

He wore my clothes. He played in my makeup. I kept saying, back then, that someone was going through my stuff. I kept saying it and saying it. I told the counselor at school. "Someone goes in my room when I'm not there, and I *know* it — goes in there and wears my clothes and goes through my stuff." I was assured by the counselor that this was not so. I was assured by my mother that this was not so. I thought my mother was doing it, snooping around for clues like mothers do. It made me a little crazy, so I started deliberately leaving things in a certain order so that I would be able to prove to myself that someone, indeed, was going through my belongings. No one, not one person, ever believed that my room was being ransacked; I was accused of just making it up. A paranoid fixation.

And all the time it was old Goldilocks.

So I tell my brother to promise me he'll see someone who counsels adult children from dysfunctional families. I tell him he needs to deal with the fact that he was physically abused on a daily basis. He tells me he doesn't remember being beaten except on three occasions. He wants me to get into a support group for families of people who are having a sex change. Support groups are people who are in the same boat. Except no one has any oars in the water.

I tell him I know how it feels to think you are in the wrong body. I tell him how I wanted my boyfriend to put a gun up inside me and blow the woman out, how I thought wearing spiked heels and low-cut dresses would somehow help my crisis, that putting on an ultrafeminine outside would mask the maleness I felt needed hiding. I tell him it's the rule, rather than the exception, that people from families like ours have very spooky sexual identity problems. He tells me that his sexuality is a birth defect. I recognize the lingo. It's support-group-for-transsexuals lingo. He tells me he sits down to pee. He told his therapist that he used to wet all over the floor. His therapist said, "You can't aim the bullets if you don't touch the gun." Lingo. My brother is hell-bent for castration, the castration that started before he had language: the castration of abuse. He will simply finish what was set in motion long ago.

I will tell my brother about the time I took ten sacks of oranges into a school so that I could teach metaphor. The school was for special students — those who were socially or intellectually impaired. I had planned to have them peel the oranges as I spoke about how much the world is like the orange. I handed out the oranges. The students refused to peel them, not because they wanted to make life difficult for me — they were enchanted with the gift. One child asked if he could have an orange to take home to his little brother. Another said he would bring me ten dollars the next day if I would give him a sack of oranges. And I knew I was at home, that these children and I shared something that *makes* the leap of mind the metaphor attempts. And something in me healed.

A neighbor of mine takes pantyhose and cuts them up and sews them up after stuffing them. Then she puts these things into Mason jars and   20 sells them, you know, to put out on the mantel for conversation. They are little penises and little scrotums, complete with hair. She calls them "Pickled Peters."

A friend of mine had a sister who had a sex change operation. This young woman had her breasts removed and ran around the house with no shirt on before the stitches were taken out. She answered the door one evening. A young man had come to call on my friend. The sex-changed sister invited him in and offered him some black bean soup as if she were perfectly normal with her red surgical wounds and her black stitches. The young man left and never went back. A couple years later, my friend's sister/brother died when s/he ran a car into a concrete bridge railing. I hope for a happier ending. For my brother, for myself, for all of us.

My brother calls. He's done his toenails: Shimmering Cinnamon. And he's left his wife and children and purchased some nightgowns at a yard sale. His hair is getting longer. He wears a special bra. Most of the people he works with know about the changes in his life. His voice is not the same voice I've heard for years; he sounds happy.

My brother calls. He's always envied me, my woman's body. The same body I live in and have cursed for its softness. He asks me how I feel about myself. He says, "You know, you are really our father's first-born son." He tells me he used to want to be me because I was the only person our father almost loved.

The drama of life. After I saw that woman in the bus station eat an orange as if it were an apple, I went out into the street and smoked a joint with some guy I'd met on the bus. Then I hailed a cab and went to a tattoo parlor. The tattoo artist tried to talk me into getting a nice bird or butterfly design; I had chosen a design on his wall that appealed to me — a symbol I didn't know the meaning of. It is the Yin-Yang, and it's tattooed above my right ankle bone. I supposed my drugged, crazed consciousness knew more than I knew: that yin combines with yang to produce all that comes to be. I am drawn to androgyny.

Of course there is the nagging possibility that my brother's dilemma is 25 genetic. Our father used to dress in drag on Halloween, and he made a beautiful woman. One year, the year my mother cut my brother's blond curls off, my father taped those curls to his own head and tied a silk scarf over the tape. Even his close friends didn't know it was him. And my youngest daughter was a body builder for a while, her lean body as muscular as a man's. And my sons are beautiful, not handsome: they look androgynous.

Then there's my grandson. I saw him when he was less than an hour old. He was naked and had hiccups. I watched as he had his first bath, and I heard him cry. He had not been named yet, but his little crib had a blue card affixed to it with tape. And on the card were the words "Baby Boy." There was no doubt in me that the words were true.

When my brother was born, my father was off flying jets in Korea. I went to the hospital with my grandfather to get my mother and this new brother. I remember how I wanted a sister, and I remember looking at him as my mother held him in the front seat of the car. I was certain he was a sister, certain that my mother was joking. She removed his diaper to show me that he was a boy. I still didn't believe her. Considering what has happened lately, I wonder if my child-skewed consciousness knew more than the anatomical proof suggested.

I try to make peace with myself. I try to understand his decision to alter himself. I try to think of him as her. I write his woman name, and I feel like I'm betraying myself. I try to be open-minded, but something in me shuts down. I think we humans are in big trouble, that many of us don't really have a clue as to what acceptable human behavior is. Something in me says no to all this, that this surgery business is the ultimate betrayal of the self. And yet, I want my brother to be happy.

It was in the city of San Antonio that my father had his surgery. I rode the bus from Kansas to Texas, and arrived at the hospital two days after the operation to find my father sitting in the solarium playing solitaire. He had a type of cancer that particularly thrived on testosterone. And so he was castrated in order to ease his pain and to stop the growth of tumors. He died six months later.

Back in the sleep of the large world of dreams, I have done surgeries   30
under water in which I float my father's testicles back into him, and he — the brutal man he was — emerges from the pool a tan and smiling man, parting the surface of the water with his perfect head. He loves all the grief away.

I will tell my brother all I know of oranges, that if you squeeze the orange peel into a flame, small fires happen because of the volatile oil in the peel. Also, if you squeeze the peel and it gets into your cat's eyes, the cat will blink and blink. I will tell him there is no perfect rhyme for the word "orange," and that if we can just make up a good word we can be immortal. We will become obsessed with finding the right word, and I will be joyous at our legitimate pursuit.

I have purchased a black camisole with lace to send to my new sister. And a card. On the outside of the card there's a drawing of a woman sitting by a pond and a zebra is off to the left. Inside are these words: "The past is ended. Be happy." And I have asked my companions to hold me and I have cried. My self is wet and small. But it is not dark. Sometimes, if no one touches me, I will die.

Sister, you are the best craziness of the family. Brother, love what you love.

The Reader's Presence

1. The essay opens with the author asleep. How do sleep and dreams figure throughout the essay? How might they help account for the odd jumps and connections that sometimes make the essay hard to follow?

2. Note the moments in the essay where Ruiz inserts paragraphs in smaller type. What are these moments? What have they to do with the main body of the essay? What do those moments have in common? How are you intended to read them?

3. In rereading the essay make a note of all references to the body. In what ways is the human body present? According to Ruiz, how does the body differ from the mind? (See paragraph 12.) How is that difference dramatized by the essay itself?

24

Scott Russell Sanders

The Men We Carry in Our Minds

Scott Russell Sanders (b. 1945) writes in a variety of genres: science fiction, realistic fiction, folktales, children's stories, essays, and historical novels. In all his work, however, he is concerned with the ways in which people live in communities. Some of his more recent books include The Paradise of Bombs *(1987), from which "The Men We Carry in Our Minds" is excerpted;* Staying Put: Making a Home in a Restless World *(1993);* Here Comes the Mystery Man *(1993); and* Writing from the Center *(1995). Sanders contributes to both literary and popular magazines. He is professor of English at Indiana University,*

Sanders has said, "I believe that a writer should be a servant of language, community, and nature. Language is the creation and sustenance of community. . . . My writing is driven by a deep regard for particular places and voices, persons and tools, plants and animals, for human skills and stories. . . . If my writing does not help my neighbors to live more alertly, pleasurably, or wisely, then it is worth little."

"This must be a hard time for women," I say to my friend Anneke. "They have so many paths to choose from, and so many voices calling them."

"I think it's a lot harder for men," she replies.

"How do you figure that?"

"The women I know feel excited, innocent, like crusaders in a just cause. The men I know are eaten up with guilt."

We are sitting at the kitchen table drinking sassafras tea, our hands   5
wrapped around the mugs because this April morning is cool and drizzly. "Like a Dutch morning," Anneke told me earlier. She is Dutch herself, a writer and midwife and peacemaker, with the round face and sad eyes of a woman in a Vermeer painting who might be waiting for the rain to stop, for a door to open. She leans over to sniff a sprig of lilac, pale lavender, that rises from a vase of cobalt blue.

"Women feel such pressure to be everything, do everything," I say. "Career, kids, art, politics. Have their babies and get back to the office a week later. It's as if they're trying to overcome a million years' worth of evolution in one lifetime."

"But we help one another. We don't try to lumber on alone, like so many wounded grizzly bears, the way men do." Anneke sips her tea. I gave her the mug with the owls on it, for wisdom. "And we have this deep-down sense that we're in the *right* — we've been held back, passed over, used — while men feel they're in the wrong. Men are the ones who've been discredited, who have to search their souls."

I search my soul. I discover guilty feelings aplenty — toward the poor, the Vietnamese, Native Americans, the whales, an endless list of debts — a guilt in each case that is as bright and (unambiguous) as a neon sign. But toward women I feel something more confused, a snarl of shame, (envy,) wary tenderness, and amazement. This muddle troubles me. To hide my unease I say, "You're right, it's tough being a man these days."

"Don't laugh." Anneke frowns at me, mournful-eyed, through the sassafras steam. "I wouldn't be a man for anything. It's much easier being the victim. All the victim has to do is break free. The (persecutor) has to live with his past."

How deep is that past? I find myself wondering after Anneke has left.   10
How much of an inheritance do I have to throw off? Is it just the beliefs I breathed in as a child? Do I have to (scour) memory back through father and grandfather? Through St. Paul? Beyond Stonehenge and into the twilit caves? I'm convinced the past we must contend with is deeper even than speech. When I think back on my childhood, on how I learned to see men and women, I have a sense of ancient, dizzying depths. The back roads of Tennessee and Ohio where I grew up were probably closer, in their sexual patterns, to the campsites of Stone Age hunters than to the genderless cities of the future into which we are rushing.

The first men, besides my father, I remember seeing were black convicts and white guards, in the cottonfield across the road from our farm on the outskirts of Memphis. I must have been three or four. The prisoners wore dingy gray-and-black zebra suits, heavy as canvas, sodden with sweat. Hatless, stooped, they chopped weeds in the fierce heat, row after row, breathing the (acrid) dust of boll-weevil poison. The (overseers) wore dazzling white shirts and broad shadowy hats. The oiled barrels of their shotguns flashed in the sunlight. Their faces in memory are (utterly) blank. Of course those men, white and black, have become for me an (emblem) of racial hatred. But they have also come to stand for the twin poles of my early vision of manhood — the (brute) toiling animal and the boss.

When I was a boy, the men I knew labored with their bodies. They were marginal farmers, just scraping by, or welders, steelworkers, carpenters; they swept floors, dug ditches, mined coal, or drove trucks, their forearms (ropy) with muscle; they trained horses, stoked furnaces, built tires, stood on assembly lines wrestling parts onto cars and refrigerators. They got up before light, worked all day long whatever the weather, and when they came home at night they looked as though somebody had been whipping them. In the evenings and on weekends they worked on their own places, tilling gardens that were lumpy with clay, fixing broken-down cars, hammering on houses that were always too drafty, too leaky, too small.

The bodies of the men I knew were twisted and (maimed) in ways visible and invisible. The nails of their hands were black and split, the hands tattooed with scars. Some had lost fingers. Heavy lifting had given many of them (finicky) backs and guts weak from hernias. Racing against conveyor belts had given them ulcers. Their ankles and knees ached from years of standing on concrete. Anyone who had worked for long around machines was hard of hearing. They squinted, and the skin of their faces was creased like the leather of old work gloves. There were times, studying them, when I dreaded growing up. Most of them coughed, from dust or cigarettes, and most of them drank cheap wine or whiskey, so their eyes looked bloodshot and bruised. The fathers of my friends always seemed older than the mothers. Men wore out sooner. Only women lived into old age.

As a boy I also knew another sort of men, who did not sweat and break down like mules. They were soldiers, and so far as I could tell they scarcely worked at all. During my early school years we lived on a military base, an arsenal in Ohio, and every day I saw GIs in the guardshacks, on the stoops of barracks, at the wheels of olive drab Chevrolets. The chief fact of their lives was boredom. Long after I left the Arsenal I came to recognize the sour smell the soldiers gave off as that of souls in limbo. They were all waiting — for wars, for transfers, for leaves, for promotions, for the end of their hitch — like so many braves waiting for the hunt to begin. Unlike the warriors of older tribes, however, they would have no say about when the battle would start or how it would be waged. Their waiting was broken only when they practiced for war. They fired guns at targets, drove tanks across the churned-up fields of the military reservation, set off bombs in the wrecks of old fighter planes. I knew this was all play. But I also felt certain that when the hour for killing arrived, they would kill. When the real shooting started, many of them would die. This was what soldiers were *for*, just as a hammer was for driving nails.

Warriors and toilers: those seemed, in my boyhood vision, to be the   15
chief destinies for men. They weren't the only destinies, as I learned from
having a few male teachers, from reading books, and from watching television. But the men on television — the politicians, the astronauts, the
generals, the savvy lawyers, the philosophical doctors, the bosses who
gave orders to both soldiers and laborers — seemed as remote and unreal
to me as the figures in tapestries. I could no more imagine growing up to
become one of these cool, potent creatures than I could imagine becoming
a prince.

A nearer and more hopeful example was that of my father, who had
escaped from a red-dirt farm to a tire factory, and from the assembly line
to the front office. Eventually he dressed in a white shirt and tie. He carried himself as if he had been born to work with his mind. But his body,
remembering the earlier years of slogging work, began to give out on him
in his fifties, and it quit on him entirely before he turned sixty-five. Even
such a partial escape from man's fate as he had accomplished did not
seem possible for most of the boys I knew. They joined the army, stood in
line for jobs in the smoky plants, helped build highways. They were
bound to work as their fathers had worked, killing themselves or preparing to kill others.

A scholarship enabled me not only to attend college, a rare enough feat
in my circle, but even to study in a university meant for the children of the
rich. Here I met for the first time young men who had assumed from birth
that they would lead lives of comfort and power. And for the first time I met
women who told me that men were guilty of having kept all the joys and
privileges of the earth for themselves. I was baffled. What privileges? What
joys? I thought about the maimed, dismal lives of most of the men back
home. What had they stolen from their wives and daughters? The right to
go five days a week, twelve months a year, for thirty or forty years to a steel
mill or a coal mine? The right to drop bombs and die in war? The right to
feel every leak in the roof, every gap in the fence, every cough in the engine,
as a wound they must mend? The right to feel, when the lay-off comes or
the plant shuts down, not only afraid but ashamed?

I was slow to understand the deep grievances of women. This was because, as a boy, I had envied them. Before college, the only people I had
ever known who were interested in art or music or literature, the only
ones who read books, the only ones who ever seemed to enjoy a sense of
ease and grace were the mothers and daughters. Like the menfolk, they
fretted about money, they scrimped and made-do. But, when the pay
stopped coming in, they were not the ones who had failed. Nor did they
have to go to war, and that seemed to me a blessed fact. By comparison
with the narrow, ironclad days of fathers, there was an expansiveness, I
thought, in the days of mothers. They went to see neighbors, to shop in
town, to run errands at school, at the library, at church. No doubt, had I
looked harder at their lives, I would have envied them less. It was not my
fate to become a woman, so it was easier for me to see the graces. Few of
them held jobs outside the home, and those who did filled thankless roles

as clerks and waitresses. I didn't see, then, what a prison a house could be, since houses seemed to me brighter, handsomer places than any factory. I did not realize — because such things were never spoken of — how often women suffered from men's bullying. I did learn about the wretchedness of abandoned wives, single mothers, widows; but I also learned about the wretchedness of lone men. Even then I could see how exhausting it was for a mother to cater all day to the needs of young children. But if I had been asked, as a boy, to choose between tending a baby and tending a machine, I think I would have chosen the baby. (Having now tended both, I know I would choose the baby.)

So I was baffled when the women at college accused me and my sex of having cornered the world's pleasures. I think something like my bafflement has been felt by other boys (and by girls as well) who grew up in dirt-poor farm country, in mining country, in black ghettos, in Hispanic barrios, in the shadows of factories, in Third World nations — any place where the fate of men is as grim and bleak as the fate of women. Toilers and warriors. I realize now how ancient these identities are, how deep the tug they exert on men, the undertow of a thousand generations. The miseries I saw, as a boy, in the lives of nearly all men I continue to see in the lives of many — the body-breaking toil, the tedium, the call to be tough, the humiliating powerlessness, the battle for a living and for territory.

When the women I met at college thought about the joys and privileges of men, they did not carry in their minds the sort of men I had known in my childhood. They thought of their fathers, who were bankers, physicians, architects, stockbrokers, the big wheels of the big cities. These fathers rode the train to work or drove cars that cost more than any of my childhood houses. They were attended from morning to night by female helpers, wives, and nurses and secretaries. They were never laid off, never short of cash at month's end, never lined up for welfare. These fathers made decisions that mattered. They ran the world.   20

The daughters of such men wanted to share in this power, this glory. So did I. They yearned for a say over their future, for jobs worthy of their abilities, for the right to live at peace, unmolested, whole. Yes, I thought, yes yes. The difference between me and these daughters was that they saw me, because of my sex, as destined from birth to become like their fathers, and therefore as an enemy to their desires. But I knew better. I wasn't an enemy, in fact or in feeling. I was an ally. If I had known, then, how to tell them so, would they have believed me? Would they now?

The Reader's Presence

1. Consider the title of the essay. Why does Sanders use the word *carry*? What image does the word convey? How is that image reinforced throughout the essay?
2. Sanders begins the essay by jumping directly into a conversation.

What effect does this conversation have on the reader? What does Sanders want you to think of him during that conversation? (See paragraphs 1–9.) Do your first impressions of Sanders remain the same throughout your reading?

3. Why did Sanders once envy women? What did women possess that men didn't? Has his impression of women's lives changed, or does he still envy them? If not, why not? If so, have his reasons changed?

25

Leslie Marmon Silko

Yellow Woman and a Beauty of the Spirit

Poet, novelist, screenwriter, and storyteller Leslie Marmon Silko (b. 1948) is of mixed heritage, part Pueblo Indian, part Mexican, and part white. She was raised on the Laguna Pueblo and educated at the University of New Mexico, where she now teaches English. Her publications include a montage of stories, legends, poems, and photographs called Storyteller *(1981), several works of fiction, the screenplay for Marlon Brando's film* Black Elks, *an illustrated autobiographical narrative called* Sacred Waters *(1993), and* Yellow Woman *and a* Beauty of the Spirit: Essays on Native American Life Today *(1996), in which the essay reprinted here appears. Her work has been extensively anthologized and published in magazines and journals. In 1981, Silko was awarded a MacArthur grant for her writing.*

When asked by an interviewer why she writes, she replied, "I don't know what I know until it comes out in narrative." Speaking specifically of the process of composing her novel Almanac of the Dead *(1991), she said, "It's like a do-it-yourself psychoanalysis. It's sort of dangerous to be a novelist . . . you're working with language and all kinds of things can escape with the words of a narrative."*

From the time I was a small child, I was aware that I was different. I looked different from my playmates. My two sisters looked different too. We didn't quite look like the other Laguna Pueblo children, but we didn't look quite white either. In the 1880s, my great-grandfather had followed his older brother west from Ohio to the New Mexico Territory to survey the land for the U.S. government. The two Marmon brothers came to the Laguna Pueblo reservation because they had an Ohio cousin who already lived there. The Ohio cousin was involved in sending Indian children thousands of miles away from their families to the War Department's big Indian boarding school in Carlisle, Pennsylvania. Both brothers married full-blood Laguna Pueblo women. My great-grandfather had first married my great-grandmother's older sister, but she died in childbirth and left two small children. My great-grandmother was fifteen or twenty years younger than my great-grandfather. She had attended Carlisle Indian School and spoke and wrote English beautifully.

I called her Grandma A'mooh because that's what I heard her say whenever she saw me. *A'mooh* means "granddaughter" in the Laguna language. I remember this word because her love and her acceptance of me as a small child were so important. I had sensed immediately that something about my appearance was not acceptable to some people, white and Indian. But I did not see any signs of that strain or anxiety in the face of my beloved Grandma A'mooh.

Younger people, people my parents' age, seemed to look at the world in a more modern way. The modern way included racism. My physical appearance seemed not to matter to the old-time people. They looked at the world very differently; a person's appearance and possessions did not matter nearly as much as a person's behavior. For them, a person's value lies in how that person interacts with other people, how that person behaves toward the animals and the earth. That is what matters most to the old-time people. The Pueblo people believed this long before the Puritans arrived with their notions of sin and damnation, and racism. The old-time beliefs persist today; thus I will refer to the old-time people in the present tense as well as the past. Many worlds may coexist here.

I spent a great deal of time with my great-grandmother. Her house was next to our house, and I used to wake up at dawn, hours before my parents or younger sisters, and I'd go wait on the porch swing or on the back steps by her kitchen door. She got up at dawn, but she was more than eighty years old, so she needed a little while to get dressed and to get the fire going in the cookstove. I had been carefully instructed by my parents not to bother her and to behave, and to try to help her any way I could. I always loved the early mornings when the air was so cool with a hint of rain smell in the breeze. In the dry New Mexico air, the least hint of dampness smells sweet.

My great-grandmother's yard was planted with lilac bushes and iris; there were four o'clocks, cosmos, morning glories, and hollyhocks, and old-fashioned rosebushes that I helped her water. If the garden hose got stuck on one of the big rocks that lined the path in the yard, I ran and pulled it free. That's what I came to do early every morning: to help Grandma water the plants before the heat of the day arrived.

Grandma A'mooh would tell about the old days, family stories about relatives who had been killed by Apache raiders who stole the sheep our relatives had been herding near Swahnee. Sometimes she read Bible sto-

5

ries that we kids liked because of the illustrations of Jonah in the mouth of a whale and Daniel surrounded by lions. Grandma A'mooh would send me home when she took her nap, but when the sun got low and the afternoon began to cool off, I would be back on the porch swing, waiting for her to come out to water the plants and to haul in firewood for the evening. When Grandma was eighty-five, she still chopped her own kindling. She used to let me carry it in the coal bucket for her, but she would not allow me to use the ax. I carried armloads of kindling too, and I learned to be proud of my strength.

I was allowed to listen quietly when Aunt Susie or Aunt Alice came to visit Grandma. When I got old enough to cross the road alone, I went and visited them almost daily. They were vigorous women who valued books and writing. They were usually busy chopping wood or cooking but never hesitated to take time to answer my questions. Best of all they told me the *hummah-hah* stories, about an earlier time when animals and humans shared a common language. In the old days, the Pueblo people had educated their children in this manner; adults took time out to talk to and teach young people. Everyone was a teacher, and every activity had the potential to teach the child.

But as soon as I started kindergarten at the Bureau of Indian Affairs day school, I began to learn more about the differences between the Laguna Pueblo world and the outside world. It was at school that I learned just how different I looked from my classmates. Sometimes tourists driving past on Route 66 would stop by Laguna Day School at recess time to take photographs of us kids. One day, when I was in the first grade, we all crowded around the smiling white tourists, who peered at our faces. We all wanted to be in the picture because afterward the tourists sometimes gave us each a penny. Just as we were all posed and ready to have our picture taken, the tourist man looked at me. "Not you," he said and motioned for me to step away from my classmates. I felt so embarrassed that I wanted to disappear. My classmates were puzzled by the tourists' behavior, but I knew the tourists didn't want me in their snapshot because I looked different, because I was part white.

In the view of the old-time people, we were all sisters and brothers because the Mother Creator made all of us — all colors and all sizes. We are sisters and brothers, clanspeople of all the living beings around us. The plants, the birds, fish, clouds, water, even the clay — they all are related to us. The old-time people believe that all things, even rocks and water, have spirit and being. They understood that all things want only to continue being as they are; they need only to be left as they are. Thus the old folks used to tell us kids not to disturb the earth unnecessarily. All things as they were created exist already in harmony with one another as long as we do not disturb them.

As the old story tells us, Tse'itsi'nako, Thought Woman, the Spider,   10
thought of her three sisters, and as she thought of them, they came into

being. Together with Thought Woman, they thought of the sun and the stars and the moon. The Mother Creators imagined the earth and the oceans, the animals and the people, and the *ka'tsina* spirits that reside in the mountains. The Mother Creators imagined all the plants that would flower and the trees that bear fruit. As Thought Woman and her sisters thought of it, the whole universe came into being. In this universe, there is no absolute good or absolute bad; there are only balances and harmonies that ebb and flow. Some years the desert receives abundant rain, other years there is too little rain, and sometimes there is so much rain that floods cause destruction. But rain itself is neither innocent nor guilty. The rain is simply itself.

My great-grandmother was dark and handsome. Her expression in photographs is one of confidence and strength. I do not know if white people then or now would consider her beautiful. I do not know if old-time Laguna Pueblo people considered her beautiful or if the old-time people even thought in those terms. To the Pueblo way of thinking, the act of comparing one living being with another was silly, because each living being or thing is unique and therefore incomparably valuable because it is the only one of its kind. The old-time people thought it was crazy to attach such importance to a person's appearance. I understood very early that there were two distinct ways of interpreting the world. There was the white people's way and there was the Laguna way. In the Laguna way, it was bad manners to make comparisons that might hurt another person's feelings.

In everyday Pueblo life, not much attention was paid to one's physical appearance or clothing. Ceremonial clothing was quite elaborate but was used only for the sacred dances. The traditional Pueblo societies were communal and strictly egalitarian, which means that no matter how well or how poorly one might have dressed, there was no social ladder to fall from. All food and other resources were strictly shared so that no one person or group had more than another. I mention social status because it seems to me that most of the definitions of beauty in contemporary Western culture are really codes for determining social status. People no longer hide their face-lifts and they discuss their liposuctions because the point of the procedures isn't just cosmetic, it is social. It says to the world, "I have enough spare cash that I can afford surgery for cosmetic purposes."

In the old-time Pueblo world, beauty was manifested in behavior and in one's relationships with other living beings. Beauty was as much a feeling of harmony as it was a visual, aural, or sensual effect. The whole person had to be beautiful, not just the face or the body; faces or bodies could not be separated from hearts and souls. Health was foremost in achieving this sense of well-being and harmony; in the old-time Pueblo world, a person who did not look healthy inspired feelings of worry and anxiety, not feelings of well-being. A healthy person, of course, is in harmony with the world around her; she is at peace with herself too. Thus an unhappy person or spiteful person would not be considered beautiful.

In the old days, sturdy women were most admired. One of my vivid preschool memories is of the crew of Laguna women, in their forties and fifties, who came to cover our house with adobe plaster. They handled the ladders with great ease, and while two women ground the adobe mud on stones and added straw, another woman loaded the hod with mud and passed it up to the two women on ladders, who were smoothing the plaster on the wall with their hands. Since women owned the houses, they did the plastering. At Laguna, men did the basket making and the weaving of fine textiles; men helped a great deal with the child care too. Because the Creator is female, there is no stigma on being female; gender is not used to control behavior. No job was a man's job or a woman's job; the most able person did the work.

My Grandma Lily had been a Ford Model A mechanic when she was   15
a teenager. I remember when I was young, she was always fixing broken lamps and appliances. She was small and wiry, but she could lift her weight in rolled roofing or boxes of nails. When she was seventy-five, she was still repairing washing machines in my uncle's coin-operated laundry.

The old-time people paid no attention to birthdays. When a person was ready to do something, she did it. When she was no longer able, she stopped. Thus the traditional Pueblo people did not worry about aging or about looking old because there were no social boundaries drawn by the passage of years. It was not remarkable for young men to marry women as old as their mothers. I never heard anyone talk about "women's work" until after I left Laguna for college. Work was there to be done by any able-bodied person who wanted to do it. At the same time, in the old-time Pueblo world, identity was acknowledged to be always in a flux; in the old stories, one minute Spider Woman is a little spider under a yucca plant, and the next instant she is a sprightly grandmother walking down the road.

When I was growing up, there was a young man from a nearby village who wore nail polish and women's blouses and permed his hair. People paid little attention to his appearance; he was always part of a group of other young men from his village. No one ever made fun of him. Pueblo communities were and still are very interdependent, but they also have to be tolerant of individual eccentricities because survival of the group means everyone has to cooperate.

In the old Pueblo world, differences were celebrated as signs of the Mother Creator's grace. Persons born with exceptional physical or sexual differences were highly respected and honored because their physical differences gave them special positions as mediators between this world and the spirit world. The great Navajo medicine man of the 1920s, the Crawler, had a hunchback and could not walk upright, but he was able to heal even the most difficult cases.

Before the arrival of Christian missionaries, a man could dress as a woman and work with women and even marry a man without any fanfare. Likewise, a woman was free to dress like a man, to hunt and go to war with the men, and to marry a woman. In the old Pueblo worldview, we are all a mixture of male and female, and this sexual identity is changing constantly. Sexual inhibition did not begin until the Christian missionaries arrived. For the old-time people, marriage was about teamwork and social relationships, not about sexual excitement. In the days before the Puritans came, marriage did not mean an end to sex with people other than your spouse. Women were just as likely as men to have a *si'ash*, or lover.

New life was so precious that pregnancy was always appropriate, and   20
pregnancy before marriage was celebrated as a good sign. Since the children belonged to the mother and her clan, and women owned and bequeathed the houses and farmland, the exact determination of paternity wasn't critical. Although fertility was prized, infertility was no problem because mothers with unplanned pregnancies gave their babies to childless couples within the clan in open adoption arrangements. Children called their mother's sisters "mother" as well, and a child became attached to a number of parent figures.

In the sacred kiva ceremonies, men mask and dress as women to pay homage and to be possessed by the female energies of the spirit beings. Because differences in physical appearance were so highly valued, surgery to change one's face and body to resemble a model's face and body would be unimaginable. To be different, to be unique was blessed and was best of all.

The traditional clothing of Pueblo women emphasized a woman's sturdiness. Buckskin leggings wrapped around the legs protected her from scratches and injuries while she worked. The more layers of buckskin, the better. All those layers gave her legs the appearance of strength, like sturdy tree trunks. To demonstrate sisterhood and brotherhood with the plants and animals, the old-time people make masks and costumes that transform the human figures of the dancers into the animal beings they portray. Dancers paint their exposed skin; their postures and motions are adapted from their observations. But the motions are stylized. The observer sees not an actual eagle or actual deer dancing, but witnesses a human being, a dancer, gradually changing into a woman/buffalo or a man/deer. Every impulse is to reaffirm the urgent relationships that human beings have with the plant and animal world.

In the high desert, all vegetation, even weeds and thorns, becomes special, and all life is precious and beautiful because without the plants, the insects, and the animals, human beings living here cannot survive. Perhaps human beings long ago noticed the devastating impact human activity can have on the plants and animals; maybe this is why tribal cultures devised the stories about humans and animals intermarrying, and the clans that bind humans to animals and plants though a whole complex of duties.

We children were always warned not to harm frogs or toads, the beloved children of the rain clouds, because terrible floods would occur. I remember in the summer the old folks used to stick big bolls of cotton on the outside of their screen doors as bait to keep the flies from going in the house when the door was opened. The old folks staunchily resisted the killing of flies because once, long, long ago, when human beings were in a great deal of trouble, a Green Bottle Fly carried desperate messages from human beings to the Mother Creator in the Fourth World, below this one. Human beings had outraged the Mother Creator by neglecting the Mother Corn altar while they dabbled with sorcery and magic. The Mother Creator disappeared, and with her disappeared the rain clouds, and the plants and the animals too. The people began to starve, and they had no way of reaching the Mother Creator down below. Green Bottle Fly took the message to the Mother Creator, and the people were saved. To show their gratitude, the old folks refused to kill any flies.

The old stories demonstrate the interrelationships that the Pueblo   25
people have maintained with their plant and animal clanspeople. Kochininako, Yellow Woman, represents all women in the old stories. Her deeds span the spectrum of human behavior and are mostly heroic acts, though in at least one story, she chooses to join the secret Destroyer Clan, which worships destruction and death. Because Laguna Pueblo cosmology features a female Creator, the status of women is equal with the status of men, and women appear as often as men in the old stories as hero figures. Yellow Woman is my favorite because she dares to cross traditional boundaries of ordinary behavior during times of crisis in order to save the Pueblo; her power lies in her courage and her uninhibited sexuality, which the old-time Pueblo stories celebrate again and again because fertility was so highly valued.

The old stories always say that Yellow Woman was beautiful, but remember that the old-time people were not so much thinking about physical appearances. In each story, the beauty that Yellow Woman possesses is the beauty of her passion, her daring, and her sheer strength to act when catastrophe is imminent.

In one story, the people are suffering during a great drought and accompanying famine. Each day, Kochininako has to walk farther and farther from the village to find fresh water for her husband and children. One day she travels far, far to the east, to the plains, and she finally locates a freshwater spring. But when she reaches the pool, the water is churning violently as if something large had just gotten out of the pool. Kochininako does not want to see what huge creature had been at the pool, but just as she fills her water jar and turns to hurry away, a strong, sexy man in buffalo-skin leggings appears by the pool. Little drops of water glisten on his chest. She cannot help but look at him because he is so strong and so good to look at. Able to transform himself from human to buffalo in the wink of an eye, Buffalo Man gallops away with her on his back. Kochininako falls in love with Buffalo Man, and because of this liaison, the Buffalo People agree to give their bodies to the hunters to feed the starving Pueblo. Thus Kochininako's fearless sensuality results in the salvation of the people of her village, who are saved by the meat the Buffalo People "give" to them.

My father taught me and my sisters to shoot .22 rifles when we were seven; I went hunting with my father when I was eight, and I killed my first mule deer buck when I was thirteen. The Kochininako stories were always my favorite because Yellow Woman had so many adventures. In one story, as she hunts rabbits to feed her family, a giant monster pursues her, but she has the courage and the presence of mind to outwit it.

In another story, Kochininako has a fling with Whirlwind Man and returns to her husband ten months later with twin baby boys. The twin boys grow up to be great heroes of the people. Once again, Kochininako's vibrant sexuality benefits her people.

The stories about Kochininako made me aware that sometimes an in- 30 dividual must act despite disapproval, or concern for appearances or what others may say. From Yellow Woman's adventures, I learned to be comfortable with my differences. I even imagined that Yellow Woman had yellow skin, brown hair, and green eyes like mine, although her name does not refer to her color, but rather to the ritual color of the east.

There have been many other moments like the one with the camera-toting tourist in the schoolyard. But the old-time people always say, remember the stories, the stories will help you be strong. So all these years I have depended on Kochininako and the stories of her adventures.

Kochininako is beautiful because she has the courage to act in times of great peril, and her triumph is achieved by her sensuality, not through violence and destruction. For these qualities of the spirit, Yellow Woman and all women are beautiful.

The Reader's Presence

1. "From the time I was a small child, I was aware that I was different," Silko begins her essay. What examples of this difference does she cite? How many kinds of difference can you find in the essay?
2. Silko makes a number of broad generalizations about beliefs among the Laguna Pueblo people, comparing them to attitudes of people living in contemporary Western culture. Do you accept her claims about the "old-time" people? How does Silko establish her authority to speak for the Laguna Pueblo people?
3. "The old-time people always say, remember the stories, the stories will help you be strong," Silko writes in paragraph 31, and she does in fact relate many stories in her essay. Do the stories seem randomly chosen, or is there a common thread to them? In what ways are they different from the kinds of stories that we learn in traditional American history (for example, Paul Revere's midnight ride or Edison's inventing the light bulb)?

26

Gary Soto

The Childhood Worries,
or Why I Became a Writer

Gary Soto (b. 1952) grew up in Fresno, California. He has published several collections of poetry, including The Elements of San Joaquin *(1977), which won the United States Award of the International Poetry Forum. His* New and Selected Poems *and* Canto Familiar/Familiar Song *were published in 1995. Soto has also written and edited several collections of essays and short stories, the most recent of which is* Jesse *(1994). His work has appeared in many literary magazines, including the* Nation, Ploughshares, Ontario Review, *and* Poetry. *"The Childhood Worries, or Why I Became a Writer" appeared in the* Iowa Review *in 1995.*

Soto writes fiction for children as well; his books include Too Many Tamales *(1993),* Chato's Kitchen *(1995), and* Old Man and His Door *(1996). He has also produced three films for television, and recently published a play,* Novio Boy *(1996). In an interview, Soto said, "I like writing. I'm fairly prolific; it's a daily activity for me. And that keeps the youth and the imagination going. If I were to stop, I'd be in serious trouble."*

As a boy growing up in Fresno I knew that disease lurked just beneath the skin, that it was possible to wake up in the morning unable to move your legs or arms or even your head, that stone on a pillow. Your eyeballs might still swim in their own liquids as they searched the ceiling, or beyond, toward heaven and whatever savage god did this to you. Frail and whimpering, you could lie in your rickety bed. You could hear the siren blast at the Sun-Maid Raisin plant, and answer that blast with your own chirp-like cry. But that was it for you, a boy now reduced to the dull activity of blinking. In the adjoining rooms, a chair scraped against the linoleum floor, the kitchen faucet ran over frozen chicken parts, the toilet flushed, the radio sputtered something in Spanish. But you were not involved. You lay useless in bed while your family prepared for the day.

Disease startled Uncle Johnnie first, a mole on his forearm having turned cancerous and bright as a red berry. He was living in Texas when he wrote my mother about his illness. We took him in in spring. He lived with us the last three months of his life, mostly lying ill on the couch, a space meant for my brother Rick and me. Before our uncle arrived, we jumped on that couch, me with a flea-like leap and my brother with the heavier bounce of a frog. Now he had the couch to himself, this uncle who was as tender as a pony.

I didn't have much memory to go on. At age six, I didn't lie in bed at night, arms folded behind my head, and savor the time when I was four and a half, a sprout of orneriness. I was too busy in my young body to consider my trail of footprints, all wiped out at the end of a day. But I re-call Uncle Johnnie and the apple pie he bought me at Charlie's Market. My greed for sweetness grinned from my sticky mouth, and we devoured the pie as we strolled home, I walking backwards and looking at the mar-ket. Later I would return to that market and let my hands settle like small crabs on two candy bars. They opened and closed around them as I de-cided whether to take them, thus steal, thus let my mouth lather itself with the creamy taste of chocolate. Charlie was probably looking at me, wagging his large Armenian head at my stupidity. But that wasn't the point: I was deciding for myself whether I should sin and then worry about this sin, the wings of my bony shoulder blades less holy.

I recall also when our television was broken and my father pulled the tube out and took it to a repair shop. The TV was eyeless, just sprouts of wires and a smothering scent of dust. While Uncle Johnnie lay on the couch, I climbed into the back of the television set and pretended to be someone funny, one of the Three Stooges, and then someone scary, like Rodan[1] with his monstrous roar. My uncle watched me with a weary smile but no joy. I told him that I could be funny or scary, but in such a small space I couldn't play a horse or an Indian shot by the calvary. He died that spring, all because of a cancerous mole, died after the tube was once again fitted into the television set. Then the couch returned to us.

For one summer disease scared me. My whiskery neighbor, whose name I have forgotten, was a talker and addressed every growing plant, chicken, and dog in his dirt yard. When he got sick , his talk increased, as if he needed to get out all the words that he had intended to use in his old age. He had to use them then or never. One afternoon he came into our yard and showed me his fingernails, yellow and hard. He held them out quivering, as if he were going to do a hocus-pocus magic trick, and when he said it was cancer, I flinched. When I looked up into his face, pale as a fistful of straw, I saw that his eyes were large and bluish, his face already sinking in disease. I was eating grapes, feeding them into my mouth, and I didn't know what to do about his dying except to offer him some of my grapes. He laughed at this. He walked away, straight as any other man, and returned to his yard where he talked to himself and revved up a boat engine clamped to a barrel. A scarf of smoke unfurled

5

---

[1] *Rodan:* A flying monster of science fiction films. — EDS.

from the engine, and the blackish water boiled. He didn't seem to be getting anywhere.

That summer we did our rough living on the street, and our dogs did too. When my uncle Junior's collie got hit by a car on Van Ness Avenue, I watched my uncle, a teenager with a flattop haircut, gather his dog into his arms. He was the bravest person I knew, for he hugged to his chest what he loved best. A few of the kids from Braly Street milled around; the barber came out of his shop, snapped his sheet as if in surrender, and stared at the commotion for a moment, his eyes the color of twilight itself.

Uncle Junior yelled at us to get away, but I shadowed him for a while, barefoot and pagan. He walked up the alley that ran along our dusty-white house. I didn't know then that he intended to wait out the last breaths and then bury his dog. I didn't know that months later at the end of this same alley we were walking down, a car would roll, its wheels in the air, the man inside dead and his hat as flat as cardboard. I would be excited. Like my uncle's collie, I panted, except from exhilaration, when the police asked if we knew the person. I pointed and said that he lived near the man with the motorboat engine and cancer.

This was the summer I began to worry about disease. My father was in road camp with my uncle Shorty. They'd gotten drunk and stolen a car, but I was behaving. I drank my milk, ate my Graham Crackers, and dutifully picked slivers from my palm, but despite my hygiene, I was involved in disease. One morning my brother woke with his throat pinched with a clot that made it difficult for him to swallow. He opened his mouth in the backyard light and, along with my mother, I looked in, worried that I would have to wallow in the same bedroom and, in time, the same disease. His mouth was like any other mouth, wet with a push of milky air. But our mother knew better: the tonsils would have to come out. Mine would have to come out, too, no matter how many times I swallowed, cried, and said, "See, Mom, I'm OK." She figured that if you do one son you might as well do two.

That night I stood by the window in our bedroom and ate M & M candies and wondered about Father and Uncle Shorty. They were in a sort of a prison camp, I knew. We had gone to see them, and father had shown me his hands, which were speckled white with paint. I rode on his knee, a camel ride of excitement because I was chewing gum and sunflower seeds at the same time. I asked him when he was coming home. Pretty soon, he answered. I didn't know that he and my uncle were painting rocks along the rural Kearny Boulevard and hoisting railroad ties that became bumpers in the gravel parking lots of Kearny Park.

I thought about them as I ate my M & Ms and touched my throat   10
when I swallowed the candy. Father wasn't there to help me. He was far away, it seemed, and I peered out the window toward the junkyard, with its silhouette of pipes, plumbing, and jagged sheet metal, the playground of my childhood. The summer wind picked up the metallic scent and

whipped it about. When a sweep of headlights from the cars that turned from Van Ness onto Braly Street frisked the junkyard, the eyes of its German Shepherd watchdog glowed orange and stared at me. I ate my candy, one last taste of sweetness on the eve of blood and gagging.

When we arrived at the community hospital, I hugged my pajamas and coloring book. I glanced nervously down the corridor. I looked at the old people's yellow fingernails, clear signs of cancer, and I peeked in a lab where I knew that blood was drawn. My brother and I walked on each side of our mother. We were led to a room where there was another child sitting up in a crib-like bed, mute as a teddy bear. He spit red into a bowl, and I immediately knew this was a scary place.

After we settled into our room, I worried not about dying, but about the filthy act of baring my bottom to a bedpan. I was in a hospital gown, not my pajamas. I held out for hours, but when I couldn't stand it anymore, I told the nurse I had to use the bathroom. She wouldn't allow me to get up from bed. I started to cry, but she scolded me, and I knew better than to carry on because she had the instruments of pain. I told my brother not to laugh, but he was too scared to entertain the thought. I squatted on the bedpan and was letting my water flow when a blind, teenage girl walked past our open door, a ghost-like figure blowing down the corridor. A nurse was helping her along, step by hesitant step. I wanted to ask the nurse if she was blind forever, or would she one day peel off that bandage and smile at every bloodshot color in the precious world. I did my number and then looked over at the boy, now asleep and pale as an angel.

I don't recall my brother and me talking much at the hospital. I lay in bed, touching the plastic wrist band with my typed name. I closed my eyes. I tried to shut out the image of the "thing" they would take out of my throat, a kidney-bean sac no longer needed. I knew that my baby teeth would eventually loosen and come out, possibly when I was biting into a peach or an apple, but I was terrified that someone behind a white mask would probe my mouth.

A few hours later, my brother was wheeled away with tears brimming in his eyes. If my big brother had dime-sized tears in his eyes, than I, his little brother with just baby teeth, would have silver dollars rolling down my cheeks. I considered crying and sobbing as pitifully as I could manage, but who would listen? My mother was gone, a tiny egg of memory living inside my head. Now my brother was gone. I looked over to where the other boy was, but his parents had come and rescued him. I didn't have anything to do except thumb through my animal coloring book and imagine what crayons I would use on the deer, elephant, giraffe, and grinning hyena. This diversion helped. But then I was wheeled away.

This was the late '50s when almost every child's tonsils were routinely clipped from his throat. I remember the room where a nurse in a mask lowered a disk-like mask onto my nose and mouth. She lowered it three times and each time said, "breathe in" as they basted my face with

15

ether. I did what I was told until my consciousness receded like a wave, and I was in a room full of testing patterns, something like television when it was still too early for cartoons. They operated, and I bled into a bowl all night, it seemed, but happily drank 7-Up with no ice, a treat that didn't cost me anything except for hoarse speech for three days.

When Rick and I got home, we were pampered with ice cream and 7-Up, a lovely blast of carbonation which singed my nostrils. I believed that we might continue to live our remaining childhood that way with mounds of ice cream, 7-Up, and cooing words from our mother. But too soon that stopped, and we were back to the usual plates of *frijoles* and tortillas. At that time, while my father and uncle were in jail, my mother worked at Readi-Spud, peeling potatoes that scurried down troughs of icy water. She would give us over to Mrs. Moreno, the mother of at least nine children and the jolliest woman in the western world. She laughed more than she spoke, and she spoke a lot. While in Mrs. Moreno's care, I became even more worried about disease because I knew roaches made a princely living in her cupboards.

Mrs. Moreno worked at a Chinese noodle factory and came to get Rick and me after work. One day, when we climbed into the back seat of her station wagon, her son Donald was standing in a cardboard tub of noodles. His feet pumped up and down and emitted a sucking sound with each marching step. When I asked Mrs. Moreno about dinner she was laughing because the baby on the front seat was crawling toward her breast. She giggled, "You like chow mein?" I slowly lowered my gaze to Donald's bare feet and felt sick.

They ate noodles right after we arrived, slurped them down so that the ends wiggled like worms into their suctioning mouths. My brother and I ate grapes and drank water. Later, all of us — eleven kids — played our version of "The Old Woman Who Lived in a Shoe." We climbed onto the roof and jumped off, a cargo of unkillable kids hitting the ground like sacks of flour. It may not have been that same evening, but I recall three babies at the end of a long, dirty hallway and some of the kids, the older ones, trying to knock them over with a real bowling ball. There was squealing and crying, but it was mostly laughter that cut through the cloistered air of a dank hallway, laughter coming even from Mrs. Moreno when one of the babies went down.

One untroubled afternoon Lloyd showed me a toy rifle, the kind that you had to crack in half to cock and which shot arrows tipped with red suction cups. He took one suction cup off, cocked the rifle, and shot the arrow into the flat spatula of his palm. "It doesn't hurt," he told me, and let me shoot the arrow repeatedly into my palm, the pressure of the arrow no more than a push. He recocked the rifle and fit the arrow into one of his nostrils. I automatically stepped back even though Lloyd was smiling. He was smiling just a moment before he pulled the trigger, before blood suddenly streamed from his nose and his eyes grew huge as two white moons and full of fright. He started crying and running around the house with the arrow in his nose, and I ran after him, almost crying. When his mother caught him by the arm, I raced out of the house, not wanting to get involved, and returned home, scared as I touched my own nose. I imagined the arrow in my own nose. I imagined blood spilling on the back porch. Later, just after I had finished dinner, I returned to Lloyd's house. He was at the table, with the threads of cotton balls hanging from his nostrils. The family was eating chow mein, piled like worms and wiggling down their throats.

The house was a poor, curled shoe, and it scared me because in its 20 carelessness lurked disease and calamity. I recall standing at their stove and asking a teenage boy who had drifted inside the house, "What's that you're making?" I looked at a large, dented kettle containing a grayish soup which Arnold was stirring with a pencil. I peeked into the soup, sipped it with a large spoon, and saw small things wheeling in the water as he stirred them — a merry-go-round of meats, I thought. When he said, "pigeons," I looked closely and could see the plucked birds bob and rise, bob and rise, and with each rise I could see the slits of their closed eyes.

The Moreno place, however, was not nearly as scary as the hospital. There were no instruments of pain, unless you counted the hive of tapeworms that showed up later because I ate raw bacon, white strips we peeled like Band-Aids from the wrapper. The Morenos taught me this too; they said it was good, and I ate my share while sitting on the roof, the sunset a stain the color of bright, bright medicine. How I would need that sun! How I would need a cure for my worry, and a cure for my brother, who was sporting on the bottom of his foot a sliver the size of a chopstick.

At age six disease scared me, and so did Grandpa, who lived just down the alley from our house on Braly Street. When I went over to eat lunch — yet another pile of *frijoles* wrapped in a diaper-sized tortilla — he was at the kitchen table playing solitaire with a big chunk of his head missing. I backed out of the house, bristling with fear, because the only thing left was his face. He looked like the poker-face card in front of him: Jack of Bad Luck, or King of Almighty Mistakes? While I backed out of the screen door, Uncle Junior caught me from behind and nudged me into the kitchen. He told me that Grandpa was wearing a nylon stocking on his head, trying to grow his hair back. A stinky concoction of *yerba buena*[2] and earthly fuels smothered his crown and temples. I sat down and ate my beans while watching Grandpa eat from his plate. I asked him if his head would grow back; he was chewing a huge amount of food like a camel. I thought I would turn seven by the time he cleared his throat and heard his answer, which was, "*Mi'jo,*[3] you got beans on your shirt. Shaddup."

---

[2] *yerba buena:* A mint tea. — EDS.
[3] *Mi'jo:* My son (*mi hijo*). — EDS.

Two kittens died from distemper and then Pete, our canary, was devoured by mama cat. A stray dog showed up outside our yard with a piece of wood in its watery eye. I touched my own eye, pulling at a tiny string of sleep. Everything seemed ill and ominous. Even our house began to slip on its foundation, which excited me because the bathroom was now at a slant. The water in the tub slouched now that one side was higher. With a scoop of my hands, it was easy to force a tidal wave on the line of ants scurrying along the baseboard.

I looked around at family and friends who were hurt or dying, but I didn't know that a year later my father would die, his neck broken in an industrial accident. This would be in August, when we were settled in a new house the color of cement. He didn't live in that house more than a week, and then he was gone. The funeral didn't mean much to me. It was the scent of flowers and the wash of tears; it was a sympathetic squeeze of my shoulders and candies slipped into the pockets of my tweed coat, which was too small because it was borrowed. After his burial I recall eating donuts at my grandparents' house. When a doctor was called because Grandma was in hysterics, I didn't stop eating. I took what was rightly mine and devoured it in the dark, near the ugly claw-like crowns of a rose bush.

I didn't know what to think except that Father was out of prison and now in the earth forever. Because he wasn't returning, I began to play with his squeaky hand drill, boring into trees and fences. I liked the smell of the blond shavings and liked to think that maybe Father used the drill in prison. He mostly painted rocks, this much I was told, but I fantasized about how he might have used it in prison to get away. I saw him poking holes in a cement wall and then pushing over that wall to get Uncle Shorty in the adjacent cell. Uncle Johnnie was there, too, a ghost-like bundle of flesh on the cot. My father was going to save not only the both of them, but in the end himself as well.

Occasionally, we would visit my father's grave, where my mother cried and set flowers, half-shadowing the oval photo on his grave. What worried me was not his death, but the gold-painted cannon on a hill that pointed at our Chevy when we drove through the cement gates. The cannon scared me because my vision of death was that when you died an angel would pick you up, place your head in the cannon, and give your neck a little twist. I was spooked by this cannon and wanted to ask my mother about it, but she was too busy in her sorrow for a straight answer. I kept quiet on the matter. I figured there was one cannon, like one God, and all graves rolled on a hill. In time, you were asked to put your head in a cannon and die as well.

I didn't realize that I was probably ill. Neither did I realize how I used my time when my mother would send me off to school. For weeks, I didn't go there. I stayed in an alley, kicking though the garbage and boredom, and returned home only after I assumed my classmates had finished with whatever the teacher had asked them to do. Sometimes I would take

25

the drill and make holes, occasionally even in the lawn. But I had grown bored with this. I had discovered how I could make a huge noise. In the empty bedroom, the one my father and mother would have used, I spent hours with fistfuls of marbles. I bounced them off the baseboard, a ricocheting clatter that I imagined were soldiers getting their fill of death. The clatter of noise busied my mind with something like hate. If I had looked into a mirror, I would have seen this hate pleated on my forehead. If anyone, including my sister or brother, had smarted off to me, I had plans to get even. I would let them go to sleep and then blast them with marbles at close range as they inhaled a simple dream.

My mother was alone, and in her loneliness she often piled us into our Chevy and drove us over to my *nina's* house on the west side of Fresno, a place that was so scary that even the blacks were afraid. My *nina* — godmother — took in identical twin boys, same age as me but filthier. Their dirty hair was like the hair Woody Woodpecker wore. They were orphans. They were sadly nicknamed "Caca" and "Peepee," and for a while they made me feel good because I knew they were poorer than me. "Peepee, is your dad dead?" I would ask. "Caca, what grade are you in?" I would inquire. They shrugged their shoulders a lot and ran when they saw my *nina*, a woman you dared not play with. Every time we visited, I took a toy to show them — plastic plane, steel car, sock of marbles, and even my brother's glow-in-the-dark statue of Jesus. I wanted them to know that even though my father was dead, I still owned things. After a few visits I didn't have anything left to share, just a ten-foot link of rubber bands. This lack made me mad, and I began to pick on them, even beat them up, in a kind of Punch-and-Judy show in the dirt driveway. When we found out that the twins were scared of ghosts, my brother and Rachel, my *nina's* daughter, told them to sit and wait in the living room because their mother and father were going to pick them up. We gave them fistfuls of raisins. Rick and Rachel then ran outside, where they scraped a bamboo rake against the window. The twins looked at me, then the curtain that was dancing like ghosts from the blast of the window cooler. Their mouths stopped churning on those raisins and the gray light of the TV flashed briefly in their eyes. When I yelled, "*La llorona*[4] is outside," they jumped and ran from the house, poor, terrified "Caca" and "Peepee" living up to their names that early evening.

I often attended church, a place that was scarier than the hospital or the Moreno's house or grandfather's head. Mother said that Jesus had been a good man, and he wanted peace and harmony in the hearts of all men. She said this while I looked at Jesus on his cross, poor Jesus who had nails and blood all over him. If they did that to someone who was so good I wondered what they might do to me. You see, I was turning out bad. I was so angry from having to worry all the time that I had become

---

[4]*La llorona:* The weeping woman; a ghost in a Mexican folk tale. — EDS.

violent. Once I stuck a broken shaft of bottle in my brother's leg for going swimming without me. Blood ran down my knuckles, and I ran away amazed that it was so calming to hurt someone who was bigger. My mother beat me with a hanger for my violence and then made me eat dinner in the bathroom. I put my bowl first on the hamper, then moved it to my knees, because I wanted a better view of the faucet dripping water. In the bathroom, then, I began to worry about our wasting water. I counted the drips to a hundred. I swallowed and pictured in my mind a pagan baby sucking a rock for moisture. Later, after I was allowed out of the bathroom, I took a pair of pliers and tried to tighten the faucet. I managed only to scratch the chrome plating on the faucets, and I went to bed worrying that my mother would conclude that it was me. I closed my eyes and let the pagan baby swallow the rock.

I asked my mother if you ever had to stop worrying, or if you had to   30
continue until you were old. I was already tired of having to learn about Jesus and the more important apostles. She answered yes and mumbled something about life not being easy. This was when I began to look at pictures in the medical dictionary: ringworms, rickets, TB, tongues with canker sores, and elephantiasis. With elephantiasis, the scariest disease, your legs swelled fat as water balloons and, I suspected, sloshed some evil liquids. I looked down at my own legs, those reeds of bone and marrow. They were skinny, but still I worried that my legs could swell and the rest of me, arms mainly, would stay thin, possibly from rickets which had made headway at school. I would be the second deformed kid on this street, the other being an older boy with one small arm that was shaped like a banana.

I knew the face of the boy in the iron lung. His hair was black and his eyes flat. He was motherless, for who could wrap a loving hug around a machine large as a barrel. I could hardly look at this boy. He might have shared my name, or my brother's name, or been related to the kid at school who had one leg shrunken from polio. I didn't like the idea of lying down for what might be forever. Still, I practiced what he lived by lying still on the couch until I fell asleep. When I woke I didn't know if I was at the new house or the old house, or if an angel had already picked me up and fit my head in the gold-painted cannon.

Then I worried about air and radiation and religious equations like the Trinity and, finally, the march of communists against our country. The hollowness in my face concerned my mother. She studied me when I did my homework at the kitchen table. She suspected that I might have ringworm because there were pale splotches on my face. It was only dirt, though, a film of dirt you could rub off with spit and a thumb.

My worry lessened when I began to understand that nothing could really hurt me. It was another summer and the beginning of the '60s. On our new street, which was green with lawns and squeaky with new trikes, I discovered my invincibility when I was running with new friends, barefoot, and with no shirt. I was particularly proud because I had hooked a screwdriver in a belt loop on my pants. I tripped and fell, and as I fell I worried for a moment, wondering if the screwdriver would drive its point into my belly. The fall was slow, like the build-up to my seven years, and the result would either be yes or no to my living.

The screwdriver kicked up sparks when it cut across the sidewalk. They were wonderful, these sparks that lasted no longer than a blink. Right then, with gravel pitted in my palm and my belly spanked by the fall, I rolled onto my back, cried, and knew that hurt and disease were way off, in another country, one that thanks to Jesus Almighty, I would never think to visit.

The Reader's Presence

1. Consider the alternate title of the essay: "Why I Became a Writer." What do the narrator's many worries about disease and encounters with death have to do with his decision to become a writer? What is the effect on the reader of the barrage of deaths — from the uncle to the neighbor to the dog, kittens, canary, ants, and the boy's own father — narrated in this essay? Identify specific passages to support your response. Which details bring home the seriousness of the losses the boy has suffered?

2. In paragraph 3, Soto writes, "I didn't have much memory to go on." He speaks of his young life as a "trail of footprints all wiped out at the end of a day." Still, this avowedly ephemeral life has left a trail of memories that informs the essay and provides its richness and texture. Discuss the role of memory in this essay. Which details are most memorable for you? Why? Which memories turn out to be touchstones for the author? How does memory transform events into prose?

3. In the child's mind, what are the causes of death and disease? What role does sin play? To what extent does the boy hold himself responsible for the calamities he faces? What role do his parents and the other adults in his life play? What lessons does he learn, directly and indirectly, from each of them? What causes the transition from his state of continuous worry to his feeling of invincibility?

27

Brent Staples

Just Walk on By: A Black Man Ponders His Power to Alter Public Space

As he describes in Parallel Time: Growing Up in Black and White *(1994), Brent Staples (b. 1951) escaped a childhood of urban poverty through success in school and his determination to be a writer. Although Staples earned a Ph.D. in psychology from the University of Chicago in 1982, his love of journalism led him to leave the field of psychology and start a career that has taken him to his current position on the editorial board of the* New York Times. *Staples contributes to several national magazines, including* Harper's, *the* New York Times Magazine, *and* Ms., *in which "Just Walk on By" appeared in 1986.*

In his autobiography, Staples remembers how in Chicago he prepared for his writing career by keeping a journal. "I wrote on buses on the Jackson Park el — though only at the stops to keep the writing legible. I traveled to distant neighborhoods, sat on their curbs, and sketched what I saw in words. Thursdays meant free admission at the Art Institute. All day I attributed motives to people in paintings, especially people in Rembrandts. At closing time I went to a nightclub in The Loop and spied on patrons, copied their conversations and speculated about their lives. The journal was more than 'a record of my inner transactions.' It was a collection of stolen souls from which I would one day construct a book."

My first victim was a woman — white, well dressed, probably in her early twenties. I came upon her late one evening on a deserted street in Hyde Park, a relatively affluent neighborhood in an otherwise mean, impoverished section of Chicago. As I swung onto the avenue behind her, there seemed to be a discreet, uninflammatory distance between us. Not so. She cast back a worried glance. To her, the youngish black man — a broad six feet two inches with a beard and billowing hair, both hands shoved into the pockets of a bulky military jacket — seemed menacingly close. After a few more quick glimpses, she picked up her pace and was soon running in earnest. Within seconds she disappeared into a cross street.

That was more than a decade ago. I was twenty-two years old, a graduate student newly arrived at the University of Chicago. It was in the

thesis

echo of that terrified woman's footfalls that I first began to know the unwieldy inheritance I'd come into — the ability to alter public space in ugly
ways. It was clear that she thought herself the quarry of a mugger, a
rapist, or worse. Suffering a bout of insomnia, however, I was stalking
sleep, not defenseless wayfarers. As a softy who is scarcely able to take a
knife to a raw chicken — let alone hold it to a person's throat — I was
surprised, embarrassed, and dismayed all at once. Her flight made me feel
like an accomplice in tyranny. It also made it clear that I was indistinguishable from the muggers who occasionally seeped into the area from
the surrounding ghetto. That first encounter, and those that followed, sig-
nified that a vast, unnerving gulf lay between nighttime pedestrians —
particularly women — and me. And I soon gathered that being perceived
as dangerous is a hazard in itself. I only needed to turn a corner into a
dicey situation, or crowd some frightened, armed person in a foyer somewhere, or make an errant move after being pulled over by a policeman.
Where fear and weapons meet — and they often do in urban America —
there is always the possibility of death.

In that first year, my first away from my hometown, I was to become
thoroughly familiar with the language of fear. At dark, shadowy intersec-
tions in Chicago, I could cross in front of a car stopped at a traffic light
and elicit the *thunk, thunk, thunk, thunk* of the driver — black, white,
male, or female — hammering down the door locks. On less traveled
streets after dark, I grew accustomed to but never comfortable with people who crossed to the other side of the street rather than pass me. Then
there were the standard unpleasantries with police, doormen, bouncers,
cabdrivers, and others whose business is to screen out troublesome individuals *before* there is any nastiness.

I moved to New York nearly two years ago and I have remained an
avid night walker. In central Manhattan, the near-constant crowd cover
minimizes tense one-on-one street encounters. Elsewhere — visiting
friends in SoHo,[1] where sidewalks are narrow and tightly spaced buildings shut out the sky — things can get very taut indeed.

Black men have a firm place in New York mugging literature. Norman Podhoretz[2] in his famed (or infamous) 1963 essay, "My Negro
Problem — And Ours," recalls growing up in terror of black males; they
"were tougher than we were, more ruthless," he writes — and as an adult
on the Upper West Side of Manhattan, he continues, he cannot constrain
his nervousness when he meets black men on certain streets. Similarly, a
decade later, the essayist and novelist Edward Hoagland extols a New
York where once "Negro bitterness bore down mainly on other Negroes." Where some see mere panhandlers, Hoagland sees "a mugger
who is clearly screwing up his nerve to do more than just *ask* for money."

5

---

[1]*Soho:* A district of lower Manhattan known for its art galleries. — EDS.
[2]*Norman Podhoretz:* A well-known literary critic and editor of *Commentary* magazine. — EDS.

But Hoagland has "the New Yorker's quick-hunch posture for broken-field maneuvering," and the bad guy swerves away.

I often witness that "hunch posture," from women after dark on the warrenlike streets of Brooklyn where I live. They seem to set their faces on neutral and, with their purse straps strung across their chests bandolier style, they forge ahead as though bracing themselves against being tackled. I understand, of course, that the danger they perceive is not a hallucination. Women are particularly vulnerable to street violence, and young black males are drastically overrepresented among the perpetrators of that violence. Yet these truths are no solace against the kind of alienation that comes of being ever the suspect, against being set apart, a fearsome entity with whom pedestrians avoid making eye contact.

It is not altogether clear to me how I reached the ripe old age of twenty-two without being conscious of the lethality nighttime pedestrians attributed to me. Perhaps it was because in Chester, Pennsylvania, the small, angry industrial town where I came of age in the 1960s, I was scarcely noticeable against a backdrop of gang warfare, street knifings, and murders. I grew up one of the good boys, had perhaps a half-dozen fistfights. In retrospect my shyness of combat has clear sources.

Many things go into the making of a young thug. One of those things is the consummation of the male romance with the power to intimidate. An infant discovers that random flailings send the baby bottle flying out of the crib and crashing to the floor. Delighted, the joyful babe repeats those motions again and again, seeking to duplicate the feat. Just so, I recall the points at which some of my boyhood friends were finally seduced by the perception of themselves as tough guys. When a mark cowered and surrendered his money without resistance, myth and reality merged — and paid off. It is, after all, only manly to embrace the power to frighten and intimidate. We, as men, are not supposed to give an inch of our lane on the highway; we are to seize the fighter's edge in work and in play and even in love; we are to be valiant in the face of hostile forces.

Unfortunately, poor and powerless young men seem to take all this nonsense literally. As a boy, I saw countless tough guys locked away; I have since buried several, too. They were babies, really — a teenage cousin, a brother of twenty-two, a childhood friend in his midtwenties — all gone down in episodes of bravado played out in the streets. I came to doubt the virtues of intimidation early on. I chose, perhaps even unconsciously, to remain a shadow — timid, but a survivor.

The fearsomeness mistakenly attributed to me in public places often   10
has a perilous flavor. The most frightening of these confusions occurred in the late 1970s and early 1980s when I worked as a journalist in Chicago. One day, rushing into the office of a magazine I was writing for with a deadline story in hand, I was mistaken for a burglar. The office manager called security and, with an ad hoc posse, pursued me through the labyrinthine halls, nearly to my editor's door. I had no way of proving who I was. I could only move briskly toward the company of someone who knew me.

Another time I was on assignment for a local paper and killing time before an interview. I entered a jewelry store on the city's affluent Near North Side. The proprietor excused herself and returned with an enormous red Doberman pinscher straining at the end of a leash. She stood, the dog extended toward me, silent to my questions, her eyes bulging nearly out of her head. I took a cursory look around, nodded, and bade her good night. Relatively speaking, however, I never fared as badly as another black male journalist. He went to nearby Waukegan, Illinois, a couple of summers ago to work on a story about a murderer who was born there. Mistaking the reporter for the killer, police hauled him from his car at gunpoint and but for his press credentials would probably have tried to book him. Such episodes are not uncommon. Black men trade tales like this all the time.

In "My Negro Problem — And Ours," Podhoretz writes that the hatred he feels for blacks makes itself known to him through a variety of avenues — one being his discomfort with that "special brand of paranoid touchiness" to which he says blacks are prone. No doubt he is speaking here of black men. In time, I learned to smother the rage I felt at so often being taken for a criminal. Not to do so would surely have led to madness — via that special "paranoid touchiness" that so annoyed Podhoretz at the time he wrote the essay.

I began to take precautions to make myself less threatening. I move about with care, particularly late in the evening. I give a wide berth to nervous people on subway platforms during the wee hours, particularly when I have exchanged business clothes for jeans. If I happen to be entering a building behind some people who appear skittish I may walk by, letting them clear the lobby before I return, so as not to seem to be following them. I have been calm and extremely congenial on those rare occasions when I've been pulled over by the police.

And on late-evening constitutionals along streets less traveled by, I employ what has proved to be an excellent tension-reducing measure: I whistle melodies from Beethoven and Vivaldi and the more popular classical composers. Even steely New Yorkers hunching toward nighttime destinations seem to relax, and occasionally they even join in the tune. Virtually everybody seems to sense that a mugger wouldn't be warbling bright, sunny selections from Vivaldi's *Four Seasons.* It is my equivalent of the cowbell that hikers wear when they know they are in bear country.

The Reader's Presence

1. Why does Staples use the word *victim* in his opening sentence? In what sense is the white woman a "victim"? How is he using the term? As readers, how might we interpret the opening sentence upon first reading? How does the meaning of the term change in rereading?

2. Does Staples blame the woman for being afraid of him? How does he deal with her anxiety? How does Staples behave on the street? How has he "altered" his own public behavior? In what ways is his behavior on the street similar to his "behavior" as a writer?

3. In rereading the essay, pay close attention to the way Staples handles point of view. When does he shift viewpoints or perspectives? What is his purpose in doing so? What are some of the connections Staples makes in this essay between the point of view one chooses and one's identity?

28

Shelby Steele

On Being Black and Middle Class

Shelby Steele (b. 1946) is professor of English at San Jose State University. He has contributed articles and reviews to periodicals such as Confrontation, Black World, Harper's, *and the* Western Humanities Review. *Steele's writings on race relations in the United States have placed him in the center of the national debate on affirmative action and other issues. "On Being Black and Middle Class" appeared in* Commentary *in 1988. Steele published his first book,* The Content of Our Character: A New Vision of Race in America, *in 1990.*

Steele told an interviewer, "Some people say I shine a harsh light on difficult problems. But I never shine a light on anything I haven't experienced or write about fears I don't see in myself first. I'm my own first target. I spill my own blood first."

Not long ago a friend of mine, black like myself, said to me that the term "black middle class" was actually a contradiction in terms. Race, he insisted, blurred class distinctions among blacks. If you were black, you were just black and that was that. When I argued, he let his eyes roll at my naiveté. Then he went on. For us, as black professionals, it was an exercise in self-flattery, a pathetic pretention, to give meaning to such a distinction. Worse, the very idea of class threatened the unity that was vital to the black community as a whole. After all, since when had white America taken note of anything but color when it came to blacks? He then reminded me of an old Malcolm X line that had been popular in the sixties. Question: What is a black man with a Ph.D.? Answer: A nigger.

For many years I had been on my friend's side of this argument. Much of my conscious thinking on the old conundrum of race and class was shaped during my high school and college years in the race-charged sixties, when the fact of my race took on an almost religious significance. Progressively, from the mid-sixties on, more and more aspects of my life found their explanation, their justification, and their motivation in race. My youthful concerns about career, romance, money, values, and even styles of dress became subject to consultation with various oracular sources of racial wisdom. And these ranged from a figure as ennobling as Martin Luther King, Jr., to the underworld elegance of dress I found in jazz clubs on the South Side of Chicago. Everywhere there were signals, and in those days I considered myself so blessed with clarity and direction that I pitied my white classmates who found more embarrassment than guidance in the face of *their* race. In 1968, inflated by my new power, I took a mischievous delight in calling them culturally disadvantaged.

But now, hearing my friend's comment was like hearing a priest from a church I'd grown disenchanted with. I understood him, but my faith was weak. What had sustained me in the sixties sounded monotonous and off the mark in the eighties. For me, race had lost much of its juju, its singular capacity to conjure meaning. And today, when I honestly look at my life and the lives of many other middle-class blacks I know, I can see that race never fully explained our situation in American society. Black though I may be, it is impossible for me to sit in my single-family house with two cars in the driveway and a swing set in the back yard and *not* see the role class has played in my life. And how can my friend, similarly raised and similarly situated, not see it?

Yet despite my certainty I felt a sharp tug of guilt as I tried to explain myself over my friend's skepticism. He is a man of many comedic facial expressions and, as I spoke, his brow lifted in extreme moral alarm as if I were uttering the unspeakable. His clear implication was that I was being elitist and possibly (dare he suggest?) antiblack — crimes for which there might well be no redemption. He pretended to fear for me. I chuckled along with him, but inwardly I did wonder at myself. Though I never doubted the validity of what I was saying, I felt guilty saying it. Why?

After he left (to retrieve his daughter from a dance lesson) I realized 5
that the trap I felt myself in had a tiresome familiarity and, in a sort of slow-motion epiphany, I began to see its outline. It was like the suddenly sharp vision one has at the end of a burdensome marriage when all the long-repressed incompatibilities come undeniably to light.

What became clear to me is that people like myself, my friend, and middle-class blacks generally are caught in a very specific double bind that keeps two equally powerful elements of our identity at odds with each other. The middle-class values by which we were raised — the work ethic, the importance of education, the value of property ownership, of respectability, of "getting ahead," of stable family life, of initiative, of self-reliance, etc. — are, in themselves, raceless and even assimilationist. They urge us toward participation in the American mainstream, toward integration, toward a strong identification with the society — and toward the entire constellation of qualities that are implied in the word "individualism." These values are almost rules for how to prosper in a democratic, free-enterprise society that admires and rewards individual effort. They tell us to work hard for ourselves and our families and to seek our opportunities whenever they appear, inside or outside the confines of whatever ethnic group we may belong to.

But the particular pattern of racial identification that emerged in the sixties and that still prevails today urges middle-class blacks (and all blacks) in the opposite direction. This pattern asks us to see ourselves as an embattled minority, and it urges an adversarial stance toward the mainstream, an emphasis on ethnic consciousness over individualism. It is organized around an implied separatism.

The opposing thrust of these two parts of our identity results in the double bind of middle-class blacks. There is no forward movement on either plane that does not constitute backward movement on the other. This was the familiar trap I felt myself in while talking with my friend. As I spoke about class, his eyes reminded me that I was betraying race. Clearly, the two indispensable parts of my identity were a threat to each other.

Of course when you think about it, class and race are both similar in some ways and also naturally opposed. They are two forms of collective identity with boundaries that intersect. But whether they clash or peacefully coexist has much to do with how they are defined. Being both black and middle class becomes a double bind when class and race are defined in sharply antagonistic terms, so that one must be repressed to appease the other.

But what is the "substance" of these two identities, and how does   10
each establish itself in an individual's overall identity? It seems to me that when we identify with any collective we are basically identifying with images that tell us what it means to be a member of that collective. Identity is not the same thing as the fact of membership in a collective; it is, rather, a form of self-definition, facilitated by images of what we wish our membership in the collective to mean. In this sense, the images we identify with may reflect the aspirations of the collective more than they reflect reality, and their content can vary with shifts in those aspirations.

But the process of identification is usually dialectical. It is just as necessary to say what we are *not* as it is to say what we are — so that finally identification comes about by embracing a polarity of positive and negative images. To identify as middle class, for example, I must have both positive and negative images of what being middle class entails; then I will know what I should and should not be doing in order to be middle class. The same goes for racial identity.

In the racially turbulent sixties the polarity of images that came to define racial identification was very antagonistic to the polarity that defined middle-class identification. One might say that the positive images of one lined up with the negative images of the other, so that to identify with both required either a contortionist's flexibility or a dangerous splitting of the self. The double bind of the black middle class was in place.

The black middle class has always defined its class identity by means of positive images gleaned from middle- and upper-class white society, and by means of negative images of lower-class blacks. This habit goes back to the institution of slavery itself, when "house" slaves both mimicked the whites they served and held themselves above the "field" slaves. But in the sixties the old bourgeois impulse to dissociate from the lower classes (the "we-they" distinction) backfired when racial identity suddenly called for the celebration of this same black lower class. One of the qualities of a double bind is that one feels it more than sees it, and I distinctly remember the tension and strange sense of dishonesty I felt in those days as I moved back and forth like a bigamist between the demands of class and race.

Though my father was born poor, he achieved middle-class standing through much hard work and sacrifice (one of his favorite words) and by identifying fully with solid middle-class values — mainly hard work, family life, property ownership, and education for his children (all four of whom have advanced degrees). In his mind these were not so much values as laws of nature. People who embodied them made up the positive images in his class polarity. The negative images came largely from the blacks he had left behind because they were "going nowhere."

No one in my family remembers how it happened, but as time went   15
on, the negative images congealed into an imaginary character named Sam, who, from the extensive service we put him to, quickly grew to mythic proportions. In our family lore he was sometimes a trickster, sometimes a boob, but always possessed of a catalogue of sly faults that gave up graphic images of everything we should not be. On sacrifice: "Sam never thinks about tomorrow. He wants it now or he doesn't care about it." On work: "Sam doesn't favor it too much." On children: "Sam likes to have them but not to raise them." On money: "Sam drinks it up and pisses it out." On fidelity: "Sam has to have two or three women." On clothes: "Sam features loud clothes. He likes to see and be seen." And so on. Sam's persona amounted to a negative instruction manual in class identity.

I don't think that any of us believed Sam's faults were accurate representations of lower-class black life. He was an instrument of self-definition, not of sociological accuracy. It never occurred to us that he looked very much like the white racist stereotype of blacks, or that he might have been a manifestation of our own racial self-hatred. He simply gave us a counterpoint against which to express our aspirations. If self-hatred was a factor, it was not, for us, a matter of hating lower-class blacks but of hating what we did not want to be.

Still, hate or love aside, it is fundamentally true that my middle-class identity involved a dissociation from images of lower-class black life and a corresponding identification with values and patterns of responsibility that are common to the middle class everywhere. These values sent me a clear message: Be both an individual and a responsible citizen; understand that the quality of your life will approximately reflect the quality of effort you put into it; know that individual responsibility is the basis of freedom and that the limitations imposed by fate (whether fair or unfair) are no excuse for passivity.

Whether I live up to these values or not, I know that my acceptance of them is the result of lifelong conditioning. I know also that I share this conditioning with middle-class people of all races and that I can no more easily be free of it than I can be free of my race. Whether all this got started because the black middle class modeled itself on the white middle class is no longer relevant. For the middle-class black, conditioned by these values from birth, the sense of meaning they provide is as immutable as the color of his skin.

I started the sixties in high school feeling that my class-conditioning was the surest way to overcome racial barriers. My racial identity was pretty much taken for granted. After all, it was obvious to the world that I was black. Yet I ended the sixties in graduate school a little embarrassed by my class background and with an almost desperate need to be "black." The tables had turned. I knew very clearly (though I struggled to repress it) that my aspirations and my sense of how to operate in the world came from my class background, yet "being black" required certain attitudes and stances that made me feel secretly a little duplicitous. The inner compatibility of class and race I had known in 1960 was gone.

For blacks, the decade between 1960 and 1969 saw racial identifica-   20
tion undergo the same sort of transformation that national identity undergoes in times of war. It became more self-conscious, more narrowly focused, more prescribed, less tolerant of opposition. It spawned an implicit party line, which tended to disallow competing forms of identity. Race-as-identity was lifted from the relative slumber it knew in the fifties and pressed into service in a social and political war against oppression. It was redefined along sharp adversarial lines and directed toward the goal of mobilizing the great mass of black Americans in this warlike effort. It was imbued with a strong moral authority, useful for denouncing those who opposed it and for celebrating those who honored it as a positive achievement rather than as a mere birthright.

The form of racial identification that quickly evolved to meet this challenge presented blacks as a racial monolith, a singular people with a common experience of oppression. Differences within the race, no matter how ineradicable, had to be minimized. Class distinctions were one of the first such differences to be sacrificed, since they not only threatened racial unity but also seemed to stand in contradiction to the principle of equality which was the announced goal of the movement for racial progress. The discomfort I felt in 1969, the vague but relentless sense of duplicity, was the result of a historical necessity that put my race and class at odds, that was asking me to cast aside the distinction of my class and identify with a monolithic view of my race.

If the form of this racial identity was the monolith, its substance was victimization. The civil rights movement and the more radical splinter groups of the late sixties were all dedicated to ending racial victimization, and the form of black identity that emerged to facilitate this goal made blackness and victimization virtually synonymous. Since it was our victimization more than any other variable that identified and unified us, moreover, it followed logically that the purest black was the poor black. It was images of him that clustered around the positive pole of the race polarity; all other blacks were, in effect, required to identify with him in order to confirm their own blackness.

Certainly there were more dimensions to the black experience than victimization, but no other had the same capacity to fire the indignation needed for war. So, again out of historical necessity, victimization became the overriding focus of racial identity. But this only deepened the double bind for middle-class blacks like me. When it came to class we were accustomed to defining ourselves against lower-class blacks and identifying with at least the values of middle-class whites; when it came to race we were now being asked to identify with images of lower-class blacks and to see whites, middle class or otherwise, as victimizers. Negative lining up with positive, we were called upon to reject what we had previously embraced and to embrace what we had previously rejected. To put it still more personally, the Sam figure I had been raised to define myself against had now become the "real" black I was expected to identify with.

The fact that the poor black's new status was only passively earned by the condition of his victimization, not by assertive, positive action made little difference. Status was status apart from the means by which it was achieved, and along with it came a certain power — the power to define the terms of access to that status, to say who was black and who was not. If a lower-class black said you were not really "black" — a sellout, an Uncle Tom — the judgment was all the more devastating because it carried the authority of his status. And this judgment soon enough came to be accepted by many whites as well.

In graduate school I was once told by a white professor, "Well,   25
but . . . you're not really black. I mean, you're not disadvantaged." In his mind my lack of victim status disqualified me from the race itself. More recently I was complimented by a black student for speaking reasonably correct English, "proper" English as he put it. "But I don't know if I really want to talk like that," he went on. "Why not?" I asked. "Because then I wouldn't be black no more," he replied without a pause.

To overcome his marginal status, the middle-class black had to identify with a degree of victimization that was beyond his actual experience. In college (and well beyond) we used to play a game called "nap matching." It was a game of one-upmanship, in which we sat around outdoing each other with stories of racial victimization, symbolically measured by the naps of our hair. Most of us were middle class and so had few personal stories to relate, but if we could not match naps with our own biographies, we would move on to those legendary tales of victimization that came to us from the public domain.

The single story that sat atop the pinnacle of racial victimization for us was that of Emmett Till, the Northern black teenager who, on a visit to the South in 1955, was killed and grotesquely mutilated for supposedly looking at or whistling at (we were never sure which, though we argued the point endlessly) a white woman. Oh, how we probed his story, finding in his youth and Northern upbringing the quintessential embodiment of black innocence, brought down by a white evil so portentous and apocalyptic, so gnarled and hideous, that it left us with a feeling not far from awe. By telling his story and others like it, we came to *feel* the immutability of our victimization, its utter indigenousness, as a thing on this earth like dirt or sand or water.

Of course, these sessions were a ritual of group identification, a means by which we, as middle-class blacks, could be at one with our race. But why were we, who had only a moderate experience of victimization (and that offset by opportunities our parents never had), so intent on assimilating or appropriating an identity that in so many ways contradicted our own? Because, I think, the sense of innocence that is always entailed in feeling victimized filled us with a corresponding feeling of entitlement, or even license, that helped us endure our vulnerability on a largely white college campus.

In my junior year in college I rode to a debate tournament with three white students and our faculty coach, an elderly English professor. The experience of being the lone black in a group of whites was so familiar to me that I thought nothing of it as our trip began. But then halfway through the trip the professor casually turned to me and, in an isn't-the-world-funny sort of tone, said that he had just refused to rent an apartment in a house he owned to a "very nice" black couple because their color would "offend" the white couple who lived downstairs. His eyebrows lifted helplessly over his hawkish nose, suggesting that he too, like me, was a victim of America's racial farce. His look assumed a kind of comradeship: he and I were above this grimy business of race, though for expediency we had occasionally to concede the world its madness.

My vulnerability in this situation came not so much from the professor's blindness to his own racism as from his assumption that I would participate in it, that I would conspire with him against my own race so that he might remain comfortably blind. Why did he think I would be amenable to this? I can only guess that he assumed my middle-class identity was so complete and all-encompassing that I would see his action as nothing more than a trifling concession to the folkways of our land, that I would in fact applaud his decision not to disturb propriety. Blind to both his own racism and to me — one blindness serving the other — he could not recognize that he was asking me to betray my race in the name of my class.

His blindness made me feel vulnerable because it threatened to expose my own repressed ambivalence. His comment pressured me to choose between my class identification, which had contributed to my being a college student and a member of the debating team, and my desperate desire to be "black." I could have one but not both; I was double-bound.

30

Because double binds are repressed there is always an element of terror in them: the terror of bringing to the conscious mind the buried duplicity, self-deception, and pretense involved in serving two masters. This terror is the stuff of vulnerability, and since vulnerability is one of the least tolerable of all human feelings, we usually transform it into an emotion that seems to restore the control of which it has robbed us; most often, that emotion is anger. And so, before the professor had even finished his little story, I had become a furnace of rage. The year was 1967, and I had been primed by endless hours of nap-matching to feel, at least consciously, completely at one with the victim-focused black identity. This identity gave me the license, and the impunity, to unleash upon this professor one of those volcanic eruptions of racial indignation familiar to us from the novels of Richard Wright. Like Cross Damon in *Outsider,* who kills in perfectly righteous anger, I tried to annihilate the man. I punished him not according to the measure of his crime but according to the measure of my vulnerability, a measure set by the cumulative tension of years of repressed terror. Soon I saw that terror in *his* face, as he stared hollow-eyed at the road ahead. My white friends in the back seat, knowing no conflict between their own class and race, were astonished that someone they had taken to be so much like themselves could harbor a rage that for all the world looked murderous.

Though my rage was triggered by the professor's comment, it was deepened and sustained by a complex of need, conflict, and repression in myself of which I had been wholly unaware. Out of my racial vulnerability I had developed the strong need of an identity with which to defend myself. The only such identity available was that of me as victim, him as victimizer. Once in the grip of this paradigm, I began to do far more damage to myself than he had done.

Seeing myself as a victim meant that I clung all the harder to my racial identity, which, in turn, meant that I suppressed my class identity. This cut me off from all the resources my class values might have offered me. In those values, for instance, I might have found the means to a more dispassionate response, the response less of a victim attacked by a victimizer than of an individual offended by a foolish old man. As an individual I might have reported this professor to the college dean. Or I might have calmly tried to reveal his blindness to him, and possibly won a convert. (The flagrancy of his remark suggested a hidden guilt and even self-recognition on which I might have capitalized. Doesn't confession usually signal a willingness to face oneself?) Or I might have simply chuckled and then let my silence serve as an answer to his provocation. Would not my composure, in any form it might take, deflect into his own heart the arrow he'd shot at me?

Instead, my anger, itself the hair-trigger expression of a long-repressed double bind, not only cut me off from the best of my own resources, it also distorted the nature of my true racial problem. The righteousness of this anger and the easy catharsis it brought buoyed the delusion of my victimization and left me as blind as the professor himself. 35

As a middle-class black I have often felt myself *contriving* to be "black." And I have noticed this same contrivance in others — a certain stretching away from the natural flow of one's life to align oneself with a victim-focused black identity. Our particular needs are out of sync with the form of identity available to meet those needs. Middle-class blacks need to identify racially; it is better to think of ourselves as black and victimized than not black at all; so we contrive (more unconsciously than consciously) to fit ourselves into an identity that denies our class and fails to address the true source of our vulnerability.

For me this once meant spending inordinate amounts of time at black faculty meetings, though these meetings had little to do with my real racial anxieties or my professional life. I was new to the university, one of two blacks in an English department of over seventy, and I felt a little isolated and vulnerable, though I did not admit it to myself. But at these meetings we discussed the problems of black faculty and students within a framework of victimization. The real vulnerability we felt was covered over by all the adversarial drama the victim/victimized polarity inspired, and hence went unseen and unassuaged. And this, I think, explains our rather chronic ineffectiveness as a group. Since victimization was not our primary problem — the university had long ago opened its doors to us — we had to contrive to make it so, and there is not much energy in contrivance. What I got at these meetings was ultimately an object lesson in how fruitless struggle can be when it is not grounded in actual need.

At our black faculty meetings, the old equation of blackness with victimization was ever present — to be black was to be a victim; therefore, not to be a victim was not to be black. As we contrived to meet the terms of this formula there was an inevitable distortion of both ourselves and the larger university. Through the prism of victimization the university seemed more impenetrable than it actually was, and we more limited in our powers. We fell prey to the victim's myopia, making the university an institution from which we could seek redress but which we could never fully join. And this mind-set often led us to look more for compensations for our supposed victimization than for opportunities we could pursue as individuals.

The discomfort and vulnerability felt by middle-class blacks in the sixties, it could be argued, was a worthwhile price to pay considering the progress achieved during that time of racial confrontation. But what may have been tolerable then is intolerable now. Though changes in American society have made it an anachronism, the monolithic form of racial identification that came out of the sixties is still very much with us. It may be more loosely held, and its power to punish heretics has probably diminished, but it continues to catch middle-class blacks in a double bind, thus impeding not only their own advancement but even, I would contend, that of blacks as a group.

The victim-focused black identity encourages the individual to feel 40 that his advancement depends almost entirely on that of the group. Thus he loses sight not only of his own possibilities but of the inextricable connection between individual effort and individual advancement. This is a profound encumbrance today, when there is more opportunity for blacks than ever before, for it reimposes limitations that can have the same oppressive effect as those the society has only recently begun to remove.

It was the emphasis on mass action in the sixties that made the victim-focused black identity a necessity. But in the eighties and beyond, when racial advancement will come only through a multitude of individual advancements, this form of identity inadvertently adds itself to the forces that hold us back. Hard work, education, individual initiative, stable family life, property ownership — these have always been the means by which ethnic groups have moved ahead in America. Regardless of past or present victimization, these "laws" of advancement apply absolutely to black Americans also. There is no getting around this. What we need is a form of racial identity that energizes the individual by putting him in touch with both his possibilities and his responsibilities.

It has always annoyed me to hear from the mouths of certain arbiters of blackness that middle-class blacks should "reach back" and pull up those blacks less fortunate than they — as though middle-class status were an unearned and essentially passive condition in which one needed a large measure of noblesse oblige to occupy one's time. My own image is of reaching back from a moving train to lift on board those who have no tickets. A noble enough sentiment — but might it not be wiser to show them the entire structure of principles, efforts, and sacrifice that puts one in a position to buy a ticket any time one likes? This, I think, is something members of the black middle class can realistically offer to other blacks. Their example is not only a testament to possibility but also a lesson in method. But they cannot lead by example until they are released from a black identity that regards that example as suspect, that sees them as "marginally" black, indeed that holds *them* back by catching them in a double bind.

To move beyond the victim-focused black identity we must learn to make a difficult but crucial distinction: between actual victimization, which we must resist with every resource, and identification with the victim's status. Until we do this we will continue to wrestle more with ourselves than with the new opportunities which so many paid so dearly to win.

The Reader's Presence

1. Steele introduces his topic by means of a reported conversation he had with a friend. What effect does this have on the reader? If you rewrote his opening paragraph and eliminated the conversational context, how would you then introduce the main topic? Try it and see how it works.

2. Why does Steele's friend maintain that class and race are antagonistic terms? Do you agree? Would his argument apply to all races and historical periods, or is it dependent only on present history? What personal experiences would you offer either to confirm or contradict Steele's friend's opening remark?
3. Steele's feeling of being in a "double bind" is seen exclusively in the context of being middle class. How does Steele define *middle class*? Would blacks from other economic groups feel differently? For example, does Steele imply that blue-collar, working-class black people feel greater racial solidarity? On the other hand, would very wealthy blacks feel a greater conflict than Steele's? Can you infer answers to these questions from Steele's essay?

29

Amy Tan

Mother Tongue

Amy Tan (b. 1952) was born in California shortly after her parents immigrated to the United States from China. She started writing as a child and won a writing contest at age eight. As an adult, Tan made her living as a free-lance business writer for many years, but started to write fiction in 1985. In 1987, Tan traveled to China for the first time, an experience that helped shape her consciousness of both her American and Chinese identities. In 1989 she published her best-selling first novel, The Joy Luck Club, *followed by* The Kitchen God's Wife *(1991), the children's books* The Moon Lady *(1992) and* The Chinese Siamese Cat *(1994), and* The Hundred Secret Senses *(1995). "Mother Tongue" originally appeared in the* Threepenny Review *in 1990.*

Commenting on the art of writing, Tan has said, "I had a very unliterary background, but I had a determination to write for myself." She believes that the goal of every serious writer of literature is "to try to find your voice and your art, because it comes from your own experiences, your own pain."

I am not a scholar of English or literature. I cannot give you much more than personal opinions on the English language and its variations in this country or others.

I am a writer. And by that definition, I am someone who has always loved language. I am fascinated by language in daily life. I spend a great deal of my time thinking about the power of language — the way it can evoke an emotion, a visual image, a complex idea, or a simple truth. Language is the tool of my trade. And I use them all — all the Englishes I grew up with.

Recently, I was made keenly aware of the different Englishes I do use. I was giving a talk to a large group of people, the same talk I had already given to half a dozen other groups. The nature of the talk was about my writing, my life, and my book, *The Joy Luck Club*. The talk was going along well enough, until I remembered one major difference that made the whole talk sound wrong. My mother was in the room. And it was perhaps the first time she had heard me give a lengthy speech, using the kind of English I have never used with her. I was saying things like "The intersection of memory upon imagination" and "There is an aspect of my fiction that relates to thus-and-thus" — a speech filled with carefully wrought grammatical phrases, burdened, it suddenly seemed to me, with nominalized forms, past perfect tenses, conditional phrases, all the forms of standard English that I had learned in school and through books, the forms of English I did not use at home with my mother.

Just last week, I was walking down the street with my mother, and I again found myself conscious of the English I was using, the English I do use with her. We were talking about the price of new and used furniture and I heard myself saying this: "Not waste money that way." My husband was with us as well, and he didn't notice any switch in my English. And then I realized why. It's because over the twenty years we've been together I've often used that same kind of English with him, and sometimes he even uses it with me. It has become our language of intimacy, a different sort of English that relates to family talk, the language I grew up with.

So you'll have some idea of what this family talk I heard sounds like,   5
I'll quote what my mother said during a recent conversation which I videotaped and then transcribed. During this conversation, my mother was talking about a political gangster in Shanghai who had the same last name as her family's, Du, and how the gangster in his early years wanted to be adopted by her family, which was rich by comparison. Later, the gangster became more powerful, far richer than my mother's family, and one day showed up at my mother's wedding to pay his respects. Here's what she said in part:

"Du Yusong having business like fruit stand. Like off the street kind. He is Du like Du Zong — but not Tsung-ming Island people. The local people call putong, the river east side, he belong to that side local people. That man want to ask Du Zong father take him in like become own family. Du Zong father wasn't look down on him, but didn't take seriously, until that man big like become a mafia. Now important person, very hard to inviting him. Chinese way, came only to show respect, don't stay for dinner. Respect for making big celebration, he shows up. Mean gives lots of respect. Chinese custom. Chinese social life that way. If too important won't have to stay too long. He come to my wedding. I didn't see, I heard it. I gone to boy's side, they have YMCA dinner. Chinese age I was nineteen."

You should know that my mother's expressive command of English belies how much she actually understands. She reads the *Forbes* report, listens to *Wall Street Week*, converses daily with her stockbroker, reads all of Shirley MacLaine's books with ease — all kinds of things I can't begin to understand. Yet some of my friends tell me they understand 50 percent of what my mother says. Some say they understand 80 to 90 percent. Some say they understand none of it, as if she were speaking pure Chinese. But to me, my mother's English is perfectly clear, perfectly natural. It's my mother tongue. Her language, as I hear it, is vivid, direct, full of observation and imagery. That was the language that helped shape the way I saw things, expressed things, made sense of the world.

Lately, I've been giving more thought to the kind of English my mother speaks. Like others, I have described it to people as "broken" or "fractured" English. But I wince when I say that. It has always bothered me that I can think of no other way to describe it other than "broken," as if it were damaged and needed to be fixed, as if it lacked a certain wholeness and soundness. I've heard other terms used, "limited English," for example. But they seem just as bad, as if everything is limited, including people's perceptions of the limited English speaker.

I know this for a fact, because when I was growing up, my mother's "limited" English limited *my* perception of her. I was ashamed of her English. I believed that her English reflected the quality of what she had to say. That is, because she expressed them imperfectly her thoughts were imperfect. And I had plenty of empirical evidence to support me: the fact that people in department stores, at banks, and at restaurants did not take her seriously, did not give her good service, pretended not to understand her, or even acted as if they did not hear her.

My mother has long realized the limitations of her English as well. When I was fifteen, she used to have me call people on the phone to pretend I was she. In this guise, I was forced to ask for information or even to complain and yell at people who had been rude to her. One time it was a call to her stockbroker in New York. She had cashed out her small portfolio and it just so happened we were going to go to New York the next week, our very first trip outside California. I had to get on the phone and say in an adolescent voice that was not very convincing, "This is Mrs. Tan." 10

And my mother was standing in the back whispering loudly, "Why he don't send me check, already two weeks late. So mad he lie to me, losing me money."

And then I said in perfect English, "Yes, I'm getting rather concerned. You had agreed to send the check two weeks ago, but it hasn't arrived."

Then she began to talk more loudly. "What he want, I come to New York tell him front of his boss, you cheating me?" And I was trying to calm her down, make her be quiet, while telling the stockbroker, "I can't tolerate any more excuses. If I don't receive the check immediately, I am going to have to speak to your manager when I'm in New York next week." And sure enough, the following week there we were in front of this astonished stockbroker, and I was sitting there red-faced and quiet, and my mother, the real Mrs. Tan, was shouting at his boss in her impeccable broken English.

We used a similar routine just five days ago, for a situation that was far less humorous. My mother had gone to the hospital for an appointment, to find out about a benign brain tumor a CAT scan had revealed a month ago. She said she had spoken very good English, her best English, no mistakes. Still, she said, the hospital did not apologize when they said they had lost the CAT scan and she had come for nothing. She said they did not seem to have any sympathy when she told them she was anxious to know the exact diagnosis, since her husband and son had both died of brain tumors. She said they would not give her any more information until the next time and she would have to make another appointment for that. So she said she would not leave until the doctor called her daughter. She wouldn't budge. And when the doctor finally called her daughter, me, who spoke in perfect English — lo and behold — we had assurances the CAT scan would be found, promises that a conference call on Monday would be held, and apologies for any suffering my mother had gone through for a most regrettable mistake.

I think my mother's English almost had an effect on limiting my possibilities in life as well. Sociologists and linguists probably will tell you that a person's developing language skills are more influenced by peers. But I do think that the language spoken in the family, especially in immigrant families which are more insular, plays a large role in shaping the language of the child. And I believe that it affected my results on achievement tests, IQ tests, and the SAT. While my English skills were never judged as poor, compared to math, English could not be considered my strong suit. In grade school I did moderately well, getting perhaps B's, sometimes B-pluses, in English and scoring perhaps in the sixtieth or seventieth percentile on achievement tests. But those scores were not good enough to override the opinion that my true abilities lay in math and science, because in those areas I achieved A's and scored in the ninetieth percentile or higher. 15

This was understandable. Math is precise; there is only one correct answer. Whereas, for me at least, the answers on English tests were always a judgment call, a matter of opinion and personal experience. Those tests were constructed around items like fill-in-the-blank sentence completion, such as "Even though Tom was _____, Mary thought he was _____." And the correct answer always seemed to be the most bland combinations of thoughts, for example, "Even though Tom was shy, Mary thought he was charming," with the grammatical structure "even though" limiting the correct answer to some sort of semantic opposites, so you wouldn't get answers like, "Even though Tom was foolish, Mary thought he was ridiculous." Well, according to my mother, there were very few limitations as to what Tom could have been and what Mary might have thought of him. So I never did well on tests like that.

The same was true with word analogies, pairs of words in which you were supposed to find some sort of logical, semantic relationship — for example, "*Sunset* is to *nightfall* as _____ is to _____." And here you would be presented with a list of four possible pairs, one of which showed the same kind of relationship: *red* is to *stoplight*, *bus* is to *arrival*, *chills* is to *fever*, *yawn* is to *boring*. Well, I could never think that way. I knew what the tests were asking, but I could not block out of my mind the images already created by the first pair, "*sunset* is to *nightfall*" — and I would see a burst of colors against a darkening sky, the moon rising, the lowering of a curtain of stars. And all the other pairs of words — red, bus, stoplight, boring — just threw up a mass of confusing images, making it impossible for me to sort out something as logical as saying: "A sunset precedes nightfall" is the same as "a chill precedes a fever." The only way I would have gotten that answer right would have been to imagine an associative situation, for example, my being disobedient and staying out past sunset, catching a chill at night, which turns into feverish pneumonia as punishment, which indeed did happen to me.

I have been thinking about all this lately, about my mother's English, about achievement tests. Because lately I've been asked, as a writer, why there are not more Asian Americans represented in American literature. Why are there few Asian Americans enrolled in creative writing programs? Why do so many Chinese students go into engineering? Well, these are broad sociological questions I can't begin to answer. But I have noticed in surveys — in fact, just last week — that Asian students, as a whole, always do significantly better on math achievement tests than in English. And this makes me think that there are other Asian-American students whose English spoken in the home might also be described as "broken" or "limited." And perhaps they also have teachers who are steering them away from writing and into math and science, which is what happened to me.

Fortunately, I happen to be rebellious in nature and enjoy the challenge of disproving assumptions made about me. I became an English major my first year in college, after being enrolled as pre-med. I started writing nonfiction as a freelancer the week after I was told by my former boss that writing was my worst skill and I should hone my talents toward account management.

But it wasn't until 1985 that I finally began to write fiction. And at first I wrote using what I thought to be wittily crafted sentences, sentences that would finally prove I had mastery over the English language. Here's an example from the first draft of a story that later made its way into *The Joy Luck Club*, but without this line: "That was my mental quandary in its nascent state." A terrible line, which I can barely pronounce.

Fortunately, for reasons I won't get into today, I later decided I should envision a reader for the stories I would write. And the reader I

20

decided upon was my mother, because these were stories about mothers. So with this reader in mind — and in fact she did read my early drafts — I began to write stories using all the Englishes I grew up with: the English I spoke to my mother, which for lack of a better term might be described as "simple": the English she used with me, which for lack of a better term might be described as "broken"; my translation of her Chinese, which could certainly be described as "watered down"; and what I imagined to be her translation of her Chinese if she could speak in perfect English, her internal language, and for that I sought to preserve the essence, but neither an English nor a Chinese structure. I wanted to capture what language ability tests can never reveal: her intent, her passion, her imagery, the rhythms of her speech, and the nature of her thoughts.

Apart from what any critic had to say about my writing, I knew I had succeeded where it counted when my mother finished reading my book and gave me her verdict: "So easy to read."

The Reader's Presence

1. In her second paragraph, Amy Tan mentions "all the Englishes" she grew up with. What were those "Englishes"? What is odd about the term? How does the oddity of the word reinforce the point of her essay?
2. What exactly is Tan's "mother tongue"? What does the phrase usually mean? How is Tan using it? How would you describe this language? Would you call it "broken English"? What does that phrase imply?
3. In paragraph 20, Tan gives an example of a sentence that she once thought showed her "mastery" of English. What does she now find wrong with that sentence? What do you think of it? What would her mother have thought of it? What sort of reader does that sentence anticipate?

30

Amy Tan

Jing-Mei Woo: Two Kinds

"Two Kinds" is one of sixteen stories that compose Amy Tan's best-selling novel, The Joy Luck Club (1989). Tan's success as a writer seemed to come about overnight, but she reminds us that writing is a process that can consume large amounts of time, energy, patience, and paper. When writing her second novel, Tan recalls, she started by writing — and throwing away — at least one thousand pages of manuscript that could have become several books. "But those books were not meant to become anything more than a lesson to me on what it takes to write fiction: persistence imposed by a limited focus. . . . The focus required of a priest, a nun, a convict serving a life's sentence."

For more information on Amy Tan, see page 196.

My mother believed you could be anything you wanted to be in America. You could open a restaurant. You could work for the government and get good retirement. You could buy a house with almost no money down. You could become rich. You could become instantly famous.

"Of course you can be prodigy, too," my mother told me when I was nine. "You can be best anything. What does Auntie Lindo know? Her daughter, she is only best tricky."

America was where all my mother's hopes lay. She had come here in 1949 after losing everything in China: her mother and father, her family home, her first husband, and two daughters, twin baby girls. But she never looked back with regret. There were so many ways for things to get better.

We didn't immediately pick the right kind of prodigy. At first my mother thought I could be a Chinese Shirley Temple. We'd watch Shirley's old movies on TV as though they were training films. My mother would poke my arm and say, *"Ni kan"* — You watch. And I would see Shirley tapping her feet, or singing a sailor song, or pursing her lips in a very round O while saying, "Oh my goodness."

"*Ni kan*," said my mother as Shirley's eyes flooded with tears. "You   5
already know how. Don't need talent for crying!"

Soon after my mother got this idea about Shirley Temple, she took
me to a beauty training school in the Mission district and put me in the
hands of a student who could barely hold the scissors without shaking.
Instead of getting big fat curls, I emerged with an uneven mass of crinkly
black fuzz. My mother dragged me off to the bathroom and tried to wet
down my hair.

"You look like Negro Chinese," she lamented, as if I had done this
on purpose.

The instructor of the beauty training school had to lop off these
soggy clumps to make my hair even again. "Peter Pan is very popular
these days," the instructor assured my mother. I now had hair the length
of a boy's, with straight-across bangs that hung at a slant two inches
above my eyebrows. I liked the haircut and it made me actually look forward to my future fame.

If fact, in the beginning, I was just as excited as my mother, maybe
even more so. I pictured this prodigy part of me as many different images,
trying each one on for size. I was a dainty ballerina girl standing by the
curtains, waiting to hear the right music that would send me floating on
my tiptoes. I was like the Christ child lifted out of the straw manger, crying with holy indignity. I was Cinderella stepping from her pumpkin carriage with sparkly cartoon music filling the air.

In all of my imaginings, I was filled with a sense that I would soon   10
become *perfect*. My mother and father would adore me. I would be beyond reproach. I would never feel the need to sulk for anything.

But sometimes the prodigy in me became impatient. "If you don't
hurry up and get me out of here, I'm disappearing for good," it warned.
"And then you'll always be nothing."

Every night after dinner, my mother and I would sit at the Formica
kitchen table. She would present new tests, taking her examples from stories of amazing children she had read in *Ripley's Believe It or Not*, or
Good Housekeeping, *Reader's Digest*, and a dozen other magazines she
kept in a pile in our bathroom. My mother got these magazines from people whose houses she cleaned. And since she cleaned many houses each
week, we had a great assortment. She would look through them all,
searching for stories about remarkable children.

The first night she brought out a story about a three-year-old boy
who knew the capitals of all the states and even most of the European
countries. A teacher was quoted as saying the little boy could also pronounce the names of the foreign cities correctly.

"What's the capital of Finland?" my mother asked me, looking at the
magazine story.

All I knew was the capital of California, because Sacramento was the   15
name of the street we lived on in Chinatown. "Nairobi!" I guessed,

saying the most foreign word I could think of. She checked to see if that was possibly one way to pronounce "Helsinki" before showing me the answer.

The tests got harder — multiplying numbers in my head, finding the queen of hearts in a deck of cards, trying to stand on my head without using my hands, predicting the daily temperatures in Los Angeles, New York, and London.

One night I had to look at a page from the Bible for three minutes and then report everything I could remember. "Now Jehoshaphat had riches and honor in abundance and . . . that's all I remember, Ma," I said.

And after seeing my mother's disappointed face once again, something inside of me began to die. I hated the tests, the raised hopes and failed expectations. Before going to bed that night, I looked in the mirror above the bathroom sink and when I saw only my face staring back — and that it would always be this ordinary face — I began to cry. Such a sad, ugly girl! I made high-pitched noises like a crazed animal, trying to scratch out the face in the mirror.

And then I saw what seemed to be the prodigy side of me — because I had never seen that face before. I looked at my reflection, blinking so I could see more clearly. The girl staring back at me was angry, powerful. This girl and I were the same. I had new thoughts, willful thoughts, or rather thoughts filled with lots of won'ts. I won't let her change me, I promised myself. I won't be what I'm not.

So now on nights when my mother presented her tests, I performed   20 listlessly, my head propped on one arm. I pretended to be bored. And I was. I got so bored I started counting the bellows of the foghorns out on the bay while my mother drilled me in other areas. The sound was comforting and reminded me of the cow jumping over the moon. And the next day, I played a game with myself, seeing if my mother would give up on me before eight bellows. After a while I usually counted only one, maybe two bellows at most. At last she was beginning to give up hope.

Two or three months had gone by without any mention of my being a prodigy again. And then one day my mother was watching *The Ed Sullivan Show* on TV. The TV was old and the sound kept shorting out. Every time my mother got halfway up from the sofa to adjust the set, the sound would go back on and Ed would be there talking. As soon as she sat down, Ed would go silent again. She got up, the TV broke into loud piano music. She sat down. Silence. Up and down, back and forth, quiet and loud. It was like a stiff embraceless dance between her and the TV set. Finally she stood by the set with her hand on the sound dial.

She seemed to be entranced by the music, a little frenzied piano piece with this mesmerizing quality, sort of quick passages and then teasing lilting ones before it returned to the quick playful parts.

"*Ni kan*," my mother said, calling me over with hurried hand gestures, "Look here."

I could see why my mother was fascinated by the music. It was being pounded out by a little Chinese girl, about nine years old, with a Peter Pan haircut. The girl had the sauciness of a Shirley Temple. She was proudly modest like a proper Chinese child. And she also did this fancy sweep of a curtsy, so that the fluffy skirt of her white dress cascaded slowly to the floor like the petals of a large carnation.

In spite of these warning signs, I wasn't worried. Our family had no piano and we couldn't afford to buy one, let alone reams of sheet music and piano lessons. So I could be generous in my comments when my mother bad-mouthed the little girl on TV.

"Play note right, but doesn't sound good! No singing sound," complained my mother.

"What are you picking on her for?" I said carelessly. "She's pretty good. Maybe she's not the best, but she's trying hard." I knew almost immediately I would be sorry I said that.

"Just like you," she said. "Not the best. Because you not trying." She gave a little huff as she let go of the sound dial and sat down on the sofa.

The little Chinese girl sat down also to play an encore of "Anitra's Dance" by Grieg. I remember the song, because later on I had to learn how to play it.

Three days after watching *The Ed Sullivan Show*, my mother told me what my schedule would be for piano lessons and piano practice. She had talked to Mr. Chong, who lived on the first floor of our apartment building. Mr. Chong was a retired piano teacher and my mother traded house-cleaning services for weekly lessons and a piano for me to practice on every day, two hours a day, from four until six.

When my mother told me this, I felt as though I had been sent to hell. I whined and then kicked my foot a little when I couldn't stand it anymore.

"Why don't you like me the way I am? I'm *not* a genius! I can't play the piano. And even if I could, I wouldn't go on TV if you paid me a million dollars!" I cried.

My mother slapped me. "Who ask you to be genius?" she shouted. "Only ask you to be your best. For your sake. You think I want you to be genius? Hnnh! What for! Who ask you!"

"So ungrateful," I heard her mutter in Chinese. "If she had as much talent as she has temper, she would be famous now."

Mr. Chong, whom I secretly nicknamed Old Chong, was very strange, always tapping his fingers to the silent music of an invisible orchestra. He looked ancient in my eyes. He had lost most of the hair on top of his head and he wore thick glasses and had eyes that always looked tired and sleepy. But he must have been younger than I thought, since he lived with his mother and was not yet married.

I met old lady Chong once and that was enough. She had this peculiar smell like a baby that had done something in its pants. And her fingers felt like a dead person's, like an old peach I once found in the back of the refrigerator, the skin just slid off the meat when I picked it up.

I soon found out why Old Chong had retired from teaching piano. He was deaf. "Like Beethoven!" he shouted to me. "We're both listening only in our head!" And he would start to conduct his frantic silent sonatas.

Our lessons went like this. He would open the book and point to different things, explaining their purpose: "Key! Treble! Bass! No sharps or flats! So this is C major! Listen now and play after me!"

And then he would play the C scale a few times, a simple chord, and then, as if inspired by an old, unreachable itch, he gradually added more notes and running trills and a pounding bass until the music was really something quite grand.

I would play after him, the simple scale, the simple chord, and then I   40
just played some nonsense that sounded like a cat running up and down on top of garbage cans. Old Chong smiled and applauded and then said, "Very good! But now you must learn to keep time!"

So that's how I discovered that Old Chong's eyes were too slow to keep up with the wrong notes I was playing. He went through the motions in half-time. To help me keep rhythm, he stood behind me, pushing down on my right shoulder for every beat. He balanced pennies on top of my wrists so I would keep them still as I slowly played scales and arpeggios. He had me curve my hand around an apple and keep that shape when playing chords. He marched stiffly to show me how to make each finger dance up and down, staccato like an obedient little soldier.

He taught me all these things, and that was how I also learned I could be lazy and get away with mistakes, lots of mistakes. If I hit the wrong notes because I hadn't practiced enough, I never corrected myself. I just kept playing in rhythm. And Old Chong kept conducting his own private reverie.

So maybe I never really gave myself a fair chance. I did pick up the basics pretty quickly, and I might have become a good pianist at that young age. But I was so determined not to try, not to be anybody different that I learned to play only the most ear-splitting preludes, the most discordant hymns.

Over the next year, I practiced like this, dutifully in my own way. And then one day I heard my mother and her friend Lindo Jong both talking in a loud bragging tone of voice so others could hear. It was after church, and I was leaning against the brick wall wearing a dress with stiff white petticoats. Auntie Lindo's daughter, Waverly, who was about my age, was standing farther down the wall about five feet away. We had grown up together and shared all the closeness of two sisters squabbling over crayons and dolls. In other words, for the most part, we hated each other. I thought she was snotty. Waverly Jong had gained a certain amount of fame as "Chinatown's Littlest Chinese Chess Champion."

"She bring home too many trophy," lamented Auntie Lindo that Sun-   45
day. "All day she play chess. All day I have no time do nothing but dust off her winnings." She threw a scolding look at Waverly, who pretended not to see her.

"You lucky you don't have this problem," said Auntie Lindo with a sigh to my mother.

And my mother squared her shoulders and bragged: "Our problem worser than yours. If we ask Jing-mei wash dish, she hear nothing but music. It's like you can't stop this natural talent."

And right then, I was determined to put a stop to her foolish pride.

A few weeks later, Old Chong and my mother conspired to have me play in a talent show which would be held in the church hall. By then, my parents had saved up enough to buy me a secondhand piano, a black Wurlitzer spinet with a scarred bench. It was the showpiece of our living room.

For the talent show, I was to play a piece called "Pleading Child" from Schumann's *Scenes from Childhood*. It was a simple, moody piece that sounded more difficult than it was. I was supposed to memorize the whole thing, playing the repeat parts twice to make the piece sound longer. But I dawdled over it, playing a few bars and then cheating, looking up to see what notes followed. I never really listened to what I was playing. I daydreamed about being somewhere else, about being someone else.

The part I liked to practice best was the fancy curtsy: right foot out, touch the rose on the carpet with a pointed foot, sweep to the side, left leg bends, look up and smile.

My parents invited all the couples from the Joy Luck Club to witness my debut. Auntie Lindo and Uncle Tin were there. Waverly and her two older brothers had also come. The first two rows were filled with children both younger and older than I was. The littlest ones got to go first. They recited simple nursery rhymes, squawked out tunes on miniature violins, twirled Hula Hoops, pranced in pink ballet tutus, and when they bowed or curtsied, the audience would sigh in unison, "Awww," and then clap enthusiastically.

When my turn came, I was very confident. I remember my childish excitement. It was as if I knew, without a doubt, that the prodigy side of me really did exist. I had no fear whatsoever, no nervousness. I remember thinking to myself, This is it! This is it! I looked out over the audience, at my mother's blank face, my father's yawn, Auntie Lindo's stiff-lipped smile, Waverly's sulky expression. I had on a white dress layered with sheets of lace, and a pink bow in my Peter Pan haircut. As I sat down I envisioned people jumping to their feet and Ed Sullivan rushing up to introduce me to everyone on TV.

And I started to play. It was so beautiful. I was so caught up in how lovely I looked that at first I didn't worry how I would sound. So it was a surprise to me when I hit the first wrong note and I realized something didn't sound quite right. And then I hit another and another followed that. A chill started at the top of my head and began to trickle down. Yet I couldn't stop playing, as though my hands were bewitched. I kept thinking my fingers would adjust themselves back, like a train switching to the right track. I played this strange jumble through two repeats, the sour notes staying with me all the way to the end.

When I stood up, I discovered my legs were shaking. Maybe I had   55
just been nervous and the audience, like Old Chong, had seen me go through the right motions and had not heard anything wrong at all. I swept my right foot out, went down on my knee, looked up and smiled. The room was quiet, except for Old Chong, who was beaming and shouting "Bravo! Bravo! Well done!" But then I saw my mother's face, her stricken face. The audience clapped weakly, and as I walked back to my chair, with my whole face quivering as I tried not to cry, I heard a little boy whisper loudly to his mother, "That was awful," and the mother whispered back, "Well, she certainly tried."

And now I realized how many people were in the audience, the whole world it seemed. I was aware of eyes burning into my back. I felt the shame of my mother and father as they sat stiffly throughout the rest of the show.

We could have escaped during the intermission. Pride and some strange sense of honor must have anchored my parents to their chairs. And so we watched it all: the eighteen-year-old boy with a fake mustache who did a magic show and juggled flaming hoops while riding a unicycle. The breasted girl with white makeup who sang from *Madama Butterfly* and got honorable mention. And the eleven-year-old boy who won first prize playing a tricky violin song that sounded like a busy bee.

After the show, the Hsus, the Jongs, and the St. Clairs from the Joy Luck Club came up to my mother and father.

"Lots of talented kids," Auntie Lindo said vaguely, smiling broadly.

"That was somethin' else," said my father, and I wondered if he was   60
referring to me in a humorous way, or whether he even remembered what I had done.

Waverly looked at me and shrugged her shoulders. "You aren't a genius like me," she said matter-of-factly. And if I hadn't felt so bad, I would have pulled her braids and punched her stomach.

But my mother's expression was what devastated me: a quiet, blank look that said she had lost everything. I felt the same way, and it seemed as if everybody were now coming up, like gawkers at the scene of an accident, to see what parts were actually missing. When we got on the bus to go home, my father was humming the busy-bee tune and my mother was silent. I kept thinking she wanted to wait until we got home before shouting at me. But when my father unlocked the door to our apartment, my mother walked in and then went to the back, into the bedroom. No accusations. No blame. And in a way, I felt disappointed. I had been waiting for her to start shouting, so I could shout back and cry and blame her for all my misery.

I assumed my talent-show fiasco meant I never had to play the piano again. But two days later, after school, my mother came out of the kitchen and saw me watching TV.

"Four clock," she reminded me as if it were any other day. I was stunned, as though she were asking me to go through the talent-show torture again. I wedged myself more tightly in front of the TV.

"Turn off TV," she called from the kitchen five minutes later.   65

I didn't budge. And then I decided. I didn't have to do what my mother said anymore. I wasn't her slave. This wasn't China. I had listened to her before and look what happened. She was the stupid one.

She came out from the kitchen and stood in the arched entryway of the living room. "Four clock," she said once again, louder.

"I'm not going to play anymore," I said nonchalantly. "Why should I? I'm not a genius."

She walked over and stood in front of the TV. I saw her chest was heaving up and down in an angry way.

"No!" I said, and I now felt stronger, as if my true self had finally   70 emerged. So this was what had been inside me all along.

"No! I won't!" I screamed.

She yanked me by the arm, pulled me off the floor, snapped off the TV. She was frighteningly strong, half pulling, half carrying me toward the piano as I kicked the throw rugs under my feet. She lifted me up and onto the hard bench. I was sobbing by now, looking at her bitterly. Her chest was heaving even more and her mouth was open, smiling crazily as if she were pleased I was crying.

"You want me to be someone that I'm not!" I sobbed. "I'll never be the kind of daughter you want me to be!"

"Only two kinds of daughters," she shouted in Chinese. "Those who are obedient and those who follow their own mind! Only one kind of daughter can live in this house! Obedient daughter!"

"Then I wish I wasn't your daughter. I wish you weren't my mother,"   75 I shouted. As I said these things I got scared. It felt like worms and toads and slimy things crawling out of my chest, but it also felt good, as if this awful side of me had surfaced, at last.

"Too late change this," said my mother shrilly.

And I could sense her anger rising to its breaking point. I wanted to see it spill over. And that's when I remembered the babies she had lost in China, the ones we never talked about. "Then I wish I'd never been born!" I shouted. "I wish I were dead! Like them."

It was as if I had said the magic words. Alakazam! — and her face went blank, her mouth closed, her arms went slack, and she backed out of the room, stunned, as if she were blowing away like a small brown leaf, thin, brittle, lifeless.

It was not the only disappointment my mother felt in me. In the years that followed, I failed her so many times, each time asserting my own will, my right to fall short of expectations. I didn't get straight As. I didn't become class president. I didn't get into Stanford. I dropped out of college.

For unlike my mother, I did not believe I could be anything I wanted   80 to be. I could only be me.

And for all those years, we never talked about the disaster at the recital or my terrible accusations afterward at the piano bench. All that remained unchecked, like a betrayal that was now unspeakable. So I never found a way to ask her why she had hoped for something so large that failure was inevitable.

And even worse, I never asked her what frightened me the most: Why had she given up hope?

For after our struggle at the piano, she never mentioned my playing again. The lessons stopped. The lid to the piano was closed, shutting out the dust, my misery, and her dreams.

So she surprised me. A few years ago, she offered to give me the piano, for my thirtieth birthday. I had not played in all those years. I saw the offer as a sign of forgiveness, a tremendous burden removed.

"Are you sure?" I asked shyly. "I mean, won't you and Dad miss it?"   85

"No, this your piano," she said firmly. "Always your piano. You only one can play."

"Well, I probably can't play anymore," I said. "It's been years."

"You pick up fast," said my mother, as if she knew this was certain. "You have natural talent. You could been genius if you want to."

"No I couldn't."

"You just not trying," said my mother. And she was neither angry   90
nor sad. She said it as if to announce a fact that could never be disproved. "Take it," she said.

But I didn't at first. It was enough that she had offered it to me. And after that, every time I saw it in my parents' living room, standing in front of the bay windows, it made me feel proud, as if it were a shiny trophy I had won back.

Last week I sent a tuner over to my parents' apartment and had the piano reconditioned, for purely sentimental reasons. My mother had died a few months before and I had been getting things in order for my father, a little bit at a time. I put the jewelry in special silk pouches. The sweaters she had knitted in yellow, pink, bright orange — all the colors I hated — I put those in moth-proof boxes. I found some old Chinese silk dresses, the kind with the little slits up the sides. I rubbed the old silk against my skin, then wrapped them in tissue and decided to take them home with me.

After I had the piano tuned, I opened the lid and touched the keys. It sounded even richer than I imagined. Really, it was a very good piano. Inside the bench were the same exercise notes with handwritten scales, the same secondhand books with their covers held together with yellow tape.

I opened up the Schumann book to the dark little piece I had played at the recital. It was on the left-hand side of the page, "Pleading Child." It looked more difficult than I remembered. I played a few bars, surprised at how easily the notes came back to me.

And for the first time, or so it seemed, I noticed the piece on the   95
right-hand side. It was called "Perfectly Contented." I tried to play this one as well. It had a lighter melody but the same flowing rhythm and

turned out to be quite easy. "Pleading Child" was shorter but slower; "Perfectly Contented" was longer, but faster. And after I played them both a few times, I realized they were two halves of the same song.

The Reader's Presence

1. Tan is able to control her reader's response by gradually shifting her point of view about the events as well as what she calls the "raised hopes and failed expectations" at the dramatic center of this story. Reread the story carefully, identify each of these shifts in point of view, and comment on the effectiveness of each. How does each shift heighten the dramatic effects Tan builds into this story? Consider, for example, the piano lessons with Mr. Chong and the mother's relation to the television set.

2. Tan begins her story with the daughter's efforts to recount and satisfy her mother's ambition — that her daughter will be recognized as a "prodigy." At what points — and with what effects — does Tan repeat this word and its synonyms for it? What are the consequences of the mother's repeating the phrase "You could"? How might this phrase serve as a commentary on both the mother's and the daughter's efforts to accept their visions of themselves and of each other? Identify — and comment on — the ways in which the daughter gradually tries to assert control over the situation by using words such as *prodigy* and *genius*.

3. Identify and comment on the effectiveness of Tan's use of similes to illustrate the daughter's states of consciousness. Consider, for example, paragraph 19. How might this dramatic moment illuminate the structure of this story about "raised hopes and failed expectations"? Trace the movements of mother and daughter away from and toward each other. When and how do mother and daughter share hopes and expectations? How does the final paragraph in the story reinforce — or further complicate — this "dance" between mother and daughter? What resolution, if any, does Tan present to the daughter's refusal to be what her mother wanted her to be?

31

Lewis Thomas

The Tucson Zoo

Lewis Thomas (1913-1993) was trained as a physician and scientist, but his intellectual curiosity and his publications took him far beyond the practice of medicine. In 1971 he became a regular contributor to the New England Journal of Medicine, *writing a column called "Notes of a Biology Watcher." Several of these essays are collected in* The Lives of the Cell *(1974), which explores the many ways in which organisms relate to one another for their mutual benefit. Joyce Carol Oates praised this book, saying that it "anticipates the kind of writing that will appear more and more frequently, as scientists take on the language of poetry in order to communicate human truths too mysterious for old-fashioned common sense."*

Thomas also published The Medusa and the Snail: More Notes of a Biology Watcher *(1979), from which "The Tucson Zoo" is excerpted. His later books expanded the range of his investigations into natural and social processes and include* Late Night Thoughts on Listening to Mahler's Ninth Symphony *(1984) and a collection of essays on language,* Et Cetera, Et Cetera: Notes of a Word Watcher *(1990).*

Science gets most of its information by the process of reductionism, exploring the details, then the details of the details, until all the smallest bits of the structure, or the smallest parts of the mechanism, are laid out for counting and scrutiny. Only when this is done can the investigation be extended to encompass the whole organism or the entire system. So we say.

Sometimes it seems that we take a loss, working this way. Much of today's public anxiety about science is the apprehension that we may forever be overlooking the whole by an endless, obsessive preoccupation with the parts. I had a brief, personal experience of this misgiving one afternoon in Tucson, where I had time on my hands and visited the zoo, just outside the city. The designers there have cut a deep pathway between two small artificial ponds, walled by clear glass, so when you stand in the center of the path you can look into the depths of each pool, and at the same time you can regard the surface. In one pool, on the right side of the path, is a family of otters; on the other side, a family of beavers. Within just a few feet of your face, on either side, beavers and otters are at play, underwater and on the surface, swimming toward your face and then away, more filled with life than any creatures I have ever seen before, in all my days. Except for the glass, you could reach across and touch them.

I was transfixed. As I now recall it, there was only one sensation in my head: pure elation mixed with amazement at such perfection. Swept off my feet, I floated from one side to the other, swiveling my brain, staring astounded at the beavers, then at the otters. I could hear shouts across my corpus callosum, from one hemisphere to the other. I remember thinking, with what was left in charge of my consciousness, that I wanted no part of the science of beavers and otters; I wanted never to know how they performed their marvels; I wished for no news about the physiology of their breathing, the coordination of their muscles, their vision, their endocrine systems, their digestive tracts. I hoped never to think of them as collections of cells. All I asked for was the full hairy complexity, then in front of my eyes, of whole, intact beavers and otters in motion.

It lasted, I regret to say, for only a few minutes, and then I was back in the late twentieth century, reductionist as ever, wondering about the details by force of habit, but not, this time, the details of otters and beavers. Instead, me. Something worth remembering had happened in my mind, I was certain of that; I would have put it somewhere in the brainstem; maybe this was my limbic system at work. I became a behavioral scientist, an experimental psychologist, an ethologist, and in the instant I lost all the wonder and the sense of being overwhelmed. I was flattened.

But I came away from the zoo with something, a piece of news about myself: I am coded, somehow, for otters and beavers. I exhibit instinctive behavior in their presence, when they are displayed close at hand behind glass, simultaneously below water and at the surface. I have receptors for this display. Beavers and otters possess a "releaser" for me, in the terminology of ethology, and the releasing was my experience. What was released? Behavior. What behavior? Standing, swiveling flabbergasted, feeling exultation and a rush of friendship. I could not, as the result of the transaction, tell you anything more about beavers and otters than you already know. I learned nothing new about them. Only about me, and I suspect also about you, maybe about human beings at large: we are endowed with genes which close out our reaction to beavers and otters, maybe our reaction to each other as well. We are stamped with stereotyped, unalterable patterns of response, ready to be released. And the behavior released in us, by such confrontations, is, essentially, a surprised affection. It is compulsory behavior and we can avoid it only by straining with the full power of our conscious minds, making up conscious excuses all the way. Left to ourselves, mechanistic and autonomic, we hanker for friends.

Everyone says, stay away from ants. They have no lessons for us; they are crazy little instruments, inhuman, incapable of controlling themselves, lacking manners, lacking souls. When they are massed together, all touching, exchanging bits of information held in their jaws like memoranda, they become a single animal. Look out for that. It is a debasement, a loss of individuality, a violation of human nature, an unnatural act.

Sometimes people argue this point of view seriously and with deep thought. Be individuals, solitary and selfish, is the message. Altruism, a jargon word for what used to be called love, is worse than weakness, it is sin, a violation of nature. Be separate. Do not be a social animal. But this is a hard argument to make convincingly when you have to depend on language to make it. You have to print up leaflets or publish books and get them bought and sent around, you have to turn up on television and catch the attention of millions of other human beings all at once, and then you have to say to all of them, all at once, all collected and paying attention: be solitary; do not depend on each other. You can't do this and keep a straight face.

Maybe altruism is our most primitive attribute, out of reach, beyond our control. Or perhaps it is immediately at hand, waiting to be released, disguised now, in our kind of civilization, as affection or friendship or attachment. I don't see why it should be unreasonable for all human beings to have strands of DNA coiled up in chromosomes, coding out instincts for usefulness and helpfulness. Usefulness may turn out to be the hardest test of fitness for survival, more important than aggression, more effective, in the long run, than grabbiness. If this is the sort of information biological science holds for the future, applying to us as well as to ants, then I am all for science.

One thing I'd like to know most of all: when those ants have made the Hill, and are all there, touching and exchanging, and the whole mass begins to behave like a single huge creature, and *thinks*, what on earth is that thought? And while you're at it, I'd like to know a second thing: when it happens, does any single ant know about it? Does his hair stand on end?

The Reader's Presence

1. Notice how Thomas uses both highly specialized terminology (for example, *corpus callosum*, a part of the brain) and informal, even conversational language ("You can't do this and keep a straight face" [paragraph 7]). Why doesn't he just stick to one or the other? Do you think Thomas expects the reader to understand all the scientific terms he uses? What effect do they have? In your opinion, do they help or hinder Thomas's argument?

2. Thomas opens his essay by describing the scientific, "reductionist" process of gathering information, but then ends the first paragraph with a disclaimer, "So we say." Who is Thomas speaking for when he uses the word *we*?

3. Do you think Thomas is suggesting that we get a better explanation of the world through nonscientific thinking? Though the essay seems critical of scientific methods, in what ways does Thomas show his own scientific predisposition?

32

Alice Walker

Beauty: When the Other Dancer Is the Self

Alice Walker (b. 1944) was awarded the Pulitzer Prize and the American Book Award for her second novel, The Color Purple *(1982), which was made into a popular film. This novel helped establish Walker's reputation as one of America's most important contemporary writers. In both her fiction and nonfiction, she shares her compassion for the black women of America whose lives have long been largely excluded from or distorted in literary representation. Walker is also the author of other novels, short stories, several volumes of poetry, a children's biography of Langston Hughes, essays, and criticism. Her most recent books are* The Temple of My Familiar *(1989),* Possessing the Secret of Joy *(1992), and* The Same River Twice *(1996). "Beauty: When the Other Dancer Is the Self" comes from her 1983 collection,* In Search of Our Mothers' Gardens.*

When asked by an interviewer about her writing habits, Walker replied, "Generally speaking I work in the morning and then I garden — I do watering. Writing is just a part of my life. I don't like to emphasize it so much it becomes a distortion. I think it was Hemingway who said that each day that you write, you don't try to write to the absolute end of what you feel and think. You leave a little, you know, so that the next day you have something else to go on. And I would take it a little further — the thing is being able to create out of fullness, and that in order to create out of fullness, you have to let it well up. You cannot do what is done so much in this culture and the world. You know, the image of what has happened to the planet is of a man and mankind just grabbing the earth by the throat and shaking it and saying 'give, give, give,' and just squeezing it until the last drop of life leaves it. That, needless to say, is very uncreative. It can only lead to death. . . . In creation you must always leave something. You have to go to the bottom of the well with creativity. You have to give it everything you've got, but at the same time you have to leave that last drop for the creative spirit or for the earth itself."

It is a bright summer day in 1947. My father, a fat, funny man with beautiful eyes and a subversive wit, is trying to decide which of his eight children he will take with him to the county fair. My mother, of course, will not go. She is knocked out from getting most of us ready: I hold my neck stiff against the pressure of her knuckles as she hastily completes the braiding and the beribboning of my hair.

My father is the driver for the rich old white lady up the road. Her name is Miss Mey. She owns all the land for miles around, as well as the house in which we live. All I remember about her is that she once offered to pay my mother thirty-five cents for cleaning her house, raking up piles of her magnolia leaves, and washing her family's clothes, and that my mother — she of no money, eight children, and a chronic earache — refused it. But I do not think of this in 1947. I am two-and-a-half years old. I want to go everywhere my daddy goes. I am excited at the prospect of riding in a car. Someone has told me fairs are fun. That there is room in the car for only three of us doesn't faze me at all. Whirling happily in my starchy frock, showing off my biscuit-polished patent-leather shoes and lavender socks, tossing my head in a way that makes my ribbons bounce, I stand, hands on hips, before my father. "Take me, Daddy," I say with assurance; "I'm the prettiest!"

Later, it does not surprise me to find myself in Miss Mey's shiny black car, sharing the back seat with the other lucky ones. Does not surprise me that I thoroughly enjoy the fair. At home that night I tell the unlucky ones all I can remember about the merry-go-round, the man who eats live chickens, and the teddy bears, until they say: that's enough, baby Alice. Shut up now, and go to sleep.

It is Easter Sunday, 1950. I am dressed in a green, flocked, scalloped-hem dress (handmade by my adoring sister, Ruth) that has its own smooth satin petticoat and tiny hot-pink roses tucked into each scallop. My shoes, new T-strap patent leather, again highly biscuit-polished. I am six years old and have learned one of the longest Easter speeches to be heard that day, totally unlike the speech I said when I was two: "Easter lilies / pure and white / blossom in / the morning light." When I rise to give my speech I do so on a great wave of love and pride and expectation. People in the church stop rustling their new crinolines. They seem to hold their breath. I can tell they admire my dress, but it is my spirit, bordering on sassiness (womanishness), they secretly applaud.

"That girl's a little *mess*," they whisper to each other, pleased.   5

Naturally I say my speech without stammer or pause, unlike those who stutter, stammer, or, worst of all, forget. This is before the word "beautiful" exists in people's vocabulary, but "Oh, isn't she the *cutest* thing!" frequently floats my way. "And got so much sense!" they gratefully add . . . for which thoughtful addition I thank them to this day.

It was great fun being cute. But then, one day, it ended.

I am eight years old and a tomboy. I have a cowboy hat, cowboy boots, checkered shirt and pants, all red. My playmates are my brothers, two and four years older than I. Their colors are black and green, the only difference in the way we are dressed. On Saturday nights we all go to the picture show, even my mother; Westerns are her favorite kind of movie. Back home, "on the ranch," we pretend we are Tom Mix, Hopalong Cassidy, Lash LaRue (we've even named one of our dogs Lash LaRue); we chase each other for hours rustling cattle, being outlaws, delivering damsels from distress. Then my parents decide to buy my brothers guns. These are not "real" guns. They shoot BBs, copper pellets my brothers say will kill birds. Because I am a girl, I do not get a gun. Instantly I am relegated to the position of Indian. Now there appears a great distance between us. They shoot and shoot at everything with their new guns. I try to keep up with my bow and arrows.

One day while I am standing on top of our makeshift "garage" — pieces of tin nailed across some poles — holding my bow and arrow and looking out toward the fields, I feel an incredible blow in my right eye. I look down just in time to see my brother lower his gun.

Both brothers rush to my side. My eye stings, and I cover it with my hand. "If you tell," they say, "we will get a whipping. You don't want that to happen, do you?" I do not. "Here is a piece of wire," says the older brother, picking it up from the roof; "say you stepped on one end of it and the other flew up and hit you." The pain is beginning to start. "Yes," I say. "Yes, I will say that is what happened." If I do not say this is what happened, I know my brothers will find ways to make me wish I had. But now I will say anything that gets me to my mother.

Confronted by our parents we stick to the lie agreed upon. They place me on a bench on the porch and I close my left eye while they examine the right. There is a tree growing from underneath the porch that climbs past the railing to the roof. It is the last thing my right eye sees. I watch as its trunk, its branches, and then its leaves are blotted out by the rising blood.

I am in shock. First there is intense fever, which my father tries to break using lily leaves bound around my head. Then there are chills: my mother tries to get me to eat soup. Eventually, I do not know how, my parents learn what has happened. A week after the "accident" they take me to see a doctor. "Why did you wait so long to come?" he asks, looking into my eye and shaking his head. "Eyes are sympathetic," he says. "If one is blind, the other will likely become blind too."

This comment of the doctor's terrifies me. But it is really how I look that bothers me most. Where the BB pellet struck there is a glob of whitish scar tissue, a hideous cataract, on my eye. Now when I stare at people — a favorite pastime, up to now — they will stare back. Not at the "cute" little girl, but at her scar. For six years I do not stare at anyone, because I do not raise my head.

Years later, in the throes of a mid-life crisis, I ask my mother and sister whether I changed after the "accident." "No," they say, puzzled. "What do you mean?"

What do I mean?   15

I am eight, and, for the first time, doing poorly in school, where I have been something of a whiz since I was four. We have just moved to the place where the "accident" occurred. We do not know any of the people around us because this is a different county. The only time I see the friends I knew is when we go back to our old church. The new school is the former state penitentiary. It is a large stone building, cold and drafty, crammed to overflowing with boisterous, ill-disciplined children. On the third floor there is a huge circular imprint of some partition that has been torn out.

"What used to be here?" I ask a sullen girl next to me on our way past it to lunch.

"The electric chair," says she.

At night I have nightmares about the electric chair, and about all the people reputedly "fried" in it. I am afraid of the school, where all the students seem to be budding criminals.

"What's the matter with your eye?" they ask, critically.   20

When I don't answer (I cannot decide whether it was an "accident" or not), they shove me, insist on a fight.

My brother, the one who created the story about the wire, comes to my rescue. But then brags so much about "protecting" me, I become sick.

After months of torture at the school, my parents decide to send me back to our old community, to my old school. I live with my grandparents and the teacher they board. But there is no room for Phoebe, my cat. By the time my grandparents decide there *is* room, and I ask for my cat, she cannot be found. Miss Yarborough, the boarding teacher, takes me under her wing, and begins to teach me to play the piano. But soon she marries an African — a "prince," she says — and is whisked away to his continent.

At my old school there is at least one teacher who loves me. She is the teacher who "knew me before I was born" and bought my first baby clothes. It is she who makes life bearable. It is her presence that finally helps me turn on the one child at the school who continually calls me "one-eyed bitch." One day I simply grab him by his coat and beat him until I am satisfied. It is my teacher who tells me my mother is ill.

My mother is lying in bed in the middle of the day, something I have   25
never seen. She is in too much pain to speak. She has an abscess in her ear. I stand looking down on her, knowing that if she dies, I cannot live. She is being treated with warm oils and hot bricks held against her cheek. Finally a doctor comes. But I must go back to my grandparents' house. The weeks pass but I am hardly aware of it. All I know is that my mother might die, my father is not so jolly, my brothers still have their guns, and I am the one sent away from home.

"You did not change," they say.

Did I imagine the anguish of never looking up?

I am twelve. When relatives come to visit I hide in my room. My cousin Brenda, just my age, whose father works in the post office and whose mother is a nurse, comes to find me. "Hello," she says. And then she asks, looking at my recent school picture, which I did not want taken, and on which the "glob," as I think of it, is clearly visible, "You still can't see out of that eye?"

"No," I say, and flop back on the bed over my book.

That night, as I do almost every night, I abuse my eye. I rant and rave   30
at it, in front of the mirror. I plead with it to clear up before morning. I tell it I hate and despise it. I do not pray for sight. I pray for beauty.

"You did not change," they say.

I am fourteen and baby-sitting for my brother Bill, who lives in Boston. He is my favorite brother and there is a strong bond between us. Understanding my feelings of shame and ugliness he and his wife take me to a local hospital, where the "glob" is removed by a doctor named O. Henry. There is still a small bluish crater where the scar tissue was, but the ugly white stuff is gone. Almost immediately I become a different person from the girl who does not raise her head. Or so I think. Now that I've raised my head I win the boyfriend of my dreams. Now that I've raised my head I have plenty of friends. Now that I've raised my head classwork comes from my lips as faultlessly as Easter speeches did, and I leave high school as valedictorian, most popular student, and *queen*, hardly believing my luck. Ironically, the girl who was voted most beautiful in our class (and was) was later shot twice through the chest by a male companion, using a "real" gun, while she was pregnant. But that's another story in itself. Or is it?

"You did not change," they say.

It is now thirty years since the "accident." A beautiful journalist comes to visit and to interview me. She is going to write a cover story for her magazine that focuses on my latest book. "Decide how you want to look on the cover," she says. "Glamorous, or whatever."

Never mind "glamorous," it is the "whatever" that I hear. Suddenly   35
all I can think of is whether I will get enough sleep the night before the photography session: If I don't, my eye will be tired and wander, as blind eyes will.

At night in bed with my lover I think up reasons why I should not appear on the cover of a magazine. "My meanest critics will say I've sold out," I say. "My family will now realize I write scandalous books."

"But what's the real reason you don't want to do this?" he asks.

"Because in all probability," I say in a rush, "my eye won't be straight."

"It will be straight enough," he says. Then, "Besides, I thought you'd made your peace with that."

And I suddenly remember that I have.   40

I remember:

I am talking to my brother Jimmy, asking if he remembers anything unusual about the day I was shot. He does not know I consider that day the last time my father, with his sweet home remedy of cool lily leaves, chose me, and that I suffered and raged inside because of this. "Well," he says, "all I remember is standing by the side of the highway with Daddy, trying to flag down a car. A white man stopped, but when Daddy said he needed somebody to take his little girl to the doctor, he drove off."

I remember:

I am in the desert for the first time. I fall totally in love with it. I am so overwhelmed by its beauty, I confront for the first time, consciously, the meaning of the doctor's words years ago: "Eyes are sympathetic. If one is blind, the other will likely become blind too." I realize I have dashed about the world madly, looking at this, looking at that, storing up images against the fading of the light. *But I might have missed seeing the desert!* The shock of that possibility — and gratitude for over twenty-five years of sight — sends me literally to my knees. Poem after poem comes — which is perhaps how poets pray.

ON SIGHT

I am so thankful I have seen
The Desert
And the creatures in the desert
And the desert Itself.

The desert has its own moon
Which I have seen
With my own eye.
There is no flag on it.

Trees of the desert have arms
All of which are always up
That is because the moon is up
The sun is up
Also the sky
The Stars
Clouds
None with flags.

If there were flags, I doubt
the trees would point.
Would you?

But mostly, I remember this: 45

I am twenty-seven, and my baby daughter is almost three. Since her birth I have worried about her discovery that her mother's eyes are different from other people's. Will she be embarrassed? I think. What will she say? Every day she watches a television program called *Big Blue Marble*. It begins with a picture of the earth as it appears from the moon. It is bluish, a little battered-looking, but full of light, with whitish clouds swirling around it. Every time I see it I weep with love, as if it is a picture of Grandma's house. One day when I am putting Rebecca down for her nap, she suddenly focuses on my eye. Something inside me cringes, gets ready to try to protect myself. All children are cruel about physical differences, I know from experience, and that they don't always mean to be is another matter. I assume Rebecca will be the same.

But no-o-o-o. She studies my face intently as we stand, her inside and me outside her crib. She even holds my face maternally between her dimpled little hands. Then, looking every bit as serious and lawyerlike as her father, she says, as if it may just possibly have slipped my attention: "Mommy, there's a *world* in your eye." (As in, "Don't be alarmed, or do anything crazy.") And then, gently, but with great interest: "Mommy, where did you *get* that world in your eye?"

For the most part, the pain left then. (So what, if my brothers grew up to buy even more powerful pellet guns for their sons and to carry real guns themselves. So what, if a young "Morehouse[1] man" once nearly fell off the steps of Trevor Arnett Library because he thought my eyes were blue.) Crying and laughing I ran to the bathroom, while Rebecca mumbled and sang herself to sleep. Yes indeed, I realized, looking into the mirror. There *was* a world in my eye. And I saw that it was possible to love it: that in fact, for all it had taught me of shame and anger and inner vision, I *did* love it. Even to see it drifting out of orbit in boredom, or rolling up out of fatigue, not to mention floating back at attention in excitement (bearing witness, a friend has called it), deeply suitable to my personality, and even characteristic of me.

That night I dream I am dancing to Stevie Wonder's song "Always" (the name of the song is really "As," but I hear it as "Always"). As I dance, whirling and joyous, happier than I've ever been in my life, another bright-faced dancer joins me. We dance and kiss each other and hold each other through the night. The other dancer has obviously come through all right, as I have done. She is beautiful, whole, and free. And she is also me.

The Reader's Presence

1. In her opening paragraph, Walker refers to her father's "beautiful eyes." How does that phrase take on more significance in rereading? Can you find other words, phrases, or images that do the same? For example, why might Walker have mentioned the pain of having her hair combed?

---

[1]*Morehouse:* Morehouse College, a black men's college in Atlanta, Georgia. — EDS.

2. Note that Walker uses the present tense throughout the essay. Why might this be unusual, given her subject? What effect does it have for both writer and reader? Try rewriting the opening paragraph in the past tense. What difference do you think it makes?

3. What is the meaning of Walker's occasional italicized comments? What do they have in common? Whose comments are they? To whom do they seem addressed? What time frame do they seem to be in? What purpose do you think they serve?

33

E. B. White

Once More to the Lake

Elwyn Brooks White (1899–1985) started contributing to the New Yorker *soon after the magazine began publication in 1925, and in the "Talk of the Town" and other columns helped establish the magazine's reputation for precise and brilliant prose. Collections of his contributions can be found in* Every Day Is Saturday *(1934),* Quo Vadimus? *(1939), and* The Wild Flag *(1946). He also wrote essays for* Harper's *on a regular basis; these essays include "Once More to the Lake" and are collected in* One Man's Meat *(1941). In his comments on this work, the critic Jonathan Yardley observed that White is "one of the few writers of this or any century who has succeeded in transforming the ephemera of journalism into something that demands to be called literature."*

Capable of brilliant satire, White could also be sad and serious, as in his compilation of forty years of writing, Essays *(1977). Among his numerous awards and honors, White received the American Academy of Arts and Letters Gold Medal (1960), a Presidential Medal of Freedom (1963), and a National Medal for Literature (1971). He made a lasting contribution to children's literature with* Stuart Little *(1945),* Charlotte's Web *(1952), and* The Trumpet of the Swan *(1970).*

White has written, "I have always felt that the first duty of a writer was to ascend — to make flights, carrying others along if he could manage it." According to White, the writer needs not only courage, but also hope and faith to accomplish this goal: "Writing itself is an act of faith, nothing else. And it must be the writer, above all others, who keeps it alive — choked with laughter, or with pain."

One summer, along about 1904, my father rented a camp on a lake in Maine and took us all there for the month of August. We all got ringworm from some kittens and had to rub Pond's Extract on our arms and legs night and morning, and my father rolled over in a canoe with all his clothes on; but outside of that the vacation was a success and from then on none of us ever thought there was any place in the world like that lake in Maine. We returned summer after summer — always on August 1st for one month. I have since become a salt-water man, but sometimes in summer there are days when the restlessness of the tides and the fearful cold of the sea water and the incessant wind that blows across the afternoon and into the evening make me wish for the placidity of a lake in the woods. A few weeks ago this feeling got so strong I bought myself a couple of bass hooks and a spinner and returned to the lake where we used to go, for a week's fishing and to revisit old haunts.

I took along my son, who had never had any fresh water up his nose and who had seen lily pads only from train windows. On the journey over to the lake I began to wonder what it would be like. I wondered how time would have marred this unique, this holy spot — the coves and streams, the hills that the sun set behind, the camps and the paths behind the camps. I was sure that the tarred road would have found it out and I wondered in what other ways it would be desolated. It is strange how much you can remember about places like that once you allow your mind to return into the grooves that lead back. You remember one thing, and that suddenly reminds you of another thing. I guess I remembered clearest of all the early mornings, when the lake was cool and motionless, remembered how the bedroom smelled of the lumber it was made of and the wet woods whose scent entered through the screen. The partitions in the camp were thin and did not extend clear to the top of the rooms, and as I was always the first up I would dress softly so as not to wake the others, and sneak out into the sweet outdoors and start out in the canoe, keeping close along the shore in the long shadows of the pines. I remembered being very careful never to rub my paddle against the gunwale for fear of disturbing the stillness of the cathedral.

The lake had never been what you would call a wild lake. There were cottages sprinkled about the shores, and it was in farming country although the shores of the lake were quite heavily wooded. Some of the cottages were owned by nearby farmers, and you would live at the shore and eat your meals at the farmhouse. That's what our family did. But although it wasn't wild, it was a fairly large and undisturbed lake and there were places in it which, to a child at least, seemed infinitely remote and primeval.

I was right about the tar: It led to within half a mile of the shore. But when I got back there, with my boy, and we settled into a camp near a farmhouse and into the kind of summertime I had known, I could tell that it was going to be pretty much the same as it had been before — I knew it, lying in bed the first morning, smelling the bedroom, and hearing the boy sneak quietly out and go off along the shore in a boat. I began to sustain the illusion that he was I, and therefore, by simple transposition, that I was my father. This sensation persisted, kept cropping up all the time we were there. It was not an entirely new feeling, but in this setting it grew much stronger. I seemed to be living a dual existence. I would be in the middle of some simple act, I would be picking up a bait box or laying down a table fork, or I would be saying something, and suddenly it would be not I but my father who was saying the words or making the gesture. It gave me a creepy sensation.

We went fishing the first morning. I felt the same damp moss cover-   5
ing the worms in the bait can, and saw the dragonfly alight on the tip of my rod as it hovered a few inches from the surface of the water. It was the arrival of this fly that convinced me beyond any doubt that everything was as it always had been, that the years were a mirage and there had been no years. The small waves were the same, chucking the rowboat under the chin as we fished at anchor, and the boat was the same boat, the same color green and the ribs broken in the same places, and under the floor-boards the same fresh-water leavings and debris — the dead hellgrammite, the wisps of moss, the rusty discarded fishhook, the dried blood from yesterday's catch. We stared silently at the tips of our rods, at the dragonflies that came and went. I lowered the tip of mine into the water, tentatively, pensively dislodging the fly, which darted two feet away, poised, darted two feet back, and came to rest again a little farther up the rod. There had been no years between the ducking of this dragon-fly and the other one — the one that was part of memory. I looked at the boy, who was silently watching his fly, and it was my hands that held his rod, my eyes watching. I felt dizzy and didn't know which rod I was at the end of.

We caught two bass, hauling them in briskly as though they were mackerel, pulling them over the side of the boat in a businesslike manner without any landing net, and stunning them with a blow on the back of the head. When we got back for a swim before lunch, the lake was ex-actly where we had left it, the same number of inches from the dock, and there was only the merest suggestion of a breeze. This seemed an utterly enchanted sea, this lake you could leave to its own devices for a few hours and come back to, and find that it had not stirred, this constant and trustworthy body of water. In the shallows, the dark, watersoaked sticks and twigs, smooth and old, were undulating in clusters on the bot-tom against the clean ribbed sand, and the track of the mussel was plain. A school of minnows swam by, each minnow with its small individual shadow, doubling the attendance, so clear and sharp in the sunlight. Some of the other campers were in swimming, along the shore, one of them with a cake of soap, and the water felt thin and clear and unsub-stantial. Over the years there had been this person with the cake of soap, this cultist, and here he was. There had been no years.

Up to the farmhouse to dinner through the teeming, dusty field, the road under our sneakers was only a two-track road. The middle track was missing, the one with the marks of the hooves and splotches of dried, flaky manure. There had always been three tracks to choose from in choosing which track to walk in; now the choice was narrowed down to two. For a moment I missed terribly the middle alternative. But the way led past the tennis court, and something about the way it lay there in the sun reassured me; the tape had loosened along the backline, the alleys were green with plantains and other weeds, and the net (installed in June and removed in September) sagged in the dry noon, and the whole place steamed with midday heat and hunger and emptiness. There was a choice of pie for dessert, and one was blueberry and one was apple, and the waitresses were the same country girls, there having been no passage of time, only the illusion of it as in a dropped curtain — the waitresses were still fifteen; their hair had been washed, that was the only difference — they had been to the movies and seen the pretty girls with the clean hair.

Summertime, oh summertime, pattern of life indelible, the fade-proof lake, the woods unshatterable, the pasture with the sweetfern and the juniper forever and ever, summer without end; this was the background, and the life along the shore was the design, the cottages with their innocent and tranquil design, their tiny docks with the flagpole and the American flag floating against the white clouds in the blue sky, the little paths over the roots of the trees leading from camp to camp and the paths leading back to the outhouses and the can of lime for sprinkling, and at the souvenir counters at the store the miniature birch-bark canoes and the post cards that showed things looking a little better than they looked. This was the American family at play, escaping the city heat, wondering whether the newcomers in the camp at the head of the cove were "common" or "nice," wondering whether it was true that the people who drove up for Sunday dinner at the farmhouse were turned away because there wasn't enough chicken.

It seemed to me, as I kept remembering all this, that those times and those summers had been infinitely precious and worth saving. There had been jollity and peace and goodness. The arriving (at the beginning of August) had been so big a business in itself, at the railway station the farm wagon drawn up, the first smell of the pine-laden air, the first glimpse of the smiling farmer, and the great importance of the trunks and your father's enormous authority in such matters, and the feel of the wagon under you for the long ten-mile haul, and at the top of the last long hill catching the first view of the lake after eleven months of not seeing this cherished body of water. The shouts and cries of the other campers when they saw you, and the trunks to be unpacked, to give up their rich burden. (Arriving was less exciting nowadays, when you sneaked up in your car and parked it under a tree near the camp and took out the bags and in five minutes it was all over, no fuss, no loud wonderful fuss about trunks).

Peace and goodness and jollity. The only thing that was wrong now,   10
really, was the sound of the place, an unfamiliar nervous sound of the outboard motors. This was the note that jarred, the one thing that would sometimes break the illusion and set the years moving. In those other

summertimes all motors were inboard; and when they were at a little distance, the noise they made was a sedative, an ingredient of summer sleep. They were one-cylinder and two-cylinder engines, and some were make-and-break and some were jump-spark, but they all made a sleepy sound across the lake. The one-lungers throbbed and fluttered, and the twin-cylinder ones purred and purred, and that was a quiet sound too. But now the campers all had outboards. In the daytime, in the hot mornings, these motors made a petulant, irritable sound; at night, in the still evening when the afterglow lit the water, they whined about one's ears like mosquitoes. My boy loved our rented outboard, and his great desire was to achieve singlehanded mastery over it, and authority, and he soon learned the trick of choking it a little (but not too much), and the adjustment of the needle valve. Watching him I would remember the things you could do with the old one-cylinder engines with the heavy flywheel, how you could have it eating out of your hand if you got really close to it spiritually. Motor boats in those days didn't have clutches, and you would make a landing by shutting off the motor at the proper time and coasting in with a dead rudder. But there was a way of reversing them, if you learned the trick, by cutting the switch and putting it on again exactly on the final dying revolution of the flywheel, so that it would kick back against compression and begin reversing. Approaching a dock in a strong following breeze, it was difficult to slow up sufficiently by the ordinary coasting method, and if a boy felt he had complete mastery over his motor, he was tempted to keep it running beyond its time and then reverse it a few feet from the dock. It took a cool nerve, because if you threw the switch a twentieth of a second too soon you could catch the flywheel when it still had speed enough to go up past center, and the boat would leap ahead, charging bull-fashion at the dock.

We had a good week at the camp. The bass were biting well and the sun shone endlessly, day after day. We would be tired at night and lie down in the accumulated heat of the little bedrooms after the long hot day and the breeze would stir almost imperceptibly outside and the smell of the swamp drift in through the rusty screens. Sleep would come easily and in the morning the red squirrel would be on the roof, tapping out his gay routine. I kept remembering everything, lying in bed in the mornings — the small steamboat that had a long rounded stern like the lip of a Ubangi, and how quietly she ran on the moonlight sails, when the older boys played their mandolins and the girls sang and we ate doughnuts dipped in sugar, and how sweet the music was on the water in the shining night, and what it had felt like to think about girls then. After breakfast we would go up to the store and the things were in the same place — the minnows in a bottle, the plugs and spinners disarranged and pawed over by the youngsters from the boys' camp, the Fig Newtons and the Beeman's gum. Outside, the road was tarred and cars stood in front of the store. Inside, all was just as it had always been, except there was more Coca-Cola and not so much Moxie and root beer and birch beer and sarsaparilla. We would walk out with a bottle of pop apiece and sometimes the pop would backfire up our noses and hurt. We explored the streams, quietly, where the turtles slid off the sunny logs and dug their way into the soft bottom; and we lay on the town wharf and fed worms to the tame bass. Everywhere we went I had trouble making out which was I, the one walking at my side, the one walking in my pants.

One afternoon while we were there at that lake a thunderstorm came up. It was like the revival of an old melodrama that I had seen long ago with childish awe. The second-act climax of the drama of the electrical disturbance over a lake in America had not changed in any important respect. This was the big scene, still the big scene. The whole thing was so familiar, the first feeling of oppression and heat and a general air around camp of not wanting to go very far away. In midafternoon (it was all the same) a curious darkening of the sky, and a lull in everything that had made life tick; and then the way the boats suddenly swung the other way at their moorings with the coming of a breeze out of the new quarter, and the premonitory rumble. Then the kettle drum, then the snare, then the bass drum and cymbals, then crackling light against the dark, and the gods grinning and licking their chops in the hills. Afterward the calm, the rain steadily rustling in the calm lake, the return of light and hope and spirits, and the campers running out in joy and relief to go swimming in the rain, their bright cries perpetuating the deathless joke about how they were getting simply drenched, and the children screaming with delight at the new sensation of bathing in the rain, and the joke about getting drenched linking the generations in a strong indestructible chain. And the comedian who waded in carrying an umbrella.

When the others went swimming my son said he was going in too. He pulled his dripping trunks from the line where they had hung all through the shower, and wrung them out. Languidly, and with no thought of going in, I watched him, his hard little body, skinny and bare, saw him wince slightly as he pulled up around his vitals the small, soggy, icy garment. As he buckled the swollen belt suddenly my groin felt the chill of death.

The Reader's Presence

1. In this essay, almost every word is deliberately chosen and intended to contribute to the meaning. Even the little words are important. For example, in paragraph 5, why does White say "*the* dragonfly" rather than "*a* dragonfly"? What difference does this word choice make?

2. In paragraph 4, White refers to a "creepy sensation." What is the basis of that sensation? Why is it "creepy"? In rereading the essay,

pay close attention to other examples of fear and anxiety. What connection do these have to White's main theme?

3. Go through the essay and identify words and images having to do with the sensory details of seeing, hearing, touching, and so on. How do these details contribute to the overall effect of the essay? How do they anticipate White's final paragraph?

Part II

Expository Writing: Shaping Information

34

Wendell Berry

The Pleasures of Eating

Wendell Berry (b. 1934) lives and farms in Kentucky. His novels, short stories, poems, and essays present his love for nature and his concerns with agriculture, the environment, and the maladies of modern industrial society. He has taught at New York University and the University of Kentucky, and his writing has been published in numerous journals, including the Nation, Prairie Schooner, *and the* Quarterly Review of Literature. *His essay "The Pleasures of Eating" comes from his book* What Are People For? *(1990). Berry's other works of nonfiction include* Standing on Earth: Selected Essays *(1991),* Sex, Economy, Freedom, and Community: Eight Essays *(1993), and* Another Turn of the Crank: Essays *(1995).* Fidelity: Five Stories *was published in 1992, and his* Collected Poems *was published in 1985.*

Like Noel Perrin, Donald Hall, and other writers with deep roots in America's rural landscape, Berry sees an intimate connection between his physical environment and his writing: "This place has become the form of my work as a poet the same way the sonnet has been the form and discipline of the work of other poets: if it doesn't fit it's not true."

Many times, after I have finished a lecture on the decline of American farming and rural life, someone in the audience has asked, "What can city people do?"

"Eat responsibly," I have usually answered. Of course, I have tried to explain what I meant, but afterward I have invariably felt that there was more to be said than I had been able to say. Now I would like to attempt a better explanation.

I begin with the proposition that eating is an agricultural act. Eating ends the annual drama of the food economy that begins with planting and birth. Most eaters, however, are no longer aware that this is true. They think of food as an agricultural product, perhaps, but they do not think of themselves as participants in agriculture. They think of themselves as "consumers." If they think beyond that, they recognize that they are passive consumers. They buy what they want — or what they have been persuaded to want — within the limits of what they can get. They pay, mostly without protest, what they are charged. And they mostly ignore certain critical questions about the quality and the cost of what they are sold: How fresh is it? How pure or clean is it, how free of dangerous chemicals? How far was it transported, and what did transportation add to the cost? How much did manufacturing or packaging or advertising add to the cost? When the food product has been "manufactured" or "processed" or "precooked," how has that affected its quality or nutritional value?

Most urban shoppers would tell you that food is processed on farms. But most of them do not know on what farms, or what kind of farms, or where the farms are, or what knowledge or skills are involved in farming. They apparently have little doubt that farms will continue to produce, but they do not know how or over what obstacles. For them, then, food is pretty much an abstract idea — something they do not know or imagine — until it appears on the grocery shelf or on the table.

The specialization of production induces specialization of consumption. Patrons of the entertainment industry, for example, entertain themselves less and less and have become more and more passively dependent on commercial suppliers. This is certainly also true of patrons of the food industry, who have tended more and more to be *mere* consumers — passive, uncritical, and dependent. Indeed, this sort of consumption may be said to be one of the chief goals of industrial production. The food industrialists have by now persuaded millions of consumers to prefer food that is already prepared. They will grow, deliver, and cook your food for you and (just like your mother) beg you to eat it. That they do not yet offer to insert it, prechewed, into your mouth is only because they have found no profitable way to do so. We may rest assured that they would be glad to find such a way. The ideal industrial food consumer would be strapped to a table with a tube running from the food factory directly into his or her stomach. (Think of the savings, the efficiency, and the effortlessness of such an arrangement!)

Perhaps I exaggerate, but not by much. The industrial eater is, in fact, one who does not know that eating is an agricultural act, who no longer knows or imagines the connections between eating and the land, and who is therefore necessarily passive and uncritical — in short, a victim. When food, in the minds of eaters, is no longer associated with farming and with the land, then the eaters are suffering a kind of cultural amnesia that is misleading and dangerous. The current version of the "dream home" of the future involves "effortless" shopping from a list of available goods on a television monitor and heating precooked food by remote control. Of course, this implies, and indeed depends on, a perfect ignorance of the history of the food that is consumed. It requires that the citizenry should give up their hereditary and sensible aversion to buying a pig in a poke. It wishes to make the selling of pigs in pokes an honorable and glamorous activity. The dreamer in this dream home will perforce know nothing about the kind or quality of this food, or where it came from, or how it was produced and prepared, or what ingredients, additives, and residues

5

it contains. Unless, that is, the dreamer undertakes a close and constant study of the food industry, in which case he or she might as well wake up and play an active and responsible part in the economy of food.

There is, then, a politics of food that, like any politics, involves our freedom. We still (sometimes) remember that we cannot be free if our minds and voices are controlled by someone else. But we have neglected to understand that neither can we be free if our food and its resources are controlled by someone else. The condition of the passive consumer of food is not a democratic condition. One reason to eat responsibly is to live free.

But, if there is a food politics, there are also food aesthetics and a food ethics, neither of which is dissociated from politics. Like industrial sex, industrial eating has become a degraded, poor, and paltry thing. Our kitchens and other eating places more and more resemble filling stations, as our homes more and more resemble motels. "Life is not very interesting," we seem to have decided. "Let its satisfactions be minimal, perfunctory, and fast." We hurry through our meals to go to work and hurry though our work in order to "recreate" ourselves in the evenings and on weekends and vacations. And then we hurry, with the greatest possible speed and noise and violence, through our recreation — for what? To eat the billionth hamburger at some fast-food joint hell-bent on increasing the "quality" of our life. And all this is carried out in a remarkable obliviousness of the causes and effects, the possibilities and the purposes of the life of the body in this world.

One will find this obliviousness represented in virgin purity in the advertisements of the food industry, in which the food wears as much makeup as the actors. If one gained one's knowledge of food — as some presumably do — from these advertisements, one would not know that the various edibles were ever living creatures, or that they all come from the soil, or that they were produced by work. The passive American consumer, sitting down to a meal of pre-prepared or fast food, confronts a platter covered with inert, anonymous substances that have been processed, dyed, breaded, sauced, gravied, ground, pulped, strained, blended, prettified, and sanitized beyond resemblance to any part of any creature that ever lived. The products of nature and agriculture have been made, to all appearances, the products of industry. Both eater and eaten are thus in exile from biological reality. And the result is a kind of solitude, unprecedented in human experience, in which the eater may think of eating as, first, a purely commercial transaction between him and a supplier, and then as a purely appetitive transaction between him and his food.

And this peculiar specialization of the act of eating is, again, of obvious benefit to the food industry, which has good reason to obscure the connection between food and farming. It would not do for the consumer to know that the hamburger she is eating came from a steer that spent much of its life standing deep in its own excrement in a feedlot, helping to

10

pollute the local streams, or that the calf that yielded the veal cutlet on her plate spent its life in a box in which it did not have room to turn around. And, though her sympathy for the coleslaw might be less tender, she should not be encouraged to meditate on the hygienic and biological implications of mile-square fields of cabbage, for vegetables grown in huge monocultures are dependent on toxic chemicals just as animals in close confinement are dependent on antibiotics and other drugs.

The consumer, that is to say, must be kept from discovering that, in the food industry — as in any other industry — the overriding concerns are not quality and health but volume and price. For decades now the entire industrial food economy, from the large farms and feedlots to the chains of fast-food restaurants and supermarkets, has been obsessed with volume. It has relentlessly increased scale in order to increase volume in order (presumably) to reduce costs. But, as scale increases, diversity declines; as diversity declines, so does health; as health declines, the dependence on drugs and chemicals necessarily increases. As capital replaces labor, it does so by substituting machines, drugs and chemicals for human workers and for the natural health and fertility of the soil. The food is produced by any means or any shortcuts that will increase profits. And the business of the cosmeticians of advertising is to persuade the consumer that food so produced is good, tasty, healthful, and a guarantee of marital fidelity and long life.

It is, then, indeed possible to be liberated from the husbandry and wifery of the old household food economy. But one can be thus liberated only by entering a trap — unless one sees ignorance and helplessness, as many people apparently do, as the signs of privilege. The trap is the ideal of industrialism: a walled city surrounded by valves that let merchandise in but no consciousness out. How does one escape this trap? Only voluntarily, the same way that one went in — by restoring one's consciousness of what is involved in eating, by reclaiming responsibility for one's own part in the food economy. One might begin with Sir Albert Howard's illuminating principle that we should understand "the whole problem of health in soil, plant, animal, and man as one great subject." Eaters, that is, must understand that eating takes place inescapably in the world, that it is inescapably an agricultural act, and that how we eat determines, to a considerable extent, the way the world is used. This is a simple way of describing a relationship that is inexpressibly complex. To eat responsibly is to understand and enact, so far as one can, this complex relationship.

What can one do? Here is a list, probably not definitive:

Participate in food production to the extent that you can. If you have a yard or even just a porch box or a pot in a sunny window, grow something to eat in it. Make a little compost of your kitchen scraps, and use it for fertilizer. Only by growing some food for yourself can you become acquainted with the beautiful energy cycle that revolves from soil to seed to flower to fruit to food to offal to decay, and around again. You will be fully responsible for any food that you grow for yourself, and you will know all about it. You will appreciate it fully, having known it all its life.

Prepare your own food. This means reviving in your own mind and life the arts of kitchen and household. This should enable you to eat more cheaply and give you a measure of "quality control." You will have some reliable knowledge of what has been added to the food you eat.

Learn the origins of the food you buy, and buy the food that is produced closest to your home. The idea that every locality should be, as much as possible, the source of its own food makes several kinds of sense. The locally produced food supply is the most secure, the freshest, and the easiest for local consumers to know about and to influence.

Whenever you can, deal directly with a local farmer, gardener, or orchardist. All the reasons listed for the previous suggestion apply here. In addition, by such dealing, you eliminate the whole pack of merchants, transporters, processors, packagers, and advertisers who thrive at the expense of both producers and consumers.

Learn, in self-defense, as much as you can of the economy and technology of industrial food production. What is added to food that is not food, and what do you pay for these additions?

Learn what is involved in the *best* farming and gardening.

Learn as much as you can, by direct observation and experience if possible, of the life histories of the food species.

The last suggestion seems particularly important to me. Many people are now as much estranged from the lives of domestic plants and animals (except for flowers and dogs and cats) as they are from the lives of the wild ones. This is regrettable, for these domestic creatures are in diverse ways attractive; there is much pleasure in knowing them. And, at their best, farming, animal husbandry, horticulture, and gardening are complex and comely arts; there is much pleasure in knowing them, too.

And it follows that there is great displeasure in knowing about a food   15
economy that degrades and abuses those arts and those plants and animals and the soil from which they come. For anyone who does know something of the modern history of food, eating away from home can be a chore. My own inclination is to eat seafood instead of red meat or poultry while I am traveling. Though I am by no means a vegetarian, I dislike the thought that some animal has been made miserable in order to feed me. If I am going to eat meat, I want it to be from an animal that has lived a pleasant, uncrowded life outdoors, on a bountiful pasture, with good water nearby and trees for shade. And I am getting almost as fussy about food plants. I like to eat vegetables and fruits that I know have lived happily and healthily in good soil — not the products of the huge, bechemicaled factory-fields that I have seen, for example, in the Central Valley of California. The industrial farm is said to have been patterned on the factory production line. In practice, it invariably looks more like a concentration camp.

The pleasure of eating should be an *extensive* pleasure, not that of the mere gourmet. People who know the garden in which their vegetables have grown and know that the garden is healthy will remember the beauty of the growing plants, perhaps in the dewy first light of morning when gardens are at their best. Such a memory involves itself with the food and is one of the pleasures of eating. The knowledge of the good health of the garden relieves and frees and comforts the eater. The same goes for eating meat. The thought of the good pasture, and of the calf contentedly grazing, flavors the steak. Some, I know, will think it blood-thirsty or worse to eat a fellow creature you have known all its life. On the contrary, I think, it means that you eat with understanding and with gratitude. A significant part of the pleasure of eating is in one's accurate consciousness of the lives and the world from which food comes. The pleasure of eating, then, may be the best available standard for our health. And this pleasure, I think, is pretty fully available to the urban consumer who will make the necessary effort.

I mentioned earlier the politics, aesthetics, and ethics of food. But to speak of the pleasure of eating is to go beyond these categories. Eating with the fullest pleasure — pleasure, that is, that does not depend on ig-norance — is perhaps the profoundest enactment of our connection with the world. In this pleasure we experience and celebrate our dependence and our gratitude, for we are living from mystery, from creatures we did not make and powers we cannot comprehend. When I think of the mean-ing of food, I always remember these lines by the poet William Carlos Williams, which seem to me merely honest:

> There is nothing to eat,
>   seek it where you will,
>   but the body of the Lord.
> The blessed plants
>   and the sea, yield it
>   to the imagination
> intact.

The Reader's Presence

1. Berry presents his essay as an answer to the question of "what city people can do" to reverse the decline of farming and rural life. To this end, he provides a list of suggestions for action. How do these suggestions relate to points Berry discusses elsewhere in the essay? Do you find his suggestions persuasive?
2. Consider the metaphors Berry brings up to describe "industrial" food production. What types of images does he invoke? How does he use these comparisons to strengthen his argument that our soci-ety's relation to food is unnatural?
3. Berry titles his essay "The Pleasures of Eating," yet he spends most of it discussing the responsibility of consumers, the "politics

of food," and the problems of the food industry. Why do you think he leaves the idea of *pleasure* until the end of the essay? How do the first few pages color your understanding of Berry's statement that "there is much pleasure in knowing" domestic animals and plants?

35

Sven Birkerts

Paging the Self: Privacies of Reading

Sven Birkerts (b. 1951) calls himself an "amateur" literary critic because he was not trained in graduate school and does not advance any particular school of literary theory. His love of reading, he says, developed when he worked as a bookstore clerk. Nonetheless, Birkerts has made his career writing critical essays and teaching. After magazines like the New Republic *and the* Boston Review *began to publish his work, Harvard University invited Birkerts to teach expository writing there. In addition to reviews and essays, Birkerts has published several books, including* An Artificial Wilderness: Essays on Twentieth-Century Literature *(1987) and* The Electric Life: Essays on Modern Poetry *(1989). He is especially interested in "the survival of print-based literary and cultural values in an age of electronic communications." The essay "Paging the Self: Privacies of Reading" comes from his book* The Gutenberg Elegies: The Fate of Reading in an Electronic Age *(1994).*

When asked about the experience of writing in today's electronic age — about writing by using computers and word processors — Birkerts responded that word processors are potentially harmful because they remove the writer from the "whole life" of the text and the process of revision. "I believe writing is something that you have to feel your way through to. In a way it's a bodily thing too — there's a kind of bodily intuition that underlies good writing, and I don't think that comes immediately. I think it finally results from many rewrites, after you've lived with a passage long enough that it takes on that life."

I'm going to take it as an axiom that the act of reading plays a vital role in the forming and conditioning of sensibility in the life of the committed reader. What interests me is to try to puzzle out the nature of that role. But before I do, I feel that I should pause over the word *sensibility*. It is, I realize, a "humanist" term that is slipping from usage; in our age of hard-edged critical terminology it suggests a fin-de-siècle preciosity. What is sensibility, besides being the counterpart to *sense?* It is neither self nor ego; neither identity nor personality. While these are designations for

reference for something

something one either *has* or *is*, sensibility is more of a construct. The old sense of the word is of a refinement or cultivation of presence; it refers to the part of the inner life that is not given but fashioned: a defining, if cloudy, complex of attitudes, predilections and honed responses. And for this very reason I want to have the term available. For while it can be many things, serious reading is above all an agency of self-making. When undertaken freely, the effort of engaging a book shows a desire to actualize and augment certain inner powers. The reader assumes the possibility of deepened self-understanding, and therefore recognizes the self as malleable. (Reading is the intimate, perhaps secret, part of a larger project, one that finally has little to do with the more societally oriented conceptions of the individual.)

thesis

progression

To talk about reading and the part it plays in developing the sensibility I will need to distinguish not only among different kinds of reading, but also to point out some ways in which reading changes across the trajectory of the reader's career. The process that begins, in most cases, with being read to, and which activates the most intense sorts of identifications in the independent reading of childhood, is something else again in adolescence, and again in full-fledged maturity, and yet again, I would guess, in later years. But because from adulthood on we are talking about sensibilities that have more or less crystallized, we may gain more by looking at the reading years of childhood and adolescence.

(1)

A Being read to, while not strictly reading, is nonetheless not an entirely passive absorption either, as any parent can tell you. The child fleshes out the narrative through imaginative projection, and questions the text constantly. "Why is he crying?" "Is she going to get hurt?" She also engages the book itself, looking at the illustrations, monitoring the momentum of the turning pages, and, with the increase of aptitude, noting the correlation between what is being read out and the placement of words on the page. I see my daughter, now five, hovering on the brink of literary independence. She still loves being read to, but she breaks the flow of the story constantly by fastening on some word and working to sound it out. I can almost see the cognitive machinery at work. My hope is that as my daughter acquires mastery over words and meanings she will also discover that specialized and self-directed inwardness that makes private reading so rewarding.

b Independent childhood reading seems to continue and elaborate upon the process of imaginative projection initiated through listening. It is, beautifully and openly, a voluntary participation in an ulterior scheme of reality. We might also call it pure escape, except that getting *away* is probably less important than getting *to*. Early childhood reading is the free indulgence of fantasy and desire, done because it feels good. I remember the sensation of reading (Freudians can note this) as one of returning to a warm and safe environment, one that I had complete control over. When I picked up a book it was as much to get back to something as it was to set off to the new. The last thing the child thinks about is self-improvement; nor is he, in any obvious sense, trying to figure out the terms of existence (though such figuring probably goes on unconsciously).

Transition

The main difference between childhood reading and reading under- 5
taken later is that in the former, futurity — the idea of one's life as a
project, or adventure, or set of possibilities — has not yet entered the
calculation. The child reads within a bubble. He is like Narcissus staring
at his lovely image in the water's mirror. He is still sealed off from any
notion of the long-term unfolding of the life, except in the perfected terms
of fantasy: *I, too, will be a pirate . . .*

The change comes during adolescence, that biological and psychological free-fire zone during which the profoundest existential questions are
not only posed, but lived. Who am I? Why am I doing what I'm doing?
What *should* I do? What will happen to me? It is in adolescence that most
of us grasp that life — our own life — is a problem to be solved, that a
set of personal unknowns must now be factored together with the frightening variables of experience. The future suddenly appears — it is the
space upon which the answers will be inscribed. The very idea of futurity
now becomes charged with electricity.

This self-intensity, which pushes toward the future as toward some
kind of release, is highly conducive to reading. The book — the novel,
that is — becomes the site for testing transformations. Indeed, whatever
else it may be, diversion or escape, the novel at this stage of life is primarily a screen that will accept various versions and projections of the self.

These projections are different from those of the child reader. The
child manipulates fantasy stuff that is still undiluted by the reality principle. The boy dreaming of river rafts or space travel is not yet constrained
by the impediments that will eventually curb and instruct his desires. Not
so for the adolescent. A different reality has announced itself. Socially,
sexually, and even within the bosom of the family, that thing grownups
call "life" has begun to bare its face.

Adolescence is the ideal laboratory for the study of reading and self-
formation. Or maybe I should say, a laboratory for studying the *ideal* impact
of reading on that formation. For of course it is no secret that fewer and
fewer adolescents now turn to reading on their own. Private reading still
exists, but more exclusively — organized sports and "lessons" as well as
seductive electronic games have made deep inroads upon the expanses of
dreamy solitude that were once the given of preadult years. And it is precisely *Transition*
this reading, not that done for school assignments, that concerns me here.

How does reading work on the psyche during what is surely its most 10
volatile period of change? There is no pinning it down, naturally, but we
might begin with the most obvious sort of answer: the role of specific
books and characters. We get reports of this influence all the time in interviews and memoirs. The subject (usually someone who has achieved
something noteworthy) tells of *living* with Tom Sawyer or David
Copperfield or Elizabeth Bennett.[1] There follows the desire to do what

---

[1]*Tom Sawyer . . . Elizabeth Bennett:* Characters from Mark Twain's *The Adventures
of Tom Sawyer* (1876), Charles Dickens's *David Copperfield* (1850), and Jane Austen's
Pride and Prejudice (1813). — Eds.

Tom did, to be like young Elizabeth. These recognitions are eventually externalized as ideals and in that form guide the behavior along after the spell of the reading passes. I vividly remember situations in which I acted in a certain way — more bravely, more recklessly — because I believed that that was what Jack London would have done (I had all but memorized Irving Stone's romantic biography *Jack London: Sailor on Horseback*). To be sure, books are not the only places where adolescents can look for role models. Ever vigilant, they pick up moves and attitude display from rock stars, athletes, and sulky actors.

But the identifications we take from books go deeper. They form the very basis of childhood play, and run like a stream alongside the less-rooted transactions of adolescence. They often function as a kind of (pardon the jargon) "meta-narrative." If one is *not* Tom Sawyer or Elizabeth Bennett or whoever (and identifications usually are not absolute) one nevertheless performs in a magnetic field that somehow contains them. The admiring reader acts in a world that is half that of the book and half that of the real life circumstance. Every action is ennobled and exaggerated in significance because the reader imagines it brightly transposed onto the field of the book — the field of a higher and more lasting reality.

Later, as adult claims displace childish needs and as the adolescent matures, reading takes on a slightly different function. Now the reader begins to borrow from the book a sense of consequential destiny that is so absent from the daily routine. For what the novel transmits, over and above its plot and character, is the bewitching assumption of connectedness. Purpose. Meaning. The characters and situations, products of the author's creative intention, are knit together into a larger wholeness. The least movement or action *tends toward;* every action is held within the larger context which is implicitly, artistically purposeful. Our own lives may drift every which way toward the future, but the lives of the characters are aimed toward determined ends. As readers we take this in, unconsciously, and we may begin to conceive of our own actions under this same aspect of fatedness. Certainly we do so while we are reading or otherwise still in thrall to the book. And we thereby become important — just when we need to most. Our lives feel pointed toward significance and resolution; we feel ourselves living toward meaning, or at least living in the light of its possibility. I don't know that this more sustained self-charge is available anywhere else but in books. Movies are too compacted and visually determinate to encourage such operations. They don't last long enough, nor do cinematic images impinge on the memory in the same way that do the images we coproduce. And certainly little in the day-to-day world conveys to the adolescent some larger momentum toward meaning. He needs something with which to fend off the most obvious version of futurity, that incarnated in his parents, whose lives must appear tyrannized by empty ritual and pettiness.

My own shields, I remember, were other alienated solitaries. I searched high and low for novels with troubled protagonists. I soothed

myself and fortified myself with novels by Thomas Wolfe, William Goldman, J.D. Salinger, and others. Their situations became the stuff of my
own cocoon; they were with me as I sharpened my grievances against the
world. When I went against my parents and teachers I was drawing
strength from their example. I took onto myself some of what I saw as
their specialness. They *had* to be special, for they were the subjects of
their own books. I was special, too — subject at least of my life.

Again, I am talking about the reading of fiction — novels and stories
that are, to a greater or lesser degree, simulations of reality. This does not
mean that I am privileging the genre above all others, but there is a very special transformation that takes place when we read fiction that is not experienced in nonfiction. This transformation, or catalyzing action, can be seen
to play a vital part in what we might call, grandly, existential self-formation.

When we read a sentence from a work of nonfiction — a history or
a study of some topic, say — the words intersect with the psychic continuum, but they do not significantly modify it. We do what we need to in
order to pay attention, to receive the information, but we do not reposi-
tion the self. Consider, for example, this straightforward sentence from
The Columbia History of the World: "When we talk about human evolution, we are dealing with two different kinds of processes: the evolution
of the human body and the evolution of human behavior." As we read
the words, we decode the syntactical logic of the statement and extract
the idea content, the sense. If there is an authorial "voice," we don't focus
upon it. The prose is a conveyor for the concept, a means to an end. We
make a place for it in that interior zone where we process verbal information, but we don't ourselves change. Unless, of course, we encounter an
idea that can be translated into relevant personal terms and thus affect
our understanding of ourselves. But even then we react less to the words
than to the implications we dig out for ourselves.

Now open a novel:

> If you really want to hear about it, the first thing you'll probably want to
> know is where I was born, and what my lousy childhood was like, and all
> that David Copperfield kind of crap, but I don't feel like going into it, if you
> want to know the truth.

This, too, is information, but it is obviously information of a very different kind. Reading the earlier sentence about evolution, we make no significant internal adjustment because it is not ourselves — as selves —
that we hear addressed. In the second sentence, the opening of J.D.
Salinger's *The Catcher in the Rye*, the voice is primary. The voice proposes a self and we must greet it accordingly. We therefore heed the casual, alienated, determinedly forthright tone and filter the sense of the
statement through that. But we cannot heed and filter so long as our own
self is in dormancy — either we decide to engage Holden Caulfield's
voice or we close the covers on the book.

Salinger, via Holden, posits a world. Holden's world. And the reader who would hear more about it is forced to open up a subjective space large enough to contain it. The opening of that space is the crucial move, for it requires the provisional loosening of whatever fixed attitudes and preconceptions we may have. In that space, two versions of reality will be stirred together — the reader's and the author's. A hybrid life will start up. Not the author's life, not fully the character's, and not quite our own though all these must be present for the mysterious catalysis of reading.

To read the book we must, in effect, bracket off our own reality and replace it with Holden's. Better, we must use what we know of our world to create his. His can only exist at the expense of ours, though — this is the law of fiction. We agree to suspend our self-grounded posture, our place in the "real" world, in order to make room for Holden's alternative sense of things. We create the textures of his reality with what we have learned from our own. But we don't disappear, either. Our awareness, our sense of life, gets filtered into the character, where it becomes strangely detached from us. The novel, in a manner of speaking, smelts its reader, extracting responsive emotions and apprehensions and then showing them forth in an aesthetic frame. Distanced from these parts of ourselves, then, we (especially as adolescents) possess them in a semiobjectified form. We begin to understand how they matter in the larger human ecology.

We don't entirely become Holden, but we abide by the terms of the world he narrates to us, agreeing to its provisions at least for the duration of our reading. We slip free from our most burdensome layer of contingent identity in order to experience the consciousness of another. This consciousness and its world are, in turn, the product of the author's consciousness. And as we read, we find that Holden's (or any character's) world manifests a kind of wholeness. This fictional world has meaning, even if Holden's own life does not appear to. Unconsciously we attune ourselves to the unitary scheme that underlies the disorder he pitches around in. This scheme, like the white page that underlies the printed words, is the surface that holds our projections. And when we close the book, we return to ourselves. Those projections stream back, only now they have been tested and modified into new shapes and they become elements in our understanding of life. We do not learn so much from the novel itself, the lessons of its situations, as we do from having stayed free of our customary boundaries. On return, those boundaries seem more articulated, more our own; we understand their degree of permeability, and this is a vital kind of knowing.

I recall from adolescent reading the powerful sensation of double consciousness, how I went about as if in the active possession of a secret. The secret had less to do with whatever specific narrative I was caught up in, and much more with the knowledge that I had a gateway out of the narrow, baffling, and often threatening world of high school.

What does all this have to do with self-formation? How does it differ from simple escape? I have to answer with my own reader's conviction, my sense that sufficient exposure to the coherent and meaningful realities represented in the pages of novels began to lay down the traces of an

20

expectation in me. They awoke a whole set of private determinations about my life in the future — the life I *had* to have. Even when the awareness of meaning or the sense of fatedness were not to be gathered from my sur- roundings, novels gave me the grounds, the incentive, to live *as if*. Indeed, more than anything else, reading created in me the awareness that life could be lived and known as a unified whole; that the patterns which make mean- ing are disclosed gradually. That awareness, I admit, gets harder to sustain with the passing of time — life feels much less concentrated as one grows away from the urgencies of adolescence — but I would not dream of sur- rendering it. Without that faith, that sense of imminent resolution, the events of the day-to-day would be like some vast assortment of colored beads without a string to hold them together.

The Reader's Presence

1. Birkerts focuses on the vital role reading plays "in the forming and conditioning of sensibility in the life of the committed reader" (paragraph 1). He admits, however, that both the word *sensibility* and the act of reading are rapidly becoming obsolete. How might you characterize Birkerts's intended audience for this essay, and what specific effect(s) does he expect to have on this audience?

2. Donald Hall's essay "On Moving One's Lips, While Reading" (page 91) also addresses the need for sustaining the art — and the pleasures — of reading. Although Hall laments the disap- pearance of the more public forms of reading and declaiming, Birkerts celebrates the "Privacies of Reading." Reread both essays carefully, and compare and contrast them in terms of the strate- gies each uses to appeal to a specific audience.

3. Birkerts explores the "ways in which reading changes across the tra- jectory of the reader's career" (paragraph 2). Identify — and ex- amine the implications of — each of the changes he notes. What seems to change more, the material that people read at each stage of their development, or their reasons and rewards for reading it? Point to and analyze specific passages to support your response.

4. At various points in the essay, the author compares serious read- ing with other pursuits, including movie viewing and the reading of nonfiction. In each case, serious reading is privileged above the other options. Which of these contrasts seem most compelling to you? Why? Did you find yourself challenging any of these com- parisons? If so, why? What counterexamples can you offer to the examples Birkerts provides? For instance, in paragraphs 15 and 16 he quotes from a history text and a novel to illustrate the rela- tive unimportance of the authorial "voice" in nonfiction. Draw on the nonfiction essays in *The Writer's Presence* as you develop counterexamples to Birkerts's claim.

36

Stephen L. Carter
The Insufficiency of Honesty

Law professor and writer Stephen L. Carter (b. 1954) is an insightful and in-cisive critic of contemporary cultural politics. His first book, Reflections of an Af-firmative Action Baby *(1992), criticizes affirmative action policies that reinforce racial stereotypes rather than break down structures of discrimination. Carter's critique emerges from his own experience as an African American student at Stan-ford University and at Yale University Law School. After graduating from Yale, he served as a law clerk for Supreme Court justice Thurgood Marshall and even-tually joined the faculty at Yale as professor of law. Carter has published widely on legal and social topics, including his books* The Culture of Disbelief: How American Law and Politics Trivialize Religious Devotion *(1993) and* The Confir-mation Mess: Cleaning Up the Federal Appointments Process *(1994). "The Insuf-ficiency of Honesty" appears in his most recent book,* Integrity *(1996).*

A couple of years ago I began a university commencement address by telling the audience that I was going to talk about integrity. The crowd broke into applause. Applause! Just because they had heard the word "in-tegrity": that's how starved for it they were. They had no idea how I was using the word, or what I was going to say about integrity, or, indeed, whether I was for it or against it. But they knew they liked the idea of talking about it.

Very well, let us consider this word "integrity." Integrity is like the weather: everybody talks about it but nobody knows what to do about it. Integrity is that stuff that we always want more of. Some say that we need to return to the good old days when we had a lot more of it. Others say that we as a nation have never really had enough of it. Hardly anybody stops to explain exactly what we mean by it, or how we know it is a good thing, or why everybody needs to have the same amount of it. Indeed, the only trouble with integrity is that everybody who uses the word seems to mean something slightly different.

For instance, when I refer to integrity, do I mean simply "honesty"? The answer is no; although honesty is a virtue of importance, it is a dif-ferent virtue from integrity. Let us, for simplicity, think of honesty as not lying; and let us further accept Sissela Bok's definition of a lie: "any intentionally deceptive message which is *stated*." Plainly, one cannot have integrity without being honest (although, as we shall see, the matter gets complicated), but one can certainly be honest and yet have little integrity.

When I refer to integrity, I have something very specific in mind. Integrity, as I will use the term, requires three steps: discerning what is right and what is wrong; acting on what you have discerned, even at personal cost; and saying openly that you are acting on your understanding of right and wrong. The first criterion captures the idea that integrity requires a degree of moral reflectiveness. The second brings in the ideal of a person of integrity as steadfast, a quality that includes keeping one's commitments. The third reminds us that a person of integrity can be trusted.

The first point to understand about the difference between honesty and integrity is that a person may be entirely honest without ever engaging in the hard work of discernment that integrity requires; she may tell us quite truthfully what she believes without ever taking the time to figure out whether what she believes is good and right and true. The problem may be as simple as someone's foolishly saying something that hurts a friend's feelings; a few moments of thought would have revealed the likelihood of the hurt and the lack of necessity for the comment. Or the problem may be more complex, as when a man who was raised from birth in a society that preaches racism states his belief in one race's inferiority as a fact, without ever really considering that perhaps this deeply held view is wrong. Certainly the racist is being honest — he is telling us what he actually thinks — but his honesty does not add up to integrity.

TELLING EVERYTHING YOU KNOW

A wonderful epigram sometimes attributed to the filmmaker Sam Goldwyn goes like this: "The most important thing in acting is honesty; once you learn to fake that, you're in." The point is that honesty can be something one *seems* to have. Without integrity, what passes for honesty often is nothing of the kind; it is fake honesty — or it is honest but irrelevant and perhaps even immoral.

Consider an example. A man who has been married for fifty years confesses to his wife on his deathbed that he was unfaithful thirty-five years earlier. The dishonesty was killing his spirit, he says. Now he has cleared his conscience and is able to die in peace.

The husband has been honest — sort of. He has certainly unburdened himself. And he has probably made his wife (soon to be his widow) quite miserable in the process, because even if she forgives him, she will not be able to remember him with quite the vivid image of love and loyalty that she had hoped for. Arranging his own emotional affairs to ease his transition to death, he has shifted to his wife the burden of confusion and pain, perhaps for the rest of her life. Moreover, he has attempted his

5

honesty at the one time in his life when it carries no risk; acting in accordance with what you think is right and risking no loss in the process is a rather thin and unadmirable form of honesty.

Besides, even though the husband has been honest in a sense, he has now twice been unfaithful to his wife: once thirty-five years ago, when he had his affair, and again when, nearing death, he decided that his own peace of mind was more important than hers. In trying to be honest he has violated his marriage vow by acting toward his wife not with love but with naked and perhaps even cruel self-interest.

As my mother used to say, you don't have to tell people everything   10
you know. Lying and nondisclosure, as the law often recognizes, are not the same thing. Sometimes it is actually illegal to tell what you know, as, for example, in the disclosure of certain financial information by market insiders. Or it may be unethical, as when a lawyer reveals a confidence entrusted to her by a client. It may be simple bad manners, as in the case of a gratuitous comment to a colleague on his or her attire. And it may be subject to religious punishment, as when a Roman Catholic priest breaks the seal of the confessional — an offense that carries automatic excommunication.

In all the cases just mentioned, the problem with telling everything you know is that somebody else is harmed. Harm may not be the intention, but it is certainly the effect. Honesty is most laudable when we risk harm to ourselves; it becomes a good deal less so if we instead risk harm to others when there is no gain to anyone other than ourselves. Integrity may counsel keeping our secrets in order to spare the feelings of others. Sometimes, as in the example of the wayward husband, the reason we want to tell what we know is precisely to shift our pain onto somebody else — a course of action dictated less by integrity than by self-interest. Fortunately, integrity and self-interest often coincide, as when a politician of integrity is rewarded with our votes. But often they do not, and it is at those moments that our integrity is truly tested.

ERROR

Another reason that honesty alone is no substitute for integrity is that if forthrightness is not preceded by discernment, it may result in the expression of an incorrect moral judgment. In other words, I may be honest about what I believe, but if I have never tested my beliefs, I may be wrong. And here I mean "wrong" in a particular sense: the proposition in question is wrong if I would change my mind about it after hard moral reflection.

Consider this example. Having been taught all his life that women are not as smart as men, a manager gives the women on his staff less-challenging assignments than he gives the men. He does this, he believes, for their own benefit: he does not want them to fail, and he believes that they will if he gives them tougher assignments. Moreover, when one of the women on his staff does poor work, he does not berate her as harshly as he would a man, because he expects nothing more. And he claims to be acting with integrity because he is acting according to his own deepest beliefs.

The manager fails the most basic test of integrity. The question is not whether his actions are consistent with what he most deeply believes but whether he has done the hard work of discerning whether what he most deeply believes is right. The manager has not taken this harder step.

Moreover, even within the universe that the manager has constructed   15
for himself, he is not acting with integrity. Although he is obviously wrong to think that the women on his staff are not as good as the men, even were he right, that would not justify applying different standards to their work. By so doing he betrays both his obligation to the institution that employs him and his duty as a manager to evaluate his employees.

The problem that the manager faces is an enormous one in our practical politics, where having the dialogue that makes democracy work can seem impossible because of our tendency to cling to our views even when we have not examined them. As Jean Bethke Elshtain has said, borrowing from John Courtney Murray, our politics are so fractured and contentious that we often cannot reach *disagreement*. Our refusal to look closely at our own most cherished principles is surely a large part of the reason. Socrates thought the unexamined life not worth living. But the unhappy truth is that few of us actually have the time for constant reflection on our views — on public or private morality. Examine them we must, however, or we will never know whether we might be wrong.

None of this should be taken to mean that integrity as I have described it presupposes a single correct truth. If, for example, your integrity-guided search tells you that affirmative action is wrong, and my integrity-guided search tells me that affirmative action is right, we need not conclude that one of us lacks integrity. As it happens, I believe — both as a Christian and as a secular citizen who struggles toward moral understanding — that we *can* find true and sound answers to our moral questions. But I do not pretend to have found very many of them, nor is an exposition of them my purpose here.

It is the case not that there aren't any right answers but that, given human fallibility, we need to be careful in assuming that we have found them. However, today's political talk about how it is wrong for the government to impose one person's morality on somebody else is just mindless chatter. *Every* law imposes one person's morality on somebody else, because law has only two functions: to tell people to do what they would rather not or to forbid them to do what they would.

And if the surveys can be believed, there is far more moral agreement in America than we sometimes allow ourselves to think. One of the reasons that character education for young people makes so much sense to so many people is precisely that there seems to be a core set of moral understandings — we might call them the American Core — that most of us accept. Some of the virtues in this American Core are, one hopes, relatively noncontroversial. About 500 American communities have signed on to Michael Josephson's program to emphasize the "six pillars" of good character: trustworthiness, respect, responsibility, caring, fairness, and citizenship. These virtues might lead to a similarly noncontroversial set of political values: having an honest regard for ourselves and others, protecting freedom of thought and religious belief, and refusing to steal or murder.

HONESTY AND COMPETING RESPONSIBILITIES

A further problem with too great an exaltation of honesty is that it   20
may allow us to escape responsibilities that morality bids us bear. If honesty is substituted for integrity, one might think that if I say I am not planning to fulfill a duty, I need not fulfill it. But it would be a peculiar morality indeed that granted us the right to avoid our moral responsibilities simply by stating our intention to ignore them. Integrity does not permit such an easy escape.

Consider an example. Before engaging in sex with a woman, her lover tells her that if she gets pregnant, it is her problem, not his. She says that she understands. In due course she does wind up pregnant. If we believe, as I hope we do, that the man would ordinarily have a moral responsibility toward both the child he will have helped to bring into the world and the child's mother, then his honest statement of what he intends does not spare him that responsibility.

This vision of responsibility assumes that not all moral obligations stem from consent or from a stated intention. The linking of obligations to promises is a rather modern and perhaps uniquely Western way of looking at life, and perhaps a luxury that the well-to-do can afford. As Fred and Shulamit Korn (a philosopher and an anthropologist) have pointed out, "If one looks at ethnographic accounts of other societies, one finds that, while obligations everywhere play a crucial role in social life, promising is not preeminent among the sources of obligation and is not even mentioned by most anthropologists." The Korns have made a study of Tonga, where promises are virtually unknown but the social order is remarkably stable. If life without any promises seems extreme, we Americans sometimes go too far the other way, parsing not only our contracts but even out marriage vows in order to discover the absolute minimum obligation that we have to others as a result of our promises.

That some societies in the world have worked out evidently functional structures of obligation without the need for promise or consent does not tell us what *we* should do. But it serves as a reminder of the basic proposition that our existence in civil society creates a set of mutual

responsibilities that philosophers used to capture in the fiction of the social contract. Nowadays, here in America, people seem to spend their
time thinking of even cleverer ways to avoid their obligations, instead of
doing what integrity commands and fulfilling them. And all too often
honesty is their excuse.

The Reader's Presence

1. If Carter intends his essay to be a discussion of honesty, why does
   he begin with a consideration of the concept of integrity? How are
   the terms related? In what important ways are they different?
   What does integrity involve that honesty doesn't?
2. Notice that in this essay Carter never once offers a dictionary definition of the words honesty or integrity. Look up each term in a
   standard dictionary. As a reader, do you think such definitions
   would have made Carter's distinctions more clear? Why do you
   think he chose not to define the words according to their common
   dictionary meanings? How does he define them?
3. Though honesty and integrity may seem to be individual, moral
   virtues, Carter concludes his essay with a discussion of practical
   American politics. How are his earlier considerations of honesty
   and integrity related to his conclusion? Explain why, in his terms,
   integrity leads to a better society than does honesty. Abraham
   Lincoln liked to say that "honesty is the best policy." Was he
   wrong?

37

Amy Cunningham

Why Women Smile

*Amy Cunningham (b. 1955) has been writing on psychological issues and
modern life for magazines such as* Redbook, Glamour, *and the* Washington Post
Magazine *since she graduated from the University of Virginia in 1977 with a
bachelor's degree in English. Cunningham says that the essay reprinted here grew
out of her own experience as an "easy to get along with person" who was raised
by Southerners in the suburbs of Chicago. She also recalls that when writing it, "I
was unhappy with myself for taking too long, for not being efficient the way
I thought a professional writer should be — but the work paid off and now I*

(handwritten top margin: Q: Is smiling an instinct on based on cultural influences?)

think it is one of the best essays I've written." "Why Women Smile" originally appeared in Lear's *in 1993.*

Looking back on her writing career, Cunningham notes, "When I was younger I thought if you had talent you would make it as a writer. I'm surprised to realize now that good writing has less to do with talent and more to do with the discipline of staying seated in the chair, by yourself, in front of the computer and getting the work done."

After smiling brilliantly for nearly four decades, I now find myself trying to quit. Or, at the very least, seeking to lower the wattage a bit.

Not everyone I know is keen on this. My smile has gleamed like a cheap plastic night-light so long and so reliably that certain friends and relatives worry that my mood will darken the moment my smile dims. "Gee," one says, "I associate you with your smile. It's the essence of you. I should think you'd want to smile more!" But the people who love me best agree that my smile — which springs forth no matter where I am or how I feel — hasn't been serving me well. Said my husband recently, "Your smiling face and unthreatening demeanor make people like you in a fuzzy way, but that doesn't seem to be what you're after these days."

(handwritten margin: What does he mean by this? / How does the sentence pump up the central purpose of the essay?)

(handwritten: Why does she use this as a signal to stop smiling for the wrong reasons?)

Smiles are not the small and innocuous things they appear to be: Too many of us smile in lieu of showing what's really on our minds. Indeed, the success of the women's movement might be measured by the sincerity — and lack of it — in our smiles. Despite all the work we American women have done to get and maintain full legal control of our bodies, not to mention our destinies, we still don't seem to be fully in charge of a couple of small muscle groups in our faces.

We smile so often and so promiscuously — when we're angry, when we're tense, when we're with children, when we're being photographed, when we're interviewing for a job, when we're meeting candidates to employ — that the Smiling Woman has become a peculiarly American archetype. This isn't entirely a bad thing, of course. A smile lightens the load, diffuses unpleasantness, redistributes nervous tension. Women doctors smile more than their male counterparts, studies show, and are better liked by their patients.

Oscar Wilde's old saw that "a woman's face is her work of fiction" is often quoted to remind us that what's on the surface may have little connection to what we're feeling. What is it in our culture that keeps our smiles on automatic pilot? The behavior seems to be an equal blend of nature and nurture. Research has demonstrated that since females often mature earlier than males and are less irritable, girls smile more than boys from the very beginning. But by adolescence, the differences in the smiling rates of boys and girls are so robust that it's clear the culture has done more than its share of the dirty work. Just think of the mothers who painstakingly embroidered the words ENTER SMILING on little samplers, and then hung their handiwork on doors by golden chains. Translation: "Your real emotions aren't welcome here."

5

Clearly, our instincts are another factor. Our smiles have their roots in the greetings of monkeys, who pull their lips up and back to show their fear of attack, as well as their reluctance to vie for a position of dominance. And like the opossum caught in the light by the clattering garbage cans, we, too, flash toothy grimaces when we make major mistakes. By declaring ourselves nonthreatening, our smiles provide an extremely versatile means of protection.

Our earliest baby smiles are involuntary reflexes having only the vaguest connection to contentment or comfort. In short, we're genetically wired to pull on our parents' heartstrings. As Desmond Morris explains in *Babywatching,* this is our way of attaching ourselves to our caretakers, as truly as baby chimps clench their mothers' fur. Even as babies we're capable of projecting onto others (in this case, our parents) the feelings we know we need to get back in return.

Bona fide social smiles occur at two-and-a-half to three months of age, usually a few weeks after we first start gazing with intense interest into the faces of our parents. By the time we are six months old, we are smiling and laughing regularly in reaction to tickling, feedings, blown raspberries, hugs, and peekaboo games. Even babies who are born blind intuitively know how to react to pleasurable changes with a smile, though their first smiles start later than those of sighted children.

Psychologists and psychiatrists have noted that babies also smile and laugh with relief when they realize that something they thought might be dangerous is not dangerous after all. Kids begin to invite their parents to indulge them with "scary" approach-avoidance games; they love to be chased or tossed up into the air. (It's interesting to note that as adults, we go through the same gosh-that's-shocking-and-dangerous-but-it's-okay-to-laugh-and-smile cycles when we listen to raunchy stand-up comics.)

From the wilds of New Guinea to the sidewalks of New York, smiles   10
are associated with joy, relief, and amusement. But smiles are by no means limited to the expression of positive emotions: People of many different cultures smile when they are frightened, embarrassed, angry, or miserable. In Japan, for instance, a smile is often used to hide pain or sorrow.

Psychologist Paul Ekman, the head of the University of California's Human Interaction Lab in San Francisco, has identified 18 distinct types of smiles, including those that show misery, compliance, fear, and contempt. The smile of true merriment, which Dr. Ekman calls the Duchenne Smile, after the 19th century French doctor who first studied it, is characterized by heightened circulation, a feeling of exhilaration, and the employment of two major facial muscles: the zygomaticus major of the lower face, and the orbicularis oculi, which crinkles the skin around the eyes. But since the average American woman's smile often has less to do with her actual state of happiness than it does with the social pressure to smile no matter what, her baseline social smile isn't apt to be a felt expression that engages the eyes like this. Ekman insists that if people learned to read smiles, they could see the sadness, misery, or pain lurking there, plain as day.

Evidently, a woman's happy, willing deference is something the world wants visibly demonstrated. Woe to the waitress, the personal assistant or receptionist, the flight attendant, or any other woman in the line of public service whose smile is not offered up to the boss or client as proof that there are no storm clouds — no kids to support, no sleep that's been missed — rolling into the sunny workplace landscape. Women are expected to smile no matter where they line up on the social, cultural, or economic ladder: College professors are criticized for not smiling, political spouses are pilloried for being too serious, and women's roles in films have historically been smiling ones. It's little wonder that men on the street still call out, "Hey, baby, smile! Life's not *that* bad, is it?" to women passing by, lost in thought.

A friend remembers being pulled aside by a teacher after class and asked, "What is wrong, dear? You sat there for the whole hour looking so sad!" "All I could figure," my friend says now, "is that I wasn't smiling. And the fact that *she* felt sorry for me for looking normal made me feel horrible."

Ironically, the social laws that govern our smiles have completely reversed themselves over the last 2,000 years. Women weren't always expected to seem animated and responsive; in fact, immoderate laughter was once considered one of the more conspicuous vices a woman could have, and mirth was downright sinful. Women were kept apart, in some cultures even veiled, so that they couldn't perpetuate Eve's seductive, evil work. The only smile deemed appropriate on a privileged woman's face was the serene, inward smile of the Virgin Mary at Christ's birth, and even that expression was best directed exclusively at young children. Cackling laughter and wicked glee were the kinds of sounds heard only in hell.

What we know of women's facial expressions in other centuries   15
comes mostly from religious writings, codes of etiquette, and portrait paintings. In 15th century Italy, it was customary for artists to paint lovely, blank-faced women in profile. A viewer could stare endlessly at such a woman, but she could not gaze back. By the Renaissance, male artists were taking some pleasure in depicting women with a semblance of complexity, Leonardo da Vinci's Mona Lisa, with her veiled enigmatic smile, being the most famous example.

The Golden Age of the Dutch Republic marks a fascinating period for studying women's facial expressions. While we might expect the drunken young whores of Amsterdam to smile devilishly (unbridled sexuality and lasciviousness were *supposed* to addle the brain), it's the faces of the Dutch women from fine families that surprise us. Considered socially more free, these women demonstrate a fuller range of facial expressions

Q: Do you think that studying painted portraits is a good way to learn actual historical developments.

than their European sisters. Frans Hals's 1622 portrait of Stephanus Geraerdt and Isabella Coymans, a married couple, is remarkable not just for the full, friendly smiles on each face, but for the frank and mutual pleasure the couple take in each other.

In the 1800s, sprightly, pretty women began appearing in advertisements for everything from beverages to those newfangled Kodak Land cameras. Women's faces were no longer impassive, and their willingness to bestow status, to offer, proffer, and yield, was most definitely promoted by their smiling images. The culture appeared to have turned the smile, originally a bond shared between intimates, into a socially required display that sold capitalist ideology as well as kitchen appliances. And female viewers soon began to emulate these highly idealized pictures. Many longed to be more like her, that perpetually smiling female. She seemed so beautiful. So content. So whole.

By the middle of the 19th century, the bulk of America's smile burden was falling primarily to women and African-American slaves, providing a very portable means of protection, a way of saying, "I'm harmless. I won't assert myself here." It reassured those in power to see signs of gratitude and contentment in the faces of subordinates. As long ago as 1963, adman David Ogilvy declared the image of a woman smiling approvingly at a product clichéd, but we've yet to get the message. Cheerful Americans still appear in ads today, smiling somewhat less disingenuously than they smiled during the middle of the century, but smiling broadly nonetheless.

Other countries have been somewhat reluctant to import our "Don't worry, be happy" American smiles. When McDonald's opened in Moscow not long ago and when EuroDisney debuted in France last year, the Americans involved in both business ventures complained that they couldn't get the natives they'd employed to smile worth a damn.

Europeans visiting the United States for the first time are often surprised at just how often Americans smile. But when you look at our history, the relentless good humor (or, at any rate, the pretense of it) falls into perspective. The American wilderness was developed on the assumption that this country had a shortage of people in relation to its possibilities. In countries with a more rigid class structure or caste system, fewer people are as captivated by the idea of quickly winning friends and influencing people. Here in the States, however, every stranger is a potential associate. Our smiles bring new people on board. The American smile is a democratic version of a curtsy or doffed hat, since, in this land of free equals, we're not especially formal about the ways we greet social superiors.

The civil rights movement never addressed the smile burden by name, but activists worked on their own to set new facial norms. African-American males stopped smiling on the streets in the 1960s, happily aware of the unsettling effect this action had on the white population. The image of the simpleminded, smiling, white-toothed black was

20

rejected as blatantly racist, and it gradually retreated into the distance. However, like the women of Sparta and the wives of samurai, who were expected to look happy upon learning their sons or husbands had died in battle, contemporary American women have yet to unilaterally declare their faces their own property.

For instance, imagine a woman at a morning business meeting being asked if she could make a spontaneous and concise summation of a complicated project she's been struggling to get under control for months. She might draw the end of her mouth back and clench her teeth — Eek! — in a protective response, a polite, restrained expression of her surprise, not unlike the expression of a conscientious young schoolgirl being told to get out paper and pencil for a pop quiz. At the same time, the woman might be feeling resentful of the supervisor who sprang the request, but she fears taking that person on. So she holds back a comment. The whole performance resolves in a weird grin collapsing into a nervous smile that conveys discomfort and unpreparedness. A pointed remark by way of explanation or self-defense might've worked better for her — but her mouth was otherwise engaged.

We'd do well to realize just how much our smiles misrepresent us, and swear off for good the self-deprecating grins and ritual displays of deference. Real smiles have beneficial physiological effects, according to Paul Ekman. False ones do nothing for us at all.

"Smiles are as important as sound bites on television," insists producer and media coach Heidi Berenson, who has worked with many of Washington's most famous faces. "And women have always been better at understanding this than men. But the smile I'm talking about is not a cutesy smile. It's an authoritative smile. A genuine smile. Properly timed, it's tremendously powerful."

To limit a woman to one expression is like editing down an orchestra to one instrument. And the search for more authentic means of expression isn't easy in a culture in which women are still expected to be magnanimous smilers, helpmates in crisis, and curators of everybody else's morale. But change is already floating in the high winds. We see a boon in assertive female comedians who are proving that women can *dish out* smiles, not just wear them. Actress Demi Moore has stated that she doesn't like to take smiling roles. Nike is running ads that show unsmiling women athletes sweating, reaching, pushing themselves. These women aren't overly concerned with issues of rapport; they're not being "nice" girls — they're working out.

If a woman's smile were truly her own, to be smiled or not, according to how the *woman* felt, rather than according to what someone else needed, she would smile more spontaneously, without ulterior, hidden motives. As Rainer Maria Rilke wrote in *The Journal of My Other Self,* "Her smile was not meant to be seen by anyone and served its whole purpose in being smiled."

That smile is my long-term aim. In the meantime, I hope to stabilize on the smile continuum somewhere between the eliciting grin of Farrah Fawcett and the haughty smirk of Jeane Kirkpatrick.

The Reader's Presence

1. Cunningham presents an informative précis of the causes and effects of smiling in Western culture. Consider the points of view from which she addresses this subject. Summarize and evaluate her treatment of smiling from a psychological, physiological, sociological, and historical point of view. Which do you find most incisive? Why? What other points of view does she introduce into her discussion of smiling? What effects do they create? What does she identify as the benefits (and the disadvantages) of smiling?

2. At what point in this essay does Cunningham address the issue of gender? Characterize the language she uses to introduce this issue. She distinguishes between the different patterns — and the consequences — experienced by men and women who smile. Summarize these differences and assess the nature and the extent of the evidence she provides for each of her points. What more general distinctions does she make about various kinds of smiles? What are their different purposes and degrees of intensity? What information does she provide about smiling as an issue of nationality and race? What is the overall purpose of this essay? Where — and how — does Cunningham create and sustain a sense of her own presence in this essay? What does she set as her personal goal in relation to smiling?

3. Cunningham presents an explanation of the causes of an activity that few of her readers think of in either scientific or historical terms. How does her audience's knowledgeability affect the nature of the metaphors and diction she uses? Point to specific words and phrases to support and develop your point. What principles of organization does she rely on to create a sequence and structure for her essay? Comment on her use of surprise in her essay — in terms of the structure, metaphors, and diction she uses to make her points.

38

Annie Dillard

Seeing

Annie Dillard (b. 1945) was awarded the Pulitzer Prize for general nonfiction in 1974 for Pilgrim at Tinker Creek, *which she describes (borrowing from Henry David Thoreau) as "a meteorological journal of the mind." She has also published poems in* Tickets for a Prayer Wheel *(1975), literary theory in* Living by Fiction *(1982), essays in* Teaching a Stone to Talk *(1982), and autobiography in* An American Childhood *(1987). Dillard published her first novel,* The Living, *in 1992, and* The Annie Dillard Reader *appeared in 1994. From 1973 to 1982 she served as contributing editor to* Harper's *magazine, and since 1979 she has taught creative writing at Wesleyan University. The essay "Seeing" is a chapter in* Pilgrim at Tinker Creek.*

In her book The Writing Life *(1989), Dillard writes, "One of the few things I know about writing is this: spend it all, shoot it, play it, lose it, all, right away, every time. . . . Something more will arise for later, something better. These things fill from behind, like well water. Similarly, the impulse to keep to yourself what you have learned is not only shameful, it is destructive. Anything you do not give freely and abundantly becomes lost to you."*

When I was six or seven years old, growing up in Pittsburgh, I used to take a precious penny of my own and hide it for someone else to find. It was a curious compulsion; sadly, I've never been seized by it since. For some reason I always "hid" the penny along the same stretch of sidewalk up the street. I would cradle it at the roots of a sycamore, say, or in a hole left by a chipped-off piece of sidewalk. Then I would take a piece of chalk, and, starting at either end of the block, draw huge arrows leading up to the penny from both directions. After I learned to write I labeled the arrows: SURPRISE AHEAD or MONEY THIS WAY. I was greatly excited, during all this arrow-drawing, at the thought of the first lucky passer-by who would receive in this way, regardless of merit, a free gift from the universe. But I never lurked about. I would go straight home and not give the matter another thought, until, some months later, I would be gripped again by the impulse to hide another penny.

It is still the first week in January, and I've got great plans. I've been thinking about seeing. There are lots of things to see, unwrapped gifts

256

and free surprises. The world is fairly studded and strewn with pennies cast broadside from a generous hand. But — and this is the point — who gets excited by a mere penny? If you follow one arrow, if you crouch motionless on a bank to watch a tremulous ripple thrill on the water and are rewarded by the sight of a muskrat kit paddling from its den, will you count that sight a chip of copper only, and go your rueful way? It is dire poverty indeed when a man is so malnourished and fatigued that he won't stoop to pick up a penny. But if you cultivate a healthy poverty and simplicity, so that finding a penny will literally make your day, then, since the world is in fact planted in pennies, you have with your poverty bought a lifetime of days. It is that simple. What you see is what you get.

I used to be able to see flying insects in the air. I'd look ahead and see, not the row of hemlocks across the road, but the air in front of it. My eyes would focus along that column of air, picking out flying insects. But I lost interest, I guess, for I dropped the habit. Now I can see birds. Probably some people can look at the grass at their feet and discover all the crawling creatures. I would like to know grasses and sedges — and care. Then my least journey into the world would be a field trip, a series of happy recognitions. Thoreau, in an expansive mood, exulted, "What a rich book might be made about buds, including, perhaps, sprouts!" It would be nice to think so. I cherish mental images I have of three perfectly happy people. One collects stones. Another — an Englishman, say — watches clouds. The third lives on a coast and collects drops of seawater which he examines microscopically and mounts. But I don't see what the specialist sees, and so I cut myself off, not only from the total picture, but from the various forms of happiness.

Unfortunately, nature is very much a now-you-see-it, now-you-don't affair. A fish flashes, then dissolves in the water before my eyes like so much salt. Deer apparently ascend bodily into heaven; the brightest oriole fades into leaves. These disappearances stun me into stillness and concentration; they say of nature that it conceals with a grand nonchalance, and they say of vision that it is a deliberate gift, the revelation of a dancer who for my eyes only flings away her seven veils. For nature does reveal as well as conceal: now-you-don't-see-it, now-you-do. For a week last September migrating red-winged blackbirds were feeding heavily down by the creek at the back of the house. One day I went out to investigate the racket; I walked up to a tree, an Osage orange, and a hundred birds flew away. They simply materialized out of the tree. I saw a tree, then a whisk of color, then a tree again. I walked closer and another hundred blackbirds took flight. Not a branch, not a twig budged: The birds were apparently weightless as well as invisible. Or, it was as if the leaves of the Osage orange had been freed from a spell in the form of red-winged blackbirds; they flew from the tree, caught my eye in the sky, and vanished. When I looked again at the tree the leaves had reassembled as if nothing had happened. Finally I walked directly to the trunk of the tree and a final hundred, the real diehards, appeared, spread, and vanished.

How could so many hide in the tree without my seeing them? The Osage orange, unruffled, looked just as it had looked from the house, when three hundred red-winged blackbirds cried from its crown. I looked downstream where they flew, and they were gone. Searching, I couldn't spot one. I wandered downstream to force them to play their hand, but they'd crossed the creek and scattered. One show to a customer. These appearances catch at my throat; they are the free gifts, the bright coppers at the roots of trees.

It's all a matter of keeping my eyes open. Nature is like one of those   5
line drawings of a tree that are puzzles for children: Can you find hidden in the leaves a duck, a house, a boy, a bucket, a zebra, and a boot? Specialists can find the most incredibly well-hidden things. A book I read when I was young recommended an easy way to find caterpillars to rear: You simply find some fresh caterpillar droppings, look up, and there's your caterpillar. More recently an author advised me to set my mind at ease about those piles of cut stems on the ground in grassy fields. Field mice make them; they cut the grass down by degrees to reach the seeds at the head. It seems that when the grass is tightly packed, as in a field of ripe grain, the blade won't topple at a single cut through the stem; instead, the cut stem simply drops vertically, held in the crush of grain. The mouse severs the bottom again and again, the stem keeps dropping an inch at a time, and finally the head is low enough for the mouse to reach the seeds. Meanwhile, the mouse is positively littering the field with its little piles of cut stems into which, presumably, the author of the book is constantly stumbling.

If I can't see these minutiae, I still try to keep my eyes open. I'm always on the lookout for antlion traps in sandy soil, monarch pupae near milkweed, skipper larvae in locust leaves. These things are utterly common, and I've not seen one. I bang on hollow trees near water, but so far no flying squirrels have appeared. In flat country I watch every sunset in hopes of seeing the green ray. The green ray is a seldom-seen streak of light that rises from the sun like a spurting fountain at the moment of sunset; it throbs into the sky for two seconds and disappears. One more reason to keep my eyes open. A photography professor at the University of Florida just happened to see a bird die in midflight; it jerked, died, dropped, and smashed on the ground. I squint at the wind because I read Stewart Edward White: "I have always maintained that if you looked closely enough you could *see* the wind — the dim, hardly-made-out, fine débris fleeing high in the air." White was an excellent observer, and devoted an entire chapter of *The Mountains* to the subject of seeing deer: "As soon as you can forget the naturally obvious and construct an artificial obvious, then you too will see deer."

But the artificial obvious is hard to see. My eyes account for less than one percent of the weight of my head; I'm bony and dense; I see what I expect. I once spent a full three minutes looking at a bullfrog that was so unexpectedly large I couldn't see it even though a dozen enthusiastic campers were shouting directions. Finally I asked, "What color am I looking for?" and a fellow said, "Green." When at last I picked out the frog, I saw what painters are up against: The thing wasn't green at all, but the color of wet hickory bark.

The lover can see, and the knowledgeable. I visited an aunt and uncle at a quarter-horse ranch in Cody, Wyoming. I couldn't do much of anything useful, but I could, I thought, draw. So, as we all sat around the kitchen table after supper, I produced a sheet of paper and drew a horse. "That's one lame horse," my aunt volunteered. The rest of the family joined in: "Only place to saddle that one is his neck"; "Looks like we better shoot the poor thing, on account of those terrible growths." Meekly, I slid the pencil and paper down the table. Everyone in that family, including my three young cousins, could draw a horse. Beautifully. When the paper came back it looked as though five shining, real quarter horses had been corraled by mistake with a papier-mâché moose; the real horses seemed to gaze at the monster with a steady, puzzled air. I stay away from horses now, but I can do a creditable goldfish. The point is that I just don't know what the lover knows; I just can't see the artificial obvious that those in the know construct. The herpetologist asks the native, "Are there snakes in that ravine?" "Nosir." And the herpetologist comes home with, yessir, three bags full. Are there butterflies on that mountain? Are the bluets in bloom, are there arrowheads here, or fossil shells in the shale?

Peeping through my keyhole I see within the range of only about thirty percent of the light that comes from the sun; the rest is infrared and some little ultraviolet, perfectly apparent to many animals, but invisible to me. A nightmare network of ganglia, charged and firing without my knowledge, cuts and splices what I do see, editing it for my brain. Donald E. Carr points out that the sense impressions of one-celled animals are *not* edited for the brain: "This is philosophically interesting in a rather mournful way, since it means that only the simplest animals perceive the universe as it is."

A fog that won't burn away drifts and flows across my field of vision.   10 When you see fog move against a backdrop of deep pines, you don't see the fog itself, but streaks of clearness floating across the air in dark shreds. So I see only tatters of clearness through a pervading obscurity. I can't distinguish the fog from the overcast sky; I can't be sure if the light is direct or reflected. Everywhere darkness and the presence of the unseen appalls. We estimate now that only one atom dances alone in every cubic meter of intergalactic space. I blink and squint. What planet or power yanks Halley's Comet out of orbit? We haven't seen that force yet; it's a question of distance, density, and the pallor of reflected light. We rock, cradled in the swaddling band of darkness. Even the simple darkness of night whispers suggestions to the mind. Last summer, in August, I stayed at the creek too late.

Where Tinker Creek flows under the sycamore log bridge to the tear-shaped island, it is slow and shallow, fringed thinly in cattail marsh. At this spot an astonishing bloom of life supports vast breeding populations of insects, fish, reptiles, birds, and mammals. On windless summer evenings I stalk along the creek bank or straddle the sycamore log in absolute stillness, watching for muskrats. The night I stayed too late I was hunched on the log staring spellbound at spreading, reflected stains of lilac on the water. A cloud in the sky suddenly lighted as if turned on by a switch; its reflection just as suddenly materialized on the water upstream, flat and floating, so that I couldn't see the creek bottom, or life in the water under the cloud. Downstream, away from the cloud on the water, water turtles smooth as beans were gliding down with the current in a series of easy, weightless push-offs, as men bound on the moon. I didn't know whether to trace the progress of one turtle I was sure of, risking sticking my face in one of the bridge's spider webs made invisible by the gathering dark, or take a chance on seeing the carp, or scan the mudbank in hope of seeing a muskrat, or follow the last of the swallows who caught at my heart and trailed it after them like streamers as they appeared from directly below, under the log, flying upstream with the tails forked, so fast.

But the shadows spread, and deepened, and stayed. After thousands of years we're still strangers to darkness, fearful aliens in an enemy camp with our arms crossed over our chests. I stirred. A land turtle on the bank, startled, hissed the air from its lungs and withdrew into its shell. An uneasy pink here, an unfathomable blue there, gave great suggestion of lurking beings. Things were going on. I couldn't see whether that sere rustle I heard was a distant rattlesnake, slit-eyed, or a nearby sparrow kicking in the dry flood debris slung at the foot of a willow. Tremendous action roiled the water everywhere I looked, big action, inexplicable. A tremor welled up beside a gaping muskrat burrow in the bank and I caught my breath, but no muskrat appeared. The ripples continued to fan upstream with a steady, powerful thrust. Night was knitting over my face an eyeless mask, and I still sat transfixed. A distant airplane, a delta wing out of nightmare, made a gliding shadow on the creek's bottom that looked like a stingray cruising upstream. At once a black fin slit the pink cloud on the water, shearing it in two. The two halves merged together and seemed to dissolve before my eyes. Darkness pooled in the cleft of the creek and rose, as water collects in a well. Untamed, dreaming lights flickered over the sky. I saw hints of hulking underwater shadows, two pale splashes out of the water, and round ripples rolling close together from a blackened center.

At last I stared upstream where only the deepest violet remained of the cloud, a cloud so high its underbelly still glowed feeble color reflected from a hidden sky lighted in turn by a sun halfway to China. And out of that violet, a sudden enormous black body arced over the water. I saw only a cylindrical sleekness. Head and tail, if there was a head and tail, were both submerged in cloud. I saw only one ebony fling, a headlong dive to darkness; then the waters closed, and the lights went out.

I walked home in a shivering daze, up hill and down. Later I lay open-mouthed in bed, my arms flung wide at my sides to steady the whirling darkness. At this latitude I'm spinning 836 miles an hour round the earth's axis; I often fancy I feel my sweeping fall as a breakneck arc like the dive of dolphins, and the hollow rushing of wind raises hair on my neck and the side of my face. In orbit around the sun I'm moving 64,800 miles an hour. The solar system as a whole, like a merry-go-round unhinged, spins, bobs, and blinks at the speed of 43,200 miles an hour along a course set east of Hercules. Someone has piped, and we are dancing a tarantella until the sweat pours. I open my eyes and I see dark, muscled forms curl out of water, with flapping gills and flattened eyes. I close my eyes and I see stars, deep stars giving way to deeper stars, deeper stars bowing to deepest stars at the crown of an infinite cone.

"Still," wrote van Gogh in a letter, "a great deal of light falls on   15
everything." If we are blinded by darkness, we are also blinded by light. When too much light falls on everything, a special terror results. Peter Freuchen describes the notorious kayak sickness to which Greenland Eskimos are prone. "The Greenland fjords are peculiar for the spells of completely quiet weather, when there is not enough wind to blow out a match and the water is like a sheet of glass. The kayak hunter must sit in his boat without stirring a finger so as not to scare the shy seals away. . . . The sun, low in the sky, sends a glare into his eyes, and the landscape around moves into the realm of the unreal. The reflex from the mirror-like water hypnotizes him, he seems to be unable to move, and all of a sudden it is as if he were floating in a bottomless void, sinking, sinking, and sinking. . . . Horror-stricken, he tries to stir, to cry out, but he cannot, he is completely paralyzed, he just falls and falls." Some hunters are especially cursed with this panic, and bring ruin and sometimes starvation to their families.

Sometimes here in Virginia at sunset low clouds on the southern or northern horizon are completely invisible in the lighted sky. I only know one is there because I can see its reflection in still water. The first time I discovered this mystery I looked from cloud to no-cloud in bewilderment, checking my bearings over and over, thinking maybe the ark of the covenant was just passing by south of Dead Man Mountain. Only much later did I read the explanation: Polarized light from the sky is very much weakened by reflection, but the light in clouds isn't polarized. So invisible clouds pass among visible clouds, till all slide over the mountains; so a greater light extinguishes a lesser as though it didn't exist.

In the great meteor shower of August, the Perseid, I wail all day for the shooting stars I miss. They're out there showering down, committing hara-kiri in a flame of fatal attraction, and hissing perhaps at last into the ocean. But at dawn what looks like a blue dome clamps down over me like a lid on a pot. The stars and planets could smash and I'd never know. Only a piece of ashen moon occasionally climbs up or down the inside of the dome, and our local star without surcease explodes on our heads. We have really only that one light, one source for all power, and yet we must turn away from it by universal decree. Nobody here on the planet seems aware of this strange, powerful taboo, that we all walk about carefully averting our faces, this way and that, lest our eyes be blasted forever.

Darkness appalls and light dazzles; the scrap of visible light that doesn't hurt my eyes hurts my brain. What I see sets me swaying. Size and distance and the sudden swelling of meanings confuse me, bowl me over. I straddle the sycamore log bridge over Tinker Creek in the summer. I look at the lighted creek bottom: Snail tracks tunnel the mud in quavering curves. A crayfish jerks, but by the time I absorb what has happened, he's gone in a billowing smokescreen of silt. I look at the water: minnows and shiners. If I'm thinking minnows, a carp will fill my brain till I scream. I look at the water's surface: skaters, bubbles, and leaves sliding down. Suddenly, my own face, reflected, startles me witless. Those snails have been tracking my face! Finally, with a shuddering wrench of the will, I see clouds, cirrus clouds. I'm dizzy, I fall in. This looking business is risky.

Once I stood on a humped rock on nearby Purgatory Mountain, watching through binoculars the great autumn hawk migration below, until I discovered that I was in danger of joining the hawks on a vertical migration of my own. I was used to binoculars, but not, apparently, to balancing on humped rocks while looking through them. I staggered. Everything advanced and receded by turns; the world was full of unexplained foreshortenings and depths. A distant huge tan object, a hawk the size of an elephant, turned out to be the browned bough of a nearby loblolly pine. I followed a sharp-shinned hawk against a featureless sky, rotating my head unawares as it flew, and when I lowered the glass a glimpse of my own looming shoulder sent me staggering. What prevents the men on Palomar from falling, voiceless and blinded, from their tiny, vaulted chairs?

I reel in confusion; I don't understand what I see. With the naked eye   20
I can see two million light-years to the Andromeda galaxy. Often I slop some creek water in a jar and when I get home I dump it in a white china bowl. After the silt settles I return and see tracings of minute snails on the bottom, a planarian or two winding round the rim of water, roundworms shimmying frantically, and finally, when my eyes have adjusted to these dimensions, amoebae. At first the amoebae look like muscae volitantes, those curled moving spots you seem to see in your eyes when you stare at a distant wall. Then I see the amoebae as drops of water congealed, bluish, translucent, like chips of sky in the bowl. At length I choose one individual and give myself over to its idea of an evening. I see it dribble a grainy foot before it on its wet, unfathomable way. Do its unedited sense impressions include the fierce focus of my eyes? Shall I take it outside and show it Andromeda, and blow its little endoplasm? I stir the water with a finger, in case it's running out of oxygen. Maybe I should get a tropical aquarium with motorized bubblers and lights, and keep this one for a pet. Yes, it would tell its fissioned descendants, the universe is two feet by five, and if you listen closely you can hear the buzzing music of the spheres.

Oh, it's mysterious lamplit evenings, here in the galaxy, one after the other. It's one of those nights when I wander from window to window, looking for a sign. But I can't see. Terror and a beauty insoluble are a ribband of blue woven into the fringes of garments of things both great and small. No culture explains, no bivouac offers real haven or rest. But it could be that we are not seeing something. Galileo thought comets were an optical illusion. This is fertile ground: Since we are certain that they're not, we can look at what our scientists have been saying with fresh hope. What if there are *really* gleaming, castellated cities hung upside-down over the desert sand? What limpid lakes and cool date palms have our caravans always passed untried? Until, one by one, by the blindest of leaps, we light on the road to these places, we must stumble in darkness and hunger. I turn from the window. I'm blind as a bat, sensing only from every direction the echo of my own thin cries.

I chanced on a wonderful book by Marius von Senden, called *Space and Light*. When Western surgeons discovered how to perform safe cataract operations, they ranged across Europe and America operating on dozens of men and women of all ages who had been blinded by cataracts since birth. Von Senden collected accounts of such cases; the histories are fascinating. Many doctors had tested their patients' sense perceptions and ideas of space both before and after the operations. The vast majority of patients, of both sexes and all ages, had, in von Senden's opinion, no idea of space whatsoever. Form, distance, and size were so many meaningless syllables. A patient "had no idea of depth, confusing it with roundness." Before the operation a doctor would give a blind patient a cube and a sphere; the patient would tongue it or feel it with his hands, and name it correctly. After the operation the doctor would show the same objects to the patient without letting him touch them; now he had no clue whatsoever what he was seeing. One patient called lemonade "square" because it pricked on his tongue as a square shape pricked on the touch of his hands. Of another postoperative patient, the doctor writes, "I have found in her no notion of size, for example, not even within the narrow limits which she might have encompassed with the aid of touch. Thus when I asked her to show me how big her mother was, she did not stretch out her hands, but set her two index-fingers a few inches apart." Other doctors reported their patients' own statements to similar effect. "The room he was in . . . he knew to be but part of the house, yet he could not conceive that the whole house could look bigger"; "Those who are blind from birth . . . have no real conception of height or distance. A house that is a mile away is thought of as nearby, but requiring the taking of a lot of steps. . . . The elevator that whizzes him up and down gives no more sense of vertical distance than does the train of horizontal."

For the newly sighted, vision is pure sensation unencumbered by meaning: "The girl went through the experience that we all go through and forget, the moment we are born. She saw, but it did not mean anything but a lot of different kinds of brightness." Again, "I asked the patient what he could see; he answered that he saw an extensive field of light, in which everything appeared dull, confused, and in motion. He could not distinguish objects." Another patient saw "nothing but a confusion of forms and colours." When a newly sighted girl saw photographs and paintings, she asked, "'Why do they put those dark marks all over them?' 'Those aren't dark marks,' her mother explained, 'those are shadows. That is one of the ways the eye knows that things have shape. If it were not for shadows many things would look flat.' 'Well, that's how things do look,' Joan answered, 'Everything looks flat with dark patches.'"

But it is the patients' concepts of space that are most revealing. One patient, according to his doctor, "practiced his vision in a strange fashion; thus he takes off one of his boots, throws it some way off in front of him, and then attempts to gauge the distance at which it lies; he takes a few steps toward the boot and tries to grasp it; on failing to reach it, he moves on a step or two and gropes for the boot until he finally gets hold of it." "But even at this stage, after three weeks' experience of seeing," von Senden goes on, "'space,' as he conceives it, ends with visual space, i.e., with color-patches that happen to bound his view. He does not yet have the notion that a larger object (a chair) can mask a smaller one (a dog), or that the latter can still be present even though it is not directly seen."

In general the newly sighted see the world as a dazzle of color-patches. 25
They are pleased by the sensation of color, and learn quickly to name the colors, but the rest of seeing is tormentingly difficult. Soon after his operation a patient "generally bumps into one of these color-patches and observes them to be substantial, since they resist him as tactual objects do. In walking about it also strikes him — or can if he pays attention — that he is continually passing in between the colors he sees, that he can go past a visual object, that a part of it then steadily disappears from view; and that in spite of this, however he twists and turns — whether entering the room from the door, for example, or returning back to it — he always has a visual space in front of him. Thus he gradually comes to realize that there is also a space behind him, which he does not see."

The mental effort involved in these reasonings proves overwhelming for many patients. It oppresses them to realize, if they ever do at all, the tremendous size of the world, which they had previously conceived of as something touchingly manageable. It oppresses them to realize that they have been visible to people all along, perhaps unattractively so, without their knowledge or consent. A disheartening number of them refuse to use their new vision, continuing to go over objects with their tongues, and lapsing into apathy and despair. "The child can see, but will not make use of his sight. Only when pressed can he with difficulty be brought to look at objects in his neighborhood; but more than a foot away it is impossible to bestir him to the necessary effort." Of a twenty-one-year-old girl, the doctor relates, "Her unfortunate father, who had hoped for so much from this operation, wrote that his daughter carefully shuts her eyes whenever she wishes to go about the house, especially when she comes to a staircase, and that she is never happier or more at ease than when, by closing her eyelids, she relapses into her former state of total blindness." A fifteen-year-old boy, who was also in love with a girl at the asylum for the blind, finally blurted out, "No, really, I can't stand it any more; I want to be sent back to the asylum again. If things aren't altered, I'll tear my eyes out."

Some do learn to see, especially the young ones. But it changes their lives. One doctor comments on "the rapid and complete loss of that striking and wonderful serenity which is characteristic only of those who have never yet seen." A blind man who learns to see is ashamed of his old habits. He dresses up, grooms himself, and tries to make a good impression. While he was blind he was indifferent to objects unless they were edible; now, "a sifting of values sets in . . . his thoughts and wishes are mightily stirred and some few of the patients are thereby led into dissimulation, envy, theft and fraud."

On the other hand, many newly sighted people speak well of the world, and teach us how dull is our own vision. To one patient, a human hand, unrecognized, is "something bright and then holes." Shown a bunch of grapes, a boy calls out, "It is dark, blue and shiny. . . . It isn't smooth, it has bumps and hollows." A little girl visits a garden. "She is greatly astonished, and can scarcely be persuaded to answer, stands speechless in front of the tree, which she only names on taking hold of it, and then as 'the tree with the lights in it.'" Some delight in their sight and give themselves over to the visual world. Of a patient just after her bandages were removed, her doctor writes, "The first things to attract her attention were her own hands; she looked at them very closely, moved them repeatedly to and fro, bent and stretched the fingers, and seemed greatly astonished at the sight." One girl was eager to tell her blind friend that "men do not really look like trees at all," and astounded to discover that her every visitor had an utterly different face. Finally, a twenty-two-year-old girl was dazzled by the world's brightness and kept her eyes shut for two weeks. When at the end of that time she opened her eyes again, she did not recognize any objects, but, "the more she now directed her gaze upon everything about her, the more it could be seen how an expression of gratification and astonishment overspread her features; she repeatedly exclaimed: 'Oh God! How beautiful!'"

I saw color-patches for weeks after I read this wonderful book. It was summer; the peaches were ripe in the valley orchards. When I woke in the morning, color-patches wrapped round my eyes, intricately, leaving not one unfilled spot. All day long I walked among shifting color-patches that parted before me like the Red Sea and closed again in silence, transfigured, wherever I looked back. Some patches swelled and loomed, while others vanished utterly, and dark marks flitted at random over the whole dazzling sweep. But I couldn't sustain the illusion of flatness. I've been around for too long. Form is condemned to an eternal danse macabre with meaning: I couldn't unpeach the peaches. Nor can I remember ever having seen without understanding; the color-patches of infancy are lost. My brain then must have been smooth as any balloon. I'm told I reached for the moon; many babies do. But the color-patches of infancy swelled as meaning filled them; they arrayed themselves in solemn ranks down distance which unrolled and stretched before me like a plain. The moon rocketed away. I live now in a world of shadows that shape and distance color, a world where space makes a kind of terrible sense. What gnosticism is this, and what physics? The fluttering patch I saw in my nursery window — silver and green and shape-shifting blue — is gone; a row of Lombardy poplars takes its place, mute, across the distant lawn. That humming oblong creature pale as light that stole along the walls of my room at night, stretching exhilaratingly around the corners, is gone, too, gone the night I ate of the bittersweet fruit, put two and two together and puckered forever my brain. Martin Buber tells this tale: "Rabbi Mendel once boasted to his teacher Rabbi Elimelekh that evenings he saw the angel who rolls away the light before the darkness, and mornings the angel who rolls away the darkness before the light. 'Yes,' said Rabbi Elimelekh, 'in my youth I saw that too. Later on you don't see these things any more.'"

Why didn't someone hand those newly sighted people paints and   30
brushes from the start, when they still didn't know what anything was? Then maybe we all could see color-patches too, the world unraveled from reason. Eden before Adam gave names. The scales would drop from my eyes; I'd see trees like men walking; I'd run down the road against all orders, hallooing and leaping.

Seeing is of course very much a matter of verbalization. Unless I call my attention to what passes before my eyes, I simply won't see it. It is, as Ruskin says, "not merely unnoticed, but in the full, clear sense of the word, unseen." My eyes alone can't solve analogy tests using figures, the ones which show, with increasing elaborations, a big square, then a small square in a big square, then a big triangle, and expect me to find a small triangle in a big triangle. I have to say the words, describe what I'm seeing. If Tinker Mountain erupted, I'd be likely to notice. But if I want to notice the lesser cataclysms of valley life, I have to maintain in my head a running description of the present. It's not that I'm observant; it's just that I talk too much. Otherwise, especially in a strange place, I'll never know what's happening. Like a blind man at the ball game, I need a radio.

When I see this way I analyze and pry. I hurl over logs and roll away stones; I study the bank a square foot at a time, probing and tilting my head. Some days when a mist covers the mountains, when the muskrats won't show and the microscope's mirror shatters, I want to climb up the blank blue dome as a man would storm the inside of a circus tent, wildly, dangling, and with a steel knife claw a rent in the top, peep, and, if I must, fall.

But there is another kind of seeing that involves a letting go. When I see this way I sway transfixed and emptied. The difference between the two ways of seeing is the difference between walking with and without a camera. When I walk with a camera I walk from shot to shot, reading the light on a calibrated meter. When I walk without a camera, my own shutter opens, and the moment's light prints on my own silver gut. When I see this second way I am above all an unscrupulous observer.

It was sunny one evening last summer at Tinker Creek; the sun was low in the sky, upstream. I was sitting on the sycamore log bridge with the sunset at my back, watching the shiners the size of minnows who were feeding over the muddy sand in skittery schools. Again and again, one fish, then another, turned for a split second across the current and flash! the sun shot out from its silver side. I couldn't watch for it. It was always just happening somewhere else, and it drew my vision just as it disappeared: flash, like a sudden dazzle of the thinnest blade, a sparking over a dun and olive ground at chance intervals from every direction. Then I noticed white specks, some sort of pale petals, small, floating from under my feet on the creek's surface, very slow and steady. So I blurred my eyes and gazed toward the brim of my hat and saw a new world. I saw the pale white circles roll up, roll up, like the world's turning, mute and perfect, and I saw the linear flashes, gleaming silver, like stars being born at random down a rolling scroll of time. Something broke and something opened. I filled up like a new wineskin. I breathed an air like light; I saw a light like water. I was the lip of a fountain the creek filled forever; I was ether, the leaf in the zephyr; I was flesh-flake, feather, bone.

When I see this way I see truly. As Thoreau says, I return to my 35 senses. I am the man who watches the baseball game in silence in an empty stadium. I see the game purely; I'm abstracted and dazed. When it's all over and the white-suited players lope off the green field to their shadowed dugouts, I leap to my feet; I cheer and cheer.

But I can't go out and try to see this way. I'll fail, I'll go mad. All I can do is try to gag the commentator, to hush the noise of useless interior babble that keeps me from seeing just as surely as a newspaper dangled before my eyes. The effort is really a discipline requiring a lifetime of dedicated struggle; it marks the literature of saints and monks of every order East and West, under every rule and no rule, discalced and shod. The world's spiritual geniuses seem to discover universally that the mind's muddy river, this ceaseless flow of trivia and trash, cannot be dammed, and that trying to dam it is a waste of effort that might lead to madness. Instead you must allow the muddy river to flow unheeded in the dim channels of consciousness; you raise your sights; you look along it, mildly, acknowledging its presence without interest and gazing beyond it into the realm of the real where subjects and objects act and rest purely, without utterance. "Launch into the deep," says Jacques Ellul, "and you shall see."

The secret of seeing is, then, the pearl of great price. If I thought he could teach me to find it and keep it forever I would stagger barefoot across a hundred deserts after any lunatic at all. But although the pearl may be found, it may not be sought. The literature of illumination reveals this above all: Although it comes to those who wait for it, it is always, even to the most practiced and adept, a gift and a total surprise. I return from one walk knowing where the killdeer nests in the field by the creek and the hour the laurel blooms. I return from the same walk a day later scarcely knowing my own name. Litanies hum in my ears; my tongue flaps in my mouth Ailinon, alleluia! I cannot cause light; the most I can do is try to put myself in the path of its beam. It is possible, in deep space, to sail on solar wind. Light, be it particle or wave, has force: you rig a giant sail and go. The secret of seeing is to sail on solar wind. Hone and spread your spirit till you yourself are a sail, whetted, translucent, broadside to the merest puff.

When her doctor took her bandages off and led her into the garden, the girl who was no longer blind saw "the tree with the lights in it." It was for this tree I searched through the peach orchards of summer, in the forests of fall and down winter and spring for years. Then one day I was walking along Tinker Creek thinking of nothing at all and I saw the tree with the lights in it. I saw the backyard cedar where the mourning doves roost charged and transfigured, each cell buzzing with flame. I stood on the grass with the lights in it, grass that was wholly fire, utterly focused and utterly dreamed. It was less like seeing than like being for the first time seen, knocked breathless by a powerful glance. The flood of fire abated, but I'm still spending the power. Gradually the lights went out in the cedar, the colors died, the cells unflamed and disappeared. I was still ringing. I had been my whole life a bell, and never knew it until at that moment I was lifted and struck. I have since only very rarely seen the tree with the lights in it. The vision comes and goes, mostly goes, but I live for it, for the moment when the mountains open and a new light roars in spate through the crack, and the mountains slam.

The Reader's Presence

1. In addition to providing a fascinating view of some overlooked aspects of nature, Annie Dillard's essay constitutes a primer on the principles and practices of observation and inference — on seeing

and coming to terms with the natural world around us. What principles about how we ought to see the world can you infer from reading this essay? Summarize the information Dillard provides about each of these principles, and show how she puts each principle into practice in her essay. What distinction, for example, does she draw between "seeing" and "observing"? between "the naturally obvious" and "the artificial obvious"? For example, what does she mean when she says: "When I see this way I see truly" (paragraph 35)?

2. Dillard is quite conscious of her readers' presence. How does this interest serve as a commentary on her statement: "Seeing is of course very much a matter of verbalization" (paragraph 31)? What does she mean here? Explain why this principle remains so important to her purpose in writing this essay. How is this statement complicated by what she says later in that same paragraph: "It's not that I'm observant; it's just that I talk too much"? In what specific ways does this sentence characterize the relationship she establishes with her readers and what she would like to see her readers learn from her essay?

3. Much of Dillard's essay is written in the form of first-person narrative. Yet Dillard also manages to convey a great deal of information about seeing and about the natural world. What advantages and disadvantages can you identify that result from this choice? What specific strategies does Dillard use to work in so much information — especially from secondary sources — about seeing and the natural world?

39

Lars Eighner

On Dumpster Diving

Lars Eighner (b. 1948) was born in Texas and attended the University of Texas at Austin. An essayist and fiction writer, he contributes regularly to the Threepenny Review, Advocate Men, The Guide, *and* Inches. *He has published a volume of stories,* Bayou Boys and Other Stories *(1985), and a book on gay erotica,* Lavender Blue: How to Write and Sell Gay Men's Erotica *(1987). More recently he has written* Whispered in the Dark *(1995) and* Gay Cosmos *(1995). Eighner became homeless in 1988, when he left his job as a mental-hospital attendant. "On Dumpster Diving" is Eighner's prize-winning essay based on this experience. It originally appeared in 1991 in the* Threepenny Review. *He has since published a full-length book about homelessness,* Travels with Lizbeth: Three Years on the Road and on the Streets *(1993). Lizbeth is Eighner's dog, with whom he currently shares an apartment in Austin.*

On what is required to find success as a writer, Eighner has said, "I was not making enough money to support myself as a housed person, but I was writing well before I became homeless. . . . A writer needs talent, luck, and persistence. You can make do with two out of three, and the more you have of one, the less you need of the others."

Long before I began Dumpster diving I was impressed with Dumpsters, enough so that I wrote the Merriam-Webster research service to discover what I could about the word "Dumpster." I learned from them that "Dumpster" is a proprietary word belonging to the Dempster Dumpster company.

Since then I have dutifully capitalized the word although it was lowercased in almost all of the citations Merriam-Webster photocopied for me. Dempster's word is too apt. I have never heard these things called anything but Dumpsters. I do not know anyone who knows the generic name for these objects. From time to time, however, I hear a wino or hobo give some corrupted credit to the original and call them Dipsy Dumpsters.

I began Dumpster diving about a year before I became homeless.

I prefer the term "scavenging" and use the word "scrounging" when I mean to be obscure. I have heard people, evidently meaning to be polite, using the word "foraging," but I prefer to reserve that word for gathering nuts and berries and such which I do also according to the season and the opportunity. "Dumpster diving" seems to me to be a little too cute and, in my case, inaccurate because I lack the athletic ability to lower myself into the Dumpsters as the true divers do, much to their increased profit.

I like the frankness of the word "scavenging," which I can hardly   5
think of without picturing a big black snail on an aquarium wall. I live from the refuse of others. I am a scavenger. I think it a sound and honorable niche, although if I could I would naturally prefer to live the comfortable consumer life, perhaps — and only perhaps — as a slightly less wasteful consumer owing to what I have learned as a scavenger.

While my dog Lizbeth and I were still living in the house on Avenue B in Austin, as my savings ran out, I put almost all my sporadic income into rent. The necessities of daily life I began to extract from Dumpsters. Yes, we ate from Dumpsters. Except for jeans, all my clothes came from Dumpsters. Boom boxes, candles, bedding, toilet paper, medicine, books, a typewriter, a virgin male love doll, change sometimes amounting to many dollars: I acquired many things from the Dumpsters.

I have learned much as a scavenger. I mean to put some of what I have learned down here, beginning with the practical art of Dumpster diving and proceeding to the abstract.

What is safe to eat?

After all, the finding of objects is becoming something of an urban art. Even respectable employed people will sometimes find something tempting sticking out of a Dumpster or standing beside one. Quite a number of people, not all of them of the bohemian type, are willing to brag that they found this or that piece in the trash. But eating from Dumpsters is the thing that separates the dilettanti from the professionals.

Eating safely from the Dumpsters involves three principles: using the senses and common sense to evaluate the condition of the found materials, knowing the Dumpsters of a given area and checking them regularly, and seeking always to answer the question "Why was this discarded?" 10

Perhaps everyone who has a kitchen and a regular supply of groceries has, at one time or another, made a sandwich and eaten half of it before discovering mold on the bread or got a mouthful of milk before realizing the milk had turned. Nothing of the sort is likely to happen to a Dumpster diver because he is constantly reminded that most food is discarded for a reason. Yet a lot of perfectly good food can be found in Dumpsters.

Canned goods, for example, turn up fairly often in the Dumpsters I frequent. All except the most phobic people would be willing to eat from a can even if it came from a Dumpster. Canned goods are among the safest of foods to be found in Dumpsters, but are not utterly foolproof.

Although very rare with modern canning methods, botulism is a possibility. Most other forms of food poisoning seldom do lasting harm to a healthy person. But botulism is almost certainly fatal and often the first symptom is death. Except for carbonated beverages, all canned goods should contain a slight vacuum and suck air when first punctured. Bulging, rusty, dented cans and cans that spew when punctured should be avoided, especially when the contents are not very acidic or syrupy.

Heat can break down the botulin, but this requires much more cooking than most people do to canned goods. To the extent that botulism occurs at all, of course, it can occur in cans on pantry shelves as well as in cans from Dumpsters. Need I say that home-canned goods found in Dumpsters are simply too risky to be recommended.

From time to time one of my companions, aware of the source of my provisions, will ask, "Do you think these crackers are really safe to eat?" For some reason it is most often the crackers they ask about. 15

This question always makes me angry. Of course I would not offer my companion anything I had doubts about. But more than that I wonder why he cannot evaluate the condition of the crackers for himself. I have no special knowledge and I have been wrong before. Since he knows where the food comes from, it seems to me he ought to assume some of the responsibility for deciding what he will put in his mouth.

For myself I have few qualms about dry foods such as crackers, cookies, cereal, chips, and pasta if they are free of visible contaminates and still dry and crisp. Most often such things are found in the original packaging, which is not so much a positive sign as it is the absence of a negative one.

Raw fruits and vegetables with intact skins seem perfectly safe to me, excluding of course the obviously rotten. Many are discarded for minor imperfections which can be pared away. Leafy vegetables, grapes, cauliflower, broccoli, and similar things may be contaminated by liquids and may be impractical to wash.

Candy, especially hard candy, is usually safe if it has not drawn ants. Chocolate is often discarded only because it has become discolored as the cocoa butter de-emulsified. Candying after all is one method of food preservation because pathogens do not like very sugary substances.

All of these foods might be found in any Dumpster and can be evaluated with some confidence largely on the basis of appearance. Beyond these are foods which cannot be correctly evaluated without additional information. 20

I began scavenging by pulling pizzas out of the Dumpster behind a pizza delivery shop. In general prepared food requires caution, but in this case I knew when the shop closed and went to the Dumpster as soon as the last of the help left.

Such shops often get prank orders, called "bogus." Because help seldom stays long at these places pizzas are often made with the wrong topping, refused on delivery for being cold, or baked incorrectly. The products to be discarded are boxed up because inventory is kept by counting boxes: A boxed pizza can be written off; an unboxed pizza does not exist.

I never placed a bogus order to increase the supply of pizzas and I believe no one else was scavenging in this Dumpster. But the people in the shop became suspicious and began to retain their garbage in the shop overnight.

While it lasted I had a steady supply of fresh, sometimes warm pizza. Because I knew the Dumpster I knew the source of the pizza, and because I visited the Dumpster regularly I knew what was fresh and what was yesterday's.

The area I frequent is inhabited by many affluent college students. I 25 am not here by chance; the Dumpsters in this area are very rich. Students throw out many good things, including food. In particular they tend to throw everything out when they move at the end of a semester, before and after breaks, and around midterm when many of them despair of college. So I find it advantageous to keep an eye on the academic calendar.

The students throw food away around the breaks because they do not know whether it has spoiled or will spoil before they return. A typical discard is a half jar of peanut butter. In fact nonorganic peanut butter does not require refrigeration and is unlikely to spoil in any reasonable time. The student does not know that, and since it is Daddy's money, the student decides not to take a chance.

Opened containers require caution and some attention to the question "Why was this discarded?" But in the case of discards from student apartments, the answer may be that the item was discarded through carelessness, ignorance, or wastefulness. This can sometimes be deduced when the item is found with many others, including some that are obviously perfectly good.

Some students, and others, approach defrosting a freezer by chucking out the whole lot. Not only do the circumstances of such a find tell the story, but also the mass of frozen goods stays cold for a long time and items may be found still frozen or freshly thawed.

Yogurt, cheese, and sour cream are items that are often thrown out while they are still good. Occasionally I find a cheese with a spot of mold, which of course I just pare off, and because it is obvious why such a cheese was discarded, I treat it with less suspicion than an apparently perfect cheese found in similar circumstances. Yogurt is often discarded, still sealed, only because the expiration date on the carton had passed. This is one of my favorite finds because yogurt will keep for several days, even in warm weather.

Students throw out canned goods and staples at the end of semesters and when they give up college at midterm. Drugs, pornography, spirits, and the like are often discarded when parents are expected — Dad's day, for example. And spirits also turn up after big party weekends, presumably discarded by the newly reformed. Wine and spirits, of course, keep perfectly well even once opened. 30

My test for carbonated soft drinks is whether they still fizz vigorously. Many juices or other beverages are too acid or too syrupy to cause much concern provided they are not visibly contaminated. Liquids, however, require some care.

One hot day I found a large jug of Pat O'Brien's Hurricane mix. The jug had been opened, but it was still ice cold. I drank three large glasses before it became apparent to me that someone had added the rum to the mix, and not a little rum. I never tasted the rum and by the time I began to feel the effects I had already ingested a very large quantity of the beverage. Some divers would have considered this a boon, but being suddenly and thoroughly intoxicated in a public place in the early afternoon is not my idea of a good time.

I have heard of people maliciously contaminating discarded food and even handouts, but mostly I have heard of this from people with vivid imaginations who have had no experience with the Dumpsters themselves. Just before the pizza shop stopped discarding its garbage at night, jalapeños began showing up on most of the discarded pizzas. If indeed this was meant to discourage me it was a wasted effort because I am native Texan.

For myself, I avoid game, poultry, pork, and egg-based foods whether I find them raw or cooked. I seldom have the means to cook what I find, but when I do I avail myself of plentiful supplies of beef which is often in very good condition. I suppose fish becomes disagreeable before it becomes dangerous. The dog is happy to have any such thing that is past its prime and, in fact, does not recognize fish as food until it is quite strong.

Home leftovers, as opposed to surpluses from restaurants, are very   35
often bad. Evidently, especially among students, there is a common type
of personality that carefully wraps up even the smallest leftover and
shoves it into the back of the refrigerator for six months or so before discarding it. Characteristic of this type are the reused jars and margarine
tubs which house the remains.

I avoid ethnic foods I am unfamiliar with. If I do not know what it is
supposed to look like when it is good, I cannot be certain I will be able to
tell if it is bad.

No matter how careful I am I still get dysentery at least once a
month, oftener in warm weather. I do not want to paint too romantic a
picture. Dumpster diving has serious drawbacks as a way of life.

I learned to scavenge gradually, on my own. Since then I have initiated several companions into the trade. I have learned that there is a predictable series of stages a person goes through in learning to scavenge.

At first the new scavenger is filled with disgust and self-loathing. He
is ashamed of being seen and may lurk around, trying to duck behind
things, or he may try to dive at night.

(In fact, most people instinctively look away from a scavenger. By   40
skulking around, the novice calls attention to himself and arouses suspicion. Diving at night is ineffective and needlessly messy.)

Every grain of rice seems to be a maggot. Everything seems to stink.
He can wipe the egg yolk off the found can, but he cannot erase the
stigma of eating garbage out of his mind.

That stage passes with experience. The scavenger finds a pair of running shoes that fit and look and smell brand new. He finds a pocket cal-
culator in perfect working order. He finds pristine ice cream, still frozen,
more than he can eat or keep. He begins to understand: People do throw
away perfectly good stuff, a lot of perfectly good stuff.

At this stage, Dumpster shyness begins to dissipate. The diver, after all,
has the last laugh. He is finding all manner of good things which are his for
the taking. Those who disparage his profession are the fools, not he.

He may begin to hang onto some perfectly good things for which he
has neither a use nor a market. Then he begins to take note of the things
which are not perfectly good but are nearly so. He mates a Walkman
with broken earphones and one that is missing a battery cover. He picks
up things which he can repair.

At this stage he may become lost and never recover. Dumpsters are   45
full of things of some potential value to someone and also of things which
never have much intrinsic value but are interesting. All the Dumpster
divers I have known come to the point of trying to acquire everything
they touch. Why not take it, they reason, since it is all free.

This is, of course, hopeless. Most divers come to realize that they
must restrict themselves to items of relatively immediate utility. But in
some cases the diver simply cannot control himself. I have met several of

these pack-rat types. Their ideas of the values of various pieces of junk verge on the psychotic. Every bit of glass may be a diamond, they think, and all that glistens, gold.

I tend to gain weight when I am scavenging. Partly this is because I always find far more pizza and doughnuts than water-packed tuna, non-fat yogurt, and fresh vegetables. Also I have not developed much faith in the reliability of Dumpsters as a food source, although it has been proven to me many times. I tend to eat as if I have no idea where my next meal is coming from. But mostly I just hate to see food go to waste and so I eat much more than I should. Something like this drives the obsession to collect junk.

As for collecting objects, I usually restrict myself to collecting one kind of small object at a time, such as pocket calculators, sunglasses, or campaign buttons. To live on the street I must anticipate my needs to a certain extent: I must pick up and save warm bedding I find in August because it will not be found in Dumpsters in November. But even if I had a home with extensive storage space I could not save everything that might be valuable in some contingency.

I have proprietary feelings about my Dumpsters. As I have suggested, it is no accident that I scavenge from Dumpsters where good finds are common. But my limited experience with Dumpsters in other areas suggests to me that it is the population of competitors rather than the affluence of the dumpers that most affects the feasibility of survival by scavenging. The large number of competitors is what puts me off the idea of trying to scavenge in places like Los Angeles.

Curiously, I do not mind my direct competition, other scavengers, so   50
much as I hate the can scroungers.

People scrounge cans because they have to have a little cash. I have tried scrounging cans with an able-bodied companion. Afoot a can scrounger simply cannot make more than a few dollars a day. One can extract the necessities of life from the Dumpsters directly with far less effort than would be required to accumulate the equivalent value in cans.

Can scroungers, then, are people who *must* have small amounts of cash. These are drug addicts and winos, mostly the latter because the amounts of cash are so small.

Spirits and drugs do, like all other commodities, turn up in Dumpsters and the scavenger will from time to time have a half bottle of a rather good wine with his dinner. But the wino cannot survive on these occasional finds; he must have his daily dose to stave off the DTs. All the cans he can carry will buy about three bottles of Wild Irish Rose.

I do not begrudge them the cans, but can scroungers tend to tear up the Dumpsters, mixing the contents and littering the area. They become so specialized that they can see only cans. They earn my contempt by passing up change, canned goods, and readily hockable items.

There are precious few courtesies among scavengers. But it is a com-   55
mon practice to set aside surplus items: pairs of shoes, clothing, canned

goods, and such. A true scavenger hates to see good stuff go to waste and what he cannot use he leaves in good condition in plain sight.

Can scroungers lay waste to everything in their path and will stir one of a pair of good shoes to the bottom of a Dumpster, to be lost or ruined in the muck. Can scroungers will even go through individual garbage cans, something I have never seen a scavenger do.

Individual garbage cans are set out on the public easement only on garbage days. On other days going through them requires trespassing close to a dwelling. Going through individual garbage cans without scattering litter is almost impossible. Litter is likely to reduce the public's tolerance of scavenging. Individual garbage cans are simply not as productive as Dumpsters; people in houses and duplexes do not move as often and for some reason do not tend to discard as much useful material. Moreover, the time required to go through one garbage can that serves one household is not much less than the time required to go through a Dumpster that contains the refuse of twenty apartments.

But my strongest reservation about going through individual garbage cans is that this seems to me a very personal kind of invasion to which I would object if I were a householder. Although many things in Dumpsters are obviously meant never to come to light, a Dumpster is somehow less personal.

I avoid trying to draw conclusions about the people who dump in the Dumpsters I frequent. I think it would be unethical to do so, although I know many people will find the idea of scavenger ethics too funny for words.

Dumpsters contain bank statements, bills, correspondence, and other documents, just as anyone might expect. But there are also less obvious sources of information. Pill bottles, for example. The labels on pill bottles contain the name of the patient, the name of the doctor, and the name of the drug. AIDS drugs and antipsychotic medicines, to name but two groups, are specific and are seldom prescribed for any other disorders. The plastic compacts for birth control pills usually have complete label information.   60

Despite all of this sensitive information, I have had only one apartment resident object to my going through the Dumpster. In that case it turned out the resident was a university athlete who was taking bets and who was afraid I would turn up his wager slips.

Occasionally a find tells a story. I once found a small paper bag containing some unused condoms, several partial tubes of flavored sexual lubricant, a partially used compact of birth control pills, and the torn pieces of a picture of a young man. Clearly she was through with him and planning to give up sex altogether.

Dumpster things are often sad — abandoned teddy bears, shredded wedding books, despaired-of sales kits. I find many pets lying in state in Dumpsters. Although I hope to get off the streets so that Lizbeth can have a long and comfortable old age, I know this hope is not very realistic. So I suppose when her time comes she too will go into a Dumpster. I will have no better place for her. And after all, for most of her life her livelihood has come from the Dumpster. When she finds something I think is safe that has been spilled from the Dumpster I let her have it. She already knows the route around the best Dumpsters. I like to think that if she survives me she will have a chance of evading the dog catcher and of finding her sustenance on the route.

Silly vanities also come to rest in the Dumpsters. I am a rather accomplished needleworker. I get a lot of materials from the Dumpsters. Evidently sorority girls, hoping to impress someone, perhaps themselves, with their mastery of a womanly art, buy a lot of embroider-by-number kits, work a few stitches horribly, and eventually discard the whole mess. I pull out their stitches, turn the canvas over, and work an original design. Do not think I refrain from chuckling as I make original gifts from these kits.

I find diaries and journals. I have often thought of compiling a book 65
of literary found objects. And perhaps I will one day. But what I find is hopelessly commonplace and bad without being, even unconsciously, camp. College students also discard their papers. I am horrified to discover the kind of paper which now merits an A in an undergraduate course. I am grateful, however, for the number of good books and magazines the students throw out.

In the area I know best I have never discovered vermin in the Dumpsters, but there are two kinds of kitty surprise. One is alley cats which I meet as they leap, claws first, out of Dumpsters. This is especially thrilling when I have Lizbeth in tow. The other kind of kitty surprise is a plastic garbage bag filled with some ponderous, amorphous mass. This always proves to be used cat litter.

City bees harvest doughnut glaze and this makes the Dumpster at the doughnut shop more interesting. My faith in the instinctive wisdom of animals is always shaken whenever I see Lizbeth attempt to catch a bee in her mouth, which she does whenever bees are present. Evidently some birds find Dumpsters profitable, for birdie surprise is almost as common as kitty surprise of the first kind. In hunting season all kinds of small game turn up in Dumpsters, some of it, sadly, not entirely dead. Curiously, summer and winter, maggots are uncommon.

The worst of the living and near-living hazards of the Dumpsters are the fire ants. The food that they claim is not much of a loss, but they are vicious and aggressive. It is very easy to brush against some surface of the Dumpster and pick up half a dozen or more fire ants, usually in some sensitive area such as the underarm. One advantage of bringing Lizbeth along as I make Dumpster rounds is that, for obvious reasons, she is very alert to ground-based fire ants. When Lizbeth recognizes the signs of fire ant infestation around our feet she does the Dance of the Zillion Fire Ants. I have learned not to ignore this warning from Lizbeth, whether I perceive the tiny ants or not, but to remove ourselves at Lizbeth's first pas de bourrée.[1] All the more so because the ants are the worst in the months I wear flip-flops, if I have them.

(Perhaps someone will misunderstand the above. Lizbeth does the Dance of the Zillion Fire Ants when she recognizes more fire ants than she cares to eat, not when she is being bitten. Since I have learned to react promptly, she does not get bitten at all. It is the isolated patrol of fire ants that falls in Lizbeth's range that deserves pity. Lizbeth finds them quite tasty.)

By far the best way to go through a Dumpster is to lower yourself   70
into it. Most of the good stuff tends to settle at the bottom because it is usually weightier than the rubbish. My more athletic companions have often demonstrated to me that they can extract much good material from a Dumpster I have already been over.

To those psychologically or physically unprepared to enter a Dumpster, I recommend a stout stick, preferably with some barb or hook at one end. The hook can be used to grab plastic garbage bags. When I find canned goods or other objects loose at the bottom of a Dumpster I usually can roll them into a small bag that I can then hoist up. Much Dumpster diving is a matter of experience for which nothing will do except practice.

Dumpster diving is outdoor work, often surprisingly pleasant. It is not entirely predictable; things of interest turn up every day and some days there are finds of great value. I am always very pleased when I can turn up exactly the thing I most wanted to find. Yet in spite of the element of change, scavenging more than most other pursuits tends to yield returns in some proportion to the effort and intelligence brought to bear. It is very sweet to turn up a few dollars in change from a Dumpster that has just been gone over by a wino.

The land is now covered with cities. The cities are full of Dumpsters. I think of scavenging as a modern form of self-reliance. In any event, after ten years of government service, where everything is geared to the lowest common denominator, I find work that rewards initiative and effort refreshing. Certainly I would be happy to have a sinecure again, but I am not heartbroken not to have one anymore.

I find from the experience of scavenging two rather deep lessons. The first is to take what I can use and let the rest go by. I have come to think that there is no value in the abstract. A thing I cannot use or make useful, perhaps by trading, has no value however fine or rare it may be. I mean useful in a broad sense — so, for example, some art I would think useful and valuable, but other art might be otherwise for me.

I was shocked to realize that some things are not worth acquiring,   75
but now I think it is so. Some material things are white elephants that eat up the possessor's substance.

---

[1]*pas de bourrée:* A transitional ballet step. — EDS.

The second lesson is of the transience of material being. This has not quite converted me to a dualist, but it has made some headway in that direction. I do not suppose that ideas are immortal, but certainly mental things are longer-lived than other material things.

Once I was the sort of person who invests material objects with sentimental value. Now I no longer have those things, but I have the sentiments yet.

Many times in my travels I have lost everything but the clothes I was wearing and Lizbeth. The things I find in Dumpsters, the love letters and ragdolls of so many lives, remind me of this lesson. Now I hardly pick up a thing without envisioning the time I will cast it away. This I think is a healthy state of mind. Almost everything I have now has already been cast out at least once, proving that what I own is valueless to someone.

Anyway, I find my desire to grab for the gaudy bauble has been largely sated. I think this is an attitude I share with the very wealthy — we both know there is plenty more where what we have came from. Between us are the rat-race millions who have confounded their selves with the objects they grasp and who nightly scavenge the cable channels looking for they know not what.

I am sorry for them.   80

The Reader's Presence

1. At the center of "On Dumpster Diving" is Lars Eighner's effort to bring out from the shadows of contemporary American life the lore and practices of scavenging, what he calls "a modern form of self-reliance." His essay also provides a compelling account of his self-education as he took to the streets for "the necessities of life." Outline the stages in this process, and summarize the ethical and moral issues and the questions of decorum that Eighner confronted along the way. Show how this process reflects the structure of his essay, "beginning with the practical art of Dumpster diving and proceeding to the abstract."

2. One of the most remarkable aspects of Eighner's essay is the tone (the attitude) he expresses toward his subject. Select a paragraph from Eighner's essay. Read it aloud. How would you characterize the sound of his voice? Does he sound, for example, tough-minded? polite? strident? experienced? cynical? something else? Consider, for example, paragraph 34, where he notes: "For myself, I avoid game, poultry, pork, and egg-based foods whether I find them raw or cooked." Where have you heard talk like this before? Do you notice any changes as the essay develops, or does Eighner maintain the same tone in discussing his subject? What

responses does he elicit from his readers when he speaks of scavenging as a "profession" and a "trade"?

3. Consider Eighner's relationship with his readers. Does he consider himself fundamentally different from or similar to his audience? In what specific ways? Consider, for example, the nature of the information Eighner provides in the essay. Does he expect his readers to be familiar with the information? How does he characterize his own knowledgeability about this often-noticed but rarely discussed activity in urban America? Comment on his use of irony in presenting information about Dumpster diving and in anticipating his readers' responses to the circumstances within which he does the work of his trade.

40

Daniel Mark Epstein

America's No. 1 Song

Daniel Mark Epstein, born in Washington, D.C. in 1948, is a poet and playwright who also writes essays that reflect upon American life and history. His poems have appeared in the New Yorker, *the* Nation, *the* Michigan Quartely Review, *and other national magazines and are collected in several books, the most recent of which is* The Boy in the Well and Other Poems *(1995). A collection of his essays is also available in* A Star of Wonder: American Stories and Memoirs *(1986). Epstein has also written a biography of the early-twentieth-century evangelist Aimee Semple McPherson,* Sister Aimee *(1993). "America's No. 1 Song" appeared in the* Atlantic *in July 1986.*

"The Star-Spangled Banner" is a sublime anthem, democratic and spacious, holding at least one note for every American. The tune is a test pattern not only for the voice but also for the human spirit. The soul singer, the rock star, and the crooner — all are humbled by the anthem. We have heard world-famous tenors and sopranos choke upon the low notes and cry out in pain at the high ones. We have seen the great Mahalia Jackson tremble.

It's unlikely that our worst enemy would have written a melody with a range more challenging to the solo performer. The melody was in fact given to us by our worst enemy at the time, the English. John Stafford Smith, an Englishman, composed the tune to which Francis Scott Key penned his lyrics a few days after the British set fire to Washington, in 1814. The capital was rebuilt, but the melody remains exactly as we received it — an inspiration and a terror. The anthem perfectly suits our collective spirit, our ambition and national range. So it ought to be sung by a crowd of Americans, to guarantee that all of the notes will be covered.

You may wonder how the national anthem achieved its election. And why, since the tune is so uncooperative, we cannot impeach the anthem and throw it out of office, like any other incompetent or mischievous official. If you are thinking such thoughts, you are in good patriotic company. House Resolution 14, which legalized the national anthem, was voted down when it was first introduced, in 1929, and hotly debated in 1931, when it passed. Every few years since then there has been an uprising, with newspaper editorials and petitions against the song and insurgents campaigning to replace "The Banner" with "America" or "This Land Is Your Land."

But it is unlikely that any new arguments will arise to unseat "The Star-Spangled Banner." Everything that could be said on the subject was said, over and over, during debates more than fifty years ago. Congressmen brought dire charges against "The Star-Spangled Banner." They denounced its ancestry, birth, and character. They dragged it through the mud.

First of all, there was the embarrassing business about the Anacreontic Society. The melody, it turned out, had been married before, to the lyrics of an English song called "To Anacreon in Heaven," which made a very different kind of anthem indeed. The ancient Greek poet Anacreon delighted in wine and lovemaking above all else. The London "gentlemen" of the Anacreontic Society in the 1770s, having chosen the poet as their patron, spent nights reviving his spirit with songs and tippling and other merrymaking.

There were other problems as well. The congressmen against "The Banner" claimed that the song was useless on the parade and battle grounds, because our soldiers could not march to it. Yet John Philip Sousa, who should have known, had once told Teddy Roosevelt that "The Star-Spangled Banner" was dandy for marching. Perhaps the soldiers weren't trying hard enough.

This leads us to the next argument against "The Star-Spangled Banner": that it is too difficult for schoolchildren to sing. An editorial in the New York *World* of March 31, 1930, answered this charge with logic and eloquence.

> What if school children could sing it? We should be so sick of it by now that we could not endure the sound of it, as the French are sick of the "Marseillaise." The virtues of "The Star-Spangled Banner" are that it does require a wide compass, so that school children cannot sing it, and that it is in three-four time, so that parades cannot march to it. So being, it has managed to remain fresh, not frayed and worn, and the citizenry still hear it with some semblance of a thrill, some touch of reverence.

And then there were the congressmen who suggested that the 1814 bombardment of Fort McHenry was too paltry a background for the national anthem. They had not read their history. If the British had gotten into Baltimore, only a few days after burning down Washington, no one can say where they might have stopped. George Washington had been dead fifteen years. Andrew Jackson was in New Orleans. If the British Navy's offensive had not been foundered at Fort McHenry, we might be singing "God Save the Queen" instead of "The Star-Spangled Banner."

Perhaps the best argument against House Resolution 14 is that it was unnecessary and therefore impertinent. In the nineteenth century Admiral George Dewey had designated "The Star-Spangled Banner" as the anthem for all Navy ceremonies. When advisors asked President Wilson, in 1916, what song should accompany state functions, he automatically replied: "The Banner." Everybody knew it was the national anthem.

But Americans do not like to be told what to eat or drink or sing.   10
Though they have eaten hot dogs and drunk beer and sung "The Star-Spangled Banner" in baseball parks for generations, try to pass a law requiring them to do so and Congress will never hear the end of it. That is the American way, and a good way. When Representative J. C. Linthicum, of Maryland, introduced a bill to make "The Star-Spangled Banner" our *official* anthem, he might have foreseen that he might be subjecting "The Banner" to a scrutiny usually reserved for presidential candidates. Congress's vote, in 1931, to give the song official status as our national anthem, despite its vocal challenges, unmarchability, and checkered past, was surely a gesture of affection with few parallels.

"The Star-Spangled Banner" deserved to win that vote. Our anthem remains one of the purest examples of unpremeditated, inspired genius in American history. Remember that Francis Scott Key, the lawyer-poet, was more lawyer than poet. Apart from the lyrics of "The Banner," and "Lord With Glowing Heart I'd Praise Thee," a hymn infrequently sung in churches, Key never wrote a line of memorable verse. Francis Scott Key was tone deaf. If anyone had told him early in September of 1814 that he was about to write the most famous song in America, the lawyer-poet would likely have laughed, with a modesty rare in poets, and gone about his business.

Key's business in September of 1814 was a matter of life and death. America had declared war upon pretexts the lawyer-poet condemned as a cover for imperialism. American privateers were looting British ships, and our troops had set Toronto on fire during a bungled attempt to annex Canada. Key was a gentle soul, so unsuited to conflict that he could never bring himself to run for political office. Yet, despite his mildness and his objections to the war, he fought dutifully in the defense of Washington. And when the British took away a civilian prisoner, Dr. William Beanes, Key begged for President Madison's commission to sail after them and plead for the doctor's release.

Key sailed down the Chesapeake in a small cartel ship, under the white flag of truce. He found the British fleet lying at anchor in the mouth of the Potomac. Admiral George Cockburn was about to hang Dr. Beanes from the ship's yardarm for acts of inhospitality to English soldiers as they passed through Upper Marlborough. The doctor had been having a garden party to celebrate the town's escape from burning, when a few straggling dragoons had come into his yard and made bold to steal the punch. Doctor Beanes had been court-martialed for not giving them any, among other discourtesies.

With the passion and eloquence of a great lawyer-poet, Francis Scott Key pleaded for Doctor Beanes's life. He argued that the detention of civilians outraged all principles of civilized warfare; if great nations could not agree on the principles of warfare, what on earth *could* they agree on? Admiral Cockburn was unmoved. What finally swayed him was certain letters, which Key was able, fortuitously, to produce from his satchel, from wounded British soldiers, showing what tender care Dr. Beanes had taken of them. After a conference the British officers announced that they would release the ill-mannered doctor the next morning.

Key's mission was badly timed for all purposes but the creation of   15
our anthem. That very night the British fleet received orders to attack Baltimore. Since the British could not conceal this from Key, they insisted that he accept their hospitality until the battle was over. They entertained the lawyer-poet on his own cartel ship. From there he had an excellent view of the contest, being right in the middle of it.

What was Francis Scott Key's state of mind as he watched the rockets' red glare and bombs bursting in air, and then saw the banner waving? He jotted notes on the back of an envelope. Later he would explain, "If it had been a hanging matter to make a poem, I must have made it." The reference to execution is not careless. It is more than likely that the gentle Key, in making his poem, was as terrified a lawyer-poet as ever held a quill in his hand.

In 1814 the rockets' red glare and bombs bursting in air were neither poetic fantasies nor Fourth of July fireworks. They were real, live bombs, screaming and whistling and exploding around the poet. Dr. Beanes, who had joined Key on the cartel's deck, must have thought that he had been saved from hanging only to be blown up.

The British rocket, a kind of primitive guided missile, was an awesome innovation in 1814. Key had watched his own men panic under bombardment from those rockets during the defense of Washington, and probably figured the Baltimoreans would do the same. The lawyer-poet must have had wildly mixed emotions as the British ships, and his cartel ship with them, approached the shore, beautifully lighted by rockets so that his fellow Americans could take better aim with their cannons. We could hardly blame Key if he had prayed for a swift surrender. He did not. He wrote a poem instead, and prayed for the sight of the flag.

The flag that flew above Fort McHenry in 1814 may be the largest battle flag ever flown. It originally was thirty feet high by forty-two feet wide — 420 square yards of red, white, and blue bunting. The flag was made to order for the defense of Fort McHenry — and, seemingly, for the

creation of our anthem. What else would possess General John Stricker
and Commodore Joshua Barney, otherwise reasonable men, to order such
a gigantic flag? They wanted to be sure that Key would see it. Although
the seamstress Mary Pickersgill snipped the stripes and stars in her tiny
workroom, she could not stitch them together there. Mary and her little
daughter worked on hands and knees, by daylight and lamplight, stitching together the Star-Spangled Banner on the malthouse floor of Claggett's
Brewery. They finished their sewing just as the British fleet was nearing
Baltimore Harbor.

The flag is surrealistically large. If you do not believe this, then go   20
and look at it, exhibited like a dinosaur in the Smithsonian Institution's
Museum of American History. That flag, flying above Fort McHenry,
must have made the fort, and the city behind it, look tiny, like a child's
sand castle. After the long night of rockets and bomb blasts and horror,
what was the author of our national anthem feeling when he saw that titanic flag flying weirdly above his homeland? Some would imagine relief.
But it was too soon for Key to feel relief — he was still a prisoner of war.
Some would imagine pride. But Key was famous for his humility — and
besides, pride does not spring readily in one's breast so soon after courage
has been shaken. After a night of unspeakable terror, with every reason to
believe that the United States would surrender in the glare of the rockets,
Francis Scott Key's emotion upon spying that bizarre flag must have been
utter amazement.

Wonder is a better word. Key could not believe his eyes, and his lyrics
reproduce in us that sense of wonder. Remember, the refrain that closes
the first stanza is a question:

> O! say does that star-spangled Banner yet wave,
> O'er the land of the free, and the home of the brave?

When we sing the anthem in the ballpark, or in school, or before the fireworks display on July 4, it is altogether fitting that we sing no more of the
lyrics after that question. The birth and survival of this nation remains
one of the wonders of the world. This was never more evident than it was
to the lawyer-poet on that cloudy morning in 1814. The flag was amazing
but undeniable. Key knew exactly how brave *he* was, having so recently
been measured for bravery. Yet he still had sensible doubts about his freedom. That is the American way, and it is a good way.

The Reader's Presence

1. What does Epstein's title suggest? If you saw only the title, what
   would you think the essay would be about? Why do you think
   Epstein, an established poet and essayist, would be especially interested in the subject and occasion he chose to write about?

2. Why do some people dislike "The Star-Spangled Banner"? Which arguments against it do you find most persuasive? Would you support a measure to replace it with another national anthem? Explain why or why not.

3. Epstein constructs his essay around information about the anthem and its author. How difficult do you think it was to obtain this information? Epstein's informal essay lists no sources; what might a few of them be? In what specific ways does Epstein's essay differ from what you might find in an encyclopedia account of the same topic? Go through the essay and identify passages you would not expect to find in an entry intended to be exclusively informative. What does Epstein bring to his information?

41

Ian Frazier

Street Scene: Minor Heroism in a Major Metropolitan Area

The journalist and essayist Ian Frazier (b. 1951) started his career on the staff of the New Yorker, *writing "Talk of the Town" pieces as well as signed essays. Many of these essays can be found in his first two books:* Dating Your Mom *(1986) and* Nobody Better, Better than Nobody *(1987). He continues to publish in the* New Yorker *and in other national magazines; "Street Scene: Minor Heroism in a Major Metropolitan Area" appeared in the* Atlantic *in 1995. In the mid-1980s Frazier left his job in New York and embarked on a journey across the North American prairies from Texas to Montana. The book that emerged after several years spent exploring this region,* Great Plains *(1989), was a great success with both critics and readers. In his most recent book,* Family *(1994), Frazier turns to a subject closer to home and tells the story of twelve generations of his family.*

In all of his writing Frazier pays close attention to detail and to location. "If you know something about a place it can save your sanity," he says, and a writer can find that knowledge through observation. "With a lot of writing, what you see is the top, the pinnacle, and the rest is invisible — all of these observations are ways of keeping yourself from flying off into space."

On a Saturday morning I left my Brooklyn apartment to shop for a dinner party and saw a crowd — baseball caps, legs straddling bicycles, an arm holding a lamp stand with a dangling price tag — around a person on the sidewalk. I was almost at my doorstep; I went closer, and saw a woman lying on her back with her lips turned into her mouth and her eyes neither open nor closed. Her hair was gray, her face the same color as the pavement. A slight, brown-haired woman was giving her mouth-to-mouth resuscitation, while a well-built brown-skinned man with hair close-cropped like a skullcap was performing chest massage. He and the woman giving mouth-to-mouth were counting, "One, two, three, four, *five*." Then he would pause and she would breathe into the woman's mouth.

A police car drove up and a young Hispanic cop got out. He went over to the woman and talked to the pair trying to revive her. Someone pointed out to him the woman's son, a tall, gangly man who stood nearby, kind of bobbing up and down and nodding to himself. The cop patted the son on the arm and spoke to him. A large, lumpy-faced man with his pants high on his waist said to me, "The ambulance will never come. They never come when you call anymore. They don't care. In New York nobody cares. People are so arrogant on the street in Manhattan. I call New York a lost city. Used to be a great city, now it's a lost city. People are nicer out west or upstate. I went to Methodist Hospital and the nurse wouldn't talk to me. I told her right to her face . . ." After a minute I realized it made no difference if I listened to him or not. The pair at work on the woman paused for a moment while the man asked if anyone had a razor so he could cut the woman's shirt. Someone found a pocket knife. He bent over his work again. Minutes passed. The cop asked if he was getting tired and he said he wasn't. Sirens rose in the distance, faded. Then one rose and didn't fade, and in the next second an Emergency Medical Service truck from Long Island College Hospital pulled up. The chest-massage guy didn't quit until the EMS paramedic took over; then he straightened up, looked at the truck, and said, "Long Island? Fuckin' Methodist is only three blocks away."

The EMS guys put the woman on a stretcher and lifted her into the back of the truck. Hands gathered up a few items the woman had dropped on the sidewalk; someone pointed out her false teeth. The woman who had been giving mouth-to-mouth bent over and picked up the teeth. She paused just a second before touching them. I thought this was from squeamishness; then I saw it was from care. Gently she handed the teeth to one of the paramedics. Then she and the chest-massage guy parted without a word, or none that I saw. The guy walked toward his car, a two-tone Pontiac. Apparently he had just been driving by; its door was still open. I went up to him and thanked him for what he had done. I shook his hand. His strength went right up my arm like a warm current. I ran after the woman, who was now well down the block. I tapped her shoulder and she turned around and I said thank you. Her eyes were full of what had just happened. There were tears on her upper cheeks. She said something like, "Oh, of course, don't mention it." She was a thin-faced white woman with Prince Valiant hair and a green windbreaker — an ordinary-looking person, but glowingly beautiful.

Is this a NY Scene or an urban one in general.

The EMS guys and the cop worked on the woman in the back of the truck with the doors open. The crowd dispersed. The son crouched inside the truck holding the IV bottle for a while; then he stood outside again. Eventually the cop got out of the back of the truck. The son climbed in, the EMS guys closed the doors, and the truck drove off with sirens going. The cop sat in his car. The window was down. I walked over and asked, "Excuse me — did they ever get a pulse?" He winced slightly at the nakedness of my question. A pause. Then he shook his head. "Nahhh. Not really."

I went to the park across the street. A bunch of kids were hanging around the entrance jawing back and forth at each other. In my neighborhood there is a gang called NAB, or Ninth Avenue Boys. Newspaper stories say they've done a lot of beatings and robberies nearby. From a few feet away I heard one kid say to another, "You shut your stupid fuckin' chicken-breath mouth." I felt as strong as the strangers I had just talked to. I walked through the kids without fear.

5 why is it important to interject this scene at the very end.

What becomes Frazier's final analysis of the situation — the event of the morning?

The Reader's Presence

1. For most of the essay, Frazier's perspective is that of a "fly on the wall": observing everything without actively taking part in the action or commenting on its meaning. How does this perspective shape your reading of the scene? Would you see the main actors differently if Frazier made a point of calling them heroes?

2. Think about how a reporter might cover the same incident for a local newspaper. How would the reporter's story differ from Frazier's account? What kinds of details about the scene does Frazier include, and what information does he omit? What can you infer about his point in writing the essay from the way he presents the incident?

3. "I felt as strong as the strangers I had just talked to. I walked through the kids without fear," says Frazier to conclude the essay. Does this seem like an appropriate ending to the piece? What do you think Frazier is saying about how life in the city shapes one's perceptions of other people?

What is the point of this essay?

Q. ① If it was entitled "Small Town Scene" would you expect story to unfold differently? — ② Where is the focus of the essay?

42

Stephen Jay Gould

Sex, Drugs, Disasters, and the Extinction of Dinosaurs

Stephen Jay Gould (b. 1941) is professor of geology and zoology at Harvard and curator of invertebrate paleontology at Harvard's Museum of Comparative Zoology. He has published widely on evolution and other topics and has earned a reputation for making technical subjects readily comprehensible to lay readers without trivializing the material. His The Panda's Thumb *(1980) won the American Book Award, and* The Mismeasure of Man *(1981) won the National Book Critics Circle Award. Gould has published over one hundred articles in scientific journals, and contributes to national magazines as well. "Sex, Drugs, Disasters, and the Extinction of Dinosaurs" appeared in* Discover *magazine in 1984. More recently, Gould has written* Bully for Brontosaurus *(1991),* Eight Little Piggies *(1993), and* Full House *(1996). Among many other honors and awards, he has been a fellow of the National Science Foundation and the MacArthur Foundation. John Updike comments that "Gould, in his scrupulous explication of [other scientists'] carefully wrought half-truths, abolishes the unnecessary distinction between the humanities and science, and honors the latter as a branch of humanistic thought, fallible and poetic."*

When asked if he finds it difficult to write about complex scientific concepts in language that is accessible to general readers, Gould replied, "I don't see why it should be that difficult. . . . Every field has its jargon. I think scientists hide behind theirs perhaps more than people in other professions do — it's part of our mythology — but I don't think the concepts of science are intrinsically more difficult than the professional notions in any other field."

Science, in its most fundamental definition, is a fruitful mode of inquiry, not a list of enticing conclusions. The conclusions are the consequence, not the essence.

My greatest unhappiness with most popular presentations of science concerns their failure to separate fascinating claims from the methods that scientists use to establish the facts of nature. Journalists, and the public, thrive on controversial and stunning statements. But science is, basically, a way of knowing — in P. B. Medawar's apt words, "the art of the soluble." If the growing corps of popular science writers would focus on *how* scientists develop and defend those fascinating claims, they would make their greatest possible contribution to public understanding.

Consider three ideas, proposed in perfect seriousness to explain that greatest of all titillating puzzles — the extinction of dinosaurs. Since these three notions invoke the primally fascinating themes of our culture — sex, drugs, and violence — they surely reside in the category of fascinating claims. I want to show why two of them rank as silly speculation, while the other represents science at its grandest and most useful.

Science works with the testable proposals. If, after much compilation and scrutiny of data, new information continues to affirm a hypothesis, we may accept it provisionally and gain confidence as further evidence mounts. We can never be completely sure that a hypothesis is right, though we may be able to show with confidence that it is wrong. The best scientific hypotheses are also generous and expansive: They suggest extensions and implications that enlighten related, and even far distant, subjects. Simply consider how the idea of evolution has influenced virtually every intellectual field.

Useless speculation, on the other hand, is restrictive. It generates no testable hypothesis, and offers no way to obtain potentially refuting evidence. Please note that I am not speaking of truth or falsity. The speculation may well be true; still, if it provides, in principle, no material for affirmation or rejection, we can make nothing of it. It must simply stand forever as an intriguing idea. Useless speculation turns in on itself and leads nowhere; good science, containing both seeds for its potential refutation and implications for more and different testable knowledge, reaches out. But, enough preaching. Let's move on to dinosaurs, and the three proposals for their extinction.

5

1. *Sex:* Testes function only in a narrow range of temperature (those of mammals hang externally in a scrotal sac because internal body temperatures are too high for their proper function). A worldwide rise in temperature at the close of the Cretaceous period caused the testes of dinosaurs to stop functioning and led to their extinction by sterilization of males.
2. *Drugs:* Angiosperms (flowering plants) first evolved toward the end of the dinosaurs' reign. Many of these plants contain psychoactive agents, avoided by mammals today as a result of their bitter taste. Dinosaurs had neither means to taste the bitterness nor livers effective enough to detoxify the substances. They died of massive overdoses.
3. *Disasters:* A large comet or asteroid struck the earth some 65 million years ago, lofting a cloud of dust into the sky and blocking sunlight, thereby suppressing photosynthesis and so drastically lowering world temperatures that dinosaurs and hosts of other creatures became extinct.

Before analyzing these three tantalizing statements, we must establish a basic ground rule often violated in proposals for the dinosaurs' demise.

There is no separate problem of the extinction of dinosaurs. Too often we divorce specific events from their wider contexts and systems of cause and effect. The fundamental fact of dinosaur extinction is its synchrony with the demise of so many other groups across a wide range of habitats, from terrestrial to marine.

The history of life has been punctuated by brief episodes of mass extinction. A recent analysis by University of Chicago paleontologists Jack Sepkoski and Dave Raup, based on the best and most exhaustive tabulation of data ever assembled, shows clearly that five episodes of mass dying stand well above the "background" extinctions of normal times (when we consider all mass extinctions, large and small, they seem to fall in a regular 26-million-year cycle). The Cretaceous debacle, occurring 65 million years ago and separating the Mesozoic and Cenozoic eras of our geological time scale, ranks prominently among the five. Nearly all the marine plankton (single-celled floating creatures) died with geological suddenness; among marine invertebrates, nearly 15 percent of all families perished, including many previously dominant groups, especially the ammonites (relatives of squids in coiled shells). On land, the dinosaurs disappeared after more than 100 million years of unchallenged domination.

In this context, speculations limited to dinosaurs alone ignore the larger phenomenon. We need a coordinated explanation for a system of events that includes the extinction of dinosaurs as one component. Thus it makes little sense, though it may fuel our desire to view mammals as inevitable inheritors of the earth, to guess that dinosaurs died because small mammals ate their eggs (a perennial favorite among untestable speculations). It seems most unlikely that some disaster peculiar to dinosaurs befell these massive beasts — and that the debacle happened to strike just when one of history's five great dyings had enveloped the earth for completely different reasons.

The testicular theory, an old favorite from the 1940s, had its root in an interesting and thoroughly respectable study of temperature tolerances in the American alligator, published in the staid *Bulletin of the American Museum of Natural History* in 1946 by three experts on living and fossil reptiles — E. H. Colbert, my own first teacher in paleontology; R. B. Cowles; and C. M. Bogert.

The first sentence of their summary reveals a purpose beyond alligators: "This report describes an attempt to infer the reactions of extinct reptiles, especially the dinosaurs, to high temperatures as based upon reactions observed in the modern alligator." They studied, by rectal thermometry, the body temperatures of alligators under changing conditions of heating and cooling. (Well, let's face it, you wouldn't want to try sticking a thermometer under a 'gator's tongue.) The predictions under test go way back to an old theory first stated by Galileo in the 1630s — the unequal scaling of surfaces and volumes. As an animal, or any object, grows (provided its shape doesn't change), surface areas must increase more slowly than volumes — since surfaces get larger as length squared, while

10

volumes increase much more rapidly, as length cubed. Therefore, small animals have high ratios of surface to volume, while large animals cover themselves with relatively little surface.

Among cold-blooded animals lacking any physiological mechanism for keeping their temperatures constant, small creatures have a hell of a time keeping warm — because they lose so much heat through their relatively large surfaces. On the other hand, large animals, with their relatively small surfaces, may lose heat so slowly that, once warm, they may maintain effectively constant temperatures against ordinary fluctuations of climate. (In fact, the resolution of the "hot-blooded dinosaur" controversy that burned so brightly a few years back may simply be that, while large dinosaurs possessed no physiological mechanism for constant temperature, and were not therefore warm-blooded in the technical sense, their large size and relatively small surface area kept them warm.)

Colbert, Cowles, and Bogert compared the warming rates of small and large alligators. As predicted, the small fellows heated up (and cooled down) more quickly. When exposed to a warm sun, a tiny 50-gram (1.76-ounce) alligator heated up one degree Celsius every minute and a half, while a large alligator, 260 times bigger at 13,000 grams (28.7 pounds), took seven and a half minutes to gain a degree. Extrapolating up to an adult 10-ton dinosaur, they concluded that a one-degree rise in body temperature would take eighty-six hours. If large animals absorb heat so slowly (through their relatively small surfaces), they will also be unable to shed any excess heat gained when temperatures rise above a favorable level.

The authors then guessed that large dinosaurs lived at or near their optimum temperatures; Cowles suggested that a rise in global temperatures just before the Cretaceous extinction caused the dinosaurs to heat up beyond their optimal tolerance — and, being so large, they couldn't shed the unwanted heat. (In a most unusual statement within a scientific paper, Colbert and Bogert then explicitly disavowed this speculative extension of their empirical work on alligators.) Cowles conceded that this excess heat probably wasn't enough to kill or even to enervate the great beasts, but since testes often function only within a narrow range of temperature, he proposed that this global rise might have sterilized all the males, causing extinction by natural contraception.

The overdose theory has recently been supported by UCLA psychiatrist Ronald K. Siegel. Siegel has gathered, he claims, more than 2,000 records of animals who, when given access, administer various drugs to themselves — from a mere swig of alcohol to massive doses of the big H. Elephants will swill the equivalent of twenty beers at a time, but do not like alcohol in concentrations greater than 7 percent. In a silly bit of anthropocentric speculation, Siegel states that "elephants drink, perhaps, to forget . . . the anxiety produced by shrinking rangeland and the competition for food."

Since fertile imaginations can apply almost any hot idea to the extinction of dinosaurs, Siegel found a way. Flowering plants did not evolve until 15 late in the dinosaurs' reign. These plants also produced an array of aromatic, amino-acid-based alkaloids — the major group of psychoactive agents. Most mammals are "smart" enough to avoid these potential poisons. The alkaloids simply don't taste good (they are bitter); in any case, we mammals have livers happily supplied with the capacity to detoxify them. But, Siegel speculates, perhaps dinosaurs could neither taste the bitterness nor detoxify the substances once ingested. He recently told members of the American Psychological Association: "I'm not suggesting that all dinosaurs OD'd on plant drugs, but it certainly was a factor." He also argued that death by overdose may help explain why so many dinosaur fossils are found in contorted positions. (Do not go gentle into that good night.)

Extraterrestrial catastrophes have long pedigrees in the popular literature of extinction, but the subject exploded again in 1979, after a long lull, when the father-son, physicist-geologist team of Luis and Walter Alvarez proposed that an asteroid, some 10 km in diameter, struck the earth 65 million years ago (comets, rather than asteroids, have since gained favor. Good science is self-corrective).

The force of such a collision would be immense, greater by far than the megatonnage of all the world's nuclear weapons. In trying to reconstruct a scenario that would explain the simultaneous dying of dinosaurs on land and so many creatures in the sea, the Alvarezes proposed that a gigantic dust cloud, generated by particles blown aloft in the impact, would so darken the earth that photosynthesis would cease and temperatures drop precipitously. (Rage, rage against the dying of the light.) The single-celled photosynthetic oceanic plankton, with life cycles measured in weeks, would perish outright, but land plants might survive through the dormancy of their seeds (land plants were not much affected by the Cretaceous extinction, and any adequate theory must account for the curious pattern of differential survival). Dinosaurs would die by starvation and freezing; small, warm-blooded mammals, with more modest requirements for food and better regulation of body temperature, would squeak through. "Let the bastards freeze in the dark," as bumper stickers of our chauvinistic neighbors in sunbelt states proclaimed several years ago during the Northeast's winter oil crisis.

All three theories, testicular malfunction, psychoactive overdosing, and asteroidal zapping, grab our attention mightily. As pure phenomenology, they rank about equally high on any hit parade of primal fascination. Yet one represents expansive science, the others restrictive and untestable speculation. The proper criterion lies in evidence and methodology; we must probe behind the superficial fascination of particular claims.

How could we possibly decide whether the hypothesis of testicular frying is right or wrong? We would have to know things that the fossil record cannot provide. What temperatures were optimal for dinosaurs? Could they avoid the absorption of excess heat by staying in the shade, or in caves? At what temperatures did their testicles cease to function? Were late Cretaceous climates ever warm enough to drive the internal temperatures of dinosaurs close to this ceiling? Testicles simply don't fossilize, and how could we infer their temperature tolerances even if they did? In short, Cowles's hypothesis is only an intriguing speculation leading nowhere. The most damning statement against it appeared right in the conclusion of Colbert, Cowles, and Bogert's paper, when they admitted: "It is difficult to advance any definite arguments against the hypothesis." My statement may seem paradoxical — isn't a hypothesis really good if you can't devise any arguments against it? Quite the contrary. It is simply untestable and unusable.

Siegel's overdosing has even less going for it. At least Cowles extrap-   20
olated his conclusion from some good data on alligators. And he didn't completely violate the primary guideline of siting dinosaur extinction in the context of a general mass dying — for rise in temperature could be the root cause of a general catastrophe, zapping dinosaurs by testicular malfunction and different groups for other reasons. But Siegel's speculation cannot touch the extinction of ammonites or oceanic plankton (diatoms make their own food with good sweet sunlight; they don't OD on the chemicals of terrestrial plants). It is simply a gratuitous, attention-grabbing guess. It cannot be tested, for how can we know what dinosaurs tasted and what their livers could do? Livers don't fossilize any better than testicles.

The hypothesis doesn't even make any sense in its own context. Angiosperms were in full flower ten million years before dinosaurs went the way of all flesh. Why did it take so long? As for the pains of a chemical death recorded in contortions of fossils, I regret to say (or rather I'm pleased to note for the dinosaurs' sake) that Siegel's knowledge of geology must be a bit deficient: muscles contract after death and geological strata rise and fall with motions of the earth's crust after burial — more than enough reason to distort a fossil's pristine appearance.

The impact story, on the other hand, has a sound basis in evidence. It can be tested, extended, refined, and, if wrong, disproved. The Alvarezes did not just construct an arresting guess for public consumption. They proposed their hypothesis after laborious geochemical studies with Frank Asaro and Helen Michael had revealed a massive increase of iridium in rocks deposited right at the time of extinction. Iridium, a rare metal of the platinum group, is virtually absent from indigenous rocks of the earth's crust; most of our iridium arrives on extraterrestrial objects that strike the earth.

The Alverez hypothesis bore immediate fruit. Based originally on evidence from two European localities, it led geochemists throughout the world to examine other sediments of the same age. They found abnormally high amounts of iridium everywhere — from continental rocks of the western United States to deep sea cores from the South Atlantic.

Cowles proposed his testicular hypothesis in the mid-1940s. Where has it gone since then? Absolutely nowhere, because scientists can do nothing with it. The hypothesis must stand as a curious appendage to a solid study of alligators. Siegel's overdose scenario will also win a few press notices and fade into oblivion. The Alvarezes' asteroid falls into a different category altogether, and much of the popular commentary has missed this essential distinction by focusing on the impact and its attendant results, and forgetting what really matters to a scientist — the iridium. If you talk just about asteroids, dust, and darkness, you tell stories no better and no more entertaining than fried testicles or terminal trips. It is the iridium — the source of testable evidence — that counts and forges the crucial distinction between speculation and science.

The proof, to twist a phrase, lies in the doing. Cowles's hypothesis has generated nothing in thirty-five years. Since its proposal in 1979, the Alvarez hypothesis has spawned hundreds of studies, a major conference, and attendant publications. Geologists are fired up. They are looking for iridium at all other extinction boundaries. Every week exposes a new wrinkle in the scientific press. Further evidence that the Cretaceous iridium represents extraterrestrial impact and not indigenous volcanism continues to accumulate. As I revise this essay in November 1984 (this paragraph will be out of date when the book is published),[1] new data include chemical "signatures" of other isotopes indicating unearthly provenance, glass spherules of a size and sort produced by impact and not by volcanic eruptions, and high-pressure varieties of silica formed (so far as we know) only under the tremendous shock of impact.

My point is simply this: Whatever the eventual outcome (I suspect it will be positive), the Alvarez hypothesis is exciting, fruitful science because it generates tests, provides us with things to do, and expands outward. We are having fun, battling back and forth, moving toward a resolution, and extending the hypothesis beyond its original scope.

As just one example of the unexpected, distant cross-fertilization that good science engenders, the Alvarez hypothesis made a major contribution to a theme that has riveted public attention in the past few months — so-called nuclear winter. In a speech delivered in April 1982, Luis Alvarez calculated the energy that a ten-kilometer asteroid would release on impact. He compared such an explosion with a full nuclear exchange and implied that all-out atomic war might unleash similar consequences.

This theme of impact leading to massive dust clouds and falling temperatures formed an important input to the decision of Carl Sagan and a group of colleagues to model the climatic consequences of nuclear holocaust. Full nuclear exchange would probably generate the same kind of dust cloud and darkening that may have wiped out the dinosaurs. Temperatures would drop precipitously and agriculture might become impossible. Avoidance of nuclear war is fundamentally an ethical and political imperative, but we must know the factual consequences to make firm judgments. I am heartened by a final link across disciplines and deep con-

25

---

[1]*The Flamingo's Smile* (1985), in which Gould collected this essay. — EDS.

cerns — another criterion, by the way, of science at its best.[2] A recognition of the very phenomenon that made our evolution possible by exterminating the previously dominant dinosaurs and clearing a way for the evolution of large mammals, including us, might actually help to save us from joining those magnificent beasts in contorted poses among the strata of the earth.

The Reader's Presence

1. Although the title of Gould's essay focuses on the extinction of dinosaurs, his overriding interest is in demonstrating the way science works, and his purpose is to make that process fully accessible and understandable to the general public. Where does he lay out this central claim, and how does he demonstrate, clarify, and complicate it as his essay proceeds?

2. What distinctions does Gould draw among "testable proposals," "intriguing ideas," and "useless speculation"? What features of each does he identify? Reread his summary of the three proposals for the extinction of dinosaurs. Which of the three terms cited above would you use to characterize this summary? In what specific ways does Gould use them to demonstrate the limitations of popular presentations of scientific theory? What crucial piece of evidence does he omit from the summary? With what effect?

3. Reread Gould's essay, with special attention to his use of tone, diction, syntax, and metaphor. How does he use these compositional strategies to make information accessible to his readers? Point to passages where Gould uses the diction and syntax of a serious scientist. When — and with what effects — does his prose sound more colloquial? Does his tone remain consistent throughout the essay? If not, when and how does it change? With what effects?

---

[2]This quirky connection so tickles my fancy that I break my own strict rule about eliminating redundancies from [this essay]. . . . — GOULD'S NOTE.

43

Pete Hamill

Crack and the Box

Pete Hamill (b. 1935) began his career in journalism by writing a letter to the editor of the New York Post *in which he criticized the lack of working-class perspectives in the paper's articles. The editor invited Hamill to write for the* Post, *and before long he was covering the major events of the 1960s: the civil rights movement, the Vietnam War, the election of 1968. In addition to publication in the* New York Post, *Hamill's award-winning columns have appeared in* Newsday, *the* New York Daily News, *the* Village Voice, *and* Esquire. *Many of those columns have been collected in* Irrational Ravings *(1971) and* The Invisible City: A New York Sketchbook *(1980). Hamill also writes short stories, screenplays, and novels, including, most recently,* The Guns of Heaven *(1983) and* Loving Women *(1989). He regularly contributes articles and essays to national magazines; "Crack and the Box" appeared in* Esquire *in 1990. His most recent book is* Piecework: Writings on Men and Women, Fools and Heroes, Lost Cities, Vanished Friends, Small Pleasures, Large Calamities and How the Weather Was *(1996).*

In 1994 Hamill published a memoir, A Drinking Life, *about his life as an alcoholic (he stopped drinking in 1973). About the experience of writing this book, Hamill says, "Writers are rememberers or they're nothing. And that remembering means remembering the pain and the grief and lousiness along with all the joys and triumphs and everything else."*

One sad rainy morning last winter, I talked to a woman who was addicted to crack cocaine. She was twenty-two, stiletto-thin, with eyes as old as tombs. She was living in two rooms in a welfare hotel with her children, who were two, three, and five years of age. Her story was the usual tangle of human woe: early pregnancy, dropping out of school, vanished men, smack and then crack, tricks with johns in parked cars to pay for the dope. I asked her why she did drugs. She shrugged in an empty way and couldn't really answer beyond "makes me feel good." While we talked and she told her tale of squalor, the children ignored us. They were watching television.

Walking back to my office in the rain, I brooded about the woman, her zombielike children, and my own callous indifference. I'd heard so

[handwritten margin notes: "Intro & background info."]

many versions of the same story that I almost never wrote them anymore; the sons of similar women, glimpsed a dozen years ago, are now in Dannemora or Soledad or Joliet; in a hundred cities, their daughters are moving into the same loveless rooms. As I walked, a series of homeless men approached me for change, most of them junkies. Others sat in doorways, staring at nothing. They were additional casualties of our time of plague, demoralized reminders that although this country holds only 2 percent of the world's population, it consumes 65 percent of the world's supply of hard drugs.

Why, for God's sake? Why do so many millions of Americans of all ages, races, and classes choose to spend all or part of their lives stupefied? I've talked to hundreds of addicts over the years; some were my friends. But none could give sensible answers. They stutter about the pain of the world, about despair or boredom, the urgent need for magic or pleasure in a society empty of both. But then they just shrug. Americans have the money to buy drugs; the supply is plentiful. But almost nobody in power asks, *Why?* Least of all, George Bush and his drug warriors.

William Bennett talks vaguely about the heritage of sixties permissiveness, the collapse of Traditional Values, and all that. But he and Bush offer the traditional American excuse: It Is Somebody Else's Fault. This posture set the stage for the self-righteous invasion of Panama, the bloodiest drug arrest in world history. Bush even accused Manuel Noriega of "poisoning our children." But he never asked *why* so many Americans demand the poison.

And then, on that rainy morning in New York, I saw another one of those ragged men staring out at the rain from a doorway. I suddenly remembered the inert postures of the children in that welfare hotel, and I thought: *television.*

Ah, no, I muttered to myself: too simple. Something as complicated as drug addiction can't be blamed on television. Come on. . . . but I remembered all those desperate places I'd visited as a reporter, where there were no books and a TV set was always playing and the older kids had gone off somewhere to shoot smack, except for the kid who was at the mortuary in a coffin. I also remembered when I was a boy in the forties and early fifties, and drugs were a minor sideshow, a kind of dark little rumor. And there was one major difference between that time and this: television.

We had unemployment then; illiteracy, poor living conditions, racism, governmental stupidity, a gap between rich and poor. We didn't have the all-consuming presence of television in our lives. Now two generations of Americans have grown up with television from their earliest moments of consciousness. Those same American generations are afflicted by the pox of drug addiction.

Only thirty-five years ago, drug addiction was not a major problem in this country. There were drug addicts. We had some at the end of the nineteenth century, hooked on the cocaine in patent medicines. During the placid fifties, Commissioner Harry Anslinger pumped up the budget

of the old Bureau of Narcotics with fantasies of reefer madness. Heroin
was sold and used in most major American cities, while the bebop generation of jazz musicians got jammed up with horse.

But until the early sixties, narcotics were still marginal to American
life; they weren't the $120-billion market they make up today. If anything,
those years have an eerie innocence. In 1955 there were 31,700,000 TV sets
in use in the country (the number is now past 184 million). But the majority of the audience had grown up without the dazzling new medium. They
embraced it, were diverted by it, perhaps even loved it, but they weren't
formed by it. That year, the New York police made a mere 1,234 felony
drug arrests; in 1988 it was 43,901. They confiscated ninety-seven ounces
of cocaine for the entire year; last year it was hundreds of pounds. During
each year of the fifties in New York, there were only about a hundred
narcotics-related deaths. But by the end of the sixties, when the first generation of children formed by television had come to maturity (and thus to
the marketplace), the number of such deaths had risen to 1,200. The same
phenomenon was true in every major American city.

In the last Nielsen survey of American viewers, the average family   10
was watching television seven hours a day. This has never happened before in history. No people has ever been entertained for seven hours a
day. The Elizabethans didn't go to the theater seven hours a day. The pre-
TV generation did not go to the movies seven hours a day. Common
sense tells us that this all-pervasive diet of instant imagery, sustained now
for forty years, must have changed us in profound ways.

Television, like drugs, dominates the lives of its addicts. And though
some lonely Americans leave their sets on without watching them, using
them as electronic companions, television usually absorbs its viewers the
way drugs absorb their users. Viewers can't work or play while watching
television; they can't read; they can't be out on the streets, falling in love
with the wrong people, learning how to quarrel and compromise with
other human beings. In short they are asocial. So are drug addicts.

One Michigan State University study in the early eighties offered a
group of four- and five-year-olds the choice of giving up television or giving up their fathers. Fully one third said they would give up Daddy. Given
a similar choice (between cocaine or heroin and father, mother, brother,
sister, wife, husband, children, job), almost every stoned junkie would do
the same.

There are other disturbing similarities. Television itself is a
consciousness-altering instrument. With the touch of a button, it takes
you out of the "real" world in which you reside and can place you at a
basketball game, the back alleys of Miami, the streets of Bucharest, or the
cartoony living rooms of Sitcom Land. Each move from channel to channel alters mood, usually with music or a laugh track. On any given
evening, you can laugh, be frightened, feel tension, thump with excitement. You can even tune in *MacNeil/Lehrer* and feel sober.

But none of these abrupt shifts in mood is earned. They are attained
as easily as popping a pill. Getting news from television, for example, is

simply not the same experience as reading it in a newspaper. Reading is *active*. The reader must decode little symbols called words, then create images or ideas and make them connect; at its most basic level, reading is an act of the imagination. But the television viewer doesn't go through that process. The words are spoken to him by Dan Rather or Tom Brokaw or Peter Jennings. There isn't much decoding to do when watching television, no time to think or ponder before the next set of images and spoken words appears to displace the present one. The reader, being active, works at his or her own pace; the viewer, being passive, proceeds at a pace determined by the show. Except at the highest levels, television never demands that its audience take part in an act of imagination. Reading always does.

In short, television works on the same imaginative and intellectual   15
level as psychoactive drugs. If prolonged television viewing makes the young passive (dozens of studies indicate that it does), then moving to drugs has a certain coherence. Drugs provide an unearned high (in contrast to the earned rush that comes from a feat accomplished, a human breakthrough earned by sweat or thought or love).

And because the television addict and the drug addict are alienated from the hard and scary world, they also feel they make no difference in its complicated events. For the junkie, the world is reduced to him and the needle, pipe, or vial; the self is absolutely isolated, with no desire for choice. The television addict lives the same way. Many Americans who fail to vote in presidential elections must believe they have no more control over such a choice than they do over the casting of *L.A. Law*.

The drug plague also coincides with the unspoken assumption of most television shows: Life should be *easy*. The most complicated events are summarized on TV news in a minute or less. Cops confront murder, chase the criminals, and bring them to justice (usually violently) within an hour. In commercials, you drink the right beer and you get the girl. *Easy!* So why should real life be a grind? Why should any American have to spend years mastering a skill or a craft, or work eight hours a day at an unpleasant job, or endure the compromises and crises of a marriage? Nobody *works* on television (except cops, doctors, and lawyers). Love stories on television are about falling in love or breaking up; the long, steady growth of a marriage — its essential *dailiness* — is seldom explored, except as comedy. Life on television is almost always simple: good guys and bad, nice girls and whores, smart guys and dumb. And if life in the real world isn't that simple, well, hey, man, have some dope, man, be happy, feel good.

The doper always whines about how he *feels*; drugs are used to enhance his feelings or obliterate them, and in this the doper is very American. No other people on earth spend so much time talking about their feelings; hundreds of thousands go to shrinks, they buy self-help books by the millions, they pour out intimate confessions to virtual strangers in bars or discos. Our political campaigns are about emotional issues now, stated in the simplicities of adolescence. Even alleged statesmen can start a sentence, "I feel that the Sandinistas should . . ." when they once might have said, "I *think* . . ." I'm convinced that this exaltation of cheap emotions over logic and reason is one by-product of hundreds of thousands of hours of television.

Most Americans under the age of fifty have now spent their lives absorbing television; that is, they've had the structures of drama pounded into them. Drama is always about conflict. So news shows, politics, and advertising are now all shaped by those structures. Nobody will pay attention to anything as complicated as the part played by Third World debt in the expanding production of cocaine; it's much easier to focus on Manuel Noriega, a character right out of *Miami Vice,* and believe that even in real life there's a Mister Big.

What is to be done? Television is certainly not going away, but its addictive qualities can be controlled. It's a lot easier to "just say no" to television than to heroin or crack. As a beginning, parents must take immediate control of the sets, teaching children to watch specific television *programs,* not "television," to get out of the house and play with other kids. Elementary and high schools must begin teaching television as a subject, the way literature is taught, showing children how shows are made, how to distinguish between the true and the false, how to recognize cheap emotional manipulation. All Americans should spend more time reading. And thinking.

For years, the defenders of television have argued that the networks are only giving the people what they want. That might be true. But so is the Medellín cartel.

The Reader's Presence

1. Hamill's attack on the addictive nature of television is grounded in his conviction that Americans — and particularly our government leaders — are asking the wrong questions about the national drug epidemic: Rather than asking why so many people are willing to sell drugs, he proposes that we ask why so many Americans are willing, even eager, to buy them. Outline each of the points Hamill makes as he unfolds this analogy, and analyze the series of connections Hamill makes between the life-style of escapism promoted on television and provided by drugs. How convincing do you find his explanations?

2. Hamill presents a great deal of statistical information to support his assertions about the causes and the effects of drug addiction in the United States. What sources does he invoke to validate his claims? What sense of authority does he create through citing this information? Explain how he reinforces this sense of authority by invoking his personal observations and experiences. See, for example, paragraphs 2 and 3. What general patterns do you notice

in the ways he introduces his personal experience in these paragraphs? Show how these patterns are sustained — or altered — in the remainder of his article.

3. Consider Hamill's point of view and his tone in criticizing television's debilitating effects on American consciousness. Can you point to any evidence in his tone to suggest that Hamill, who makes his living writing newspaper columns and magazine articles, bears a prejudice toward television, especially toward its popularity? What assumptions about the relative cultural value of newspapers, magazines, and television does Hamill express in the article? What is their effect?

44

Linda M. Hasselstrom

Why One Peaceful Woman Carries a Pistol

Linda M. Hasselstrom (b. 1943) is a rancher and writer who splits her time between her home in Cheyenne, Wyoming, and her ranch in western South Dakota. She has written about her experiences as a rancher in Windbreak: A Woman Rancher on the Northern Plains *(1987) and* Going over East: Reflections of a Woman Rancher *(1987). Hasselstrom's poetry can be found in* Dakota Bones *(1992) and in a collection of poems and essays,* Land Circle: Writings Collected from the Land *(1991), in which "Why One Peaceful Woman Carries a Pistol" appears. She continues to write essays on ranching and the environment and recently published* Roadside History of South Dakota *(1994). She also enjoys teaching writing workshops to writers of all ages and from diverse backgrounds.*

Hasselstrom's writing is strongly connected to the natural environment in which she lives. "All parts of life need to come together, and I have tried to make my life into a circle," she says. "I write, do ranch work, garden, and they all fit together. I take care of the land and it takes care of me. It provides me with inspiration for my writing on many topics: on people, on animals, on the environment — and of course you can't separate them. It is important for me to be connected to country, to place, *in order to keep writing."*

I'm a peace-loving woman. I also carry a pistol. For years, I've written about my decision in an effort to help other women make intelligent choices about gun ownership, but editors rejected the articles. Between 1983 and 1986, however, when gun sales to men held steady, gun ownership among women rose fifty-three percent, to more than twelve million.

We learned that any female over the age of twelve can expect to be criminally assaulted some time in her life, that women aged thirty have a fifty-fifty chance of being raped, robbed, or attacked, and that many police officials say flatly that they cannot protect citizens from crime. During the same period, the number of women considering gun ownership quadrupled to nearly two million. Manufacturers began showing lightweight weapons with small grips, and purses with built-in holsters. A new magazine is called *Guns and Women,* and more than eight thousand copies of the video *A Woman's Guide to Firearms* were sold by 1988. Experts say female gun buyers are not limited to any particular age group, profession, social class, or area of the country, and most are buying guns to protect themselves. Shooting instructors say women view guns with more caution than do men, and may make better shots.

I decided to buy a handgun for several reasons. During one four-year period, I drove more than a hundred thousand miles alone, giving speeches, readings, and workshops. A woman is advised, usually by men, to protect herself by avoiding bars, by approaching her car like an Indian scout, by locking doors and windows. But these precautions aren't always enough. And the logic angers me: *Because* I am female, it is my responsibility to be extra careful.

As a responsible environmentalist, I choose to recycle, avoid chemicals on my land, minimize waste. As an informed woman alone, I choose to be as responsible for my own safety as possible: I keep my car running well, use caution in where I go and what I do. And I learned about self-protection — not an easy or quick decision. I developed a strategy of protection that includes handgun possession. The following incidents, chosen from a larger number because I think they could happen to anyone, helped make up my mind.

When I camped with another woman for several weeks, she didn't want to carry a pistol, and police told us Mace was illegal. We tucked spray deodorant into our sleeping bags, theorizing that any man crawling into our tent at night would be nervous anyway; anything sprayed in his face would slow him down until we could hit him with a frying pan, or escape. We never used our improvised weapon, because we were lucky enough to camp beside people who came to our aid when we needed them. I returned from that trip determined to reconsider.

At that time, I lived alone and taught night classes in town. Along a city street I often traveled, a woman had a flat tire, called for help on her CB, and got a rapist; he didn't fix the tire either. She was afraid to call for help again and stayed in her car until morning. Also, CBs work best along line-of-sight; I ruled them out.

As I drove home one night, a car followed me, lights bright. It passed on a narrow bridge, while a passenger flashed a spotlight in my face, blinding me. I braked sharply. The car stopped, angled across the bridge, and four men jumped out. I realized the locked doors were useless if they broke my car windows. I started forward, hoping to knock their car aside

5

so I could pass. Just then, another car appeared, and the men got back in their car, but continued to follow me, passing and repassing. I dared not go home. I passed no lighted houses. Finally, they pulled to the roadside, and I decided to use their tactic: fear. I roared past them inches away, horn blaring. It worked; they turned off the highway. But it was desperate and foolish, and I was frightened and angry. Even in my vehicle I was too vulnerable.

Other incidents followed. One day I saw a man in the field near my house, carrying a shotgun and heading for a pond full of ducks. I drove to meet him, and politely explained that the land was posted. He stared at me, and the muzzle of his shotgun rose. I realized that if he simply shot me and drove away, I would be a statistic. The moment passed; the man left.

One night, I returned home from class to find deep tire ruts on the lawn, a large gas tank empty, garbage in the driveway. A light shone in the house; I couldn't remember leaving it on. I was too embarrassed to wake the neighbors. An hour of cautious exploration convinced me the house was safe, but once inside, with the doors locked, I was still afraid. I put a .22 rifle by my bed, but I kept thinking of how naked I felt, prowling around my own house in the dark.

It was time to consider self-defense. I took a kung fu class and learned to define the distance to maintain between myself and a stranger. Once someone enters that space without permission, kung fu teaches appropriate evasive or protective action. I learned to move confidently, scanning for possible attack. I learned how to assess danger, and techniques for avoiding it without combat.

I also learned that one must practice several hours every day to be good at kung fu. By that time I had married George; when I practiced with him, I learned how *close* you must be to your attacker to use martial arts, and decided a 120-pound woman dare not let a six-foot, 220-pound attacker get that close unless she is very, very good at self-defense. Some women who are well trained in martial arts have been raped and beaten anyway.

Reluctantly I decided to carry a pistol. George helped me practice with his .357 and .22. I disliked the .357's recoil, though I later became comfortable with it. I bought a .22 at a pawn shop. A standard .22 bullet, fired at close range, can kill, but news reports tell of attackers advancing with five such bullets in them. I bought magnum shells, with more power, and practiced until I could hit someone close enough to endanger me. Then I bought a license making it legal for me to carry the gun concealed.

George taught me that the most important preparation was mental: convincing myself I could shoot someone. Few of us really wish to hurt or kill another human being. But there is no point in having a gun — in fact, gun possession might increase your danger — unless you know you can use it against another human being. A good training course includes mental preparation, as well as training in safety. As I drive or walk, I often rehearse the conditions which would cause me to shoot. Men grow up handling firearms, and learn controlled violence in contact sports, but women grow up learning to be subservient and vulnerable. To make ourselves comfortable with the idea that we are capable of protecting ourselves requires effort. But it need not turn us into macho, gun-fighting broads. We must simply learn to do as men do from an early age: believe in, and rely on, *ourselves* for protection. The pistol only adds an extra edge, an attention-getter; it is a weapon of last resort.

Because shooting at another person means shooting to kill. It's impossible even for seasoned police officers to be sure of only wounding an assailant. If I shot an attacking man, I would aim at the largest target, the chest. This is not an easy choice, but for me it would be better than rape.

In my car, my pistol is within instant reach. When I enter a deserted rest stop at night, it's in my purse, my hand on the grip. When I walk from a dark parking lot into a motel, it's in my hand, under a coat. When I walk my dog in the deserted lots around most motels, the pistol is in a shoulder holster, and I am always aware of my surroundings. In my motel room, it lies on the bedside table. At home, it's on the headboard.

Just carrying a pistol is not protection. Avoidance is still the best approach to trouble; watch for danger signs, and practice avoiding them. Develop your instinct for danger.   15

One day while driving to the highway mailbox, I saw a vehicle parked about halfway to the house. Several men were standing in the ditch, relieving themselves. I have no objection to emergency urination; we always need moisture. But they'd also dumped several dozen beer cans, which blow into pastures and can slash a cow's legs or stomach.

As I slowly drove closer, the men zipped their trousers (ostentatiously) while walking toward me. Four men gathered around my small foreign car, making remarks they wouldn't make to their mothers, and one of them demanded what the hell I wanted.

"This is private land; I'd like you to pick up the beer cans."

"What beer cans?" said the belligerent one, putting both hands on the car door, and leaning in my window. His face was inches from mine, the beer fumes were strong, and he looked angry. The others laughed. One tried the passenger door, locked; another put his foot on the hood and rocked the car. They circled, lightly thumping the roof, discussing my good fortune in meeting them, and the benefits they were likely to (bestow) upon me. I felt small and trapped; they knew it.

"The ones you just threw out," I said politely.   20

"I don't see no beer cans. Why don't you get out here and show them to me, honey?" said the belligerent one, reaching for the handle inside my door.

"Right over there," I said, still being polite, "there and over there." I pointed with the pistol, which had been under my thigh. Within one minute the cans and the men were back in the car, and headed down the road.

I believe this small incident illustrates several principles. The men were trespassing and knew it; their judgment may have been impaired by alcohol. Their response to the polite request of a woman alone was to use their size and numbers to inspire fear. The pistol was a response in the same language. Politeness didn't work; I couldn't intimidate them. Out of the car, I'd have been more vulnerable. The pistol just changed the balance of power.

My husband, George, asked one question when I told him. "What would you have done if he'd grabbed for the pistol?"

"I had the car in reverse; I'd have hit the accelerator, and backed up; if he'd kept coming, I'd have fired straight at him." He nodded.

In fact, the sight of the pistol made the man straighten up; he cracked his head on the door frame. He and the two in front of the car stepped backward, catching the attention of the fourth, who joined them. They were all in front of me then, and as the car was still running and in reverse gear, my options had multiplied. If they'd advanced again, I'd have backed away, turning to keep the open window toward them. Given time, I'd have put the first shot into the ground in front of them, the second into the belligerent leader. It might have been better to wait until they were gone, pick up the beer cans, and avoid confrontation, but I believed it was reasonable and my right to make a polite request to strangers littering my property. Showing the pistol worked on another occasion when I was driving in a desolate part of Wyoming. A man played cat-and-mouse with me for thirty miles, ultimately trying to run my car off the road. When his car was only two inches from mine, I pointed my pistol at him, and he disappeared.

I believe that a handgun is like a car; both are tools for specific purposes; both can be lethal if used improperly. Both require a license, training, and alertness. Both require you to be aware of what is happening before and behind you. Driving becomes almost instinctive; so does handgun use. When I've drawn my gun for protection, I simply found it in my hand. Instinct told me a situation was dangerous before my conscious mind reacted; I've felt the same while driving. Most good drivers react to emergencies by instinct.

Knives are another useful tool often misunderstood and misused; some people acquire knives mostly for display, either on a wall or on a belt, and such knives are often so large as to serve no useful purpose. My pocket knives are always razor sharp, because a small, sharp knife will do most jobs. Skinning blades serve for cutting meat and splitting small kindling in camp. A *sgian dubh,* a four-inch flat blade in a wooden sheath, was easily concealed inside a Scotsman's high socks, and slips into my dress or work boots as well. Some buckskinners keep what they call a "grace knife" on a thong around their necks; the name may derive from *coup de grâce,* the welcome throat-slash a wounded knight asked from his closest friend, to keep him from falling alive into the hands of his enemies. I also have a push dagger, with a blade only three inches long, attached to a handle that fits into the fist so well that the knife would be hard to lose even in hand-to-hand combat. When I first showed it, without explanation, to an older woman who would never consider carrying a knife, she took one look and said, "Why, you could push that right into someone's stomach," and demonstrated with a flourish. That's what it's for. I wear it for decoration, because it was handmade by Jerry and fits my hand perfectly, but I am intently aware of its purpose. I like my knives, not because they are weapons, but because they are well designed, and beautiful, and because each is a tool with a specific purpose.

Women didn't always have jobs, or drive cars or heavy equipment, though western women did many of those things almost as soon as they arrived here. Men in authority argued that their attempt to do so would unravel the fabric of society. Women, they said, would become less feminine; they hadn't the intelligence to cope with the mechanics of a car, or the judgment to cope with emergencies. Since these ideas were so wrong, perhaps it is time women brought a new dimension to the wise use of handguns as well.

We can and should educate ourselves in how to travel safely, take   30
self-defense courses, reason, plead, or avoid trouble in other ways. But some men cannot be stopped by those methods; they understand only power. A man who is committing an attack already knows he's breaking laws; he has no concern for someone else's rights. A pistol is a woman's answer to his greater power. It makes her equally frightening. I have thought of revising the old Colt slogan: "God made man, but Sam Colt made them equal" to read "God made men *and women* but Sam Colt made them equal." Recently I have seen an ad for a popular gunmaker with a similar sentiment; perhaps this is an idea whose time has come, though the pacifist inside me will be saddened if the only way women can achieve equality is by carrying a weapon.

As a society, we were shocked in early 1989 when a female jogger in New York's Central Park was beaten and raped savagely and left in a coma. I was even more shocked when reporters interviewed children who lived near the victim and quoted a twelve-year-old as saying, "She had nothing to guard herself; she didn't have no man with her; she didn't have no Mace." And another sixth-grader said, "It is like she committed suicide." Surely this is not a majority opinion, but I think it is not so unusual, either, even in this liberated age. Yet there is no city or county in the nation where law officers can relax because all the criminals are in jail. Some authorities say citizens armed with handguns stop almost as many crimes annually as armed criminals succeed in committing, and that people defending themselves kill three times more attackers and robbers than police do. I don't suggest all criminals should be killed, but some can be stopped only by death or permanent incarceration. Law enforcement officials can't prevent crimes; later punishment may be of little comfort to the victim. A society so controlled that no crime existed would probably be too confined for most of us, and is not likely to exist any time soon.

Therefore, many of us should be ready and able to protect ourselves, and the intelligent use of firearms is one way.

We must treat a firearm's power with caution. "Power tends to corrupt, and absolute power corrupts absolutely," as a man (Lord Acton) once said. A pistol is not the only way to avoid being raped or murdered in today's world, but a firearm, intelligently wielded, can shift the balance and provide a measure of safety.

The Reader's Presence

Group Work

1. The title of Hasselstrom's essay announces her purpose. Outline each of the points she highlights in her defense of carrying a firearm. What alternatives to a handgun does she consider, and why does she reject each? How does she anticipate objections to her explanation? What kinds of preparation does she think necessary in order to "ready" herself to carry a pistol? What, finally, does she see as the most effective form of protection against trouble?

2. In what specific ways does Hasselstrom address the conventional perception that men are more likely to bear arms than women? When — and in what terms — does she make gender an issue in carrying a firearm? What specific words and phrases does she repeat to emphasize her own vulnerability and that of other women?

3. In the opening paragraphs of her detailed explanation of why she carries a gun, Hasselstrom announces to her readers the point of view from which she speaks: a "peace-loving woman," a freelance writer who lives on a ranch in western South Dakota. Recognizing that "handgun possession is a controversial subject," she immediately expresses her overall aim in writing: "perhaps my reasoning will interest others." Who might be included in the "others" she mentions here? Is there any evidence to suggest, for example, that she has women primarily in mind as her audience? If so, what evidence validates your reading? If, however, you believe that gender is not an important factor in determining who might be included in her audience for this article, what factors in her explanation might help you to identify her intended audience?

45

Linda Hogan

Dwellings

The writer and educator Linda Hogan was born in Colorado in 1947. A member of the Chickasaw tribe, she is active in Native American communities and in environmental politics. Hogan has published essays, plays, short stories, and many volumes of poetry, including most recently The Book of Medicines *(1993). Her novels* Mean Spirit *(1990) and* Solar Storms *(1995) have been celebrated for their complex and compelling representation of Native Americans. Hogan's interests in narrative and the natural environment are represented in the essay included here, which appears in her book* Dwellings: Reflections on the Natural World *(1995). She has taught at the University of Minnesota and is currently professor of English at the University of Colorado at Boulder.*

Hogan has said, "My writing comes from and goes back to the community, both the human and the global community. I am interested in the deepest questions, those of spirit, of shelter, of growth and movement toward peace and liberation, inner and outer."

Not far from where I live is a hill that was cut into by the moving water of a creek. Eroded this way, all that's left of it is a broken wall of earth that contains old roots and pebbles woven together and exposed. Seen from a distance, it is only a rise of raw earth. But up close it is something wonderful, a small cliff dwelling that looks almost as intricate and well made as those the Anasazi left behind when they vanished mysteriously centuries ago. This hill is a place that could be the starry skies at night turned inward into the thousand round holes where solitary bees have lived and died. It is a hill of tunneling rooms. At the mouths of some of the excavations, half-circles of clay beetle out like awnings shading a doorway. It is earth that was turned to clay in the mouths of the bees and spit out as they mined deeper into their dwelling places.

This place is where the bees reside at an angle safe from rain. It faces the southern sun. It is a warm and intelligent architecture of memory, learned by whatever memory lives in the blood. Many of the holes still contain gold husks of dead bees, their faces dry and gone, their flat eyes gazing out from death's land toward the other uninhabited half of the hill that is across the creek from the catacombs.

The first time I found the residence of the bees, it was dusty summer. The sun was hot, and land was the dry color of rust. Now and then a car rumbled along the dirt road and dust rose up behind it before settling back down on older dust. In the silence, the bees made a soft droning hum. They were alive then, and working the hill, going out and returning with pollen, in and out through the holes, back and forth between daylight and the cooler, darker regions of the inner earth. They were flying an invisible map through air, a map charted by landmarks, the slant of light, and a circling story they told one another about the direction of food held inside the center of yellow flowers.

Sitting in the hot sun, watching the small bees fly in and out around the hill, hearing the summer birds, the light breeze, I felt right in the world. I belonged there. I thought of my own dwelling places, those real and those imagined. Once I lived in a town called Manitou, which means "Great Spirit," and where hot mineral springwater gurgled beneath the streets and rose into open wells. I felt safe there. With the underground movement of water and heat a constant reminder of other life, of what lives beneath us, it seemed to be the center of the world.

A few years after that, I wanted silence. My daydreams were full of places I longed to be, shelters and solitudes. I wanted a room apart from others, a hidden cabin to rest in. I wanted to be in a redwood forest with trees so tall the owls called out in the daytime. I daydreamed of living in a vapor cave a few hours away from here. Underground, warm, and moist, I thought it would be the perfect world for staying out of cold winter, for escaping the noise of living.   5

And how often I've wanted to escape to a wilderness where a human hand has not been in everything. But those were only dreams of peace, of comfort, of a nest inside stone or woods, a sanctuary where a dream or life wouldn't be invaded.

Years ago, in the next canyon west of here, there was a man who followed one of those dreams and moved into a cave that could only be reached by climbing down a rope. For years he lived there in comfort, like a troglodyte. The inner weather was stable, never too hot, too cold, too wet, or too dry. But then he felt lonely. His utopia needed a woman. He went to town until he found a wife. For a while after the marriage, his wife climbed down the rope along with him, but before long she didn't want the mice scurrying about in the cave, or the untidy bats that wanted to hang from the stones of the ceiling. So they built a door. Because of the closed entryway, the temperature changed. They had to put in heat. Then the inner moisture of earth warped the door, so they had to have air-conditioning, and after that the earth wanted to go about life in its own way and it didn't give in to the people.

In other days and places, people paid more attention to the strong-headed will of earth. Once homes were built of wood that had been felled from a single region in a forest. That way, it was thought, the house would hold together more harmoniously, and the family of walls would not fall or lend themselves to the unhappiness or arguments of the inhabitants.

An Italian immigrant to Chicago, Aldo Piacenzi, built birdhouses that were dwellings of harmony and peace. They were the incredible spired shapes of cathedrals in Italy. They housed not only the birds, but also his memories, his own past. He painted them the watery blue of his Mediterranean, the wild rose of flowers in a summer field. Inside them was straw and the droppings of lives that layed eggs, fledglings who grew there. What places to inhabit, the bright and sunny birdhouses in dreary alleyways of the city.

One beautiful afternoon, cool and moist, with the kind of yellow   10
light that falls on earth in these arid regions, I waited for barn swallows to return from their daily work of food gathering. Inside the tunnel where they live, hundreds of swallows had mixed their saliva with mud and clay, much like the solitary bees, and formed nests that were perfect as a potter's bowl. At five in the evening, they returned all at once, a dark, flying shadow. Despite their enormous numbers and the crowding together of nests, they didn't pause for even a moment before entering the nests, nor did they crowd one another. Instantly they vanished into the nests. The tunnel went silent. It held no outward signs of life.

But I knew they were there, filled with the fire of living. And what a marriage of elements was in those nests. Not only mud's earth and water, the fire of sun and dry air, but even the elements contained one another. The bodies of prophets and crazy men were broken down in that soil.

I've noticed often how when a house is abandoned, it begins to sag. Without a tenant, it has no need to go on. If it were a person, we'd say it is depressed or lonely. The roof settles in, the paint cracks, the walls and floorboards warp and slope downward in their own natural ways, telling us that life must stay in everything as the world whirls and tilts and moves through boundless space.

One summer day, cleaning up after long-eared owls where I work at a rehabilitation facility for birds of prey, I was raking the gravel floor of a flight cage. Down on the ground, something looked like it was moving. I bent over to look into the pile of bones and pellets I'd just raked together. There, close to the ground, were two fetal mice. They were new to the planet, pink and hairless. They were so tenderly young. Their faces had swollen blue-veined eyes. They were nestled in a mound of feathers, soft as velvet, each one curled up smaller than an infant's ear, listening to the first sounds of earth. But the ants were biting them. They turned in agony, unable to pull away, not yet having the arms or legs to move, but feeling, twisting away from, the pain of the bites. I was horrified to see them bitten out of life that way. I dipped them in water, as if to take away the sting, and let the ants fall in the bucket. Then I held the tiny mice in the palm of my hand. Some of ants were drowning in the water. I was trading one life for another, exchanging the lives of the ants for those of mice, but I hated their suffering, and hated even more that they had not yet grown to a life, and already they inhabited the miserable world of pain. Death and life feed each other. I know that.

Inside these rooms where birds are healed, there are other lives besides those of mice. There are fine gray globes the wasps have woven together, the white cocoons of spiders in a corner, the downward tunneling anthills. All these dwellings are inside one small walled space, but I think most about the mice. Sometimes the downy nests fall out of the walls where their mothers have placed them out of the way of their enemies. When one of the nests falls, they are so well made and soft, woven mostly from the chest feathers of birds. Sometimes the leg of a small quail holds the nest together like a slender cornerstone with dry, bent claws. The mice have adapted to life in the presence of their enemies, adapted to living in the thin wall between beak and beak, claw and claw. They move their nests often, as if a new rafter or wall will protect them from the inevitable fate of all our returns home to the deeper, wider nests of earth that houses us all.

One August at Zia Pueblo during the corn dance I noticed tourists picking up shards of all the old pottery that had been made and broken there. The residents of Zia know not to take the bowls and pots left behind by the older ones. They know that the fragments of those earlier lives need to be smoothed back to earth, but younger nations, travelers from continents across the world who have come to inhabit this land, have little of their own to grow on. The pieces of earth that were formed into bowls, even on their way home to dust, provide the new people a lifeline to an unknown land, help them remember that they live in the old nest of earth.   15

It was in early February, during the mating season of the great horned owl. It was dusk, and I hiked up the back of a mountain to where I'd heard the owls a year before. I wanted to hear them again, the voices so tender, so deep, like a memory of comfort. I was halfway up the trail when I found a soft, round nest. It had fallen from one of the bare-branched trees. It was a delicate nest, woven together of feathers, sage, and strands of wild grass. Holding it in my hand in the rosy twilight, I noticed that a blue thread was entwined with the other gatherings there. I pulled at the thread a little, and then I recognized it. It was a thread from one of my skirts. It was blue cotton. It was the unmistakable color and shape of a pattern I knew. I liked it, that a thread of my life was in an abandoned nest, one that had held eggs and new life. I took the nest home. At home, I held it to the light and looked more closely. There, to my surprise, nestled into the gray-green sage, was a gnarl of black hair. It was also unmistakable. It was my daughter's hair, cleaned from a brush and picked up out in the sun beneath the maple tree, or the pit cherry where the birds eat from the overladen, fertile branches until only the seeds remain on the trees.

I didn't know what kind of nest it was, or who had lived there. It didn't matter. I thought of the remnants of our lives carried up the hill that way and turned into shelter. That night, resting inside the walls of our home, the world outside weighed so heavily against the thin wood of the house. The sloped roof was the only thing between us and the universe. Everything outside of our wooden boundaries seemed so large. Filled with the night's citizens, it all came alive. The world opened in the thickets of the dark. The wild grapes would soon ripen on the vines. The burrowing ones were emerging. Horned owls sat in treetops. Mice scurried here and there. Skunks, fox, the slow and holy porcupine, all were passing by this way. The young of the solitary bees were feeding on the pollen in the dark. The whole world was a nest on its humble tilt, in the maze of the universe, holding us.

The Reader's Presence

1. In each of the vignettes that make up this essay, Hogan contemplates the meaning of various dwellings. What are the specific characteristics of a dwelling place for Hogan? Who lives there? How does each dwelling suit and serve its inhabitants? Why does Hogan describe dwellings for animals as well as dwellings for humans? With what effect(s)? To what extent and in what ways do the two overlap? What are the advantages — and the disadvantages — of Hogan's having chosen to contemplate death as well as life in this essay about where we live? How would you characterize the vision of life, death, and the universe that emerges from this essay?

2. Reread carefully the story about the cave dweller and his wife told in paragraph 7. To what extent does Hogan encourage her readers to take the story literally? At what point does it begin to take on the qualities of myth or fable? Compare and contrast this story with the biblical story of Adam and Eve, and their fall from the Garden of Eden. To whom, or to what impulse(s), can each fall be attributed? How are women characterized in the respective stories? How are the endings similar, and where do they diverge? Based on your comparative analysis of these stories, what inferences might you draw about the Native American and Judeo-Christian worldviews?

3. Identify and discuss the various analogies Hogan draws throughout the essay. Where does she compare dwellings made by animals
   to human-made artifacts? human-made dwellings to natural phenomena? the animate to the inanimate? With what effects? Where
   are analogies between the various vignettes implied, and what do
   you infer from those implied analogies? For example, how do the
   narrator's own actions in paragraph 15 echo the actions of the
   tourists in paragraph 14, and how do these echoes contribute to
   the overall effect of the essay? Examine, too, the remarkable shifts
   in scale, from the very small tunnels dug by the bees to the starry
   skies (paragraph 1), that Hogan weaves into this essay. How do
   these analogies between the very large and the very small contribute to the sense of a palpable universe, "the whole world" as
   "a nest on its humble tilt" (paragraph 16)?

46

John Hollander

Mess

*John Hollander (b. 1929) is one of the leading poets in the United States
today. His poems and prose appear regularly in the* New Yorker, *the* Partisan Review, Esquire, *and other popular and scholarly magazines. The essay "Mess" appeared in the* Yale Review *in 1995. Hollander is professor of English at Yale University, and he has written and edited numerous scholarly works and anthologies.
He has published over twenty volumes of poetry, including most recently his* Selected Poetry *(1993) and a volume called* Animal Poems *(1994).*

*Commenting on the experience of writing both poetry and prose, Hollander
notes, "Ordinarily, the prose I write is critical or scholarly, where there is some
occasion (a lecture to be given, a longish review to be done, etc.) to elicit the piece
of writing. My most important writing is my poetry, which is not occasional in
these ways. . . . This brief essay was generated more from within, like a poem,
than most other prose of mine — nobody asked me to write it, but I felt impelled
to observe something about one aspect of life that tends to get swept under the
rug, as it were."*

Mess is a state of mind. Or rather, messiness is a particular relation
between the state of arrangement of a collection of things and a state of
mind that contemplates it in its containing space. For example, X's mess
may be Y's delight — sheer profusion, uncompromised by any apparent
structure even in the representation of it. Or there may be some inner

order or logic to A's mess that B cannot possibly perceive. Consider: someone — Alpha — rearranges all the books on Beta's library shelf, which have been piled or stacked, sometimes properly, sometimes not, but all in relevant sequence (by author and, within that, by date of publication), and rearranges them neatly, by size and color. Beta surveys the result, and can only feel, if not blurt out, "WHAT A MESS!" This situation often occurs with respect to messes of the workplace generally.

For there are many kinds of mess, both within walls and outside them: neglected gardens and the aftermath of tropical storms, and the indoor kinds of disorder peculiar to specific areas of our life with, and in and among, *things*. There are messes of one's own making, messes not even of one's own person, places or things. There are personal states of mind about common areas of messiness — those of the kitchen, the bedroom, the bathroom, the salon (of whatever sort, from half a bed-sitter[1] to some grand public parlor), or those of personal appearance (clothes, hair, etc.). Then, for all those who are in any way self-employed or whose avocations are practiced in some private space — a workshop, a darkroom, a study or a studio — there is a mess of the workplace. It's not the most common kind of mess, but it's exemplary: the eye surveying it is sickened by the rollercoaster of scanning the scene. And, alas, it's the one I'm most afflicted with.

I know that things are really in a mess when — as about ninety seconds ago — I reach for the mouse on my Macintosh and find instead a thick layer of old envelopes, manuscript notes consulted three weeks ago, favorite pens and inoperative ones, folders used hastily and not replaced, and so forth. In order to start working, I brush these accumulated impedimenta aside, thus creating a new mess. But this is, worse yet, absorbed by the general condition of my study: piles of thin books and thick books, green volumes of the Loeb Classical Library and slimy paperbacks of ephemeral spy-thrillers, mostly used notepads, bills paid and unpaid, immortal letters from beloved friends, unopened and untrashed folders stuffed with things that should be in various other folders, book-mailing envelopes, unanswered mail whose cries for help and attention are muffled by three months' worth of bank statements enshrouding them in the gloom of continued neglect. Even this fairly orderly inventory seems to simplify the confusion: in actuality, searching for a letter or a page of manuscript in this state of things involves crouching down with my head on one side and searching vertically along the outside of a teetering pile for what may be a thin, hidden layer of it.

Displacement, and lack of design, are obscured in the origins of our very word *mess*. The famous biblical "mess of red pottage" (lentil mush or dal) for which Esau sold his birthright wasn't "messy" in our sense (unless, or course, in the not very interesting case of Esau having dribbled it on his clothing). The word meant a serving of food, or a course in a meal: something *placed* in front of you (from the Latin *missis*, put or placed), hence

---

[1]*bed-sitter:* A combined bedroom and sitting room. — EDS.

"messmates" (dining companions) and ultimately "officers' mess" and the like. It also came to mean a dish of prepared mixed food — like an *olla podrida* or a minestrone — then by extension (but only from the early nineteenth century on) any hodge-podge: inedible, and outside the neat confines of a bowl or pot, and thus unpleasant, confusing, and agitating or depressing to contemplate. But for us, the association with food perhaps remains only in how much the state of mind of being messy is like that of being fat: for example, X says, "God, I'm getting gross! I'll have to diet!" Y, *really* fat, cringes on hearing this, and feels that for the slender X to talk that way is an obscenity. Similarly, X: "God, this place is a pigsty!" Y: (ditto). For a person prone to messiness, Cyril Connolly's celebrated observation about fat people is projected onto the world itself: inside every neat arrangement is a mess struggling to break out, like some kind of statue of chaos lying implicit in the marble of apparent organization.

In Paradise, there was no such thing as messiness. This was partly because unfallen, ideal life needed no supplemental *things* — objects of use and artifice, elements of any sort of technology. Thus there was nothing to leave lying around, messily or even neatly, by Adam and Eve — according to Milton — "at their savory dinner set / Of herbs and other country messes." But it was also because order, hence orderliness, was itself so natural that whatever bit of nature Adam and Eve might have been occupied with, or even using in a momentary tool-like way, flew or leapt or crept into place in some sort of reasonable arrangement, even as in our unparadised state things *fall* under the joyless tug of gravity. But messiness may seem to be an inevitable state of the condition of having so many *things*, precious or disposable, in one's life.

As I observed before, even to describe a mess is to impose order on it. The ancient Greek vision of primal chaos, even, was not *messy* in that it was pre-messy: there weren't any categories by which to define order, so that there could be no disorder — no nextness or betweenness, no above, below, here, there, and so forth. *"Let there be light"* meant "Let there be perception of something," and it was then that order became possible, and mess possibly implied. Now, a list or inventory is in itself an orderly literary form, and even incoherent assemblages of items fall too easily into some other kind of order: in *Through the Looking-Glass*, the Walrus's "Of shoes and ships, and sealing wax, / Of cabbages, and kings," is given a harmonious structure by the pairs of alliterative words, and even by the half-punning association of "ships, [sailing] sealing wax." The wonderful catalogue in *Tom Sawyer* of the elements of what must have been, pocketed or piled on the ground, a mess of splendid proportions, is a poem of its own. The objects of barter for a stint of fence whitewashing (Tom, it will be remembered, turns *having* to do a chore into *getting* to do it by sheer con-man's insouciance) comprise

> twelve marbles, part of a jewsharp, a piece of blue bottle-glass to look through, a spool cannon, a key that wouldn't unlock anything, a fragment of chalk, a glass stopper of a decanter, a tin soldier, a couple of tadpoles, six

fire-crackers, a kitten with only one eye, a brass door-knob, a dog collar — but no dog — the handle of a knife, four pieces of orange peel, and a dilapidated old window sash.

Thus such representations of disorder as lists, paintings, photos, etc., all compromise the purity of true messiness by the verbal or visual order they impose on the confusion. To get at the mess in my study, for example, a movie might serve best, alternately mixing mid-shot and zoom on a particular portion of the disaster, which would, in an almost fractal way, seem to be a mini-disaster of its own. There are even neatly conventionalized emblems of messiness that are, after all, all too neat: thus, whenever a movie wants to show an apartment or office that has been ransacked by Baddies (cop Baddies or baddy Baddies or whatever) in search of the Thing They Want, the designer is always careful to show at least one picture on the wall hanging carefully askew. All this could possibly tell us about a degree of messiness is that the searchers were so messy (at another level of application of the term) in their technique that they violated their search agenda to run over to the wall and tilt the picture (very messy procedure indeed), or that, hastily leaving the scene to avoid detection, they nonetheless took a final revenge against the Occupant for not having the Thing on his or her premises, and tilted the picture in a fit of pique. And yet a tilted picture gives good cueing mileage: it can present a good bit of disorder at the expense of a minimum of misalignment, after all.

A meditation on mess could be endless. As I struggle to conclude this one, one of my cats regards me from her nest in and among one of the disaster areas that all surfaces in my study soon become. Cats disdain messes in several ways. First, they are proverbially neat about their shit and the condition of their fur. Second, the pick their way so elegantly among my piles of books, papers, and ancillary objects (dishes of paper clips, scissors, functional and dried-out pens, crumpled envelopes, outmoded postage stamps, boxes of slides and disks, staplers, glue bottles, tape dispensers — *you* know) that they cannot even be said to acknowledge the mess's existence. The gray familiar creature currently making her own order out of a region of mess on my desk — carefully disposing herself around and over and among piles and bunches and stacks and crazily oblique layers and thereby reinterpreting it as natural landscape — makes me further despair until I realize that what she does with her body, I must do with my perception of this inevitable disorder — shaping its forms to the disorder and thereby shaping the disorder to its forms. She has taught me resignation.

The Reader's Presence

1. In the second sentence of his essay, Hollander defines "mess" as "a particular relation between the state of arrangement of a collection of things and a state of mind that contemplates it in its

containing space." How would you paraphrase Hollander's definition? To what extent does his definition echo proverbs and traditional sayings such as "beauty is in the eye of the beholder"?
What does Hollander's definition add to this kind of general insight about the observer? What role do the "things" play in messiness, and what role is played by the person who contemplates
them? Examine carefully the many observers mentioned in this
essay, from the hypothetical X and Y in the first paragraph to the
real cat in the final paragraph. What are their various reactions to
the seeming disorder around them?

2. Hollander traces the origins of the word *mess* in paragraph 4.
What is the connection between its original meaning and the
meaning it took on "by extension" in the nineteenth century? According to Hollander, how does the state of mind of being messy
correspond to the state of mind of being fat? He follows this association with yet another: the sculpture lying latent within the marble. Examine carefully — and then comment on — the way each
analogy leads by association into the next and the effect of this series of associations.

3. Hollander's project is complicated by the fact that he has chosen a
word to define that is enmeshed in his own writing process and
product. How does the act of describing the "mess" on his desk
(paragraph 3) alter the nature of the scene he describes? Is it, according to the author, even possible to do justice to a mess in written terms? Consider the fluctuation between control and lack of
control manifested not only in the subject of the essay but in the
essay itself. Where, for example, does the moment of his writing
erupt into the text itself? Why does Hollander find himself struggling to conclude the essay (paragraph 8)? How would you characterize the overall structure of Hollander's essay? Based on your
analysis, how would you compare and contrast the degree of
order in his study and in his writing? In what specific ways might
there be a cause-and-effect relationship between the two?

47

Pico Iyer

In Praise of the Humble Comma

Pico Iyer was born in 1957 in England to Indian parents. He firmly established his reputation as an essayist with his acclaimed travel book, Video Night in Kathmandu: And Other Reports from the Not-So-Far East *(1988), a reflection on the impact global consumer culture has on traditional societies. He has written two other travel books,* The Lady and the Monk: Four Seasons in Kyoto *(1991) and* Falling off the Map *(1993). In 1995 Iyer published his first novel,* Cuba and the Night. *Since 1982 he has written essays for* Time *magazine, where "In Praise of the Humble Comma" first appeared.*

Iyer has said that "writing should be an act of communication more than of mere self-expression — a telling of a story rather than a flourishing of skills. . . . Writing, in fact, should, ideally, be as spontaneous and urgent as a letter to a lover, or a message to a friend who has just lost a parent."

The gods, they say, give breath, and they take it away. But the same could be said — could it not? — of the humble comma. Add it to the present clause, and, of a sudden, the mind is, quite literally, given pause to think; take it out if you wish or forget it and the mind is deprived of a resting place. Yet still the comma gets no respect. It seems just a slip of a thing, a pedant's tick, a blip on the edge of our consciousness, a kind of printer's smudge almost. Small, we claim, is beautiful (especially in the age of the microchip). Yet what is so often used, and so rarely recalled, as the comma — unless it be breath itself?

Punctuation, one is taught, has a point: to keep up law and order. Punctuation marks are the road signs placed along the highway of our communications — to control speeds, provide directions and prevent head-on collisions. A period has the unblinking finality of a red light; the comma is a flashing yellow light that asks us only to slow down; and the semicolon is a stop sign that tells us to ease gradually to a halt, before gradually starting up again. By establishing the relations between words, punctuation establishes the relations between people using words. That may be one reason why schoolteachers exalt it and lovers defy it ("We love each other and belong to each other let's don't ever hurt each other

Nicole let's don't ever hurt each other," wrote Gary Gilmore[1] to his girl-friend). A comma, he must have known, "separates inseparables," in the clinching words of H. W. Fowler, King of English Usage.

Punctuation, then, is a civic prop, a pillar that holds society upright. (A run-on sentence, its phrases piling up without division, is as unsightly as a sink piled high with dirty dishes.) Small wonder, then, that punctuation was one of the first proprieties of the Victorian age, the age of the corset, that the modernists threw off: the sexual revolution might be said to have begun when Joyce's Molly Bloom spilled out all her private thoughts in 36 pages of unbridled, almost unperioded and officially censored prose; and another rebellion was surely marked when E. E. Cummings first felt free to commit "God" to the lower case.

Punctuation thus becomes the signature of cultures. The hot-blooded Spaniard seems to be revealed in the passion and urgency of his doubled exclamation points and question marks ("*¡Caramba!*" *¿Quien sabe?*"), while the impassive Chinese traditionally added to his so-called inscrutability by omitting directions from his ideograms. The anarchy and commotion of the '60s were given voice in the exploding exclamation marks, riotous capital letters and Day-Glo italics of Tom Wolfe's spray-paint prose; and in Communist societies, where the State is absolute, the dignity — and divinity — of capital letters is reserved for Ministries, Sub-Committees and Secretariats.

Yet punctuation is something more than a culture's birthmark; it   5 scores the music in our minds, gets our thoughts moving to the rhythm of our hearts. Punctuation is the notation in the sheet music of our words, telling us where to rest, or when to raise our voices; it acknowledges that the meaning of our discourse as of any symphonic composition, lies not in the units but in the pauses, the pacing and the phrasing. Punctuation is the way one bats one's eyes, lowers one's voice or blushes demurely. Punctuation adjusts the tone and color and volume till the feeling comes into perfect focus, not disgust exactly, but distaste; not lust, or like, but love.

Punctuation, in short, gives us the human voice, and all the meanings that lie between the words. "You aren't young, are you?" loses its innocence when it loses the question mark. Every child knows the menace of a dropped apostrophe (the parents, "Don't do that" shifting to the more enunciated "Do not do that"), and every believer, the ignominy of having his faith reduced to "faith." Add an exclamation point to "To be or not to be . . ." and the gloomy Dane has all the resolve he needs; add a comma, and the noble sobriety of "God save the Queen" becomes a cry of desperation bordering on double sacrilege.

Sometimes, of course, our markings may be simply a matter of aesthetics. Popping in a comma can be like slipping on the necklace that gives an

---

[1] *Gary Gilmore:* Utah serial murderer who was executed in 1977 and who was the subject of Norman Mailer's documentary novel, *The Executioner's Song.* — EDS.

outfit quiet elegance, or like catching the sound of running water that complements, as it completes, the silence of the Japanese landscape. When V. S. Naipaul, in his latest novel, writes, "He was a middle-aged man, with glasses," the first comma can seem a little precious. Yet it gives the description a spin, as well as a subtlety, that it otherwise lacks, and it shows that the glasses are not part of the middle-agedness, but something else.

Thus all these tiny scratches give us breadth and heft and depth. A world that only has periods is a world without inflections. It is a world without shade. It has a music without sharps and flats. It is a martial music. It has a jackboot rhythm. Words cannot bend and curve. A comma, by comparison, catches the gentle drift of the mind in thought, turning in on itself and back on itself, reversing, redoubling and returning along the course of its own sweet river music; while the semicolon brings clauses and thoughts together with all the silent discretion of a hostess arranging guests around her dinner table.

Punctuation, then, is a matter of care. Care for words, yes, but also, and more important, for what the words imply. Only a lover notices the small things: the way the afternoon light catches the nape of the neck, or how a strand of hair slips out from behind an ear, or the way a finger curls around a cup. And no one scans a letter so closely as a lover, searching for its small print, straining to hear its nuances, its gasps, its sighs and hesitation, poring over the secret messages that lie in every cadence. The difference between "Jane (whom I adore)" and "Jane, whom I adore," and the difference between them both and "Jane — whom I adore —" marks all the distance between ecstasy and heartache. "No iron can pierce the heart with such force as a period put at just the right place," in Isaac Babel's lovely words: a comma can let us hear a voice break, or a heart. Punctuation, in fact, is a labor of love. Which brings us back, in a way, to gods.

The Reader's Presence

1. Identify and comment on the effectiveness of each simile and metaphor Iyer uses in this essay. At what specific points in the essay does he introduce analogy? With what effects? How does Iyer's sentence structure exemplify each of the points he makes about the function and the consequences of using "the humble comma" to shape a sentence and the reader's reaction to it?

2. Outline the points Iyer makes in this essay. At what points does the focus of the essay expand and contract? What other subjects does he explore? With what effect(s)? In what specific ways does Iyer illustrate that punctuation has become "the signature of cultures," both historically and ethnically? How do Iyer's explanations reinforce or complicate national and racial stereotypes? Point to specific words and phrases to support your response.

3. In paragraph 8, Iyer presents several examples of how introducing a comma significantly changes the meaning of well-known sentences and phrases such as "God save the Queen." Think of other examples, and demonstrate how placing a comma somewhere in that sentence or phrase dramatically redirects its focus and meaning. What, in effect, can punctuation do that words alone aren't able to accomplish?

48

Maxine Hong Kingston
No Name Woman

Maxine Hong Kingston (b. 1940) won the National Book Critics Circle Award for nonfiction with her first book, The Woman Warrior: Memoirs of a Girlhood among Ghosts *(1976). "No Name Woman" is a chapter of this book, which* Time *magazine named one of the top ten nonfiction works of the 1970s. Her second book,* China Men *(1980), won the American Book Award and is also considered nonfiction, though Kingston's writing often blurs the distinction between fiction and nonfiction. Her narratives blend autobiography, history, myth, and legend, drawing on the stories she remembers from her childhood in the Chinese American community of Stockton, California. Kingston's essays, stories, and poems also appear in numerous magazines. She currently teaches at the University of California, Berkeley.*

Kingston has said that before writing The Woman Warrior, *"My life as a writer had been a long struggle with pronouns. For 30 years I wrote in the first person singular. At a certain point I was thinking that I was self-centered and egotistical, solipsistic, and not very developed as a human being, nor as an artist, because I could only see from this one point of view." She began to write in the third person because "I thought I had to overcome this self-centeredness." As she wrote her third novel, Kingston experienced the disappearance of her authorial voice. "I feel that this is an artistic as well as psychological improvement on my part. Because I am now a much less selfish person."*

"You must not tell anyone," my mother said, "what I am about to tell you. In China your father had a sister who killed herself. She jumped into the family well. We say that your father has all brothers because it is as if she had never been born.

"In 1924 just a few days after our village celebrated seventeen hurry-up weddings — to make sure that every young man who went 'out on the road' would responsibly come home — your father and his brothers and

your grandfather and his brothers and your aunt's new husband sailed for
America, the Gold Mountain. It was your grandfather's last trip. Those
lucky enough to get contracts waved good-bye from the decks. They fed
and guarded the stowaways and helped them off in Cuba, New York,
Bali, Hawaii. 'We'll meet in California next year,' they said. All of them
sent money home.

"I remember looking at your aunt one day when she and I were
dressing; I had not noticed before that she had such a protruding melon
of a stomach. But I did not think, 'She's pregnant,' until she began to
look like other pregnant women, her shirt pulling and the white tops of
her black pants showing. She could not have been pregnant, you see, because her husband had been gone for years. No one said anything. We
did not discuss it. In early summer she was ready to have the child, long
after the time when it could have been possible.

"The village had also been counting. On the night the baby was to be
born the villagers raided our house. Some were crying. Like a great saw,
teeth strung with lights, files of people walked zigzag across our land,
tearing the rice. Their lanterns doubled in the disturbed black water,
which drained away through the broken bunds. As the villagers closed in,
we could see that some of them, probably men and women we knew well,
wore white masks. The people with long hair hung it over their faces.
Women with short hair made it stand up on end. Some had tied white
bands around their foreheads, arms, and legs.

"At first they threw mud and rocks at the house. Then they threw   5
eggs and began slaughtering our stock. We could hear the animals scream
their deaths — the roosters, the pigs, a last great roar from the ox. Familiar wild heads flared in our night windows; the villagers encircled us.
Some of the faces stopped to peer at us, their eyes rushing like search-
lights. The hands flattened against the panes, framed heads, and left red
prints.

"The villagers broke in the front and the back doors at the same time,
even though we had not locked the doors against them. Their knives
dripped with the blood of our animals. They smeared blood on the doors
and walls. One woman swung a chicken, whose throat she had slit, splat-
tering blood in red arcs about her. We stood together in the middle of our
house, in the family hall with the pictures and tables of the ancestors
around us, and looked straight ahead.

"At that time the house had only two wings. When the men came
back we would build two more to enclose our courtyard and a third one
to begin a second courtyard. The villagers pushed through both wings,
even your grandparents' rooms, to find your aunt's, which was also mine
until the men returned. From this room a new wing for one of the
younger families would grow. They ripped up her clothes and shoes and
broke her combs, grinding them underfoot. They tore her work from the
loom. They scattered the cooking fire and rolled the new weaving in it.
We could hear them in the kitchen breaking our bowls and banging the

pots. They overturned the great waist-high earthenware jugs; duck eggs, pickled fruits, vegetables burst out and mixed in acrid torrents. The old woman from the next field swept a broom through the air and loosed the spirits-of-the-broom over our heads. 'Pig.' 'Ghost.' 'Pig,' they sobbed and scolded while they ruined our house.

"When they left, they took sugar and oranges to bless themselves. They cut pieces from the dead animals. Some of them took bowls that were not broken and clothes that were not torn. Afterward we swept up the rice and sewed it back up into sacks. But the smells from the spilled preserves lasted. Your aunt gave birth in the pigsty that night. The next morning when I went up for the water, I found her and the baby plugging up the family well.

"Don't let your father know that I told you. He denies her. Now that you have started to menstruate, what happened to her could happen to you. Don't humiliate us. You wouldn't like to be forgotten as if you had never been born. The villagers are watchful."

Whenever she had to warn us about life, my mother told stories that   10 ran like this one, a story to grow up on. She tested our strength to establish realities. Those in the emigrant generations who could not reassert brute survival died young and far from home. Those of us in the first American generations have had to figure out how the invisible world the emigrants built around our childhoods fit in solid America.

The emigrants confused the gods by diverting their curses, misleading them with crooked streets and false names. They must try to confuse their offspring as well, who, I suppose, threaten them in similar ways — always trying to get things straight, always trying to name the unspeakable. The Chinese I know hide their names; sojourners take new names when their lives change and guard their real names with silence.

Chinese-Americans, when you try to understand what things in you are Chinese, how do you separate what is peculiar to childhood, to poverty, insanities, one family, your mother who marked your growing with stories, from what is Chinese? What is Chinese tradition and what is the movies?

If I want to learn what clothes my aunt wore, whether flashy or ordinary, I would have to begin, "Remember Father's drowned-in-the-well sister?" I cannot ask that. My mother has told me once and for all the useful parts. She will add nothing unless powered by Necessity, a riverbank that guides her life. She plants vegetable gardens rather than lawns; she carries the odd-shaped tomatoes home from the fields and eats food left for the gods.

Whenever we did frivolous things, we used up energy; we flew high kites. We children came up off the ground over the melting cones our parents brought home from work and the American movie on New Years' Day — *Oh, You Beautiful Doll* with Betty Grable one year, and *She Wore a Yellow Ribbon* with John Wayne another year. After the one carnival ride each, we paid in guilt; our tired father counted his change on the dark walk home.

Adultery is extravagance. Could people who hatch their own chicks
and eat the embryos and the heads for delicacies and boil the feet in vine-
gar for party food, leaving only the gravel, eating even the gizzard lining — could such people engender a prodigal aunt? To be a woman, to
have a daughter in starvation time was a waste enough. My aunt could
not have been the lone romantic who gave up everything for sex. Women
in the old China did not choose. Some man had commanded her to lie
with him and be his secret evil. I wonder whether he masked himself
when he joined the raid on her family.

Perhaps she encountered him in the fields or on the mountain where
the daughters-in-law collected fuel. Or perhaps he first noticed her in the
marketplace. He was not a stranger because the village housed no
strangers. She had to have dealings with him other than sex. Perhaps he
worked an adjoining field, or he sold her the cloth for the dress she sewed
and wore. His demand must have surprised, then terrified her. She obeyed
him; she always did as she was told.

When the family found a young man in the next village to be her husband, she stood tractably beside the best rooster, his proxy, and promised
before they met that she would be his forever. She was lucky that he was
her age and she would be the first wife, an advantage secure now. The
night she first saw him, he had sex with her. Then he left for America. She
had almost forgotten what he looked like. When she tried to envision
him, she only saw the black and white face in the group photograph the
men had had taken before leaving.

The other man was not, after all, much different from her husband.
They both gave orders: she followed. "If you tell your family, I'll beat
you. I'll kill you. Be here again next week." No one talked sex, ever. And
she might have separated the rapes from the rest of living if only she did
not have to buy her oil from him or gather wood in the same forest. I
want her fear to have lasted just as long as rape lasted so that the fear
could have been contained. No drawn-out fear. But women at sex haz-
arded birth and hence lifetimes. The fear did not stop but permeated
everywhere. She told the man, "I think I'm pregnant." He organized the
raid against her.

On nights when my mother and father talked about their life back
home, sometimes they mentioned an "outcast table" whose business they
still seemed to be settling, their voices tight. In a commensal tradition,
where food is precious, the powerful older people made wrongdoers eat
alone. Instead of letting them start separate new lives like the Japanese,
who could become samurais and geishas, the Chinese family, faces
averted but eyes glowering sideways, hung on to the offenders and fed
them leftovers. My aunt must have lived in the same house as my parents
and eaten at an outcast table. My mother spoke about the raid as if she
had seen it, when she and my aunt, a daughter-in-law to a different
household, should not have been living together at all. Daughters-in-law
lived with their husbands' parents, not their own; a synonym for marriage

in Chinese is "taking a daughter-in-law." Her husband's parents could have sold her, mortgaged her, stoned her. But they had sent her back to her own mother and father, a mysterious act hinting at disgraces not told me. Perhaps they had thrown her out to deflect the avengers.

She was the only daughter; her four brothers went with her father, husband, and uncles "out on the road" and for some years became western men. When the goods were divided among the family, three of the brothers took land, and the youngest, my father, chose an education. After my grandparents gave their daughter away to her husband's family, they had dispensed all the adventure and all the property. They expected her alone to keep the traditional ways, which her brothers, now among the barbarians, could fumble without detection. The heavy, deep-rooted women were to maintain the past against the flood, safe for returning. But the rare urge west had fixed upon our family, and so my aunt crossed boundaries not delineated in space.

The work of preservation demands that the feelings playing about in one's guts not be turned into action. Just watch their passing like cherry blossoms. But perhaps my aunt, my forerunner, caught in a slow life, let dreams grow and fade and after some months or years went toward what persisted. Fear at the enormities of the forbidden kept her desires delicate, wire and bone. She looked at a man because she liked the way the hair was tucked behind his ears, or she liked the question-mark line of a long torso curving at the shoulder and straight at the hip. For warm eyes or a soft voice or a slow walk — that's all — a few hairs, a line, a brightness, a sound, a pace, she gave up family. She offered us up for a charm that vanished with tiredness, a pigtail that didn't toss when the wind died. Why, the wrong lighting could erase the dearest thing about him.

It could very well have been, however, that my aunt did not take subtle enjoyment of her friend, but, a wild woman, kept rollicking company. Imagining her free with sex doesn't fit, though. I don't know any women like that, or men either. Unless I see her life branching into mine, she gives me no ancestral help.

To sustain her being in love, she often worked at herself in the mirror, guessing at the colors and shapes that would interest him, changing them frequently in order to hit on the right combination. She wanted to look back.

On a farm near the sea, a woman who tended her appearance reaped a reputation for eccentricity. All the married women blunt-cut their hair in flaps about their ears or pulled it back in tight buns. No nonsense. Neither style blew easily into heart-catching tangles. And at their weddings they displayed themselves in their long hair for the last time. "It brushed the backs of my knees," my mother tells me. "It was braided, and even so, it brushed the backs of my knees."

At the mirror my aunt combed individuality into her bob. A bun could have been contrived to escape into black streamers blowing in the wind or in quiet wisps about her face, but only the older women in our picture album wear buns. She brushed her hair back from her forehead, tucking the flaps behind her ears. She looped a piece of thread, knotted into a circle between her index fingers and thumbs, and ran the double strand across her forehead. When she closed her fingers as if she were making a pair of shadow geese bite, the string twisted together catching the little hairs. Then she pulled the thread away from her skin, ripping the hairs out neatly, her eyes watering from the needles of pain. Opening her fingers, she cleaned the thread, then rolled it along her hairline and the tops of the eyebrows. My mother did the same to me and my sisters and herself. I used to believe that the expression "caught by the short hairs" meant a captive held with a depilatory string. It especially hurt at the temples, but my mother said we were lucky we didn't have to have our feet bound when we were seven. Sisters used to sit on their beds and cry together, she said, as their mothers or their slave removed the bandages for a few minutes each night and let the blood gush back into their veins. I hope that the man my aunt loved appreciated a smooth brow, that he wasn't just a tits-and-ass man.

Once my aunt found a freckle on her chin, at a spot that the almanac said predestined her for unhappiness. She dug it out with a hot needle and washed the wound with peroxide.

More attention to her looks than these pullings of hairs and pickings at spots would have caused gossip among the villagers. They owned work clothes and good clothes, and they wore good clothes for feasting the new seasons. But since a woman combing her hair hexes beginnings, my aunt rarely found an occasion to look her best. Women looked like great sea snails — the corded wood, babies, and laundry they carried were the whorls on their backs. The Chinese did not admire a bent back; goddesses and warriors stood straight. Still there must have been a marvelous freeing of beauty when a worker laid down her burden and stretched and arched.

Such commonplace loveliness, however, was not enough for my aunt. She dreamed of a lover for the fifteen days of New Year's, the time for families to exchange visits, money, and food. She plied her secret comb. And sure enough she cursed the year, the family, the village, and herself.

Even as her hair lured her imminent lover, many other men looked at her. Uncles, cousins, nephews, brothers would have looked, too, had they been home between journeys. Perhaps they had already been restraining their curiosity, and they left, fearful that their glances, like a field of nesting birds, might be startled and caught. Poverty hurt, and that was their first reason for leaving. But another, final reason for leaving the crowded house was the never-said.

She may have been unusually beloved, the precious only daughter, 30 spoiled and mirror-gazing because of the affection the family lavished on her. When her husband left, they welcomed the chance to take her back from the in-laws; she could live like the little daughter for just a while longer. There are stories that my grandfather was different from other people, "crazy ever since the little Jap bayoneted him in the head." He used to put his naked penis on the dinner table, laughing. And one day he brought home a baby girl, wrapped up inside his brown western-style greatcoat. He had traded one of his sons, probably my father, the youngest, for her. My grandmother made him trade back. When he finally got a daughter of his own, he doted on her. They must have all loved her, except perhaps my father, the only brother who never went back to China, having once been traded for a girl.

Brothers and sisters, newly men and women, had to efface their sexual color and present plain miens. Disturbing hair and eyes, a smile like no other, threatened the ideal of five generations living under one roof. To focus blurs, people shouted face to face and yelled from room to room. The immigrants I know have loud voices, unmodulated to American tones even after years away from the village where they called their friendships out across the fields. I have not been able to stop my mother's screams in public libraries or over telephones. Walking erect (knees straight, toes pointed forward, not pigeon-toed, which is Chinese-feminine) and speaking in an inaudible voice, I have tried to turn myself American-feminine. Chinese communication was loud, public. Only sick people had to whisper. But at the dinner table, where the family members came nearest one another, no one could talk, not the outcasts nor any eaters. Every word that falls from the mouth is a coin lost. Silently they gave and accepted food with both hands. A preoccupied child who took his bowl with one hand got a sideways glare. A complete moment of total attention is due everyone alike. Children and lovers have no singularity here, but my aunt used a secret voice, a separate attentiveness.

She kept the man's name to herself throughout her labor and dying; she did not accuse him that he be punished with her. To save her inseminator's name she gave silent birth.

He may have been somebody in her own household, but intercourse with a man outside the family would have been no less abhorrent. All the village were kinsmen, and the titles shouted in loud country voices never let kinship be forgotten. Any man within visiting distance would have been neutralized as a lover — "brother," "younger brother," "older brother" — 115 relationship titles. Parents researched birth charts probably not so much to assure good fortune as to circumvent incest in a population that has but one hundred surnames. Everybody has eight million relatives. How useless then sexual mannerisms, how dangerous.

As if it came from an atavism deeper than fear, I used to add "brother" silently to boys' names. It hexed the boys, who would or would not ask me to dance, and made them less scary and as familiar and deserving of benevolence as girls.

But, of course, I hexed myself also — no dates. I should have stood up, both arms waving, and shouted out across libraries, "Hey, you! Love me back." I had no idea, though, how to make attraction selective, how to control its direction and magnitude. If I made myself American-pretty so that the five or six Chinese boys in the class fell in love with me, everyone else — the Caucasian, Negro, and Japanese boys — would too. Sisterliness, dignified and honorable, made much more sense.

35

Attraction eludes control so stubbornly that whole societies designed to organize relationships among people cannot keep order, not even when they bind people to one another from childhood and raise them together. Among the very poor and the wealthy, brothers married their adopted sisters, like doves. Our family allowed some romance, paying adult brides' prices and providing dowries so that their sons and daughters could marry strangers. Marriage promises to turn strangers into friendly relatives — a nation of siblings.

In the village structure, spirits shimmered among the live creatures, balanced and held in equilibrium by time and land. But one human being flaring up into violence could open up a black hole, a maelstrom that pulled in the sky. The frightened villagers, who depended on one another to maintain the real, went to my aunt to show her a personal, physical representation of the break she made in the "roundness." Misallying couples snapped off the future, which was to be embodied in true offspring. The villagers punished her for acting as if she could have a private life, secret and apart from them.

If my aunt had betrayed the family at a time of large grain yields and peace, when many boys were born, and wings were being built on many houses, perhaps she might have escaped such severe punishment. But the men — hungry, greedy, tired of planting in dry soil, cuckolded — had been forced to leave the village in order to send food-money home. There were ghost plagues, bandit plagues, wars with the Japanese, floods. My Chinese brother and sister had died of an unknown sickness. Adultery, perhaps only a mistake during good times, became a crime when the village needed food.

The round moon cakes and round doorways, the round tables of graduated size that fit one roundness inside another, round windows and rice bowls — these talismans had lost their power to warn this family of the law: A family must be whole, faithfully keeping the descent line by having sons to feed the old and the dead who in turn look after the family. The villagers came to show my aunt and lover-in-hiding a broken house. The villagers were speeding up the circling of events because she was too shortsighted to see that her infidelity had already harmed the village, that waves of consequences would return unpredictably, sometimes in disguise, as now, to hurt her. This roundness had to be made coin-sized so that she would see its circumference: Punish her at the birth of her baby. Awaken her to the inexorable. People who refused fatalism because they could invent small resources insisted on culpability. Deny accidents and wrest fault from the stars.

After the villagers left, their lanterns now scattering in various directions toward home, the family broke their silence and cursed her. "Aiaa, we're going to die. Death is coming. Death is coming. Look what you've done. You've killed us. Ghost! Dead Ghost! Ghost! You've never been born." She ran out into the fields, far enough from the house so that she could no longer hear their voices, and pressed herself against the earth, her own land no more. When she felt the birth coming, she thought that she had been hurt. Her body seized together. "They've hurt me too

40

much," she thought. "This is gall, and it will kill me." With forehead and knees against the earth, her body convulsed and then relaxed. She turned on her back, lay on the ground. The black well of sky and stars went out and out forever; her body and her complexity seemed to disappear. She was one of the stars, a bright dot in blackness, without home, without a companion, in eternal cold and silence. An agoraphobia rose in her, speeding higher and higher, bigger and bigger; she would not be able to contain it; there would be no end to fear.

Flayed, unprotected against space, she felt pain return, focusing her body. This pain chilled her — a cold, steady kind of surface pain. Inside, spasmodically, the other pain, the pain of the child, heated her. For hours she lay on the ground, alternately body and space. Sometimes a vision of normal comfort obliterated reality: She saw the family in the evening gambling at the dinner table, the young people massaging their elders' backs. She saw them congratulating one another, high joy on the mornings the rice shoots came up. When these pictures burst, the stars drew yet further apart. Black space opened.

She got to her feet to fight better and remembered that old-fashioned women gave birth in their pigsties to fool the jealous, pain-dealing gods, who do not snatch piglets. Before the next spasms could stop her, she ran to the pigsty, each step a rushing out into emptiness. She climbed over the fence and knelt in the dirt. It was good to have a fence enclosing her, a tribal person alone.

Laboring, this woman who had carried her child as a foreign growth that sickened her every day, expelled it at last. She reached down to touch the hot, wet, moving mass, surely smaller than anything human, and could feel that it was human after all — fingers, toes, nails, nose. She pulled it up on to her belly, and it lay curled there, butt in the air, feet precisely tucked one under the other. She opened her loose shirt and buttoned the child inside. After resting, it squirmed and thrashed and she pushed it up to her breast. It turned its head this way and that until it found her nipple. There, it made little snuffling noises. She clenched her teeth at its preciousness, lovely as a young calf, a piglet, a little dog.

She may have gone to the pigsty as a last act of responsibility: She would protect this child as she had protected its father. It would look after her soul, leaving supplies on her grave. But how would this tiny child without family find her grave when there would be no marker for her anywhere, neither in the earth nor the family hall? No one would give her a family hall name. She had taken the child with her into the wastes. At its birth the two of them had felt the same raw pain of separation, a wound that only the family pressing tight could close. A child with no descent line would not soften her life but only trail after her, ghostlike, begging her to give it purpose. At dawn the villagers on their way to the fields would stand around the fence and look.

Full of milk, the little ghost slept. When it awoke, she hardened her breasts against the milk that crying loosens. Toward morning she picked up the baby and walked to the well.

Carrying the baby to the well shows loving. Otherwise abandon it. Turn its face into the mud. Mothers who love their children take them along. It was probably a girl; there is some hope of forgiveness for boys.

"Don't tell anyone you had an aunt. Your father does not want to hear her name. She has never been born." I have believed that sex was unspeakable and words so strong and fathers so frail that "aunt" would do my father mysterious harm. I have thought that my family, having settled among immigrants who had also been their neighbors in the ancestral land, needed to clean their name, and a wrong word would incite the kinspeople even here. But there is more to this silence: They want me to participate in her punishment. And I have.

In the twenty years since I heard this story I have not asked for details nor said my aunt's name; I do not know it. People who comfort the dead can also chase after them to hurt them further — a reverse ancestor worship. The real punishment was not the raid swiftly inflicted by the villagers, but the family's deliberately forgetting her. Her betrayal so maddened them, they saw to it that she would suffer forever, even after death. Always hungry, always needing, she would have to beg food from other ghosts, snatch and steal it from those whose living descendants give them gifts. She would have to fight the ghosts massed at crossroads for the buns a few thoughtful citizens leave to decoy her away from village and home so that the ancestral spirits could feast unharassed. At peace, they could act like gods, not ghosts, their descent lines providing them with paper suits and dresses, spirit money, paper houses, paper automobiles, chicken, meat, and rice into eternity — essences delivered up in smoke and flames, steam and incense rising from each rice bowl. In an attempt to make the Chinese care for people outside the family, Chairman Mao encourages us now to give our paper replicas to the spirits of outstanding soldiers and workers, no matter whose ancestors they may be. My aunt remains forever hungry. Goods are not distributed evenly among the dead.

My aunt haunts me — her ghost drawn to me because now, after fifty years of neglect, I alone devote pages of paper to her, though not origamied into houses and clothes. I do not think she always means me well. I am telling on her, and she was a spite suicide, drowning herself in the drinking water. The Chinese are always very frightened of the drowned one, whose weeping ghost, wet hair hanging and skin bloated, waits silently by the water to pull down a substitute.

The Reader's Presence

1. Kingston's account of her aunt's life and death is a remarkable blend of fact and speculation. Consider the overall structure of "No Name Woman." How many versions of the aunt's story do we hear? Where, for example, does the mother's story end? Where

does the narrator's begin? Which version do you find more compelling? Why? What does the narrator mean when she says that
her mother's stories "tested our strength to establish realities"
(paragraph 10)?

2. The narrator's version of her aunt's story is replete with such words
   and phrases as *perhaps* and *It could very well have been.* The narrator seems far more speculative about her aunt's life than her mother
   is. At what point does the narrator raise doubts about the veracity
   of her mother's version of the aunt's story? What purpose does the
   mother espouse in telling the aunt's story? Is it meant primarily to
   express family lore? to issue a warning? Point to specific passages to
   verify your response. What is the proposed moral of the story? Is
   that moral the same for the mother as for the narrator? Explain.

3. What does the narrator mean when she says "They must try to
   confuse their offspring as well, who, I suppose, threaten them in
   similar ways — always trying to get things straight, always trying
   to name the unspeakable" (paragraph 11)? What line does
   Kingston draw between the two cultures represented in the story:
   between the mother, a superstitious, cautious Chinese woman,
   and the narrator, an American-born child trying to "straighten
   out" her mother's confusing story? How does the narrator resolve
   the issue by thinking of herself as neither Chinese nor American,
   but as a Chinese American? How are these issues made matters of
   gender? Judging from the evidence in this story, how would you
   summarize — and characterize — Chinese expectations of men?
   of women? How much does the story depend on gender stereotypes, and how does the narrator explore the complexity of those
   roles in her version of her aunt's story?

49

Marvin Minsky

Will Robots Inherit the Earth?

*Professor of electrical engineering at the Massachusetts Institute of Technol-
ogy, Marvin Minsky (b. 1927) is a pioneer in the field of artificial intelligence. He
defines this field as "research concerned with making machines do things that
people consider to require intelligence," and in this field Minsky has had some notable success. In 1951, together with a colleague, he assembled 400 vacuum tubes
in the first neural network learning machine. In order to build a computer capable
of thinking like a human mind, Minsky believes that it is first necessary to under-*

stand how the human mind works. He advances a theory about the processes of thought in his book The Society of Mind *(1988). Minsky has written numerous books and articles concerned with artificial intelligence, mathematics, electronics, and computing, and has also co-authored a science-fiction novel,* The Turing Option *(1992). "Will Robots Inherit the Earth?" appeared in* Scientific American *in 1994.*

Concerning his own thought processes, Minsky has said, "It is largely during writing that I work out my ideas and theories. (I usually get the basic ideas themselves while giving deliberately unprepared lectures, or in arguing with people with whom I strongly disagree.) When I'm writing an essay it grows large, cluttered with fragments of theories and bits of text, which get rearranged, destroyed, and revised dozens of times. I envy writers who 'have the whole thing' planned out in their minds, and know where they're going at almost every step, but that's a different world to me. If I actually understand anything that well, it just seems too trivial to talk about."

> Early to bed and early to rise,
> Makes a man healthy, wealthy, and wise.
>
> —Benjamin Franklin

Everyone wants wisdom and wealth. Nevertheless, our health often gives out before we achieve them. To lengthen our lives and improve our minds, we will need to change our bodies and brains. To that end, we first must consider how traditional Darwinian evolution brought us to where we are. Then we must imagine ways in which novel replacements for worn body parts might solve our problems of failing health. Next we must invent strategies to augment our brains and gain greater wisdom. Eventually, using nanotechnology, we will entirely replace our brains. Once delivered from the limitations of biology, we will decide the length of our lives — with the option of immortality — and choose among other, unimagined capabilities as well.

In such a future, attaining wealth will be easy; the trouble will be in controlling it. Obviously, such changes are difficult to envision, and many thinkers still argue that these advances are impossible, particularly in the domain of artificial intelligence. But the sciences needed to enact this transition are already in the making, and it is time to consider what this new world will be like.

Such a future cannot be realized through biology. In recent times we have learned much about health and how to maintain it. We have devised thousands of specific treatments for specific diseases and disabilities. Yet we do not seem to have increased the maximum length of our life span. Benjamin Franklin lived for 84 years, and except in popular legends and myths no one has ever lived twice that long. According to the estimates of Roy L. Walford, professor of pathology at the University of California at Los Angeles School of Medicine, the average human lifetime was about 22 years in ancient Rome, was about 50 in the developed countries in 1900, and today stands at about 75 in the U.S. Despite this increase, each of those curves seems to terminate sharply near 115 years. Centuries of improvements in health care have had no effect on that maximum.

Why are our life spans so limited? The answer is simple: natural selection favors the genes of those with the most descendants. Those numbers tend to grow exponentially with the number of generations, and so natural selection prefers the genes of those who reproduce at earlier ages. Evolution does not usually preserve genes that lengthen lives beyond that amount adults need to care for their young. Indeed, it may even favor offspring who do not have to compete with living parents. Such competition could promote the accretion of genes that cause death. For example, after spawning, the Mediterranean octopus promptly stops eating and starves itself. If a certain gland is removed, the octopus continues to eat and lives twice as long. Many other animals are programmed to die soon after they cease reproducing. Exceptions to this phenomenon include animals such as ourselves and elephants, whose progeny learn a great deal from the social transmission of accumulated knowledge.

We humans appear to be the longest-lived warm-blooded animals. What selective pressure might have led to our present longevity, which is almost twice that of our other primate relatives? The answer is related to wisdom. Among all mammals our infants are the most poorly equipped to survive by themselves. Perhaps we need not only parents but grandparents, too, to care for us and to pass on precious survival tips.

5

Even with such advice there are many causes of mortality to which we might succumb. Some deaths result from infections. Our immune systems have evolved versatile ways to cope with most such diseases. Unhappily, those very same immune systems often injure us by treating various parts of ourselves as though they, too, were infectious invaders. This autoimmune blindness leads to diseases such as diabetes, multiple sclerosis, rheumatoid arthritis and many others.

We are also subject to injuries that our bodies cannot repair: accidents, dietary imbalances, chemical poisons, heat, radiation and sundry other influences can deform or chemically alter the molecules of our cells so that they are unable to function. Some of these errors get corrected by replacing defective molecules. Nevertheless, when the replacement rate is too low, errors build up. For example, when the proteins of the eyes' lenses lose their elasticity, we lose our ability to focus and need bifocal spectacles — a Franklin invention.

The major natural causes of death stem from the effects of inherited genes. These genes include those that seem to be largely responsible for heart disease and cancer, the two biggest causes of mortality, as well as countless other disorders, such as cystic fibrosis and sickle cell anemia. New technologies should be able to prevent some of these disorders by replacing those genes.

Most likely, senescence is inevitable in all biological organisms. To be sure, certain species (including some varieties of fish, tortoises and lobster) do not appear to show any systematic increase in mortality as they age. These animals seem to die mainly from external causes, such as predators or starvation. All the same, we have no records of animals that have lived for as long as 200 years — although this lack does not prove that none exist. Walford and many others believe a carefully designed diet, one seriously restricted in calories, can significantly increase a human's life span but cannot ultimately prevent death.

By learning more about our genes, we should be able to correct or at   10
least postpone many conditions that still plague our later years. Yet even if we found a cure for each specific disease, we would still have to face the general problem of "wearing out." The normal function of every cell involves thousands of chemical processes, each of which sometimes makes random mistakes. Our bodies use many kinds of correction techniques, each triggered by a specific type of mistake. But those random errors happen in so many different ways that no low-level scheme can correct them all.

The problem is that out genetic systems were not designed for very long term maintenance. The relation between genes and cells is exceedingly indirect; there are no blueprints or maps to guide our genes as they build or rebuild the body. To repair defects on larger scales, a body would need some kind of catalogue that specified which types of cells should be located where. In computer programs it is easy to install such redundancy. Many computers maintain unused copies of their most critical system programs and routinely check their integrity. No animals have evolved similar schemes, presumably because such algorithms cannot develop through natural selection. The trouble is that error correction would stop mutation, which would ultimately slow the rate of evolution of an animal's descendants so much that they would be unable to adapt to changes in their environments.

Could we live for several centuries simply by changing some number of genes? After all, we now differ from our relatives, the gorillas and chimpanzees, by only a few thousand genes — and yet we live almost twice as long. If we assume that only a small fraction of those new genes caused the increase in life span, then perhaps no more than 100 or so of those genes were involved. Even if this turned out to be true, though, it would not guarantee that we could gain another century by changing another 100 genes. We might need to change just a few of them — or we might have to change a good many more.

Making new genes and installing them are slowly becoming feasible. But we are already exploiting another approach to combat biological wear and tear: replacing each organ that threatens to fail with a biological or artificial substitute. Some replacements are already routine. Others are on the horizon. Hearts are merely clever pumps. Muscles and bones are motors and beams. Digestive systems are chemical reactors. Eventually, we will find ways to transplant or replace all these parts. But when it comes to the brain, a transplant will not work. You cannot simply exchange your brain for another and remain the same person. You would lose the knowledge and the processes that constitute your identity. Nevertheless, we might be able to replace certain worn-out parts of brains by transplanting tissue-cultured fetal cells. This procedure would not restore lost knowledge, but that might not matter as much as it seems. We probably store each fragment of knowledge in several different places, in different forms. New parts of the brain could be retrained and reintegrated with the rest, and some of that might even happen spontaneously.

Even before our bodies wear out, I suspect that we often run into limitations in our brain's abilities. As a species, we seem to have reached a plateau in our intellectual development. There is no sign that we are getting smarter. Was Albert Einstein a better scientist than Isaac Newton or Archimedes? Has any playwright in recent years topped William Shakespeare or Euripides? We have learned a lot in 2,000 years, yet much ancient wisdom still seems sound, which makes me think we have not been making much progress. We still do not know how to resolve conflicts between individual goals and global interests. We are so bad at making important decisions that, whenever we can, we leave to chance what we are unsure about.

Why is our wisdom so limited? Is it because we do not have the time to learn very much or that we lack enough capacity? Is it because, according to popular accounts, we use only a fraction of our brains? Could better education help? Of course, but only to a point. Even our best prodigies learn no more than twice as quickly as the rest. Everything takes us too long to learn because our brains are so terribly slow. It would certainly help to have more time, but longevity is not enough. The brain, like other finite things, must reach some limits to what it can learn. We do not know what those limits are; perhaps our brains could keep learning for several more centuries. But at some point, we will need to increase their capacity.

The more we learn about our brains, the more ways we will find to improve them. Each brain has hundreds of specialized regions. We only know a little about what each one does or how it does it, but as soon as we find out how any one part works, researchers will try to devise ways to extend that part's capacity. They will also conceive of entirely new abilities that biology has never provided. As these inventions grow ever more prevalent, we will try to connect them to our brains, perhaps though millions of microscopic electrodes inserted into the great nerve bundle called the corpus callosum, the largest databus in the brain. With further advances, no part of the brain will be out-of-bounds for attaching new accessories. In the end, we will find ways to replace every part of the body and brain and thus repair all the defects and injuries that make our lives so brief.

Needless to say, in doing so we will be making ourselves into machines. Does this mean machines will replace us? I do not feel that it makes much sense to think in terms of "us" and "them." I much prefer

15

the attitude of Hans P. Moravec of Carnegie Mellon University, who suggests that we think of these future intelligent machines as our own "mind-children."

In the past we have tended to see ourselves as a final product of evolution, but our evolution has not ceased. Indeed, we are now evolving more rapidly, though not in the familiar, slow Darwinian way. It is time that we started to think about our new emerging identities. We can begin to design systems based on inventive kinds of "unnatural selection" that can advance explicit plans and goals and can also exploit the inheritance of acquired characteristics. It took a century for evolutionists to train themselves to avoid such ideas — biologists call them "teleological" and "Lamarckian"[1] — but now we may have to change those rules.

Almost all the knowledge we amass is embodied in various networks   20
inside our brains. These networks consist of huge numbers of tiny nerve cells and smaller structures, called synapses, that control how signals jump from one nerve cell to another. To make a replacement of a human brain, we would need to know something about how each of the synapses relates to the two cells it joins. We would also have to know how each of those structures responds to the various electric fields, hormones, neurotransmitters, nutrients, and other chemicals that are active in its neighborhood. A human brain contains trillions of synapses, so this is no small requirement.

Fortunately, we would not need to know every minute detail. If details were important, our brains would not work in the first place. In biological organisms, each system has generally evolved to be insensitive to most of what goes on in the smaller subsystems on which it depends. Therefore, to copy a functional brain it should suffice to replicate just enough of the function of each part to produce its important effects on other parts.

Suppose we wanted to copy a machine, such as a brain, that contained a trillion components. Today we could not do such a thing (even with the necessary knowledge) if we had to build each component separately. But if we had a million construction machines that could each build 1,000 parts per second, our task would take mere minutes. In the decades to come, new fabrication machines will make this possible. Most present-day manufacturing is based on shaping bulk materials. In contrast, nanotechnologists aim to build materials and machinery by placing each atom and molecule precisely where they want it.

By such methods we could make truly identical parts and thus escape from the randomness that hinders conventionally made machines. Today, for example, when we try to etch very small circuits, the sizes of the wires vary so much that we cannot predict their electrical properties. If we can locate each atom exactly, however, the behavior of those wires would be indistinguishable. This capability would lead to new kinds of materials that current techniques could never make; we could endow them with enormous

---

[1]*Lamarckian:* The early evolutionary theory of the French scientist Jean Baptiste Lamarck (1744–1829) held that acquired characteristics could be inherited. — Eds.

strength or novel quantum properties. These products in turn could lead to computers as small as synapses, having unparalleled speed and efficiency.

Once we can use these techniques to construct a general-purpose assembly machine that operates on atomic scales, further progress should be swift. If it took one week for such a machine to make a copy of itself, we could have a billion copies in less than a year. These devices would transform our world. For example, we could program them to fabricate efficient solar-energy collecting devices and attach these to nearby surfaces. Hence, the devices could power themselves. We would be able to grow fields of microfactories in much the same way that we now grow trees. In such a future we will have little trouble attaining wealth; our trouble will be in learning how to control it. In particular, we must always take care to maintain control over those things (such as ourselves) that might be able to reproduce themselves.

If we want to consider augmenting our brains, we might first ask how much a person knows today. Thomas K. Landauer of Bellcore reviewed many experiments in which people were asked to read text, look at pictures and listen to words, sentences, short passages of music and nonsense syllables. They were later tested to see how much they remembered. In none of these situations were people able to learn, and later remember for any extended period, more than about two bits per second. If one could maintain that rate for 12 hours every day for 100 years, the total would be about three billion bits — less than what we can currently store on a regular five-inch compact disc. In a decade or so that amount should fit on a single computer chip.

Although these experiments do not much resemble what we do in real life, we do not have any hard evidence that people can learn more quickly. Despite common reports about people with "photographic memories," no one seems to have mastered, word for word, the contents of as few as 100 books or of a single major encyclopedia. The complete works of Shakespeare come to about 130 million bits. Landauer's limit implies that a person would need at least four years to memorize them. We have no well-founded estimates of how much information we require to perform skills such as painting or skiing, but I do not see any reason why these activities should not be similarly limited.

The brain is believed to contain on the order of 100 trillion synapses, which should leave plenty of room for those few billion bits of reproducible memories. Someday, using nanotechnology, it should be feasible to build that much storage space into a package as small as a pea.

Once we know what we need to do, our nanotechnologies should enable us to construct replacement bodies and brains that will not be constrained to work at the crawling pace of "real time." The events in our computer chips already happen millions of times faster than those in brain cells. Hence, we could design our "mind-children" to think a million times faster than we do. To such a being, half a minute might seem as long as one of our years and each hour as long as an entire human lifetime.

But could such beings really exist? Many scholars from a variety of disciplines firmly maintain that machines will never have thoughts like ours, because no matter how we build them, they will always lack some vital ingredient. These thinkers refer to this missing essence by various names: sentience, consciousness, spirit or soul. Philosophers write entire books to prove that because of this deficiency, machines can never feel or understand the kinds of things that people do. Yet every proof in each of those books is flawed by assuming, in one way or another, what it purports to prove — the existence of some magical spark that has no detectable properties. I have no patience with such arguments. We should not be searching for any single missing part. Human thought has many ingredients, and every machine that we have ever built is missing dozens or hundreds of them! Compare what computers do today with what we call "thinking." Clearly, human thinking is far more flexible, resourceful and adaptable. When anything goes even slightly wrong within a present-day computer program, the machine will either come to a halt or generate worthless results. When a person thinks, things are constantly going wrong as well, yet such troubles rarely thwart us. Instead we simply try something else. We look at our problem differently and switch to another strategy. What empowers us to do this?

On my desk lies a textbook about the brain. Its index has approxi-   30
mately 6,000 lines that refer to hundreds of specialized structures. If you happen to injure some of these components, you could lose your ability to remember the names of animals. Another injury might leave you unable to make long-range plans. Another impairment could render you prone to suddenly utter dirty words because of damage to the machinery that normally censors that type of expression. We know from thousands of similar facts that the brain contains diverse machinery. Thus, your knowledge is represented in various forms that are stored in different regions of the brain, to be used by different processes. What are those representations like? We do not yet know.

But in the field of artificial intelligence, researchers have found several useful means to represent knowledge, each better suited to some purposes than to others. The most popular ones use collections of "if-then" rules. Other systems use structures called frames, which resemble forms that are to be filled out. Yet other programs use weblike networks or schemes that resemble trees or sequences of planlike scripts. Some systems store knowledge in languagelike sentences or in expressions of mathematical logic. A programmer starts any new job by trying to decide which representation will best accomplish the task at hand. Typically a computer program uses a single representation, which, should it fail, can cause the system to break down. This shortcoming justifies the common complaint that computers do not really "understand" what they are doing.

What does it mean to understand? Many philosophers have declared that understanding (or meaning or consciousness) must be a basic, elemental ability that only a living mind can possess. To me, this claim appears to be a symptom of "physics envy" — that is, they are jealous of how well physical science has explained so much in terms of so few principles. Physicists have done very well by rejecting all explanations that seem too complicated and then searching instead for simple ones. Still, this method does not work when we are addressing the full complexity of the brain. Here is an abridgment of what I said about the ability to understand in my book *The Society of Mind:*

> If you understand something in only one way, then you do not really understand it at all. This is because if something goes wrong you get stuck with a thought that just sits in your mind with nowhere to go. The secret of what anything means to us depends on how we have connected it to all the other things we know. This is why, when someone learns "by rote," we say that they do not really understand. However, if you have several different representations, when one approach fails you can try another. Of course, making too many indiscriminate connections will turn a mind to mush. But well-connected representations let you turn ideas around in your mind, to envision things from many perspectives, until you find one that works for you. And that is what we mean by thinking!

I think flexibility explains why, at the moment, thinking is easy for us and hard for computers. In *The Society of Mind*, I suggest that the brain rarely uses a single representation. Instead it always runs several scenarios in parallel so that multiple viewpoints are always available. Furthermore, each system is supervised by other, higher-level ones that keep track of their performance and reformulate problems when necessary. Because each part and process in the brain may have deficiencies, we should expect to find other parts that try to detect and correct such bugs.

In order to think effectively, you need multiple processes to help you describe, predict, explain, abstract and plan what your mind should do next. The reason we can think so well is not because we house mysterious sparklike talents and gifts but because we employ societies of agencies that work in concert to keep us from getting stuck. When we discover how these societies work, we can put them inside computers, too. Then if one procedure in a program gets stuck, another might suggest an alternative approach. If you saw a machine do things like that, you would certainly think it was conscious.

This article bears on our rights to have children, to change our genes and to die if we so wish. No popular ethical system yet, be it humanist or religion-based, has shown itself able to face the challenges that already confront us. How many people should occupy the earth? What sorts of people should they be? How should we share the available space? Clearly, we must change our ideas about making additional children. Individuals now are conceived by chance. Someday, instead, they could be "composed" in accord with considered desires and designs. Furthermore, when we build new brains, these need not start out the way ours do, with so little knowledge about the world. What kinds of things should our "mind-children" know? How many of them should we produce, and who should decide their attributes?

Traditional systems of ethical thought are focused mainly on individuals, as though they were the only entities of value. Obviously, we must also consider the rights and the roles of larger-scale beings — such as the superpersons we term cultures and the great, growing systems called sciences — that help us understand the world. How many such entities do we want? Which are the kinds that we most need? We ought to be wary of ones that get locked into forms that resist all further growth. Some future options have never been seen: imagine a scheme that could review both your mentality and mine and then compile a new, merged mind based on that shared experience.

Whatever the unknown future may bring, we are already changing the rules that made us. Most of us will fear change, but others will surely want to escape from our present limitations. When I decided to write this article, I tried these ideas out on several groups. I was amazed to find that at least three quarters of the individuals with whom I spoke seemed to feel our lifespans were already too long. "Why would anyone want to live for 500 years? Wouldn't it be boring? What if you outlived all your friends? What would you do with all that time?" they asked. It seemed as though they secretly feared that they did not deserve to live so long. I find it rather worrisome that so many people are resigned to die. Might not such people, who feel that they do not have much to lose, be dangerous?

My scientist friends showed few such concerns. "There are countless things that I want to find out and so many problems I want to solve that I could use many centuries," they said. Certainly immortality would seem unattractive if it mean endless infirmity, debility and dependency on others, but we are assuming a state of perfect health. Some people expressed a sounder concern — that the old ones must die because young ones are needed to weed out their worn-out ideas. Yet if it is true, as I fear, that we are approaching our intellectual limits, then that response is not a good answer. We would still be cut off from the larger ideas in those oceans of wisdom beyond our grasp.

Will robots inherit the earth? Yes, but they will be our children. We owe our minds to the deaths and lives of all the creatures that were ever engaged in the struggle called evolution. Our job is to see that all this work shall not end up in meaningless waste.

The Reader's Presence

1. Throughout this essay, Minsky compares the human brain and the computer. What advantage does the brain have over the computer? What advantages does the computer have over the brain? How does Minsky refute the "missing essence" theory proposed by some philosophers (paragraph 29)? How might those philosophers counter his argument?

2. Minsky provides an optimistic look into the future. If this were science fiction rather than an article in *Scientific American*, the author might have chosen a more negative set of predictions, if only to add an element of conflict to the narrative. Which of Minsky's predictions seem to have the most potential as the basis for a good disaster film or novel? What ideas does Minsky leave out in his attempt to paint a positive vision of the future? Where, for instance, does he address the question of who will maintain control of the scientific process he describes (paragraph 23)? Who does Minsky include in the "we" in paragraph 35? How might the "mind-children" and their parents get along? How does he answer the ethical questions he raises in paragraph 34?

3. Consider the intended audience for this article. What specific compositional strategies does Minsky use to make complex scientific concepts accessible to this audience? Point to specific rhetorical strategies as well as words and phrases that Minsky uses to aid his audience in comprehending the ideas he unfolds. How does Minsky help to shape the audience's reaction to his argument? Where did you position yourself when you read the closing paragraphs, in which he writes of the informal poll he took among his acquaintances? Did the reported results change your reaction?

50

Gloria Naylor

A Question of Language

Gloria Naylor (b. 1950) won an American Book Award for her first novel, The Women of Brewster Place *(1982). Her other works of fiction include* Linden Hills *(1985),* Mama Day *(1988), and* Bailey's Café *(1992), and her nonfiction has been published in* Centennial *(1986). In addition to these books, Naylor contributes essays and articles to many periodicals, including* Southern Review, Essence, Ms., Life, Callaloo, *and the* Ontario Review. *Also, she recently founded One Way Productions, an independent film company that she established to bring the novel* Mama Day *to the screen. Naylor has worked as the "Hers" columnist for the* New York Times *and as a visiting professor and writer at Princeton University, New York University, the University of Pennsylvania, Boston University, and Brandeis University. In addition, Naylor was a cultural exchange lecturer in India in 1985 and a senior fellow at the Society for the Humanities, Cornell University, in 1988. The article "A Question of Language" first appeared in the* New York Times *in 1986.*

Naylor credits her mother's inspiration for her love of books and writing: "Realizing that I was a painfully shy child, she gave me my first diary and told me to write my feelings down in there. Over the years that diary was followed by reams and reams of paper that eventually culminated in The Women of Brewster Place. *And I wrote that book as a tribute to her and other black women who, in spite of very limited personal circumstances, somehow manage to hold fierce belief in the limitless possibilities of the human spirit."*

Language is the subject. It is the written form with which I've managed to keep the wolf away from the door and, in diaries, to keep my sanity. In spite of this, I consider the written word inferior to the spoken, and much of the frustration experienced by novelists is the awareness that whatever we manage to capture in even the most transcendent passages falls far short of the richness of life. Dialogue achieves its power in the dynamics of a fleeting moment of sight, sound, smell, and touch.

I'm not going to enter the debate here about whether it is language that shapes reality or vice versa. That battle is doomed to be waged whenever we seek intermittent reprieve from the chicken and egg dispute. I will simply take the position that the spoken word, like the written word, amounts to a nonsensical arrangement of sounds or letters without a consensus that assigns "meaning." And building from the meanings of what we hear, we order reality. Words themselves are innocuous; it is the consensus that gives them true power.

I remember the first time I heard the word *nigger*. In my third-grade class, our math tests were being passed down the rows, and as I handed the papers to a little boy in back of me, I remarked that once again he had received a much lower mark than I did. He snatched his test from me and spit out that word. Had he called me a nymphomaniac or a necrophiliac, I couldn't have been more puzzled. I didn't know what a nigger was, but I knew that whatever it meant, it was something he shouldn't have called me. This was verified when I raised my hand, and in a loud voice repeated what he had said and watched the teacher scold him for using a "bad" word. I was later to go home and ask the inevitable question that every black parent must face — "Mommy, what does 'nigger' mean?"

And what exactly did it mean? Thinking back, I realize that this could not have been the first time the word was used in my presence. I was part of a large extended family that had migrated from the rural South after World War II and formed a close-knit network that gravitated around my maternal grandparents. Their ground-floor apartment in one of the buildings they owned in Harlem was a weekend mecca for my immediate family, along with countless aunts, uncles, and cousins who brought along assorted friends. It was a bustling and open house with assorted neighbors and tenants popping in and out to exchange bits of gossip, pick up an old quarrel, or referee the ongoing checkers game in which my grandmother cheated shamelessly. They were all there to let down their hair and put up their feet after a week of labor in the factories, laundries, and shipyards of New York.

Amid the clamor, which could reach deafening proportions — two or three conversations going on simultaneously, punctuated by the sound of a baby's crying somewhere in the back rooms or out on the street — there was still a rigid set of rules about what was said and how. Older children were sent out of the living room when it was time to get into the juicy details about "you-know-who" up on the third floor who had gone and gotten herself "p-r-e-g-n-a-n-t!" But my parents, knowing that I could spell well beyond my years, always demanded that I follow the others out to play. Beyond sexual misconduct and death, everything else was considered harmless for our young ears. And so among the anecdotes of the triumphs and disappointments in the various workings of their lives, the word *nigger* was used in my presence, but it was set within contexts and inflections that caused it to register in my mind as something else.

In the singular, the word was always applied to a man who had distinguished himself in some situation that brought their approval for his strength, intelligence, or drive:

"Did Johnny really do that?"

"I'm telling you, that nigger pulled in $6,000 of overtime last year. Said he got enough for a down payment on a house."

When used with a possessive adjective by a woman — "my nigger" — it became a term of endearment for husband or boyfriend. But it could be more than just a term applied to a man. In their mouths it became the pure essence of manhood — a disembodied force that channeled their past history of struggle and present survival against the odds into a victorious statement of being: "Yeah, that old foreman found out quick enough — you don't mess with a nigger."

In the plural, it became a description of some group within the community that had overstepped the bounds of decency as my family defined it: Parents who neglected their children, a drunken couple who fought in public, people who simply refused to look for work, those with excessively dirty mouths or unkempt households were all "trifling niggers." This particular circle could forgive hard times, unemployment, the occasional bout of depression — they had gone through all of that themselves — but the unforgivable sin was lack of self-respect.

A woman could never be a *nigger* in the singular, with its connotation of confirming worth. The noun *girl* was its closest equivalent in that sense, but only when used in direct address and regardless of the gender doing the addressing. *Girl* was a token of respect for a woman. The one-syllable word was drawn out to sound like three in recognition of the extra ounce of wit, nerve, or daring that the woman had shown in the situation under discussion.

"G-i-r-l, stop. You mean you said that to his face?"

But if the word was used in a third-person reference or shortened so that it almost snapped out of the mouth, it always involved some element of communal disapproval. And age became an important factor in these exchanges. It was only between individuals of the same generation, or from an older person to a younger (but never the other way around), that "girl" would be considered a compliment.

I don't agree with the argument that use of the word *nigger* at this social stratum of the black community was an internalization of racism. The dynamics were the exact opposite: the people in my grandmother's living room took a word that whites used to signify worthlessness or degradation and rendered it impotent. Gathering there together, they transformed *nigger* to signify the varied and complex human beings they knew themselves to be. If the word was to disappear totally from the mouths of even the most liberal of white society, no one in that room was naïve enough to believe it would disappear from white minds. Meeting the word head-on, they proved it had absolutely nothing to do with the way they were determined to live their lives.

So there must have been dozens of times that the word *nigger* was   15
spoken in front of me before I reached the third grade. But I didn't "hear" it until it was said by a small pair of lips that had already learned it could be a way to humiliate me. That was the word I went home and asked my mother about. And since she knew that I had to grow up in America, she took me in her lap and explained.

The Reader's Presence

1. Naylor analyzes the various meanings of the word *nigger,* meanings that are agreed to by consensus and that vary according to the speaker, the audience, and the context within which the word is spoken. Outline the different meanings of *nigger,* and evaluate the effectiveness of the example she provides to illustrate each definition. Do the same for her definitions of *girl.* Can you think of any other examples to reinforce the points she makes in each definition, or any examples that challenge her definitions?

2. Where — and how — does Naylor make her own point of view clear in this essay? How does she reveal her personal stake in the issues addressed in the essay? Consider her use of personal narrative. Comment, for example, on the effectiveness of paragraphs 4 and 5. What do they contribute to the overall point of her essay? What does this description of the circumstances of her extended family in Harlem add to the essay?

3. Naylor creates a two-part structure for her essay: two generalized, abstract opening paragraphs, followed by a series of extended illustrations of her definitions of the words *nigger* and *girl.* In the first paragraph she talks about the nature of language and its

inadequacy in conveying the fullness and complexity of an experience. In the second she asserts the need for consensus in order to
establish meaning. Where does she announce the overriding point
of her essay? Review the different definitions she provides. What
inferences can you draw from these definitions about the values of
the communities she describes? What do these definitions tell us
about what is important to these communities? about what kinds
of behavior are to be avoided and censured?

51

Joyce Carol Oates

They All Just Went Away

*The novelist, essayist, playwright, and poet Joyce Carol Oates (b. 1938) has
published over two dozen novels and countless collections of poems, essays, short
stories, and plays. She has received nominations for nearly every prestigious literary prize in the United States, and at age thirty-one was the youngest author ever
to receive the National Book Award for fiction, awarded for her novel* them
*(1969). Oates writes comfortably in many different styles, voices, and moods, but
she is especially celebrated for her talent to conjure suspense and terror in the
gothic tradition. Two of her recent titles demonstrate this talent:* Haunted: Tales
of the Grotesque *(1995) and* American Gothic Tales *(1996). Oates has also recently published* What I Lived For *(1995) and* Will You Always Love Me? *(1996).
Henry Louis Gates, Jr., comments about Oates that "a future archeologist
equipped with only her* oeuvre *could easily piece together the whole of postwar
America." The essay "They All Just Went Away" appeared in the* New Yorker *in
1995.*

*When asked what advice she might give to young writers, Oates replied,
"Just to write. The literal practice of writing, putting words down, getting a first
draft. If you get a first draft, then you start feeling a little surge of power. You feel
kind of happy about it, so you'll go on to the second draft. . . . Have an open and
free attitude because writing should be playful and fun."*

I must have been a lonely child. Until the age of twelve or thirteen,
my most intense, happiest hours were spent tramping desolate fields,
woods, and creek banks near my family's farmhouse in Millersport, New
York. No one knew where I went. My father, working most of the day at
Harrison's, a division of General Motors in Lockport, and at other times
preoccupied, would not have asked; if my mother asked, I might have answered in a way that would deflect curiosity. I was an articulate, verbal

child. Yet I could not have explained what drew me to the abandoned houses, barns, silos, corncribs. A hike of miles through fields of spiky grass, across outcroppings of shale as steeply angled as stairs, was a lark if the reward was an empty house.

Some of these houses had been inhabited as "homes" fairly recently — they had not yet reverted to the wild. Others, abandoned during the Depression, had long since begun to rot and collapse, engulfed by vegetation (trumpet vine, wisteria, rose of Sharon, willow) that elsewhere, on our property, for instance, were kept neatly trimmed. I was drawn to both kinds of houses, though the more recently inhabited were more forbidding and therefore more inviting.

To push open a door into such silence: the absolute emptiness of a house whose occupants have departed. Often, the crack of broken glass underfoot. A startled buzzing of flies, hornets. The slithering, ticklish sensation of a garter snake crawling across floorboards.

Left behind, as if in haste, were remnants of a lost household. A broken toy on the floor, a baby's bottle. A rain-soaked sofa, looking as if it had been gutted with a hunter's skilled knife. Strips of wallpaper like shredded skin. Smashed crockery, piles of tin cans; soda, beer, whiskey bottles. An icebox, its door yawning open. Once, on a counter, a dirt-stiffened rag that, unfolded like a precious cloth, revealed itself to be a woman's cheaply glamorous "see-through" blouse, threaded with glitter-strips of gold.

This was a long time ago, yet it is more vivid to me than anything now.   5

This was when I was too young to think the house is the mother's body; you have been expelled and are forbidden now to reënter.

Always, I was prepared to see a face at a high, empty window. A woman's hand uplifted in greeting, or in warning. *Hello! Come in! Stay away! Run! Who are you?* A movement in the corner of my eye: the blurred motion of a person passing through a doorway, or glimpsed through a window. There might be a single shriek of laughter from a barn — piercing as a bird's cry. Murmurous, teasing voices confused with wind rippling through tall, coarse, gone-to-seed grass. Voices that, when you pause to listen, fade immediately and are gone.

The sky in such places of abandonment was always of the hue and brightness of tin, as if the melancholy rural poverty of tin roofs reflected upward.

A house: a structural arrangement of space, geometrically laid out to provide what are called rooms, these divided from one another by verticals and horizontals called walls, ceilings, floors. The house contains the home but is not identical with it. The house anticipates the home and will very likely survive it, reverting again simply to house when home (that is, life) departs. For only where there is life can there be home.

I have never found the visual equivalent of these abandoned farm-   10
houses of upstate New York, of northern Erie County, in the area of the

long, meandering Tonawanda Creek and the Barge Canal. You think most immediately of the canvases of Edward Hopper: those dreamily stylized visions of a lost America, houses never depicted as homes, and human beings, if you look closer, never depicted as other than mannequins. For Hopper is not a realist but a surrealist. His dreams are of the ordinary, as if, even in imagination, the artist were trapped in an unyielding daylight consciousness. There seems almost a kind of rage, a revenge against such restraints, in Hopper's studied, endlessly repeated *simplicity*. By contrast, Charles Burchfield, with his numerous oils and watercolors — frequently of upstate New York landscapes, houses, and farms — rendered the real as visionary and luminous, suffused with a Blakean rapture and a kind of radical simplicity, too. Then there are the shimmering New England barns, fields, and skies of our contemporary Wolf Kahn — images evoked by memory, almost on the verge of dissolution. But the "real" — what assaults the eye before the eye begins its work of selection — is never on the verge of dissolution, still less of appropriation. The real is raw, jarring, unexpected, sometimes trashy, sometimes luminous. Above all, the real is arbitrary. For to be a realist (in art or in life) is to acknowledge that all things might be other than they are. That there is no design, no intention, no aesthetic or moral or teleological imprimatur but, rather, the equivalent of Darwin's great vision of a blind, purposeless, ceaseless evolutionary process that yields no "products" — only temporary strategies against extinction.

Yet, being human, we think, To what purpose these broken-off things, if not to be gathered up, at last, in a single ecstatic vision?

There is a strange and profound and unknowable reality to these abandoned houses where jealously guarded, even prized possessions have become mere trash: windowpanes long ago smashed, and the spaces where they had been festooned with cobwebs, and cobwebs brushing against your face, catching in your hair like caresses. The peculiar, dank smell of wood rot and mildew, in one of the houses I most recall that had partly burned down, the smell of smoke and scorch, in early summer pervading even the lyric smell of honeysuckle — these haunting smells, never, at the time of experiencing, given specific sources, names.

Where a house has been abandoned — unworthy of being sold to new tenants, very likely seized by the county for default on taxes and the property held in escrow — you can be sure there has been a sad story. There have been devastated lives. Lives to be spoken of pityingly. How they went wrong. Why did she marry him, why did she stay with him? Just desperate people. Ignorant. Poor white trash. Runs in the family. A wrong turn.

Shall I say for the record that ours was a happy, close-knit, and unextraordinary family for our time, place, and economic status? Yet what was vividly real in the solid-built old farmhouse that contained my home (my family consisted of my father, mother, younger brother, grandfather, and grandmother, who owned the property — a slow-failing farm whose principal crop had become Bartlett pears by the time I was a girl) was of far less significance to me than what was real elsewhere. A gone-to-seed landscape had an authority that seemed to me incontestable: the powerful authority of silence in houses from which the human voice had vanished. For the abandoned house contained the future of any house — the lilac tree pushing through the rotted veranda, hornets' nests beneath eaves, windows smashed by vandals, human excrement left to dry on a parlor floor once scrubbed on hands and knees.

The abandoned, the devastated, was the profound experience,   15
whereas involvement in family life — the fever, the bliss, the abrasions, the infinite distractions of human love — was so clearly temporary. Like a television screen upon which antic images (at this time, in the fifties, minimally varying gradations of gray) appear fleetingly and are gone.

I have seemed to suggest that the abandoned houses were all distant from our house, but in fact the one that had been partly gutted by fire — which I will call the Weidel house — was perhaps a half mile away. If you drove, turning right off Transit Road, which was our road, onto the old Creek Road, it would have been a distance of a mile or more, but if you crossed through our back potato field and through the marshy woods which no one seemed to own, it was a quick walk.

The Weidels' dog, Slossie, a mixed breed with a stumpy, energetic tail and a sweet disposition, sand-colored, rheumy-eyed, as hungry for affection as for the scraps we sometimes fed her, trotted over frequently to play with my brother and me. Though, strictly speaking, Slossie was not wanted at our house. None of the Weidels were wanted.

The "Weidel house," it would be called for years. The "Weidel property." As if the very land — which the family had not owned in any case, but only rented, partly with county-welfare support — were somehow imprinted with that name, a man's identity. Or infamy.

For tales were told of the father who drank, beat and terrorized his family, "did things to" his daughters, and finally set the house on fire and fled and was arrested, disappearing forever from the proper, decent life of our community. There was no romance in Mr. Weidel, whom my father knew only slightly and despised as a drinker, and as a wife- and child-beater. Mr. Weidel was a railway worker in Lockport, or perhaps an ex-railway worker, for he seemed to work only sporadically, though he always wore a railwayman's cap. He and his elder sons were hunters, owning a shotgun among them, and one or two deer rifles. His face was broad, fair, vein-swollen, with a look of flushed, alcoholic reproach. He was tall and heavyset, with graying black whiskers that sprouted like quills. His eyes had a way of swerving in their sockets, seeking you out when you could not slip away quickly enough. *H'lo there, little Joyce! Joycie! Joycie Oates, h'lo!* He wore rubber boots that flapped, unbuckled, about his feet.

Mrs. Weidel was a faded-pretty, apologetic woman with a body that   20
seemed to have become bloated, as with perpetual pregnancy. Her bosom

had sunk to her waist. Her legs were encased, sausagelike, in flesh-colored support hose. *How can that woman live with him? That pig.* There was disdain, disgust, in this frequent refrain. *Why doesn't she leave him? Did you see that black eye? Did you hear her the other night? Take the girls away, at least.* It was thought that she could, for Mrs. Weidel was the only one in the family who seemed to work at all regularly. She was hired for seasonal canning in a tomato factory in lower Lockport and may have done housecleaning in the city.

A shifting household of relatives and rumored "boarders" lived in the Weidel house. There were six Weidel children, four sons and two daughters. Ruth was a year older than I, and Dorothy two years younger. There was an older brother of Mr. Weidel's, who walked with a cane and was said to be an ex-convict, from Attica. The eldest Weidel son, Roy, owned a motorcycle, and friends of his often visited, fellow-bikers. There were loud parties, frequent disputes, and tales of Mr. Weidel's chasing his wife with a butcher knife, a claw hammer, the shotgun, threatening to "blow her head off." Mrs. Weidel and the younger children fled outdoors in terror and hid in the hayloft. Sheriff's deputies drove out to the house, but no charges were ever pressed against Mr. Weidel. Until the fire, which was so public it couldn't be denied.

There was the summer day — I was eleven years old — that Mr. Weidel shot Slossie. We heard the poor creature yelping and whimpering for what seemed like hours. When my father came home from work, he went to speak to Mr. Weidel, though my mother begged him not to. By this time, the dog had dragged herself beneath the Weidels' house to die. Mr. Weidel was furious at the intrusion, drunk, defensive — Slossie was his goddam dog, he said, she'd been getting in the way, she was "old." But my father convinced him to put the poor dog out of her misery. So Mr. Weidel made one of his sons drag Slossie out from beneath the house, and he straddled her and shot her a second time, and a third, at close range. My father, who'd never hunted, who'd never owned a gun, backed off, a hand over his eyes.

Afterward, my father would say of that day that walking away from that drunken son of a bitch with a rifle in his hands was about the hardest thing he'd ever done. He'd expected a shot between his shoulders.

The fire was the following year, around Thanksgiving.

After the Weidels were gone from Millersport and the house stood empty, I discovered Slossie's grave. I'm sure it was Slossie's grave. It was beyond the dog hutch, in the weedy back yard, a sunken patch of earth measuring about three feet by four with one of Mrs. Weidel's big white-washed rocks at the head.

Morning glories grew in clusters on the posts of the front porch. Mrs. Weidel had planted hollyhocks, sunflowers, and trumpet vine in the yard. Tough, weed-like flowers that would survive for years.

It had been said of Ruth and her sister Dorothy that they were "slow." Yet Ruth was never slow to fly into a rage when she was teased by neighborhood boys or by her older brothers. She waved her fists and stammered obscenities, words that stung like hail. Her face darkened with blood, and her full, thick lips quivered with a strange sort of pleasure. How you loved to see Ruth Weidel fly into one of her rages; it was like holding a lighted match to flammable material.

The Weidel house was like any other run-down wood-frame house, said by my grandfather to have been "thrown up" in the nineteen-twenties. It had no cellar, only a concrete-block foundation — an emptiness that gradually filled with debris. It had an upstairs with several small bedrooms. There was no attic. No insulation. Steep, almost vertical stairs. The previous tenant had started to construct a front porch of raw planks, never completed or painted. (Though Mrs. Weidel added "touches" to the porch — chairs, a woven-rush rug, geraniums in flowerpots.) The roof of the house was made of sheets of tin, scarred and scabbed like skin, and the front was covered in simulated-brick asphalt siding pieced together from lumberyard scraps. All year round, a number of the windows were covered in transparent duct tape and never opened. From a distance, the house was the fading dun color of a deer's winter coat.

Our house had an attic and a cellar and a deep well and a solid cement foundation. My father did all the carpentry on our house, most of the shingling, the painting, the masonry. I would not know until I was an adult that he'd come from what's called a "broken home" himself — what an image, luridly visual, of a house literally broken, split in two, its secrets spilled out onto the ground for all to see, like entrails.

My mother, unlike Mrs. Weidel, had time to houseclean. It was a continuous task, a mother's responsibility. My mother planted vegetables, strawberries, beds of flowers. Petunias and pansies and zinnias. Crimson peonies that flowered for my birthday, in mid-June.   30

I remember the night of the fire vividly, as if it had been a festive affair to which I'd been invited.

There was the sound of a siren on the Creek Road. There were shouts, and an astonishing burst of flame in the night, in the direction of the Weidel house. The air was moist, and reflected and magnified the fire, surrounding it like a nimbus. My grandparents would claim there had never been such excitement in Millersport, and perhaps that was true. My father dressed hurriedly and went to help the firefighters, and my mother and the rest of us watched from upstairs windows. The fire began at about 1 A.M., and it would be past 4 A.M. before my seven-year-old brother and I got back to bed.

Yet what was so exciting an event was, in fact, an ending, with nothing to follow. Immediately afterward, the Weidels disappeared from Millersport and from our lives. It was said that Mr. Weidel fled "as a fugitive" but was captured and arrested the next day, in Buffalo. The family was broken up, scattered, the younger children placed in foster homes. That quickly, the Weidels were gone.

For a long time, the smell of wood smoke, scorch, pervaded the air of Millersport, the fresh, damp smell of earth sullied by its presence. Neighbors complained that the Weidel house should be razed at the county's expense, bulldozed over, and the property sold. But nothing was done for years. Who knows why? When I went away to college, the old falling-down house was still there.

How swiftly, in a single season, a human habitation can turn wild.   35
The bumpy cinder driveway over which the eldest Weidel had ridden his motorcycle was soon stippled with tall reeds.

What had happened to Roy Weidel? It was said he'd joined the Navy. No, he had a police record and could not have joined the Navy. He'd disappeared. Asked by the police to give a sworn statement about the night of his father's "arson," he'd panicked and fled.

Signs were posted — "NO TRESPASSING," "THIS PROPERTY CONDEMNED BY ERIE CO." — and they, too, over a period of months, became shabby and faded. My parents warned me never to wander onto the Weidel property. There was a well with a loose-fitting cover, among other dangers. As if *I* would fall into a well! I smiled to think how little my parents knew me. How little anyone knew me.

Have I said that my father never struck his children, as Mr. Weidel struck his? And did worse things to them, the girls sometimes, it was whispered? Yes, and Mrs. Weidel, who seemed so soft and apologetic and sad, she, too, had beaten the younger children when she'd been drinking. County social workers came around to question neighbors, and spread the story of what they learned along the way.

In fact, I may have been disciplined, spanked, a few times. Like most children, I don't remember. I remember Mr. Weidel spanking his children until they screamed (though I wasn't a witness, was I?), but I don't remember being spanked by my parents, and in any case, if I was, it was no more than I deserved.

I'd seen Mr. Weidel urinating once at the roadside. The loose-flying   40
skein of the kerosene he'd flung around the house before setting the fire must have resembled the stream of his urine, transparent and glittering. But they laughed, saying Mr. Weidel had been too drunk, or too careless, to have done an adequate job of sprinkling kerosene through the downstairs of the house. Wasn't it like him, such a slovenly job. Only part of the house had burned, a wall of the kitchen and an adjoining woodshed.

Had Mr. Weidel wanted to burn his family alive in their beds? Mrs. Weidel testified no, they'd all been awake, they'd run out into the yard before the fire began. They'd never been in any danger, she swore. But Mr. Weidel was indicted on several counts of attempted murder, along with other charges.

For so many years the Weidel house remained standing. There was something defiant about it, like someone who has been mortally wounded but will not die. In the weedy front yard, Mrs. Weidel's display of whitewashed rocks and plaster-of-Paris gnomes and the clay pedestal with the shiny blue glass ball disappeared from view within a year or so. Brambles grew everywhere. I forced myself to taste a small bitter red berry but spat it out, it made my mouth pucker so.

What did it mean that Erie County had "condemned" the Weidel property? The downstairs windows were carelessly boarded over, and both the front and rear doors were unlocked, collapsing on their hinges. Broken glass underfoot and a sickening stench of burn, mildew, decay. Yet there were "touches" — on what remained of a kitchen wall, a Holstein calendar from a local feed store, a child's crayon drawing. Upstairs, children's clothes, socks and old shoes heaped on the floor. I recognized with a thrill of repugnance an old red sweater of Ruth's, angora-fuzzy. There were broken Christmas-tree ornaments, a naked pink plastic doll. Toppled bedsprings, filthy mattresses streaked with yellow and rust-colored stains. The mattresses looked as if they'd been gutted, their stuffing strewn about. The most terrible punishment, I thought, would be to be forced to lie down on such a mattress.

I thought of Mrs. Weidel, her swollen, blackened eyes, her bruised face. Shouts and sirens in the night, the sheriff's patrol car. But no charges filed. The social worker told my mother how Mrs. Weidel had screamed at the county people, insisting her husband hadn't done anything wrong and shouldn't go to jail. The names she'd called them! Unrepeatable!

She was the wife of that man, they'd had babies together. The law had no right to interfere. The law had nothing to do with them.   45

As a woman and as a writer, I have long wondered at the wellsprings of female masochism. Or what, in despair of a more subtle, less reductive phrase, we can call the congeries of predilections toward self-hurt, self-erasure, self-repudiation in women. These predilections are presumably "learned" — "acquired" — but perhaps also imprinted in our genes, of biological necessity, neurophysiological fate, predilections that predate culture. Indeed, may shape culture. Do not say, "Yes, but these are isolated, peripheral examples. These are marginal Americans, uneducated. They tell us nothing about ourselves." They tell us everything about ourselves, and even the telling, the exposure, is a kind of cutting, an inscription in the flesh.

Yet what could possibly be the evolutionary advantage of self-hurt in the female? Abnegation in the face of another's cruelty? Acquiescence to another's will? This loathsome secret that women do not care to speak of, or even acknowledge.

Two or three years later, in high school, twelve miles away in a consolidated district school to which, as a sophomore, I went by school bus, Ruth Weidel appeared. She was living now with relatives in Lockport. She looked, at sixteen, like a woman in her twenties; big-breasted, with full, strong thighs and burnished-brown hair inexpertly bleached. Ruth's homeroom was "special education," but she took some classes with the rest of us. If she recognized me, in our home-economics class, she was careful to give no sign.

There was a tacit understanding that "something had happened" to Ruth Weidel, and her teachers treated her guardedly. Ruth was special, the way a handicapped person is special. She was withdrawn, quiet; if still prone to violent outbursts of rage, she might have been on medication to control it. Her eyes, like her father's, seemed always about to swerve in their sockets. Her face was round, fleshy, like a pudding, her nose oily-pored. Yet she wore lipstick, she was "glamorous" — almost. In gym class, Ruth's large breasts straining against her T-shirt and the shining rippled muscles and fatty flesh of her thighs were amazing to us; we were so much thinner and less female, so much younger.

I believed that I should protect Ruth Weidel, so I told none of the other students about her family. Even to Ruth, for a long time I pretended not to know who she was. I can't explain how Ruth could have possibly believed me, yet this seems to be so. Quite purposefully, I befriended Ruth. I thought her face would lose its sallow hardness if she could be made to smile, and so it became a kind of challenge to me to induce Ruth Weidel to smile. She was lonely and miserable at school, and flattered by my attention. For so few "normal" girls sought out "special-ed" girls. At first she may have been suspicious, but by degrees she became trusting. I thought of Slossie: trust shows in the eyes.

I sat with Ruth at lunch in the cafeteria and eventually I asked her about the house on the old Creek Road, and she lied bluntly, to my face, insisting that an uncle of hers had owned that house. She'd only visited a few times. She and her family. I asked, "How did the fire start?" and Ruth said, slowly, each word sucked like a pebble in the mouth, "Lightning. Lightning hit it. One night in a storm." I asked, "Are you living with your mother now, Ruth?" and Ruth shrugged, made a face, and said "She's O.K. I see her sometimes." I asked about Dorothy. I asked where Mrs. Weidel was. I said that my mother had always liked her mother, and missed her when she went away. But Ruth seemed not to hear. Her gaze had drifted. I said, "Why did you all move away?" Ruth did not reply, though I could hear her breathing hard. "Why did you abandon your house? It could have been fixed. It's still there. Your mom's hollyhocks are still there. You should come out and see it sometime. You could visit me." Ruth shrugged, and laughed. She gave me a sidelong glance, almost flirtatiously. It was startling to see how good-looking she could be, how sullen-sexy; to know how men would stare at her who would never so much as glance at a girl like me. Ruth said slowly, as if she'd come to a final, adamant conclusion to a problem that had long vexed her, "They all just went away."

Another time, after lunch with Ruth, I left a plastic change purse with a few coins in it on the ledge in one of the girls' lavatories, where Ruth was washing her hands. I don't recall whether I left it on purpose or not. But when I returned, after waiting for Ruth to leave the lavatory, the change purse was gone.

Once or twice, I invited Ruth Weidel to come home with me on the school bus some afternoon, to Millersport, to have supper with my family and stay the night. I must not have truly believed she might accept, for my mother would have been horrified and would have forced me to rescind the invitation. Ruth had hesitated, as if she wanted to say yes, wanted very badly to say yes, but finally she said, "No. I guess I better not."

The Reader's Presence

1. The author begins by telling us she "could not have explained" what attracted her to abandoned houses. After finishing the essay, what explanations can you offer? What psychological clues does Oates provide to help the reader construct an explanation?
2. Note the author's remarks about painters in paragraphs 9–11. Why does she introduce this material? Of what relevance is it to the reader's understanding of her subject?
3. Toward the end of the essay, Oates concentrates on a particular family, the Weidels. How does this family differ from her own? What explicit comparisons does she make between her family and the Weidels? Why does the author seem fascinated by this family? In what ways does her attraction to them resemble her attraction to abandoned houses?

52

Joyce Carol Oates

Christmas Night 1962

The story "Christmas Night 1962" can be found in Will You Always Love Me? *and Other Stories (1996). Since Joyce Carol Oates has published so widely, she is often asked how she goes about the process of writing. One interviewer asked her if she wrote best in any particular mood. "One must be pitiless about this matter of 'mood,'" she replied. "In a sense the writing will create the mood. If art is, as I believe it to be, a genuinely transcendental function — a means by which we rise out of limited, parochial states of mind — then it should not matter very much what states of mind or emotion we are in. Generally I've found this to be true: I have forced myself to begin writing when I've been utterly exhausted, when I've felt my soul as thin as a playing-card, when nothing has seemed worth*

*enduring for another five minutes . . . and somehow the activity of writing
changes everything."*

For more information on Oates, see page 345.

Come on then! he said. Goddamn you I'll take you.

My mother was in the back bedroom crying. Christmas night, you
wouldn't think it could still be the same day. She'd been crying seeing the
raggedy doll thrown across the room. She'd been drinking too except
with her, unlike the men, it made the freckles come out in her face, and
the skin beneath like skim milk. It made her walk strange like the floor
was tilted and laugh when nothing was funny and rub her knuckles into
her eyes like she was trying to wake up and not succeeding. Her hair red-
frizzed like mine except it was coarser than mine which was so fine I'd
squirm and whimper when she ran the hairbrush through, then the steel
comb. Frantic to get every last one of the snarls out she said, damn you
hush! don't be a baby.

It started after we got home from Grandpa's. He was on the sofa
watching the same TV football they'd had on at the other house then he
said something making her laugh that sharp laugh like scraping your finger on a blackboard and that was the mistake. For always there was a
mistake you could point to. First he slapped her with his open hand and
she screamed and turned over the table where some of the presents were
from that morning, and his beer, and somehow it happened the raggedy
doll that was Grandma's present for me went flying across the room hitting the doorframe banging its head *crack!*

She'd tried to stop him but she'd run into his fist — more than his
fist. When it happens it happens fast. Like the boxing he took us to in
Port Oriskany, the men up in the ring in the lights coming at each other
slow and wary so you think nothing's going to happen you could shut
your eyes seeing something far away but suddenly people are yelling and
it's happening faster than you can see so you have to invent what it was
to account for one of the boxers down on the canvas, blood leaking from
his mouth. Just like that, that fast, in the living room with the TV on high
and the Christmas tree in the corner knocked now on its side and some of
the glass bulbs shattered.

I cried, I wasn't to blame. I knew I would be blamed.   5

The red-swirled glass bulbs shaped like pears, that Grandma gave us,
the ones that were so beautiful. And the frosted white ones with the glitter dust. Home by myself I'd drag the cardboard box of ornaments out of
the closet just to look through them, touch them. The tinsel for looping
over the tree branches, the colored lights in the shape of candles, the
angel for the top of the tree with her pretty painted-on face and gold halo
like the statue of the Blessed Virgin Mary in church. Where the tree was
fallen over, the angel hung upside down like something in a cartoon.

Come on Honey, he said, wiping his mouth, squatting over where the
raggedy doll was broken on the floor. You know you're okay.

If you'd stop that goddamn fucking crying, he said. His face going white like the blood was being squeezed out of it.

My mother came out of the back bedroom running with towels and a blanket and she screamed at him to get away, she was going to take me to Yewville to the hospital and he shoved at her saying she was too pissed to drive and she screamed *he* was too pissed, *he* was the crazy one, if he took me out of the house she'd call the police. He said, You call the police and I'll rip you apart, go for that phone to call anybody you'll wish you were never born, nor her either. She was trying to wrap the towel around my head where I was bleeding and they both pulled at me, *he* was going to take me he said, he guessed my leg might be broken, and my mother ran back into the bedroom then returned with the gun waving it at him, holding it in both hands waving it at him, You think I won't? You bastard, you think I won't?

This pistol he'd brought home last summer, he'd won playing poker. 10
My mother was scared to have it in the house but later on, back in the woods, he'd target practice shooting bottles and got my mother to try it too, giggling and nervous and I'd crouch behind them pressing my hands against my ears as he held her with his right arm around her to steady her, helping her aim, pull the trigger, absorb the kick. And her hiding her face in his neck afterward, breathless from what she'd done.

Now my mother in a velour shirt the color of crushed strawberries ripped off the shoulder from where he'd grabbed her and her black slacks glistening with blood holding that pistol trembling in her hands. Screaming and waving it her eyes wild so he backed off on his haunches, Okay Anna, okay just don't pull that trigger, you're crazy enough to do it, and she said, That's right! I am! Just try me, mister, I *am*!

So she lifted me and wrapped me in the blanket holding him off with the gun. The blood soaked into the gray wool making it wet. I was crying, I couldn't stop, like hiccups when you can't stop. She was sobbing too saying, Don't fight me, Honey, you're going to be all right but it hurt so when she lifted me I had to scream.

That Christmas night. Snow blowing gritty as sand. She had to carry me, I couldn't walk where the bone was cracked. My left leg below the knee where I'd hit against the doorframe, and my forehead bleeding and swollen already to the size of a hen's egg. And my mouth, there was something wrong with my mouth Mommy was trying to hold the towel against slipping and sliding out to the car. Oh! oh! oh! our breaths were steaming, she'd grabbed her coat but hadn't time to put on boots. Saying, Honey don't cry Mommy has you safe now okay? trying to fit me in the front seat but I screamed with the pain so she had to put me in the back laying me out flat wrapped in the blanket. I screamed and held onto her not wanting to let go.

Christmas night, and the morning so long ago. Snowdrifts up to the windows, taller than a man by the garage, giant icicles glittering like knife blades hanging down from the roof's edge frozen solid in the minus-ten-degree-fahrenheit cold. That morning the windows were blinding with snow-light and now it was dark, snowflakes swirling in the car headlights like something you could stare and stare into and lose your way not remembering who you are.

I can't tell this. I don't have the words. I remember everything but I don't have the words. Even when I say them, the words are not the right ones.

The raggedy doll sewed by my grandmother, it was big enough for me to need both arms to carry it. A floppy head with shiny black button eyes and a button nose and a smile and orange-red pigtails braided out of yarn. Her top was cotton printed in tiny flowers and her bottom was cotton printed in bright yellow checks and her legs which had no bones were white wool stockings and she was stuffed with something soft like cotton batting. Every year for all the years I could remember Grandma sewed me a Christmas doll, and things to wear.

I loved Grandma so much. She was his mother so she had to take his side. My other grandmother wasn't here they said and when I asked where was she they said with God in Heaven. But I knew what that was — buried in the cemetery that's just a hilly field behind the church.

That morning my mother dressed me for Christmas before she dressed herself. Only a few times a year we'd go to church and Christmas morning was one but *he* didn't go. Mommy brushed my hair wetting and shaping the curls into corkscrew-curls around her fingers then tickling blowing in my ear, Pretty girl! who's my pretty girl! Mommy loves you so. She pulled on over my head the new jumper Grandma had sewed for me for Christmas, soft velour to match Mommy's shirt she'd sewed too with a big patch pocket green like a strawberry leaf. White woolly socks, black patent-leather shoes but the same old scuffed boots to fit over them.

A little velour bow too in my hair. A row of bobby pins, barrettes. Corkscrew curls to my shoulders so I'd turn my head and feel them moving, tickling. Before Mommy and I went to church he squatted down in front of me staring at me. Cupped my face in his hands looking at me for a long time his eyes like that kind of marble with a glaze to them so the colors inside look cracked. That way I knew he wasn't seeing me though he said, Merry Christmas, sweetheart! The big day's here, eh?

Mommy said in her careful voice, Don't scare her. You scare her looking at her like that.

Like what? he said. Now straightening up, and taking Mommy's chin in his hand, holding her so she had to look at him. Like this?

He used to be Daddy but says not to call him that anymore but sometimes I forget. But after Christmas night I won't forget.

It was at my grandparents' place the drinking started. The big old farmhouse, the long table for Christmas dinner. So much food at two in the afternoon, your stomach isn't ready for it. The men were playing poker and they were loud and laughing and my father was loud winning a hand but louder losing, red-faced and squinting up his eyes laughing

15

20

like it was a joke only he got. Uncle Dwight who's married to Aunt Helen, Uncle Marcus who's married to Auntie Irene, Uncle Bud who used to be married but isn't now and you're not to ask why, you never ask *why* of adults. Grandpa and Uncle Dwight worked in the gypsum plant on the Jamestown Road where my father did except they were laid off through January. How long after that nobody knew. They'd been laid off, the factory gates chained shut, since before the first snow.

Who can you believe, they said. What any one of them tells you, or you read in the paper, if it's somebody in a suit and tie for sure he's lying to you because he makes his money off you. And if it's a politician he's already lied to get where he is. So fuck it.

Once when I was real little I said that word. My cousins whispered it   25
in my ear and afterward when I said it some people laughed except not Grandma, and nòt Mommy. Mommy scolded saying that's not a nice word, nice little girls don't say that word. I giggled saying Yes they do! yes they do! and said the word again running around the table where she couldn't catch me. Except this time the way she looked at me I was sorry so I didn't say it ever again, that Mommy could hear.

My mother was driving our old 1957 Chevy along the Canal Road trying to keep the car's tires in the ruts in the snow made by other cars. The snow plow had come by in the morning and all day it had been snowing and now in the night the narrow road was drifting over and she was praying Holy Mary Mother of God! Holy Mary Mother of God! and in the back seat the limp sobbing raggedy doll. Leg cracked below the knee, bleeding from a swelling cut above her eye. And vomit, and the stink of vomit, on the gray blanket. No other cars were on the road. The headlights swung and lurched, snowflakes rushed at the windshield, the car's stops and starts and skids and jolts were stabs of pain Oh! oh! oh! At the steep ramp to the Yewville bridge the drifts are so high the car's front wheels get stuck. Back up, go forward, back up, go forward rocking the car until momentum carries it onto the ramp.

Honey, are you all right? — Honey? — your Mommy's going to take care of you. Don't cry! Don't cry!

Then scared and angry-sounding as the car moves slowly so slowly not five miles an hour across the high windblown shaky plank-floored bridge, Holy Mary Mother of God have mercy on us!

The water tower at the top of Church Street. The steep drop to Memorial Avenue, the ice-slick pavement where the car skids, begins to slide. The front tire jolting against the curb Oh! oh! Seneca Street, Ontario, Locust. The redbrick Episcopal Church with the high tower, the big stained-glass window. Bell Telephone Co. where my mother worked as an operator before she fell in love with and married the man who would be my father. Before she came to live in the country nine miles north of Yewville where I was born, where she became a woman who was a mother and where her life changed and could never return to what it was. And now at Locust near

Main there are cars moving with painstaking slowness in the blizzard and my mother has no choice but to follow behind them sobbing Holy Mary help us! help us! God help us! like it was a curse.

At Providence Hospital on Locust and Van Buren there's a Christmas   30
tree blinking red lights over the front entrance and the parking lot is two-thirds empty, drifted over in snow but my mother parks the car and carries me through the snow stinging gritty as sand in our faces and into the brightly lit reception area where there's only a single nurse behind the counter whose eyes swing onto us startled and disapproving. My mother begins to speak and the nurse cuts her off saying there's no emergency room in this hospital you'll have to go to Yewville General don't you know this isn't that kind of hospital, and my mother says, My little girl's hurt, she fell and hurt herself and I think her leg is broken, I think she's hurt her head bad, please can we see a doctor? please is there a doctor? I'll pay — and another nurse comes out and says in a loud voice like my mother might be hard of hearing, Ma'am? would you like us to call ahead to Yewville General? would you like us to call an ambulance to take you there? the two nurses staring at us, keeping their distance. My young mother with her windblown red-frizzed hair, her white skin splotched with freckles like tiny rust-stains, a purplish bruise swelling the right side of her face. Shivering, swaying with the weight of the child in her arms, a girl of about four years of age, wrapped in a blanket stained with blood and vomit. And my mother asks again for a doctor raising her voice and again the nurses raising their voices say you'll have to go to Yewville General, there's no doctor on duty here tonight and there are no emergency room facilities in this hospital and my mother says begging will you look at her, then? please help us will you please help us? coming forward so the nurses speak more sharply saying Sorry ma'am, sorry you'll have to go to Yewville General, we have no emergency room facilities in this hospital ma'am, and my mother begins to shout, Aren't you nurses? what the hell are you if you aren't nurses? my little girl's hurt, my little girl's in pain Goddamn you! and the older nurse says angrily, Ma'am, we'll have to ask you to leave these premises, picks up a telephone receiver threatening to call the police. So my mother backs off, sobbing and cursing carrying me back outside to the car where the headlights are on, the back door's wide open, the back seat already filling up with snow.

Driving then along Van Buren skidding through a red light then stuck behind a sanding truck moving at five miles an hour all the way to East Avenue where the big hospital Yewville General is. Where Auntie Irene was for her surgery and I was brought to visit one Sunday but we don't go to the front entrance, my mother drives around to the rear where the parking lot is filled with snow and almost empty of cars too and she parks at the curb and carries me half-staggering into another bright-lit reception area larger than the other but there's no one in the waiting room and just one woman at the desk saying Yes? What is it? How can we help you? and Mommy says, quick and scared like she knows she's going to be turned away, It's my little girl, she's hurt, I need to see a doctor! — coming forward past the desk toward the double swinging doors NO ADMITTANCE EMERGENCY and the woman calls out, Ma'am! Stop! and a young man in a white uniform appears to block her way and Mommy is saying, We need a doctor, please help us, my little girl is hurt bad, her head! her leg! I think her leg is broken please help us! her voice shrill and her eyes wild like she's been drinking. There's a nurse too saying, You'll have to check in at reception first, ma'am, ma'am? — you have to check in at reception first. My mother is pleading with the young man, Doctor? help us please, will you examine my little girl? she hit her head running, she fell down and I think her leg is broken, please Doctor? her voice rising as if to prevent the young man from interrupting saying he isn't a doctor, he isn't in charge.

Mommy is a thin woman, you wouldn't think she'd be strong enough to carry me, to hold me like this in her arms. The tight hard muscles tensing in her upper arms and shoulders like it's lifting from the bone.

And everybody in this bright lit place staring at the limp raggedy doll, bleeding from a cut about the left eye. Wrapped in a filthy blanket. Frizzy red corkscrew curls messy as a rat's nest.

The strong smell pierces my nostrils like the dentist's office to make me gag. Mommy hugs me, whispering Honey it's all right, Honey you're safe now, but there's a woman's voice running on and on repeating no patients can be treated at Yewville General Hospital without first filling out the proper forms at reception, yes and you need insurance identification, this is hospital policy, this is New York State law. There's an artificial silver-tinsel Christmas tree, three feet high, on a table, glittery sequin-snow sprinkled onto the green cloth beneath. And brightly wrapped Christmas presents, the kind of presents that if you lift them are just empty boxes. At the reception desk there's a radio playing "Rudolph the Red-Nosed Reindeer." My mother is saying, pleading, I don't know about our insurance, I don't know the name of the insurance, I came out without my wallet and I.D. speaking fast so they can't interrupt, then angry, saying, You're going to take this child! this is a hurt child, an injured child, Goddamn you! And a nurse, an older woman with peach-colored hair and a little fringe of bangs says making her voice steely calm, Ma'am, this is a private hospital and we are not obliged to accept any patient not adequately covered by hospital and medical insurance so if you will please cooperate —, and my mother says screaming, I told you! I don't have my wallet! There isn't time! This is an emergency! Her arms are weakening and give way and she almost drops me on the floor carrying me to a couch in the waiting room, now the voices are louder, there are more of them and more disapproving and Mommy is saying, furious, You think we're trash, is that it, we're white trash is that it! We're poor, we're from the country, we don't count, we're shit on your shoes is that it! Now there's another, older man wearing a white coat, a doctor this time asking what's going on here, and the nurse tells him, and my mother interrupts, You're not going to let my daughter die, Goddamn you, you sons of bitches you're not going to let my daughter die, taking the pistol out of her coat pocket and waving it in their faces her hand trembling and her eyes wild and frightened as everybody goes Oh! oh! shrinking back in astonishment and the quick terror of animals you see in their eyes in a car's headlights at night but my mother lets the pistol fall, she's sobbing Goddamn you, Goddamn you, letting it fall clattering onto the floor and for a long moment there's no sound except over the radio the tinkly jingly "Rudolph the Red-Nosed Reindeer" coming to an end.

Then the older man, the doctor, stoops quickly to pick up the pistol. He hands it to the young man saying call the police, please.

And Mommy is standing there panting like she's been running, turning her head from side to side like she's trying to clear it, to wake up. And the doctor says, Yes, I will examine your little girl but you'll remain out here until the police arrive. Do you understand, ma'am? — you will remain out here. And Mommy says her lips moving slow, Yes Doctor.

There's a stretcher brought out to where I'm lying and they lift me onto it and Mommy wants to help but they make her stand back. Staring at me seeing the ugly bruised cut on my forehead, the slack wet mouth and the bloody root of a missing front tooth, the blanket falls open showing the surprise of the strawberry-red velour jumper sewed by Grandma who loves me. White woolly socks and shiny patent-leather shoes and the skinny leg hanging limp, swelling below the knee like a giant bee had stung it.

On the radio, a woman's happy voice singing "Walking in the Winter Wonder-Land."

This woman who's my mother stands watching as I'm carried into the emergency room of Yewville General Hospital, Yewville, New York, 9:25 P.M. of Christmas night 1962. Standing clenching her fingers into fists her head slightly lowered as if to hide her own injuries and her lips moving and she begins to cry giving herself up to hoarse racking angry sobs, helpless sobs as if, now she's got what she has wanted, now she sees her child taken from her by strangers, now these strangers have yielded as if by magic to her desperate will, bearing me through the doors below NO ADMITTANCE EMERGENCY, she's surrendered me forever. It's over.

The Reader's Presence

1. The narrator is often quite specific about clothing. Why do you think details of dress are so important to the emotional impact of the story?
2. Consider carefully the story's point of view. From whose perspective is it told? Do you think the narrative truly reflects a child's point of view? Why, or why not?
3. Could the family in this story be the Weidels of "They All Just Went Away" (page 345)? What similarities do you find significant? What differences? How is the author's theme of abuse handled differently in fiction and nonfiction? Which version do you personally find more compelling? Why?

53

Susan Orlean

The American Man at Age Ten

The journalist and essayist Susan Orlean (b. 1955) began her career writing for the Willamette Week *in Portland, Oregon, before moving to the* Boston Phoenix *and then to the* Boston Globe. *Her first book,* Red Sox, Bluefish, and Other Things That Make New England New England *(1987), collects the columns she published at the* Globe. *From 1987 to 1991, Orlean was a contributing editor at* Rolling Stone *magazine, and since 1987 she has been a staff writer at the* New Yorker. *"The American Man at Age Ten" appeared in* Esquire *in 1992. Her most recent book,* Saturday Night *(1990), describes the various activities and entertainments pursued by all kinds of Americans on their Saturday nights, and is based on her extensive travels and interviews across the country.*

"For me the biggest step in the writing process," says Orlean, "is to peel away all of the expectations I brought to the story — all of the preconceptions about the subject or the person I'm writing about — and to really find in my heart what I felt like in the moment of reporting. You need to dig into yourself to find your true emotions and thoughts and responses to what you have seen and felt and experienced. . . . Writing is a process of unlearning expectations and paying attention to the genuineness of the moment. How you do that is to reconsider, rethink, recollect, and talk about what you are trying to say. Eventually the writing will emerge out of that — the real thread of truth."

If Colin Duffy and I were to get married, we would have matching superhero notebooks. We would wear shorts, big sneakers, and long, baggy T-shirts depicting famous athletes every single day, even in the winter. We would sleep in our clothes. We would both be good at Nintendo Street Fighter II, but Colin would be better than me. We would have some homework, but it would not be too hard and we would always have just finished it. We would eat pizza and candy for all of our meals. We wouldn't have sex, but we would have crushes on each other and, magically, babies would appear in our home. We would win the lottery and then buy land in Wyoming, where we would have one of every kind of cute animal. All the while, Colin would be working in law enforcement — probably the FBI. Our favorite movie star, Morgan Freeman, would visit us occasionally. We would listen to the same Eurythmics song ("Here Comes the Rain Again") over and over again and watch two hours of television every Friday night. We would both be good at football, have best friends, and know how to drive; we would cure AIDS and the garbage problem and everything that hurts animals. We would hang out a lot with Colin's dad. For fun, we would load a slingshot with dog food and shoot it at my butt. We would have a very good life.

Here are the particulars about Colin Duffy: He is ten years old, on the nose. He is four feet eight inches high, weighs seventy-five pounds, and appears to be mostly leg and shoulder blade. He is a handsome kid. He has a broad forehead, dark eyes with dense lashes, and a sharp, dimply smile. I have rarely seen him without a baseball cap. He owns several, but favors a University of Michigan Wolverines model, on account of its pleasing colors. The hat styles his hair into wild disarray. If you ever managed to get the hat off his head, you would see a boy with a nimbus of golden-brown hair, dented in the back, where the hat hits him.

Colin lives with his mother, Elaine; his father, Jim; his older sister, Megan; and his little brother, Chris, in a pretty pale-blue Victorian house on a bosky street in Glen Ridge, New Jersey. Glen Ridge is a serene and civilized old town twenty miles west of New York City. It does not have much of a commercial district, but it is a town of amazing lawns. Most of the houses were built around the turn of the century and are set back a gracious, green distance from the street. The rest of the town seems to consist of parks and playing fields and sidewalks and backyards — in other words, it is a far cry from South-Central Los Angeles and from Bedford-Stuyvesant and other, grimmer parts of the country where a very different ten-year-old American man is growing up today.

There is a fine school system in Glen Ridge, but Elaine and Jim, who are both schoolteachers, choose to send their children to a parents' cooperative elementary school in Montclair, a neighboring suburb. Currently, Colin is in fifth grade. He is a good student. He plans to go to college, to a place he says is called Oklahoma City State College University. OCSCU satisfies his desire to live out west, to attend a small college, and to study law enforcement, which OCSCU apparently offers as a major. After four years at Oklahoma City State College University, he plans to work for the FBI. He says that getting to be a police officer involves tons of hard work, but working for the FBI will be a cinch, because all you have to do is fill out one form, which he has already gotten from the head FBI office. Colin is quiet in class but loud on the playground. He has a great throwing arm, significant foot speed, and a lot of physical confidence. He is also brave. Huge wild cats with rabies and gross stuff dripping from their teeth, which he says run rampant throughout his neighborhood, do not scare him. Otherwise, he is slightly bashful. This combination of athletic grace and valor and personal reserve accounts for considerable popularity. He has a fluid relationship to many social groups, including the superbright nerds, the ultrajocks, the flashy kids who will someday be-come extremely popular and socially successful juvenile delinquents, and the kids who will be elected president of the student body. In his opinion, the most popular boy in his class is Christian, who happens to be black, and Colin's favorite television character is Steve Urkel on *Family Matters*, who is black, too, but otherwise he seems uninterested in or oblivious to race. Until this year, he was a Boy Scout. Now he is planning to begin karate lessons. His favorite schoolyard game is football, followed closely by prison dodge ball, blob tag, and bombardo. He's crazy about athletes, although sometimes it isn't clear if he is absolutely sure of the difference between human athletes and Marvel Comics action figures. His current athletic hero is Dave Meggett. His current best friend is named Japeth. He used to have another best friend named Ozzie. According to Colin, Ozzie was found on a doorstep, then changed his name to Michael and moved to Massachusetts, and then Colin never saw him or heard from him again.

He has had other losses in his life. He is old enough to know people   5 who have died and to know things about the world that are worrisome. When he dreams, he dreams about moving to Wyoming, which he has visited with his family. His plan is to buy land there and have some sort of ranch that would definitely include horses. Sometimes when he talks about this, it sounds as ordinary and hard-boiled as a real estate ap-praisal; other times it can sound fantastical and wifty and achingly naive, informed by the last inklings of childhood — the musings of a balmy real estate appraiser assaying a wonderful and magical landscape that erodes from memory a little bit every day. The collision in his mind of what he understands, what he hears, what he figures out, what popular culture pours into him, what he knows, what he pretends to know, and what he imagines, makes an interesting mess. The mess often has the form of what he will probably think like when he is a grown man, but the content of what he is like as a little boy.

He is old enough to begin imagining that he will someday get mar-ried, but at ten he is still convinced that the best thing about being mar-ried will be that he will be allowed to sleep in his clothes. His father once observed that living with Colin was like living with a Martian who had done some reading on American culture. As it happens, Colin is not espe-cially sad or worried about the prospect of growing up, although he sometimes frets over whether he should be called a kid or a grown-up; he has settled on the word *kid-up*. Once I asked him what the biggest advan-tage to adulthood will be, and he said, "The best thing is that grown-ups can go wherever they want." I asked him what he meant, exactly, and he said, "Well, if you're grown-up, you'd have a car, and whenever you felt like it, you could get into your car and drive somewhere and get candy."

Colin loves recycling. He loves it even more than, say, playing with little birds. That ten-year-olds feel the weight of the world and consider it their mission to shoulder it came as a surprise to me. I had gone with Colin one Monday to his classroom at Montclair Cooperative School. The Coop is in a steep, old, sharp-angled brick building that had served for many years as a public school until a group of parents in the area took it over and made it into a private, progressive elementary school. The fifth-grade classroom is on the top floor, under the dormers, which gives the room the eccentric shape and closeness of an attic. It is a rather informal environment. There are computers lined up in an adjoining room and instructions spelled out on the chalkboard — BRING IN: 1) A CUBBY WITH YOUR NAME ON IT, 2) A TRAPPER WITH A 5-POCKET ENVELOPE LABELED SCIENCE, SOCIAL STUDIES, READING/LANGUAGE ARTS, MATH, MATH LAB/COMPUTER; WHITE LINED PAPER; A PLASTIC PENCIL BAG; A SMALL HOMEWORK PAD, 3) LARGE BROWN GROCERY BAGS — but there is also a couch in the center of the classroom, which the kids take turns occupying, a rocking chair, and three canaries in cages near the door.

It happened to be Colin's first day in fifth grade. Before class began, there was a lot of horsing around, but there were also a lot of conversations about whether Magic Johnson had AIDS or just HIV and whether someone falling in a pool of blood from a cut of his would get the disease. These jolts of sobriety in the midst of rank goofiness are a ten-year-old's specialty. Each one comes as a fresh, hard surprise, like finding a razor blade in a candy apple. One day, Colin and I had been discussing horses or dogs or something, and out of the blue he said, "What do you think is better, to dump garbage in the ocean, to dump it on land, or to burn it?" Another time, he asked me if I planned to have children. I had just spent an evening with him and his friend Japeth, during which they put every small, movable object in the house into Japeth's slingshot and fired it at me, so I told him I wanted children but that I hoped they would all be girls, and he said, "Will you have an abortion if you find out you have a boy?"

At school, after discussing summer vacation, the kids began choosing the jobs they would do to help out around the classroom. Most of the jobs are humdrum — putting the chairs up on the tables, washing the chalkboard, turning the computers off or on. Five of the most humdrum tasks are recycling chores — for example, taking bottles or stacks of paper down to the basement, where they would be sorted and prepared for pickup. Two children would be assigned to feed the birds and cover their cages at the end of the day.

I expected the bird jobs to be the first to go. Everyone loved the birds;   10 they'd spent an hour that morning voting on names for them (Tweetie, Montgomery, and Rose narrowly beating out Axl Rose, Bugs, Ol' Yeller, Fido, Slim, Lucy, and Chirpie). Instead, they all wanted to recycle. The recycling jobs were claimed by the first five kids called by Suzanne Nakamura, the fifth-grade teacher; each kid called after that responded by groaning, "Suzanne, aren't there any more recycling jobs?" Colin ended up with the job of taking down the chairs each morning. He accepted the task with a sort of resignation — this was just going to be a job rather than a mission.

On the way home that day, I was quizzing Colin about his world views.

"Who's the coolest person in the world?"

"Morgan Freeman."

"What's the best sport?"

"Football."   15

"Who's the coolest woman?"

"None. I don't know."

"What's the most important thing in the world?"

"Game Boy." Pause. "No, the world. The world is the most important thing in the world."

Danny's Pizzeria is a dark little shop next door to the Montclair Co-   20
operative School. It is not much to look at. Outside, the brick facing is painted muddy brown. Inside, there are some saggy counters, a splintered bench, and enough room for either six teenagers or about a dozen ten-year-olds who happen to be getting along well. The light is low. The air is oily. At Danny's, you will find pizza, candy, Nintendo, and very few girls. To a ten-year-old boy, it is the most beautiful place in the world.

One afternoon, after class was dismissed, we went to Danny's with Colin's friend Japeth to play Nintendo. Danny's has only one game, Street Fighter II Champion Edition. Some teenage boys from a nearby middle school had gotten there first and were standing in a tall, impenetrable thicket around the machine.

"Next game," Colin said. The teenagers ignored him.

"Hey, we get next game," Japeth said. He is smaller than Colin, scrappy, and, as he explained to me once, famous for wearing his hat backward all the time and having a huge wristwatch and a huge bedroom. He stamped his foot and announced again, "Hey, we get next game."

One of the teenagers turned around and said, "Fuck you, *next game*," and then turned back to the machine.

"Whoa," Japeth said.   25

He and Colin went outside, where they felt bigger.

"Which street fighter are you going to be?" Colin asked Japeth.

"Blanka," Japeth said. "I know how to do his head-butt."

"I hate that! I hate the head-butt," Colin said. He dropped his voice a little and growled, "I'm going to be Ken, and I will kill you with my dragon punch."

"Yeah, right, and monkeys will fly out of my butt," Japeth said.   30

Street Fighter II is a video game in which two characters have an explosive brawl in a scenic international setting. It is currently the most popular video-arcade game in America. This is not an insignificant amount of popularity. Most arcade versions of video games, which end up in pizza parlors, malls, and arcades, sell about two thousand units. So far, some fifty thousand Street Fighter II and Street Fighter II Championship Edition arcade games have been sold. Not since Pac-Man, which was released the year before Colin was born, has there been a video game as popular as Street Fighter. The home version of Street Fighter is the most popular home video game in the country, and that, too, is not an insignificant thing. Thirty-two million Nintendo home systems have been sold since 1986, when it was introduced in this country. There is a Nintendo system in seven of every ten homes in America in which a child between the ages of eight and twelve resides. By the time a boy in America turns ten, he will almost certainly have been exposed to Nintendo home games, Nintendo arcade games, and Game Boy, the hand-held version. He will probably own a system and dozens of games. By ten, according to Nintendo studies, teachers, and psychologists, game prowess becomes a fundamental, essential male social marker and a schoolyard boast.

The Street Fighter characters are Dhalsim, Ken, Guile, Blanka, E. Honda, Ryu, Zangief, and Chun Li. Each represents a different country, and they each have their own special weapon. Chun Li, for instance, is from China and possesses a devastating whirlwind kick that is triggered if you push the control pad down for two seconds and then up for two seconds, and then you hit the kick button. Chun Li's kick is money in the bank, because most of the other fighters do not have a good defense against it. By the way, Chun Li happens to be a girl — the only female Street Fighter character.

I asked Colin if he was interested in being Chun Li. There was a long pause. "I'd rather be Ken," he said.

The girls in Colin's class at school are named Cortnerd, Terror, Spacey, Lizard, Maggot, and Diarrhea. "They do have other names, but that's what we call them," Colin told me. "The girls aren't very popular."

"They are about as popular as a piece of dirt," Japeth said. "Or, you 35
know that couch in the classroom? That couch is more popular than any girl. A thousand times more." They talked for a minute about one of the girls in their class, a tall blonde with cheerleader genetic material, who they allowed was not quite as gross as some of the other girls. Japeth said that a chubby, awkward boy in their class was boasting that this girl liked him.

"No way," Colin said. "She would never like him. I mean, not that he's so . . . I don't know. I don't hate him because he's fat, anyway. I hate him because he's nasty."

"Well, she doesn't like him," Japeth said. "She's been really mean to me lately, so I'm pretty sure she likes me."

"Girls are different," Colin said. He hopped up and down on the balls of his feet, wrinkling his nose. "Girls are stupid and weird."

"I have a lot of girlfriends, about six or so," Japeth said, turning contemplative. "I don't exactly remember their names, though."

The teenagers came crashing out of Danny's and jostled past us, so 40
we went inside. The man who runs Danny's, whose name is Tom, was

leaning across the counter on his elbows, looking exhausted. Two little boys, holding Slush Puppies, shuffled toward the Nintendo, but Colin and Japeth elbowed them aside and slammed their quarters down on the machine. The little boys shuffled back toward the counter and stood gawking at them, sucking on their drinks.

"You want to know how to tell if a girl likes you?" Japeth said. "She'll act really mean to you. That's a sure sign. I don't know why they do it, but it's always a sure sign. It gets your attention. You know how I show a girl I like her? I steal something from her and then run away. I do it to get their attention, and it works."

They played four quarters' worth of games. During the last one, a teenager with a quilted leather jacket and a fade haircut came in, pushed his arm between them, and put a quarter down on the deck of the machine.

Japeth said, "Hey, what's that?"

The teenager said, "I get next game. I've marked it now. Everyone knows this secret sign for next game. It's a universal thing."

"So now we know," Japeth said. "Colin, let's get out of here and go   45
bother Maggie. I mean Maggot. Okay?" They picked up their backpacks and headed out the door.

Psychologists identify ten as roughly the age at which many boys experience the gender-linked normative developmental trauma that leaves them, as adult men, at risk for specific psychological sequelae often manifest as deficits in the arenas of intimacy, empathy, and struggles with commitment in relationships. In other words, this is around the age when guys get screwed up about girls. Elaine and Jim Duffy, and probably most of the parents who send their kids to Montclair Cooperative School, have done a lot of stuff to try to avoid this. They gave Colin dolls as well as guns. (He preferred guns.) Japeth's father has three motorcycles and two dirt bikes but does most of the cooking and cleaning in their home. Suzanne, Colin's teacher, is careful to avoid sexist references in her presentations. After school, the yard at Montclair Cooperative is filled with as many fathers as mothers — fathers who hug their kids when they come prancing out of the building and are dismayed when their sons clamor for Supersoaker water guns and war toys or take pleasure in beating up girls.

In a study of adolescents conducted by the Gesell Institute of Human Development, nearly half the ten-year-old boys questioned said they thought they had inadequate information about sex. Nevertheless, most ten-year-old boys across the country are subjected to a few months of sex education in school. Colin and his class will get their dose next spring. It is yet another installment in a plan to make them into new, improved men with reconstructed notions of sex and male-female relationships. One afternoon I asked Philip, a schoolmate of Colin's, whether he was looking forward to sex education, and he said, "No, because I think it'll probably make me really, really hyper. I have a feeling it's going to be just like what it was like when some television reporters came to school last year and filmed us in class and I got really hyper. They stood around with all these cameras and asked us questions. I think that's what sex education is probably like."

At a class meeting earlier in the day:

Suzanne: "Today was our first swimming class, and I have one observation to make. The girls went to their locker room, got dressed without a lot of fuss, and came into the pool area. The boys, on the other hand, the *boys* had some sort of problem doing that rather simple task. Can someone tell me exactly what went on in the locker room?"

Keith: "There was a lot of shouting."

Suzanne: "Okay, I hear you saying that people were being noisy and shouting. Anything else?"

Christian: "Some people were screaming so much that my ears were killing me. It gave me, like, a huge headache. Also, some of the boys were taking their towels, I mean, after they had taken their clothes off, they had their towels around their waists and then they would drop them really fast and then pull them back up, really fast."

Suzanne: "Okay, you're saying some people were being silly about their bodies."

Christian: "Well, yeah, but it was more like they were being silly about their pants."

Colin's bedroom is decorated simply. He has a cage with his pet parakeet, Dude, on his dresser, a lot of recently worn clothing piled haphazardly on the floor, and a husky brown teddy bear sitting upright in a chair near the foot of his bed. The walls are mostly bare, except for a Spiderman poster and a few ads torn out of magazines he has thumbtacked up. One of the ads is for a cologne, illustrated with several small photographs of cowboy hats; another, a feverish portrait of a woman on a horse, is an ad for blue jeans. These inspire him sometimes when he lies in bed and makes plans for the move to Wyoming. Also, he happens to like ads. He also likes television commercials. Generally speaking, he likes consumer products and popular culture. He partakes avidly but not indiscriminately. In fact, during the time we spent together, he provided a running commentary on merchandise, media, and entertainment:

"The only shoes anyone will wear are Reebok Pumps. Big T-shirts are cool, not the kind that are sticky and close to you, but big and baggy and long, not the kind that stop at your stomach."

"The best food is Chicken McNuggets and Life cereal and Frosted Flakes."

"Don't go to Blimpie's. They have the worst service."

"I'm not into Teenage Mutant Ninja Turtles anymore. I grew out of that. I like Donatello, but I'm not a fan. I don't buy the figures anymore."

"The best television shows are on Friday night on ABC. It's called TGIF, and it's *Family Matters, Step by Step, Dinosaurs,* and *Perfect Strangers,* where the guy has a funny accent."

"The best candy is Skittles and Symphony bars and Crybabies and Warheads. Crybabies are great because if you eat a lot of them at once you feel so sour."

"Hyundais are Korean cars. It's the only Korean car. They're not that good because Koreans don't have a lot of experience building cars."

"The best movie is *City Slickers,* and the best part was when he saved his little cow in the river."

"The Giants really need to get rid of Ray Handley. They have to get somebody who has real coaching experience. He's just no good."

"My dog, Sally, costs seventy-two dollars. That sounds like a lot of money but it's a really good price because you get a flea bath with your dog." 65

"The best magazines are *Nintendo Power,* because they tell you how to do the secret moves in the video games, and also *Mad* magazine and *Money Guide* — I really like that one."

"The best artist in the world is Jim Davis."

"The most beautiful woman in the world is not Madonna! Only Wayne and Garth think that! She looks like maybe a . . . a . . . slut or something. Cindy Crawford looks like she would look good, but if you see her on an awards program on TV she doesn't look that good. I think the most beautiful woman in the world probably is my mom."

Colin thinks a lot about money. This started when he was about nine and a half, which is when a lot of other things started — a new way of walking that has a little macho hitch and swagger, a decision about the Teenage Mutant Ninja Turtles (con) and Eurythmics (pro), and a persistent curiosity about a certain girl whose name he will not reveal. He knows the price of everything he encounters. He knows how much college costs and what someone might earn performing different jobs. Once, he asked me what my husband did; when I answered that he was a lawyer, he snapped, "You must be a rich family. Lawyers make $400,000 a year." His preoccupation with money baffles his family. They are not struggling, so this is not the anxiety of deprivation; they are not rich, so he is not responding to an elegant, advantaged world. His allowance is five dollars a week. It seems sufficient for his needs, which consist chiefly of quarters for Nintendo and candy money. The remainder is put into his Wyoming fund. His fascination is not just specific to needing money or having plans for money: It is as if money itself, and the way it makes the world work, and the realization that almost everything in the world can be assigned a price, has possessed him. "I just pay attention to things like that," Colin says. "It's really very interesting."

He is looking for a windfall. He tells me his mother has been notified 70 that she is in the fourth and final round of the Publisher's Clearinghouse Sweepstakes. This is not an ironic observation. He plays the New Jersey lottery every Thursday night. He knows the weekly jackpot; he knows the number to call to find out if he has won. I do not think this presages a future for Colin as a high-stakes gambler; I think it says more about the powerful grasp that money has on imagination and what a large percentage of a ten-year-old's mind is made up of imaginings. One Friday, we were at school together, and one of his friends was asking him about the lottery, and he said, "This week it was $4 million. That would be I forget how much every year for the rest of your life. It's a lot, I think. You should play. All it takes is a dollar and a dream."

Until the lottery comes through and he starts putting together the Wyoming land deal, Colin can be found most of the time in the backyard. Often, he will have friends come over. Regularly, children from the neighborhood will gravitate to the backyard, too. As a technical matter of real-property law, title to the house and yard belongs to Jim and Elaine Duffy, but Colin adversely possesses the backyard, at least from 4:00 each afternoon until it gets dark. As yet, the fixtures of teenage life — malls, video arcades, friends' basements, automobiles — either hold little interest for him or are not his to have.

He is, at the moment, very content with his backyard. For most intents and purposes, it is as big as Wyoming. One day, certainly, he will grow and it will shrink, and it will become simply a suburban backyard and it won't be big enough for him anymore. This will happen so fast that one night he will be in the backyard, believing it a perfect place, and by the next night he will have changed and the yard as he imagined it will be gone, and this era of his life will be behind him forever.

Most days, he spends hours in the backyard building an Evil Spider-Web Trap. This entails running a spool of Jim's fishing line from every surface in the yard until it forms a huge web. Once a garbageman picking up the Duffys' trash got caught in the trap. Otherwise, the Evil Spider-Web Trap mostly has a deterrent effect, because the kids in the neighborhood who might roam over know that Colin builds it back there. "I do it all the time," he says. "First I plan who I'd like to catch in it, and then we get started. Trespassers have to beware."

One afternoon when I came over for a few rounds of Street Fighter at Danny's, Colin started building a trap. He selected a victim for inspiration — a boy in his class who had been pestering him — and began wrapping. He was entirely absorbed. He moved from tree to tree, wrapping; he laced fishing line through the railing of the deck and then back to the shed; he circled an old jungle gym, something he'd outgrown and abandoned a few years ago, and then crossed over to a bush at the back of the yard. Briefly, he contemplated making his dog, Sally, part of the web. Dusk fell. He kept wrapping, paying out fishing line an inch at a time. We could hear mothers up and down the block hooting for their kids; two tiny children from next door stood transfixed at the edge of the yard,

uncertain whether they would end up inside or outside the web. After a
while, the spool spun around in Colin's hands one more time and then
stopped; he was out of line.

It was almost too dark to see much of anything, although now and   75
again the light from the deck would glance off a length of line, and it
would glint and sparkle. "That's the point," he said. "You could do it
with thread, but the fishing line is invisible. Now I have this perfect thing
and the only one who knows about it is me." With that, he dropped the
spool, skipped up the stairs of the deck, threw open the screen door, and
then bounded into the house, leaving me and Sally the dog trapped in his
web.

The Reader's Presence

1. Orlean begins the essay with a description of what life would be
   like if she and Colin Duffy got married. From whose perspective is
   she writing? How does this introduction set the tone for the rest of
   the essay?

2. Consider the role of gender in the essay. Do you think it makes
   any difference that the author is a woman? How might her tone
   and approach be different if Orlean had once been a ten-year-old
   boy? Why do you think she chose to title the essay "The American
   Man at Age Ten" rather than "The American *Boy* at Age Ten"?
   What is Orlean trying to say about the way that men learn cultural attitudes and beliefs?

3. By most standards, Colin Duffy's life is relatively privileged. How
   does Orlean acknowledge this fact? Is she presenting Colin as a
   representative ten-year-old boy? Which elements of his life do you
   see as universal, and which are specific to his situation?

54

George Orwell

Politics and the English Language

During his lifetime, George Orwell was well known for the political positions he laid out in his essays. The events that inspired Orwell to write his essays have long since passed, but his writing continues to be read and enjoyed. Orwell demonstrates that political writing need not be narrowly topical — it can speak to enduring issues and concerns. He suggested as much in 1946 when he wrote, "What I have most wanted to do throughout the past ten years is to make political writing into an art. My starting point is always a feeling of partisanship, a feeling of injustice. . . . But I could not do the work of writing a book, or even a long magazine article, if it were not also an aesthetic experience." "Politics and the English Language" appears in Shooting an Elephant and Other Essays (1950)*
For more information about Orwell, see page 126.*

Most people who bother with the matter at all would admit that the English language is in a bad way, but it is generally assumed that we cannot by conscious action do anything about it. Our civilization is decadent and our language — so the argument runs — must inevitably share in the general collapse. It follows that any struggle against the abuse of language is a sentimental archaism, like preferring candles to electric light or hansom cabs to airplanes. Underneath this lies the half-conscious belief that language is a natural growth and not an instrument which we shape for our own purposes.

Now, it is clear that the decline of a language must ultimately have political and economic causes: It is not due simply to the bad influence of this or that individual writer. But an effect can become a cause, reinforcing the original cause and producing the same effect in an intensified form, and so on indefinitely. A man may take to drink because he feels himself to be a failure, and then fail all the more completely because he drinks. It is rather the same thing that is happening to the English language. It becomes ugly and inaccurate because our thoughts are foolish, but the slovenliness of our language makes it easier for us to have foolish thoughts. The point is that the process is reversible. Modern English, especially written English, is full of bad habits which spread by imitation and which can be avoided if one is willing to take the necessary trouble. If one gets rid of these habits one can think more clearly, and to think clearly is a necessary first step towards political regeneration: so that the fight against bad English is not frivolous and is not the exclusive concern of professional writers. I will come back to this presently, and I hope that by that time the meaning of what I have said here will have become clearer. Meanwhile, here are five specimens of the English language as it is now habitually written.

These five passages have not been picked out because they are especially bad — I could have quoted far worse if I had chosen — but because they illustrate various of the mental vices from which we now suffer. They are a little below the average, but are fairly representative samples. I number them so that I can refer back to them when necessary:

(1) I am not, indeed, sure whether it is not true to say that the Milton who once seemed not unlike a seventeenth-century Shelley had not become, out of an experience ever more bitter in each year, more alien [*sic*] to the founder of that Jesuit sect which nothing could induce him to tolerate.

Professor Harold Laski (Essay in *Freedom of Expression*).

(2) Above all, we cannot play ducks and drakes with a native battery of idioms which prescribes such egregious collections of vocables as the Basic *put up with* for *tolerate* or *put at a loss* for *bewilder*.

Professor Lancelot Hogben (*Interglossa*).

(3) On the one side we have the free personality: By definition it is not neurotic, for it has neither conflict nor dream. Its desires, such as they are, are transparent, for they are just what institutional approval keeps in the forefront of consciousness; another institutional pattern would alter their number and intensity; there is little in them that is natural, irreducible, or culturally dangerous. But *on the other side,* the social bond itself is nothing but the mutual reflection of these self-secure integrities. Recall the definition of love. Is not this the very picture of a small academic? Where is there a place in this hall of mirrors for either personality or fraternity?

Essay on psychology in *Politics* (New York).

(4) All the "best people" from the gentlemen's clubs, and all the frantic fascist captains, united in common hatred of Socialism and bestial horror of the rising tide of the mass revolutionary movement, have turned to acts of provocation, to foul incendiarism, to medieval legends of poisoned wells, to legalize their own destruction of proletarian organizations, and rouse the agitated petty-bourgeoisie to chauvinistic fervor on behalf of the fight against the revolutionary way out of the crisis.

Communist pamphlet.

(5) If a new spirit *is* to be infused into this old country, there is one thorny and contentious reform which must be tackled, and that is the humanization and galvanization of the B.B.C. Timidity here will bespeak cancer and atrophy of the soul. The heart of Britain may be sound and of strong beat, for instance, but the British lion's roar at present is like that of Bottom in Shakespeare's *Midsummer Night's Dream* — as gentle as any sucking dove. A virile

new Britain cannot continue indefinitely to be traduced in the eyes or rather ears, of the world by the effete languors of Langham Place, brazenly masquerading as "standard English." When the Voice of Britain is heard at nine o'clock, better far and infinitely less ludicrous to hear aitches honestly dropped than the present priggish, inflated, inhibited, school-ma'amish arch braying of blameless bashful mewing maidens!

Letter in *Tribune*.

Each of these passages has faults of its own, but, quite apart from avoidable ugliness, two qualities are common to all of them. The first is staleness of imagery: The other is lack of precision. The writer either has a meaning and cannot express it, or he inadvertently says something else, or he is almost indifferent as to whether his words mean anything or not. This mixture of vagueness and sheer incompetence is the most marked characteristic of modern English prose, and especially of any kind of political writing. As soon as certain topics are raised, the concrete melts into the abstract and no one seems able to think of turns of speech that are not hackneyed: Prose consists less and less of *words* chosen for the sake of their meaning, and more and more of *phrases* tacked together like the sections of a prefabricated hen-house. I list below, with notes and examples, various of the tricks by means of which the work of prose-construction is habitually dodged:

Dying Metaphors. A newly invented metaphor assists thought by evoking a visual image, while on the other hand a metaphor which is technically "dead" (e.g., *iron resolution*) has in effect reverted to being an ordinary word and can generally be used without loss of vividness. But in between these two classes there is a huge dump of worn-out metaphors which have lost all evocative power and are merely used because they save people the trouble of inventing phrases for themselves. Examples are: *Ring the changes on, take up the cudgels for, toe the line, ride roughshod over, stand shoulder to shoulder with, play into the hands of, no axe to grind, grist to the mill, fishing in troubled waters, rift within the lute, on the order of the day, Achilles' heel, swan song, hotbed.* Many of these are used without knowledge of their meaning (what is a "rift," for instance?), and incompatible metaphors are frequently mixed, a sure sign that the writer is not interested in what he is saying. Some metaphors now current have been twisted out of their original meaning without those who use them even being aware of the fact. For example, *toe the line* is sometimes written *tow the line.* Another example is *the hammer and the anvil*, now always used with the implication that the anvil gets the worst of it. In real life it is always the anvil that breaks the hammer, never the other way about: A writer who stopped to think what he was saying would be aware of this, and would avoid perverting the original phrase.

Operators or Verbal False Limbs. These save the trouble of picking out appropriate verbs and nouns, and at the same time pad each sentence with extra syllables which give it an appearance of symmetry. Characteristic phrases are *render inoperative, militate against, make contact with, be subjected to, give rise to, give grounds for, have the effect of, play a leading part (role) in, make itself felt, take effect, exhibit a tendency to, serve the purpose of, etc., etc.* The keynote is the elimination of simple verbs. Instead of being a single word, such as *break, stop, spoil, mend, kill,* a verb becomes a *phrase,* made up of a noun or adjective tacked on to some general-purpose verb such as *prove, serve, form, play, render.* In addition, the passive voice is wherever possible used in preference to the active, and noun constructions are used instead of gerunds (*by examination of* instead of *by examining*). The range of verbs is further cut down by means of the *-ize* and *de-* formation, and the banal statements are given an appearance of profundity by means of the *not un-* formation. Simple conjunctions and prepositions are replaced by such phrases as *with respect to, having regard to, the fact that, by dint of, in view of, in the interests of, on the hypothesis that;* and the ends of sentences are saved from anticlimax by such resounding commonplaces as *greatly to be desired, cannot be left out of account, a development to be expected in the near future, deserving of serious consideration, brought to a satisfactory conclusion,* and so on and so forth.

Pretentious Diction. Words like *phenomenon, element, individual* (as noun), *objective, categorical, effective, virtual, basic, primary, promote, constitute, exhibit, exploit, utilize, eliminate, liquidate,* are used to dress up simple statements and give an air of scientific impartiality to biased judgments. Adjectives like *epoch-making, epic, historic, unforgettable, triumphant, age-old, inevitable, inexorable, veritable,* are used to dignify the sordid processes of international politics, while writing that aims at glorifying war usually takes on an archaic color, its characteristic words being: *realm, throne, chariot, mailed fist, trident, sword, shield, buckler, banner, jackboot, clarion.* Foreign words and expressions such as *cul de sac, ancien régime, deus ex machina, mutatis mutandis, status quo, gleichschaltung, weltanschauung,* are used to give an air of culture and elegance. Except for the useful abbreviations *i.e., e.g.,* and *etc.,* there is no real need for any of the hundreds of foreign phrases now current in English. Bad writers, and especially scientific, political, and sociological writers, are nearly always haunted by the notion that Latin or Greek words are grander than Saxon ones, and unnecessary words like *expedite, ameliorate, predict, extraneous, deracinated, clandestine, subaqueous,* and hundreds of others constantly gain ground from their Anglo-Saxon opposite numbers.[1] The jargon peculiar to Marxist writing (*hyena, hangman, can-*

---

[1]An interesting illustration of this is the way in which the English flower names which were in use till very recently are being ousted by Greek ones, *snapdragon* becoming *antirrhinum, forget-me-not* becoming *myosotis,* etc. It is hard to see any practical reason for this change of fashion: It is probably due to an instinctive turning away from the more homely word and a vague feeling that the Greek word is scientific. — ORWELL'S NOTE.

nibal, petty bourgeois, these gentry, lackey, flunkey, mad dog, White Guard, etc.) consists largely of words and phrases translated from Russian, German, or French; but the normal way of coining a new word is to use a Latin or Greek root with the appropriate affix and, where necessary, the *-ize* formation. It is often easier to make up words of this kind (*deregionalize, impermissible, extramarital, nonfragmentatory,* and so forth) than to think up the English words that will cover one's meaning. The result, in general, is an increase in slovenliness and vagueness.

Meaningless Words. In certain kinds of writing, particularly in art criticism and literary criticism, it is normal to come across long passages which are almost completely lacking in meaning.[2] Words like *romantic, plastic, values, human, dead, sentimental, natural, vitality,* as used in art criticism, are strictly meaningless, in the sense that they not only do not point to any discoverable object, but are hardly ever expected to do so by the reader. When one critic writes, "The outstanding feature of Mr. X's work is its living quality," while another writes, "The immediately striking thing about Mr. X's work is its peculiar deadness," the reader accepts this as a simple difference of opinion. If words like *black* and *white* were involved, instead of the jargon words *dead* and *living*, he would see at once that language was being used in an improper way. Many political words are similarly abused. The word *Fascism* has now no meaning except in so far as it signifies "something not desirable." The words *democracy, socialism, freedom, patriotic, realistic, justice,* have each of them several different meanings which cannot be reconciled with one another. In the case of a word like *democracy,* not only is there no agreed definition, but the attempt to make one is resisted from all sides. It is almost universally felt that when we call a country democratic we are praising it: Consequently the defenders of every kind of regime claim that it is a democracy, and fear that they might have to stop using the word if it were tied down to any one meaning. Words of this kind are often used in a consciously dishonest way. That is, the person who uses them has his own private definition, but allows his hearer to think he means something quite different. Statements like *Marshal Pétain[3] was a true patriot, The Soviet Press is the freest in the world, The Catholic Church is opposed to persecution,* are almost always made with intent to deceive. Other words

---

[2]Example: "Comfort's catholicity of perception and image, strangely Whitmanesque in range, almost the exact opposite in aesthetic compulsion, continues to evoke that trembling atmospheric accumulative hinting at a cruel, an inexorably serene timelessness. . . . Wrey Gardiner scores by aiming at simple bull's-eyes with precision. Only they are not so simple, and through this contented sadness runs more than the surface bitter-sweet of resignation." (*Poetry Quarterly.*) — ORWELL'S NOTE.

[3]*Pétain:* Henry Philippe Pétain was a World War I French military hero who served as chief of state in France from 1940 to 1945, after France surrendered to Germany. A controversial figure, Pétain was regarded by some to be a patriot who had sacrificed himself for his country, while others considered him to be a traitor. He was sentenced to life imprisonment in 1945, the year before Orwell wrote his essay. — EDS.

used in variable meanings, in most cases more or less dishonestly, are: *class, totalitarian, science, progressive, reactionary, bourgeois, equality.*

Now that I have made this catalogue of swindles and perversions, let me give another example of the kind of writing that they lead to. This time it must of its nature be an imaginary one. I am going to translate a passage of good English into modern English of the worst sort. Here is a well-known verse from *Ecclesiastes:*

> I returned and saw under the sun, that the race is not to the swift, nor the battle to the strong, neither yet bread to the wise, nor yet riches to men of understanding, nor yet favor to men of skill; but time and chance happeneth to them all.

Here it is in modern English:

> Objective consideration of contemporary phenomena compels the conclusion that success or failure in competitive activities exhibits no tendency to be commensurate with innate capacity, but that a considerable element of the unpredictable must invariably be taken into account.

This is a parody, but not a very gross one. Exhibit (3), above, for instance, contains several patches of the same kind of English. It will be seen that I have not made a full translation. The beginning and ending of the sentence follow the original meaning fairly closely, but in the middle the concrete illustrations — race, battle, bread — dissolve into the vague phrase "success or failure in competitive activities." This had to be so, because no modern writer of the kind I am discussing — no one capable of using phrases like "objective consideration of contemporary phenomena" — would ever tabulate his thoughts in that precise and detailed way. The whole tendency of modern prose is away from concreteness. Now analyze these two sentences a little more closely. The first contains forty-nine words but only sixty syllables, and all its words are those of everyday life. The second contains thirty-eight words of ninety syllables: Eighteen of its words are from Latin roots, and one from Greek. The first sentence contains six vivid images, and only one phrase ("time and chance") that could be called vague. The second contains not a single fresh, arresting phrase, and in spite of its ninety syllables it gives only a shortened version of the meaning contained in the first. Yet without a doubt it is the second kind of sentence that is gaining ground in modern English. I do not want to exaggerate. This kind of writing is not yet universal, and outcrops of simplicity will occur here and there in the worst-written page. Still, if you or I were told to write a few lines on the uncertainty of human fortunes, we should probably come much nearer to my imaginary sentence than to the one from *Ecclesiastes.*

As I have tried to show, modern writing at its worst does not consist in picking out words for the sake of their meaning and inventing images in order to make the meaning clearer. It consists in gumming together

10

long strips of words which have already been set in order by someone else, and making the results presentable by sheer humbug. The attraction of this way of writing is that it is easy. It is easier — even quicker once you have the habit — to say *In my opinion it is a not unjustifiable assumption that* than to say *I think*. If you use ready-made phrases, you not only don't have to hunt about for words; you also don't have to bother with the rhythms of your sentences, since these phrases are generally so arranged as to be more or less euphonious. When you are composing in a hurry — when you are dictating to a stenographer, for instance, or making a public speech — it is natural to fall into a pretentious, Latinized style. Tags like *a consideration which we should do well to bear in mind* or *a conclusion to which all of us would readily assent* will save many a sentence from coming down with a bump. By using stale metaphors, similes, and idioms, you save much mental effort, at the cost of leaving your meaning vague, not only for your reader but for yourself. This is the significance of mixed metaphors. The sole aim of a metaphor is to call up a visual image. When these images clash — as in *The Fascist octopus has sung its swan song, the jackboot is thrown into the melting pot* — it can be taken as certain that the writer is not seeing a mental image of the objects he is naming; in other words he is not really thinking. Look again at the examples I gave at the beginning of this essay. Professor Laski (1) uses five negatives in fifty-three words. One of these is superfluous, making nonsense of the whole passage, and in addition there is the slip — *alien* for akin — making further nonsense, and several avoidable pieces of clumsiness which increase the general vagueness. Professor Hogben (2) plays ducks and drakes with a battery which is able to write prescriptions, and, while disapproving of the everyday phrase *put up with*, is unwilling to look *egregious* up in the dictionary and see what it means; (3), if one takes an uncharitable attitude towards it, is simply meaningless: Probably one could work out its intended meaning by reading the whole of the article in which it occurs. In (4), the writer knows more or less what he wants to say, but an accumulation of stale phrases chokes him like tea leaves blocking a sink. In (5), words and meaning have almost parted company. People who write in this manner usually have a general emotional meaning — they dislike one thing and want to express solidarity with another — but they are not interested in the detail of what they are saying. A scrupulous writer, in every sentence that he writes, will ask himself at least four questions, thus: What am I trying to say? What words will express it? What image or idiom will make it clearer? Is this image fresh enough to have an effect? And he will probably ask himself two more: Could I put it more shortly? Have I said anything that is avoidably ugly? But you are not obliged to go to all this trouble. You can shirk it by simply throwing your mind open and letting the ready-made phrases come crowding in. They will construct your sentences for you — even think your thoughts for you, to a certain extent — and at need they will perform the important service of partially concealing your meaning even from yourself. It is at this point that the special connection between politics and the debasement of language becomes clear.

In our time it is broadly true that political writing is bad writing. Where it is not true, it will generally be found that the writer is some kind of rebel, expressing his private opinions and not a "party line." Orthodoxy, of whatever color, seems to demand a lifeless, imitative style. The political dialects to be found in pamphlets, leading articles, manifestos, White Papers, and the speeches of under-secretaries do, of course, vary from party to party, but they are all alike in that one almost never finds in them a fresh, vivid, home-made turn of speech. When one watches some tired hack on the platform mechanically repeating the familiar phrases — *bestial atrocities, iron heel, bloodstained tyranny, free peoples of the world, stand shoulder to shoulder* — one often has a curious feeling that one is not watching a live human being but some kind of dummy: a feeling which suddenly becomes stronger at moments when the light catches the speaker's spectacles and turns them into blank discs which seem to have no eyes behind them. And this is not altogether fanciful. A speaker who uses that kind of phraseology has gone some distance towards turning himself into a machine. The appropriate noises are coming out of his larynx, but his brain is not involved as it would be if he were choosing his words for himself. If the speech he is making is one that he is accustomed to make over and over again, he may be almost unconscious of what he is saying, as one is when one utters the responses in church. And this reduced state of consciousness, if not indispensable, is at any rate favorable to political conformity.

In our time, political speech and writing are largely the defense of the indefensible. Things like the continuance of British rule in India, the Russian purges and deportations, the dropping of the atom bombs on Japan, can indeed be defended, but only by arguments which are too brutal for most people to face, and which do not square with the professed aims of political parties. Thus political language has to consist largely of euphemism, question-begging, and sheer cloudy vagueness. Defenseless villages are bombarded from the air, the inhabitants driven out into the countryside, the cattle machine-gunned, the huts set on fire with incendiary bullets: This is called *pacification*. Millions of peasants are robbed of their farms and sent trudging along the roads with no more than they can carry: This is called *transfer of population* or *rectification of frontiers*. People are imprisoned for years without trial, or shot in the back of the neck or sent to die of scurvy in Arctic lumber camps:[4] This is called *elimination of unreliable elements*. Such phraseology is needed if one wants to name things without calling up mental pictures of them. Consider for instance some comfortable English professor defending Russian totalitari-

---

[4]*People . . . camps:* Though Orwell is decrying all totalitarian abuse of language, his examples are mainly pointed at the Soviet purges under Stalin. — EDS.

anism. He cannot say outright, "I believe in killing off your opponents when you get good results by doing so." Probably, therefore, he will say something like this:

"While freely conceding that the Soviet régime exhibits certain features which the humanitarian may be inclined to deplore, we must, I think, agree that a certain curtailment of the right to political opposition is an unavoidable concomitant of transitional periods, and that the rigors which the Russian people have been called upon to undergo have been amply justified in the sphere of concrete achievement."

The inflated style is itself a kind of euphemism. A mass of Latin words falls upon the facts like soft snow, blurring the outlines and covering up all the details. The great enemy of clear language is insincerity. When there is a gap between one's real and one's declared aims, one turns as it were instinctively to long words and exhausted idioms, like a cuttlefish squirting out ink. In our age there is no such thing as "keeping out of politics." All issues are political issues, and politics itself is a mass of lies, evasions, folly, hatred, and schizophrenia. When the general atmosphere is bad, language must suffer. I should expect to find — this is a guess which I have not sufficient knowledge to verify — that the German, Russian, and Italian languages have all deteriorated in the last ten or fifteen years, as a result of dictatorship.

But if thought corrupts language, language can also corrupt thought. A bad usage can spread by tradition and imitation, even among people who should and do know better. The debased language that I have been discussing is in some ways very convenient. Phrases like *a not unjustifiable assumption, leaves much to be desired, would serve no good purpose, a consideration which we should do well to bear in mind,* are a continuous temptation, a packet of aspirins always at one's elbow. Look back through this essay, and for certain you will find that I have again and again committed the very faults I am protesting against. By this morning's post I have received a pamphlet dealing with conditions in Germany. The author tells me that he "felt impelled" to write it. I open it at random, and here is almost the first sentence that I see: "(The Allies) have an opportunity not only of achieving a radical transformation of Germany's social and political structure in such a way as to avoid a nationalistic reaction in Germany itself, but at the same time of laying the foundations of a co-operative and unified Europe." You see, he "feels impelled" to write — feels, presumably, that he has something new to say — and yet his words, like cavalry horses answering the bugle, group themselves automatically into the familiar dreary pattern. This invasion of one's mind by ready-made phrases (*lay the foundations, achieve a radical transformation*) can only be prevented if one is constantly on guard against them, and every such phrase anaesthetizes a portion of one's brain.

I said earlier that the decadence of our language is probably curable. Those who deny this would argue, if they produced an argument at all, that language merely reflects existing social conditions, and that we cannot influence its development by any direct tinkering with words and constructions. So far as the general tone or spirit of a language goes, this may be true, but it is not true in detail. Silly words and expressions have often disappeared, not through any evolutionary process but owing to the conscious action of a minority. Two recent examples were *explore every avenue* and *leave no stone unturned,* which were killed by the jeers of a few journalists. There is a long list of flyblown metaphors which could similarly be got rid of if enough people would interest themselves in the job; and it should also be possible to laugh the *not un-* formation out of existence,[5] to reduce the amount of Latin and Greek in the average sentence, to drive out foreign phrases and strayed scientific words, and, in general, to make pretentiousness unfashionable. But all these are minor points. The defense of the English language implies more than this, and perhaps it is best to start by saying what it does *not* imply.

To begin with it has nothing to do with archaism, with the salvaging of obsolete words and turns of speech, or with the setting up of a "standard English" which must never be departed from. On the contrary, it is especially concerned with the scrapping of every word or idiom which has outworn its usefulness. It has nothing to do with correct grammar and syntax, which are of no importance so long as one makes one's meaning clear, or with the avoidance of Americanisms, or with having what is called a "good prose style." On the other hand it is not concerned with fake simplicity and the attempt to make written English colloquial. Nor does it even imply in every case preferring the Saxon word to the Latin one, though it does imply using the fewest and shortest words that will cover one's meaning. What is above all needed is to let the meaning choose the word, and not the other way about. In prose, the worst thing one can do with words is to surrender to them. When you think of a concrete object, you think wordlessly, and then, if you want to describe the thing you have been visualizing you probably hunt about till you find the exact words that seem to fit. When you think of something abstract you are more inclined to use words from the start, and unless you make a conscious effort to prevent it, the existing dialect will come rushing in and do the job for you, at the expense of blurring or even changing your meaning. Probably it is better to put off using words as long as possible and get one's meaning as clear as one can through pictures or sensations. Afterwards one can choose — not simply *accept* — the phrases that will best cover the meaning, and then switch round and decide what impression one's words are likely to make on another person. This last effort of the mind cuts out all stale or mixed images, all prefabricated phrases, needless repetitions, and humbug and vagueness generally. But one can often be in doubt about the effect of a word or a phrase, and one needs

---

[5]One can cure oneself of the *not un-* formation by memorizing this sentence: *A not un-black dog was chasing a not unsmall rabbit across a not ungreen field.* — ORWELL'S NOTE.

rules that one can rely on when instinct fails. I think the following rules will cover most cases:

(i) Never use a metaphor, simile, or other figure of speech which you are used to seeing in print.
(ii) Never use a long word where a short one will do.
(iii) If it is possible to cut a word out, always cut it out.
(iv) Never use the passive where you can use the active.
(v) Never use a foreign phrase, a scientific word, or a jargon word if you can think of an everyday English equivalent.
(vi) Break any of these rules sooner than say anything outright barbarous.

These rules sound elementary, and so they are, but they demand a deep change in attitude in anyone who has grown used to writing in the style now fashionable. One could keep all of them and still write bad English, but one could not write the kind of stuff that I quoted in those five specimens at the beginning of this article.

I have not here been considering the literary use of language, but merely language as an instrument for expressing and not for concealing or preventing thought. Stuart Chase and others have come near to claiming that all abstract words are meaningless, and have used this as a pretext for advocating a kind of political quietism. Since you don't know what Fascism is, how can you struggle against Fascism? One need not swallow such absurdities as these, but one ought to recognize that the present political chaos is connected with the decay of language, and that one can probably bring about some improvement by starting at the verbal end. If you simplify your English, you are freed from the worst follies of orthodoxy. You cannot speak any of the necessary dialects, and when you make a stupid remark its stupidity will be obvious, even to yourself. Political language — and with variations this is true of all political parties, from Conservatives to Anarchists — is designed to make lies sound truthful and murder respectable, and to give an appearance of solidity to pure wind. One cannot change this all in a moment, but one can at least change one's own habits, and from time to time one can even, if one jeers loudly enough, send some worn-out and useless phrase — some *jackboot, Achilles' heel, hotbed, melting pot, acid test, veritable inferno,* or other lump of verbal refuse — into the dustbin where it belongs.

The Reader's Presence

1. Look carefully at Orwell's five examples of bad prose. Would you have identified this writing as "bad" writing if you had come across it in the course of your college reading? What do the examples remind you of?

2. What characteristics of Orwell's own writing demonstrate his six rules for writing good prose? Can you identify five examples in which Orwell practices what he preaches? Can you identify any moments when he seems to slip?

3. Note that Orwell does not provide *positive* examples of political expression. Why do you think this is so? Is Orwell implying that all political language — regardless of party or position — is corrupt? From this essay can you infer his political philosophy? Explain your answer.

55

Walker Percy

The Loss of the Creature

Walker Percy (1916-1990) received his M.D. in 1941 and began a career practicing and teaching medicine shortly thereafter. However, as a resident physician he contracted tuberculosis, and the disease changed the course of his life. During his recovery he read extensively in literature, philosophy, and theology, and this reading program became the basis for a new career of reading and writing. His first novel, The Moviegoer *(1961), won a National Book Award. He wrote a number of other novels, including* The Thanatos Syndrome *(1987), as well as works of nonfiction such as* Lost in the Cosmos *(1983) and* The Message in the Bottle *(1975). The latter work contains the essay "The Loss of the Creature."*

Percy believed in the ability of writing "to affirm people, to affirm the reader." In an age dominated by scientific ways of thinking, Percy once said, people are left asking questions that science cannot answer. "But the role of a novelist, or an artist, for that matter, is to tell the truth, and to convey a kind of knowledge which cannot be conveyed by science, or psychology, or newspapers."

I

Every explorer names his island Formosa, beautiful. To him it is beautiful because, being first, he has access to it and can see it for what it is. But to no one else is it ever as beautiful — except the rare man who manages to recover it, who knows that it has to be recovered.

Garcia López de Cárdenas discovered the Grand Canyon and was amazed at the sight. It can be imagined: One crosses miles of desert, breaks through the mesquite, and there it is at one's feet. Later the government set the place aside as a national park, hoping to pass along to millions the experience of Cárdenas. Does not one see the same sight from the Bright Angel Lodge that Cárdenas saw?

The assumption is that the Grand Canyon is a remarkably interesting and beautiful place and that if it had a certain value P for Cárdenas, the same value P may be transmitted to any number of sightseers — just as Banting's discovery of insulin can be transmitted to any number of diabetics. A counterinfluence is at work, however, and it would be nearer the truth to say that if the place is seen by a million sightseers, a single sightseer does not receive value P but a millionth part of value P.

It is assumed that since the Grand Canyon has the fixed interest value P, tours can be organized for any number of people. A man in Boston decides to spend his vacation at the Grand Canyon. He visits his travel bureau, looks at the folder, signs up for a two-week tour. He and his family take the tour, see the Grand Canyon, and return to Boston. May we say that this man has seen the Grand Canyon? Possibly he has. But it is more likely that what he has done is the one sure way not to see the canyon.

Why is it almost impossible to gaze directly at the Grand Canyon under these circumstances and see it for what it is — as one picks up a strange object from one's back yard and gazes directly at it? It is almost impossible because the Grand Canyon, the thing as it is, has been appropriated by the symbolic complex which has already been formed in the sightseer's mind. Seeing the canyon under approved circumstances is seeing the symbolic complex head on. The thing is no longer the thing as it confronted the Spaniard; it is rather that which has already been formulated — by picture postcard, geography book, tourist folders, and the words *Grand Canyon*. As a result of this preformulation, the source of the sightseer's pleasure undergoes a shift. Where the wonder and delight of the Spaniard arose from his penetration of the thing itself, from a progressive discovery of depths, patterns, colors, shadows, etc., now the sightseer measures his satisfaction *by the degree to which the canyon conforms to the preformed complex.* If it does so, if it looks just like the postcard, he is pleased; he might even say, "Why it is every bit as beautiful as a picture postcard!" He feels he has not been cheated. But if it does not conform, if the colors are somber, he will not be able to see it directly; he will only be conscious of the disparity between what it is and what it is supposed to be. He will say later that he was unlucky in not being there at the right time. The highest point, the term of the sightseer's satisfaction, is not the sovereign discovery of the thing before him; it is rather the measuring up of the thing to the criterion of the preformed symbolic complex.

Seeing the canyon is made even more difficult by what the sightseer does when the moment arrives, when sovereign knower confronts the thing to be known. Instead of looking at it, he photographs it. There is no confrontation at all. At the end of forty years of preformulation and with the Grand Canyon yawning at his feet, what does he do? He waives his right of seeing and knowing and records symbols for the next forty years.

For him there is no present; there is only the past of what has been formulated and seen and the future of what has been formulated and not seen.
The present is surrendered to the past and the future.

The sightseer may be aware that something is wrong. He may simply
be bored; or he may be conscious of the difficulty: that the great thing
yawning at his feet somehow eludes him. The harder he looks at it, the
less he can see. It eludes everybody. The tourist cannot see it; the bellboy
at the Angel Lodge cannot see it: For him it is only one side of the space
he lives in, like one wall of a room; to the ranger it is a tissue of everyday
signs relevant to his own prospects — the blue haze down there means
that he will probably get rained on during the donkey ride.

How can the sightseer recover the Grand Canyon? He can recover it
in any number of ways, all sharing in common the stratagem of avoiding
the approved confrontation of the tour and the Park Service.

It may be recovered by leaving the beaten track. The tourist leaves the
tour, camps in the back country. He arises before dawn and approaches
the South Rim through a wild terrain where there are no trails and no
railed-in lookout points. In other words, he sees the canyon by avoiding
all the facilities for seeing the canyon. If the benevolent Park Service hears
about this fellow and thinks he has a good idea and places the following
notice in the Bright Angel Lodge: *Consult ranger for information on getting off the beaten track* — the end result will only be the closing of another access to the canyon.

It may be recovered by a dialectical movement which brings one back   10
to the beaten track but at a level above it. For example, after a lifetime of
avoiding the beaten track and guided tours, a man may deliberately seek
out the most beaten track of all, the most commonplace tour imaginable:
He may visit the canyon by a Greyhound tour in the company of a party
from Terre Haute — just as a man who has lived in New York all his life
may visit the Statue of Liberty. (Such dialectical savorings of the *familiar*
as the familiar are, of course, a favorite stratagem of *The New Yorker*
magazine.) The thing is recovered from familiarity by means of an exercise in familiarity. Our complex friend stands behind the fellow tourists at
the Bright Angel Lodge and sees the canyon through them and their
predicament, their picture taking and busy disregard. In a sense, he ex-
ploits his fellow tourists; he stands on their shoulders to see the canyon.

Such a man is far more advanced in the dialectic than the sightseer
who is trying to get off the beaten track — getting up at dawn and approaching the canyon through the mesquite. This stratagem is, in fact, for
our complex man the weariest, most beaten track of all.

It may be recovered as a consequence of a breakdown of the symbolic
machinery by which the experts present the experience to the consumer.
A family visits the canyon in the usual way. But shortly after their arrival,
the park is closed by an outbreak of typhus in the south. They have the
canyon to themselves. What do they mean when they tell the home folks
of their good luck: "We had the whole place to ourselves"? How does

one see the thing better when the others are absent? Is looking like sucking: the more lookers, the less there is to see? They could hardly answer,
but by saying this they testify to a state of affairs which is considerably
more complex than the simple statement of the schoolbook about the
Spaniard and the millions who followed him. It is a state in which there is
a complex distribution of sovereignty, of zoning.

It may be recovered in a time of national disaster. The Bright Angel
Lodge is converted into a rest home, a function that has nothing to do
with the canyon a few yards away. A wounded man is brought in. He re-
gains consciousness; there outside his window is the canyon.

The most extreme case of access by privilege conferred by disaster is
the Huxleyan[1] novel of the adventures of the surviving remnant after the
great wars of the twentieth century. An expedition from Australia lands
in Southern California and heads east. They stumble across the Bright
Angel Lodge, now fallen into ruins. The trails are grown over, the guard
rails fallen away, the dime telescope at Battleship Point rusted. But there
is the canyon, exposed at last. Exposed by what? By the decay of those facilities which were designed to help the sightseer.

This dialectic of sightseeing cannot be taken into account by plan-   15
ners, for the object of the dialectic is nothing other than the subversion of
the efforts of the planners.

The dialectic is not known to objective theorists, psychologists, and
the like. Yet it is quite well known in the fantasy-consciousness of the
popular arts. The devices by which the museum exhibit, the Grand
Canyon, the ordinary thing, is recovered have long since been stumbled
upon. A movie shows a man visiting the Grand Canyon. But the
moviemaker knows something the planner does not know. He knows
that one cannot take the sight frontally. The canyon must be approached
by the stratagems we have mentioned: the Inside Track, the Familiar Re-
visited, the Accidental Encounter. Who is the stranger at the Bright Angel
Lodge? Is he the ordinary tourist from Terre Haute that he makes himself
out to be? He is not. He has another objective in mind, to revenge his
wronged brother, counterespionage, etc. By virtue of the fact that he has
other fish to fry, he may take a stroll along the rim after supper and then
we can see the canyon through him. The movie accomplishes its purpose
by concealing it. Overtly the characters (the American family marooned
by typhus) and we the onlookers experience pity for the sufferers, and the
family experience anxiety for themselves; covertly and in truth they are
the happiest of people and we are happy through them, for we have the
canyon to ourselves. The movie cashes in on the recovery of sovereignty
through disaster. Not only is the canyon now accessible to the remnant:
The members of the remnant are now accessible to each other; a whole
new ensemble of relations becomes possible — friendship, love, hatred,

---

[1]*Huxleyan:* A reference to the English novelist Aldous Huxley (1894–1963), best
known for his anti-utopian novel, *Brave New World* (1932). — EDS.

clandestine sexual adventures. In a movie when a man sits next to a woman on a bus, it is necessary either that the bus break down or that the woman lose her memory. (The question occurs to one: Do you imagine there are sightseers who see sights just as they are supposed to? a family who live in Terre Haute, who decide to take the canyon tour, who go there, see it, enjoy it immensely, and go home content? a family who are entirely innocent of all the barriers, zones, losses of sovereignty I have been talking about? Wouldn't most people be sorry if Battleship Point fell into the canyon, carrying all one's fellow passengers to their death, leaving one alone on the South Rim? I cannot answer this. Perhaps there are such people. Certainly a great many American families would swear they had no such problems, that they came, saw, and went away happy. Yet it is just these families who would be happiest if they had gotten the Inside Track and been among the surviving remnant.)

It is now apparent that as between the many measures which may be taken to overcome the opacity, the boredom, of the direct confrontation of the thing or creature in its citadel of symbolic investiture, some are less authentic than others. That is to say, some stratagems obviously serve other purposes than that of providing access to being — for example, various unconscious motivations which it is not necessary to go into here.

Let us take an example in which the recovery of being is ambiguous, where it may under the same circumstances contain both authentic and unauthentic components. An American couple, we will say, drives down into Mexico. They see the usual sights and have a fair time of it. Yet they are never without the sense of missing something. Although Taxco and Cuernavaca are interesting and picturesque as advertised, they fall short of "it." What do the couple have in mind by "it"? What do they really hope for? What sort of experience could they have in Mexico so that upon their return, they would feel that "it" had happened? We have a clue: Their hope has something to do with their own role as tourists in a foreign country and the way in which they conceive this role. It has something to do with other American tourists. Certainly they feel that they are very far from "it" when, after traveling five thousand miles, they arrive at the plaza in Guanajuato only to find themselves surrounded by a dozen other couples from the Midwest.

Already we may distinguish authentic and unauthentic elements. First, we see the problem the couple faces and we understand their efforts to surmount it. The problem is to find an "unspoiled" place. "Unspoiled" does not mean only that a place is left physically intact; it means also that it is not encrusted by renown and by the familiar (as in Taxco), that it has not been discovered by others. We understand that the couple really want to get at the place and enjoy it. Yet at the same time we wonder if there is not something wrong in their dislike of their compatriots. Does access to the place require the exclusion of others?

Let us see what happens.   20

The couple decide to drive from Guanajuato to Mexico City. On the

way they get lost. After hours on a rocky mountain road, they find themselves in a tiny valley not even marked on the map. There they discover
an Indian village. Some sort of religious festival is going on. It is apparently a corn dance in supplication of the rain god.

The couple know at once that this is "it." They are entranced. They
spend several days in the village, observing the Indians and being themselves observed with friendly curiosity.

Now may we not say that the sightseers have at last come face to face
with an authentic sight, a sight which is charming, quaint, picturesque,
unspoiled, and that they see the sight and come away rewarded? Possibly
this may occur. Yet it is more likely that what happens is a far cry indeed
from an immediate encounter with being, that the experience, while masquerading as such, is in truth a rather desperate impersonation. I use the
word *desperate* advisedly to signify an actual loss of hope.

The clue to the spuriousness of their enjoyment of the village and the
festival is a certain restiveness in the sightseers themselves. It is given expression by their repeated exclamations that "this is too good to be true,"
and by their anxiety that it may not prove to be so perfect, and finally by
their downright relief at leaving the valley and having the experience in
the bag, so to speak — that is, safely embalmed in memory and movie
film.

What is the source of their anxiety during the visit? Does it not mean   25
that the couple are looking at the place with a certain standard of performance in mind? Are they like Fabre,[2] who gazed at the world about him
with wonder, letting it be what it is; or are they not like the overanxious
mother who sees her child as one performing, now doing badly, now
doing well? The village is their child and their love for it is an anxious
love because they are afraid that at any moment it might fail them.

We have another clue in their subsequent remark to an ethnologist
friend. "How we wished you had been there with us! What a perfect
goldmine of folkways! Every minute we would say to each other, if only
you were here! You must return with us." This surely testifies to a generosity of spirit, a willingness to share their experience with others, not
at all like their feelings toward their fellow Iowans on the plaza at
Guanajuato!

I am afraid this is not the case at all. It is true that they longed for
their ethnologist friend, but it was for an entirely different reason. They
wanted him, not to share their experience, but to certify their experience
as genuine.

"This is it" and "Now we are really living" do not necessarily refer to
the sovereign encounter of the person with the sight that enlivens the
mind and gladdens the heart. It means that now at last we are having the

---

[2]*Fabre:* Jean-Henri Fabre (1823–1913), French scientist who wrote numerous books
on insects (*The Life of the Fly, The Life of the Spider,* etc.) based on careful observation. —
EDS.

acceptable experience. The present experience is always measured by a prototype, the "it" of their dreams. "Now I am really living" means that now I am filling the role of sightseer and the sight is living up to the prototype of sights. This quaint and picturesque village is measured by a Platonic ideal of the Quaint and the Picturesque.

Hence their anxiety during the encounter. For at any minute something could go wrong. A fellow Iowan might emerge from a 'dobe hut; the chief might show them his Sears catalogue. (If the failures are "wrong" enough, as these are, they might still be turned to account as rueful conversation pieces: "There we were expecting the chief to bring us a churinga and he shows up with a Sears catalogue!") They have snatched victory from disaster, but their experience always runs the danger of failure.

They need the ethnologist to certify their experience as genuine. This   30
is borne out by their behavior when the three of them return for the next corn dance. During the dance, the couple do not watch the goings-on; instead they watch the ethnologist! Their highest hope is that their friend should find the dance interesting. And if he should show signs of true absorption, an interest in the goings-on so powerful that he becomes oblivious of his friends — then their cup is full. "Didn't we tell you?" they say at last. What they want from him is not ethnological explanations; all they want is his approval.

What has taken place is a radical loss of sovereignty over that which is as much theirs as it is the ethnologist's. The fault does not lie with the ethnologist. He has no wish to stake a claim to the village; in fact, he desires the opposite: He will bore his friends to death by telling them about the village and the meaning of the folkways. A degree of sovereignty has been surrendered by the couple. It is the nature of the loss, moreover, that they are not aware of the loss, beyond a certain uneasiness. (Even if they read this and admitted it, it would be very difficult for them to bridge the gap in their confrontation of the world. Their consciousness of the corn dance cannot escape their consciousness of their consciousness, so that with the onset of the first direct enjoyment, their higher consciousness pounces and certifies: "Now you are doing it! Now you are really living!" and, in certifying the experience, sets it at nought.)

Their basic placement in the world is such that they recognize a priority of title of the expert over his particular department of being. The whole horizon of being is staked out by "them," the experts. The highest satisfaction of the sightseer (not merely the tourist but any layman seer of sights) is that his sight should be certified as genuine. The worst of this impoverishment is that there is no sense of impoverishment. The surrender of title is so complete that it never even occurs to one to reassert title. A poor man may envy the rich man, but the sightseer does not envy the expert. When a caste system becomes absolute, envy disappears. Yet the caste of layman-expert is not the fault of the expert. It is due altogether to the eager surrender of sovereignty by the layman so that he may take up the role not of the person but of the consumer.

I do not refer only to the special relation of layman to theorist. I refer to the general situation in which sovereignty is surrendered to a class of privileged knowers, whether these be theorists or artists. A reader may surrender sovereignty over that which has been written about, just as a consumer may surrender sovereignty over a thing which has been theorized about. The consumer is content to receive an experience just as it has been presented to him by theorists and planners. The reader may also be content to judge life by whether it has or has not been formulated by those who know and write about life. A young man goes to France. He too has a fair time of it, sees the sights, enjoys the food. On his last day, in fact as he sits in a restaurant in Le Havre waiting for his boat, something happens. A group of French students in the restaurant get into an impassioned argument over a recent play. A riot takes place. Madame la concierge joins in, swinging her mop at the rioters. Our young American is transported. This is "it." And he had almost left France without seeing "it"!

But the young man's delight is ambiguous. On the one hand, it is a pleasure for him to encounter the same Gallic temperament he had heard about from Puccini and Rolland.[3] But on the other hand, the source of his pleasure testifies to a certain alienation. For the young man is actually barred from a direct encounter with anything French excepting only that which has been set forth, authenticated by Puccini and Rolland — those who know. If he had encountered the restaurant scene without reading Hemingway, without knowing that the performance was so typically, charmingly French, he would not have been delighted. He would only have been anxious at seeing things get out of hand. The source of his delight is the sanction of those who know.

This loss of sovereignty is not a marginal process, as might appear   35
from my example of estranged sightseers. It is a generalized surrender of the horizon to those experts within whose competence a particular segment of the horizon is thought to lie. Kwakiutls are surrendered to Franz Boas;[4] decaying Southern mansions are surrendered to Faulkner and Tennessee Williams. So that, although it is by no means the intention of the expert to expropriate sovereignty — in fact he would not even know what sovereignty meant in this context — the danger of theory and consumption is a seduction and deprivation of the consumer.

In the New Mexican desert, natives occasionally come across strange-looking artifacts which have fallen from the skies and which are stenciled: *Return to U.S. Experimental Project, Alamogordo. Reward.* The finder returns the object and is rewarded. He knows nothing of the nature of the

[3]*Puccini:* Giacomo Puccini (1853–1924), the Italian composer of such well-known operas as *La Bohème* (1896) and *Madama Butterfly* (1904); *Rolland:* Romain Rolland (1866–1944), Nobel Prize–winning French novelist and dramatist. — Eds.

[4]*Boas:* Franz Boas (1858–1942), influential German-born American anthropologist who specialized in the languages of and cultures of Native Americans; in 1886 he began studying the Kwakiutl tribe of British Columbia. — Eds.

object he has found and does not care to know. The sole role of the native, the highest role he can play, is that of finder and returner of the mysterious equipment.

The same is true of the layman's relation to *natural* objects in a modern technical society. No matter what the object or event is, whether it is a star, a swallow, a Kwakiutl, a "psychological phenomenon," the layman who confronts it does not confront it as a sovereign person, as Crusoe confronts a seashell he finds on the beach. The highest role he can conceive himself as playing is to be able to recognize the title of the object, to return it to the appropriate expert, and have it certified as a genuine find. He does not even permit himself to see the thing — as Gerard Hopkins[5] could see a rock or a cloud or a field. If anyone asks him why he doesn't look, he may reply that he didn't take that subject in college (or he hasn't read Faulkner).

This loss of sovereignty extends even to oneself. There is the neurotic who asks nothing more of his doctor than that his symptoms should prove interesting. When all else fails, the poor fellow has nothing to offer but his own neurosis. But even this is sufficient if only the doctor will show interest when he says, "Last night I had a curious sort of dream; perhaps it will be significant to one who knows about such things. It seems I was standing in a sort of alley —" (I have nothing else to offer you but my own unhappiness. Please say that it, at least, measures up, that it is a *proper* sort of unhappiness.)

II

A young Falkland Islander walking along a beach and spying a dead dogfish and going to work on it with his jackknife has, in a fashion wholly unprovided in modern educational theory, a great advantage over the Scarsdale high-school pupil who finds the dogfish on his laboratory desk. Similarly the citizen of Huxley's *Brave New World* who stumbles across a volume of Shakespeare in some vine-grown ruins and squats on a potsherd to read it is in a fairer way of getting at a sonnet than the Harvard sophomore taking English Poetry II.

The educator whose business it is to teach students biology or poetry   40
is unaware of a whole ensemble of relations which exist between the student and the dogfish and between the student and the Shakespeare sonnet. To put it bluntly: A student who has the desire to get at a dogfish or a Shakespeare sonnet may have the greatest difficulty in salvaging the creature itself from the educational package in which it is presented. The great difficulty is that he is not aware that there is a difficulty; surely, he

---

[5]*Hopkins:* Gerard Manley Hopkins (1844–1889), English poet admired for his observations of nature and his innovative use of rhythm and metrics. — EDS.

thinks, in such a fine classroom, with such a fine textbook, the sonnet must come across! What's wrong with me?

The sonnet and the dogfish are obscured by two different processes. The sonnet is obscured by the symbolic package which is formulated not by the sonnet itself but by the *media* through which the sonnet is transmitted, the media which the educators believe for some reason to be transparent. The new textbook, the type, the smell of the page, the classroom, the aluminum windows and the winter sky, the personality of Miss Hawkins — these media which are supposed to transmit the sonnet may only succeed in transmitting themselves. It is only the hardiest and cleverest of students who can salvage the sonnet from this many-tissued package. It is only the rarest student who knows that the sonnet must be salvaged from the package. (The educator is well aware that something is wrong, that there is a fatal gap between the student's learning and the student's life: The student reads the poem, appears to understand it, and gives all the answers. But what does he recall if he should happen to read a Shakespeare sonnet twenty years later? Does he recall the poem or does he recall the smell of the page and the smell of Miss Hawkins?)

One might object, point out that Huxley's citizen reading his sonnet in the ruins and the Falkland Islander looking at his dogfish on the beach also receive them in a certain package. Yes, but the difference lies in the fundamental placement of the student in the world, a placement which makes it possible to extract the thing from the package. The pupil at Scarsdale High sees himself placed as a consumer receiving an experience-package; but the Falkland Islander exploring his dogfish is a person exercising the sovereign right of a person in his lordship and mastery of creation. He too could use an instructor and a book and a technique, but he would use them as his subordinates, just as he uses his jackknife. The biology student does not use his scalpel as an instrument; he uses it as a magic wand! Since it is a "scientific instrument," it should do "scientific things."

The dogfish is concealed in the same symbolic package as the sonnet. But the dogfish suffers an additional loss. As a consequence of this double deprivation, the Sarah Lawrence student who scores A in zoology is apt to know very little about a dogfish. She is twice removed from the dogfish, once by the symbolic complex by which the dogfish is concealed, once again by the spoliation of the dogfish by theory which renders it invisible. Through no fault of zoology instructors, it is nevertheless a fact that the zoology laboratory at Sarah Lawrence College is one of the few places in the world where it is all but impossible to see a dogfish.

The dogfish, the tree, the seashell, the American Negro, the dream, are rendered invisible by a shift of reality from concrete thing to theory which Whitehead[6] has called the fallacy of misplaced concreteness. It is

---

[6]*Whitehead:* Alfred North Whitehead (1861–1947), prominent British philosopher and mathematician. — EDS.

the mistaking of an idea, a principle, an abstraction, for the real. As a consequence of the shift, the "specimen" is seen as less real than the theory of the specimen. As Kierkegaard[7] said, once a person is seen as a specimen of a race or a species, at that very moment he ceases to be an individual. Then there are no more individuals but only specimens.

To illustrate: A student enters a laboratory which, in the pragmatic   45 view, offers the student the optimum conditions under which an educational experience may be had. In the existential view, however — that view of the student in which he is regarded not as a receptacle of experience but as a knowing being whose peculiar property it is to see himself as being in a certain situation — the modern laboratory could not have been more effectively designed to conceal the dogfish forever.

The student comes to his desk. On it, neatly arranged by his instructor, he finds his laboratory manual, a dissecting board, instruments, and a mimeographed list:

Exercise 22: Materials
1 dissecting board
1 scalpel
1 forceps
1 probe
1 bottle india ink and syringe
1 specimen of *Squalus acanthias*

The clue to the situation in which the student finds himself is to be found in the last item: 1 specimen of *Squalus acanthias*.

The phrase *specimen of* expresses in the most succinct way imaginable the radical character of the loss of being which has occurred under his very nose. To refer to the dogfish, the unique concrete existent before him, as a "specimen of *Squalus acanthias*" reveals by its grammar the spoliation of the dogfish by the theoretical method. This phrase, *specimen of*, example of, instance of, indicates the ontological status of the individual creature in the eyes of the theorist. The dogfish itself is seen as a rather shabby expression of an ideal reality, the species *Squalus acanthias*. The result is the radical devaluation of the individual dogfish. (The *reductio ad absurdum*[8] of Whitehead's shift is Toynbee's[9] employment of it in his historical method. If a gram of NaCl is referred to by the chemist as a "sample of" NaCl, one may think of it as such and not much is missed by the oversight of the act of being of this particular pinch of salt,

---

[7]*Kierkegaard:* Sören Aabye Kierkegaard (1813–1855), Danish philosopher and theologian. — EDS.

[8]*reductio ad absurdum:* "A reduction to absurdity" (Latin); the argumentative method by which one shows that a statement carried to its logical conclusion leads to an absurdity. — EDS.

[9]*Toynbee:* Arnold Toynbee (1889–1975), British historian who believed that civilizations were formed out of responses to adversity. — EDS.

but when the Jews, and the Jewish religion are understood as — in Toynbee's favorite phrase — a "classical example of" such and such a kind of
Voelkerwanderung,[10] we begin to suspect that something is being left
out.)

If we look into the ways in which the student can recover the dogfish
(or the sonnet), we will see that they have in common the stratagem of
avoiding the educator's direct presentation of the object as a lesson to be
learned and restoring access to sonnet and dogfish as beings to be known,
reasserting the sovereignty of knower over known.

In truth, the biography of scientists and poets is usually the story of   50
the discovery of the indirect approach, the circumvention of the educator's presentation — the young man who was sent to the *Technikum*[11]
and on his way fell into the habit of loitering in book stores and reading
poetry; or the young man dutifully attending law school who on the way
became curious about the comings and goings of ants. One remembers
the scene in *The Heart Is a Lonely Hunter*[12] where the girl hides in the
bushes to hear the Capehart in the big house play Beethoven. Perhaps she
was the lucky one after all. Think of the unhappy souls inside, who see
the record, worry about scratches, and most of all worry about whether
they are *getting it*, whether they are bona fide music lovers. What is the
best way to hear Beethoven: sitting in a proper silence around the Capehart or eavesdropping from an azalea bush?

However it may come about, we notice two traits of the second situation: (1) an openness of the thing before one — instead of being an exercise to be learned according to an approved mode, it is a garden of de-
lights which beckons to one; (2) a sovereignty of the knower — instead of
being a consumer of a prepared experience, I am a sovereign wayfarer, a
wanderer in the neighborhood of being who stumbles into the garden.

One can think of two sorts of circumstances through which the thing
may be restored to the person. (There is always, of course, the direct recovery: A student may simply be strong enough, brave enough, clever
enough to take the dogfish and the sonnet by storm, to wrest control of it
from the educators and the educational package.) First by ordeal: The
Bomb falls; when the young man recovers consciousness in the shambles
of the biology laboratory, there not ten inches from his nose lies the dogfish. Now all at once he can see it, directly and without let,[13] just as the
exile or the prisoner or the sick man sees the sparrow at his window in all
its inexhaustibility; just as the commuter who has had a heart attack sees
his own hand for the first time. In these cases, the simulacrum of every-

[10]*Voelkerwanderung:* Barbarian invasion (German). — EDS.

[11]*Technikum:* Technical school (German). — EDS.

[12]*The Heart Is a Lonely Hunter:* A 1940 novel by Carson McCullers (1917–1967). —
EDS.

[13]*let:* Hindrance. Used here in its older sense: The dogfish is seen "without hindrance."
Related to the tennis call "let ball," meaning the net interfered with (hindered) the ball. —
EDS.

dayness and of consumption has been destroyed by disaster; in the case of
the bomb, literally destroyed. Secondly, by apprenticeship to a great man:
One day a great biologist walks into the laboratory; he stops in front of
our student's desk; he leans over, picks up the dogfish, and ignoring instruments and procedure, probes with a broken fingernail into the little
carcass. "Now here is a curious business," he says, ignoring also the
proper jargon of the specialty. "Look here how this little duct reverses its
direction and drops into the pelvis. Now if you would look into a coela-
canth, you would see that it —" And all at once the student can see. The
technician and the sophomore who loves his textbooks are always offended by the genuine research man because the latter is usually a little
vague and always humble before the thing; he doesn't have much use for
the equipment or the jargon. Whereas the technician is never vague and
never humble before the thing; he holds the thing disposed of by the principle, the formula, the textbook outline; and he thinks a great deal of
equipment and jargon.

But since neither of these methods of recovering the dogfish is peda-
gogically feasible — perhaps the great man even less so than the Bomb —
I wish to propose the following educational technique which should
prove equally effective for Harvard and Shreveport High School. I propose that English poetry and biology should be taught as usual, but that
at irregular intervals, poetry students should find dogfishes on their desks
and biology students should find Shakespeare sonnets on their dissection
boards. I am serious in declaring that a Sarah Lawrence English major
who began poking about in a dogfish with a bobby pin would learn more
in thirty minutes than a biology major in a whole semester; and that the
latter upon reading on her dissecting board

> That time of year Thou may'st in me behold
> When yellow leaves, or none, or few, do hang
> Upon those boughs which shake against the cold —
> Bare ruin'd choirs where late the sweet birds sang.[14]

might catch fire at the beauty of it.

The situation of the tourist at the Grand Canyon and the biology student are special cases of a predicament in which everyone finds himself in
a modern technical society — a society, that is, in which there is a division between expert and layman, planner and consumer, in which experts
and planners take special measures to teach and edify the consumer. The
measures taken are measures appropriate to the consumer: The expert
and the planner *know* and *plan*, but the consumer *needs* and *experiences*.

There is a double deprivation. First, the thing is lost through its pack-   55
aging. The very means by which the thing is presented for consumption,
the very techniques by which the thing is made available as an item of

---

[14]The opening lines of William Shakespeare's Sonnet 73. — EDS.

need-satisfaction, these very means operate to remove the thing from the sovereignty of the knower. A loss of title occurs. The measures which the museum curator takes to present the thing to the public are self-liquidating. The upshot of the curator's efforts are not that everyone can see the exhibit but that no one can see it. The curator protests: Why are they so indifferent? Why do they even deface the exhibit? Don't they know it is theirs? But it is not theirs. It is his, the curator's. By the most exclusive sort of zoning, the museum exhibit, the park oak tree, is part of an ensemble, a package, which is almost impenetrable to them. The archaeologist who puts his find in a museum so that everyone can see it accomplishes the reverse of his expectations. The result of his action is that no one can see it now but the archaeologist. He would have done better to keep it in his pocket and show it now and then to strangers.

The tourist who carves his initials in a public place, which is theoretically "his" in the first place, has good reasons for doing so, reasons which the exhibitor and planner know nothing about. He does so because in his role of consumer of an experience (a "recreational experience" to satisfy a "recreational need") he knows that he is disinherited. He is deprived of his title over being. He knows very well that he is in a very special sort of zone in which his only rights are the rights of a consumer. He moves like a ghost through schoolroom, city streets, trains, parks, movies. He carves his initials as a last desperate measure to escape his ghostly role of consumer. He is saying in effect: I am not a ghost after all; I am a sovereign person. And he establishes title the only way remaining to him, by staking his claim over one square inch of wood or stone.

Does this mean that we should get rid of museums? No, but it means that the sightseer should be prepared to enter into a struggle to recover a sight from a museum.

The second loss is the spoliation of the thing, the tree, the rock, the swallow, by the layman's misunderstanding of scientific theory. He believes that the thing is *disposed of* by theory, that it stands in the Platonic relation of being a *specimen of* such and such an underlying principle. In the transmission of scientific theory from theorist to layman, the expectation of the theorist is reversed. Instead of the marvels of the universe being made available to the public, the universe is disposed of by theory. The loss of sovereignty takes this form: As a result of the science of botany, trees are not made available to every man. On the contrary. The tree loses its proper density and mystery as a concrete existent and, as merely another *specimen of* a species, becomes itself nugatory.

Does this mean that there is no use taking biology at Harvard and Shreveport High? No, but it means that the student should know what a fight he has on his hands to rescue the specimen from the educational package. The educator is only partly to blame. For there is nothing the educator can do to provide for this need of the student. Everything the educator does only succeeds in becoming, for the student, part of the educational package. The highest role of the educator is the maieutic role of

Socrates: to help the student come to himself not as a consumer of experience but as a sovereign individual.

The thing is twice lost to the consumer. First, sovereignty is lost: It is   60
theirs, not his. Second, it is radically devalued by theory. This is a loss
which has been brought about by science but through no fault of the scientist and through no fault of scientific theory. The loss has come about
as a consequence of the seduction of the layman by science. The layman
will be seduced as long as he regards beings as consumer items to be experienced rather than prizes to be won, and as long as he waives his sovereign rights as a person and accepts his role of consumer as the highest
estate to which the layman can aspire.

As Mounier said, the person is not something one can study and provide for; he is something one struggles for. But unless he also struggles for
himself, unless he knows that there is a struggle, he is going to be just
what the planners think he is.

The Reader's Presence

1. Percy's essay is about the difficulties of seeing the world around
   us. At the beginning of paragraph 5, Percy asks: "Why is it almost
   impossible to gaze directly at the Grand Canyon under these circumstances and see it for what it is . . . ? . . . because the Grand
   Canyon . . . has been appropriated by the symbolic complex
   which has already been formed in the sightseer's mind." What
   does he mean when he talks about "these circumstances" and "the
   symbolic complex"? In the next sentence Percy mentions seeing
   the Grand Canyon "under approved circumstances." What does
   he mean here, and how does he extend this point beyond seeing to
   learning as well?

2. What would you identify as Percy's overall purpose in writing this
   essay? Where does he announce this purpose? With what terms?
   Consider Percy's diction. From what sources does he derive his
   vocabulary? What, for example, do such terms as *authenticity, appropriation, expropriate,* and *sovereignty* have in common? What
   point of view does he express about each of these terms and, more
   generally, about seeing the world directly? How would you characterize Percy's tone of voice in this essay? Is it, for example, pessimistic or optimistic? What attitude does he finally express about
   the individual's ability to discover and/or recover the world?
   Where is this theme of discovery and recovery first introduced in
   the essay? How is it developed?

3. Outline the structure of Percy's essay. In what specific ways does
   the structure of the first part of his essay reappear in the second

part? What is the general subject of the second part, and how does
Percy connect it to the subject of the first part? Percy builds his
case for experiencing the world first-hand by exploring a series of
examples. Work through several of these examples, and show
how they not only support the points he makes but eventually
take on a life of their own. Consider, for example, the moment in
paragraph 53 when he announces: "I propose that English poetry
and biology should be taught as usual, but that at irregular intervals, poetry students should find dogfishes on their desks and biology students should find Shakespeare sonnets on their dissection
boards." What sense do you make of this statement? How does it
represent Percy's attitude about education? about seeing the
world?

56

Katha Pollitt

Why Boys Don't Play with Dolls

*Katha Pollitt was born in 1949 in New York City and is considered one of
the leading poets of her generation. Her 1982 collection of poetry,* Antarctic
Traveller, *won a National Book Critics Circle Award. Her poetry has received
many other honors and has appeared in the* Atlantic *and the* New Yorker. *Pollitt
also writes essays, and she has gained a reputation for incisive analysis and persuasive argument. She contributes reviews and essays to many national magazines
including the* Nation *and* Mother Jones. *"Why Boys Don't Play with Dolls" appeared in the* New York Times Magazine *in 1995. Her essays can also be found
in* Reasonable Creatures: Feminism and Society in American Culture at the End of
the Twentieth Century *(1994).*

*Pollitt thinks of writing poems and political essays as two distinct endeavors.
"What I want in a poem — one that I read or one that I write — is not an argument, it's not a statement, it has to do with language. . . . There isn't that much
political poetry that I find I even want to read once, and almost none that I would
want to read again."*

It's 28 years since the founding of NOW, and boys still like trucks
and girls still like dolls. Increasingly, we are told that the source of these
robust preferences must lie outside society — in prenatal hormonal influences, brain chemistry, genes — and that feminism has reached its natural
limits. What else could possibly explain the love of preschool girls for

party dresses or the desire of toddler boys to own more guns than Mark from Michigan.[1]

True, recent studies claim to show small cognitive differences between the sexes: he gets around by orienting himself in space, she does it by remembering landmarks. Time will tell if any deserve the hoopla with which each is invariably greeted, over the protests of the researchers themselves. But even if the results hold up (and the history of such research is not encouraging), we don't need studies of sex-differentiated brain activity in reading, say, to understand why boys and girls still seem so unalike.

The feminist movement has done much for some women, and something for every woman, but it has hardly turned America into a playground free of sex roles. It hasn't even got women to stop dieting or men to stop interrupting them.

Instead of looking at kids to "prove" that differences in behavior by sex are innate, we can look at the ways we raise kids as an index to how unfinished the feminist revolution really is, and how tentatively it is embraced even by adults who fully expect their daughters to enter previously male-dominated professions and their sons to change diapers.

I'm at a children's birthday party. "I'm sorry," one mom silently   5
mouths to the mother of the birthday girl, who has just torn open her present — Tropical Splash Barbie. Now, you can love Barbie or you can hate Barbie, and there are feminists in both camps. But *apologize* for Barbie? Inflict Barbie, against your own convictions, on the child of a friend you know will be none too pleased?

Every mother in that room had spent years becoming a person who had to be taken seriously, not least by herself. Even the most attractive, I'm willing to bet, had suffered over her body's failure to fit the impossible American ideal. Given all that, it seems crazy to transmit Barbie to the next generation. Yet to reject her is to say that what Barbie represents — being sexy, thin, stylish — is unimportant, which is obviously not true, and children know it's not true.

Women's looks matter terribly in this society, and so Barbie, however ambivalently, must be passed along. After all, there are worse toys. The Cut and Style Barbie styling head, for example, a grotesque object intended to encourage "hair play." The grown-ups who give that probably apologize, too.

How happy would most parents be to have a child who flouted sex conventions? I know a lot of women, feminists, who complain in a comical, eyeball-rolling way about their sons' passion for sports: the ruined weekends, obnoxious coaches, macho values. But they would not think of discouraging their sons from participating in this activity they find so foolish. Or do they? Their husbands are sports fans, too, and they like their husbands a lot.

---

[1]***Mark from Michigan:*** Mark Koernke, a former right-wing talk-show host who supports the militia movement's resistance to federal government. — EDS.

Could it be that even sports-resistant moms see athletics as part of manliness? That if their sons wanted to spend the weekend writing up their diaries, or reading, or baking, they'd find it disturbing? Too antisocial? Too lonely? Too gay?

Theories of innate differences in behavior are appealing. They let parents off the hook — no small recommendation in a culture that holds moms, and sometimes even dads, responsible for their children's every misstep on the road to bliss and success. 10

They allow grown-ups to take the path of least resistance to the dominant culture, which always requires less psychic effort, even if it means more actual work: just ask the working mother who comes home exhausted and nonetheless finds it easier to pick up her son's socks than make him do it himself. They let families buy for their children, without *too* much guilt, the unbelievably sexist junk that the kids, who have been watching commercials since birth, understandably crave.

But the thing the theories do most of all is tell adults that the *adult* world — in which moms and dads still play by many of the old rules even as they question and fidget and chafe against them — is the way it's supposed to be. A girl with a doll and a boy with a truck "explain" why men are from Mars and women are from Venus, why wives do housework and husbands just don't understand.

The paradox is that the world of rigid and hierarchical sex roles evoked by determinist theories is already passing away. Three-year-olds may indeed insist that doctors are male and nurses female, even if their own mother is a physician. Six-year-olds know better. These days, something like half of all medical students are female, and male applications to nursing school are inching upward. When tomorrow's 3-year-olds play doctor, who's to say how they'll assign the roles?

With sex roles, as in every area of life, people aspire to what is possible, and conform to what is necessary. But these are not fixed, especially today. Biological determinism may reassure some adults about their present, but it is feminism, the ideology of flexible and converging sex roles, that fits our children's future. And the kids, somehow, know this.

That's why, if you look carefully, you'll find that for every kid who fits 15 a stereotype, there's another who's breaking one down. Sometimes it's the same kid — the boy who skateboards *and* takes cooking in his afterschool program; the girl who collects stuffed animals *and* A-pluses in science.

Feminists are often accused of imposing their "agenda" on children. Isn't that what adults always do, consciously and unconsciously? Kids aren't born religious, or polite, or kind, or able to remember where they put their sneakers. Inculcating these behaviors, and the values behind them, is a tremendous amount of work, involving many adults. We don't have a choice, really, about *whether* we should give our children messages about what it means to be male and female — they're bombarded with them from morning till night.

The question, as always, is what do we want those messages to be?

The Reader's Presence

1. Pollitt notes in her opening paragraph that "it's 28 years since the founding of NOW, and boys still like trucks and girls still like dolls." What does Pollitt identify as the competing theories to explain these differences between boys and girls? Which theory does Pollitt prefer, and how does she express her support of it?

2. How would you characterize Pollitt's stance toward today's parents? What are some of the reasons Pollitt gives to explain parents' choices and actions? What incentives does she offer, implicitly or explicitly, for them to alter those choices and behaviors?

3. As you reread the essay, consider carefully the role of the media in upholding the status quo with regard to differentiated roles for girls and boys. As you develop a response to this question, examine carefully both the media directed principally to children and the media targeted at adults. In the latter category, for instance, Pollitt refers to the media version of scientific research studies into gender differences (paragraph 2) and alludes to popular books that discuss the differences between men and women, such as *Men Are from Mars, Women Are from Venus* and *You Just Don't Understand* (paragraph 12). Drawing on Pollitt's essay and on your own experience, identify — and discuss — the specific social responsibilities you would like to see America's mass media take more seriously.

57

Richard Selzer

The Language of Pain

Richard Selzer (b. 1928), like Anton Chekhov, W. Somerset Maugham, and William Carlos Williams, is that rare breed of doctor who is also a writer. Both careers cross-pollinated each other for a long time, and Selzer has said that "a doctor walks in and out of a dozen stories a day. It is irresistible to write them down." Before leaving medicine to write full-time, Richard Selzer spent fifteen years teaching surgery at the Yale School of Medicine and running a private surgical practice. Selzer has published several books, including Confessions of a Knife *(1979),* Letters to a Young Doctor *(1982), and* Raising the Dead *(Selzer's 1993 account of his near-death experience from Legionnaires' disease and his slow recovery). His essays have appeared in* Harper's, Esquire, Antaeus, *and many* other magazines. "The Language of Pain" appeared in the Wilson Quarterly in 1994.

In an interview, Selzer explained how he taught himself to write: "The way a surgeon would prepare himself for a new operation was exactly the way I approached the task of writing, and since words were to be my new instruments, I had to learn them, learn how to use them, put them down in order, suture them together, as it were." He continued by comparing the scalpel and the pen: "Since the new instrument I had picked up was a pen, I immediately felt at home with it. It's about the same size as a scalpel, has the same circumference, if you will. It sits differently in the hand; nevertheless it was an instrument so like the one I had used all my life that it was not a stranger, but a distant cousin of the knife. In the use of each, something is shed. When you use the scalpel, blood is shed; when you use the pen, ink is shed. I liked holding the instrument in my hand rather than typing because I was able to watch the word issuing from the end of my hand, as though it were a secretion from my own body, something that I had not only made, but done, as if it were coming out of me. And that intimacy with the word as it was being written became very important to me."

Why do you write so much about pain? they ask me. To give it a name, I reply. And I am not sure what I mean. I try again: In October, when the leaves have fallen from the trees, you can see farther into the forest. Now do you see? No? Well, what is your notion of pain? Pain is fire, a ravening, insatiable thing that insists upon utter domination; it is the occasion when the body reasserts itself over the mind; the universe contracts about the part that hurts; if the pain is not placated with analgesics, it will devour the whole organism. Only then will it too be snuffed. Still, pain is revelatory; in the blaze of it, one might catch a glimpse of the truth about human existence.

It was the poet Rilke who wrote that the events of the body cannot be rendered in language. Surely this is so with pain as with its opposite, orgasm. These extremes of sensation remain beyond the power of language to express. Say that a doctor is examining a patient who is in pain. The doctor needs to know the exact location of the pain and its nature. Is the pain sharp or dull? Steady or intermittent? Does it throb or pulse? Is it stabbing? A heavy pressure? Crampy? Does it burn? Sting? All these questions the doctor asks of the patient. But there is no wholly adequate way for the sufferer to portray his pain other than to cry out. In order to convey his pain, the patient, like the writer, must resort to metaphor, simile, imagery: "You want to know what it's like? It's as if someone were digging in my ribs with a shovel." "It feels as if there's a heavy rock on my chest."

Years ago as a doctor and more recently as a writer, I declared my faith in images — the human fact placed near a superhuman mystery, even if both are illusions of the senses. Diagnosis, like writing, calls for the imagination and the skill to discover things not seen, things that hide themselves under the shadow of natural objects. It is the purpose of the writer and the doctor to fix these unseen phenomena in words, thereby presenting to plain sight what did not actually exist until he arrived. Much as a footprint hides beneath a foot until a step is taken.

By using metaphor and imagery, the patient brings the doctor into a state of partial understanding of his pain. In order to express it fully, he would have to cry out in a language that is incomprehensible to anyone else. This language of pain has no consonants, but consists only of vowels: ow! aiee! oy! oh! These are the sounds the sufferer makes, each punctuated by grunts, hiccoughs, sobs, moans, gasps. It is a self-absorbed language that might have been the first ever uttered by prehistoric man. Perhaps it was learned from animals. These howled vowels have the eloquence of the wild, the uncivilized, the atavistic. Comprehension is instantaneous, despite the absence of what we call words. It is a mode of expression beyond normal language. Nor could it be made more passionate or revelatory by the most gifted writer. Not even by Shakespeare.

But what is the purpose of these cries of pain? Wouldn't silence be as   5
eloquent? For one thing, the loud, unrestrained pouring forth of vowels is useful in attracting the attention of anyone within earshot who might come to the assistance of the sufferer. Vowels carry farther than consonants and are easier to mouth, requiring only the widely opened jaws, without the more complex involvement of tongue, teeth, and palate that the speaking of consonants requires. Giuseppe Verdi[1] knew that and made his librettist write lines full of easily singable vowels and diphthongs. It is the sung vowel that carries to the last row of La Scala.[2] The consonants are often elided or faked by the singers who know that consonants are confined to the immediate vicinity of the stage and are altogether less able to be infused with emotive force. It comes as no surprise that the greatest opera singers are in the Italian repertoire — Italian, a language dripping with vowels and in which there is scarcely a word that does not end in one. "Mille serpi divoranmi il petto," sings the anguished Alfredo upon learning of the sacrifice made by his beloved Violetta in *La Traviata*. The translation — "A thousand snakes are eating my breast" — simply won't do.

One purpose of these cries of pain, then, might be to summon help, to notify fellow members of the tribe of one's predicament so that they will come running. But I think there is more to it than that. For the sufferer, these outcries have a kind of magical property of their own, offering not only an outlet for the emotion but a means of letting out the pain. Hollering, all by itself, gives a measure of relief. To cry out ow! or aiee! requires that the noise be carried away from the body on a cloud of warm, humid air that had been within the lungs of the sufferer. The expulsion of this air, and with it, the sound, is an attempt to exteriorize the

---

[1] *Giuseppe Verdi* (1813–1901): An Italian composer of opera, whose works such as *La Traviata* (1853) remain among the most popular of all operas. — EDS.

[2] *La Scala:* The famous 18th century opera house in Milan, Italy, where many of Verdi's operas had their premieres. — EDS.

pain, to dispossess oneself of it, as though the vowels of pain were, in some magical way, the pain itself. It is not hard to see why the medieval church came to believe that a body, writhing and wracked and uttering unearthly, primitive cries, was possessed by devils. Faced with such a sufferer, authorities of the church deemed exorcism both necessary and compassionate.

"Go ahead and holler," says the nurse to the patient. "You'll feel better. Don't hold it in." It is wise advice that has been passed down through the millennia of human suffering. But even these ululations cannot really convey to the reader what the sufferer is feeling, for they are not literature. To write *ow* or *aiee* on a page is not an art. The language of pain, then, is the most exclusive of tongues, spoken and understood by an elite of one. Hearing it, we shudder, out of sympathy for the sufferer, but just as much out of the premonition that each of us shall know this language in our time. Our turn will come. It is a fact that within moments of having been relieved of this pain, sufferers are no longer fluent in this language. They have already forgotten it, all but an inkling or two, and are left with a vague sense of dread, a recollection that the pain was awful, a fear that it might return.

In lieu of language, the doctor seems to diagnose by examining the body and its secretions — urine, blood, spinal fluid — and by using a number of ingenious photographic instruments. A last resort would be the laying open of the body for exploratory surgery. Fifty years ago, it was to the corpse that the doctor went for answers. Ironic that life should have provided concealment and death be revelatory. Even now, it is only in the autopsy room that the true courage of the human body is apparent, the way it carries on in the face of all odds: arteriosclerosis, calculi, pulmonary fibrosis, softening of the brain. And still the body goes on day after day, bearing its burdens, if not jauntily, at least with acceptance and obedience until at last it must sink beneath the weight of those burdens and come to the morgue where its faithfulness can be observed and granted homage.

There is about pain that which exhilarates even as it appalls, as Emily Dickinson has written. Pain is the expression of the dark underside of the body. As such, the sight of the wound, the sound of the outcry it produces, stir the imagination in a way that pleasure never can. We are drawn to the vicinity of pain by the hint of danger and death, as much as by the human desire to compare our fortunate state to that of those unluckier. Then, too, there is the undeniable relation of pain and beauty, brought to artistic flower during the Renaissance and later by the 19th-century Romantic poets. It is the writhen Christ slumping on the cross that is the emblematic vision of pain from which has come the word *excruciating*. It was Christianity that first tried to wrest meaning from pain. "Offer it up," say the Catholics, as if suffering, boredom, or even annoyance were currency to be paid on the road to sanctity. Simone Weil turned affliction into evidence of God's tenderness. Affliction is love, she wrote. To some, this represents a perversion of the senses, not unlike the masochism that welcomes pain as pleasure. To welcome pain as an approach to God is to negate mercy as proof of His love for human beings. It is an elite band of saints that can achieve ecstasy through pain. Even Christ cried out from the cross: Why hast thou forsaken me?

The artist who would prettify or soften the Crucifixion is missing the point. The aim was to kill horribly and to subject the victim to the utmost humiliation. It involved a preliminary whipping with the dreaded Roman *flagrum,* a leather whip with three tails. At the tip of each tail there was tied a small dumbbell-shaped weight of iron or bone. With each lash of the whip, the three bits dug into the flesh. The victim was tied or chained to a post and two centurions stood on either side. The wounds extended around to the chest and abdomen. Profuse bleeding ensued. Then the condemned was beaten on the face with reeds so that his face was bruised, his nose broken. To ensure maximum humiliation, the cross was set up in a public place or on an elevation of land such as the hill of Calvary. In the case of Jesus, in order to deride him further and to mock his appellation of King of the Jews, a crown of thorns was placed on his brow. Jesus, weakened by a night of fasting and prayer, as well as by the flogging and the blood loss, was not able to carry his own cross to the place of execution as the punishment required. Simon of Cyrene did it for him. Then Jesus' hands were nailed to the crosspiece, which was raised and set into a groove on the vertical piece. The height was approximately seven and a half feet. At one point, a Roman soldier hurled a spear that opened the wound in his side. To add to Christ's suffering, he was assailed by extreme thirst, as is usual in instances of severe blood loss and dehydration. Once, a disciple was able to reach up and give him a drink through a hollow straw. Death came slowly, from shock, both traumatic and hypovolemic, and from respiratory failure due to the difficulty of expelling air from the lungs in the upright and suspended position when the diaphragm does not easily rise.

I wonder whether man has not lost the ability to withstand pain, what with the proliferation of pain-killing drugs and anesthetic agents. Physical pain has become a once-in-a-while experience for most of the industrialized world. Resistance to pain, like any other unused talent, atrophies, leaving one all the more vulnerable. What to a woman of the late 19th century might have been bearable is insupportable to her great-great-granddaughter. Still, for some, chronic pain is an old adversary, one whose cunning can be, if not negated, at least balanced, by hypnosis, acupuncture, biofeedback, exercise, practice of ritual, and other techniques not well understood. There is that pain which cannot be relieved by any means short of death and which must be lived *against*. Such was the pain of Montaigne who, tortured by bladder stones that occluded the outflow of urine, had to write *against* the pain. On the other hand, Aristotle was unable to philosophize because of his toothache.

Is the pain experienced in a dream any less than the pain experienced while awake? I think it is not. I have a dream that has recurred many times: I am standing alone in the middle of a great empty amphitheater. It is midnight and the scene is bathed in bluish moonlight. The city is European; Milan, I think. At either end of the amphitheater, a statue stands upon a marble pedestal. One is of Caesar wearing a toga and holding up a sheaf of wheat. The other is a great marble tiger. All at once, the tiger stirs, rises to its feet, then rears as if to spring. Yes, it is about to spring! I turn to run in the opposite direction, toward Caesar, but my feet are heavy, so heavy that I cannot lift them. Already I can sense the nearness of the beast, feel its hot breath upon my neck. A moment later there is the pressure of its fangs in the supraclavicular fossa on the left — and again in the nape. And there is pain. I look down to see my shadow bearing the burden of the huge cat on its back. At that instant, I wake up. My heart is pounding; I am gasping; the bed is drenched with sweat. And in the left side of my neck there is pain as if that area had been badly bruised. The pressure of my fingers intensifies the pain that I have brought back with me from the dream, the pain that has crossed from dream to wakefulness. Slowly, my pulse returns to normal; the pain dissipates and I begin to regain a measure of equanimity. But only a measure, for I know that I shall have this dream again, that its pain and horror will be undiminished.

Lying there in the ecstasy of having survived, I wonder: Had I died in the jaws of that tiger, died of a heart attack or sudden arrhythmia, died of fright, doubtless my next of kin would comfort themselves with the knowledge that I had died peacefully in my sleep. "He died the death of a righteous man," they would murmur to one another. Had I the breath for it, I would sit up in the coffin and shout: "No! No! It wasn't like that at all!"

Pain. The very word carries its own linguistic baggage, coming down to us from the Latin *poena* — punishment. It is the penalty for misdeeds; one is placed in a penitentiary and made to do penance. The pain of childbirth was inflicted upon Eve for her act of disobedience, and from her upon all those who follow. Immediately upon delivery of her young, a woman begins to distance herself from the pain which she experienced during childbirth. Such forgetfulness is nature's way of assuring the continuation of the human race.

It is at the very least curious that Milton in *Paradise Lost*, reinventing the birth of Eve, has the masculine effrontery to anesthetize Adam during the rib resection. In Book 8, Adam has just finished telling God of his loneliness, his sense of incompleteness. God has promised the solution. Here is Adam describing the birth of Eve:

> Dazzl'd and spent, sunk down, [I] sought repair
> Of sleep, which instantly fell on me, call'd

15

By Nature as in aid, and clos'd mine eyes.
Mine eyes he clos'd, but op'n left the Cell
Of Fancy my internal sight, by which
Abstract as in a trance methought I saw,
Though sleeping where I lay, and saw the shape
Still glorious before whom awake I stood;
Who stooping op'n'd my left side, and took
From thence a Rib, with cordial spirits warm,
And Life-blood streaming fresh; wide was the wound,
But suddenly with flesh fill'd up and heal'd:
The Rib he form'd and fashion'd with his hands;
Under his forming hands a Creature grew,
Manlike, but different sex, so lovely fair. . . .

Milton's act of anesthesia is evidence, if any further were needed, that a man cannot imagine, nor can he admit, the pain of giving birth. It is outside the precincts of his understanding. Had *Paradise Lost* been written by a woman, doubtless Adam would have felt each and every twinge.

Many is the writer who has tried to make the reader *feel* pain in a fictional character. I among them, in this passage from an essay on the subject of kidney stones:

Whom the stone grips is transformed in one instant from man to shark; and like the shark that must remain in perpetual motion, fins and tail moving lest it sink to terrible black depths of pressure, so the harborer of stone writhes and twists, bending and unbending in ceaseless turmoil. Now he straightens, stretches his limbs, only to draw them upon his trunk the next moment and fling his body from one side to the other, finding ease in neither. From between his teeth come sounds so primitive as to trigger the skin to creep. He shudders and vomits as though to cast forth the rock that grinds within. He would sell his birthright, forfeit his honor, his name, even kill to rid him of it. He toils in bed, pronged and spiked from within. Seed pearls of sweat break upon his face. In a moment his hair is heavy with it. His fingers scrabble against the bed, the wall, his own flesh to tear relief from these surfaces. But it does not pass. The impacted stone cannot push through into the lake, and from there voided. Like some terrible work of art, insatiable it screams to be extruded, let out into the air and light so as to be seen, touched, venerated. Never mind that the very act of deliverance will tear apart its creator.

At last he is able to force a few drops of bloody urine and the pain subsides. The stone has fallen away from the point of impaction, washed loose into the bladder. He is miraculously free of the pain. It is no less than being touched by the hand of God. Still, he is afraid to move lest the lightest change of position should sink the craggy thing into some new part and the hell be reenacted. It has not passed. It lies within him yet, malevolent, scorpioid. It is only a matter of time before the beast will rise again.

Does this convey the pain of colic? I think it does not. No matter the metaphor and simile, all the pomp of language falls short in transmitting pain, that private corporeal experience, to the reader. It is beyond the reach of words; it is subverbal. Just as well, for to convey pain exactly would be to relive it and to suffer anew. In the matter of pain, it is better to experience it metaphorically than to know it directly.

The Reader's Presence

1. Selzer opens this essay by admitting, first, that he is not sure why pain fascinates him, and second, that pain is indescribable. In the first paragraph he is asked, "Why do you write so much about pain?" What reasons can you infer from his essay? In the second paragraph he states, "These extremes of sensation remain beyond the power of language to express." In what specific ways does this statement of the futility of his essay-writing project turn out to be true or false? What techniques does he employ in his quest to describe the indescribable?

2. At various points in his essay, Selzer (a doctor himself) compares the writer to the suffering patient and to the doctor. In what specific ways does the writer resemble each? What is the significance of comparing the writer to both halves of the patient-doctor pair? Which of the author's insights in this essay have their source in his profession, and which have their source in his experience as a human being who occasionally suffers pain himself?

3. The title of this essay is "The Language of Pain." Focus for a moment on the word *language*. What kinds of language does Selzer use in this essay? Where do you find evidence of his medical vocabulary? What is the effect of that vocabulary in these contexts? Where does his language become more literary? With what effect(s)? Similarly, look at the disciplines Selzer draws on in the course of this essay. Where is his perspective more scientific, and where does it draw on the humanities? Does he privilege one at the expense of the other? If so, why, and to what effect? If not, what is gained by the conjunction of these disciplinary perspectives?

58

Deborah Tannen

Gender Gap in Cyberspace

Deborah Tannen (b. 1945) is University Professor of Linguistics at George-town University. She writes both for general and academic readers, and her many books and articles have been popular with both audiences. Her specialty is socio-linguistics, and in her research Tannen focuses on the different ways men and women communicate — and on the difficulties of communicating across gender. Her 1990 book You Just Don't Understand: Women and Men in Conversation *was a best-seller and has been translated into eighteen languages. In spite of the title, the book was written with the faith that men and women can understand each other better if they take the time to consider how gender influences commu-nication styles. More recently she published* Gender and Conversational Interac-tion *(1993),* Gender and Discourse *(1994) and* Talking from 9 to 5: Women and Men in the Workplace *(1995). "Gender Gap in Cyberspace" appeared in* Newsweek *in 1994.*

Reflecting on the experience of writing, Tannen says, "Writing is hard to begin — it's much easier to return a phone call or check E-mail for messages — but once underway, if it's going well, it's joy, exhilaration, intense pleasure."

I was a computer pioneer, but I'm still something of a novice. That paradox is telling.

I was the second person on my block to get a computer. The first was my colleague Ralph. It was 1980. Ralph got a Radio Shack TRS-80, I got a used Apple II+. He helped me get started and went on to become a maven, reading computer magazines, hungering for the new technology he read about, and buying and mastering it as quickly as he could afford. I hung on to old equipment far too long because I dislike giving up what I'm used to, fear making the wrong decision about what to buy, and re-sent the time it takes to install and learn a new system.

My first Apple came with videogames; I gave them away. Playing games on the computer didn't interest me. If I had free time I'd spend it talking on the telephone to friends.

Ralph got hooked. His wife was often annoyed by the hours he spent at his computer and the money he spent upgrading it. My marriage had no such strains — until I discovered E-mail. Then I got hooked. E-mail draws me the same way the phone does: it's a souped-up conversation.

E-mail deepened my friendship with Ralph. Though his office was   5 next to mine, we rarely had extended conversations because he is shy. Face to face he mumbled so, I could barely tell he was speaking. But when we both got on E-mail, I started receiving long, self-revealing messages; we poured our hearts out to each other. A friend discovered that E-mail opened up that kind of communication with her father. He would never talk much on the phone (as her mother would), but they have become close since they both got on line.

Why, I wondered, would some men find it easier to open up on E-mail? It's a combination of the technology (which they enjoy) and the obliqueness of the written word, just as many men will reveal feelings in dribs and drabs while riding in the car or doing something, which they'd never talk about sitting face to face. It's too intense, too bearing-down on them, and once you start you have to keep going. With a computer in between, it's safer.

It was on E-mail, in fact, that I described to Ralph how boys in groups often struggle to get the upper hand whereas girls tend to maintain an appearance of cooperation. And he pointed out that this explained why boys are more likely to be captivated by computers than girls are. Boys are typically motivated by a social structure that says if you don't dominate you will be dominated. Computers, by their nature, balk; you type a perfectly appropriate command and it refuses to do what it should. Many boys and men are incited by this defiance: "I'm going to whip this into line and teach it who's boss! I'll get it to do what I say!" (and if they work hard enough, they always can). Girls and women are more likely to respond, "This thing won't cooperate. Get it away from me!"

Although no one wants to think of herself as "typical" — how much nicer to be *sui generis*[1] — my relationship to my computer is — gulp — fairly typical for a woman. Most women (with plenty of exceptions) aren't excited by tinkering with the technology, grappling with the challenge of eliminating bugs or getting the biggest and best computer. These dynamics appeal to many men's interest in making sure they're on the top side of the inevitable who's-up-who's-down struggle that life is for them. E-mail appeals to my view of life as a contest for connections to others. When I see that I have fifteen messages, I feel loved.

I once posted a technical question on a computer network for linguists and was flooded with long dispositions, some pages long. I was staggered by the generosity and the expertise, but wondered where these guys found the time — and why all the answers I got were from men.

Like coed classrooms and meetings, discussions on E-mail networks   10

---

[1] *Sui generis:* Latin, meaning "of its own kind," "unique." — EDS.

tend to be dominated by male voices, unless they're specifically women-only, like single-sex schools. On line, women don't have to worry about getting the floor (you just send a message when you feel like it), but, according to linguists Susan Herring and Laurel Sutton, who have studied this, they have the usual problems of having their messages ignored or attacked. The anonymity of public networks frees a small number of men to send long, vituperative, sarcastic messages that many other men either can tolerate or actually enjoy, but that turn most women off.

The anonymity of networks leads to another sad part of the E-mail story: there are men who deluge women with questions about their appearance and invitations to sex. On college campuses, as soon as women students log on, they are bombarded by references to sex, like going to work and finding pornographic posters adorning the walls.

Most women want one thing from a computer — to work. This is significant counterevidence to the claim that men want to focus on information while women are interested in rapport. That claim I found was often true in casual conversation, in which there is no particular information to be conveyed. But with computers, it is often women who are more focused on information, because they don't respond to the challenge of getting equipment to submit.

Once I had learned the basics, my interest in computers waned. I use it to write books (though I never mastered having it do bibliographies or tables of contents) and write checks (but not balance my checkbook). Much as I'd like to use it to do more, I begrudge the time it would take to learn.

Ralph's computer expertise costs him a lot of time. Chivalry requires that he rescue novices in need, and he is called upon by damsel novices far more often than knaves. More men would rather study the instruction booklet than ask directions, as it were, from another person. "When I do help men," Ralph wrote (on E-mail, of course), "they want to be more involved. I once installed a hard drive for a guy, and he wanted to be there with me, wielding the screwdriver and giving his own advice where he could." Women, he finds, usually are not interested in what he's doing; they just want him to get the computer to the point where they can do what they want.

Which pretty much explains how I managed to be a pioneer without   15
becoming an expert.

The Reader's Presence

1. The author makes her case about gender and computers mainly through the use of two instances — her own and her friend Ralph's experiences. To what extent does this allow her to assume that they are representative of men and women in general? Where

do you find Tannen's generalization strongest? Where do you think she is weakest?

2. Tannen's essay focuses more on electronic mail than on computer technology. Does her enthusiasm for E-mail contradict her point about women and computers? How does she confront this problem?

3. A built-in problem with making comparisons — even if we want to be neutral — is that the writer often favors one side over another. As a reader, do you find that Tannen is neutral in her assessment of gender, or do you think she believes that one sex is superior to another in its relation to computer technology? Explain what elements of her comparison most affect your response.

59

Sallie Tisdale

A Weight That Women Carry

Sallie Tisdale was born in 1957 in California and has lived in Oregon for many years. A nurse by profession, her medical training has shaped her career as a writer. Her first books, The Sorcerer's Apprentice: Tales of the Modern Hospital *(1986) and* Harvest Moon: Portrait of a Nursing Home *(1987), discuss the complex ethical issues that complicate the relationship between caregivers and patients. Tisdale takes up the subject of health from quite a different angle in her book* Lot's Wife: Salt and the Human Condition *(1988). This book uses the issue of salt consumption to reflect on the interconnections between people and the natural environment they inhabit. Tisdale's thoughts on these matters are further developed in* Stepping Westward: The Long Search for Home in the Pacific Northwest *(1991). More recently she has published* Talk Dirty to Me: An Intimate Philosophy of Sex *(1994). Tisdale has taught writing at the University of Portland and the University of California at Davis. "A Weight That Women Carry" appeared in* Harper's *in 1993.*

Tisdale has said, "My love of writing is at its heart a love of language and words, the joy of the successful search for the proper word, the joy of the process of expression itself. . . . I have a particular love for the prose form, which can contain everything we imagine."

I don't know how much I weigh these days, though I can make a good guess. For years I'd known that number, sometimes within a quarter pound, known how it changed from day to day and hour to hour. I want to weigh myself now; I lean toward the scale in the next room, imagine standing there, lining up the balance. But I don't do it. Going this long, starting to break the scale's spell — it's like waking up suddenly sober.

By the time I was sixteen years old I had reached my adult height of five feet six inches and weighed 164 pounds. I weighed 164 pounds before and after a healthy pregnancy. I assume I weigh about the same now; nothing significant seems to have happened to my body, this same old body I've had all these years. I usually wear a size 14, a common clothing size for American women. On bad days I think my body looks lumpy and misshapen. On my good days, which are more frequent lately, I think I look plush and strong; I think I look like a lot of women whose bodies and lives I admire.

I'm not sure when the word "fat" first sounded pejorative to me, or when I first applied it to myself. My grandmother was a petite woman, the only one in my family. She stole food from other people's plates, and hid the debris of her own meals so that no one would know how much she ate. My mother was a size 14, like me, all her adult life; we shared clothes. She fretted endlessly over food scales, calorie counters, and diet books. She didn't want to quit smoking because she was afraid she would gain weight, and she worried about her weight until she died of cancer five years ago. Dieting was always in my mother's way, always there in the conversations above my head, the dialogue of stocky women. But I was strong and healthy and didn't pay too much attention to my weight until I was grown.

It probably wouldn't have been possible for me to escape forever. It doesn't matter that whole human epochs have celebrated big men and women, because the brief period in which I live does not; since I was born, even the voluptuous calendar girl has gone. Today's models, the women whose pictures I see constantly, unavoidably, grow more minimal by the day. When I berate myself for not looking like — whomever I think I should look like that day, I don't really care that no one looks like that. I don't care that Michelle Pfeiffer doesn't look like the photographs I see of Michelle Pfeiffer, I want to look — think I should look — like the photographs. I want her little miracles; the makeup artists, photographers, and computer imagers who can add a mole, remove a scar, lift the breasts, widen the eyes, narrow the hips, flatten the curves. The final product is what I see, have seen my whole adult life. And I've seen this: Even when big people become celebrities, their weight is constantly remarked upon and scrutinized; their successes seem always to be *in spite of* their weight. I thought my successes must be, too.

I feel myself expand and diminish from day to day, sometimes from hour to hour. If I tell someone my weight, I change in their eyes: I become bigger or smaller, better or worse, depending on what that number, my weight, means to them. I know many men and women, young and old, gay and straight, who look fine, whom I love to see and whose faces and forms I cherish, who despise themselves for their weight. For their ordinary, human bodies. They and I are simply bigger than we think we should be. We always talk about weight in terms of gains and losses, and

5

How does she use totem here?
What lens?

don't wonder at the strangeness of the words. In trying always to lose weight, we've lost hope of simply being seen for ourselves.

My weight has never actually affected anything — it's never seemed to mean anything one way or the other to how I lived. Yet for the last ten years I've felt quite bad about it. After a time, the number on the scale became my totem, more important than my experience — it was layered, metaphorical, *metaphysical,* and it had bewitching power. I thought if I could change that number I could change my life.

In my mid-twenties I started secretly taking diet pills. They made me feel strange, half-crazed, vaguely nauseated. I lost about twenty-five pounds, dropped two sizes, and bought new clothes. I developed rituals and taboos around food, ate very little, and continued to lose weight. For a long time afterward I thought it only coincidental that with every passing week I also grew more depressed and irritable.

I could recite the details, but they're remarkable only for being so common. I lost more weight until I was rather thin, and then I gained it all back. It came back slowly, pound by pound, in spite of erratic and melancholy and sometimes frantic dieting, dieting I clung to even though being thin had changed nothing, had meant nothing to my life except that I was thin. Looking back, I remember blinding moments of shame and lightning-bright moments of clearheadedness, which inevitably gave way to rage at the time I'd wasted — rage that eventually would become, once again, self-disgust and the urge to lose weight. So it went, until I weighed exactly what I'd weighed when I began.

I used to be attracted to the sharp angles of the chronic dieter — the caffeine-wild, chain-smoking, skinny women I see sometimes. I considered them a pinnacle not of beauty but of will. Even after I gained back my weight, I wanted to be like that, controlled and persevering, live that underfed life so unlike my own rather sensual and disorderly existence. I felt I should always be dieting, for the dieting of it; dieting had become a rule, a given, a constant. Every ordinary value is distorted in this lens. I felt guilty for not being completely absorbed in my diet, for getting distracted, for not caring enough all the time. The fat person's character flaw is a lack of narcissism. She's let herself go.

So I would begin again — and at first it would all seem so . . . easy.   10
Simple arithmetic. After all, 3,500 calories equal one pound of fat — so the books and articles by the thousands say. I would calculate how long it would take to achieve the magic number on the scale, to succeed, to win. All past failures were suppressed. If 3,500 calories equal one pound, all I needed to do was cut 3,500 calories out of my intake every week. The first few days of a new diet would be colored with a sense of control — organization and planning, power over the self. Then the basic futile misery took over.

I would weigh myself with foreboding, and my weight would determine how went the rest of my day, my week, my life. When 3,500 calories didn't equal one pound lost after all, I figured it was my body that was flawed, not the theory. One friend, who had tried for years to lose weight following prescribed diets, made what she called "an amazing discovery." The real secret to a diet, she said, was that you had to be willing to be hungry *all the time.* You had to eat even less than the diet allowed.

I believed that being thin would make me happy. Such a pernicious, enduring belief. I lost weight and wasn't happy and saw that elusive happiness disappear in a vanishing point, requiring more — more self-disgust, more of the misery of dieting. Knowing all that I know now about the biology and anthropology of weight, knowing that people naturally come in many shapes and sizes, knowing that diets are bad for me and won't make me thin — sometimes none of this matters. I look in the mirror and think: Who am I kidding? *I've got to do something about myself.* Only then will this vague discontent disappear. Then I'll be loved. *Thin = Love?*

For ages humans believed that the body helped create the personality, from the humors of Galen to W. H. Sheldon's somatotypes. Sheldon distinguished between three templates — endomorph, mesomorph, and ectomorph — and combined them into hundreds of variations with physical, emotional, and psychological characteristics. When I read about weight now, I see the potent shift in the last few decades: The modern culture of dieting is based on the idea that the personality creates the body. Our size must be in some way voluntary, or else it wouldn't be subject to change. A lot of my misery over my weight wasn't about how I looked at all. I was miserable because I believed *I* was bad, not my body. I felt truly reduced then, reduced to being just a body and nothing more.

Fat is perceived as an *act* rather than a thing. It is antisocial, and curable through the application of social controls. Even the feminist revisions of dieting, so powerful in themselves, pick up the theme: the hungry, empty heart; the woman seeking release from sexual assault, or the man from the loss of the mother, through food and fat. Fat is now a symbol not of the personality but of the soul — the cluttered, neurotic, and immature soul.

Fat people eat for "mere gratification," I read, as though no one else   15
does. Their weight is *intentioned,* they simply eat "too much," their flesh is lazy flesh. Whenever I went on a diet, eating became cheating. One pretzel was cheating. Two apples instead of one was cheating — a large potato instead of a small, carrots instead of broccoli. It didn't matter which diet I was on; diets have failure built in, failure is in the definition. Every substitution — even carrots for broccoli — was a triumph of desire over will. When I dieted, I didn't feel pious just for sticking to the rules. I felt condemned for the act of eating itself, as though my hunger were never normal. My penance was to not eat at all.

My attitude toward food became quite corrupt. I came, in fact, to subconsciously believe food itself was corrupt. Diet books often distinguish between "real" and "unreal" hunger, so that *correct* eating is hollowed out, unemotional. A friend of mine who thinks of herself as a compulsive eater says she feels bad only when she eats for pleasure. "Why?" I ask, and she says, "Because I'm eating food I don't need." A few years ago I might have admired that. Now I try to imagine a world where we eat only food we need, and it seems inhuman. I imagine a world devoid of holidays and wedding feasts, wakes and reunions, a unique shared joy. "What's wrong with eating a cookie because you like cookies?" I ask her, and she hasn't got an answer. These aren't rational beliefs, any more than the unnecessary pleasure of ice cream is rational. Dieting presumes pleasure to be an insignificant, or at least malleable, human motive.

I felt no joy in being thin — it was just work, something I had to do. But when I began to gain back the weight, I felt despair. I started reading about the "recidivism" of dieting. I wondered if I had myself to blame not only for needing to diet in the first place but for dieting itself, the weight inevitably regained. I joined organized weight-loss programs, spent a lot of money, listened to lectures I didn't believe on quack nutrition, ate awful, processed diet foods. I sat in groups and applauded people who'd lost a half pound, feeling smug because I'd lost a pound and a half. I felt ill much of the time, found exercise increasingly difficult, cried often. And I thought that if I could only lose a little weight, everything would be all right.

When I say to someone, "I'm fat," I hear, "Oh, no! You're not *fat*! You're just —" What? Plump? Big-boned? Rubenesque? I'm just *not thin*. That's crime enough. I began this story by stating my weight. I said it all at once, trying to forget it and take away its power; I said it to be done being scared. Doing so, saying it out loud like that, felt like confessing a mortal sin. I have to bite my tongue not to seek reassurance, not to defend myself, not to plead. I see an old friend for the first time in years, and she comments on how much my fourteen-year-old son looks like me — "except, of course, he's not chubby." "Look who's talking," I reply, through clenched teeth. This pettiness is never far away; concern with my weight evokes the smallest, meanest parts of me. I look at another woman passing on the street and think, "At least I'm not *that* fat."

Recently I was talking with a friend who is naturally slender about a mutual acquaintance who is quite large. To my surprise my friend reproached this woman because she had seen her eating a cookie at lunchtime. "How is she going to lose weight that way?" my friend wondered. When you are as fat as our acquaintance is, you are primarily, fundamentally, seen as fat. It is your essential characteristic. There are so many presumptions in my friend's casual, cruel remark. She assumes that this woman should diet all the time — and that she *can*. She pronounces whole categories of food to be denied her. She sees her unwillingness to behave in this externally prescribed way, even for a moment, as an act of rebellion. In his story "A Hunger Artist," Kafka writes that the guards of the fasting man were "usually butchers, strangely enough." Not so strange, I think.

I know that the world, even if it views me as overweight (and I'm not sure it really does), clearly makes a distinction between me and this very   20 big woman. I would rather stand with her and not against her, see her for all she is besides fat. But I know our experiences aren't the same. My thin friend assumes my fat friend is unhappy because she is fat: Therefore, if she loses weight she will be happy. My fat friend has a happy marriage and family and a good career, but insofar as her weight is a source of misery, I think she would be much happier if she could eat her cookie in peace, if people would shut up and leave her weight alone. But the world never lets up when you are her size; she cannot walk to the bank without risking insult. Her fat is seen as perverse bad manners. I have no doubt she would be rid of the fat if she could be. If my left-handedness invited the criticism her weight does, I would want to cut that hand off.

In these last several years I seem to have had an infinite number of conversations about dieting. They are really all the same conversation — weight is lost, then weight is gained back. This repetition finally began to sink in. Why did everyone sooner or later have the same experience? (My friend who had learned to be hungry all the time gained back all the weight she had lost and more, just like the rest of us.) Was it really our bodies that were flawed? I began reading the biology of weight more carefully, reading the fine print in the endless studies. There is, in fact, a preponderance of evidence disputing our commonly held assumptions about weight.

The predominant biological myth of weight is that thin people live longer than fat people. The truth is far more complicated. (Some deaths of fat people attributed to heart disease seem actually to have been the result of radical dieting.) If health were our real concern, it would be dieting we questioned, not weight. The current ideal of thinness has never been held before, except as a religious ideal; the underfed body is the martyr's body. Even if people can lose weight, maintaining an artificially low weight for any period of time requires a kind of starvation. Lots of people are naturally thin, but for those who are not, dieting is an unnatural act; biology rebels. The metabolism of the hungry body can change inalterably, making it ever harder and harder to stay thin. I think chronic dieting made me gain weight — not only pounds, but fat. This equation seemed so strange at first that I couldn't believe it. But the weight I put back on after losing was much more stubborn than the original weight. I had lost it by taking diet pills and not eating much of anything at all for quite a long time. I haven't touched the pills again, but not eating much of anything no longer works.

When Oprah Winfrey first revealed her lost weight, I didn't envy her. I thought, She's in trouble now. I knew, I was certain, she would gain it back; I believed she was biologically destined to do so. The tabloid headlines blamed it on a cheeseburger or mashed potatoes, they screamed OPRAH PASSES 200 POUNDS, and I cringed at her misery and how the world wouldn't let up, wouldn't leave her alone, wouldn't let her be anything else. How dare the world do this to anyone? I thought, and then realized I did it to myself.

The "Ideal Weight" charts my mother used were at their lowest acceptable-weight ranges in the 1950s, when I was a child. They were based on sketchy and often inaccurate actuarial evidence, using, for the most part, data on northern Europeans and allowing for the most minimal differences in size for a population of less than half a billion people. I never fit those weight charts, I was always just outside the pale. As an adult, when I would join an organized diet program, I accepted their version of my Weight Goal as gospel, knowing it would be virtually impossible to reach. But reach I tried; that's what one does with gospel. Only in the last few years have the weight tables begun to climb back into the world of the average human. The newest ones distinguish by gender, frame, and age. And suddenly I'm not off the charts anymore. I have a place.

A man who is attracted to fat women says, "I actually have less specific physical criteria than most men. I'm attracted to women who weigh 170 or 270 or 370. Most men are only attracted to women who weigh between 100 and 135. So who's got more of a fetish?" We look at fat as a problem of the fat person. Rarely do the tables get turned, rarely do we imagine that it might be the viewer, not the viewed, who is limited. What the hell is wrong with *them,* anyway? Do they believe everything they see on television?

My friend Phil, who is chronically and almost painfully thin, admitted that in his search for a partner he finds himself prejudiced against fat women. He seemed genuinely bewildered by this. I didn't jump to reassure him that such prejudice is hard to resist. What I did was bite my tongue at my urge to be reassured by him, to be told that I, at least, wasn't fat. That over the centuries humans have been inclined to prefer extra flesh rather than the other way around seems unimportant. All we see now tells us otherwise. Why does my kindhearted friend criticize another woman for eating a cookie when she would never dream of commenting in such a way on another person's race or sexual orientation or disability? Deprivation is the dystopian idea.

My mother called her endless diets "reducing plans." Reduction, the diminution of women, is the opposite of feminism, as Kim Chernin points out in *The Obsession.* Smallness is what feminism strives against, the smallness that women confront everywhere. All of women's spaces are smaller than those of men, often inadequate, without privacy. Furniture designers distinguish between a man's and a woman's chair, because women don't spread out like men. (A sprawling woman means only one thing.) Even our voices are kept down. By embracing dieting I was rejecting a lot I held dear, and the emotional dissonance that created just seemed like one more necessary evil.

A fashion magazine recently celebrated the return of the "well-fed" body; a particular model was said to be "the archetype of the new womanly woman . . . stately, powerful." She is a size 8. The images of women presented to us, images claiming so maliciously to be the images of women's whole lives, are not merely social fictions. They are *absolute*

fictions; they can't exist. How would it feel, I began to wonder, to cultivate my own real womanliness rather than despise it? Because it was my
fleshy curves I wanted to be rid of, after all. I dreamed of having a boy's
body, smooth, hipless, lean. A body rapt with possibility, a receptive
body suspended before the storms of maturity. A dear friend of mine,
nursing her second child, weeps at her newly voluptuous body. She loves
her children and hates her own motherliness, wanting to be unripened
again, to be a bud and not a flower.

Recently I've started shopping occasionally at stores for "large
women," where the smallest size is a 14. In department stores the size 12
and 14 and 16 clothes are kept in a ghetto called the Women's Department. (And who would want that, to be the size of a woman? We all
dream of being "juniors" instead.) In the specialty stores the clerks are
usually big women and the customers are big, too, big like a lot of
women in my life — friends, my sister, my mother and aunts. Not long
ago I bought a pair of jeans at Lane Bryant and then walked through the
mall to the Gap, with its shelves of generic clothing. I flicked through the
clearance rack and suddenly remembered the Lane Bryant shopping bag
in my hand and its enormous weight, the sheer heaviness of that brand
name shouting to the world. The shout is that I've let myself go. I still feel
like crying out sometimes: Can't I feel *satisfied?* But I am not supposed to
be satisfied, not allowed to be satisfied. My discontent fuels the market; I
need to be afraid in order to fully participate.

American culture, which has produced our dieting mania, does more   30
than reward <u>privation</u> and <u>acquisition</u> at the same time: it actually associates them with each other. Read the ads: the virtuous runner's reward is a
new pair of $180 running shoes. The fat person is thought to be impul-
sive, indulgent, but insufficiently or incorrectly greedy, greedy for the
wrong thing. The fat person lacks ambition. The young executive is complimented for being "hungry"; he is "starved for success." We are teased
with what we will *have* if we are willing to *have not* for a time. A dieting
friend, avoiding the food on my table, says, "I'm just dying for a bite of
that."

Dieters are the perfect consumers: They never get enough. The dieter
wistfully imagines food without substance, food that is not food, that
begs the definition of food, because food is the problem. Even the ways
we *don't eat* are based in class. The middle class don't eat in support
groups. The poor can't afford not to eat at all. The rich hire someone to
not eat with them in private. Dieting is an emblem of capitalism. It has a
venal heart.

The possibility of living another way, living without dieting, began to
take root in my mind a few years ago, and finally my second trip through
Weight Watchers ended dieting for me. This last time I just couldn't stand
the details, the same kind of details I'd seen and despised in other pro-

grams, on other diets: the scent of resignation, the weighing-in by the quarter pound, the before and after photographs of group leaders prominently displayed. Jean Nidetch, the founder of Weight Watchers, says, "Most fat people need to be hurt badly before they do something about themselves." She mocks every aspect of our need for food, of a person's sense of entitlement to food, of daring to *eat what we want*. Weight Watchers refuses to release its own weight charts except to say they make no distinction for frame size; neither has the organization ever released statistics on how many people who lose weight on the program eventually gain it back. I hated the endlessness of it, the turning of food into portions and exchanges, everything measured out, permitted, denied. I hated the very idea of "maintenance." Finally I realized I didn't just hate the diet. I was sick of the way I acted on a diet, the way I whined, my niggardly, penny-pinching behavior. What I liked in myself seemed to shrivel and disappear when I dieted. Slowly, slowly I saw these things. I saw that my pain was cut from whole cloth, imaginary, my own invention. I saw how much time I'd spent on something ephemeral, something that simply wasn't important, didn't matter. I saw that the real point of dieting is dieting — to not be done with it, ever.

I looked in the mirror and saw a woman, with flesh, curves, muscles, a few stretch marks, the beginnings of wrinkles, with strength and softness in equal measure. My body is the one part of me that is always, undeniably, here. To like myself means to be, literally, shameless, to be wanton in the pleasures of being inside a body. I feel *loose* this way, a little abandoned, a little dangerous. That first feeling of liking my body — not being resigned to it or despairing of change, but actually *liking* it — was tentative and guilty and frightening. It was alarming, because it was the way I'd felt as a child, before the world had interfered. Because surely I was wrong; I knew, I'd known for so long, that my body wasn't all right this way. I was afraid even to act as though I were all right: I was afraid that by doing so I'd be acting a fool.

For a time I was thin, I remember — and what I remember is nothing special — strain, a kind of hollowness, the same troubles and fears, and no magic. So I imagine losing weight again. If the world applauded, would this comfort me? Or would it only compromise whatever approval the world gives me now? What else will be required of me besides thinness? What will happen to me if I get sick, or lose the use of a limb, or, God forbid, grow old?

By fussing endlessly over my body, I've ceased to inhabit it. I'm trying to reverse this equation now, to trust my body and enter it again with a whole heart. I know more now than I used to about what constitutes "happy" and "unhappy," what the depths and textures of contentment are like. By letting go of dieting, I free up mental and emotional room. I have more space, I can move. The pursuit of another, elusive body, the body someone else says I should have, is a terrible distraction, a sidetracking that might have lasted my whole life long. By letting myself go, I go places.

35

Each of us in this culture, this twisted, <u>inchoate</u> culture, has to choose between battles: one battle is against the cultural ideal, and the other is against ourselves. I've chosen to stop fighting myself. Maybe I'm tilting at windmills; the cultural ideal is ever-changing, out of my control. It's not a cerebral journey, except insofar as I have to remind myself to stop counting, to stop thinking in terms of numbers. I know, even now that I've quit dieting and eat what I want, how many calories I take in every day. If I eat as I please, I eat a lot one day and very little the next; I skip meals and snack at odd times. My nourishment is good — as far as nutrition is concerned. I'm in much better shape than when I was dieting. I know that the small losses and gains in my weight over a period of time aren't simply related to the number of calories I eat. Someone asked me not long ago how I could possibly know my calorie intake if I'm not dieting (the implication being, perhaps, that I'm dieting secretly). I know because calorie counts and grams of fat and fiber are embedded in me. I have to work to *not* think of them, and I have to learn to not think of them in order to really live without fear.

When I look, *really* look, at the people I see every day on the street, I see a jungle of bodies, a community of women and men growing every which way like lush plants, growing tall and short and slender and round, hairy and hairless, dark and pale and soft and hard and glorious. Do I look around at the multitudes and think all these people — all these people who are like me and not like me, who are various and different — are not loved or lovable? Lately, everyone's body interests me, every body is desirable in some way. I see how muscles and skin shift with movement; I sense a cornucopia of flesh in the world. In the midst of it I am a little capacious and unruly.

I repeat with Walt Whitman, "I <u>dote</u> on myself . . . there is that lot of me, and all so luscious." I'm eating better, exercising more, feeling fine — and then I catch myself thinking, *Maybe I'll lose some weight.* But my mood changes or my attention is caught by something else, something deeper, more lingering. Then I can catch a glimpse of myself by accident and think only: That's me. My face, my hips, my hands. Myself.

The Reader's Presence

1. Tisdale's essay on the compulsion to diet in American society offers a revealing look at the prejudices, standards, and values associated with being "fat" and "thin" in contemporary life. Summarize the stereotypes Tisdale presents about "fat" people. How are they characterized by others, and especially by thin people? What assumptions about their personalities are embedded in these stereotypes? For example, what does Tisdale mean when she says: "Fat is perceived as an *act* rather than a thing" (paragraph 14)?

What, more generally, does she offer as the "preponderance of evidence disputing our commonly held assumptions about weight" (paragraph 21)?

2. What does Tisdale mean when, at the end of paragraph 5, she reminds her readers that "We always talk about weight in terms of gains and losses, and don't wonder at the strangeness of the words"? What is so "strange" about the language of dieting? What metaphors are most often used to talk about dieting? To what extent do irony and paradox play important roles in the ways in which Americans are encouraged to think and talk about dieting? Point to specific examples to support your response. At what point does Tisdale suggest that one's perspective on being fat is finally quite relative, a matter of point of view? How convincing do you find her analysis at this point and at related moments?

3. Tisdale shapes her information into a series of illustrative anecdotes about fat people and the American mania about dieting. What patterns do you notice in the sequence of examples she presents? Does the fact that Tisdale announces that she is five foot six inches and weighs 164 pounds make it easier — or more difficult — for you as a reader to be drawn to and convinced by her analysis of dieting, its mythology, and its social and individual consequences? What does she "gain" and "lose" by providing us with this information in the first paragraph? How persuasive do you find the alternatives to dieting that she presents in the conclusion of her essay? What, finally, is the overriding purpose of her essay?

60

Calvin Trillin

A Traditional Family

The journalist, critic, novelist, and humorist Calvin Trillin was born in Kansas City in 1935, but has lived in New York City for many years. He works as a staff writer at the New Yorker *and contributes to many other magazines, including the* Atlantic, Harper's, Life, *and the* Nation. *Trillin is a successful novelist and short story writer, and he is especially well known for his nonfiction. His magazine columns are collected in* Uncivil Liberties *(1982),* With All Disrespect: More Uncivil Liberties *(1985),* If You Can't Say Something Nice *(1987), and* Enough's Enough *(1990). Trillin has also published a series of very popular books dealing with food and eating. In* American Fried *(1974) he paints a revealing portrait of American life through his discussion of regional and national eating habits. His love of traveling and eating in the company of his wife Alice also led him to write* Alice, Let's Eat *(1978),* Third Helpings *(1983), and* Travels with Alice *(1989). More recently Trillin has forsworn the temptation to eat for a living and has taken his keen sense of humor to the stage in one-man shows. "A Traditional Family" is excerpted from his book* Too Soon to Tell *(1995); his other recent publications include* Deadline Poet: My Life as a Doggerelist *(1994) and* Messages from My Father *(1996).*

When asked to describe the process he goes through when writing factual as opposed to imaginative columns, Trillin replied, "In a non-fiction piece . . . you really have to carry around a lot of baggage. You have what happened, your understanding of what happened, what you want to get across about what happened, all kinds of burdens of being fair to whatever sides there are. The facts are terribly restricting." Trillin typically writes at least four drafts of nonfiction articles, but finds that imaginative writing is less predictable. When writing his humor columns, for example, "it's a much less rigid system than that of writing non-fiction. Sometimes it only takes two drafts; sometimes it takes five."

I just found out that our family is no longer what the Census Bureau calls a traditional American family, and I want everyone to know that this is not our fault.

We now find ourselves included in the statistics that are used constantly to show the lamentable decline of the typical American household from something like Ozzie and Harriet and the kids to something like a bunch of kooks and hippies.

I want everyone to know right at the start that we are not kooks. Oh sure, we have our peculiarities, but we are not kooks. Also, we are not hippies. We have no children named Goodness. I am the first one to admit that reasonable people may differ on how to characterize a couple of my veteran sportcoats, and there may have been a remark or two passed in the neighborhood from time to time about the state of our front lawn. But no one has ever seriously suggested that we are hippies.

In fact, most people find us rather traditional. My wife and I have a marriage certificate, although I can't say I know exactly where to put my hands on it right at the moment. We have two children. We have a big meal on Christmas. We put on costumes at Halloween. (What about the fact that I always wear an ax murderer's mask on Halloween? That happens to be one of the peculiarities.) We make family decisions in the traditional American family way, which is to say the father is manipulated by the wife and the children. We lose a lot of socks in the wash. At our house, the dishes are done and the garbage is taken out regularly — after the glass and cans and other recyclable materials have been separated out. We're not talking about a commune here.

So why has the Census Bureau begun listing us with households that   5
consist of, say, the ex-stepchild of someone's former marriage living with someone who is under the mistaken impression that she is the aunt of somebody or other? Because the official definition of a traditional Ameri-

can family is two parents and one or more children under age eighteen. Our younger daughter just turned nineteen. Is that our fault?

As it happens, I did everything in my power to keep her from turning nineteen. When our daughters were about two and five, I decided that they were the perfect age, and I looked around for some sort of freezing process that might keep them there. I discovered that there was no such freezing process on the market. Assuming, in the traditional American way, that the technology would come along by and by, I renewed my investigation several times during their childhoods — they always seemed to be at the perfect age — but the freezing process never surfaced. Meanwhile, they kept getting older at what seemed to me a constantly accelerating rate. Before you could say "Zip up your jacket," the baby turned nineteen. What's a parent to do?

Ask for an easement. That's what a parent's to do. When I learned about the Census Bureau's definition of a traditional family — it was mentioned in an Associated Press story about how the latest census shows the traditional family declining at a more moderate pace than "the rapid and destabilizing rate" at which it declined between 1970 and 1980 — it occurred to me that we could simply explain the situation to the Census Bureau and ask that an exception be made in our case.

I realize that the Census Bureau would probably want to send out an inspector. I would acknowledge to him that our daughters are more or less away from home, but remind him that we have been assured by more experienced parents that we can absolutely count on their return. I would take the position, in other words, that we are just as traditional as any American family, just slightly undermanned at the moment — like a hockey team that has a couple of guys in the penalty box but is still a presence on the ice. We could show the official our Christmas tree decorations and our Halloween costumes and a lot of single socks. We might, in the traditional American way, offer him a cup of coffee and a small bribe.

I haven't decided for sure to approach the Census Bureau. For one thing, someone might whisper in the inspector's ear that I have been heard to refer to my older daughter's room — the room where we now keep the exercise bike — as "the gym," and that might take some explaining. Also, I haven't discussed the matter with my wife. I would, of course, abide by her wishes. It's traditional.

The Reader's Presence

1. According to Trillin, how does the Census Bureau define "a traditional American family"? How does Trillin discover that his family would no longer be included in the Census Bureau's statistical compilations about "traditional" American families? Why does

his family no longer satisfy the Census Bureau's criteria? What does Trillin try to do about this "problem"?

2. What characteristics of his family's behavior does Trillin identify as "traditional"? Examine the effect(s) of Trillin's verb choices. What patterns do you notice? What other patterns do you notice that he has woven into his word choices? When — and how — does Trillin poke fun at himself and the members of his family? To what extent does his humor depend on irony? on wit? Point to specific words and phrases to support your response.

3. When — and how — does Trillin use gender and familial stereotypes to reinforce the points he makes? What significance do you attach to the attention to "fault" Trillin weaves into the essay? Identify — and then comment on the effectiveness of — how his examples subtly reinforce his concern about fault and responsibility.

61

John Updike

The Mystery of Mickey Mouse

Over the course of his career as a novelist, short story writer, poet, essayist, and dramatist, John Updike (b. 1932) has been awarded every major American literary award. For one novel alone, Rabbit Is Rich *(1981), he won the Pulitzer Prize, the American Book Award, and the National Book Critics Circle Award. Among over a dozen published novels, his recurring themes include religion, sexuality, and middle-class experience. In his essays, Updike's concerns range widely over literary and cultural issues. One volume of his collected essays,* Hugging the Shore: Essays and Criticism *(1983), was awarded a National Book Critics Circle Award. His most recent publications include* The Afterlife and Other Stories *(1994), the novel* Brazil *(1994),* Collected Poems *(1995), and the novel* In the Beauty of the Lilies *(1996). "The Mystery of Mickey Mouse" first appeared in* Arts and Antiques *in 1991.*

Updike has said, "I began my writing career with a fairly distinct set of principles which, one by one, have eroded into something approaching shapelessness." He does maintain one principle, however: "You should attempt to write things that you would like to read." Writing, he continues, is a process of rendering "your vision of reality into the written symbol. Out of this, living art will come."

It's all in the ears. When Mickey Mouse was born, in 1927, the world of early cartoon animation was filled with two-legged zoomorphic humanoids, whose strange half-black faces were distinguished one from another chiefly by the ears. Felix the Cat had pointed triangular ears and

Oswald the Rabbit — Walt Disney's first successful cartoon creation, which he abandoned when his New York distributor, Charles Mintz, attempted to swindle him — had long floppy ears, with a few notches in the end to suggest fur. Disney's Oswald films, and the Alice animations that preceded them, had mice in them, with linear limbs, wiry tails, and ears that are oblong, yet not round. On the way back to California from New York by train, having left Oswald enmeshed for good in the machinations of Mr. Mintz, Walt and his wife Lillian invented another character based — the genesis legend claims — on the tame field mice that used to wander into Disney's old studio in Kansas City. His first thought was to call the mouse Mortimer; Lillian proposed instead the less pretentious name Mickey. Somewhere between Chicago and Los Angeles, the young couple concocted the plot of Mickey's first cartoon short, *Plane Crazy,* costarring Minnie and capitalizing on 1927's Lindbergh craze. The next short produced by Disney's fledgling studio — which included, besides himself and Lillian, his brother Roy and his old Kansas City associate Ub Iwerks — was *Gallopin' Gaucho,* and introduced a fat and wicked cat who did not yet wear the prosthesis that would give him his name of Pegleg Pete. The third short, *Steamboat Willie,* incorporated that brand-new novelty, a sound track, and was released first, in 1928. Mickey Mouse entered history, as the most persistent and pervasive figment of American popular culture in this century.

His ears are two solid black circles, no matter the angle at which he holds his head. Three-dimensional images of Mickey Mouse — toy dolls, or the papier-mâché heads the grotesque Disneyland Mickeys wear — make us uneasy, since the ears inevitably exist edgewise as well as frontally. These ears properly belong not to three-dimensional space but to an ideal realm of notation, of symbolization, of cartoon resilience and indestructibility. In drawings, when Mickey is in profile, one ear is at the back of his head like a spherical ponytail, or like a secondary bubble in a computer-generated Mandelbrot[1] set. We accept it, as we accepted Li'l Abner's hair always being parted on the side facing the viewer. A surreal optical consistency is part of the cartoon world, halfway between our world and the plane of pure signs, of alphabets and trademarks.

In the sixty-four years since Mickey Mouse's image was promulgated, the ears, though a bit more organically irregular and flexible than the classic 1930s appendages, have not been essentially modified. Many other modifications have, however, overtaken that first crude cartoon, born of an era of starker stylizations. White gloves, like the gloves worn in minstrel shows, appeared after those first, to cover the black hands. The infantile bare chest and shorts with two buttons were phased out in the forties. The eyes have undergone a number of changes, most drastically in

[1]*Benoit B. Mandelbrot* (b. 1924): A Polish-born mathematician who investigated sets of self-repeating geometrical patterns now regularly studied with the aid of computer graphics. — EDS.

the late thirties, when, some historians mistakenly claim, they acquired pupils. Not so: the old eyes, the black oblongs that acquired a nick of reflection in the sides, *were* the pupils; the eye whites filled the entire space beneath Mickey's cap of black, its widow's peak marking the division between these enormous oculi. This can be seen clearly in the face of the classic Minnie; when she bats her eyelids, their lashed shades cover over the full width of what might be thought to be her brow. But all the old animated animals were built this way from Felix the Cat on; Felix had lower lids, and the Mickey of *Plane Crazy* also. So it was an evolutionary misstep that, beginning in 1938, replaced the shiny black pupils with entire oval eyes, containing pupils of their own. No such mutation has overtaken Pluto, Goofy, or Donald Duck. The change brought Mickey closer to us humans, but also took away something of his vitality, his alertness, his bug-eyed cartoon readiness for adventure. It made him less abstract, less iconic, more merely cute and dwarfish. The original Mickey, as he scuttles and bounces through those early animated shorts, was angular and wiry, with much of the impudence and desperation of a true rodent. He was gradually rounded to the proportions of a child, a regression sealed by his fifties manifestation as the genius of the children's television show *The Mickey Mouse Club*, with its live Mouseketeers. Most of the artists who depict Mickey today, though too young to have grown up, as I did, with his old form, have instinctively reverted to it; it is the bare-chested basic Mickey, with his yellow shoes and oval buttons on his shorts, who is the icon, beside whom his modified later version is a mere mousy trousered pipsqueak.

His first, iconic manifestation had something of Chaplin to it; he was the little guy, just over the border of respectable. His circular ears, like two minimal cents, bespeak the smallest economic unit, the overlookable democratic man. His name has passed into the language as a byword for the small, the weak — a "Mickey Mouse operation" means an undercapitalized company or minor surgery. Children of my generation — wearing our Mickey Mouse watches, prying pennies from our Mickey Mouse piggy banks (I won one in a third-grade spelling bee, my first intellectual triumph), following his running combat with Pegleg Pete in the daily funnies, going to the local movie-house movies every Saturday afternoon and cheering when his smiling visage burst onto the screen to introduce a cartoon — felt Mickey was one of us, a bridge to the adult world of which Donald Duck was, for all of his childish sailor suit, an irascible, tyrannical member. Mickey didn't seek trouble, and he didn't complain; he rolled with the punches, and surprised himself as much as us when, as in *The Little Tailor*, he showed warrior resourcefulness and won, once again, a blushing kiss from dear, all but identical Minnie. His minimal, decent nature meant that he would yield, in the Disney animated cartoons, the starring role to combative, sputtering Donald Duck and even to Goofy, with his "gawshes" and Gary Cooper–like gawkiness. But for an occasional comeback like the "Sorcerer's Apprentice" episode of *Fan-*

tasia, and last year's rather souped-up *The Prince and the Pauper*, Mickey was through as a star by 1940. But as with Marilyn Monroe when her career was over, his life as an icon gathered strength. The America that is not symbolized by that imperial Yankee Uncle Sam is symbolized by Mickey Mouse. He is America as it feels to itself — plucky, put-on, inventive, resilient, good-natured, game.

Like America, Mickey has a lot of black blood. This fact was revealed   5
to me in a conversation by Saul Steinberg, who, in attempting to depict the racially mixed reality of New York streets for the supersensitive and race-blind *New Yorker* of the sixties and seventies, hit upon scribbling numerous Mickeys as a way of representing what was jauntily and scruffily and unignorably there. From just the way Mickey swings along in his classic, trademark pose, one three-fingered gloved hand held on high, he is jiving. Along with round black ears and yellow shoes, Mickey has soul. Looking back to such early animations as the early Looney Tunes' Bosko and Honey series (1930–36) and the Arab figures in Disney's own *Mickey in Arabia* of 1932, we see that blacks were drawn much like cartoon animals, with round button noses and great white eyes creating the double arch of the curious peaked skullcaps. Cartoon characters' rubberiness, their jazziness, their cheerful bouyance and idleness, all chimed with popular images of African Americans, earlier embodied in minstrel shows and in Joel Chandler Harris's tales of Uncle Remus, which Disney was to make into an animated feature, *Song of the South*, in 1946.

Up to 1950, animated cartoons, like films in general, contained caricatures of blacks that would be unacceptable now; in fact, *Song of the South* raised objections from the NAACP when it was released. In recent issues of *Fantasia*, two Nubian centaurettes and a pickaninny centaurette who shines the others' hooves have been edited out. Not even the superb crows section of *Dumbo* would be made now. But there is a sense in which all animated cartoon characters are more or less black. Steven Spielberg's hectic tribute to animation, *Who Framed Roger Rabbit?*, has them all, from the singing trees of Silly Symphonies to Daffy Duck and Woody Woodpecker, living in a Los Angeles ghetto, Toonville. As blacks were second-class citizens with entertaining qualities, so the animated shorts were second-class movies, with unreal actors who mocked and illuminated from underneath the real world, the live-actor cinema. Of course, even in a ghetto there are class distinctions. Porky Pig and Bugs Bunny have homes that they tend and defend, whereas Mickey started out, like those other raffish stick figures and dancing blots from the twenties, as a free spirit, a wanderer. As Richard Schnickel has pointed out, "The locales of his adventures throughout the 1930s ranged from the South Seas to the Alps to the deserts of Africa. He was, at various times, a gaucho, teamster, explorer, swimmer, cowboy, fireman, convict, pioneer, taxi driver, castaway, fisherman, cyclist, Arab, football player, inventor, jockey, storekeeper, camper, sailor, Gulliver, boxer," and so forth. He was, in short, a rootless vaudevillian who would play any part that the bosses at Disney Studios assigned him. And though the comic strip, which still persists, has fitted him with all of a white man's household comforts and headaches, it is as an unencumbered drifter whistling along the road of hard knocks, ready for whatever adventure waits at the next turning, that he lives in our minds.

Cartoon characters have soul as Carl Jung defined it in his *Archetypes and the Collective Unconscious:* "soul is a life-giving demon who plays his elfin game above and below human existence." Without the "leaping and twinkling of the soul," Jung says, "man would rot away in his greatest passion, idleness." The Mickey Mouse of the thirties shorts was a whirlwind of activity, with a host of unsuspected skills and a reluctant heroism that rose to every occasion. Like Chaplin and Douglas Fairbanks and Fred Astaire, he acted out our fantasies of endless nimbleness, of perfect weightlessness. Yet withal, there was nothing aggressive or self-promoting about him, as there was about Popeye. Disney, interviewed in the thirties, said, "Sometimes I've tried to figure out why Mickey appealed to the whole world. Everybody's tried to figure it out. So far as I know, nobody has. He's a pretty nice fellow who never does anybody any harm, who gets into scrapes through no fault of his own, but always manages to come up grinning." This was perhaps Disney's image of himself: for twenty years he did Mickey's voice in the films, and would often say, "There's a lot of the Mouse in me." Mickey was a character created with his own pen, and nurtured on Disney's memories of his mouse-ridden Kansas City studio and of the Missouri farm where his struggling father tried for a time to make a living. Walt's humble, scrambling beginnings remained embodied in the mouse, whom the Nazis, in a fury against the Mickey-inspired Allied legions (the Allied code word on D-Day was "Mickey Mouse"), called "the most miserable ideal ever revealed . . . mice are dirty."

But was Disney, like Mickey, just "a pretty nice fellow"? He was until crossed in his driving perfectionism, his Napoleonic capacity to marshal men and take risks in the service of an artistic and entrepreneurial vision. He was one of those great Americans, like Edison and Henry Ford, who invented themselves in terms of a new technology. The technology — in Disney's case, film animation — would have been there anyway, but only a few driven men seized the full possibilities and made empires. In the dozen years between *Steamboat Willie* and *Fantasia*, the Disney studios took the art of animation to heights of ambition and accomplishment it would never have reached otherwise, and Disney's personal zeal was the animating force. He created an empire of the mind, and its emperor was Mickey Mouse.

The thirties were Mickey's conquering decade. His image circled the globe. In Africa, tribesman painfully had tiny mosaic Mickey Mouses inset into their front teeth, and a South African tribe refused to buy soap unless the cakes were embossed with Mickey's image, and a revolt of some native bearers was quelled when the safari masters projected some Mickey Mouse cartoons for them. Nor were the high and mighty immune to Mickey's elemental appeal — King George V and Franklin Roosevelt insisted that all film showings they attended include a dose of Mickey Mouse. But other popular phantoms, like Felix the Cat, have faded, where Mickey has settled into the national collective consciousness. The television program revived him for my children's generation, and the theme parks make him live for my grandchildren's. Yet survival cannot be imposed through weight of publicity; Mickey's persistence springs from something unhyped, something timeless in the image that has allowed it to pass in status from a fad to an icon.

To take a bite out of our imaginations, an icon must be simple. The 10 ears, the wiggly tail, the red shorts, give us a Mickey. Donald Duck and Goofy, Bugs Bunny and Woody Woodpecker are inextricably bound up with the draftsmanship of the artists who make them move and squawk, but Mickey floats free. It was Claes Oldenburg's pop art that first alerted me to the fact that Mickey Mouse had passed out of the realm of commercially generated image into that of artifact. A new Disney gadget, advertised on television, is a camera-like box that spouts bubbles when a key is turned; the key consists of three circles, two mounted on a larger one, and the image is unmistakably Mickey. Like yin and yang, like the Christian cross and the star of Israel, Mickey can be seen everywhere — a sign, a rune, a hieroglyphic trace of a secret power, an electricity we want to plug into. Like totem poles, like African masks, Mickey stands at that intersection of abstraction and representation where magic connects.

Usually cartoon figures do not age, and yet their audience does age, as generation succeeds generation, so that a weight of allusion and sentimental reference increases. To the movie audiences of the early thirties, Mickey Mouse was a piping-voiced live wire, the latest thing in entertainment; by the time of *Fantasia* he was already a sentimental figure, welcomed back. *The Mickey Mouse Club*, with its slightly melancholy pack leader, Jimmie Dodd, created a Mickey more removed and marginal than in his first incarnation. The generation that watched it grew up into the rebels of the sixties, to whom Mickey became camp, a symbol of U.S. cultural fast food, with a touch of the old rodent raffishness. Politically, Walt, stung by the studio strike of 1940, moved to the right, but Mickey remains one of the thirties proletariat, not uncomfortable in the cartoon-rickety, cheerfully verminous crash pads of the counterculture. At the Florida and California theme parks, Mickey manifests himself as a short real person wearing an awkward giant head, costumed as a ringmaster; he is in danger, in these nineties, of seeming not merely venerable kitsch but part of the great trash problem, one more piece of visual litter being moved back and forth by the bulldozers of consumerism.

But never fear, his basic goodness will shine through. Beyond recall, perhaps, is the simple love felt by us of the generation that grew up with him. He was five years my senior and felt like a playmate. I remember crying when the local newspaper, cutting down its comics page to help us win World War II, eliminated the Mickey Mouse strip. I was old enough, nine or ten, to write an angry letter to the editor. In fact, the strips had been eliminated by the votes of a readership poll, and my indignation and sorrow stemmed from my incredulous realization that not everybody loved Mickey Mouse as I did. In an account of my boyhood written over thirty years ago, "The Dogwood Tree," I find these sentences concerning another boy, a rival: "When we both collected Big Little Books, he outbid me for my supreme find (in the attic of a third boy), the first Mickey Mouse. I can still see that book. I wanted it so badly, its paper tan with age and its drawings done in Disney's primitive style, when Mickey's black chest is naked like a child's and his eyes are two nicked oblongs." And I once tried to write a short story called "A Sensation of Mickey Mouse," trying to superimpose on adult experience, as a shiver-inducing revenant, that indescribable childhood sensation — a rubbery taste, a licorice smell, a feeling of supernatural clarity and close-in excitation that Mickey Mouse gave me, and gives me, much dimmed by the years, still. He is a "genius" in the primary dictionary sense of "an attendant spirit," with his vulnerable bare black chest, his touchingly big yellow shoes, the mysterious place at the back of his shorts where his tail came out, the little cleft cushion of a tongue, red as a valentine and glossy as candy, always peeping through the catenary curves of his undiscourageable smile. Not to mention his ears.

The Reader's Presence

1. Updike begins and ends his essay with a reference to Mickey Mouse's ears. Of what importance are they to Updike's entire interpretation? How have the ears contributed to the cartoon's status as a cultural icon?
2. Do you find it surprising to think of Mickey Mouse as black? Does Updike want us to see him as an African American? What evidence does he supply for considering Mickey in this light? How persuasive do you find his view? Do you think his creator, Walt Disney, intended this identity?
3. Why is Mickey Mouse a cultural icon? In what ways does a character become an icon? Does it take more than enormous popularity? Would Mickey Mouse be an icon even if he weren't globally marketed by the Disney Corporation? How does Updike answer these questions?

62

Alice Walker

In Search of Our Mothers' Gardens

"In Search of Our Mothers' Gardens" is the title essay from the collection
Alice Walker published in 1983. Reflecting on what inspires her writing, Walker
once said, "If I spend a long time in silence, which I really love, that's very good
for my writing. The main thing is just to live intensely and to feel. If there's the
slightest little bubble from the spring coming up, I try to go with the bubble until
it gets to the top of the water and then try to be there for it so that I can begin to
understand what is happening down in the depths." For more information on
Walker, see page 215.

> I described her own nature and temperament. Told how they
> needed a larger life for their expression. . . . I pointed out that in lieu of
> proper channels, her emotions had overflowed into paths that dissipated
> them. I talked, beautifully I thought, about an art that would be born,
> an art that would open the way for women the likes of her. I asked her
> to hope, and build up an inner life against the coming of that day. . . . I
> sang, with a strange quiver in my voice, a promise song.
>
> —"Avey," JEAN TOOMER, CANE
> The poet speaking to a prostitute who
> falls asleep while he's talking.

When the poet Jean Toomer[1] walked through the South in the early
twenties, he discovered a curious thing: black women whose spirituality
were so intense, so deep, so *unconscious,* they were themselves unaware
of the richness they held. They stumbled blindly through their lives: creatures so abused and mutilated in body, so dimmed and confused by pain,
that they considered themselves unworthy even of hope. In the selfless abstractions their bodies became to the men who used them, they became
more than "sexual objects," more even than mere women: They became

---

[1]*Jean Toomer* (1894–1967): A black poet, novelist, and leading figure of the Harlem
Renaissance who wrote *Cane* in 1923. — EDS.

"Saints." Instead of being perceived as whole persons, their bodies became shrines: What was thought to be their minds became temples suitable for worship. These crazy Saints stared out at the world, wildly, like lunatics — or quietly, like suicides; and the "God" that was in their gaze was as mute as a great stone.

Who were these Saints? These crazy, loony, pitiful women?

Some of them, without a doubt, were our mothers and grandmothers.

In the still heat of the post-Reconstruction South, this is how they seemed to Jean Toomer: exquisite butterflies trapped in an evil honey, toiling away their lives in an era, a century, that did not acknowledge them, except as "the *mule* of the world." They dreamed dreams that no one knew — not even themselves, in any coherent fashion — and saw visions no one could understand. They wandered or sat about the countryside crooning lullabies to ghosts, and drawing the mother of Christ in charcoal on courthouse walls.

They forced their minds to desert their bodies and their striving spirits   5
sought to rise, like frail whirlwinds from the hard red clay. And when those frail whirlwinds fell, in scattered particles, upon the ground, no one mourned. Instead, men lit candles to celebrate the emptiness that remained, as people do who enter a beautiful but vacant space to resurrect a God.

Our mothers and grandmothers, some of them: moving to music not yet written. And they waited.

They waited for a day when the unknown thing that was in them would be made known; but guessed, somehow in their darkness, that on the day of their revelation they would be long dead. Therefore to Toomer they walked, and even ran, in slow motion. For they were going nowhere immediate, and the future was not yet within their grasp. And men took our mothers and grandmothers, "but got no pleasure from it." So complex was their passion and their calm.

To Toomer, they lay vacant and fallow as autumn fields, with harvest time never in sight: and he saw them enter loveless marriages, without joy; and become prostitutes, without resistance; and become mothers of children, without fulfillment.

For these grandmothers and mothers of ours were not Saints, but Artists; driven to a numb and bleeding madness by the springs of creativity in them for which there was no release. They were Creators, who lived lives of spiritual waste, because they were so rich in spirituality — which is the basis of Art — that the strain of enduring their unused and unwanted talent drove them insane. Throwing away this spirituality was their pathetic attempt to lighten the soul to a weight their work-worn, sexually abused bodies could bear.

What did it mean for a black woman to be an artist in our grand-   10
mothers' time? In our great-grandmothers' day? It is a question with an answer cruel enough to stop the blood.

Did you have a genius of a great-great-grandmother who died under some ignorant and depraved white overseer's lash? Or was she required to bake biscuits for a lazy backwater tramp, when she cried out in her soul to paint watercolors of sunsets, or the rain falling on the green and peaceful pasturelands? Or was her body broken and forced to bear children (who were more often than not sold away from her) — eight, ten, fifteen, twenty children — when her one joy was the thought of modeling heroic figures of rebellion, in stone or clay?

How was the creativity of the black woman kept alive, year after year and century after century, when for most of the years black people have been in America, it was a punishable crime for a black person to read or write? And the freedom to paint, to sculpt, to expand the mind with action did not exist. Consider, if you can bear to imagine it, what might have been the result if singing, too, had been forbidden by law. Listen to the voices of Bessie Smith, Billie Holiday, Nina Simone, Roberta Flack, and Aretha Franklin, among others and imagine those voices muzzled for life. Then you may begin to comprehend the lives of our "crazy," "Sainted" mothers and grandmothers. The agony of the lives of women who might have been Poets, Novelists, Essayists, and Short-Story Writers (over a period of centuries), who died with their real gifts stifled within them.

And, if this were the end of the story, we would have cause to cry out in my paraphrase of Okot p'Bitek's great poem:

> *O, my clanswomen*
> *Let us all cry together!*
> *Come,*
> *Let us mourn the death of our mother,*
> *The death of a Queen*
> *The ash that was produced*
> *By a great fire!*
> *O, this homestead is utterly dead*
> *Close the gates*
> *With* lacari *thorns,*
> *For our mother*
> *The creator of the Stool is lost!*
> *And all the young men*
> *Have perished in the wilderness!*

But this is not the end of the story, for all the young women — our mothers and grandmothers, *ourselves* — have not perished in the wilderness. And if we ask ourselves why, and search for and find the answer, we will know beyond all efforts to erase it from our minds, just exactly who, and of what, we black American women are.

One example, perhaps the most pathetic, most misunderstood one, can provide a backdrop for our mothers' work: Phillis Wheatley,[2] a slave in the 1700s. 15

---

[2]*Phillis Wheatley* (ca. 1754–1784): A slave in a prosperous Boston family; published her first poetry at the age of thirteen and enjoyed an international reputation, acclaimed by such figures as Voltaire, George Washington, and Benjamin Franklin. She died, however, in poverty and obscurity. — EDS.

Virginia Woolf, in her book *A Room of One's Own,* wrote that in order for a woman to write fiction she must have two things, certainly: a room of her own (with key and lock) and enough money to support herself.

What then are we to make of Phillis Wheatley, a slave, who owned not even herself? This sickly, frail black girl who required a servant of her own at times — her health was so precarious — and who, had she been white, would have been easily considered the intellectual superior of all the women and most of the men in the society of her day.

Virginia Woolf wrote further, speaking of course not of our Phillis, that "any woman born with a great gift in the sixteenth century [insert "eighteenth century," insert "black woman," insert "born or made a slave"] would certainly have gone crazed, shot herself, or ended her days in some lonely cottage outside the village, half witch, half wizard [insert "Saint"], feared and mocked at. For it needs little skill and psychology to be sure that a highly gifted girl who had tried to use her gift of poetry would have been so thwarted and hindered by contrary instincts [add "chains, guns, the lash, the ownership of one's body by someone else, submission to an alien religion"], that she must have lost her health and sanity to a certainty."

The key words, as they relate to Phillis, are "contrary instincts." For when we read the poetry of Phillis Wheatley — as when we read the novels of Nella Larsen or the oddly false-sounding autobiography of that freest of all black women writers, Zora Hurston — evidence of "contrary instincts" is everywhere. Her loyalties were completely divided, as was, without question, her mind.

But how could this be otherwise? Captured at seven, a slave of wealthy, doting whites who instilled in her the "savagery" of the Africa they "rescued" her from . . . one wonders if she was even able to remember her homeland as she had known it, or as it really was.

Yet, because she did try to use her gift for poetry in a world that made her a slave, she was "so thwarted and hindered by . . . contrary instincts, that she . . . lost her health . . ." In the last years of her brief life, burdened not only with the need to express her gift but also with a penniless, friendless "freedom" and several small children for whom she was forced to do strenuous work to feed, she lost her health, certainly. Suffering from malnutrition and neglect and who knows what mental agonies, Phillis Wheatley died.

So torn by "contrary instincts" was black, kidnapped, enslaved Phillis that her description of "the Goddess" — as she poetically called the Liberty she did not have — is ironically, cruelly humorous. And, in fact, has held Phillis up to ridicule for more than a century. It is usually read prior to hanging Phillis's memory as that of a fool. She wrote:

20

> *The Goddess comes, she moves divinely fair,*
> *Olive and laurel binds her golden hair.*
> *Wherever shines this native of the skies,*
> *Unnumber'd charms and recent graces rise.* [My emphasis]

It is obvious that Phillis, the slave, combed the "Goddess's" hair every morning; prior, perhaps, to bringing in the milk, or fixing her mistress's lunch. She took her imagery from the one thing she saw elevated above all others.

With the benefit of hindsight we ask, "How could she?"

But at last, Phillis, we understand. No more snickering when your   25
stiff, struggling, ambivalent lines are forced on us. We know now that you were not an idiot or a traitor; only a sickly little black girl, snatched from your home and country and made a slave; a woman who still struggled to sing the song that was your gift, although in a land of barbarians who praised you for your bewildered tongue. It is not so much what you sang, as that you kept alive, in so many of our ancestors, *the notion of song*.

Black women are called, in the folklore that so aptly identifies one's status in society, "the *mule* of the world," because we have been handed the burdens that everyone else — *everyone* else — refused to carry. We have also been called "Matriarchs," "Superwomen," and "Mean and Evil Bitches." Not to mention "Castraters" and "Sapphire's Mama." When we have pleaded for understanding, our character has been distorted; when we have asked for simple caring, we have been handed empty inspirational appellations, then stuck in the farthest corner. When we have asked for love, we have been given children. In short, even our plainer gifts, our labors of fidelity and love, have been knocked down our throats. To be an artist and a black woman, even today, lowers our status in many respects, rather than raises it: And yet, artists we will be.

Therefore we must fearlessly pull out of ourselves and look at and identify with our lives the living creativity some of our great-grandmothers were not allowed to know. I stress *some* of them because it is well known that the majority of our great-grandmothers knew, even without "knowing" it, the reality of their spirituality, even if they didn't recognize it beyond what happened in the singing at church — and they never had any intention of giving it up.

How they did it — those millions of black women who were not Phillis Wheatley, or Lucy Terry or Frances Harper or Zora Hurston or Nella Larsen or Bessie Smith; or Elizabeth Catlett, or Katherine Dunham, either — brings me to the title of this essay, "In Search of Our Mothers' Gardens," which is a personal account that is yet shared, in its theme and its meaning, by all of us. I found, while thinking about the far-reaching world of the creative black woman, that often the truest answer to a question that really matters can be found very close.

In the late 1920s my mother ran away from home to marry my father. Marriage, if not running away, was expected of seventeen-year-old girls. By the time she was twenty, she had two children and was pregnant with a third. Five children later, I was born. And this is how I came to know my mother: She seemed a large, soft, loving-eyed woman who was rarely impatient in our home. Her quick, violent temper was on view only a few times a year, when she battled with the white landlord who had the misfortune to suggest to her that her children did not need to go to school.

She made all the clothes we wore, even my brothers' overalls. She   30
made all the towels and sheets we used. She spent the summers canning vegetables and fruits. She spent the winter evenings making quilts enough to cover our beds.

During the "working" day, she labored beside — not behind — my father in the fields. Her day began before sunup, and did not end until late at night. There was never a moment for her to sit down, undisturbed, to unravel her own private thoughts; never a time free from interruption — by work or the noisy inquiries of her many children. And yet, it is to my mother — and all our mothers who were not famous — that I went in search of the secret of what has fed that muzzled and often mutilated, but vibrant, creative spirit that the black woman has inherited, and that pops out in wild and unlikely places to this day.

But when, you will ask, did my overworked mother have time to know or care about feeding the creative spirit?

The answer is so simple that many of us have spent years discovering it. We have constantly looked high, when we should have looked high — and low.

For example: In the Smithsonian Institution in Washington, D.C., there hangs a quilt unlike any other in the world. In fanciful, inspired, and yet simple and identifiable figures, it portrays the story of the Crucifixion. It is considered rare, beyond price. Though it follows no known pattern of quilt-making, and though it is made of bits and pieces of worthless rags, it is obviously the work of a person of powerful imagination and deep spiritual feeling. Below this quilt I saw a note that says it was made by "an anonymous Black woman in Alabama, a hundred years ago."

If we could locate this "anonymous" black woman from Alabama,   35
she would turn out to be one of our grandmothers — an artist who left her mark in the only materials she could afford, and in the only medium her position in society allowed her to use.

As Virginia Woolf wrote further, in *A Room of One's Own*:

> Yet genius of a sort must have existed among women as it must have existed among the working class. [Change this to "slaves" and "the wives and daughters of sharecroppers."] Now and again an Emily Brontë or a Robert Burns [change this to "a Zora Hurston or a Richard Wright"] blazes out and proves its presence. But certainly it never got itself on to paper. When, however, one reads of a witch being ducked, of a woman possessed by devils [or "Sainthood"], of a wise woman selling herbs [our root workers], or even a very remarkable man who had a mother, then I think we are on the track of a lost novelist, a suppressed poet, or some

mute and inglorious Jane Austen. . . . Indeed, I would venture to guess that Anon, who wrote so many poems without signing them, was often a woman. . . .

And so our mothers and grandmothers have, more often than not anonymously, handed on the creative spark, the seed of the flower they themselves never hoped to see: or like a sealed letter they could not plainly read.

And so it is, certainly, with my own mother. Unlike "Ma" Rainey's songs, which retained their creator's name even while blasting forth from Bessie Smith's mouth, no song or poem will bear my mother's name. Yet so many of the stories that I write, that we all write, are my mother's stories. Only recently did I fully realize this: That through years of listening to my mother's stories of her life, I have absorbed not only the stories themselves, but something of the manner in which she spoke, something of the urgency that involves the knowledge that her stories — like her life — must be recorded. It is probably for this reason that so much of what I have written is about characters whose counterparts in real life are so much older than I am.

But the telling of these stories, which came from my mother's lips as naturally as breathing, was not the only way my mother showed herself as an artist. For stories, too, were subject to being distracted, to dying without conclusion. Dinners must be started, and cotton must be gathered before the big rains. The artist that was and is my mother showed itself to me only after many years. This is what I finally noticed:

Like Mem, a character in *The Third Life of Grange Copeland*,[3] my   40
mother adorned with flowers whatever shabby house we were forced to live in. And not just your typical straggly country stand of zinnias, either. She planted ambitious gardens — and still does — with over fifty different varieties of plants that bloom profusely from early March until late November. Before she left home for the fields, she watered her flowers, chopped up the grass, and laid out new beds. When she returned from the fields, she might divide clumps of bulbs, dig a cold pit, uproot and replant roses, or prune branches from her taller bushes or trees — until night came and it was too dark to see.

Whatever she planted grew as if by magic, and her fame as a grower of flowers spread over three counties. Because of her creativity with her flowers, even my memories of poverty are seen through a screen of blooms — sunflowers, petunias, roses, dahlias, forsythia, spirea, delphiniums, verbena . . . and on and on.

And I remember people coming to my mother's yard to be given cuttings from her flowers; I hear again the praise showered on her because whatever rocky soil she landed on, she turned into a garden. A garden so

---

[3] *The Third Life of Grange Copeland:* Walker's first novel, published in 1970. — EDS.

brilliant with colors, so original in its design, so magnificent with life and creativity, that to this day people drive by our house in Georgia — perfect strangers and imperfect strangers — and ask to stand or walk among my mother's art.

I notice that it is only when my mother is working in her flowers that she is radiant, almost to the point of being invisible — except as Creator: hand and eye. She is involved in work her soul must have. Ordering the universe in the image of her personal conception of Beauty.

Her face, as she prepares the Art that is her gift, is a legacy of respect she leaves to me, for all that illuminates and cherishes life. She has handed down respect for the possibilities — and the will to grasp them.

For her, so hindered and intruded upon in so many ways, being an artist has still been a daily part of her life. This ability to hold on, even in very simple ways, is work black women have done for a very long time.   45

This poem is not enough, but it is something, for the woman who literally covered the holes in our walls with sunflowers:

> They were women then
> My mamma's generation
> Husky of voice — Stout of
> Step
> With fists as well as
> Hands
> How they battered down
> Doors
> And ironed
> Starched white
> Shirts
> How they led
> Armies
> Headragged Generals
> Across mined
> Fields
> Booby-trapped
> Kitchens
> To discover books
> Desks
> A place for us
> How they knew what we
> Must *know*
> Without knowing a page
> Of it
> Themselves

Guided by my heritage of a love of beauty and a respect for strength — in search of my mother's garden, I found my own.

And perhaps in Africa over two hundred years ago, there was just such a mother; perhaps she painted vivid and daring decorations in oranges and yellows and greens on the walls of her hut; perhaps she sang —

in a voice like Roberta Flack's — *sweetly* over the compounds of her village; perhaps she wove the most stunning mats or told the most ingenious
stories of all the village storytellers. Perhaps she was herself a poet —
though only her daughter's name is signed to the poems that we know.

Perhaps Phillis Wheatley's mother was also an artist.

Perhaps in more than Phillis Wheatley's biological life is her mother's   50
signature made clear.

The Reader's Presence

1. The *our* of the essay's title signals an identification of the author
   with an audience. Why didn't Walker title her essay "In Search of
   My Mother's Garden"? Does Walker's *our* include everyone who
   reads the essay — or is her audience more restricted? Explain your
   answer.
2. Consider carefully Walker's image of the garden. What does it
   mean both to her and to other women? What is the connection between gardens and a woman's "living creativity"? What other objects or activities in the essay are related to the idea of gardens?
3. In rereading the essay, note the many quotations throughout.
   Consider the way Walker uses quotation in general. Can you detect any patterns? What sort of "presence" do they convey? Why
   do you think she brought in so many quotations in an essay about
   silence? How does her use of quotations contribute to her overall
   theme?

63

George Will

Printed Noise

Through his syndicated columns in the Washington Post *and* Newsweek, *and
through his commentary on ABC-TV's "This Week with David Brinkley" and
"World News Tonight," George Will (b. 1941) is one of the most visible and influential political commentators in the United States today. Will began his career
as a professor of politics at Michigan State University and the University of
Toronto. In 1970 he moved to Washington, D.C., to work as a congressional
aide, and in 1972 he became the Washington editor of the* National Review. *His
columns have appeared in the* Washington Post *since 1974, and he has been a
contributing editor at* Newsweek *since 1976. "Printed Noise" appears in Will's*

first book, The Pursuit of Happiness and Other Sobering Thoughts *(1978), in which over one hundred of his essays and columns are collected. Celebrated for their subtlety, sophistication, and elegance, Will's essays can also be found in* The Morning After: American Successes and Excesses *(1986) and* The New Season: A Spectator's Guide to the 1988 Elections *(1987). In 1977 Will was awarded a Pulitzer Prize for distinguished commentary. His recent books include* Restoration: Congress Term Limits and the Recovery of Deliberative Democracy *(1993) and* The Leveling Wind: Politics, the Culture, and Other News *(1994).*

Will believes not only in the conservative viewpoint from which he writes, but also in the important role that writing plays in civil society. "There is a scarcity of reasoned, civilized discourse in the world," Will says. "With such discourse we can stand anything. Without it we are doomed."

The flavor list at the local Baskin-Robbins ice cream shop is an anarchy of names like "Peanut Butter 'N Chocolate" and "Strawberry Rhubarb Sherbert." These are not the names of things that reasonable people consider consuming, but the names are admirably businesslike, briskly descriptive.

Unfortunately, my favorite delight (chocolate-coated vanilla flecked with nuts) bears the unutterable name "Hot Fudge Nutty Buddy," an example of the plague of cuteness in commerce. There are some things a gentleman simply will not do, and one is announce in public a desire for a "Nutty Buddy." So I usually settle for a plain vanilla cone.

I am not the only person suffering for immutable standards of propriety. The May issue of *Atlantic* contains an absorbing tale of lonely heroism at a Burger King. A gentleman requested a ham and cheese sandwich that the Burger King calls a Yumbo. The girl taking orders was bewildered.

"Oh," she eventually exclaimed, "you mean a Yumbo."

Gentleman: "The ham and cheese. Yes."   5

Girl, nettled: "It's called a Yumbo. Now, do you want a Yumbo or not?"

Gentleman, teeth clenched: "Yes, thank you, the ham and cheese."

Girl: "Look, I've got to have an order here. You're holding up the line. You want a Yumbo, don't you? You want a Yumbo!"

Whereupon the gentleman chose the straight and narrow path of virtue. He walked out rather than call a ham and cheese a Yumbo. His principles are anachronisms but his prejudices are impeccable, and he is on my short list of civilization's friends.

That list includes the Cambridge don who would not appear out-   10
doors without a top hat, not even when routed by fire at 3 A.M., and who refused to read another line of Tennyson after he saw the poet put water in fine port. The list includes another don who, although devoutly Tory, voted Liberal during Gladstone's day because the duties of prime minister kept Gladstone too busy to declaim on Holy Scripture. And high on the list is the grammarian whose last words were: "I am about to — or I am going to — die: either expression is correct."

Gentle reader, can you imagine any of these magnificent persons asking a teenage girl for a "Yumbo"? Or uttering "Fishamagig" or "Egg Mc-Muffin" or "Fribble" (that's a milk shake, sort of)?

At one point in the evolution of American taste, restaurants that were relentlessly fun, fun, fun were built to look like lemons or bananas. I am told that in Los Angeles there was the Toed Inn, a strange spelling for a strange place shaped like a giant toad. Customers entered through the mouth, like flies being swallowed.

But the mature nation has put away such childish things in favor of menus that are fun, fun, fun. Seafood is "From Neptune's Pantry" or "Denizens of the Briny Deep." And "Surf 'N Turf," which you might think is fish and horsemeat, actually is lobster and beef.

To be fair, there are practical considerations behind the asphyxiatingly cute names given hamburgers. Many hamburgers are made from portions of the cow that the cow had no reason to boast about. So sellers invent distracting names to give hamburgers cachet. Hence "Whoppers" and "Heroburgers."

But there is no excuse for Howard Johnson's menu. In a just society it   15 would be a flogging offense to speak of "steerburgers," clams "fried to order" (which probably means they don't fry clams for you unless you order fried clams), a "natural cut" (what is an "unnatural" cut?) of sirloin, "oven-baked" meatloaf, chicken pot pie with "flaky crust," "golden croquettes," "grilled-in-butter Frankforts [sic]," "liver with smothered onions" (smothered by onions?), and a "hearty" Reuben sandwich.

America is marred by scores of Dew Drop Inns serving "crispy green" salads, "garden fresh" vegetables, "succulent" lamb, "savory" pork, "sizzling" steaks, and "creamy" or "tangy" coleslaw. I've nothing against Homeric adjectives ("wine-dark sea," "wing-footed Achilles") but isn't coleslaw just coleslaw? Americans hear the incessant roar of commerce without listening to it, and read the written roar without really noticing it. Who would notice if a menu proclaimed "creamy" steaks and "sizzling" coleslaw? Such verbal litter is to language as Muzak is to music. As advertising blather becomes the nation's normal idiom, language becomes printed noise.

The Reader's Presence

1. The primary target of Will's wit and invective here is "printed noise," "verbal litter," "advertising blather" (paragraph 16). What, according to Will, are the dangers of such abuses of language? In paragraph 15 he lists several items from a Howard Johnson's menu. Identify the specific ways in which each one offends his sensibilities. What seem to be Will's criteria for the proper use of language? Compare and contrast Will's own

language, in particular his diction, with the language of the advertisements he cites.

2. At the opposite end of the spectrum from the advertising industry,
   Will posits a "short list of civilization's friends" (paragraph 9).
   How might you characterize the values of those on the short list?
   What phrases does Will use to describe them? What "immutable
   standards of propriety" do they uphold (paragraph 3)? How would
   you describe the tone he takes toward those on the "short list"?

3. Many of Will's examples concern food and restaurants. He critiques "American taste" (paragraph 12), but reserves most of his
   contempt for our breaches of taste in descriptions of food rather
   than our taste in food itself. Comment on the intersection between
   these related but not identical definitions of "taste" in Will's essay.

64

Virginia Woolf

The Death of the Moth

*One of the most important writers of the twentieth century, Virginia Woolf
(1882–1941) explored innovations in indirect narration and the impressionistic
use of language that are now considered hallmarks of the modern novel and continue to influence novelists on both sides of the Atlantic. Together with her husband, Leonard Woolf, she founded the Hogarth Press, which published many experimental works that have now become classics, including her own. A central
figure in the Bloomsbury group of writers, Woolf established her reputation with
the novels* Mrs. Dalloway *(1925),* To the Lighthouse *(1927), and* The Waves
*(1931). The feminist movement has helped to focus attention on her work, and
Woolf's nonfiction has provided the basis for several important lines of argument
in contemporary feminist theory.* A Room of One's Own *(1929),* Three Guineas
(1938), and The Common Reader *(1938) are the major works of nonfiction published in Woolf's lifetime; posthumously, her essays have been gathered together
in* The Death of the Moth *(where the essay reprinted here appears) and in the
four-volume* Collected Essays.

*Reflecting on her own writing life, Woolf wrote, "The novelist — it is his dis-
tinction and his danger — is terribly exposed to life. . . . He can no more cease to
receive impressions than a fish in mid-ocean can cease to let the water rush
through his gills." To turn those impressions into writing, Woolf maintained, requires solitude and the time for thoughtful selection. Given tranquillity, a writer
can, with effort, discover art in experience. "There emerges from the mist something stark, formidable and enduring, the bone and substance upon which our
rush of indiscriminating emotion was founded."*

Moths that fly by day are not properly to be called moths; they do not excite that pleasant sense of dark autumn nights and ivy-blossom which the commonest yellow-underwing asleep in the shadow of the curtain never fails to rouse in us. They are hybrid creatures, neither gay like butterflies nor somber like their own species. Nevertheless the present specimen, with his narrow hay-colored wings, fringed with a tassel of the same color, seemed to be content with life. It was a pleasant morning, mid-September, mild, benignant, yet with a keener breath than that of the summer months. The plough was already scoring the field opposite the window, and where the share had been, the earth was pressed flat and gleamed with moisture. Such vigor came rolling in from the fields and the down beyond that it was difficult to keep the eyes strictly turned upon the book. The rooks too were keeping one of their annual festivities; soaring round the tree tops until it looked as if a vast net with thousands of black knots in it had been cast up into the air; which, after a few moments sank slowly down upon the trees until every twig seemed to have a knot at the end of it. Then, suddenly, the net would be thrown into the air again in a wider circle this time, with the utmost clamor and vociferation, as though to be thrown into the air and settle slowly down upon the tree tops were a tremendously exciting experience.

The same energy which inspired the rooks, the ploughmen, the horses, and even, it seemed, the lean bare-backed downs, sent the moth fluttering from side to side of his square of the windowpane. One could not help watching him. One, was, indeed, conscious of a queer feeling of pity for him. The possibilities of pleasure seemed that morning so enormous and so various that to have only a moth's part in life, and a day moth's at that, appeared a hard fate, and his zest in enjoying his meager opportunities to the full, pathetic. He flew vigorously to one corner of his compartment, and after waiting there a second, flew across to the other. What remained for him but to fly to a third corner and then to a fourth? That was all he could do, in spite of the size of the downs, the width of the sky, the far-off smoke of houses, and the romantic voice, now and then, of a steamer out at sea. What he could do he did. Watching him, it seemed as if a fiber, very thin but pure, of the enormous energy of the world had been thrust into his frail and diminutive body. As often as he crossed the pane, I could fancy that a thread of vital light became visible. He was little or nothing but life.

Yet, because he was so small, and so simple a form of the energy that was rolling in at the open window and driving its way through so many narrow and intricate corridors in my own brain and in those of other human beings, there was something marvelous as well as pathetic about him. It was as if someone had taken a tiny bead of pure life and decking it as lightly as possible with down and feathers, had set it dancing and zigzagging to show us the true nature of life. Thus displayed one could not get over the strangeness of it. One is apt to forget all about life, seeing it humped and bossed and garnished and cumbered so that it has to move with the greatest circumspection and dignity. Again, the thought of all that life might have been had he been born in any other shape caused one to view his simple activities with a kind of pity.

After a time, tired by his dancing apparently, he settled on the window ledge in the sun, and, the queer spectacle being at an end, I forgot about him. Then, looking up, my eye was caught by him. He was trying to resume his dancing, but seemed either so stiff or so awkward that he could only flutter to the bottom of the windowpane; and when he tried to fly across it he failed. Being intent on other matters I watched these futile attempts for a time without thinking, unconsciously waiting for him to resume his flight, as one waits for a machine, that has stopped momentarily, to start again without considering the reason of its failure. After perhaps a seventh attempt he slipped from the wooden ledge and fell, fluttering his wings, on to his back on the windowsill. The helplessness of his attitude roused me. It flashed upon me that he was in difficulties; he could no longer raise himself; his legs struggled vainly. But, as I stretched out a pencil, meaning to help him to right himself, it came over me that the failure and awkwardness were the approach of death. I laid the pencil down again.

The legs agitated themselves once more. I looked as if for the enemy against which he struggled. I looked out of doors. What had happened there? Presumably it was midday, and work in the fields had stopped. Stillness and quiet had replaced the previous animation. The birds had taken themselves off to feed in the brooks. The horses stood still. Yet the power was there all the same, massed outside, indifferent, impersonal, not attending to anything in particular. Somehow it was opposed to the little hay-colored moth. It was useless to try to do anything. One could only watch the extraordinary efforts made by those tiny legs against an oncoming doom which could, had it chosen, have submerged an entire city, not merely a city, but masses of human beings; nothing, I knew had any chance against death. Nevertheless after a pause of exhaustion the legs fluttered again. It was superb this last protest, and so frantic that he succeeded at last in righting himself. One's sympathies, of course, were all on the side of life. Also, when there was nobody to care or to know, this gigantic effort on the part of an insignificant little moth, against a power of such magnitude, to retain what no one else valued or desired to keep, moved one strangely. Again, somehow, one saw life, a pure bead. I lifted the pencil again, useless though I knew it to be. But even as I did so, the unmistakable tokens of death showed themselves. The body relaxed, and instantly grew stiff. The struggle was over. The insignificant little creature now knew death. As I looked at the dead moth, this minute wayside triumph of so great a force over so mean an antagonist filled me with wonder. Just as life had been strange a few minutes before, so death was now as strange. The moth having righted himself now lay most decently and uncomplainingly composed. O yes, he seemed to say, death is stronger than I am.

The Reader's Presence

1. Woolf calls her essay "The Death of *the* Moth" rather than "The Death of *a* Moth." Describe what difference this makes. What quality does the definite article add to the essay?

2. Can you find any connections between what happens to the moth and what happens outside the window? Why do you think Woolf brings in the outside world? Of what importance is it to the essay?

3. Reread the essay, paying special attention not to the moth but to the writer. What presence does Woolf establish for herself in the essay? How does the act of writing itself get introduced? Of what significance is the pencil? Can you discover any connection between the essay's subject and its composition?

Part III

Argumentative Writing: Contending with Issues

65

James Baldwin

Stranger in the Village

James Baldwin (1924–1987) grew up in New York City but moved to France in 1948 because he felt personally and artistically stifled as a gay African American man in the United States. His first novels, Go Tell It on the Mountain *(1956) and* Giovanni's Room *(1956), and his first collection of essays,* Notes of a Native Son *(1955), were published during Baldwin's first stay abroad, where he was able to write critically about race, sexual identity, and social injustice in America. The essay "Stranger in the Village" appears in* Notes of a Native Son. *After nearly a decade in France, he returned to New York and became a national figure in the civil rights movement. Henry Louis Gates Jr. eulogized Baldwin as the conscience of the nation, for he "educated an entire generation of Americans about the civil-rights struggle and the sensibility of Afro-Americans as we faced and conquered the final barriers in our long quest for civil rights." Baldwin continues to educate through his essays, collected in* The Price of the Ticket: Collected Nonfiction *(1985).*

When asked if he approached the writing of fiction and nonfiction in different ways, Baldwin responded, "Every form is different, no one is easier than another. . . . An essay is not simpler, though it may seem so. An essay is clearly an argument. The writer's point of view in an essay is always absolutely clear. The writer is trying to make the readers see something, trying to convince them of something. In a novel or a play you're trying to show them something. The risks, in any case, are exactly the same."

From all available evidence no black man had ever set foot in this tiny Swiss village before I came. I was told before arriving that I would probably be a "sight" for the village; I took this to mean that people of my complexion were rarely seen in Switzerland, and also that city people are always something of a "sight" outside of the city. It did not occur to me — possibly because I am an American — that there could be people anywhere who had never seen a Negro.

It is a fact that cannot be explained on the basis of the inaccessibility of the village. The village is very high, but it is only four hours from Milan and three hours from Lausanne. It is true that it is virtually unknown. Few people making plans for a holiday would elect to come here. On the other hand, the villagers are able, presumably, to come and go as they please — which they do: to another town at the foot of the mountain, with a population of approximately five thousand, the nearest place to see a movie or go to the bank. In the village there is no movie house, no bank, no library, no theater; very few radios, one jeep, one station wagon; and, at the moment, one typewriter, mine, an invention which the woman next door to me here had never seen. There are about six hundred people living here, all Catholic — I conclude this from the fact that the Catholic church is open all year round, whereas the Protestant chapel, set off on a hill a little removed from the village, is open only in the summertime when the tourists arrive. There are four or five hotels, all closed now, and four or five bistros, of which, however, only two do any business during the winter. These two do not do a great deal, for life in the village seems to end around nine or ten o'clock. There are a few stores, butcher, baker, *épicerie*,[1] a hardware store, and a money-changer — who cannot change travelers' checks, but must send them down to the bank, an operation which takes two or three days. There is something called the *Ballet Haus,* closed in the winter and used for God knows what, certainly not ballet, during the summer. There seems to be only one schoolhouse in the village, and this for the quite young children; I suppose this to mean that their older brothers and sisters at some point descend from these mountains in order to complete their education — possibly, again, to the town just below. The landscape is absolutely forbidding, mountains towering on all four sides, ice and snow as far as the eye can reach. In this white wilderness, men and women and children move all day, carrying washing, wood, buckets of milk or water, sometimes skiing on Sunday afternoons. All week long boys and young men are to be seen shoveling snow off the rooftops, or dragging wood down from the forest in sleds.

   The village's only real attraction, which explains the tourist season, is the hot spring water. A disquietingly high proportion of these tourists are cripples, or semi-cripples, who come year after year — from other parts of Switzerland, usually — to take the waters. This lends the village, at the height of the season, a rather terrifying air of sanctity, as though it were a lesser Lourdes. There is often something beautiful, there is always something awful, in the spectacle of a person who has lost one of his faculties, a faculty he never questioned until it was gone, and who struggles to recover it. Yet people remain people, on crutches or indeed on deathbeds; and wherever I passed, the first summer I was here, among the native villagers or among the lame, a wind passed with me — of astonishment, curiosity, amusement, and outrage. That first summer I stayed two weeks and never intended to return. But I did return in the winter, to work; the village offers, obviously, no distractions whatever and has the further ad-

---

[1]*épicerie:* A grocery store (French). — EDS.

vantage of being extremely cheap. Now it is winter again, a year later, and I am here again. Everyone in the village knows my name, though they scarcely ever use it, knows that I come from America — though, this, apparently, they will never really believe: black men come from Africa — and everyone knows that I am the friend of the son of a woman who was born here, and that I am staying in their chalet. But I remain as much a stranger today as I was the first day I arrived, and the children shout *Neger! Neger!* as I walk along the streets.

It must be admitted that in the beginning I was far too shocked to have any real reaction. In so far as I reacted at all, I reacted by trying to be pleasant — it being a great part of the American Negro's education (long before he goes to school) that he must make people "like" him. This smile-and-the-world-smiles-with-you routine worked about as well in this situation as it had in the situation for which it was designed, which is to say that it did not work at all. No one, after all, can be liked whose human weight and complexity cannot be, or has not been, admitted. My smile was simply another unheard-of phenomenon which allowed them to see my teeth — they did not, really, see my smile and I began to think that, should I take to snarling, no one would notice any difference. All of the physical characteristics of the Negro which had caused me, in America, a very different and almost forgotten pain were nothing less than miraculous — or infernal — in the eyes of the village people. Some thought my hair was the color of tar, that it had the texture of wire, or the texture of cotton. It was jocularly suggested that I might let it all grow long and make myself a winter coat. If I sat in the sun for more than five minutes some daring creature was certain to come along and gingerly put his fingers on my hair, as though he were afraid of an electric shock, or put his hand on my hand, astonished that the color did not rub off. In all of this, in which it must be conceded there was the charm of genuine wonder and in which there was certainly no element of intentional unkindness, there was yet no suggestion that I was human: I was simply a living wonder.

I knew that they did not mean to be unkind, and I know it now; it is 5 necessary, nevertheless, for me to repeat this to myself each time I walk out of the chalet. The children who shout *Neger!* have no way of knowing the echoes this sound raises in me. They are brimming with good humor and the more daring swell with pride when I stop to speak with them. Just the same, there are days when I cannot pause and smile, when I have no heart to play with them; when, indeed, I mutter sourly to myself, exactly as I muttered on the streets of a city these children have never seen, when I was no bigger than these children are now: *Your* mother *was a nigger.* Joyce is right about history being a nightmare — but it may be the nightmare from which no one *can* awaken. People are trapped in history and history is trapped in them.

There is a custom in the village — I am told it is repeated in many villages — of "buying" African natives for the purpose of converting them to Christianity. There stands in the church all year round a small box with a slot for money, decorated with a black figurine, and into this box the villagers drop their francs. During the *carnaval* which precedes Lent, two village children have their faces blackened — out of which bloodless darkness their blue eyes shine like ice — and fantastic horsehair wigs are placed on their blond heads; thus disguised, they solicit among the villagers for money for the missionaries in Africa. Between the box in the church and the blackened children, the village "bought" last year six or eight African natives. This was reported to me with pride by the wife of one of the bistro owners and I was careful to express astonishment and pleasure at the solicitude shown by the village for the souls of black folk. The bistro owner's wife beamed with a pleasure far more genuine than my own and seemed to feel that I might now breathe more easily concerning the souls of at least six of my kinsmen.

I tried not to think of these so lately baptized kinsmen, of the price paid for them, or the peculiar price they themselves would pay, and said nothing about my father, who having taken his own conversion too literally never, at bottom, forgave the white world (which he described as heathen) for having saddled him with a Christ in whom, to judge at least from their treatment of him, they themselves no longer believed. I thought of white men arriving for the first time in an African village, strangers there, as I am a stranger here, and tried to imagine the astounded populace touching their hair and marveling at the color of their skin. But there is a great difference between being the first white man to be seen by Africans and being the first black man to be seen by whites. The white man takes the astonishment as tribute, for he arrives to conquer and to convert the natives, whose inferiority in relation to himself is not even to be questioned; whereas I, without a thought of conquest, find myself among a people whose culture controls me, has even, in a sense, created me, people who have cost me more in anguish and rage than they will ever know, who yet do not even know of my existence. The astonishment with which I might have greeted them, should they have stumbled into my African village a few hundred years ago, might have rejoiced their hearts. But the astonishment with which they greet me today can only poison mine.

And this is so despite everything I may do to feel differently, despite my friendly conversations with the bistro owner's wife, despite their three-year-old son who has at last become my friend, despite the *saluts* and *bonsoirs* which I exchange with people as I walk, despite the fact that I know that no individual can be taken to task for what history is doing, or has done. I say that the culture of these people controls me — but they can scarcely be held responsible for European culture. America comes out of Europe, but these people have never seen America, nor have most of them seen more of Europe than the hamlet at the foot of their mountain. Yet they move with an authority which I shall never have; and they regard me, quite rightly, not only as a stranger in their village but as a suspect latecomer, bearing no credentials, to everything they have — however unconsciously — inherited.

For this village, even were it incomparably more remote and incredibly more primitive, is the West, the West onto which I have been so strangely grafted. These people cannot be, from the point of view of power, strangers anywhere in the world; they have made the modern world, in effect, even if they do not know it. The most illiterate among them is related, in a way that I am not, to Dante, Shakespeare, Michelangelo, Aeschylus, Da Vinci, Rembrandt, and Racine; the cathedral at Chartres says something to them which it cannot say to me, as indeed would New York's Empire State Building, should anyone here ever see it. Out of their hymns and dances come Beethoven and Bach. Go back a few centuries and they are in their full glory — but I am in Africa, watching the conquerors arrive.

The rage of the disesteemed is personally fruitless, but it is also absolutely inevitable; this rage, so generally discounted, so little understood even among the people whose daily bread it is, is one of the things that makes history. Rage can only with difficulty, and never entirely, be brought under the domination of the intelligence and is therefore not susceptible to any arguments whatever. This is a fact which ordinary representatives of the *Herrenvolk*, having never felt this rage and being unable to imagine it, quite fail to understand. Also, rage cannot be hidden, it can only be dissembled. This dissembling deludes the thoughtless, and strengthens rage, and adds, to rage, contempt. There are, no doubt, as many ways of coping with the resulting complex of tensions as there are black men in the world, but no black man can hope ever to be entirely liberated from this internal warfare — rage, dissembling, and contempt having inevitably accompanied his first realization of the power of white men. What is crucial here is that, since white men represent in the black man's world so heavy a weight, white men have for black men a reality which is far from being reciprocal; and hence all black men have toward all white men an attitude which is designed, really, either to rob the white man of the jewel of his naïveté, or else to make it cost him dear. 10

The black man insists, by whatever means he finds at his disposal, that the white man cease to regard him as an exotic rarity and recognize him as a human being. This is a very charged and difficult moment, for there is a great deal of will power involved in the white man's naïveté. Most people are not naturally reflective any more than they are naturally malicious, and the white man prefers to keep the black man at a certain human remove because it is easier for him thus to preserve his simplicity and avoid being called to account for crimes committed by his forefathers, or his neighbors. He is inescapably aware, nevertheless, that he is in a better position in the world than black men are, nor can he quite put to death the suspicion that he is hated by black men therefor. He does not wish to be hated, neither does he wish to change places, and at this point in his uneasiness he can scarcely avoid having recourse to those legends which white men have created about black men, the most usual effect of which is that the white man finds himself enmeshed, so to speak, in his own language which describes hell, as well as the attributes which lead one to hell, as being as black as night.

Every legend, moreover, contains its residuum of truth, and the root function of language is to control the universe by describing it. It is of quite considerable significance that black men remain, in the imagination, and in overwhelming numbers in fact, beyond the disciplines of salvation; and this despite the fact that the West has been "buying" African natives for centuries. There is, I should hazard, an instantaneous necessity to be divorced from this so visibly unsaved stranger, in whose heart, moreover, one cannot guess what dreams of vengeance are being nourished; and, at the same time, there are few things on earth more attractive than the idea of the unspeakable liberty which is allowed the unredeemed. When, beneath the black mask, a human being begins to make himself felt one cannot escape a certain awful wonder as to what kind of human being it is. What one's imagination makes of other people is dictated, of course, by the laws of one's own personality and it is one of the ironies of black-white relations that, by means of what the white man imagines the black man to be, the black man is enabled to know who the white man is.

I have said, for example, that I am as much a stranger in this village today as I was the first summer I arrived, but this is not quite true. The villagers wonder less about the texture of my hair than they did then, and wonder rather more about me. And the fact that their wonder now exists on another level is reflected in their attitudes and in their eyes. There are the children who make those delightful, hilarious, sometimes astonishing grave overtures of friendship in the unpredictable fashion of children; other children, having been taught that the devil is a black man, scream in genuine anguish as I approach. Some of the older women never pass without a friendly greeting, never pass, indeed, if it seems that they will be able to engage me in conversation; other women look down or look away or rather contemptuously smirk. Some of the men drink with me and suggest that I learn how to ski — partly, I gather, because they cannot imagine what I would look like on skis — and want to know if I am married, and ask questions about my métier. But some of the men have accused *le sale négre* — behind my back — of stealing wood and there is already in the eyes of some of them that peculiar intent, paranoiac malevolence which one sometimes surprises in the eyes of American white men when, out walking with their Sunday girl, they see a Negro male approach.

There is a dreadful abyss between the streets of this village and the streets of the city in which I was born, between the children who shout *Neger!* today and those who shouted *Nigger!* yesterday — the abyss is experience, the American experience. The syllable hurled behind me today expresses, above all, wonder: I am a stranger here. But I am not a stranger in America and the same syllable riding on the American air expresses the war my presence has occasioned in the American soul.

For this village brings home to me this fact: that there was a day, and   15
not really a very distant day, when Americans were scarcely Americans at
all but discontented Europeans, facing a great unconquered continent and
strolling, say, into a marketplace and seeing black men for the first time.
The shock this spectacle afforded is suggested, surely, by the promptness
with which they decided that these black men were not really men but
cattle. It is true that the necessity on the part of the settlers of the New
World of reconciling their moral assumptions with the fact — and the necessity — of slavery enhanced immensely the charm of this idea, and it is
also true that this idea expresses, with a truly American bluntness, the attitude which to varying extents all masters have had toward all slaves.

But between all former slaves and slave-owners and the drama which
begins for Americans over three hundred years ago at Jamestown, there
are at least two differences to be observed. The American Negro slave
could not suppose, for one thing, as slaves in past epochs had supposed
and often done, that he would ever be able to wrest the power from his
master's hands. This was a supposition which the modern era, which was
to bring about such vast changes in the aims and dimensions of power,
put to death; it only begins, in unprecedented fashion, and with dreadful
implications, to be resurrected today. But even had this supposition persisted with undiminished force, the American Negro slave could not have
used it to lend his condition dignity, for the reason that this supposition
rests on another: that the slave in exile yet remains related to his past, has
some means — if only in memory — of revering and sustaining the forms
of his former life, is able, in short, to maintain his identity.

This was not the case with the American Negro slave. His is unique
among the black men of the world in that his past was taken from him,
almost literally, at one blow. One wonders what on earth the first slave
found to say to the first dark child he bore. I am told that there are
Haitians able to trace their ancestry back to African kings, but any American Negro wishing to go back so far will find his journey through time
abruptly arrested by the signature on the bill of sale which served as the
entrance paper for his ancestor. At the time — to say nothing of the circumstances — of the enslavement of the captive black man who was to
become the American Negro, there was not the remotest possibility that
he would ever take power from his master's hands. There was no reason
to suppose that his situation would ever change, nor was there, shortly,
anything to indicate that his situation had ever been different. It was his
necessity, in the words of E. Franklin Frazier, to find a "motive for living
under American culture or die." The identity of the American Negro
comes out of this extreme situation, and the evolution of this identity was
a source of the most intolerable anxiety in the minds and the lives of his
masters.

For the history of the American Negro is unique also in this: that the
question of his humanity, and of his rights therefore as a human being,
became a burning one for several generations of Americans, so burning a

question that it ultimately became one of those used to divide the nation. It is out of this argument that the venom of the epithet *Nigger!* is derived. It is an argument which Europe has never had, and hence Europe quite sincerely fails to understand how or why the argument arose in the first place, why its effects are so frequently disastrous and always so unpredictable, why it refuses until today to be entirely settled. Europe's black possessions remained — and do remain — in Europe's colonies, at which remove they represented no threat to European identity. If they posed any problem at all for the European conscience, it was a problem which remained comfortably abstract: in effect, the black man, *as a man,* did not exist for Europe. But in America, even as a slave, he was an inescapable part of the general social fabric and no American could escape having an attitude toward him. Americans attempt until today to make an abstraction of the Negro, but the very nature of these abstractions reveals the tremendous effects the presence of the Negro has had on the American character.

When one considers the history of the Negro in America it is of the greatest importance to recognize that the moral beliefs of a person, or a people, are never really as tenuous as life — which is not moral — very often causes them to appear; these create for them a frame of reference and a necessary hope, the hope being that when life has done its worst they will be enabled to rise above themselves and to triumph over life. Life would scarcely be bearable if this hope did not exist. Again, even when the worst has been said, to betray a belief is not by any means to have put oneself beyond its power; the betrayal of a belief is not the same thing as ceasing to believe. If this were not so there would be no moral standards in the world at all. Yet one must also recognize that morality is based on ideas and that all ideas are dangerous — dangerous because ideas can only lead to action and where the action leads no man can say. And dangerous in this respect: that confronted with the impossibility of remaining faithful to one's beliefs, and the equal impossibility of becoming free of them, one can be driven to the most inhuman excesses. The ideas on which American beliefs are based are not, though Americans often seem to think so, ideas which originated in America. They came out of Europe. And the establishment of democracy on the American continent was scarcely as radical a break with the past as was the necessity, which Americans faced, of broadening this concept to include black men.

This was, literally, a hard necessity. It was impossible, for one thing, 20 for Americans to abandon their beliefs, not only because these beliefs alone seemed able to justify the sacrifices they had endured and the blood that they had spilled, but also because these beliefs afforded them their only bulwark against a moral chaos as absolute as the physical chaos of the continent it was their destiny to conquer. But in the situation in which Americans found themselves, these beliefs threatened an idea which, whether or not one likes to think so, is the very warp and woof of the heritage of the West, the idea of white supremacy.

Americans have made themselves notorious by the shrillness and the brutality with which they have insisted on this idea, but they did not invent it; and it has escaped the world's notice that those very excesses of which Americans have been guilty imply a certain, unprecedented uneasiness over the idea's life and power, if not, indeed, the idea's validity. The idea of white supremacy rests simply on the fact that white men are the creators of civilization (the present civilization, which is the only one that matters; all previous civilizations are simply "contributions" to our own) and are therefore civilization's guardians and defenders. Thus it was impossible for Americans to accept the black man as one of themselves, for to do so was to jeopardize their status as white men. But not so to accept him was to deny his human reality, his human weight and complexity, and the strain of denying the overwhelmingly undeniable forced Americans into rationalizations so fantastic that they approached the pathological.

At the root of the American Negro problem is the necessity of the American white man to find a way of living with the Negro in order to be able to live with himself. And the history of this problem can be reduced to the means used by Americans — lynch law and law, segregation and legal acceptance, terrorization and concession — either to come to terms with this necessity, or to find a way around it, or (most usually) to find a way of doing both these things at once. The resulting spectacle, at once foolish and dreadful, led someone to make the quite accurate observation that "the Negro-in-America is a form of insanity which overtakes white men."

In this long battle, a battle by no means finished, the unforeseeable effects of which will be felt by many future generations, the white man's motive was the protection of his identity; the black man was motivated by the need to establish an identity. And despite the terrorization which the Negro in America endured and endures sporadically until today, despite the cruel and totally inescapable ambivalence of his status in his country, the battle for his identity has long ago been won. He is not a visitor to the West, but a citizen there, an American, as American as the Americans who despise him, the Americans who fear him, the Americans who love him — the Americans who became less than themselves, or rose to be greater than themselves by virtue of the fact that the challenge he represented was inescapable. He is perhaps the only black man in the world whose relationship to white men is more terrible, more subtle, and more meaningful than the relationship of bitter possessed to uncertain possessor. His survival depended, and his development depends, on his ability to turn his peculiar status in the Western world to his own advantage and, it may be, to the very great advantage of that world. It remains for him to fashion out of his experience that which will give him sustenance, and a voice.

The cathedral of Chartres, I have said, says something to the people of this village which it cannot say to me; but it is important to understand that this cathedral says something to me which it cannot say to them. Perhaps they are struck by the power of the spires, the glory of the windows; but they have known God, after all, longer than I have known him, and in a different way, and I am terrified by the slippery bottomless well to be found in the crypt, down which heretics were hurled to death, and by the obscene, inescapable gargoyles jutting out of the stone and seeming to say that God and the devil can never be divorced. I doubt that the villagers think of the devil when they face a cathedral because they have never been identified with the devil. But I must accept the status which myth, if nothing else, gives me in the West before I can hope to change the myth.

Yet, if the American Negro has arrived at his identity by virtue of the   25
absoluteness of his estrangement from his past, American white men still nourish the illusion that there is some means of recovering the European innocence, of returning to a state in which black men do not exist. This is one of the greatest errors Americans can make. The identity they fought so hard to protect has, by virtue of that battle, undergone a change: Americans are as unlike any other white people in the world as it is possible to be. I do not think, for example, that it is too much to suggest that the American vision of the world — which allows so little reality, generally speaking, for any of the darker forces in human life, which tends until today to paint moral issues in glaring black and white — owes a great deal to the battle waged by Americans to maintain between themselves and black men a human separation which could not be bridged. It is only now beginning to be borne in on us — very faintly, it must be admitted, very slowly, and very much against our will — that this vision of the world is dangerously inaccurate, and perfectly useless. For it protects our moral high-mindedness at the terrible expense of weakening our grasp of reality. People who shut their eyes to reality simply invite their own destruction, and anyone who insists on remaining in a state of innocence long after that innocence is dead turns himself into a monster.

The time has come to realize that the interracial drama acted out on the American continent has not only created a new black man, it has created a new white man, too. No road whatever will lead Americans back to the simplicity of this European village where white men still have the luxury of looking on me as a stranger. I am not, really, a stranger any longer for any American alive. One of the things that distinguishes Americans from other people is that no other people has ever been so deeply involved in the lives of black men, and vice versa. This fact faced, with all its implications, it can be seen that the history of the American Negro problem is not merely shameful, it is also something of an achievement. For even when the worst has been said, it must also be added that the perpetual challenge posed by this problem was always, somehow, perpetually met. It is precisely this black-white experience which may prove of indispensable value to us in the world we face today. This world is white no longer, and it will never be white again.

The Reader's Presence

1. Baldwin opens the essay with an account of himself as a stranger in an actual Swiss village. But how do we begin to see him as a stranger in more general ways? What does the village come to represent? What is the relation of the Swiss village to Baldwin's America?
2. This is an essay that moves from autobiography to argument. In rereading it, can you find the place where Baldwin's autobiography begins to disappear and where his argument begins to take over? Try stating Baldwin's central argument in your own terms. To what extent is his argument historical?
3. In paragraph 21, Baldwin writes about the denial of "human weight and complexity." What role does such complexity play in this essay? In rereading the essay, locate several sentences in which you think Baldwin's ideas resist simplification. Study these sentences carefully. What do they have in common? How do they illustrate the kind of complexity that Baldwin sees as essentially human?

66

Stanley Crouch

The Good News:
The O. J. Simpson Verdict

Stanley Crouch (b. 1945) has worked as a playwright and actor, a drummer and band leader, and a teacher of drama, literature, and jazz history. He is best known to the literary world as a jazz critic and essayist; for many years he wrote on jazz for the Village Voice, *and his social commentary has appeared in the* New York Times *and* Esquire, *among other periodicals. Crouch's criticism is noted for its independent spirit and is collected in two books,* Notes of a Hanging Judge: Essays and Reviews *(1990) and* The All-American Skin Game, or, The Decoy of Race *(1995). He is a contributing editor to the* New Republic, *a Sunday columnist for the* New York Daily News, *and a frequent panelist on the* Charlie Rose Show. *"The Good News: The O. J. Simpson Verdict" appeared in* Esquire *in 1995.*

Responding to the observation that many of his opinions are controversial and that his essays criticize both left-wing and right-wing political positions, Crouch replies, "I usually write something I think is true, and if in the process it's provocative, it's too bad."

Race is such a large (decoy) that it almost causes us to get very important things wrong. That is why I don't accept the idea that the verdict in the O.J. Simpson double-murder case, and the heated counterpoint of celebration and (condemnation) mean the country is now in greater racial trouble. As Americans, we are all members of an improvising social experiment that is always is in some sort of trouble. Ours is a country that learns whatever it learns by bruising its ideals in combat with human shortcomings, from the public to the private sector, the mass to the individual. In the long goodbye to those no-good things that we are eventually forced to address, context by context, nothing slips the noose forever. This means that we have serious scars and lumps on our heads from the crashing of idols in every line of high-profile endeavor. "Say it ain't so" is the dark, hot, minor strain of the national anthem.

Yet we always cool off. That's part of our style and part of the heroic drama that defines the evolution of our nation. It happens once the sort of emotion we feel for our individual and group of identities wears itself away. We then cease hiding under our beds, where we try to ignore the mature responsibilities demanded by the blues that periodically knocks at the national door, the blues dressed up in new duds and full of classic devilment. So what we are facing is just another situation in which those looking for something to get happy about and those looking for the opportunity to express their rage about some condition of the purported oppression have gotten their moment. Such occasions inevitably work out for the national good because they demand that we face the complexities of our nation and grow up.

A chance to mature is exactly what was put before us in the case that began in a high-rent district with Nicole Brown Simpson's nearly decapitated corpse lying in sticky red death not far from the body of Ronald Goldman, the male model and weight-lifting waiter who came to deliver sunglasses and found himself in a losing struggle with the savage blade of murder. We were given fresh access to the kind of human tragedy that is not limited by race or social class or profession or good looks or athletic prowess or intelligence or sex or, apparently, golden luck. As the media lapped up every drop of blood, fingered every swelling, sniffed out every scent of illicit sex, and listened for every puff and snort of drugs, we came to know brutal and decadent secrets that were bribed or coaxed or forced up from the world of whispers.

In terms of our human understanding, the Simpson verdict crosses a terrain in which something is both amiss and affirmed in our national mythology. Once we cut ourselves loose from Europe, we made that mythology up as we went along. It had to stretch from the backwoods to the cities to the plains, North, South, East, and West. It had to be big enough to handle people from backgrounds as different as those of Jefferson, Lincoln, Douglass, Edison, and so on. We needed a cultural myth to explain the flesh-and-blood illumination that arrived from the crude background as well as the smooth. But what we have settled for in our weakest moments may well have put far too much emphasis on squeaky-clean human symbols, since we are almost always pulled up short by the tattling of private tales or by the public exposure of caked or fresh dung in the drawers of widely admired figures.

Fused to our human symbols were our newspapers, which, if they weren't muckraking, did their assumed duty by hiding that dung from us. People in the business figured we couldn't stand the truth, and they didn't mind reporting only as much as they thought we could take. Censorship functioned in the name of "good taste." Whenever in doubt, we moved into the recasting of a basic American vision, which is that the common person, the innocent, the mistreated or the misunderstood, will pick up where others have failed at truly realizing the meanings of our democratic ideals. This person will not be corrupted by the narcissism that comes with large monetary success, excessive power, and inordinate admiration by the mob. This person, one callused big toe standing on pointe at the peak of the moral pyramid, will have a messianic effect on our belief in our system.

That is where the Negro comes in, and where, at our moments of greatest desperation, we secretly make our most serious bets on something better rising out of something bad. If the Negro can stand the pressure of sustained and unfair opposition, then we all can. If the Negro can get up to the top and hold in place everything this culture has found so charismatic, we have a much greater chance of bringing off this social experiment, especially since the Afro-American's history on this land reaches back beyond the Mayflower. The patience, the grace, the rhythm, the humor, the discipline, and the heroic majesty historically found in the best of Negro life have always provided some sort of an antidote to the disorder that, as Ralph Ellison observed, is ever a danger to our society. That is why identification with Negro aspirations and Negro style has been so important to the development of this country's democracy and its culture. The Negro has tested our democracy and been central to what we mean by the spirit of America when it sings, when it dances, when it talks to the cosmos, when it gives a certain texture of rhythm to English or exhibits the long memory so essential to our recognition of the tragic losses that have formed the hill of corpses upon which we stand and are able to see beyond the worst of our human limitations while acknowledging their every nuance.

The Simpson case tested all of our contemporary democratic mythologies about good and evil, about race and fairness, about law enforcement and the criminal courts and justice. The Negroes who disturbed so many by celebrating, by cheering, and by dancing were responding to a dream of American possibility quite different from that assumed by the media. It was all, given the brilliance of the defense, much, much deeper than "a brother beating the system." The multiethnic selection of citizens that magically disappeared and conveniently became an all-black jury — even in the mind of outraged liberals — delivered a verdict that had nothing to do with racial solidarity or jury nullification.

Those jury members were neither that simpleminded nor that incapable of understanding what was on display as evidence. The jurors might well have recognized that they were in the presence of a level of lawyering that none will probably ever see in the flesh again, day by day, witness by witness, exhibit by exhibit. That, above all else, is what they responded to in such a quick stroke.

As far as color goes, we all saw just what our country has come down to, which is not some imbecilic racial divide but interracial teams working both sides of the basic arguments. Just as there are now highly visible so-called minorities in both major political parties and either heading or inside the administrations of almost every important city, the prosecution and the defense in this epic trial comprised integrated teams. For all of the discussion about sinister developments in black and Jewish relations, we saw prosecutor Marcia Clark, a Jewish woman, whose central partner was Christopher Darden, an unarguably grassroots Negro, both backed up by a remarkably diverse group of people appearing as witnesses, police officers, and experts. The same was true of the defense team, which was first headed by the extremely smooth Robert Shapiro, whose demotion in favor of Johnnie Cochran may reveal as much about his post-trial sour grapes as anything else. If, say, Shapiro is the kind of guy who is accustomed to being far brighter than most people he encounters, it must have been quite an experience for him to observe in Cochran a level of argument, eloquence, delineated passion, and superbly paced execution that he will never feel or hear coming out of his own body. He might have smarted quite deeply as his initial celebrity was gradually but completely overshadowed by Cochran's. That smarting might have reached its supreme intensity near the end, when Shapiro found himself so far down in the public polls that he was loudly booed at a basketball game and approached in restaurants by social wild cards ranting about his betraying the genocidal horrors of World War II.

In fact, there may have been no issue larger in the overview of it all than betrayal. Riled feminists ideologues freely accused Negro females — on and off the jury — of betraying their battered and butchered blond sister. (This uncriticized demand for solidarity is ironic, given that Negroes were condemned for their purported racial unanimity in the wake of the verdict.) The solidarity of victimhood should have transcended the looming presence of a remarkable doubt. The dark welts on the souls of the athletic heroes and media figures are not new to us, whether we are talking about an O. J. Simpson or a Jessica Savitch.[1] But this time, we had our sensibilities and whatever innocence we could claim pushed right into hard facts about law enforcement, about the risky deals a prosecution team will make with the devil, about the kind of sloppiness in evidence collection that seems to pass by quite easily in most instances. In the af-

[1] *Jessica Savitch:* A popular TV newscaster with drug problems who died at age 35 in 1983. Her life became the subject of television movies and docu-dramas. — EDS.

termath, we got a chance to see how all of those people who so cynically dismiss "the system" with examples like Watergate, FBI hanky-panky, the serpentine antics of the CIA, Oliver North, the savings-and-loan scandal, the Clarence Thomas–Anita Hill hearings, and so on were suddenly and haughtily able to set aside every example of police misconduct and suspicious evidence in the Simpson case.

Those same people — *all of whom should know that juries almost*   10 *automatically acquit when the police are caught lying or red-handed —* turned in the other direction, dropped their pants, and contemptuously mooned the verdict. Turning back around, these people asserted that the forensic evidence should have transcended everything else. They seemed to forget that Americans have a dual attitude toward the kind of technology that lay beneath DNA evidence. We suspect machinery just as much as we love it, primarily because our society is one at war with the potential anonymity imposed by our technology. So when a good-enough lawyer plays into that aversion to the technological, he or she isn't so much summoning up the ignorant impatience of the jury as pulling forth a basic aspect of its American feeling: our fear that our humanity will be compromised by our toys of mathematical definition and measurement. As lovers of the underdog, as people from one group or another who have had the deck stacked against us at some distant or recent time, we don't take too kindly to statistics and often refuse to be bullied by experts.

Sometimes, like the sort of farm boys whose down-home logic thwarts city slickers, we just want to know why some blood left on a fence for several weeks contains a chemical found in police labs. (Is that a statement on the preservative powers of smoggy Los Angeles weather?) We just want to know why there is no blood trail leading to or away from the infamous bloody glove, which was described by Mark Fuhrman as being "moist or sticky" when it was found during his foraging for evidence all by his lonesome — seven and a half hours after it was supposedly dropped by the murderer. We would like to know how even a former superathlete and seriously mediocre actor could park, leap over a fence, bang into a wall three times, drop a glove, run upstairs, shower, change clothes, and come downstairs deporting himself as just another guy a little late for a limousine ride to the airport. As a deeply disturbed Mario Cuomo observed, there was more than enough to raise a "reasonable doubt," but endless white Americans were distraught because the jury took that doubt's specifically instructed meaning so seriously. Those howlers would have preferred that the jurors ignore the law. They felt betrayed.

There are those who feel betrayed by Simpson's upper-class life to such an extent that a special kind of racism has been put back into play, one that used to slither off the term *uppity*. It now allows William Safire to write in *The New York Times*, "The wealthy celebrity who lived white, spoke white, and married white wrapped himself in the rags of social

injustice and told his black counsel to move black jurors to vote black."
Safire was following the pompous lead of *Time* magazine's Jack E. White,
head mulatto in charge of darky corrections, who wrote, "Never one to
speak out on civil rights, [Simpson] seemed to shed his racial identity,
crossing over into a sort of colorless minor celebrity as easily as he escaped from tacklers — or from the black wife he traded in for a white
teenager."

Twenty-five years ago, no writer, black or white, would have been allowed to impose such a limited vision of "authenticity" on a Negro. Individual freedom was then the issue, not joining a movement, not maintaining a style that would make certain white people feel more comfortable in
the exclusive and fraudulent franchise of their "whiteness," which includes the expensive property, privilege upon privilege, the money to do
battle with the legal system on equal ground, the proper enunciation of
the English language, and freedom of social choice. In this era, when
Woody Allen was in the middle of his big mess with Mia Farrow, he
wasn't asked to reinstate his foreskin because of the women he's chosen
over the years. No one asks Allen to suppress his urban neurosis in favor
of the elegant worldliness of Richard Bernstein. Nor is Susan Sontag told
to emulate Fanny Brice[2] in order to truly represent the group. Sylvester
Stallone isn't under attack for his lovers or where he lives or whose company he travels in. The only ethnic under that pressure is the Negro,
whose unlimited variations on Americanness must now meet not the infinite meanings of our national humanity but some short-order ethnic
recipe written up and agreed on by supposed insiders and outsiders.

As we look back on this trial from some point in the future, we will
see beyond such recipes and remember certain purely American things
that are signal examples of the way our country is going. Ours is no
longer a culture dominated by one race taking up all the seats in the high
places. We will remember Judge Lance Ito — Eagle Scout and son of parents who did time in American concentration camps — letting both sides
have a lot of rope but surely favoring a prosecution that still couldn't
serve Simpson's head on a platter. We will remember Johnnie Cochran
doing an extremely witty variation on Marc Antony's speech over
Caesar's body, pivoting on the phrase "but Christopher Darden loves
me." We will remember Marcia Clark coddling Mark Fuhrman through
his testimony and F. Lee Bailey getting the rogue cop to say things under
oath that would make him unarguably a perjurer. We will remember
Rosa Lopez cringing under Darden's smoldering questions. We will remember Dennis Fung's perfectly modulated voice losing all confidence
and starting to quaver as Barry Scheck systematically turned his expertise
into confetti. We will remember the way Henry Lee sat there and spun

---

[2] ***Susan Sontag . . . Fanny Brice:*** Sontag (b. 1933) is a prominent author and intellectual; Brice (1891–1951) was a famous Vaudeville entertainer. Crouch's point, apparently, is
that they are both Jewish. — EDS.

out parables while speaking with such clear, technical authority that it seemed as though the ghost of Charlie Chan[3] had been brought to life with a deeply human three-dimensionality the Hollywood scriptwriters never achieved. We will remember the enlarging pie pans under Marcia Clark's eyes as the months passed and then the extremely chilling way she ended her summation with the voice of Nicole Brown Simpson calling 911 for help. We will remember the rising and falling of the case, each side seeming to be losing at one point, winning at another. Then we will remember the final arguments.

By the end, it came down to black and white, Negro and Jew,   15 Christopher Darden and Marcia Clark up against Johnnie Cochran and Barry Scheck. The astonishing one was Cochran. Whatever we must say about this lawyer so foolishly allowing Nation of Islam goons to guard him, or his demagogically attempting to recruit black reporters for the defense point of view, we should also remember that, in the heat of battle, especially during the ninety minutes that followed the dinner break on the first two days of defense summations, the man was so extraordinary that Brooklyn district attorney Joe Hynes said that, in thirty years as a professional, he had never witnessed such a tour de force in the arena of advocacy.

Cochran's command of American sound and rhythm was perfectly orchestrated within the context of an argument that tore down the prosecution's case as he ripped apart the state's speculative logic and showed how the testimony of one police officer after another was full of specious contradictions. He convincingly revealed the holes in certain evidence and unmasked the potentially sleazy motives behind the actions of the cops at Simpson's mansion. Part of his compelling virtuosity was the way in which he mixed various straight and street accents, crossing and recrossing the ethnic divide, reaching for an idealistic judicial diction, parodying the voices of the cops and backing things up with superb pauses and brilliant emphasis, then closing out with the repetitions and inflections of the best and more subtle Afro-American pulpit talk. Cochran was so remarkable that, at one point, Ito himself repressed a smile at the quality of the summation he was hearing. The dark-skinned and handsome Cochran, ever immaculately dressed, jumped froggy and brought that Negro American swing to court. One understood right then why Los Angeles lawyer Mike Yamamoto says that to bellow and whine about "the race card" is to deny the fact that this man proved, day by day, that he is the best lawyer in the whole town.

For all that we might find fault with on either side, there is no denying the bottomless humanity we witnessed. There is no denying that if all we learned as a nation about police misconduct, irresponsible prosecution teams, and sloppy crime laboratories moves us closer to bettering the

---

[3]***Charlie Chan:*** The Chinese detective, Charlie Chan, was a popular fictional and film hero of the 1930s and '40s. The Charlie Chan series consists of some forty films. — EDS.

liberty of the people through the agencies created to protect them, then Nicole Brown Simpson and Ronald Goldman will not have died in vain, regardless of who may have killed them. Lying murdered in Beverly Hills, their bodies brought elements into play that let us see how vulnerable we all are to the most brutal treatment, and how much we still have to do if we want to move this country closer and closer to justice. Along the way, we will continue to grow up, since the immature can never handle the inevitable blows of the blues. However we get there, as the trial never failed to let us know, we will achieve our American ideals only through multiracial teams of both sexes, calling upon the fullest range of our national humanity.

The Reader's Presence

1. Crouch refers several times in the essay to America as a "social experiment." What do you think he means by this? What is experimental about American society? Why is this concept important to Crouch's argument about the O.J. Simpson trial?

2. Note that Crouch uses the term *Negro* throughout. Though the word was used by civil rights leaders as late as Martin Luther King, Jr., it became socially and politically taboo by 1970. Why do you think Crouch reintroduces the word? What point is he making? Do you think he wants the term to replace *black* or *African American*?

3. Crouch believes that the O. J. Simpson verdict will help the nation mature. In what way will this occur? What does Crouch find immature about the country? Does Crouch's point have anything to do with whether one thinks O. J. Simpson is guilty or not?

1) What is Crouch's purpose?

2) Exactly what is he writing about / the trial on the crime / the trial or the crime? Do you feel frustrated or angry with just the portions of the text? Identify not just how Crouch's content to which you object, but to how closely at the P's) working as a writer. (Look closely at the P's)

67

Barbara Ehrenreich

The Naked Truth about Fitness

The writer, feminist, and socialist party leader Barbara Ehrenreich (b. 1941) wrote some of her first articles and books on the inefficiency and inhumanity of the American health care system. In Complaints and Disorders: The Sexual Politics of Sickness *(co-authored with Deirdre English, 1973) she critiques the unjust and unequal treatment women receive in the medical system. She has written a dozen books, among them* The Hearts of Men: American Dreams and the Flight from Commitment *(1983) and* The Worst Years of Our Lives: Irreverent Notes from a Decade of Greed *(1990). Ehrenreich is a contributing editor at* Ms. *and* Mother Jones, *and her essays also appear regularly in magazines as varied as* Radical America, Time, Vogue, *and the* New York Times Magazine. *Her most recent books are* Kipper's Game *(1993) and* The Snarling Citizen: Essays *(1995), in which "The Naked Truth about Fitness" appears.*

Asked whether she writes in a different voice for the alternative and the mainstream press, Ehrenreich replied, "I don't think it's really a different voice. . . . Obviously I assume more political sympathy for my views if I'm writing for Z *or the* Guardian *in England or the* Nation *than* Time, *but it might be the exact basic argument." She added, "An essay is like a little story, a short story, and I will obsess about what is the real point, what are the real connections, a long time before I ever put finger to keyboard."*

The conversation has all the earmarks of a serious moral debate. The man is holding out for the pleasures of this life, few as they are and short as it is. The woman (we assume his wife, since they are having breakfast together and this is a prime-time television commercial) defends the high road of virtue and self-denial. We know there will be a solution, that it will taste like fresh-baked cookies and will simultaneously lower cholesterol, fight osteoporosis, and melt off unwholesome flab. We *know* this. What we have almost forgotten to wonder about is this: since when is breakfast cereal a *moral* issue?

Morality is no longer a prominent feature of civil society. In the 1980s, politicians abandoned it, Wall Street discarded it, televangelists defiled it. Figuratively speaking, we went for the sucrose rush and forgot the challenge of fiber. But only figuratively. For as virtue drained out of our public lives, it reappeared in our cereal bowls, our exercise regimens, and our militant responses to cigarette smoke, strong drink, and greasy food.

We redefined virtue as health. And considering the probable state of our souls, this was not a bad move. By relocating the seat of virtue from the soul to the pecs, the abs, and the coronary arteries, we may not have become the most virtuous people on earth, but we surely became the most desperate for grace. We spend $5 billion a year on our health-club memberships, $2 billion on vitamins, nearly $1 billion on home-exercise equipment, and $6 billion on sneakers to wear out on our treadmills and StairMasters. We rejoice in activities that leave a hangover of muscle pain and in foods that might, in more temperate times, have been classified as fodder. To say we want to be healthy is to gravely understate the case. We want to be *good*.

Consider my own breakfast cereal, a tasteless, colorless substance that clings to the stomach lining with the avidity of Krazy Glue. Quite wisely, the box makes no promise of good taste or visual charm. Even the supposed health benefits are modestly outlined in tiny print. No, the incentive here is of a higher nature. "It is the right thing to do," the manufacturer intones on the back of the box, knowing that, however alluring our temptations to evil, we all want to do the right thing.

The same confusion of the moral and the physical pervades my health club. "Commit to get fit!" is the current slogan, the verb reminding us of the moral tenacity that has become so elusive in our human relationships. In the locker room we sound like the inmates of a miraculously rehabilitative women's prison, always repenting, forever resolving: "I shouldn't have had that doughnut this morning." "I wasn't here for two weeks and now I'm going to pay the price." Ours is a hierarchy of hardness. The soft, the slow, the easily tired rate no compassion, only the coldest of snubs.

Health is almost universally recognized as a *kind* of virtue. At least, most cultures strong enough to leave an ethnographic trace have discouraged forms of behavior that are believed to be unhealthy. Nevertheless, most of us recognize that health is not an accomplishment so much as it is a *potential*. My upper-body musculature, developed largely on Nautilus machines, means that I probably *can* chop wood or unload trucks, not that I ever *will*. Human cultures have valued many things — courage, fertility, craftsmanship, and deadly aim among them — but ours is almost alone in valuing not the deed itself but the mere capacity to perform it.

So what is it that drives us to run, lift, strain, and monitor our metabolisms as if we were really accomplishing something — something pure, that is, and noble? Sociologist Robert Crawford argues that outbreaks of American "healthism" coincide with bouts of middle-class anxiety. It was near the turn of the century, a time of economic turmoil and violent labor struggles, that white-collar Americans embarked on their first 1980s-style health craze. They hiked, rode bikes, lifted weights, and otherwise heeded Teddy Roosevelt's call for "the strenuous life." They filtered their water and fussed about bran (though sweets were heavily favored as a source of energy). On the loonier fringe, they tried "electric belts," vibrating chairs, testicle supporters, "water cures," prolonged mastication, and copious enemas — moralizing all the while about "right living" and "the divine laws of health."

Our own health-and-fitness craze began in another period of economic anxiety — the 1970s, when the economy slid into "stagflation" and a college degree suddenly ceased to guarantee a career above the cab-driving level. In another decade — say in the 1930s or the 1960s — we might have mobilized for economic change. But the 1970s was the era of *How to Be Your Own Best Friend* and *Looking Out for Number One*, a time in which it seemed more important, or more feasible, to reform our bodies than to change the world. Bit by bit and with the best of intentions, we began to set aside the public morality of participation and protest for the personal morality of health.

Our fascination with fitness has paid off. Fewer Americans smoke than did fifteen years ago; they drink less hard liquor, eat more fiber and less fat. Our rate of heart disease keeps declining, our life expectancy is on the rise. We are less dependent on doctors, more aware of our responsibility for health. No doubt we feel better too, at least those of us who have the means and the motivation to give up bourbon for Evian and poker for raquetball. I personally am more confident and probably more durable as a fitness devotee than I ever was in my former life as a chairwarmer.

But there's a difference between health and health*ism*, between health   10
as a reasonable goal and health as a transcendent value. By confusing health and virtue, we've gotten testier, less tolerant, and ultimately less capable of confronting the sources of disease that do *not* lie within our individual control. Victim blaming, for example, is an almost inevitable side effect of healthism. If health is our personal responsibility, the reasoning goes, then disease must be *our* fault.

I think of the friend — a thoroughly intelligent, compassionate, and (need I say?) ultrafit person — who called to tell me that her sister was facing surgery for a uterine tumor. "I can't understand it," my friend confided. "I'm sure she's been working out." *Not quite enough* was the implication, however, despite the absence of even the frailest connection between fibroids and muscle tone. But like the pretechnological tribalists, we've come to see every illness as a punishment for past transgressions. When Chicago mayor Harold Washington died of a heart attack almost three years ago, some eulogizers offered baleful mutterings about his penchant for unreformed, high-cholesterol soul food. When we hear of someone getting cancer, we mentally scan their lifestyle for the fatal flaw — fatty foods, smoking, even "repressed anger."

There are whole categories of disease that cannot, in good conscience, be blamed on the lifestyles or moral shortcomings of their victims. An estimated 25,000 cancer deaths a year, for example, result from exposure to the pesticides applied so lavishly in agribusiness. Ten thousand Americans are killed every year in industrial accidents; an estimated 20,000 more die from exposure to carcinogens in the workplace — asbestos, toxic solvents, radiation. These deaths are preventable, but not with any amount of oat bran or low-impact aerobics. Environmental and occupational diseases will require a far more rigorous social and political regimen of citizen action, legislation, and enforcement.

Even unhealthy lifestyles can have "environmental" as well as personal origins. Take the matter of diet and smoking. It's easy for the middle-class fiber enthusiast to look down on the ghetto dweller who smokes cigarettes and spends her food stamps on Doritos and soda pop. But in low-income neighborhoods convenience stores and fast-food joints are often the only sources of food, while billboards and TV commercials are the primary sources of nutritional "information." Motivation is another problem. It's one thing to give up smoking and sucrose when life seems long and promising, quite another when it might well be short and brutal.

Statistically speaking, the joggers and bran eaters are concentrated in the white-collar upper-middle class. Blue- and pink-collar people still tend to prefer Bud to Evian and meat loaf to poached salmon. And they still smoke — at a rate of 51 percent, compared with 35 percent for people in professional and managerial occupations. These facts should excite our concern: Why not special cardiovascular-fitness programs for the assembly-line worker as well as the executive? Reduced-rate health-club memberships for truck drivers and typists? Nutritional supplements for the down-and-out? Instead, healthism tends to reinforce longstanding prejudices. If healthy habits are an expression of moral excellence, then the working class is not only "tacky," ill-mannered, or whatever else we've been encouraged to believe — it's morally deficient.

Thus, perversely, does healthism ease the anxieties of the affluent. No   15
amount of straining against muscle machines could have saved Drexel Burnham[1] operatives from unemployment; no aerobic exercises can reduce the price of a private-school education. But fitness *can* give its practitioners a sense of superiority over the potbellied masses. On the other side of victim blaming is an odious mood of self-congratulation: "We" may not be any smarter or more secure about our futures. But surely we are more disciplined and pure.

In the end, though — and the end does come — no one is well served by victim blaming. The victim isn't always "someone else," someone fatter, lazier, or more addicted to smoke and grease. The fact is that we do die, all of us, and that almost all of us will encounter disease, disability, and considerable discomfort either in the process or along the way. The

---

[1]*Drexel Burnham:* An investment firm notorious for its junk bond trading in the 1980s. — EDS.

final tragedy of healthism is that it leaves us so ill prepared for the inevitable. If we believe that health is a sign of moral purity and anything less is a species of sin, then death condemns us all as failures. Longevity is not a resoundingly interesting lifetime achievement, just as working out is not exactly a life's work.

Somehow, we need to find our way back to being healthy without being health*ist*. Health is great. It makes us bouncier and probably happier. Better yet, it can make us fit *for* something: strong enough to fight the big-time polluters, for example, the corporate waste dumpers; tough enough to take on economic arrangements that condemn so many to poverty and to dangerous occupations; lean and powerful enough to demand a more nurturing, less anxiety-ridden social order.

Health is good. But it is not, as even the ancient and athletic Greeks would have said, *the* good.

The Reader's Presence

1. In paragraph 1, Ehrenreich wonders: "Since when is breakfast cereal a *moral* issue?" What does she mean by this remark? Can you find historical evidence in the essay that supplies an answer?

2. How does Ehrenreich use the words *morality* and *virtue*? Does she draw distinctions between the two terms, or does she use them as synonyms? How would you define them?

3. Why does Ehrenreich discuss illnesses (such as cancer) in terms of environment or social class and not in terms of genetics or chronic conditions? Where does Ehrenreich want to place the blame for poor health? Where does "healthism" place the blame? Can you think of alternative ways to determine who's at fault?

68

Susan Faludi

Blame It on Feminism

Susan Faludi's best-selling book Backlash: The Undeclared War against American Women *(1991) became a cause célèbre because of her controversial assertion that the social, economic, and political advances of women and feminism were subtly being attacked throughout the 1980s by media armed with skewed statistics and a conservative ideology. Praised as "feminism's new manifesto" by Eleanor Smeal of the National Organization for Women and denounced as a "conspiracy theory" in a* New Republic *review, the highly publicized, hotly debated* Backlash *turned Faludi into what she self-deprecatingly referred to as the "feminist du jour." Faludi (b. 1959) contributes regularly to* Mother Jones, Ms., *and* California West. *The essay reprinted here, "Blame It on Feminism," appeared in* Mother Jones *shortly before Crown Publishers rushed* Backlash *to bookstores in October 1991 — a moment when, Faludi observed, "women were ready to wake up." The book arrived as abortion rights were being threatened and Americans were watching the Clarence Thomas hearings and the William Kennedy Smith rape case trial. Faludi currently lives in the Haight Ashbury district of San Francisco.*

Faludi finds that celebrity has its disadvantages. She believes that the best journalism relentlessly reports the truth, and for a writer that means "if you're worth anything, you want to offend as many people as possible." However, "when you go from being the anonymous journalist to being a public figure . . . you're suddenly worried about whom you are going to offend." Nonetheless, she continues to offer public criticism of feminists with whom she disagrees because "by censoring our disagreements or papering them over, we ultimately set ourselves back."

To be a woman in America at the close of the twentieth century — what good fortune. That's what we keep hearing anyway. The barricades have fallen, politicians assure us. Women have "made it," Madison Avenue cheers. Women's fight for equality has "largely been won," *Time* magazine announces. Enroll at any university, join any law firm, apply for credit at any bank. Women have so many opportunities now, corporate leaders say, that they don't really need opportunity policies. Women are so equal now, lawmakers say, that they no longer need an Equal Rights Amendment. Women have "so much," former president Ronald

Reagan says, that the White House no longer needs to appoint them to high office. Even American Express ads are saluting a woman's right to charge it. At last, women have received their full citizenship papers.

And yet . . .

Behind this celebration of the American woman's victory, behind the news, cheerfully and endlessly repeated, that the struggle for women's rights is won, another message flashes: You may be free and equal now, but you have never been more miserable.

This bulletin of despair is posted everywhere — at the newsstand, on the TV set, at the movies, in advertisements and doctors' offices and academic journals. Professional women are suffering "burnout" and succumbing to an "infertility epidemic." Single women are grieving from a "man shortage." The *New York Times* reports: Childless women are "depressed and confused" and their ranks are swelling. *Newsweek* says: Unwed women are "hysterical" and crumbling under a "profound crisis of confidence." The health-advice manuals inform: High-powered career women are stricken with unprecedented outbreaks of "stress-induced disorders," hair loss, bad nerves, alcoholism, and even heart attacks. The psychology books advise: Independent women's loneliness represents "a major mental-health problem today." Even founding feminist Betty Friedan has been spreading the word: She warns that women now suffer from "new problems that have no name."

How can American women be in so much trouble at the same time   5
that they are supposed to be so blessed? If women got what they asked for, what could possibly be the matter now?

The prevailing wisdom of the past decade has supported one, and only one, answer to this riddle: It must be all that equality that's causing all that pain. Women are unhappy precisely because they are free. Women are enslaved by their own liberation. They have grabbed at the gold ring of independence, only to miss the one ring that really matters. They have gained control of their fertility, only to destroy it. They have pursued their own professional dreams — and lost out on romance, the greatest female adventure. "Our generation was the human sacrifice" to the women's movement, writer Elizabeth Mehren contends in a *Time* cover story. Baby-boom women, like her, she says, have been duped by feminism: "We believed the rhetoric." In *Newsweek*, writer Kay Ebeling dubs feminism the "Great Experiment That Failed" and asserts, "Women in my generation, its perpetrators, are the casualties."

In the eighties, publications from the *New York Times* to *Vanity Fair* to *The Nation* have issued a steady stream of indictments against the women's movement, with such headlines as "When Feminism Failed" or "The Awful Truth About Women's Lib." They hold the campaign for women's equality responsible for nearly every woe besetting women, from depression to meager savings accounts, from teenage suicides to eating disorders to bad complexions. The *Today* show says women's liberation is to blame for bag ladies. A guest columnist in the *Baltimore Sun* even proposes that feminists produced the rise in slasher movies. By making the "violence" of abortion more acceptable, the author reasons, women's rights activists made it all right to show graphic murders on screen.

At the same time, other outlets of popular culture have been forging the same connection: in Hollywood films, of which *Fatal Attraction* is only the most famous, emancipated women with condominiums of their own slink wild-eyed between bare walls, paying for their liberty with an empty bed, a barren womb. "My biological clock is ticking so loud it keeps me awake at night," Sally Field cries in the film *Surrender,* as, in an all-too-common transformation in the cinema of the eighties, an actress who once played scrappy working heroines is now showcased groveling for a groom. In prime-time television shows, from *thirtysomething* to *Family Man,* single, professional, and feminist women are humiliated, turned into harpies, or hit by nervous breakdowns; the wise ones recant their independent ways by the closing sequence. In popular novels, from Gail Parent's *A Sign of the Eighties* to Stephen King's *Misery,* unwed women shrink to sniveling spinsters or inflate to fire-breathing she-devils; renouncing all aspirations but marriage, they beg for wedding bands from strangers or swing axes at reluctant bachelors. Even Erica Jong's high-flying independent heroine literally crashes by the end of the decade, as the author supplants *Fear of Flying*'s saucy Isadora Wing, an exuberant symbol of female sexual emancipation in the seventies, with an embittered careerist-turned-recovering "codependent" in *Any Woman's Blues* — a book that is intended, as the narrator bluntly states, "to demonstrate what a dead end the so-called sexual revolution had become and how desperate so-called free women were in the last few years of our decadent epoch."

Popular psychology manuals peddle the same diagnosis for contemporary female distress. "Feminism, having promised her a stronger sense of her own identity, has given her little more than an identity *crisis,*" the best-selling advice manual *Being a Woman* asserts. The authors of the era's self-help classic, *Smart Women/Foolish Choices,* proclaim that women's distress was "an unfortunate consequence of feminism" because "it created a myth among women that the apex of self-realization could be achieved only through autonomy, independence, and career."

In the Reagan and Bush years, government officials have needed no prompting to endorse this thesis. Reagan spokeswoman Faith Ryan Whittlesey declared feminism a "straitjacket" for women, in one of the White House's only policy speeches on the status of the American female population — entitled "Radical Feminism in Retreat." The U.S. attorney general's Commission on Pornography even proposed that women's professional advancement might be responsible for rising rape rates: With more women in college and at work now, the commission members reasoned in their report, women just have more opportunities to be raped.   10

Legal scholars have railed against the "equality trap." Sociologists have claimed that "feminist-inspired" legislative reforms have stripped women of special "protections." Economists have argued that well-paid working women have created a "less stable American family." And demographers, with greatest fanfare, have legitimated the prevailing wisdom with so-called neutral data on sex ratios and fertility trends; they say they actually have the numbers to prove that equality doesn't mix with marriage and motherhood.

Finally, some "liberated" women themselves have joined the lamentations. In *The Cost of Loving: Women and the New Fear of Intimacy*, Megan Marshall, a Harvard-pedigreed writer, asserts that the feminist "Myth of Independence" has turned her generation into unloved and unhappy fast-trackers, "dehumanized" by careers and "uncertain of their gender identity." Other diaries of mad Superwomen charge that "the hard-core feminist viewpoint," as one of them puts it, has relegated educated executive achievers to solitary nights of frozen dinners and closet drinking. The triumph of equality, they report, has merely given women hives, stomach cramps, eye "twitching" disorders, even comas.

But what "equality" are all these authorities talking about?

If American women are so equal, why do they represent two-thirds of all poor adults? Why are more than 70 percent of full-time working women making less than twenty-five thousand dollars a year, nearly double the number of men at that level? Why are they still far more likely than men to live in poor housing, and twice as likely to draw no pension? If women "have it all," then why don't they have the most basic requirements to achieve equality in the work force: Unlike that of virtually all other industrialized nations, the U.S. government still has no family-leave and child-care programs.

If women are so "free," why are their reproductive freedoms in   15 greater jeopardy today than a decade earlier? Why, in their own homes, do they still shoulder 70 percent of the household duties — while the only major change in the last fifteen years is that now men *think* they do more around the house? In thirty states, it is still generally legal for husbands to rape their wives; and only ten states have laws mandating arrest for domestic violence — even though battering is the leading cause of injury to women (greater than rapes, muggings, and auto accidents combined).

The word may be that women have been "liberated," but women themselves seem to feel otherwise. Repeatedly in national surveys, majorities of women say they are still far from equality. In poll after poll in the decade, overwhelming majorities of women said they need equal pay and equal job opportunities, they need an Equal Rights Amendment, they need the right to an abortion without government interference, they need a federal law guaranteeing maternity leave, they need decent child-care services. They have none of these. So how exactly have women "won" the war for women's rights?

Seen against this background, the much ballyhooed claim that feminism is responsible for making women miserable becomes absurd — and irrelevant. The afflictions ascribed to feminism, from "the man shortage" to "the infertility epidemic" to "female burnout" to "toxic day care," have had their origins not in the actual conditions of women's lives but rather in a closed system that starts and ends in the media, popular culture, and advertising — an endless feedback loop that perpetuates and exaggerates its own false images of womanhood. And women don't see feminism as their enemy, either. In fact, in national surveys, 75 to 95 percent of women credit the feminist campaign with *improving* their lives, and a similar proportion say that the women's movement should keep pushing for change.

If the many ponderers of the Woman Question really wanted to know what is troubling the American female population, they might have asked their subjects. In public-opinion surveys, women consistently rank their own *inequality*, at work and at home, among their most urgent concerns. Over and over, women complain to pollsters of a lack of economic, not marital, opportunities; they protest that working men, not working women, fail to spend time in the nursery and the kitchen. It is justice for their gender, not wedding rings and bassinets, that women believe to be in desperately short supply.

As the last decade ran its course, the monitors that serve to track slippage in women's status have been working overtime. Government and private surveys are showing that women's already vast representation in the lowliest occupations is rising, their tiny presence in higher-paying trade and craft jobs stalled or backsliding, their minuscule representation in upper management posts stagnant or falling, and their pay dropping in the very occupations where they have made the most "progress."

In national politics, the already small numbers of women in both   20
elective posts and political appointments fell during the eighties. In private life, the average amount that a divorced man paid in child support fell by about 25 percent from the late seventies to the mid-eighties (to a mere $140 a month). And government records chronicled a spectacular rise in sexual violence against women. Reported rapes more than doubled from the early seventies — at nearly twice the rate of all other violent crimes and four times the overall crime rate in the United States.

The truth is that the last decade has seen a powerful counterassault on women's rights, a backlash, an attempt to retract the handful of small and hard-won victories that the feminist movement did manage to win for women. This counterassault is largely insidious: In a kind of pop-culture version of the big lie, it stands the truth boldly on its head and proclaims that the very steps that have elevated women's position have actually led to their downfall.

The backlash is at once sophisticated and banal, deceptively "progressive" and proudly backward. It deploys both the "new" findings of "scientific research" and the dime-store moralism of yesteryear; it turns into media sound bites both the glib pronouncements of pop-psych trend-watchers and the frenzied rhetoric of New Right preachers. The backlash has succeeded in framing virtually the whole issue of women's rights in its own language. Just as Reaganism shifted political discourse far to the right and demonized liberalism, so the backlash convinced the public that women's "liberation" was the true contemporary American scourge — the source of an endless laundry list of personal, social, and economic problems.

But what has made women unhappy in the last decade is not their "equality" — which they don't yet have — but the rising pressure to halt, and even reverse, women's quest for that equality. The "man shortage" and the "infertility epidemic" are not the price of liberation; in fact, they do not even exist. But these chimeras are part of a relentless whittling-down process — much of it amounting to outright propaganda — that has served to stir women's private anxieties and break their political wills. Identifying feminism as women's enemy only furthers the ends of a backlash against women's equality by simultaneously deflecting attention from the backlash's central role and recruiting women to attack their own cause.

Some social observers may well ask whether the current pressures on women actually constitute a backlash — or just a continuation of American society's long-standing resistance to women's equal rights. Certainly hostility to female independence has always been with us. But if fear and loathing of feminism is a sort of perpetual viral condition in our culture, it is not always in an acute stage; its symptoms subside and resurface periodically. And it is these episodes of resurgence, such as the one we face now, that can accurately be termed "backlashes" to women's advancement. If we trace these occurrences in American history, we find such flare-ups are hardly random; they have always been triggered by the perception — accurate or not — that women are making great strides. These outbreaks are backlashes because they have always arisen in reaction to women's "progress," caused not simply by a bedrock of misogyny but by the specific efforts of contemporary women to improve their status, efforts that have been interpreted time and again by men — especially men grappling with real threats to their economic and social well-being on other fronts — as spelling their own masculine doom.

The most recent round of backlash first surfaced in the late seventies on the fringes, among the evangelical Right. By the early eighties, the fundamentalist ideology had shouldered its way into the White House. By the mid-eighties, as resistance to women's rights acquired political and social acceptability, it passed into the popular culture. And in every case, the timing coincided with signs that women were believed to be on the verge of a breakthrough.

Just when the women's quest for equal rights seemed closest to achieving its objectives, the backlash struck it down. Just when a "gender gap" at the voting booth surfaced in 1980, and women in politics began to talk of capitalizing on it, the Republican party elevated Ronald Reagan and both political parties began to shunt women's rights off their platforms. Just when support for feminism and the Equal Rights Amendment reached a record high in 1981, the amendment was defeated the following year. Just when women were starting to mobilize against battering and sexual assaults, the federal government cut funding for battered-women's programs, defeated bills to fund shelters, and shut down its Office of Domestic Violence — only two years after opening it in 1979. Just when record numbers of younger women were supporting feminist goals in the mid-eighties (more of them, in fact, than older women) and a majority of all women were calling themselves feminists, the media declared the advent of a younger "postfeminist generation" that supposedly reviled the women's movement. Just when women racked up their largest percentage ever supporting the right to abortion, the U.S. Supreme Court moved toward reconsidering it.

In other words, the antifeminist backlash has been set off not by women's achievement of full equality but by the increased possibility that they might win it. It is a preemptive strike that stops women long before they reach the finish line. "A backlash may be an indication that women really have had an effect," feminist psychiatrist Dr. Jean Baker Miller has written, "but backlashes occur when advances have been small, before changes are sufficient to help many people. . . . It is almost as if the leaders of backlashes use the fear of change as a threat before major change has occurred." In the last decade, some women did make substantial advances before the backlash hit, but millions of others were left behind, stranded. Some women now enjoy the right to legal abortion — but not the forty-four million women, from the indigent to the military worker, who depend on the federal government for their medical care. Some women can now walk into high-paying professional careers — but not the millions still in the typing pools or behind the department-store sales counters. (Contrary to popular myth about the "have-it-all" baby-boom women, the largest percentage of women in this generation remain in office support roles.)

As the backlash has gathered force, it has cut off the few from the many — and the few women who have advanced seek to prove, as a social survival tactic, that they aren't so interested in advancement after all. Some of them parade their defection from the women's movement, while their working-class peers founder and cling to the splintered remains of the feminist cause. While a very few affluent and celebrity women who are showcased in news stories boast about going home to "bake bread," the many working-class women appeal for their economic rights — flocking to unions in record numbers, striking on their own for pay equity, and establishing their own fledgling groups for working-women's rights. In 1986, while 41 percent of upper-income women were claiming in the Gallup poll that they were not feminists, only 26 percent of low-income women were making the same claim.

Women's advances and retreats are generally described in military terms: battles won, battles lost, points and territory gained and surrendered. The metaphor of combat is not without its merits in this context, and, clearly, the same sort of martial accounting and vocabulary is already surfacing here. But by imagining the conflict as two battalions neatly arrayed on either side of the line, we miss the entangled nature, the locked embrace, of a "war" between women and the male culture they inhabit. We miss the reactive nature of a backlash, which, by definition, can exist only in response to another force.

In times when feminism is at a low ebb, women assume the reactive   30
role — privately and, most often, covertly struggling to assert themselves against the dominant cultural tide. But when feminism itself becomes the tide, the opposition doesn't simply go along with the reversal: It digs in its heels, brandishes its fists, builds walls and dams. And its resistance creates countercurrents and treacherous undertows.

The force and furor of the backlash churn beneath the surface, largely invisible to the public eye. On occasion in the last decade, they have burst into view. We have seen New Right politicians condemn women's independence, antiabortion protesters firebomb women's clinics, fundamentalist preachers damn feminists as "whores." Other signs of the backlash's wrath, by their sheer brutality, can push their way into public consciousness for a time — the sharp increase in rape, for example, or the rise in pornography that depicts extreme violence against women.

More subtle indicators in popular culture may receive momentary, and often bemused, media notice, then quickly slip from social awareness: a report, for instance, that the image of women on prime-time TV shows has suddenly degenerated. A survey of mystery fiction finding the number of tortured and mutilated female characters mysteriously multiplying. The puzzling news that, as one commentator put it, "so many hit songs have the B word [bitch] to refer to women that some rap music seems to be veering toward rape music." The ascendancy of violently misogynist comics like Andrew Dice Clay, who calls women "pigs" and "sluts," or radio hosts like Rush Limbaugh, whose broadsides against "femi-Nazi" feminists helped make his syndicated program the most popular radio talk show in the nation. Or word that, in 1987, the American Women in Radio and Television couldn't award its annual prize to ads that feature women positively: It could find no ad that qualified.

These phenomena are all related, but that doesn't mean they are somehow coordinated. The backlash is not a conspiracy, with a council dispatching agents from some central control room, nor are the people who serve its ends often aware of their role; some even consider themselves feminists. For the most part, its workings are encoded and internalized, diffuse and chameleonic. Not all of the manifestations of the backlash are of equal weight or significance, either; some are mere ephemera thrown up by a culture machine that is always scrounging for a "fresh" angle. Taken as a whole, however, these codes and cajolings, these whispers and threats and myths, move overwhelmingly in one direction: They try to push women back into their "acceptable" roles — whether as Daddy's girl or fluttery romantic, active nester or passive love object.

Although the backlash is not an organized movement, that doesn't make it any less destructive. In fact, the lack of orchestration, the absence of a single string-puller, only makes it harder to see — and perhaps more effective. A backlash against women's rights succeeds to a degree that it appears *not* to be political, that it appears not to be a struggle at all. It is most powerful when it goes private, when it lodges inside a woman's mind and turns her vision inward, until she imagines the pressure is all in her head, until she begins to enforce the backlash, too — on herself.

In the last decade, the backlash has moved through the culture's se-   35
cret chambers, traveling through passageways of flattery and fear. Along the way, it has adopted disguises: a mask of mild derision or the painted face of deep "concern." Its lips profess pity for any woman who won't fit the mold, while it tries to clamp the mold around her ears. It pursues a divide-and-conquer strategy: single versus married women, working women versus homemakers, middle versus working class. It manipulates a system of rewards and punishments, elevating women who follow its rules, isolating those who don't. The backlash remarkets old myths about women as new facts and ignores all appeals to reason. Cornered, it denies its own existence, points an accusatory finger at feminism, and burrows deeper underground.

Backlash happens to be the title of a 1947 Hollywood movie in which a man frames his wife for a murder he's committed. The backlash against women's rights works in much the same way: Its rhetoric charges feminists with all the crimes it perpetrates. The backlash line blames the women's movement for the "feminization of poverty" — while the backlash's own instigators in Washington have pushed through the budget cuts that have helped impoverish millions of women, have fought pay-equity proposals, and undermined equal-opportunity laws. The backlash line claims the women's movement cares nothing for children's rights — while its own representatives in the capital and state legislatures have blocked one bill after another to improve child care, slashed billions of dollars in aid for children, and relaxed state licensing standards for day-care centers. The backlash line accuses the women's movement of creating a generation of unhappy single and childless women — but its purveyors in the media are the ones guilty of making single and childless women feel like circus freaks.

To blame feminism for women's "lesser life" is to miss its point entirely, which is to win women a wider range of experience. Feminism remains a pretty simple concept, despite repeated — and enormously effective — efforts to dress it up in greasepaint and turn its proponents into gargoyles. As Rebecca West wrote sardonically in 1913, "I myself have never been able to find out precisely what feminism is: I only know that people call me a feminist whenever I express sentiments that differentiate me from a doormat."

The meaning of the word "feminism" has not really changed since it first appeared in a book review in *The Athenaeum* on April 27, 1895, describing a woman who "has in her the capacity of fighting her way back to independence." It is the basic proposition that, as Nora put it in Ibsen's *A Doll's House* a century ago, "Before everything else I'm a human being." It is the simply worded sign hoisted by a little girl in the 1970 Women's Strike for Equality: "I AM NOT A BARBIE DOLL." Feminism asks the world to recognize at long last that women aren't decorative ornaments, worthy vessels, members of a "special-interest group." They are half (in fact, now more than half) of the national population, and just as deserving of rights and opportunities, just as capable of participating in the world's events, as the other half. Feminism's agenda is basic: It asks that women not be forced to "choose" between public justice and private happiness. It asks that women be free to define themselves — instead of having their identity defined for them, time and again, by their culture and their men.

The fact that these are still such incendiary notions should tell us that American women have a way to go before they enter the promised land of equality.

The Reader's Presence

1. How would you describe the tone of voice Faludi adopts in her opening paragraph? What is her attitude toward the opinions she cites? Do you think she wants her readers to recognize her attitude immediately? Is it possible to read the paragraph and think she agrees with all of the opinions she cites? What sort of reader is she counting on?

2. What is a backlash? How does Faludi use the term? What proof does she offer that a backlash against feminism is occurring? To what extent does she hold women themselves responsible? Which groups does she view as most responsible for the backlash? Why?

3. In rereading the essay, take careful note of the way Faludi supports her contention that a backlash is occurring. List all of the evidence she offers. Can you find any similarities among her sources? To what extent does she depend upon personal experience? upon interviews? upon experts? upon research? upon inference? Which evidence strikes you as the strongest? as the weakest?

69

Paul Fussell

A Well-Regulated Militia

A well-established English professor who taught at Rutgers before accepting a distinguished professorship at the University of Pennsylvania in 1983, Paul Fussell (b. 1924) did not successfully break with academic prose until he tired of writing what he was "supposed to write." After twenty years of writing critical works such as Poetic Meter and Poetic Form *(1965) and* The Rhetorical World of Augustan Humanism *(1965), Fussell published his first work of nonfiction for a general audience.* The Great War and Modern Memory *(1975) won the National Book Award and the National Book Critics Circle Award and received wide critical acclaim for its examination of how World War I changed what Frank Kermode called "the texture of our culture." Fussell continued to touch upon the subject of war in his subsequent books,* Abroad: British Literary Traveling between the Wars *(1980) and* The Boy Scout Handbook and Other Observations *(1982). Fussell then wrote* Class: A Guide through the American Status System *(1983) and edited* The Norton Book of Travel *(1987). Fussell returned to his favorite subject in his collection of essays* Thank God for the Atom Bomb and Other Essays *(1988), from which this selection is taken. Fussell's most recent publications are* Bad, or The Dumbing of America *(1991), and* The Anti-Egoist, Kingsley Amis, Man of Letters *(1994).*

In the spring Washington swarms with high school graduating classes. They come to the great pulsating heart of the Republic — which no one has yet told them is Wall Street — to be impressed by the White House and the Capitol and the monuments and the Smithsonian and the space capsules. Given the state of public secondary education, I doubt if many of these young people are at all interested in language and rhetoric, and I imagine few are fascinated by such attendants of power and pressure as verbal misrepresentation and disingenuous quotation. But any who are can profit from a stroll past the headquarters of the National Rifle Association of America, its slick marble façade conspicuous at 1600 Rhode Island Avenue, NW.

There they would see an entrance flanked by two marble panels offering language, and language more dignified and traditional than that customarily associated with the Association's gun-freak constituency, with its T-shirts reading GUNS, GUTS, AND GLORY ARE WHAT MADE AMERICA GREAT and its belt buckles proclaiming I'LL GIVE UP MY GUN WHEN THEY PRY MY COLD DEAD FINGERS FROM AROUND IT. The marble panel on the right reads, "The right of the people to keep and bear arms shall not be infringed," which sounds familiar. So familiar that the student naturally expects the left-hand panel to honor the principle of symmetry by presenting the first half of the quotation, namely: "A well-regulated Militia, being necessary to the security of a free state, . . ." But looking to the left, the inquirer discovers not that clause at all but rather this lame list of NRA functions and specializations: "Firearms Safety Education. Marksmanship Training. Shooting for Recreation." It's as if in presenting its well-washed, shiny public face the NRA doesn't want to remind anyone of the crucial dependent clause of the Second Amendment, whose latter half alone it is so fond of invoking to urge its prerogatives. (Some legible belt buckles of members retreat further into a seductive vagueness, reading only, "Our American Heritage: the Second Amendment.") We infer that for the Association, the less emphasis on the clause about the militia, the better. Hence its pretence on the front of its premises that the quoted main clause is not crucially dependent on the now unadvertised subordinate clause — indeed, it's meaningless without it.

Because flying .38- and .45-caliber bullets rank close to cancer, heart disease, and AIDS as menaces to public health in this country, the firearm lobby, led by the NRA, comes under liberal attack regularly, and with special vigor immediately after an assault on some conspicuous person like Ronald Reagan or John Lennon. Thus *The New Republic,* in April 1981, deplored the state of things but offered as a solution only the suggestion that the whole Second Amendment be perceived as obsolete and amended out of the Constitution. This would leave the NRA with not a leg to stand on.

But here as elsewhere a better solution would be not to fiddle with the Constitution but to take it seriously, the way we've done with the First Amendment, say, or with the Thirteenth, the one forbidding open and avowed slavery. And by taking the Second Amendment seriously I mean taking it literally. We should "close read" it and thus focus lots of attention on the grammatical reasoning of its two clauses. This might shame the NRA into pulling the dependent clause out of the closet, displaying it on its façade, and accepting its not entirely pleasant implications. These could be particularized in an Act of Congress providing:

(1) that the Militia shall now, after these many years, be "well-regulated," as the Constitution requires.

(2) that any person who has chosen to possess at home a gun of any kind, and who is not a member of the police or the military or an appropriate government agency, shall be deemed to have enrolled

automatically in the Militia of the United States. Members of the Militia, who will be issued identifying badges, will be organized in units of battalion, company, or platoon size representing counties, towns, or boroughs. If they bear arms while not proceeding to or from scheduled exercises of the Militia, they will be punished "as a court martial may direct."

(3) that any gun owner who declines to join the regulated Militia may opt out by selling his firearms to the federal government for $1,000 each. He will sign an undertaking that if he ever again owns firearms he will be considered to have enlisted in the Militia.

(4) that because the Constitution specifically requires that the Militia shall be "well regulated," a regular training program, of the sort familiar to all who have belonged to military units charged with the orderly management of small arms, shall be instituted. This will require at least eight hours of drill each Saturday at some convenient field or park, rain or shine or snow or ice. There will be weekly supervised target practice (separation from the service, publicly announced, for those who can't hit a barn door). And there will be ample practice in digging simple defense works, like foxholes and trenches, as well as necessary sanitary installations like field latrines and straddle trenches. Each summer there will be a six-week bivouac (without spouses), and this, like all the other exercises, will be under the close supervision of long-service noncommissioned officers of the United States Army and the Marine Corps. On bivouac, liquor will be forbidden under extreme penalty, but there will be an issue every Friday night of two cans of 3.2 beer, and feeding will follow traditional military lines, the cuisine consisting largely of shit-on-a-shingle, sandwiches made of bull dick (baloney) and choke-ass (cheese), beans, and fatty pork. On Sundays and holidays, powdered eggs for breakfast. Chlorinated water will often be available, in Lister Bags. Further obligatory exercises designed to toughen up the Militia will include twenty-five-mile hikes and the negotiation of obstacle courses. In addition, there will be instruction of the sort appropriate to other lightly armed, well-regulated military units: in map-reading, the erection of double-apron barbed-wire fences, and the rudiments of military courtesy and the traditions of the Militia, beginning with the Minute Men. Per diem payments will be made to those participating in these exercises.

(5) that since the purpose of the Militia is, as the Constitution says, to safeguard "the security of a free state," at times when invasion threatens (perhaps now the threat will come from Nicaragua, national security no longer being menaced by North Vietnam) all units of the Militia will be trucked to the borders for the duration of the emergency, there to remain in field conditions (here's

where the practice in latrine-digging pays off) until Congress declares that the emergency has passed. Congress may also order the Militia to perform other duties consistent with its constitutional identity as a regulated volunteer force: for example, flood and emergency and disaster service (digging, sandbag filling, rescuing old people); patrolling angry or incinerated cities; or controlling crowds at large public events like patriotic parades, motor races, and professional football games.

(6) that failure to appear for these scheduled drills, practices, bivouacs, and mobilizations shall result in the Militiaperson's dismissal from the service and forfeiture of badge, pay, and firearm.

Why did the Framers of the Constitution add the word *bear* to the phrase "keep and bear arms?" Because they conceived that keeping arms at home implied the public obligation to bear them in a regulated way for "the security of" not a private household but "a free state." If interstate bus fares can be regulated, it is hard to see why the Militia can't be, especially since the Constitution says it must be. *The New Republic* has recognized that "the Second Amendment to the Constitution clearly connects the right to bear arms to the 18th-century national need to raise a militia." But it goes on: "That need is now obsolete, and so is the amendment." And it concludes: "If the only way this country can get control of firearms is to amend the Constitution, then it's time for Congress to get the process under way."

I think not. Rather, it's time not to amend Article II of the Bill of Rights (and Obligations) but to read it, publicize it, embrace it, and enforce it. That the Second Amendment stems from concerns that can be stigmatized as "18th-century" cuts little ice. The First Amendment stems precisely from such concerns, and no one but Yahoos wants to amend it. Also "18th-century" is that lovely bit in Section 9 of Article I forbidding any "Title of Nobility" to be granted by the United States. That's why we've been spared Lord Annenberg and Sir Leonard Bernstein, Knight. Thank God for the eighteenth century, I say. It understood not just what a firearm is and what a Militia is. It also understood what "well regulated" means. It knew how to compose a constitutional article and it knew how to read it. And it assumed that everyone, gun lobbyists and touring students alike, would understand and correctly quote it. Both halves of it.

The Reader's Presence

1. Here is the Second Amendment of the Bill of Rights: "A well-regulated Militia being necessary to the security of a free state, the right of the people to keep and bear arms shall not be infringed." Why does Fussell point out that the first part of the amendment

does not appear on the marble facade of the National Rifle Association headquarters in Washington, D.C.? Why does he believe that the first half of the amendment is crucial to a correct understanding of the second half? Do you agree? Can you think of an alternative interpretation?

2. Though he is a proponent of gun control, why doesn't Fussell believe the Second Amendment should be repealed or revised? In what ways does his interpretation preserve the Second Amendment? Do you think the National Rifle Association would endorse Fussell's proposal? Do you think it would support any aspects of it? Explain.

3. Suppose Congress took Fussell's proposal seriously. Could it enact the kind of regulations Fussell recommends? What practical problems might arise? For example, how would the Militia be maintained? How expensive would it be? What parts of Fussell's plan do you think are meant to be taken seriously? What parts are intended as humorous? How can you tell the difference?

70

June Jordan

Nobody Mean More to Me than You[1] *and the Future Life of Willie Jordan*

June Jordan (b. 1936) is professor of African American studies at the University of California, Berkeley. She is the author of novels, short stories, poetry, children's fiction, and biography. Her essays can be found in collections such as On Call *(1986),* Moving Toward Home: Political Essays *(1989) and* Technical Difficulties: African American Notes on the State of the Union *(1992). Jordan's most recent work is a musical,* I Was Looking at the Ceiling and Then I Saw the Sky: Earthquake-Romance *(1995), for which John Adams wrote the music. The essay "Nobody Mean More to Me than You and the Future Life of Willie Jordan" is found in* On Call. *She has also published stories and poems in numerous national magazines.*

Jordan thinks of writing, and especially of poetry, as a way toward empowerment. "Why should power and language coalesce in poetry? Because poetry is the medium for telling the truth, and because a poem is antithetical to lies/evasions and superficiality, anyone who becomes a practicing poet has an excellent chance of becoming somebody real, somebody known, self-defined and attuned to and listening and hungering for kindred real voices utterly/articulately different from his or her own voice."

---

[1]Black English aphorism crafted by Monica Morris, a junior at S.U.N.Y. at Stony Brook, October, 1984. — JORDAN'S NOTE.

Black English is not exactly a linguistic buffalo; as children, most of the thirty-five million Afro-Americans living here depend on this language for our discovery of the world. But then we approach our maturity inside a larger social body that will not support our efforts to become anything other than the clones of those who are neither our mothers nor our fathers. We begin to grow up in a house where every true mirror shows us the face of somebody who does not belong there, whose walk and whose talk will never look or sound "right," because that house was meant to shelter a family that is alien and hostile to us. As we learn our way around this environment, either we hide our original word habits, or we completely surrender our own voice, hoping to please those who will never respect anyone different from themselves: Black English is not exactly a linguistic buffalo, but we should understand its status as an endangered species, as a perishing, irreplaceable system of community intelligence, or we should expect its extinction, and, along with that, the extinguishing of much that constitutes our own proud, and singular identity.

What we casually call "English," less and less defers to England and its "gentlemen." "English" is no longer a specific matter of geography or an element of class privilege; more than thirty-three countries use this tool as a means of "intranational communication."[2] Countries as disparate as Zimbabwe and Malaysia, or Israel and Uganda, use it as their non-native currency of convenience. Obviously, this tool, this "English," cannot function inside thirty-three discrete societies on the basis of rules and values absolutely determined somewhere else, in a thirty-fourth other country, for example.

In addition to that staggering congeries of non-native users of English, there are five countries, or 333,746,000 people, for whom this thing called "English" serves as a native tongue.[3] Approximately ten percent of these native speakers of "English" are Afro-American citizens of the U.S.A. I cite these numbers and varieties of human beings dependent on "English" in order, quickly, to suggest how strange and how tenuous is any concept of "Standard English." Obviously, numerous forms of English now operate inside a natural, an uncontrollable, continuum of development. I would suppose "the standard" for English in Malaysia is not the same as "the standard" in Zimbabwe. I know that standard forms of English for Black people in this country do not copy that of whites. And, in fact, the structural differences between these two kinds of English have intensified, becoming more Black, or less white, despite the expected homogenizing effects of television[4] and other mass media.

---

[2]*English Is Spreading, but What Is English?* A presentation by Professor S. N. Sridahr, Dept. Of Linguistics, S.U.N.Y. at Stony Brook, April 9, 1985; Dean's Conversation among the Disciplines. — JORDAN'S NOTE.

[3]Ibid. — JORDAN'S NOTE.

[4]*New York Times*, March 15, 1985, Section One, p. 14: Report on study by Linguistics at the University of Pennsylvania. — JORDAN'S NOTE.

Nonetheless, white standards of English persist, supreme and unquestioned, in these United States. Despite our multilingual population, and despite the deepening Black and white cleavage within that conglomerate, white standards control our official and popular judgments of verbal proficiency and correct, or incorrect, language skills, including speech. In contrast to India, where at least fourteen languages co-exist as legitimate Indian languages, in contrast to Nicaragua, where all citizens are legally entitled to formal school instruction in their regional or tribal languages, compulsory education in America compels accommodation to exclusively white forms of "English." White English, in America, is "Standard English."

This story begins two years ago. I was teaching a new course, "In   5
Search of the Invisible Black Woman," and my rather large class seemed evenly divided between young Black women and men. Five or six white students also sat in attendance. With unexpected speed and enthusiasm we had moved through historical narratives of the 19th century to literature by and about Black women, in the 20th. I had assigned the first forty pages of Alice Walker's *The Color Purple,* and I came, eagerly, to class that morning:

"So!" I exclaimed, aloud. "What did you think? How did you like it?"

The students studied their hands, or the floor. There was no response. The tense, resistant feeling in the room fairly astounded me.

At last, one student, a young woman still not meeting my eyes, muttered something in my direction:

"What did you say?" I prompted her.

"Why she have them talk so funny. It don't sound right."   10

"You mean the language?"

Another student lifted his head: "It don't look right, neither. I couldn't hardly read it."

At this, several students dumped on the book. Just about unanimously, their criticisms targeted the language. I listened to what they wanted to say and silently marveled at the similarities between their casual speech patterns and Alice Walker's written version of Black English.

But I decided against pointing to these identical traits of syntax; I wanted not to make them self-conscious about their own spoken language — not while they clearly felt it was "wrong." Instead I decided to swallow my astonishment. Here was a negative Black reaction to a prize winning accomplishment of Black literature that white readers across the country had selected as a best seller. Black rejection was aimed at the one irreducibly Black element of Walker's work: the language — Celie's Black English. I wrote the opening lines of *The Color Purple* on the blackboard and asked the students to help me translate these sentences into Standard English:

You better not never tell nobody but God. It'd kill your mammy.
Dear God,

   I am fourteen years old. I have always been a good girl. Maybe you
can give me a sign letting me know what is happening to me.

   Last spring after Little Lucious come I heard them fussing. He was
pulling on her arm. She say it too soon, Fonso. I aint well. Finally he leave
her alone. A week go by, he pulling on her arm again. She say, Naw, I
ain't gonna. Can't you see I'm already half dead, an all of the children.[5]

Our process of translation exploded with hilarity and even hysterical,
shocked laughter: The Black writer, Alice Walker, knew what she was
doing! If rudimentary criteria for good fiction includes the manipulation
of language so that the syntax and diction of sentences will tell you the
identity of speakers, the probable age and sex and class of speakers, and
even the locale — urban/rural/southern/western — then Walker had written, perfectly. This is the translation into Standard English that our class
produced:

   Absolutely, one should never confide in anybody besides God. Your
   secrets could prove devastating to your mother.
   Dear God,

   I am fourteen years old, I have always been good. But now, could you
help me to understand what is happening to me?

   Last spring, after my little brother, Lucious, was born, I heard my
parents fighting. My father kept pulling at my mother's arm. But she told
him, "It's too soon for sex, Alfonso. I am still not feeling well." Finally,
my father left her alone. A week went by, and then he began bothering my
mother, again: Pulling her arm. She told him, "No, I won't! Can't you see
I'm already exhausted from all of these children?"

(Our favorite line was "It's too soon for sex, Alphonso.")   15

   Once we could stop laughing, once we could stop our exponentially
wild improvisations on the theme of Translated Black English, the students pushed me to explain their own negative first reactions to their spoken language on the printed page. I thought it was probably akin to the
shock of seeing yourself in a photograph for the first time. Most of the
students had never before seen a written facsimile of the way they talk.
None of the students had ever learned how to read and write their own
verbal system of communication: Black English. Alternatively, this fact
began to baffle or else bemuse and then infuriate my students. Why not?
Was it too late? Could they learn how to do it, now? And, ultimately, the
final test question, the one testing my sincerity: Could I teach them? Because I had never taught anyone Black English and, as far as I knew, no
one, anywhere in the United States, had ever offered such a course, the
best I could say was "I'll try."

---

[5]Alice Walker, *The Color Purple*, p. 11, Harcourt Brace, N.Y. — JORDAN'S NOTE.

He looked like a wrestler.

He sat dead center in the packed room and, every time our eyes met, he quickly nodded his head as though anxious to reassure, and encourage, me.

Short, with strikingly broad shoulders and long arms, he spoke with a surprisingly high, soft voice that matched the soft bright movement of his eyes. His name was Willie Jordan. He would have seemed even more unlikely in the context of Contemporary Women's Poetry, except that ten or twelve other Black men were taking the course, as well. Still, Willie was conspicuous. His extreme fitness, the muscular density of his presence underscored the riveted, gentle attention that he gave to anything anyone said. Generally, he did not join the loud and rowdy dialogue flying back and forth, but there could be no doubt about his interest in our discussions. And, when he stood to present an argument he'd prepared, overnight, that nervous smile of his vanished and an irregular stammering replaced it, as he spoke with visceral sincerity, word by word.

That was how I met Willie Jordan. It was in between "In Search of   20
the Invisible Black Woman" and "The Art of Black English." I was waiting for Departmental approval and I supposed that Willie might be, so to speak, killing time until he, too, could study Black English. But Willie really did want to explore Contemporary Women's poetry and, to that end, volunteered for extra research and never missed a class.

Towards the end of that semester, Willie approached me for an independent study project on South Africa. It would commence the next semester. I thought Willie's writing needed the kind of improvement only intense practice will yield. I knew his intelligence was outstanding. But he'd wholeheartedly opted for "Standard English" at a rather late age, and the results were stilted and frequently polysyllabic, simply for the sake of having more syllables. Willie's unnatural formality of language seemed to me consistent with the formality of his research into South African apartheid. As he projected his studies, he would have little time, indeed, for newspapers. Instead, more than 90 percent of his research would mean saturation in strictly historical, if not archival, material. I was certainly interested. It would be tricky to guide him into a more confident and spontaneous relationship both with language and apartheid. It was going to be wonderful to see what happened when he could catch up with himself, entirely, and talk back to the world.

September, 1984: Breezy fall weather and much excitement! My class, "The Art of Black English," was full to the limit of the fire laws. And, in Independent Study, Willie Jordan showed up, weekly, fifteen minutes early for each of our sessions. I was pretty happy to be teaching, altogether!

I remember an early class when a young brother, replete with his ever present pork-pie hat, raised his hand and then told us that most of what he'd heard was "all right" except it was "too clean." "The brothers on the street," he continued, "they mix it up more. Like 'fuck' and 'motherfuck.' Or like 'shit.'" He waited, I waited. Then all of us laughed a good while, and we got into a brawl about "correct" and "realistic" Black English that led to Rule 1.

Rule 1: *Black English is about a whole lot more than mothafuckin.*

As a criterion, we decided, "realistic" could take you anywhere you   25
want to go. Artful places. Angry places. Eloquent and sweetalkin places. Polemical places. Church. And the local Bar & Grill. We were checking out a language, not a mood or a scene or one guy's forgettable mouthing off.

It was hard. For most of the students, learning Black English required a fallback to patterns and rhythms of speech that many of their parents had beaten out of them. I mean *beaten.* And, in a majority of cases, correct Black English could be achieved only by striving for *incorrect* Standard English, something they were still pushing at, quite uncertainly. This state of affairs led to Rule 2.

Rule 2: *If it's wrong in Standard English it's probably right in Black English, or, at least, you're hot.*

It was hard. Roommates and family members ridiculed their studies, or remained incredulous, "You *studying* that shit? At school?" But we were beginning to feel the companionship of pioneers. And we decided that we needed another rule that would establish each one of us as equally important to our success. This was Rule 3.

Rule 3: *If it don't sound like something that come out somebody mouth then it don't sound right. If it don't sound right then it ain't hardly right. Period.*

This rule produced two weeks of compositions in which the students   30
agonizingly tried to spell the sound of the Black English sentence they wanted to convey. But Black English is, preeminently, an oral/spoken means of communication. *And spelling don't talk.* So we needed Rule 4.

Rule 4: *Forget about the spelling. Let the syntax carry you.*

Once we arrived at Rule 4 we started to fly because syntax, the structure of an idea, leads you to the world view of the speaker and reveals her values. The syntax of a sentence equals the structure of your consciousness. If we insisted that the language of Black English adheres to a distinctive Black syntax, then we were postulating a profound difference between white and Black people, *per se.* Was it a difference to prize or to obliterate?

There are three qualities of Black English — the presence of life, voice, and clarity — that testify to a distinctive Black value system that we became excited about and self-consciously tried to maintain.

1. Black English has been produced by a pre-technocratic, if not anti-technological, culture. More, our culture has been constantly threatened by annihilation or, at least, the swallowed blurring of assimilation. Therefore, our language is a system constructed by people constantly needing to insist that we exist, that we are present. Our language devolves from a culture that abhors all abstraction, or anything tending to obscure or

delete the fact of the human being who is here and now/the truth of the person who is speaking or listening. Consequently, *there is no passive voice construction possible in Black English*. For example, you cannot say, "Black English is being eliminated." You must say, instead, "White people eliminating Black English." The assumption of the presence of life governs all of Black English. Therefore, overwhelmingly, *all action takes place in the language of the present indicative*. And every sentence assumes the living and active participation of at least two human beings, the speaker and the listener.

2. A primary consequence of the person-centered values of Black 35
English is the delivery of voice. If you speak or write Black English, your ideas will necessarily possess that otherwise elusive attribute, *voice*.

3. One main benefit following from the person-centered values of Black English is that of *clarity*. If your idea, your sentence, assumes the presence of at least two living and active people, you will make it understandable because the motivation behind every sentence is the wish to say something real to somebody real.

As the weeks piled up, translation from Standard English into Black English or vice versa occupied a hefty part of our course work.

> Standard English (hereafter S.E.): "In considering the idea of studying Black English those questioned suggested —"
>> (What's the subject? Where's the person? Is anybody alive in there, in that idea?)
>> Black English (hereafter B.E.): "I been asking people what you think about somebody studying Black English and they answer me like this."

But there were interesting limits. You cannot "translate" instances of Standard English preoccupied with abstraction or with nothing/nobody evidently alive, into Black English. That would warp the language into uses antithetical to the guiding perspective of its community of users. Rather you must first change those Standard English sentences, themselves, into ideas consistent with the person-centered assumptions of Black English.

GUIDELINES FOR BLACK ENGLISH

1. Minimal number of words for every idea: This is the source for the aphoristic and/or poetic force of the language; eliminate every possible word.

2. Clarity: If the sentence is not clear it's not Black English.

3. Eliminate use of the verb *to be* whenever possible. This leads to the 40
deployment of more descriptive and, therefore, more precise verbs.

4. Use *be* or *been* only when you want to describe a chronic, ongoing state of things.

He *be* at the office, by 9. (He is always at the office by 9.)
He *been* with her since forever.

5. Zero copula: Always eliminate the verb *to be* whenever it would combine with another verb in Standard English.

S.E.: She is going out with him.
B.E.: She going out with him.

6. Eliminate *do* as in:

S.E.: What do you think? What do you want?
B.E.: What you think? What you want?

Rules number 3, 4, 5, and 6 provide for the use of the minimal number of verbs per idea and, therefore, greater accuracy in the choice of verb.

7. In general, if you wish to say something really positive, try to formulate the idea using emphatic negative structure. 45

S.E.: He's fabulous.
B.E.: He bad.

8. Use double or triple negatives for dramatic emphasis.

S.E.: Tina Turner sings out of this world.
B.E.: Ain nobody sing like Tina.

9. Never use the *-ed* suffix to indicate the past tense of a verb.

S.E.: She closed the door.
B.E.: She close the door. Or, she have close the door.

10. Regardless of intentional verb time, only use the third person singular, present indicative, for use of the verb *to have,* as an auxiliary.

S.E.: He had his wallet then he lost it.
B.E.: He have him wallet then he lose it.
S.E.: He had seen that movie.
B.E.: We seen that movie. Or, we have see that movie.

11. Observe a minimal inflection of verbs. Particularly, never change from the first person singular forms to the third person singular.

S.E.: Present Tense Forms: He goes to the store.
B.E.: He go to the store.
S.E.: Past Tense Forms: He went to the store.
B.E.: He go to the store. Or, he gone to the store. Or, he been to the store.

12. The possessive case scarcely ever appears in Black English. Never 50 use an apostrophe ('s) construction. If you wander into a possessive case component of an idea, then keep logically consistent: ours, *his, theirs, mines.* But, most likely, if you bump into such a component, you have wandered outside the underlying world-view of Black English.

S.E.: He will take their car tomorrow.
B.E.: He taking they car tomorrow.

13. Plurality: Logical consistency, continued: If the modifier indicates plurality then the noun remains in the singular case.

S.E.: He ate twelve doughnuts.
B.E.: He eat twelve doughnut.
S.E.: She has many books.
B.E.: She have many book.

14. Listen for, or invent, special Black English forms of the past tense, such as: "He losted it. That what she felted." If they are clear and readily understood, then use them.

15. Do not hesitate to play with words, sometimes inventing them: e.g. "astropotomous" means huge like a hippo plus astronomical and, therefore, signifies real big.

16. In Black English, unless you keenly want to underscore the past tense nature of an action, stay in the present tense and rely on the overall context of your ideas for the conveyance of time and sequence.

17. Never use the suffix -*ly* form of an adverb in Black English.   55

S.E.: The rain came down rather quickly.
B.E.: The rain come down pretty quick.

18. Never use the indefinite article *an* in Black English.

S.E.: He wanted to ride an elephant.
B.E.: He want to ride him a elephant.

19. Invariant syntax: in correct Black English it is possible to formulate an imperative, an interrogative, and a simple declarative idea with the same syntax:

B.E.: You going to the store?
    You going to the store.
    You going to the store!

Where was Willie Jordan? We'd reached the mid-term of the semester. Students had formulated Black English guidelines, by consensus, and they were now writing with remarkable beauty, purpose, and enjoyment:

I ain hardly speakin for everybody but myself so understan that. — Kim Parks

Samples from student writings:

Janie have a great big ole hole inside her. Tea Cake the only thing that fit that hole . . .

    That pear tree beautiful to Janie, especial when bees fiddlin with the blossomin pear there growing large and lovely. But personal speakin, the love she get from staring at that tree ain the love what starin back at her in them relationship. (Monica Morris)

Love is a big theme in, *They Eye Was Watching God*. Love show people new corners inside theyself. It pull out good stuff and stuff back bad stuff . . . Joe worship the doing uh his own hand and need other people to worship him too. But he ain't think about Janie that she a person and ought to live like anybody common do. Queen life not for Janie. (Monica Morris)

In both life and writin, Black womens have varietous experience of love that be cold like a iceberg or fiery like a inferno. Passion got for the other partner involve, man or woman, seem as shallow, ankle-deep water or the most profoundest abyss. (Constance Evans)

Family love another bond that ain't never break under no pressure. (Constance Evans)

You know it really cold / When the friend you / Always get out the fire / Act like they don't know you / When you in the heat. (Constance Evans)

Big classroom discussion bout love at this time. I never take no class where us have any long arguin for and against for two or three day. New to me and great. I find the class time talkin a million time more interestin than detail bout the book. (Kathy Esseks)

As these examples suggest, Black English no longer limited the students, in any way. In fact, one of them, Philip Garfield, would shortly "translate" a pivotal scene from Ibsen's *Doll House,* as his final term paper.

NORA: I didn't gived no shit. I thinked you a asshole back then, too, you make it so hard for me save mines husband life.
KROGSTAD: Girl, it clear you ain't any idea what you done. You done exact what once done, and I losed my reputation over it.
NORA: You asks me believe you once act brave save you wife life?
KROGSTAD: Law care less why you done it.
NORA: Law must suck.
KROGSTAD: Suck or no, if I wants, judge screw you wid dis paper.
NORA: No way, man. (Philip Garfield)

But where was Willie? Compulsively punctual, and always thoroughly prepared with neatly typed compositions, he had disappeared. He failed to show up for our regularly scheduled conference, and I received neither a note nor a phone call of explanation. A whole week went by. I wondered if Willie had finally been captured by the extremely current happenings in South Africa: passage of a new constitution that did not enfranchise the Black majority, and militant Black South African reaction to that affront. I wondered if he'd been hurt, somewhere. I wondered if the serious workload of weekly readings and writings had overwhelmed him and changed his mind about independent study. Where was Willie Jordan?

One week after the first conference that Willie missed, he called: "Hello, Professor Jordan? This is Willie. I'm sorry I wasn't there last week. But something has come up and I'm pretty upset. I'm sorry but I really can't deal right now."

I asked Willie to drop by my office and just let me see that he was okay. He agreed to do that. When I saw him I knew something hideous had happened. Something had hurt him and scared him to the marrow. He was all agitated and stammering and terse and incoherent. At last, his sadly jumbled account let me surmise, as follows: Brooklyn police had murdered his unarmed, twenty-five-year-old brother, Reggie Jordan. Neither Willie nor his elderly parents knew what to do about it. Nobody from the press was interested. His folks had no money. Police ran his family around and around, to no point. And Reggie was really dead. And Willie wanted to fight, but he felt helpless.

With Willie's permission I began to try to secure legal counsel for the Jordan family. Unfortunately Black victims of police violence are truly numerous while the resources available to prosecute their killers are truly scarce. A friend of mine at the Center for Constitutional Rights estimated that just the preparatory costs for bringing the cops into court normally approaches $180,000. Unless the execution of Reggie Jordan became a major community cause for organizing, and protest, his murder would simply become a statistical item.

Again, with Willie's permission, I contacted every newspaper and media person I could think of. But the William Bastone feature article in *The Village Voice* was the only result from that canvassing.

Again, with Willie's permission, I presented the case to my class in   65
Black English. We had talked about the politics of language. We had talked about love and sex and child abuse and men and women. But the murder of Reggie Jordan broke like a hurricane across the room.

There are few "issues" as endemic to Black life as police violence. Most of the students knew and respected and liked Jordan. Many of them came from the very neighborhood where the murder had occurred. All of the students had known somebody close to them who had been killed by police, or had known frightening moments of gratuitous confrontation with the cops. They wanted to do everything at once to avenge death. Number One: They decided to compose personal statements of condolence to Willie Jordan and his family written in Black English. Number Two: They decided to compose individual messages to the police, in Black English. These should be prefaced by an explanatory paragraph composed by the entire group. Number Three: These individual messages, with their lead paragraph, should be sent to *Newsday*.

The morning after we agreed on these objectives, one of the young women students appeared with an unidentified visitor, who sat through the class, smiling in a peculiar, comfortable way.

Now we had to make more tactical decisions. Because we wanted the messages published, and because we thought it imperative that our outrage be known by the police, the tactical question was this: Should the opening, group paragraph be written in Black English or Standard English?

I have seldom been privy to a discussion with so much heart at the dead heat of it. I will never forget the eloquence, the sudden haltings of speech, the fierce struggle against tears, the furious throwaway, and useless explosions that this question elicited.

That one question contained several others, each of them extraordinarily painful to even contemplate. How best to serve the memory of Reggie Jordan? Should we use the language of the killers — Standard English — in order to make our ideas acceptable to those controlling the killers? But wouldn't what we had to say be rejected, summarily, if we said it in our own language, the language of the victim, Reggie Jordan? But if we sought to express ourselves by abandoning our language wouldn't that mean our suicide on top of Reggie's murder? But if we expressed ourselves in our own language wouldn't that be suicidal to the wish to communicate with those who, evidently, did not give a damn about us/Reggie/police violence in the Black community?

At the end of one of the longest, most difficult hours of my own life, the students voted, unanimously, to preface their individual messages with a paragraph composed in the language of Reggie Jordan. "*At least we don't give up nothing else. At least we stick to the truth: Be who we been. And stay all the way with Reggie.*"

It was heartbreaking to proceed, from that point. Everyone in the room realized that our decision in favor of Black English had doomed our writings, even as the distinctive reality of our Black lives always has doomed our efforts to "be who we been" in this country.

I went to the blackboard and took down this paragraph, dictated by the class:

. . . YOU COPS!
WE THE BROTHER AND SISTER OF WILLIE JORDAN, A FELLOW STONY BROOK STUDENT WHO THE BROTHER OF THE DEAD REGGIE JORDAN. REGGIE, LIKE MANY BROTHER AND SISTER, HE A VICTIM OF BRUTAL RACIST POLICE, OCTOBER 25, 1984. US APPALL, FED UP, BECAUSE THAT ANOTHER SENSELESS DEATH WHAT OCCUR IN OUR COMMUNITY. THIS WHAT WE FEEL, THIS, FROM OUR HEART, FOR WE AIN'T STAYIN' SILENT NO MORE.

With the completion of this introduction, nobody said anything. I asked for comments. At this invitation, the unidentified visitor, a young Black man, ceaselessly smiling, raised his hand. He was, it so happens, a rookie cop. He had just joined the force in September and, he said he thought he should clarify a few things. So he came forward and sprawled easily into a posture of barroom, or fireside, nostalgia:

"See," Officer Charles enlightened us, "most times when you out on the street and something come down you do one of two things. Over-react or under-react. Now, if you under-react then you can get yourself kilt. And if you over-react then maybe you kill somebody. Fortunately it's about nine times out of ten and you will over-react. So the brother got kilt. And I'm sorry about that, believe me. But what you have to understand is what kilt him: Over-reaction. That's all. Now you talk about Black people and white police but see, now, I'm a cop myself. And (big smile) I'm Black. And just a couple months ago I was on the other side. But see it's the same for me. You a cop, you the ultimate authority: the Ultimate Authority. And you on the street, most of the time you can only do one of two things: over-react or under-react. That's all it is with the brother. Over-reaction. Didn't have nothing to do with race."

That morning Officer Charles had the good fortune to escape without being boiled alive. But barely. And I remember the pride of his smile when I read about the fate of Black policemen and other collaborators, in South Africa. I remember him, and I remember the shock and palpable feeling of shame that filled the room. It was as though that foolish, and deadly, young man had just relieved himself of his foolish, and deadly, explanation, face to face with the grief of Reggie Jordan's father and Reggie Jordan's mother. Class ended quietly. I copied the paragraph from the blackboard, collected the individual messages and left to type them up.

Newsday rejected the piece.

The Village Voice could not find room in their "Letters" section to print the individual messages from the students to the police.

None of the TV news reporters picked up the story.

Nobody raised $180,000 to prosecute the murder of Reggie Jordan.   80

Reggie Jordan is really dead.

I asked Willie Jordan to write an essay pulling together everything important to him from that semester. He was still deeply beside himself with frustration and amazement and loss. This is what he wrote, unedited, and in its entirety:

> Throughout the course of this semester I have been researching the effects of oppression and exploitation along racial lines in South Africa and its neighboring countries. I have become aware of South African police brutalization of native Africans beyond the extent of the law, even though the laws themselves are catalyst affliction upon Black men, women, and children. Many Africans die each year as a result of the deliberate use of police force to protect the white power structure.
>
> Social control agents in South Africa, such as policemen, are also used to force compliance among citizens through both overt and covert tactics. It is not uncommon to find bold-faced coercion and cold-blooded killings of Blacks by South African police for undetermined and/or inadequate reasons. Perhaps the truth is that the only reasons for this heinous treatment of Blacks rests in racial differences. We should also understand that what is conveyed through the media is not always accurate and may sometimes be construed as the tip of the iceberg at best.
>
> I recently received a painful reminder that racism, poverty, and the abuse of power are global problems which are by no means unique to South Africa. On October 25, 1984, at approximately 3:00 P.M. my brother, Mr. Reginald Jordan, was shot and killed by two New York

City policemen from the 75th precinct in the East New York section of Brooklyn. His life ended at the age of twenty-five. Even up to this current point in time the Police Department has failed to provide my family, which consists of five brothers, eight sisters, and two parents, with a plausible reason for Reggie's death. Out of the many stories that were given to my family by the Police Department, not one of them seems to hold water. In fact, I honestly believe that the Police Department's assessment of my brother's murder is nothing short of ABSOLUTE BULLSHIT, and thus far no evidence had been produced to alter perception of the situation.

Furthermore, I believe that one of three cases may have occurred in this incident. First, Reggie's death may have been the desired outcome of the police officer's action, in which case the killing was premeditated. Or, it was a case of mistaken identity, which clarifies the fact that the two officers who killed my brother and their commanding parties are all grossly incompetent. Or, both of the above cases are correct, i.e., Reggie's murderers intended to kill him and the Police Department behaved insubordinately.

Part of the argument of the officers who shot Reggie was that he had attacked one of them and took his gun. This was their major claim. They also said that only one of them had actually shot Reggie. The facts, however, speak for themselves. According to the Death Certificate and autopsy report, Reggie was shot eight times from point-blank range. The Doctor who performed the autopsy told me himself that two bullets entered the side of my brother's head, four bullets were sprayed into his back, and two bullets struck him in the back of his legs. It is obvious that unnecessary force was used by the police and that it is extremely difficult to shoot someone in his back when he is attacking or approaching you.

After experiencing a situation like this and researching South Africa I believe that to a large degree, justice may only exist as rhetoric. I find it difficult to talk of true justice when the oppression of my people both at home and abroad attests to the fact that inequality and injustice are serious problems whereby Blacks and Third World people are perpetually short-changed by society. Something has to be done about the way in which this world is set up. Although it is a difficult task, we do have the power to make a change.

— Willie J. Jordan, Jr.
EGL 487, Section 58, November 14, 1984

It is my privilege to dedicate this book to the future life of Willie J. Jordan, Jr.

August 8, 1985

The Reader's Presence

1. How would you characterize Jordan's tone at the outset of this essay? When and how does her tone of voice change as the essay proceeds? How, for example, would you describe her voice when she takes up the subject of Black English, and more particularly its

history and grammar? In what specific ways does her tone change when she discusses her class and her experiences with them? when she discusses Willie Jordan and her course in contemporary women's poetry? In what specific ways does her diction change in each of these parts of her essay? What, more specifically, do you make of the section where Jordan experiments with "translating" Alice Walker? What point does she make here about the adequacy of Standard English to represent the nuances of an important dimension of American culture?

2. Consider the "Rules and Guidelines" Jordan and her students formulate about Black English. Summarize the rationale for each, and comment on the extent to which you are convinced by the logic of each proposition. Assess the specific strengths and weaknesses of the examples Jordan presents from her students' own writing. Explain why the question of how the students should write their group preface to their message of protest is so sensitive. What sorts of issues are at stake in such a decision? What does Jordan mean when she says "our decision in favor of Black English had doomed our writings" (paragraph 72)? In what sense was the decision to write the protest in Black English courageous?

3. Reread the scene in which Officer Charles explains Reggie Jordan's death. What responses does this account elicit from the author? from her students? What diction and tone of voice does Jordan use to convey her attitude toward Officer Charles's apology for the system? What conclusions does Jordan draw from her experiences with this class? What connections does she make between the students' work with Black English and their response to Reggie Jordan's death?

71

Jamaica Kincaid

On Seeing England for the First Time

Jamaica Kincaid was born in Antigua in 1949 and came to the United States at the age of seventeen to work for a New York family as an au pair. Her novel Lucy *(1990) is an imaginative account of her experience of coming into adulthood in a foreign country and continues the narrative of her personal history begun in the novel* Annie John *(1985). She has also published a collection of short stories,* At the Bottom of the River *(1983), a collection of essays,* A Small Place *(1988), and a third novel,* The Autobiography of My Mother *(1995). Her writing also appears in national magazines, especially the* New Yorker, *where she has worked as a staff writer. "On Seeing England for the First Time" first appeared in* Transition *in 1991.*

"I'm someone who writes to save her life," Kincaid says. "I mean, I can't imagine what I would do if I didn't write. I would be dead or I would be in jail because — what else could I do? I can't really do anything but write. All the things that were available to someone in my position involved being a subject person. And I'm very bad at being a subject person."

When I saw England for the first time, I was a child in school sitting at a desk. The England I was looking at was laid out on a map gently, beautifully, delicately, a very special jewel; it lay on a bed of sky blue — the background of the map — its yellow form mysterious, because though it looked like a leg of mutton, it could not really look like anything so familiar as a leg of mutton because it was England — with shadings of pink and green, unlike any shadings of pink and green I had seen before, squiggly veins of red running in every direction. England was a special jewel all right, and only special people got to wear it. The people who got to wear England were English people. They wore it well and they wore it everywhere: in jungles, in deserts, on plains, on top of the highest mountains, on all the oceans, on all the seas, in places where they were not welcome, in places they should not have been. When my teacher had pinned this map up on the blackboard, she said, "This is England" — and she said it with authority, seriousness, and adoration, and we all sat up. It was as if she had said, "This is Jerusalem, the place you will go to when you die but only if you have been good." We understood then — we were meant to understand then — that England was to be our source of myth and the source from which we got our sense of reality, our sense of what was meaningful, our sense of what was meaningless — and much about our own lives and much about the very idea of us headed that last list.

At the time I was a child sitting at my desk seeing England for the first time, I was already very familiar with the greatness of it. Each morning before I left for school, I ate a breakfast of half a grapefruit, an egg, bread and butter and a slice of cheese, and a cup of cocoa; or half a grapefruit, a bowl of oat porridge, bread and butter and a slice of cheese, and a cup of cocoa. The can of cocoa was often left on the table in front of me. It had written on it the name of the company, the year the company was established, and the words "Made in England." Those words, "Made in England," were written on the box the oats came in too. They would also have been written on the box the shoes I was wearing came in; a bolt of gray linen cloth lying on the shelf of a store from which my mother had bought three yards to make the uniform that I was wearing had written along its edge those three words. The shoes I wore were made in England; so were my socks and cotton undergarments and the satin ribbons I wore tied at the end of two plaits of my hair. My father, who might have sat next to me at breakfast, was a carpenter and cabinet maker. The shoes he wore to work would have been made in England, as were his khaki shirt and trousers, his underpants and undershirt, his socks and brown felt hat. Felt was not the proper material from which a hat that was expected to provide shade from the hot sun should be made, but my father must have seen and admired a picture of an Englishman wearing such a hat in England, and this picture that he saw must have been so compelling that it caused him to wear the wrong hat for a hot climate most of his long life. And this hat — a brown felt hat — became so central to his character that it was the first thing he put on in the morning as he stepped out of bed and the last thing he took off before he stepped back into bed at night. As we sat at breakfast a car might go by. The car, a Hillman or a Zephyr, was made in England. The very idea of the meal itself, breakfast, and its substantial quality and quantity was an idea from England; we somehow knew that in England they began the day with this meal called breakfast and a proper breakfast was a big breakfast. No one I knew liked eating so much food so early in the day; it made us feel sleepy, tired. But this breakfast business was Made in England like almost everything else that surrounded us, the exceptions being the sea, the sky, and the air we breathed.

At the time I saw this map — seeing England for the first time — I did not say to myself, "Ah, so that's what it looks like," because there was no longing in me to put a shape to those three words that ran through every part of my life, no matter how small; for me to have had such a longing would have meant that I lived in a certain atmosphere, an atmosphere in which those three words were felt as a burden. But I did not live in such an atmosphere. My father's brown felt hat would develop a hole in its crown, the lining would separate from the hat itself, and six weeks before he thought that he could not be seen wearing it — he was a very vain man — he would order another hat from England. And my mother taught me to eat my food in the English way: the knife in the right hand, the fork in the left, my elbows held still close to my side, the food carefully balanced on my fork and then brought up to my mouth. When I had finally mastered it, I overheard her saying to a friend, "Did you see how nicely she can eat?" But I knew then that I enjoyed my food more when I ate it with my bare hands, and I continued to do so when she wasn't looking. And when my teacher showed us the map, she asked us to study it carefully, because no test we would ever take would be complete without this statement: "Draw a map of England."

I did not know then that the statement "Draw a map of England" was something far worse than a declaration of war, for in fact a flat-out declaration of war would have put me on alert, and again in fact, there was no need for war — I had long ago been conquered. I did not know then that this statement was part of a process that would result in my erasure, not my physical erasure, but my erasure all the same. I did not know then that this statement was meant to make me feel in awe and small whenever I heard the word "England": awe at its existence, small because I was not from it. I did not know very much of anything then — certainly not what a blessing it was that I was unable to draw a map of England correctly.

After that there were many times of seeing England for the first time. I saw England in history. I knew the names of all the kings of England. I knew the names of their children, their wives, their disappointments, their triumphs, the names of people who betrayed them, I knew the dates on which they were born and the dates they died. I knew their conquests and was made to feel glad if I figured in them; I knew their defeats. I knew the details of the year 1066 (the Battle of Hastings, the end of the reign of the Anglo-Saxon kings) before I knew the details of the year 1832 (the year slavery was abolished). It wasn't as bad as I make it sound now; it was worse. I did like so much hearing again and again how Alfred the Great, traveling in disguise, had been left to watch cakes, and because he wasn't used to this the cakes got burned, and Alfred burned his hands pulling them out of the fire, and the woman who had left him to watch the cakes screamed at him. I loved King Alfred. My grandfather was named after him; his son, my uncle, was named after King Alfred; my brother is named after King Alfred. And so there are three people in my family named after a man they have never met, a man who died over ten centuries ago. The first view I got of England then was not unlike the first view received by the person who named my grandfather.

This view, though — the naming of the kings, their deeds, their disappointments — was the vivid view, the forceful view. There were other views, subtler ones, softer, almost not there — but these were the ones that made the most lasting impression on me, these were the ones that made me really feel like nothing. "When morning touched the sky" was one phrase, for no morning touched the sky where I lived. The mornings where I lived came on abruptly, with a shock of heat and loud noises. "Evening approaches" was another, but the evenings where I lived did not approach; in fact, I had no evening — I had night and I had day and they came and went in a mechanical way: on, off; on, off. And then there were gentle mountains and low blue skies and moors over which people took walks for nothing but pleasure, when where I lived a walk was an act of labor, a burden, something only death or the automobile could relieve. And there were things that a small turn of a head could convey — entire worlds, whole lives would depend on this thing, a certain turn of a head. Everyday life could be quite tiring, more tiring than anything I was told not to do. I was told not to gossip, but they did that all the time. And they ate so much food, violating another of those rules they taught me: Do not indulge in gluttony. And the foods they ate actually: If only sometime I could eat cold cuts after theater, cold cuts of lamb and mint sauce, and Yorkshire pudding and scones, and clotted cream, and sausages that came from up-country (imagine, "up-country"). And having troubling thoughts at twilight, a good time to have troubling thoughts, apparently; and servants who stole and left in the middle of a crisis, who were born with a limp or some other kind of deformity, not nourished properly in their mother's womb (that last part I figured out for myself; the point was, oh to have an untrustworthy servant); and wonderful cobbled streets onto which solid front doors opened; and people whose eyes were blue and who had fair skins and who smelled only of lavender, or sometimes sweet pea or primrose. And those flowers with those names: delphiniums, foxgloves, tulips, daffodils, floribunda, peonies: in bloom, a striking display, being cut and placed in large glass bowls, crystal, decorating rooms so large twenty families the size of mine could fit in comfortably but used only for passing through. And the weather was so remarkable because the rain fell gently always, only occasionally in deep gusts, and it colored the air various shades of gray, each an appealing shade for a dress to be worn when a portrait was being painted; and when it rained at twilight, wonderful things happened: People bumped into each other unexpectedly and that would lead to all sorts of turns of events — a plot, the mere weather caused plots. I saw that people rushed: They rushed to catch trains, they rushed toward each other and away from each other; they rushed and rushed and rushed. That word: rushed! I did not know what it was to do that. It was too hot to do that, and so I came to envy people who would rush, even though it had no meaning to me to do such a thing. But there they are again. They loved their children; their children were sent to their own rooms as a punishment, rooms larger than my entire house. They were special, everything about them said so, even their clothes; their clothes rustled, swished, soothed. The world was theirs, not mine; everything told me so.

If now as I speak of all this I give the impression of someone on the outside looking in, nose pressed up against a glass window, that is wrong. My nose was pressed up against a glass window all right, but there was an iron vise at the back of my neck forcing my head to stay in place. To avert my gaze was to fall back into something from which I had been rescued, a hole filled with nothing, and that was the word for everything about me, nothing. The reality of my life was conquests, subjugation, humiliation, enforced amnesia. I was forced to forget. Just for instance, this: I lived in a part of St. John's, Antigua, called Ovals. Ovals was made up of five streets, each of them named after a famous English seaman — to be quite frank, an officially sanctioned criminal: Rodney Street (after George Rodney), Nelson Street (after Horatio Nelson), Drake Street (after Francis Drake), Hood Street, and Hawkins Street (after John Hawkins). But John Hawkins was knighted after a trip he made to Africa, opening up a new trade, the slave trade. He was then entitled to wear as his crest a Negro bound with a cord. Every single person living on Hawkins Street was descended from a slave. John Hawkins's ship, the one in which he transported the people he had bought and kidnapped, was called *The Jesus*. He later became the treasurer of the Royal Navy and rear admiral.

Again, the reality of my life, the life I led at the time I was being shown these views of England for the first time, for the second time, for the one-hundred-millionth time, was this: The sun shone with what sometimes seemed to be a deliberate cruelty; we must have done something to deserve that. My dresses did not rustle in the evening air as I strolled to the theater (I had no evening, I had no theater; my dresses were made of a cheap cotton, the weave of which would give way after not too many washings). I got up in the morning, I did my chores (fetched water from the public pipe for my mother, swept the yard), I washed myself, I went to a woman to have my hair combed freshly every day (because before we were allowed into our classroom our teachers would inspect us, and children who had not bathed that day, or had dirt under their fingernails, or whose hair had not been combed anew that day, might not be allowed to attend class). I ate that breakfast. I walked to school. At school we gathered in an auditorium and sang a hymn, "All Things Bright and Beautiful," and looking down on us as we sang were portraits of the Queen of England and her husband; they wore jewels and medals and they smiled. I was a Brownie. At each meeting we would form a little group around a flagpole, and after raising the Union Jack, we would say, "I promise to do my best, to do my duty to God and the Queen, to help other people every day and obey the scouts' law."

Who were these people and why had I never seen them, I mean really seen them, in the place where they lived? I had never been to England. No one I knew had ever been to England, or I should say, no one I knew had ever been and returned to tell me about it. All the people I knew who had gone to England had stayed there. Sometimes they left behind them their small children, never to see them again. England! I had seen England's representatives. I had seen the governor general at the public grounds at a ceremony celebrating the Queen's birthday. I had seen an old princess and I had seen a young princess. They had both been extremely not beautiful, but who of us would have told them that? I had never seen England, really seen it, I had only met a representative, seen a picture, read books, memorized its history. I had never set foot, my own foot, in it.

The space between the idea of something and its reality is always   10
wide and deep and dark. The longer they are kept apart — idea of thing, reality of thing — the wider the width, the deeper the depth, the thicker and darker the darkness. This space starts out empty, there is nothing in it, but it rapidly becomes filled up with obsession or desire or hatred or love — sometimes all of these things, sometimes some of these things, sometimes only one of these things. The existence of the world as I came to know it was a result of this: idea of thing over here, reality of thing way, way over there. There was Christopher Columbus, an unlikable man, an unpleasant man, a liar (and so, of course, a thief) surrounded by maps and schemes and plans, and there was the reality on the other side of that width, that depth, that darkness. He became obsessed, he became filled with desire, the hatred came later, love was never a part of it. Eventually, his idea met the longed-for reality. That the idea of something and its reality are often two completely different things is something no one ever remembers; and so when they meet and find that they are not compatible, the weaker of the two, idea or reality, dies. That idea Christopher Columbus had was more powerful than the reality he met, and so the reality he met died.

And so finally, when I was a grown-up woman, the mother of two children, the wife of someone, a person who resides in a powerful country that takes up more than its fair share of a continent, the owner of a house with many rooms in it and of two automobiles, with the desire and will (which I very much act upon) to take from the world more than I give back to it, more than I deserve, more than I need, finally then, I saw England, the real England, not a picture, not a painting, not through a story in a book, but England, for the first time. In me, the space between the idea of it and its reality had become filled with hatred, and so when at last I saw it I wanted to take it into my hands and tear it into little pieces and then crumble it up as if it were clay, child's clay. That was impossible, and so I could only indulge in not-favorable opinions.

There were monuments everywhere; they commemorated victories, battles fought between them and the people who lived across the sea from them, all vile people, fought over which of them would have dominion over the people who looked like me. The monuments were useless to them now, people sat on them and ate their lunch. They were like markers on an old useless trail, like a piece of old string tied to a finger to jog the memory, like old decoration in an old house, dirty, useless, in the way. Their skins were so pale, it made them look so fragile, so weak, so ugly. What if I had the power to simply banish them from their land, send boat after boatload of them on a voyage that in fact had no destination, force them to live in a place where the sun's presence was a constant? This would rid them of their pale complexion and make them look more like me, make them look more like the people I love and treasure and hold dear, and more like the people who occupy the near and far reaches of my imagination, my history, my geography, and reduce them and everything they have ever known to figurines as evidence that I was in divine favor, what if all this was in my power? Could I resist it? No one ever has.

And they were rude, they were rude to each other. They didn't like each other very much. They didn't like each other in the way they didn't like me, and it occurred to me that their dislike for me was one of the few things they agreed on.

I was on a train in England with a friend, an English woman. Before we were in England she liked me very much. In England she didn't like me at all. She didn't like the claim I said I had on England, she didn't like the views I had of England. I didn't like England, she didn't like England, but she didn't like me not liking it too. She said, "I want to show you my England, I want to show you the England that I know and love." I had told her many times before that I knew England and I didn't want to love it anyway. She no longer lived in England; it was her own country, but it had not been kind to her, so she left. On the train, the conductor was rude to her; she asked something, and he responded in a rude way. She became ashamed. She was ashamed at the way he treated her; she was ashamed at the way he behaved. "This is the new England," she said. But I liked the conductor being rude; his behavior seemed quite appropriate. Earlier this had happened: We had gone to a store to buy a shirt for my husband; it was meant to be a special present, a special shirt to wear on special occasions. This was a store where the Prince of Wales has his shirts made, but the shirts sold in this store are beautiful all the same. I found a shirt I thought my husband would like and I wanted to buy him a tie to go with it. When I couldn't decide which one to choose, the salesman showed me a new set. He was very pleased with these, he said, because they bore the crest of the Prince of Wales, and the Prince of Wales had never allowed his crest to decorate an article of clothing before. There was something in the way he said it; his tone was slavish, reverential, awed. It made me feel angry; I wanted to hit him. I didn't do that. I said, my husband and I hate princes, my husband would never wear anything that had a prince's anything on it. My friend stiffened. The salesman stiffened. They both drew themselves in, away from me. My friend told me that the prince was a symbol of her Englishness, and I could see that I had caused offense. I looked at her. She was an English person, the sort of English person I used to know at home, the sort who was nobody in England but somebody when they came to live among the people like me. There were many people I could have seen England with; that I was seeing it with this particular person, a person who reminded me of the people who showed me England long ago as I sat in church or at my desk, made me feel silent and afraid, for I wondered if, all these years of our friendship, I had had a friend or had been in the thrall of a racial memory.

I went to Bath — we, my friend and I, did this, but though we were together, I was no longer with her. The landscape was almost as familiar as my own hand, but I had never been in this place before, so how could that be again? And the streets of Bath were familiar, too, but I had never walked on them before. It was all those years of reading, starting with Roman Britain. Why did I have to know about Roman Britain? It was of no real use to me, a person living on a hot, drought-ridden island, and it is of no use to me now, and yet my head is filled with this nonsense, Roman Britain. In Bath, I drank tea in a room I had read about in a novel written in the eighteenth century. In this very same room, young women wearing those dresses that rustled and so on danced and flirted and sometimes disgraced themselves with young men, soldiers, sailors, who were on their way to Bristol or someplace like that, so many places like that where so many adventures, the outcome of which was not good for me, began. Bristol, England. A sentence that began "That night the ship sailed from Bristol, England" would end not so good for me. And then I was driving through the countryside in an English motorcar, on narrow winding roads, and they were so familiar, though I had never been on them before; and through little villages the names of which I somehow knew so well though I had never been there before. And the countryside did have all those hedges and hedges, fields hedged in. I was marveling at all the toil of it, the planting of the hedges to begin with and then the care of it, all that clipping, year after year of clipping, and I wondered at the lives of the people who would have to do this, because wherever I see and feel the hands that hold up the world, I see and feel myself and all the people who look like me. And I said, "Those hedges" and my friend said that someone, a woman named Mrs. Rothchild, worried that the hedges weren't being taken care of properly; the farmers couldn't afford or find the help to keep up the hedges, and often they replaced them with wire fencing. I might have said to that, well if Mrs. Rothchild doesn't like the wire fencing, why doesn't she take care of the hedges herself, but I didn't. And then in those fields that were now hemmed in by wire fencing that a privileged woman didn't like was planted a vile yellow flowering bush that produced an oil, and my friend said that Mrs. Rothchild didn't like this either; it ruined the English countryside, it ruined the traditional look of the English countryside.

It was not at that moment that I wished every sentence, everything I knew, that began with England would end with "and then it all died; we don't know how, it just all died." At that moment, I was thinking, who are these people who forced me to think of them all the time, who forced me to think that the world I knew was incomplete, or without substance, or did not measure up because it was not England; that I was incomplete, or without substance, and did not measure up because I was not English. Who were these people? The person sitting next to me couldn't give me a clue; no one person could. In any case, if I had said to her, I find England ugly, I hate England; the weather is like a jail sentence, the English are a very ugly people, the food in England is like a jail sentence, the hair of English people is so straight, so dead looking, the English have an unbearable smell so different from the smell of people I know, real people of course, she would have said that I was a person full of prejudice. Apart from the fact that it is I — that is, the people who look like me — who made her aware of the unpleasantness of such a thing, the idea of such a thing, prejudice, she would have been only partly right, sort of right: I may be capable of prejudice, but my prejudices have no weight to them, my prejudices have no force behind them, my prejudices remain opinions, my prejudices remain my personal opinion. And a great feeling of rage and disappointment came over me as I looked at England, my head full of personal opinions that could not have public, my public, approval. The people I come from are powerless to do evil on grand scale.

The moment I wished every sentence, everything I knew, that began with England would end with "and then it all died, we don't know how, it just all died" was when I saw the white cliffs of Dover. I had sung hymns and recited poems that were about a longing to see the white cliffs of Dover again. At the time I sang the hymns and recited the poems, I could really long to see them again because I had never seen them at all, nor had anyone around me at the time. But there we were, groups of people longing for something we had never seen. And so there they were, the white cliffs, but they were not that pearly majestic thing I used to sing about, that thing that created such a feeling in these people that when they died in the place where I lived they had themselves buried facing a direction that would allow them to see the white cliffs of Dover when they were resurrected, as surely they would be. The white cliffs of Dover, when finally I saw them, were cliffs, but they were not white; you would only call them that if the word "white" meant something special to you; they were dirty and they were steep; they were so steep, the correct height from which all my views of England, starting with the map before me in my classroom and ending with the trip I had just taken, should jump and die and disappear forever.

The Reader's Presence

1. What twist does Kincaid give the word *seeing* throughout the first half of her essay? What England does she see? For example, why doesn't she see the slums of London or the industrial squalor of

Manchester? How might these sights have affected her point of view? Where does her information come from?

2. Note the details Kincaid provides in paragraph 6. Where do these details come from? Where do the quotations come from? How do you think she wants her readers to see and hear these details? What have they to do with the "idea of England" as opposed to the reality?

3. Note that Kincaid does not include the English language among the many things she hates about England and the English. Do you think she regards the language as one of the few satisfactory parts of England? Or do you think she resents the language as well? In rereading the essay, consider her use of English. Given her overall hostility to England, what can you infer about her attitude toward the language itself?

72

Jamaica Kincaid

Girl

Jamaica Kincaid became a professional writer almost by accident. Living in New York City in the 1970s, she befriended one of the staff writers at the New Yorker *and began to accompany him as he conducted research for the "Talk of the Town" section. Before long, she discovered that she could write and that her writing impressed the editors of the magazine. When her first piece of nonfiction was published, Kincaid remembers, "That is when I realized what my writing was. My writing was the thing that I thought. Not something else. Just what I thought." After working as a staff writer at the* New Yorker *for four years, she began to turn to fiction. "Girl" is the first piece of fiction she published; it appeared in the* New Yorker *in 1978.*

For more information on Jamaica Kincaid, see page 503.

Wash the white clothes on Monday and put them on the stone heap; wash the color clothes on Tuesday and put them on the clothesline to dry; don't walk barehead in the hot sun; cook pumpkin fritters in very hot sweet oil; soak your little clothes right after you take them off; when buying cotton to make yourself a nice blouse, be sure that it doesn't have gum on it, because that way it won't hold up well after a wash; soak salt fish overnight before you cook it; is it true that you sing benna in Sunday School?; always eat your food in such a way that it won't turn someone else's stomach; on Sundays try to walk like a lady and not like the slut you are so bent on becoming; don't sing benna in Sunday School; you mustn't speak to wharf-rat boys, not even to give directions; don't eat fruits on the street — flies will follow you; *but I don't sing benna*[1] *on Sundays at all and never in Sunday School*; this is how to sew on a button; this is how to make a buttonhole for the button you have just sewed on; this is how to hem a dress when you see the hem coming down and so to prevent yourself from looking like the slut I know you are so bent on becoming; this is how you iron your father's khaki shirt so that it doesn't have a crease; this is how you iron your father's khaki pants so that they don't have a crease; this is how you grow okra — far from the house, because okra tree harbors red ants; when you are growing dasheen,[2] make sure it gets plenty of water or else it makes your throat itch when you are eating it; this is how you sweep a corner; this is how you sweep a whole house; this is how you sweep a yard; this is how you smile to someone you don't like too much; this is how you smile to someone you don't like at all; this is how you smile to someone you like completely; this is how you set a table for tea; this is how you set a table for dinner; this is how you set a table for dinner with an important guest; this is how you set a table for lunch; this is how you set a table for breakfast; this is how to behave in the presence of men who don't know you very well, and this way they won't recognize immediately the slut I have warned you against becoming; be sure to wash every day, even if it is with your own spit; don't squat down to play marbles — you are not a boy, you know; don't pick people's flowers — you might catch something; don't throw stones at blackbirds, because it might not be a blackbird at all; this is how to make a bread pudding; this is how to make doukona;[3] this is how to make pepper pot; this is how to make a good medicine for a cold; this is how to make a good medicine to throw away a child before it even becomes a child; this is how to catch a fish; this is how to throw back a fish you don't like, and that way something bad won't fall on you; this is how to bully a man; this is how a man bullies you; this is how to love a man, and if this doesn't work there are other ways, and if they don't work don't feel too bad about giving up; this is how to spit up in the air if you feel like it, and this is how to move quick so that it doesn't fall on you; this is how to make ends meet; always squeeze bread to make sure it's fresh; *but what if the baker won't let me feel the bread?*; you mean to say that after all you are really going to be the kind of woman who the baker won't let near the bread?

---

[1]*benna:* Popular calypso-like music. — EDS.
[2]*dasheen:* A starchy vegetable. — EDS.
[3]*doukona:* Cornmeal. — EDS.

The Reader's Presence

1. Whose voice dominates this story? To whom is the monologue addressed? What effect(s) does the speaker seek to have on the listener? Where does the speaker appear to have acquired her values? Categorize the kinds of advice you find in the story. Identify sentences in which one category of advice merges into another. How are the different kinds of advice alike, and to what extent are they contradictory?

2. "Girl" speaks only two lines, both of which are italicized. In each case, what prompts her to speak? What is the result? Stories generally create the expectation that at least one main character will undergo a change. What differences, if any, do you notice between her first and second lines of dialogue (and the replies she elicits), differences that might suggest that such a change has taken place? If so, in whom? Analyze the girl's character based not only on what she says but on what she hears (if one can assume that this monologue was not delivered all in one sitting, but is rather the distillation of years' worth of advice, as heard by the girl).

3. Discuss the role of gender in this story. What gender stereotypes are accepted and perpetuated by the main speaker? Look not only at the stereotypes that affect women, but also those that define the roles of men. Find the references to men and boys in the story. What can you infer about the males, who remain behind the scenes? What can you infer about the balance of power between the genders in the community in which "girl" is being raised? What can you infer about the author's (as opposed to the narrator's) attitude toward these gender issues?

73

Martin Luther King Jr.

Letter from Birmingham Jail

Martin Luther King Jr. (1929–1968) was born in Atlanta, Georgia, and after training for the ministry became pastor of the Dexler Avenue Baptist Church in Montgomery, Alabama. He became active in the civil rights movement in 1956 when he was elected president of the Montgomery Improvement Association, the group which organized a transportation boycott in response to the arrest of Rosa Parks. King later became president of the Southern Christian Leadership Conference, and under his philosophy of nonviolent direct action he led marches and protests throughout the South, to Chicago, and to Washington, D.C. In 1963 King delivered his most famous speech, "I Have a Dream," before 200,000 people in front of the Lincoln Memorial in Washington, D.C., and in 1964 he was awarded the Nobel Peace Prize. King was assassinated on April 3, 1968, in Memphis, Tennessee.

King was a masterful orator and a powerful writer. As well as his many speeches, King wrote several books, including Why We Can't Wait *(1963),* Where Do We Go from Here: Chaos or Community? *(1967),* The Measure of a Man *(1968), and* Trumpet of Conscience *(1968). "Letter from Birmingham Jail" appeared in* Why We Can't Wait.

King's best-known writings and speeches, including the letter reprinted here, are designed to educate his audiences and inspire them to act. "Through education we seek to break down the spiritual barriers to integration," he once said, and "through legislation and court orders we seek to break down the physical barriers to integration. One method is not a substitute for the other, but a meaningful and necessary supplement."

MARTIN LUTHER KING JR.
Birmingham City Jail
April 16, 1963

Bishop C. C. J. CARPENTER
Bishop JOSEPH A. DURICK
Rabbi MILTON L. GRAFMAN
Bishop PAUL HARDIN
Bishop NOLAN B. HARMON
The Rev. GEORGE M. MURRAY
The Rev. EDWARD V. RAMAGE
The Rev. EARL STALLINGS

My dear Fellow Clergymen,

While confined here in the Birmingham City Jail, I came across your recent statement calling our present activities "unwise and untimely." Seldom, if ever, do I pause to answer criticism of my work and ideas. If I sought to answer all of the criticisms that cross my desk, my secretaries would be engaged in little else in the course of the day and I would have no time for constructive work. But since I feel that you are men of genuine good will and your criticisms are sincerely set forth, I would like to answer your statement in what I hope will be patient and reasonable terms.

I think I should give the reason for my being in Birmingham, since you have been influenced by the argument of "outsiders coming in." I have the honor of serving as president of the Southern Christian Leadership Conference, an organization operating in every Southern state with headquarters in Atlanta, Georgia. We have some eighty-five affiliate organizations all across the South — one being the Alabama Christian Movement for Human Rights. Whenever necessary and possible we share staff, educational, and financial resources with our affiliates. Several months

ago our local affiliate here in Birmingham invited us to be on call to engage in a nonviolent direct action program if such were deemed necessary. We readily consented and when the hour came we lived up to our
promises. So I am here, along with several members of my staff, because
we were invited here. I am here because I have basic organizational ties
here. Beyond this, I am in Birmingham because injustice is here. Just as
the eighth century prophets left their little villages and carried their "thus
saith the Lord" far beyond the boundaries of their home town, and just
as the Apostle Paul left his little village of Tarsus and carried the gospel of
Jesus Christ to practically every hamlet and city of the Graeco-Roman
world, I too am compelled to carry the gospel of freedom beyond my particular home town. Like Paul, I must constantly respond to the Macedon-
ian call for aid.

Moreover, I am cognizant of the interrelatedness of all communities
and states. I cannot sit idly by in Atlanta and not be concerned about
what happens in Birmingham. Injustice anywhere is a threat to justice
everywhere. We are caught in an inescapable network of mutuality tied in
a single garment of destiny. Whatever affects one directly affects all indirectly. Never again can we afford to live with the narrow, provincial
"outside agitator" idea. Anyone who lives inside the United States can
never be considered an outsider anywhere in this country.

You deplore the demonstrations that are presently taking place in
Birmingham. But I am sorry that your statement did not express a similar
concern for the conditions that brought the demonstrations into being. I
am sure that each of you would want to go beyond the superficial social
analyst who looks merely at effects, and does not grapple with underlying
causes. I would not hesitate to say that it is unfortunate that so-called
demonstrations are taking place in Birmingham at this time, but I would
say in more emphatic terms that it is even more unfortunate that the
white power structure of this city left the Negro community with no other
alternative.

In any nonviolent campaign there are four basic steps: (1) collection   5
of the facts to determine whether injustices are alive; (2) negotiation;
(3) self-purification; and (4) direct action. We have gone through all of
these steps in Birmingham. There can be no gainsaying of the fact that
racial injustice engulfs this community. Birmingham is probably the most
thoroughly segregated city in the United States. Its ugly record of police
brutality is known in every section of this country. Its unjust treatment of
Negroes in the courts is a notorious reality. There have been more un-
solved bombings of Negro homes and churches in Birmingham than any
city in this nation. These are the hard, brutal, and unbelievable facts. On
the basis of these conditions Negro leaders sought to negotiate with the
city fathers. But the political leaders consistently refused to engage in
good faith negotiation.

Then came the opportunity last September to talk with some of the
leaders of the economic community. In these negotiating sessions certain

promises were made by the merchants — such as the promise to remove the humiliating racial signs from the stores. On the basis of these promises Rev. Shuttlesworth and the leaders of the Alabama Christian Movement for Human Rights agreed to call a moratorium on any type of demonstrations. As the weeks and months unfolded we realized that we were the victims of a broken promise. The signs remained. As in so many experiences of the past we were confronted with blasted hopes, and the dark shadow of a deep disappointment settled upon us. So we had no alternative except that of preparing for direct action, whereby we would present our very bodies as a means of laying our case before the conscience of the local and national community. We were not unmindful of the difficulties involved. So we decided to go through a process of self-purification. We started having workshops on nonviolence and repeatedly asked ourselves the questions, "Are you able to accept blows without retaliating?" "Are you able to endure the ordeals of jail?"

We decided to set our direct action program around the Easter season, realizing that with the exception of Christmas, this was the largest shopping period of the year. Knowing that a strong economic withdrawal program would be the by-product of direct action, we felt that this was the best time to bring pressure on the merchants for the needed changes. Then it occurred to us that the March election was ahead, and so we speedily decided to postpone action until after election day. When we discovered that Mr. Connor[1] was in the run-off, we decided again to postpone so that the demonstrations could not be used to cloud the issues. At this time we agreed to begin our nonviolent witness the day after the run-off.

This reveals that we did not move irresponsibly into direct action. We too wanted to see Mr. Connor defeated; so we went through postponement after postponement to aid in this community need. After this we felt that direct action could be delayed no longer.

You may well ask, "Why direct action? Why sit-ins, marches, etc.? Isn't negotiation a better path?" You are exactly right in your call for negotiation. Indeed, this is the purpose of direct action. Nonviolent direct action seeks to create such a crisis and establish such creative tension that a community that has constantly refused to negotiate is forced to confront the issue. It seeks so to dramatize the issue that it can no longer be ignored. I just referred to the creation of tension as a part of the work of the nonviolent resister. This may sound rather shocking. But I must confess that I am not afraid of the word tension. I have earnestly worked and

---

[1]**Mr. Connor:** Eugene "Bull" Connor and Albert Boutwell ran for mayor of Birmingham, Alabama, in 1963. Although Boutwell, the more moderate candidate, was declared the winner, Connor, the city commissioner of public safety, refused to leave office, claiming that he had been elected to serve until 1965. While the issue was debated in the courts, Connor was on the street ordering the police to use force to suppress demonstrations against segregation. — EDS.

preached against violent tension, but there is a type of constructive nonviolent tension that is necessary for growth. Just as Socrates felt that it was necessary to create a tension in the mind so that individuals could rise from the bondage of myths and half-truths to the unfettered realm of creative analysis and objective appraisal, we must see the need of having nonviolent gadflies to create the kind of tension in society that will help men rise from the dark depths of prejudice and racism to the majestic heights of understanding and brotherhood. So the purpose of the direct action is to create a situation so crisis-packed that it will inevitably open the door to negotiation. We, therefore, concur with you in your call for negotiation. Too long has our beloved Southland been bogged down in the tragic attempt to live in monologue rather than dialogue.

One of the basic points in your statement is that our acts are un-   10
timely. Some have asked, "Why didn't you give the new administration time to act?" The only answer that I can give to this inquiry is that the new administration must be prodded about as much as the outgoing one before it acts. We will be sadly mistaken if we feel that the election of Mr. Boutwell will bring the millennium to Birmingham. While Mr. Boutwell is much more articulate and gentle than Mr. Connor, they are both segregationists dedicated to the task of maintaining the status quo. The hope I see in Mr. Boutwell is that he will be reasonable enough to see the futility of massive resistance to desegregation. But he will not see this without pressure from the devotees of civil rights. My friends, I must say to you that we have not made a single gain in civil rights without determined legal and nonviolent pressure. History is the long and tragic story of the fact that privileged groups seldom give up their privileges voluntarily. Individuals may see the moral light and voluntarily give up their unjust posture; but as Reinhold Niebuhr has reminded us, groups are more immoral than individuals.

We know through painful experience that freedom is never voluntarily given by the oppressor; it must be demanded by the oppressed. Frankly I have never yet engaged in a direct action movement that was "well timed," according to the timetable of those who have not suffered unduly from the disease of segregation. For years now I have heard the word "Wait!" It rings in the ear of every Negro with a piercing familiarity. This "wait" has almost always meant "never." It has been a tranquilizing thalidomide, relieving the emotional stress for a moment, only to give birth to an ill-formed infant of frustration. We must come to see with the distinguished jurist of yesterday that "justice too long delayed is justice denied." We have waited for more than three hundred and forty years for our constitutional and God-given rights. The nations of Asia and Africa are moving with jet-like speed toward the goal of political independence, and we still creep at horse and buggy pace toward the gaining of a cup of coffee at a lunch counter.

I guess it is easy for those who have never felt the stinging darts of segregation to say wait. But when you have seen vicious mobs lynch your mothers and fathers at will and drown your sisters and brothers at whim; when you have seen hate-filled policemen curse, kick, brutalize, and even kill your black brothers and sisters with impunity; when you see the vast majority of your twenty million Negro brothers smothering in an air-tight cage of poverty in the midst of an affluent society; when you suddenly find your tongue twisted and your speech stammering as you seek to explain to your six-year-old daughter why she can't go to the public amusement park that has just been advertised on television, and see tears welling up in her little eyes when she is told that Funtown is closed to colored children, and see the depressing clouds of inferiority begin to form in her little mental sky, and see her begin to distort her little personality by unconsciously developing a bitterness toward white people; when you have to concoct an answer for a five-year-old son asking in agonizing pathos: "Daddy, why do white people treat colored people so mean?"; when you take a cross country drive and find it necessary to sleep night after night in the uncomfortable corners of your automobile because no motel will accept you; when you are humiliated day in and day out by nagging signs reading "white" men and "colored"; when your first name becomes "nigger" and your middle name becomes "boy" (however old you are) and your last name becomes "John," and when your wife and mother are never given the respected title "Mrs."; when you are harried by day and haunted by night by the fact that you are a Negro, living constantly at tip-toe stance never quite knowing what to expect next, and plagued with inner fears and outer resentments; when you are forever fighting a degenerating sense of "nobodiness"; — then you will understand why we find it difficult to wait. There comes a time when the cup of endurance runs over, and men are no longer willing to be plunged into an abyss of injustice where they experience the bleakness of corroding despair. I hope, sirs, you can understand our legitimate and unavoidable impatience.

You express a great deal of anxiety over our willingness to break laws. This is certainly a legitimate concern. Since we so diligently urge people to obey the Supreme Court's decision of 1954 outlawing segregation in the public schools, it is rather strange and paradoxical to find us consciously breaking laws. One may well ask, "How can you advocate breaking some laws and obeying others?" The answer is found in the fact that there are two types of laws. There are *just* laws and there are *unjust* laws. I would be the first to advocate obeying just laws. One has not only a legal but moral responsibility to obey just laws. Conversely, one has a moral responsibility to disobey unjust laws. I would agree with Saint Augustine that "An unjust law is no law at all."

Now what is the difference between the two? How does one determine when a law is just or unjust? A just law is a man-made code that squares with the moral law or the law of God. An unjust law is a code that is out of harmony with the moral law. To put it in the terms of Saint Thomas Aquinas, an unjust law is a human law that is not rooted in eternal and natural law. Any law that uplifts human personality is just. Any law that degrades human personality is unjust. All segregation statutes are unjust because segregation distorts the soul and damages the personality. It gives the segregator a false sense of superiority and the segregated a false sense of inferiority. To use the words of Martin Buber, the great Jewish philosopher, segregation substitutes an "I-it" relationship for the "I-thou" relationship, and ends up relegating persons to the status of things. So segregation is not only politically, economically, and sociologically unsound, but it is morally wrong and sinful. Paul Tillich[2] has said that sin is separation. Isn't segregation an existential expression of man's tragic separation, an expression of his awful estrangement, his terrible sinfulness? So I can urge men to obey the 1954 decision of the Supreme Court[3] because it is morally right, and I can urge them to disobey segregation ordinances because they are morally wrong.

Let us turn to a more concrete example of just and unjust laws. An   15
unjust law is a code that a majority inflicts on a minority that is not binding on itself. This is *difference* made legal. On the other hand a just law is a code that a majority compels a minority to follow that it is willing to follow itself. This is *sameness* made legal.

Let me give another explanation. An unjust law is a code inflicted upon a minority which that minority had no part in enacting or creating because they did not have the unhampered right to vote. Who can say the legislature of Alabama which set up the segregation laws was democratically elected? Throughout the state of Alabama all types of conniving methods are used to prevent Negroes from becoming registered voters and there are some counties without a single Negro registered to vote despite the fact that the Negro constitutes a majority of the population. Can any law set up in such a state be considered democratically structured?

These are just a few examples of unjust and just laws. There are some instances when a law is just on its face but unjust in its application. For instance, I was arrested Friday on a charge of parading without a permit. Now there is nothing wrong with an ordinance which requires a permit for a parade, but when the ordinance is used to preserve segregation and to deny citizens the First Amendment privilege of peaceful assembly and peaceful protest, then it becomes unjust.

I hope you can see the distinction I am trying to point out. In no sense do I advocate evading or defying the law as the rabid segregationist would do. This would lead to anarchy. One who breaks an unjust law must do it *openly, lovingly* (not hatefully as the white mothers did in New Orleans when they were seen on television screaming "nigger, nigger, nigger") and with a willingness to accept the penalty. I submit that

[2]*Paul Tillich* (1886–1965): Theologian and philosopher. — EDS.
[3]*1954 decision of the Supreme Court: Brown v. Board of Education,* the case in which the Supreme Court ruled racial segregation in the nation's public schools unconstitutional. — EDS.

an individual who breaks a law that conscience tells him is unjust, and willingly accepts the penalty by staying in jail to arouse the conscience of the community over its injustice, is in reality expressing the very highest respect for law.

Of course there is nothing new about this kind of civil disobedience. It was seen sublimely in the refusal of Shadrach, Meshach, and Abednego to obey the laws of Nebuchadnezzar because a higher moral law was involved. It was practiced superbly by the early Christians who were willing to face hungry lions and the excruciating pain of chopping blocks, before submitting to certain unjust laws of the Roman Empire. To a degree academic freedom is a reality today because Socrates practiced civil disobedience.

We can never forget that everything Hitler did in Germany was "legal" and everything the Hungarian freedom fighters[4] did in Hungary was "illegal." It was "illegal" to aid and comfort a Jew in Hitler's Germany. But I am sure that, if I had lived in Germany during that time, I would have aided and comforted my Jewish brothers even though it was illegal. If I lived in a communist country today where certain principles dear to the Christian faith are suppressed, I believe I would openly advocate disobeying those antireligious laws.

I must make two honest confessions to you, my Christian and Jewish brothers. First I must confess that over the last few years I have been gravely disappointed with the white moderate. I have almost reached the regrettable conclusion that the Negroes' great stumbling block in the stride toward freedom is not the White Citizens' "Counciler" or the Ku Klux Klanner, but the white moderate who is more devoted to "order" than to justice; who prefers a negative peace which is the absence of tension to a positive peace which is the presence of justice; who constantly says "I agree with you in the goal you seek, but I can't agree with your methods of direct action"; who paternalistically feels that he can set the timetable for another man's freedom; who lives by the myth of time and who constantly advises the Negro to wait until a "more convenient season." Shallow understanding from people of good will is more frustrating than absolute misunderstanding from people of ill will. Lukewarm acceptance is much more bewildering than outright rejection.

I had hoped that the white moderate would understand that law and order exist for the purpose of establishing justice, and that when they fail to do this they become the dangerously structured dams that block the flow of social progress. I had hoped that the white moderate would understand that the present tension in the South is merely a necessary phase of the transition from an obnoxious negative peace, where the Negro passively accepted his unjust plight, to a substance-filled positive peace, where all men will respect the dignity and worth of human personality.

20

---

[4]*Hungarian freedom fighters:* Those who fought in the unsuccessful 1956 revolt against Soviet oppression. — EDS.

Actually, we who engage in nonviolent direct action are not the creators of tension. We merely bring to the surface the hidden tension that is already alive. We bring it out in the open where it can be seen and dealt with. Like a boil that can never be cured as long as it is covered up but must be opened with all its pus-flowing ugliness to the natural medicines of air and light, injustice must likewise be exposed, with all of the tension its exposing creates, to the light of human conscience and the air of national opinion before it can be cured.

In your statement you asserted that our actions, even though peaceful, must be condemned because they precipitate violence. But can this assertion be logically made? Isn't this like condemning the robbed man because his possession of money precipitated the evil act of robbery? Isn't this like condemning Socrates because his unswerving commitment to truth and his philosophical delvings precipitated the misguided popular mind to make him drink the hemlock? Isn't this like condemning Jesus because His unique God consciousness and never-ceasing devotion to His will precipitated the evil act of crucifixion? We must come to see, as federal courts have consistently affirmed, that it is immoral to urge an individual to withdraw his efforts to gain his basic constitutional rights because the quest precipitates violence. Society must protect the robbed and punish the robber.

I had also hoped that the white moderate would reject the myth of time. I received a letter this morning from a white brother in Texas which said: "All Christians know that the colored people will receive equal rights eventually, but is it possible that you are in too great of a religious hurry? It has taken Christianity almost 2000 years to accomplish what it has. The teachings of Christ take time to come to earth." All that is said here grows out of a tragic misconception of time. It is the strangely irrational notion that there is something in the very flow of time that will inevitably cure all ills. Actually time is neutral. It can be used either destructively or constructively. I am coming to feel that the people of ill will have used time much more effectively than the people of good will. We will have to repent in this generation not merely for the vitriolic words and actions of the bad people, but for the appalling silence of the good people. We must come to see that human progress never rolls in on wheels of inevitability. It comes through the tireless efforts and persistent work of men willing to be co-workers with God, and without this hard work time itself becomes an ally of the forces of social stagnation.

We must use time creatively, and forever realize that the time is always ripe to do right. Now is the time to make real the promise of democracy, and transform our pending national elegy into a creative psalm of brotherhood. Now is the time to lift our national policy from the quicksand of racial injustice to the solid rock of human dignity.

You spoke of our activity in Birmingham as extreme. At first I was rather disappointed that fellow clergymen would see my nonviolent ef-

25

forts as those of the extremist. I started thinking about the fact that I stand in the middle of two opposing forces in the Negro community. One is a force of complacency made up of Negroes who, as a result of long years of oppression, have been so completely drained of self-respect and a sense of "somebodiness" that they have adjusted to segregation, and of a few Negroes in the middle class who, because of a degree of academic and economic security, and because at points they profit by segregation, have unconsciously become insensitive to the problems of the masses. The other force is one of bitterness and hatred and comes perilously close to advocating violence. It is expressed in the various black nationalist groups that are springing up over the nation, the largest and best known being Elijah Muhammad's Muslim movement.[5] This movement is nourished by the contemporary frustration over the continued existence of racial discrimination. It is made up of people who have lost faith in America, who have absolutely repudiated Christianity, and who have concluded that the white man is an incurable "devil." I have tried to stand between these two forces saying that we need not follow the "do-nothing-ism" of the complacent or the hatred and despair of the black nationalist. There is the more excellent way of love and nonviolent protest. I'm grateful to God that, through the Negro church, the dimension of nonviolence entered our struggle. If this philosophy had not emerged I am convinced that by now many streets of the South would be flowing with floods of blood. And I am further convinced that if our white brothers dismiss us as "rabble rousers" and "outside agitators" — those of us who are working through the channels of nonviolent direct action — and refuse to support our nonviolent efforts, millions of Negroes, out of frustration and despair, will seek solace and security in black nationalist ideologies, a development that will lead inevitably to a frightening racial nightmare.

Oppressed people cannot remain oppressed forever. The urge for freedom will eventually come. This is what has happened to the American Negro. Something within has reminded him of his birthright of freedom; something without has reminded him that he can gain it. Consciously and unconsciously, he has been swept in by what the Germans call the *Zeitgeist*,[6] and with his black brothers of Africa, and his brown and yellow brothers of Asia, South America, and the Caribbean, he is moving with a sense of cosmic urgency toward the promised land of racial justice. Recognizing this vital urge that has engulfed the Negro community, one should readily understand public demonstrations. The Negro has many pent-up resentments and latent frustrations. He has to get them out. So let him march sometime; let him have his prayer pilgrimages to the city

---

[5]***Elijah Muhammad's Muslim Movement:*** Led by Elijah Muhammad, the Black Muslims opposed integration and promoted the creation of a black nation within the United States. — EDS.

[6]***Zeitgeist:*** A German word meaning "spirit of the time." — EDS.

hall; understand why he must have sit-ins and freedom rides. If his re-pressed emotions do not come out in these nonviolent ways, they will come out in ominous expressions of violence. This is not a threat; it is a fact of history. So I have not said to my people, "Get rid of your discon-tent." But I have tried to say that this normal and healthy discontent can be channeled through the creative outlet of nonviolent direct action. Now this approach is being dismissed as extremist. I must admit that I was ini-tially disappointed in being so categorized.

But as I continued to think about the matter I gradually gained a bit of satisfaction from being considered an extremist. Was not Jesus an ex-tremist in love? "Love your enemies, bless them that curse you, pray for them that despitefully use you." Was not Amos an extremist for justice — "Let justice roll down like waters and righteousness like a mighty stream." Was not Paul an extremist for the gospel of Jesus Christ — "I bear in my body the marks of the Lord Jesus." Was not Martin Luther an extremist — "Here I stand; I can do none other so help me God." Was not John Bunyan an extremist — "I will stay in jail to the end of my days before I make a butchery of my conscience." Was not Abraham Lincoln an extremist — "This nation cannot survive half slave and half free." Was not Thomas Jefferson an extremist — "We hold these truths to be self evident that all men are created equal." So the question is not whether we will be extremist but what kind of extremist will we be. Will we be extremists for hate or will we be extremists for love? Will we be ex-tremists for the preservation of injustice — or will we be extremists for the cause of justice? In that dramatic scene on Calvary's hill three men were crucified. We must never forget that all three were crucified for the same crime — the crime of extremism. Two were extremists for immoral-ity, and thus fell below their environment. The other, Jesus Christ, was an extremist for love, truth, and goodness, and thereby rose above His envi-ronment. So, after all, maybe the South, the nation, and the world are in dire need of creative extremists.

I had hoped that the white moderate would see this. Maybe I was too optimistic. Maybe I expected too much. I guess I should have realized that few members of a race that has oppressed another race can under-stand or appreciate the deep groans and passionate yearnings of those that have been oppressed, and still fewer have the vision to see that injus-tice must be rooted out by strong, persistent, and determined action. I am thankful, however, that some of our white brothers have grasped the meaning of this social revolution and committed themselves to it. They are still all too small in quantity, but they are big in quality. Some like Ralph McGill, Lillian Smith, Harry Golden, and James Dabbs have writ-ten about our struggle in eloquent, prophetic, and understanding terms. Others have marched with us down nameless streets of the South. They have languished in filthy, roach-infested jails, suffering the abuse and bru-tality of angry policemen who see them as "dirty nigger lovers." They, unlike so many of their moderate brothers and sisters, have recognized the urgency of the moment and sensed the need for powerful "action" antidotes to combat the disease of segregation.

Let me rush on to mention my other disappointment. I have been so greatly disappointed with the white Church and its leadership. Of course there are some notable exceptions. I am not unmindful of the fact that each of you has taken some significant stands on this issue. I commend you, Rev. Stallings, for your Christian stand on this past Sunday, in welcoming Negroes to your worship service on a nonsegregated basis. I commend the Catholic leaders of this state for integrating Springhill College several years ago. 30

But despite these notable exceptions I must honestly reiterate that I have been disappointed with the Church. I do not say that as one of those negative critics who can always find something wrong with the Church. I say it as a minister of the gospel, who loves the Church; who was nurtured in its bosom; who has been sustained by its spiritual blessings and who will remain true to it as long as the cord of life shall lengthen.

I had the strange feeling when I was suddenly catapulted into the leadership of the bus protest in Montgomery[7] several years ago that we would have the support of the white Church. I felt that the white ministers, priests, and rabbis of the South would be some of our strongest allies. Instead, some have been outright opponents, refusing to understand the freedom movement and misrepresenting its leaders; all too many others have been more cautious than courageous and have remained silent behind the anesthetizing security of stained glass windows.

In spite of my shattered dreams of the past, I came to Birmingham with the hope that the white religious leadership of the community would see the justice of our cause and, with deep moral concern, serve as the channel through which our just grievances could get to the power structure. I had hoped that each of you would understand. But again I have been disappointed.

I have heard numerous religious leaders of the South call upon their worshippers to comply with a desegregation decision because it is the law, but I have longed to hear white ministers say follow this decree because integration is morally right and the Negro is your brother. In the midst of blatant injustices inflicted upon the Negro, I have watched white churches stand on the sideline and merely mouth pious irrelevancies and sanctimonious trivialities. In the midst of a mighty struggle to rid our nation of racial and economic injustice, I have heard so many ministers say, "Those are social issues with which the Gospel has no real concern," and I have watched so many churches commit themselves to a completely

---

[7]*bus protest in Montgomery:* After Rosa Parks was arrested on December 1, 1955, in Montgomery, Alabama, for refusing to give her seat on a bus to a white male passenger, a bus boycott began, which lasted nearly one year and was supported by nearly all of the city's black residents. — EDS.

otherworldly religion which made a strange distinction between body and soul, the sacred and the secular.

So here we are moving toward the exit of the twentieth century with   35
a religious community largely adjusted to the status quo, standing as a tail-light behind other community agencies rather than a headlight leading men to higher levels of justice.

I have travelled the length and breadth of Alabama, Mississippi, and all the other Southern states. On sweltering summer days and crisp autumn mornings I have looked at her beautiful churches with their spires pointing heavenward. I have beheld the impressive outlay of her massive religious education buildings. Over and over again I have found myself asking: "Who worships here? Who is their God? Where were their voices when the lips of Governor Barnett[8] dripped with words of interposition and nullification? Where were they when Governor Wallace[9] gave the clarion call for defiance and hatred? Where were their voices of support when tired, bruised, and weary Negro men and women decided to rise from the dark dungeons of complacency to the bright hills of creative protest?"

Yes, these questions are still in my mind. In deep disappointment, I have wept over the laxity of the Church. But be assured that my tears have been tears of love. There can be no deep disappointment where there is not deep love. Yes, I love the Church; I love her sacred walls. How could I do otherwise? I am in the rather unique position of being the son, the grandson, and the great grandson of preachers. Yes, I see the Church as the body of Christ. But, oh! How we have blemished and scarred that body through social neglect and fear of being nonconformists.

There was a time when the Church was very powerful. It was during that period when the early Christians rejoiced when they were deemed worthy to suffer for what they believed. In those days the Church was not merely a thermometer that recorded the ideas and principles of popular opinion; it was a thermostat that transformed the mores of society. Wherever the early Christians entered a town the power structure got disturbed and immediately sought to convict them for being "disturbers of the peace" and "outside agitators." But they went on with the conviction that they were a "colony of heaven" and had to obey God rather than man. They were small in number but big in commitment. They were too God-intoxicated to be "astronomically intimidated." They brought an end to such ancient evils as infanticide and gladiatorial contest.

Things are different now. The contemporary Church is so often a weak, ineffectual voice with an uncertain sound. It is so often the arch-supporter of the status quo. Far from being disturbed by the presence of

---

[8]*Governor Barnett:* Ross R. Barnett, governor of Mississippi from 1960 to 1964. — EDS.
    [9]*Governor Wallace:* George C. Wallace served as governor of Alabama from 1963 to 1966, 1971 to 1979, and 1983 to 1987. — EDS.

the Church, the power structure of the average community is consoled by the Church's silent and often vocal sanction of things as they are.

But the judgment of God is upon the Church as never before. If the Church of today does not recapture the sacrificial spirit of the early Church, it will lose its authentic ring, forfeit the loyalty of millions, and be dismissed as an irrelevant social club with no meaning for the twentieth century. I am meeting young people every day whose disappointment with the Church has risen to outright disgust.   40

Maybe again I have been too optimistic. Is organized religion too inextricably bound to the status quo to save our nation and the world? Maybe I must turn my faith to the inner spiritual Church, the church within the Church, as the true *ecclesia*[10] and the hope of the world. But again I am thankful to God that some noble souls from the ranks of organized religion have broken loose from the paralyzing chains of conformity and joined us as active partners in the struggle for freedom. They have left their secure congregations and walked the streets of Albany, Georgia, with us. They have gone through the highways of the South on torturous rides for freedom. Yes, they have gone to jail with us. Some have been kicked out of their churches and lost the support of their bishops and fellow ministers. But they have gone with the faith that right defeated is stronger than evil triumphant. These men have been the leaven in the lump of the race. Their witness has been the spiritual salt that has preserved the true meaning of the Gospel in these troubled times. They have carved a tunnel of hope through the dark mountain of disappointment.

I hope the Church as a whole will meet the challenge of this decisive hour. But even if the Church does not come to the aid of justice, I have no despair about the future. I have no fear about the outcome of our struggle in Birmingham, even if our motives are presently misunderstood. We will reach the goal of freedom in Birmingham and all over the nation, because the goal of America is freedom. Abused and scorned though we may be, our destiny is tied up with the destiny of America. Before the pilgrims landed at Plymouth, we were here. Before the pen of Jefferson etched across the pages of history the majestic words of the Declaration of Independence, we were here. For more than two centuries our foreparents labored in this country without wages; they made cotton "king"; and they built the homes of their masters in the midst of brutal injustice and shameful humiliation — and yet out of a bottomless vitality they continued to thrive and develop. If the inexpressible cruelties of slavery could not stop us, the opposition we now face will surely fail. We will win our freedom because the sacred heritage of our nation and the eternal will of God are embodied in our echoing demands.

I must close now. But before closing I am impelled to mention one other point in your statement that troubled me profoundly. You warmly

---

[10]*ecclesia:* The Latin word for church. — EDS.

commended the Birmingham police force for keeping "order" and "preventing violence." I don't believe you would have so warmly commended the police force if you had seen its angry violent dogs literally biting six unarmed, nonviolent Negroes. I don't believe you would so quickly commend the policemen if you would observe their ugly and inhuman treatment of Negroes here in the city jail; if you would watch them push and curse old Negro women and young Negro girls; if you would see them slap and kick old Negro men and young Negro boys; if you will observe them, as they did on two occasions, refuse to give us food because we wanted to sing our grace together. I'm sorry that I can't join you in your praise for the police department.

It is true that they have been rather disciplined in their public handling of the demonstrators. In this sense they have been rather publicly "nonviolent." But for what purpose? To preserve the evil system of segregation. Over the last few years I have consistently preached that nonviolence demands that the means we use must be as pure as the ends we seek. So I have tried to make it clear that it is wrong to use immoral means to attain moral ends. But now I must affirm that it is just as wrong, or even more so, to use moral means to preserve immoral ends. Maybe Mr. Connor and his policemen have been rather publicly nonviolent, as Chief Pritchett[11] was in Albany, Georgia, but they have used the moral means of nonviolence to maintain the immoral end of flagrant racial injustice. T. S. Eliot has said that there is no greater treason than to do the right deed for the wrong reason.

I wish you had commended the Negro sit-inners and demonstrators   45
of Birmingham for their sublime courage, their willingness to suffer, and their amazing discipline in the midst of the most inhuman provocation. One day the South will recognize its real heroes. They will be the James Merediths,[12] courageously and with a majestic sense of purpose, facing jeering and hostile mobs and the agonizing loneliness that characterizes the life of the pioneer. They will be old, oppressed, battered Negro women, symbolized in a seventy-two year old woman of Montgomery, Alabama, who rose up with a sense of dignity and with her people decided not to ride the segregated buses, and responded to one who inquired about her tiredness with ungrammatical profundity: "My feets is tired, but my soul is rested." They will be young high school and college students, young ministers of the gospel and a host of the elders, courageously and nonviolently sitting in at lunch counters and willingly going to jail for conscience sake. One day the South will know that when these

[11]*Chief Pritchett:* Pritchett served as police chief in Albany, Georgia, during nonviolent demonstrations in 1961 and 1962. Chief Pritchett responded to the nonviolent demonstrations with nonviolence, refusing to allow his officers to physically or verbally abuse the demonstrators. — EDS.

[12]*James Merediths:* Under the protection of federal marshals and the National Guard in 1962, James Meredith was the first black man to enroll at the University of Mississippi. — EDS.

disinherited children of God sat down at lunch counters they were in reality standing up for the best in the American dream and the most sacred values in our Judeo-Christian heritage, and thus carrying our whole nation back to great wells of democracy which were dug deep by the founding fathers in the formulation of the Constitution and the Declaration of Independence.

Never before have I written a letter this long (or should I say a book?). I'm afraid that it is much too long to take your precious time. I can assure you that it would have been much shorter if I had been writing from a comfortable desk, but what else is there to do when you are alone for days in the dull monotony of a narrow jail cell other than write long letters, think strange thoughts, and pray long prayers?

If I have said anything in this letter that is an overstatement of the truth and is indicative of an unreasonable impatience, I beg you to forgive me. If I have said anything in this letter that is an understatement of the truth and is indicative of my having a patience that makes me patient with anything less than brotherhood, I beg God to forgive me.

I hope this letter finds you strong in the faith. I also hope that circumstances will soon make it possible for me to meet each of you, not as an integrationist or a civil rights leader, but as a fellow clergyman and a Christian brother. Let us all hope that the dark clouds of racial prejudice will soon pass away and the deep fog of misunderstanding will be lifted from our fear-drenched communities and in some not too distant tomorrow the radiant stars of love and brotherhood will shine over our great nation with all of their scintillating beauty.

Yours for the cause of
Peace and Brotherhood
MARTIN LUTHER KING JR.

The Reader's Presence

1. King wrote this letter in response to the eight clergymen identified at the beginning of the letter, who had declared that the civil rights activities of King and his associates were "unwise and untimely." What does King gain by characterizing his "Fellow Clergymen" as "men of genuine good will," whose criticisms are "sincerely set forth"? What evidence can you point to in King's letter to verify the claim that his audience extends far beyond the eight clergymen he explicitly addresses? Comment on the overall structure of King's letter. What principle of composition underpins the structure of his response?

2. King establishes the tone of his response to the criticisms of the clergymen at the end of the opening paragraph: "I would like to answer your statement in what I hope will be patient and reasonable

terms." As you reread his letter, identify specific words and phrases — as well as argumentative strategies — that satisfy these self-imposed criteria. In what specific sense does King use the word *hope* here? As you reread his letter, point to each subsequent reference to hope. How does King emphasize the different meanings and connotations of the word as he unfolds his argument? Do the same for his use of the word *disappointment.* What distinctions does he draw about the word *tension?* How are these distinctions related to his argument?

3. On what historical sources does King rely to create a precedent for his actions in Birmingham? With what religious figure does King most closely identify? With what effects? What more general analogy does he draw between the circumstances in Birmingham and elsewhere? What argument does he offer in support of this specific claim? Comment on the nature — and the extent — of his use of metaphors. Does he use metaphor primarily to clarify and reinforce a point? to introduce an element of emotion? some combination of these? something else? In what ways does King base his argument on an appeal to his readers' emotions? Point to particular examples to clarify and support your response. What purposes does he identify in his definition of — and justification of — "nonviolent direct action"?

74

Barbara Kingsolver

Stone Soup

Barbara Kingsolver (b. 1955) writes about middle-American lives, and in both her fiction and her essays she searches for the common threads that bind people together. She has published stories in Homeland *(1989), poetry in* Another America *(1994), and three novels,* The Bean Trees *(1988),* Animal Dreams *(1990), and* Pigs in Heaven *(1993). She also contributes to numerous periodicals, including the* Progressive, Smithsonian, *the* New York Times Book Review, *and the* Los Angeles Times Book Review. *Her nonfiction works include* Holding the Line: Women in the Great Arizona Mine Strike of 1983 *(1989) and* High Tide in Tucson: Essays for Now or Never *(1995), in which "Stone Soup" appears.*

Regarding her work, Kingsolver remarks, "To me, writing is writing. . . . I believe there are some truths that are better told as fiction, and other truths that are most jarring and moving when you know they really did happen — like the Holding the Line *strike. There are moments of light that are best revealed in a poem, or a short story. . . . But the techniques, for me, remain the same."*

In the catalog of family values, where do we rank an occasion like this? A curly-haired boy who wanted to run before he walked, age seven now, a soccer player scoring a winning goal. He turns to the bleachers with his fists in the air and a smile wide as a gap-toothed galaxy. His own cheering section of grown-ups and kids all leap to their feet and hug each other, delirious with love for this boy. He's Andy, my best friend's son. The cheering section includes his mother and her friends, his brother, his father and stepmother, a stepbrother and stepsister, and a grandparent. Lucky is the child with this many relatives on hand to hail a proud accomplishment. I'm there too, witnessing a family fortune. But in spite of myself, defensive words take shape in my head. I am thinking: I dare *anybody* to call this a broken home.

Families change, and remain the same. Why are our names for home so slow to catch up to the truth of where we live?

When I was a child, I had two parents who loved me without cease. One of them attended every excuse for attention I ever contrived, and the other made it to the ones with higher production values, like piano recitals and appendicitis. So I was a lucky child too. I played with a set of paper dolls called "The Family of Dolls," four in number, who came with the factory-assigned names of Dad, Mom, Sis, and Junior. I think you know what they looked like, at least before I loved them to death and their heads fell off.

Now I've replaced the dolls with a life. I knit my days around my daughter's survival and happiness, and am proud to say her head is still on. But we aren't the Family of Dolls. Maybe you're not, either. And if not, even though you are statistically no oddity, it's probably been suggested to you in a hundred ways that yours isn't exactly a real family, but an impostor family, a harbinger of cultural ruin, a slapdash substitute — something like counterfeit money. Here at the tail end of our century, most of us are up to our ears in the noisy business of trying to support and love a thing called family. But there's a current in the air with ferocious moral force that finds its way even into political campaigns, claiming there is only one right way to do it, the Way It Has Always Been.

In the face of a thriving, particolored world, this narrow view is so pickled and absurd I'm astonished that it gets airplay. And I'm astonished that it still stings. 5

Every parent has endured the arrogance of a child-unfriendly grump sitting in judgment, explaining what those kids of ours really need (for example, "a good licking"). If we're polite, we move our crew to another bench in the park. If we're forthright (as I am in my mind, only, for the rest of the day), we fix them with a sweet imperious stare and say, "Come back and let's talk about it after you've changed a thousand diapers."

But it's harder somehow to shrug off the Family-of-Dolls Family Values crew when they judge (from their safe distance) that divorced people, blended families, gay families, and single parents are failures. That our children are at risk, and the whole arrangement is messy and embarrassing.

A marriage that ends is not called "finished," it's called *failed*. The children of this family may have been born to a happy union, but now they are called *the children of divorce*.

I had no idea how thoroughly these assumptions overlaid my culture until I went through divorce myself. I wrote to a friend: "This might be worse than being widowed. Overnight I've suffered the same losses — companionship, financial and practical support, my identity as a wife and partner, the future I'd taken for granted. I am lonely, grieving, and hard-pressed to take care of my household alone. But instead of bringing casseroles, people are acting like I had a fit and broke up the family china."

Once upon a time I held these beliefs about divorce: that everyone who does it could have chosen not to do it. That it's a lazy way out of marital problems. That it selfishly puts personal happiness ahead of family integrity. Now I tremble for my ignorance. It's easy, in fortunate times, to forget about the ambush that could leave your head reeling: serious mental or physical illness, death in the family, abandonment, financial calamity, humiliation, violence, despair.

I started out like any child, intent on being the Family of Dolls. I set   10
upon young womanhood believing in most of the doctrines of my generation: I wore my skirts four inches above the knee. I had that Barbie with her zebra-striped swimsuit and a figure unlike anything found in nature. And I understood the Prince Charming Theory of Marriage, a quest for Mr. Right that ends smack dab where you find him. I did not completely understand that another whole story *begins* there, and no fairy tale prepared me for the combination of bad luck and persistent hope that would interrupt my dream and lead me to other arrangements. Like a cancer diagnosis, a dying marriage is a thing to fight, to deny, and finally, when there's no choice left, to dig in and survive. Casseroles would help. Likewise, I imagine it must be a painful reckoning in adolescence (or later on) to realize one's own true love will never look like the soft-focus fragrance ads because Prince Charming (surprise!) is a princess. Or vice versa. Or has skin the color your parents didn't want you messing with, except in the Crayola box.

It's awfully easy to hold in contempt the straw broken home, and that mythical category of persons who toss away nuclear family for the sheer fun of it. Even the legal terms we use have a suggestion of caprice. I resent the phrase "irreconcilable differences," which suggests a stubborn refusal to accept a spouse's little quirks. This is specious. Every happily married couple I know has loads of irreconcilable differences. Negotiating where to set the thermostat is not the point. A nonfunctioning marriage is a slow asphyxiation. It is waking up despised each morning, listening to the pulse of your own loneliness before the radio begins to blare its raucous gospel that you're nothing if you aren't loved. It is sharing your airless house with the threat of suicide or other kinds of violence, while the ghost that whispers, "Leave here and destroy your children," has passed over every door and nailed it shut. Disassembling a marriage in these circumstances is as much *fun* as amputating your own gangrenous leg. You do it, if you can, to save a life — or two, or more.

I know of no one who really went looking to hoe the harder row, especially the daunting one of single parenthood. Yet it seems to be the most American of customs to blame the burdened for their destiny. We'd like so desperately to believe in freedom and justice for all, we can hardly name that rogue bad luck, even when he's a close enough snake to bite us. In the wake of my divorce, some friends (even a few close ones) chose to vanish, rather than linger within striking distance of misfortune.

But most stuck around, bless their hearts, and if I'm any the wiser for my trials, it's from having learned the worth of steadfast friendship. And also, what not to say. The least helpful question is: "Did you want the divorce, or didn't you?" Did I want to keep that gangrenous leg, or not? How to explain, in a culture that venerates choice: two terrifying options are much worse than none at all. Give me any day the quick hand of cruel fate that will leave me scarred but blameless. As it was, I kept thinking of that wicked third-grade joke in which some boy comes up behind you and grabs your ear, starts in with a prolonged tug, and asks, "Do you want this ear any longer?"

Still, the friend who holds your hand and says the wrong thing is made of dearer stuff than the one who stays away. And generally, through all of it, you live. My favorite fictional character, Kate Vaiden (in the novel by Reynolds Price), advises: "Strength just comes in one brand — you stand up at sunrise and meet what they send you and keep your hair combed."

Once you've weathered the straits, you get to cross the tricky juncture from casualty to survivor. If you're on your feet at the end of a year or two, and have begun putting together a happy new existence, those friends who were kind enough to feel sorry for you when you needed it must now accept you back to the ranks of the living. If you're truly blessed, they will dance at your second wedding. Everybody else, for heaven's sake, should stop throwing stones. 15

Arguing about whether nontraditional families deserve pity or tolerance is a little like the medieval debate about left-handedness as a mark of the devil. Divorce, remarriage, single parenthood, gay parents, and blended families simply are. They're facts of our time. Some of the reasons listed by sociologists for these family reconstructions are: the idea of marriage as a romantic partnership rather than a pragmatic one; a shift in women's expectations, from servility to self-respect and independence; and longevity (prior to antibiotics no marriage was expected to last many decades — in Colonial days the average couple lived to be married less than twelve years). Add to all this, our growing sense of entitlement to happiness and safety from abuse. Most would agree these are all good things. Yet their result — a culture in which serial monogamy and the consequent reshaping of families are the norm — gets diagnosed as "failing."

For many of us, once we have put ourselves Humpty-Dumpty-wise back together again, the main problem with our reorganized family is that other people think we have a problem. My daughter tells me the only time she's uncomfortable about being the child of divorced parents is when her friends say they feel sorry for her. It's a bizarre sympathy, given that half the kids in her school and nation are in the same boat, pursuing childish happiness with the same energy as their married-parent peers. When anyone asks how *she* feels about it, she spontaneously lists the benefits: our house is in the country and we have a dog, but she can go to her dad's neighborhood for the urban thrills of a pool and sidewalks for roller-skating. What's more, she has three sets of grandparents!

Why is it surprising that a child would revel in a widened family and the right to feel at home in more than one house? Isn't it the opposite that should worry us — a child with no home at all, or too few resources to feel safe? The child at risk is the one whose parents are too immature themselves to guide wisely; too diminished by poverty to nurture; too far from opportunity to offer hope. The number of children in the U.S. living in poverty at this moment is almost unfathomably large: twenty percent. There are families among us that need help all right, and by no means are they new on the landscape. The rate at which teenage girls had babies in 1957 (ninety-six per thousand) was twice what it is now. That remarkable statistic is ignored by the religious right — probably because the teen birth rate was cut in half mainly by legalized abortion. In fact, the policy gatekeepers who coined the phrase "family values" have steadfastly ignored the desperation of too-small families, and since 1979 have steadily reduced the amount of financial support available to a single parent. But, this camp's most outspoken attacks seem aimed at the notion of families getting too complex, with add-ons and extras such as a gay parent's partner, or a remarried mother's new husband and his children.

To judge a family's value by its tidy symmetry is to purchase a book for its cover. There's no moral authority there. The famous family comprised of Dad, Mom, Sis, and Junior living as an isolated economic unit is not built on historical bedrock. In *The Way We Never Were*, Stephanie Coontz writes, "Whenever people propose that we go back to the traditional family, I always suggest that they pick a ballpark date for the family they have in mind." Colonial families were tidily disciplined, but their members (meaning everyone but infants) labored incessantly and died young. Then the Victorian family adopted a new division of labor, in which women's role was domestic and children were allowed time for study and play, but this was an upper-class construct supported by myriad slaves. Coontz writes, "For every nineteenth-century middle-class family that protected its wife and child within the family circle, there was an Irish or German girl scrubbing floors . . . a Welsh boy mining coal to keep the home-baked goodies warm, a black girl doing the family laundry, a black mother and child picking cotton to be made into clothes for the family, and a Jewish or an Italian daughter in a sweatshop making 'ladies' dresses or artificial flowers for the family to purchase."

The abolition of slavery brought slightly more democratic arrangements, in which extended families were harnessed together in cottage industries; at the turn of the century came a steep rise in child labor in mines and sweatshops. Twenty percent of American children lived in orphanages at the time; their parents were not necessarily dead, but couldn't afford to keep them.

During the Depression and up to the end of World War II, many millions of U.S. households were more multigenerational than nuclear. Women my grandmother's age were likely to live with a fluid assortment of elderly relatives, in-laws, siblings, and children. In many cases they spent virtually every waking hour working in the company of other women — a companionable scenario in which it would be easier, I imagine, to tolerate an estranged or difficult spouse. I'm reluctant to idealize a life of so much hard work and so little spousal intimacy, but its advantage may have been resilience. A family so large and varied would not easily be brought down by a single blow: it could absorb a death, long illness, an abandonment here or there, and any number of irreconcilable differences.

The Family of Dolls came along midcentury as a great American experiment. A booming economy required a mobile labor force and demanded that women surrender jobs to returning soldiers. Families came to be defined by a single breadwinner. They struck out for single-family homes at an earlier age than ever before, and in unprecedented numbers they raised children in suburban isolation. The nuclear family was launched to sink or swim.

More than a few sank. Social historians corroborate that the suburban family of the postwar economic boom, which we have recently selected as our definition of "traditional," was no panacea. Twenty-five percent of Americans were poor in the mid-1950s, and as yet there were no food stamps. Sixty percent of the elderly lived on less than $1,000 a year, and most had no medical insurance. In the sequestered suburbs, alcoholism and sexual abuse of children were far more widespread than anyone imagined.

Expectations soared, and the economy sagged. It's hard to depend on one other adult for everything, come what may. In the last three decades, that amorphous, adaptable structure we call "family" has been reshaped once more by economic tides. Compared with fifties families, mothers are far more likely now to be employed. We are statistically more likely to divorce, and to live in blended families or other extranuclear arrangements. We are also more likely to plan and space our children, and to rate our marriages as "happy." We are less likely to suffer abuse without recourse, or to stare out at our lives through a glaze of prescription tranquilizers. Our aged parents are less likely to become destitute, and we're half as likely to have a teenage daughter turn up a mother herself. All in all, I would say that if "intact" in modern family-values jargon means living quietly desperate in the bell jar, then hip-hip-hooray for "broken." A neat family model constructed to service the Baby Boom economy seems to be returning gradually to a grand, lumpy shape that human families apparently have tended toward since they first took root in the Olduvai Gorge. We're social animals, deeply fond of companionship, and children love best to run in packs. If there is a *normal* for humans, at all, I expect it looks like two or three Families of Dolls, connected variously by kinship and passion, shuffled like cards and strewn over several shoeboxes.

The sooner we can let go the fairy tale of families functioning perfectly in isolation, the better we might embrace the relief of community. Even the admirable parents who've stayed married through thick and thin are very likely, at present, to incorporate other adults into their families — household help and baby-sitters if they can afford them, or neighbors and grandparents if they can't. For single parents, this support is the rock-bottom definition of family. And most parents who have split apart, however painfully, still manage to maintain family continuity for their children, creating in many cases a boisterous phenomenon that Constance Ahrons in her book *The Good Divorce* calls the "binuclear family." Call it what you will — when ex-spouses beat swords into plowshares and jump up and down at a soccer game together, it makes for happy kids.

Cinderella, look, who needs her? All those evil stepsisters? That story always seemed like too much cotton-picking fuss over clothes. A childhood tale that fascinated me more was the one called "Stone Soup," and the gist of it is this: Once upon a time, a pair of beleaguered soldiers straggled home to a village empty-handed, in a land ruined by war. They were famished, but the villagers had so little they shouted evil words and slammed their doors. So the soldiers dragged out a big kettle, filled it with water, and put it on a fire to boil. They rolled a clean round stone into the pot, while the villagers peered through their curtains in amazement.

"What kind of soup is that?" they hooted.

"Stone soup," the soldiers replied. "Everybody can have some when it's done."

"Well, thanks," one matron grumbled, coming out with a shriveled carrot. "But it'd be better if you threw this in."

And so on, of course, a vegetable at a time, until the whole suspicious village managed to feed itself grandly.

Any family is a big empty pot, save for what gets thrown in. Each stew turns out different. Generosity, a resolve to turn bad luck into good, and re-spect for variety — these things will nourish a nation of children. Name-calling and suspicion will not. My soup contains a rock or two of hard times, and maybe yours does too. I expect it's a heck of a bouillabaisse.

The Reader's Presence

1. In paragraph 2, Kingsolver asks, "Why are our names for home so slow to catch up to the truth of where we live?" What are some of the old, outworn labels or buzzwords that Kingsolver identifies directly or indirectly in this essay? What are some of the phrases she offers to replace them? What difference(s) might these new terms make?

2. Kingsolver draws on Stephanie Koontz's book *The Way We Never Were* to support her idea that the good old days for which many feel nostalgic were not really all that "good." What are some of the advantages, according to Kingsolver, of living in the contemporary world as opposed to in the past? In what particular ways have women's and children's lives changed for the better? What are some of the remaining social problems that Kingsolver believes the "policy gatekeepers" (paragraph 18) would do better to address?

3. Examine carefully the metaphors and analogies Kingsolver employs in this essay. Where, for instance, do comparisons with death and dismemberment arise, and to what effect(s)? What are some of the analogies she employs to describe the traditional and the modern family? Some of the analogies will require more interpretation than others. What, for example, does she mean when she writes that "arguing about whether nontraditional families deserve pity or tolerance is a little like the medieval debate about left-handedness as a mark of the devil" (paragraph 16)?

75

Nancy Mairs

A Letter to Matthew

Nancy Mairs (b. 1943) has contributed poetry, short stories, articles, and essays to numerous journals. The collection of her essays from which "A Letter to Matthew" comes, Plaintext, *was published in 1986. More recent publications include* Remembering the Bone House: An Erotics of Time and Space *(1989),* Carnal Acts: Essays *(1990), and* Ordinary Time: Cycles in Marriage, Faith, and Renewal *(1993). From 1983 to 1985 she served as assistant director of the Southwest Institute for Research on Women in Tucson, and has also taught at the University of Arizona and at UCLA.*

In Voice Lessons: On Becoming a (Woman) Writer *(1994), she writes, "I want a prose that is allusive and translucent, that eases you into me and embraces you, not one that baffles you or bounces you around so that you can't even tell where I am. And so I have chosen to work, very, very carefully, with the language we share, faults and all, choosing each word for its capacity, its ambiguity, the space it provides for me to live my life within it, relating rather than opposing each word to the next, each sentence to the next, 'starting on all sides at once . . . twenty times, thirty times, over': the stuttering adventure of the essay."*

July 1983

My Dear Child —

Last night Daddy and I watched, on William F. Buckley, Jr.'s *Firing Line*, a debate whether women "have it as good as men," and I have been talking to you in my head ever since. Odd not to be able to talk with you in person — I'm not yet used to your absence — but I thought I would put onto paper some of the things I would say if you were here. They are not the sort of things I would say to Mr. Buckley if ever I met him. Mr. Buckley is an elderly man, fixed by his circumstances within a range of experiences so narrow that new ideas and new behaviors cannot squeeze through the boundaries. He is complete as he is. But you are just emerging into young manhood, still fluid, still making the choices that will determine the shape that manhood will take. I, as your mother and as a feminist, hope that the choices you make — you individually and your generation as a whole — will be transformative, that the manhood you

538

develop will be so radically new that the question in Mr. Buckley's debate, smacking as it does of competition for goods and goodness, will no longer have any more meaning than questions like "Do pigs have it as good as fiddlehead ferns?" or, more aptly, "Do pigs have it as good as pigs?"

In many ways, of course, you've dashed my hopes already. You have, after all, lived for fourteen years in a dangerously patriarchal society, and you have put on much of the purple that Mr. Buckley wears with such aplomb. When I find myself disliking you — and I find myself disliking you with about the same regularity, I imagine, as you find yourself disliking me — I can usually tell that I'm responding to some behavior that I identify as peculiarly "masculine." I dislike your cockiness, for instance. When you first began to work with computers, I remember, you immediately assumed the attitude that you knew all that was worth knowing about computers; when you took up racquetball, right away you set yourself up as a champion. This kind of swaggering strikes me as a very old pattern of masculine behavior (I think of Beowulf and Unferth at Heorot), the boast designed to establish superiority and domination, which trigger challenge and thus conflict. Related to your cockiness is your quickness to generalize and, from your generalizations, to pronounce judgments: Calculus is a waste of time; Christians are stupidly superstitious; classical music is boring; Jerry Falwell and the Moral Majority are idiots. This is just the kind of uninformed thinking that empowers Jerry Falwell and the Moral Majority in the first place, of course, this refusal to experience and explore the ambiguities of whatever one is quick to condemn. More seriously, such a pattern of response enables men to create the distinctions between Us and Them — the good guys and the bad guys, the left wing and the right, the Americans and the Russians — that lead to suspicion, fear, hatred, and finally the casting of stones.

Well then, have you shattered *all* my hopes? By no means. For you are not merely arrogant and opinionated. These qualities are overshadowed by another, one I have seldom seen in men: your extraordinary empathic capacity, your willingness to listen for and try to fulfill the needs of others. When Sean was threatening suicide, you were genuinely engaged in his pain. When Katherine needed a male model to encourage her creepy little fifth-grade boys to dance, you leaped in with psychological (if not physical!) grace. When Anne left us for good, I felt your presence supporting and soothing me despite your relief at being an only child at last. Women have long been schooled in this sensitivity to others; but men have been trained to hold themselves aloof, to leave the emotional business of life to their mothers and sisters and wives. I think you are learning to conduct some of that business on your own.

Clearly I believe that the ability to do so is a benefit and not the curse our patriarchal culture has made it out to be. In fact, in an ironic way the answer to Mr. Buckley's question might be that women have it better than men, and it is the fear of such an answer that keeps men nervously posing the question in the first place. You'll remember that Freud ascribed to women a problem he called "penis envy"; a later psychoanalyst, Lacan, called it a "lack." If I've learned anything during the years I've spent in psychotherapy, I've learned that the feelings and motives I ascribe to others tell me little about them but much about myself, for I am projecting my own feelings and motives onto them. Freud ascribed to women penis envy; ascription = projection; therefore Freud was really suffering from womb envy. QED. A man, lacking the womb and yearning to return to his early identity with the mother, tries to hide his pain by denigrating everything associated with the womb: the blood, the babies, the intuitive and nurturing behaviors of child-rearing. The very condition of having a womb in the first place he labels a pathology: hysteria. If I haven't got it, he tells himself, it can't be worth having. (But maybe, he whispers so softly that even he can't hear, maybe it *is*.)

I'm more than half serious, you know, amid this high-flown silliness.   5
But I don't seriously believe, despite some psychological advantages, that in the "real world" women have it as good as men. In some highly visible ways they have it very bad indeed: They are raped, battered, prostituted, abandoned to raise their children in poverty. Less visibly but no less ruinously, they are brainwashed (often by their mothers and sisters as well as their fathers, brothers, lovers, and husbands) into believing that whatever they get is what they deserve, being only women. Imagine this, Matthew, if you can — and maybe you can, since you are just emerging from childhood, and children are often treated like women in our society. Imagine thinking yourself lucky to get *any* job, no matter how servile or poorly paid, *any* partner, no matter how brutal or dull, *any* roof over your head, no matter how costly the psychic mortgage payment. Imagine believing that's what you deserve. Imagine feeling guilty if you fail to feel grateful.

If you have trouble imagining such conditions, I'm not surprised. I have trouble too; and for many years I held back from calling myself a feminist because I couldn't conceive problems I hadn't experienced. The men in our family do not smack their women and children around. They seldom raise their voices, let alone their palms. They are gentle, courteous, witty, companionable, solicitous. And yet, of late, I've begun to recognize in them certain behaviors and attitudes which suggest that they, too, share a set of cultural assumptions about male power and rights which devalue women's lives. But our men worship their women, you may say; they put them right up on what one of my students once called a "pedastool." True enough, but tell me, how much actual living could you get done confined to a tiny platform several feet above the ground, especially if you had acrophobia?

Look, now that you're staying with them, at Aunt Helen and Uncle Ted, for instance. For forty-eight years they have sustained a relationship founded on domination and submission if ever there was one. Daddy has often insisted that their relationship is fine as long as it works for them.

For a long time I tried to accept it too, because I believed that he must be right. I tend, as you know, to believe that Daddy is always right: I'm the product of a patriarchal society too, after all. But now I believe that he's wrong. Although I admire much about their marriage, especially its durability and friendliness, I balk at its basis in a kind of human sacrifice. Trying, I suppose, to compensate for not having graduated from high school, Uncle Ted kept Aunt Helen, a college graduate, confined in a life containing only himself, their one son, and the housework to maintain them. She could have worked, of course — she had the education, and they always needed the money — but Uncle Ted's manly pride insisted on his being the breadwinner, and her job became to stretch the crusts and crumbs from one meager meal to the next. So little had she to occupy her that she grieved for years after her child left for college, and clung to her housework to give her days meaning. Once, in the late sixties, I asked her why she didn't replace her old-fashioned washing machine with an automatic (my mother had had one since 1952), and she replied, "But then what would I do on Mondays?" Worse than the deprivation of stimulating activity has been the undermining of her self-confidence. Even her statements sound like questions, and she repeatedly turns to her husband: "Isn't that right, Ted?" She tiptoes through space as through conversation like our Lionel Tigress, cautious, timorous, whiskers twitching, ready to dash under the bed at a strange voice or a heavy footfall. I like to watch her bake a cake. There in her kitchen she plants her feet firmly and even, sometimes, rattles the pans.

Is Uncle Ted then a monster, some Bluebeard glowering and dangling the incriminating key that represents some independent act that will cost Aunt Helen her head? Hardly. He is a man of sincerity and rectitude, who has lived scrupulously, at considerable cost to himself, according to the code by which he was raised, a code that Rudyard Kipling, whom he admires, described as the "white man's burden." In it, women (among others, such as our "darker brethren") require the kind of protection and control they are unable, being more "natural" creatures, to provide themselves. He adores Aunt Helen, I do believe, and wants to do only what's best for her. But he assumes that he knows what's best for her, and so does she. In the name of manhood, he has taken from her the only authentic power a human being can hold: that of knowing and choosing the good. Such theft of power results in mastery. There is no mistressy.

I've been uneasy, as you know, about your spending this summer with them, largely, I suppose, because I don't want Uncle Ted to make a "man" of you. And I've encouraged you to subvert their patterns of interaction in a small way, by helping Aunt Helen with her chores just as you help Uncle Ted with his, even when he tries to divert you and she tells you to run along with him, not so that you can change those patterns (you can't) but so that you'll remain aware of them. You may well be tempted to fall into them because what Uncle Ted construes as "men's work" is infinitely more interesting than "women's work." You already know what a drag it is to set the table knowing that within an hour the dishes will be streaked and gummy, to wash those dishes knowing that they'll go right back on the table for breakfast, to fold a whole line of clothes that will crawl straight back into the hamper, muddy and limp, to be washed and hung out again. How much more pleasant and heartening to tramp through the woods checking the line from the brook, to ride the lawn mower round and round on the sweet falling grass, to plot traps for porcupines and saw down trees and paddle the canoe across the pond spreading algicide and possibly falling in. If everyone washed the dishes together, of course, everyone could go for a walk in the woods. How one would tell the men from the women, though, I'm not sure.

But then, so what if you do fall into the patterns? Surely the world   10 won't end if you and Uncle Ted take the fishing rods down to the Battenkill to catch a few trout for breakfast, leaving Aunt Helen to make the beds? Well yes, I think in a way it will, and that's why I'm writing you this letter. For Aunt Helen and Uncle Ted's marriage is not in the least extraordinary. On the contrary, the interactions between them, despite some idiosyncracies, are being played out in millions of relationships throughout the world, including, in its own way, Daddy's and mine, within which you have lived your whole life. One partner is telling the other (though seldom in words) that she is weaker physically and intellectually, that her concerns are less meaningful to the world at large, that she is better suited (or even formed by God) to serve his needs in the privacy of his home than to confront the tangled problems of the public sphere. And instead of ignoring his transparent tactics for enhancing his uncertain self-image and increasing his own comfort, she is subordinating her needs to his, accepting the limits he decrees, and thereby bolstering the artificial pride that enables him to believe himself a "superior" creature. As soon as he feels superiority, he is capable of dividing his fellow creatures into Us and Them and of trying to dominate Them. That is, he is ready to make war.

This connection — between the private male who rules his roost and keeps his woman, however lovingly, in her place and the public male who imposes his will by keeping blacks poor and pacifying Vietnamese villages and shipping arms and men to Central America — is far from new. Virginia Woolf made it in *Three Guineas* nearly fifty years ago. "The public and the private worlds are inseparably connected," she wrote; "the tyrannies and servilities of the one are the tyrannies and servilities of the other." But *Three Guineas* has been largely ignored or denigrated: One male critic called it "neurotic," "morbid"; another, "cantankerous." (You know, I am sure, that when a man speaks out, he is assertive, forthright; when a woman speaks her "mind," she is sick or bitchy.) Moreover, its feminism has been labeled "old-fashioned," as though already in 1938 the problems Woolf named had been solved. If so, why do we stand today in the same spot she stood then, looking at the same photographs of dead bodies and burned villages? No, her feminism isn't out of date, though such a label shows a desperate attempt to set it aside. Rather, it says something, valid today, that men still do not want to hear: that if humanity — men and women — is to have it any good at all, men must give up their pleasure in domination, their belief in their superiority, the adulation of their fellow creatures, at the personal and private level of their lives. Now. They must stop believing that whoever they love will perish without their "protection," for the act of protecting leads to a sense of possession, and it necessitates enemies to protect from. They must completely and radically revise their relationships with themselves, their wives and children, their business associates, the men and women in the next block, the next city, the next country. They must learn to say to every other who enters their lives not, "You're over there, and you're bad," but, "You're over there, and you're me."

Can they do it? Some feminists think not. They say that we should simply kill men off (except perhaps for the babies) and start fresh. I understand the anger that fuels such a proposal and the desire to sweep the rubbishy world clean. But I reject it because it perpetuates the violence that distinguishes masculine solutions to conflict. Our cultural heritage would still be based on killing, our mythology rooted in massacre.

No, I think that I will let you live. Will you let me live? If so, the terms of your existence must be transformed. What's been good enough for Aunt Helen and Uncle Ted, for Mr. Buckley, for Ronald Reagan and the other men who govern us and every other nation, for the Catholic Church, for the medical and legal professions, for the universities, for all the patriarchy, cannot be good enough for you. (And I address you personally, though obviously I mean all young men everywhere, because moral choice is always a lonely matter. You may all encourage one another — in fact, if the transformation is working, you will — but each will have to choose his way of being for himself.) You must learn to develop your identity through exploring the ways you are like, not different from or better than, others. You must learn to experience power through your connections with people, your ability to support their growth, not through weakening them by ridicule or patronage or deprivation. If this means dancing with the little boys, then dance your heart out; they'll dance on into the future with more assurance because of you. And who can shoot straight while he's dancing?

I am demanding something of you that takes more courage than entering a battle: not to enter the battle. I am asking you to say *no* to the values that have defined manhood through the ages — prowess, competition, victory — and to grow into a manhood that has not existed before. If you do, some men and women will ridicule and even despise you. They may call you spineless, possibly even (harshest of curses) womanish. But your life depends on it. My life depends on it. I wish you well.

Now go help Aunt Helen with the dishes.   15

> I love you —
> *Mother*

The Reader's Presence

1. Essays in the form of letters are usually addressed to one person; thus we can specifically identify Mairs's intended reader. But are there indications in the essay to show that Mairs wants a wider readership than one other person? In other words, do you think this was a "real" letter that she sent her son — or one she intended to be a published essay? What aspects of the selection make you feel one way or the other about this question?

2. The recipient of this letter is fourteen years old. In what ways do you think Mairs takes the age of her son into account? Are there times when you think she doesn't make adjustments because of age? How do her adjustments or lack of adjustments reflect her overall purpose in writing the letter?

3. What is Mairs attempting to persuade her son to do? How would you describe her persuasive efforts? What does she appeal to? How does she use both criticism and praise? How does her son's immediate situation — that he is staying with relatives — affect the terms of her appeal? Put yourself in Matthew's place as the reader. Explain whether this letter would transform your behavior or not.

76

Paul Monette

Can Gays and Straights Be Friends?

A passionate advocate for a humane, swift, and urgent response to the AIDS crisis, Paul Monette (1945–1995) first became a national literary figure with his book Borrowed Time: An AIDS Memoir *(1988). In this book and in a collection of poems,* Love Alone: Eighteen Elegies for Rog *(1988), he mourned the loss of his partner Roger Horwitz and chronicled the early years of the epidemic. He continued to explore his rage against the AIDS crisis in two novels —* Afterlife *(1990) and* Halfway Home *(1991) — in which he also affirmed the experience of living with AIDS and fighting back against ignorance, prejudice, and fear. In 1992 Monette received a National Book Award for his autobiography,* Becoming a Man: Half a Life Story, *and shortly before his death from the disease he completed a collection of essays,* Last Watch of the Night: Essays Too Personal and Otherwise *(1994). "Can Gays and Straights Be Friends?" appeared in* Playboy *in 1993.*

Monette published a number of novels and volumes of poetry during the 1970s and 1980s, but endured many rejection notices in the process. In Last Watch of the

Night *he wrote, "I spent twenty years being turned down because my work was considered 'too gay.' Which I came to regard as a compliment, and proof I was on the right track." Even after receiving his National Book Award, some of his essays were turned down by publishers because they were considered "too personal," which, Monette wrote, "I couldn't help but feel was even better than a compliment. For I grew up in a culture in which the personal was* verboten, *especially in polite company — a company I've long since sold my stock in."*

Radio call-ins are the worst, especially during drive time. Commuters sit gridlocked in traffic, their only way out by cellular phone to the local radio show. Some callers practically foam at the mouth, saying I deserve to die and my kind makes them want to puke. Usually, I've been talking about the skyrocketing rates of teen suicide, a third of which involve gays and lesbians. Or I'm describing the tyranny of the closet, the stunting of the heart by cruel stereotypes. "Excuse me," I said to the caller in Houston, "do I make you want to puke because I'm gay or because I have AIDS?"

It's not a meaningful distinction to your weed-variety homophobe. Over my desk hangs a picture of a young woman whose wet T-shirt reads: THANK GOD FOR AIDS. Such hatred pours across the airwaves daily from preachers wringing their hands over the sins of Sodom. Their diatribes rarely mention lesbians. To them it is a fight unto death between two breeds of men — the "real" ones and the "sick" ones.

Where do they come by this virulence? Is it an inherent code of pumped-up self-regard passed from dugout and locker room to cover a straight man's fear of being misperceived as queer? Is it a primal fear of being penetrated? A Seattle boy called in once, so cocksure at the age of 11, and asked with disdain, "Why would anyone want to be gay?" All he thought he needed was to score with a girl and his sexual issues would be eternally resolved. "In ten or fifteen years," I promised him, "you will grapple as hard as anyone, gay or straight, with problems of intimacy" — the lifelong struggle to somehow integrate *fuck* and *love*.

As for wanting to be gay, every young man who knows that he's "different" has already internalized society's ugly message. Gay kids become locked in a self-hatred that renders them meek, apologetic and invisible — their only safety the prison walls of their secret.

It's crucial to understand the difference between homophobia and   5
what I call homo-ignorance. There's much more of the latter, especially as gay and lesbian issues have surfaced more prominently in the news. Instinctively, people of goodwill rejected the paranoid philippic delivered in Houston by Pat Buchanan — a walking hate crime all by himself.

A straight friend of mine considers himself completely unhomophobic, he's that secure in his own manhood. Yet, when pinned down, he'll admit that the tactics of Queer Nation and Act Up make him, well, uncomfortable.

Uncomfortable is how the activists want him to feel. Even gays and lesbians juggle conflicting feelings about the guerrilla warriors in our midst.

Sometimes I'm engulfed in the minutiae of political correctness, labeled an enemy of my own people because I'm white, prosperous and published. But I also feel juiced to have been part of the FDA takeover action in 1988 demanding the release of AIDS drugs. Our movement is only a generation old, and we've done it almost entirely without role models. Harvey Milk[1] was our Martin Luther King, but history texts have erased him. I studied Whitman at Yale for two years without hearing a mention of his homosexuality. Let alone Eleanor Roosevelt's. Or J. Edgar Hoover's.

It's easy to stay ignorant if gay never speaks its name. We need our straight allies to understand the nature of our struggle. It used to be said that a faggot was a homosexual gentleman who had just left the room. That can cease if enough heteros speak up and say "That's not funny" to fag jokes. Our families raise us the best they can, but it's a rare man who reaches adulthood without some legacy of racism, sexism and homophobia. We must confront these demons in ourselves, tolerance being the minimum goal of self-examination.

There's this thing that many straight men have about being on the team, one of the guys. This is the argument of the military brass who want to keep us out. What they really want is for us to continue hiding and lying. While the Joint Chiefs of Staff deliberate the earth-shattering problem of queers taking showers with straight men, the Armed Forces drown in sexual-harassment cover-ups. And the only thing they can offer by way of sensitivity training is "Don't bend over to pick up the soap."

I don't want to do it with a straight man any more than I want to "indoctrinate" his sons. I have no problem with straight men's sexuality, unless it harms or belittles women. I experience none of the homophobe's obsession with what others do in bed. That's a sexual compulsion all its own, as if gay or lesbian had only carnal meaning. I think what disorients straight men today is how happy and fulfilled many gay lives are. We're supposed to be miserable, after all.   10

We all have closets to come out of. Gay isn't the enemy of straight. Heterosexual men have told me for years that, since college, they have no male friends to talk with. The emotional isolation caused by fear of intimacy is indifferent to sexual orientation. We're not boys anymore, trapped in the insecurities of the schoolyard. Our common enemy is ignorance, a sex-phobic bitterness and name-calling purveyed by those who are jealous of the joy of others because they have none of their own.

Nothing is more important to me than the freedom of being "out." I won't live to see 50, yet not even that can take away the happiness of having lived my life for real. Of course, you must realize you are in a closet before you can open the door. As gay and straight men, we can

---

[1]*Harvey Milk* (1930–1978): An openly gay politician, Milk was elected to the San Francisco Board of Supervisors in 1977. He and Mayor George Moscone were assassinated in 1978 by former city supervisor and police officer Don White. — EDS.

help one another over the great divide. We make terrific friends, we queers, perhaps because we have traveled so far to reach the free country of the heart. All men deserve to live there.

The Reader's Presence

1. The title of this essay poses a question: "Can Gays and Straights Be Friends?" How and where does Monette answer this question? What are some of the common grounds between gays and straights that Monette mentions or implies in his essay? What actions might heterosexual people take to ease gay-straight relations? What might homosexuals do? In what ways does Monette's essay itself further the cause of gay-straight friendships?

2. What are the causes of homophobia? In developing your response, draw on both the essay and on your own personal experience. This essay was first published in *Playboy* magazine, which caters to heterosexual men. What signs do you find in the essay to suggest that Monette anticipates a measure of potential homophobia in his readers? Point to specific words and phrases to support your response. How effectively do you think he deals with the possible homophobia of his readers? Compare and contrast, for example, the discomfort felt by the radio call-ins in paragraph 1 and the discomfort intentionally caused by gay activists discussed in paragraph 7.

3. A popular gay slogan reads "Silence = Death." Comment on the kinds of silences that Monette refers or alludes to in this essay. When does silence very literally lead to death? What less literal consequences does it have?

77 ———————————————————————

Toni Morrison

Nobel Lecture, 7 December 1993

One of the most celebrated living American novelists, Toni Morrison (b. 1931) was awarded the Nobel Prize for literature in 1993. Her acceptance speech for this award is reprinted here as it appeared in the Georgia Review *in 1995. In extending this honor, the Nobel Committee applauded Morrison for eloquently and imaginatively exploring African American experience in her six novels, although Henry Louis Gates Jr. notes that the award would be deserved had she written only* Beloved *(1987). Morrison was born in Ohio, and the state figures prominently in her fiction, especially in* Beloved *and* Sula *(1973). Her most recent novel,* Jazz *(1992), centers on characters from the rural South who settle in Harlem in the 1920s. In addition to writing novels, Morrison teaches at Princeton University, writes literary criticism, and lectures widely.*

She has written that fiction "should be beautiful, and powerful, but it should also work. It should have something in it that enlightens; something in it that opens the door and points the way. Something in it that suggests what the conflicts are, what the problems are. But it need not solve those problems because it is not a case study, it is not a recipe."

Members of the Swedish Academy, Ladies and Gentlemen:

Narrative has never been merely entertainment for me. It is, I believe, one of the principal ways in which we absorb knowledge. I hope you will understand, then, why I begin these remarks with the opening phrase of what must be the oldest sentence in the world, and the earliest one we remember from childhood: "Once upon a time . . ."

"Once upon a time there was an old woman. Blind but wise." Or was it an old man? A guru, perhaps. Or a *griot*[1] soothing restless children. I have heard this story, or one exactly like it, in the lore of several cultures.

"Once upon a time there was an old woman. Blind. Wise."

In the version I know the woman is the daughter of slaves, black, American, and lives alone in a small house outside of town. Her reputation for wisdom is without peer and without question. Among her people she is both the law and its transgression. The honor she is paid and the awe in which she is held reach beyond her neighborhood to places far away; to the city where the intelligence of rural prophets is the source of much amusement.   5

One day the woman is visited by some young people who seem to be bent on disproving her clairvoyance and showing her up for the fraud they believe she is. Their plan is simple: they enter her house and ask the one question the answer to which rides solely on her difference from them, a difference they regard as a profound disability: her blindness. They stand before her, and one of them says,

"Old woman, I hold in my hand a bird. Tell me whether it is living or dead."

She does not answer, and the question is repeated. "Is the bird I am holding living or dead?"

Still she does not answer. She is blind and cannot see her visitors, let alone what is in their hands. She does not know their color, gender, or homeland. She knows only their motive.

The old woman's silence is so long, the young people have trouble holding their laughter.   10

---

[1]*griot:* a storyteller in western Africa. — EDS.

Finally she speaks, and her voice is soft but stern. "I don't know," she says. "I don't know whether the bird you are holding is dead or alive, but what I do know is that it is in your hands. It is in your hands."

Her answer can be taken to mean: if it is dead, you have either found it that way or you have killed it. If it is alive, you can still kill it. Whether it is to stay alive is your decision. Whatever the case, it is your responsibility.

For parading their power and her helplessness, the young visitors are reprimanded, told they are responsible not only for the act of mockery but also for the small bundle of life sacrificed to achieve its aims. The blind woman shifts attention away from assertions of power to the instrument through which that power is exercised.

Speculation on what (other than its own frail body) that bird in the hand might signify has always been attractive to me, but especially so now, thinking as I have been about the work I do that has brought me to this company. So I choose to read the bird as language and the woman as a practiced writer.

She is worried about how the language she dreams in, given to her at birth, is handled, put into service, even withheld from her for certain nefarious purposes. Being a writer, she thinks of language partly as a system, partly as a living thing over which one has control, but mostly as agency — as an act with consequences. So the question the children put to her, "Is it living or dead?," is not unreal, because she thinks of language as susceptible to death, erasure; certainly imperiled and salvageable only by an effort of the will. She believes that if the bird in the hands of her visitors is dead, the custodians are responsible for the corpse. For her a dead language is not only one no longer spoken or written, it is unyielding language content to admire its own paralysis. Like statist language, censored and censoring. Ruthless in its policing duties, it has no desire or purpose other than to maintain the free range of its own narcotic narcissism, its own exclusivity and dominance. However, moribund, it is not without effect, for it actively thwarts the intellect, stalls conscience, suppresses human potential. Unreceptive to interrogation, it cannot form or tolerate new ideas, shape other thoughts, tell another story, fill baffling silences. Official language smitheried to sanction ignorance and preserve privilege is a suit of armor, polished to shocking glitter, a husk from which the knight departed long ago. Yet there it is; dumb, predatory, sentimental. Exciting reverence in schoolchildren, providing shelter for despots, summoning false memories of stability, harmony among the public.

She is convinced that when language dies, out of carelessness, disuse, indifference, and absence of esteem, or killed by fiat, not only she herself but all users and makers are accountable for its demise. In her country children have bitten their tongues off and use bullets instead to iterate the void of speechlessness, of disabled and disabling language, of language adults have abandoned altogether as a device for grappling with meaning, providing guidance, or expressing love. But she knows tongue-suicide is

15

not only the choice of children. It is common among the infantile heads of state and power merchants whose evacuated language leaves them with no access to what is left of their human instincts, for they speak only to those who obey, or in order to force obedience.

The systematic looting of language can be recognized by the tendency of its users to forgo its nuanced, complex, midwifery properties, replacing them with menace and subjugation. Oppressive language does more than represent violence; it is violence; does more than represent the limits of knowledge; it limits knowledge. Whether it is obscuring state language or the faux language of mindless media; whether it is the proud but calcified language of the academy or the commodity-driven language of science; whether it is the malign language of law-without-ethics, or language designed for the estrangement of minorities, hiding its racist plunder in its literary cheek — it must be rejected, altered, and exposed. It is the language that drinks blood, laps vulnerabilities, tucks its fascist boots under crinolines of respectability and patriotism as it moves relentlessly toward the bottom line and the bottomed-out mind. Sexist language, racist language, theistic language — all are typical of the policing languages of mastery, and cannot, do not, permit new knowledge or encourage the mutual exchange of ideas.

The old woman is keenly aware that no intellectual mercenary or insatiable dictator, no paid-for politician or demagogue, no counterfeit journalist would be persuaded by her thoughts. There is and will be rousing language to keep citizens armed and arming; slaughtered and slaughtering in the malls, courthouses, post offices, playgrounds, bedrooms, and boulevards; stirring, memorializing language to mask the pity and waste of needless death. There will be more diplomatic language to countenance rape, torture, assassination. There is and will be more seductive, mutant language designed to throttle women, to pack their throats like pâté-producing geese with their own unsayable, transgressive words; there will be more of the language of surveillance disguised as research; of politics and history calculated to render the suffering of millions mute; language glamorized to thrill the dissatisfied and bereft into assaulting their neighbors; arrogant pseudo-empirical language crafted to lock creative people into cages of inferiority and hopelessness.

Underneath the eloquence, the glamour, the scholarly associations, however stirring or seductive, the heart of such language is languishing, or perhaps not beating at all — if the bird is already dead.

She has thought about what could have been the intellectual history   20
of any discipline if it had not insisted upon, or been forced into, the waste of time and life that rationalizations for and representations of dominance required — lethal discourses of exclusion blocking access to cognition for both the excluder and the excluded.

The conventional wisdom of the Tower of Babel story is that the collapse was a misfortune. That it was the distraction or the weight of many languages that precipitated the tower's failed architecture. That one monolithic language would have expedited the building, and heaven would have been reached. Whose heaven, she wonders? And what kind? Perhaps the achievement of Paradise was premature, a little hasty if no one could take the time to understand other languages, other views, other narratives. Had they, the heaven they imagined might have been found at their feet. Complicated, demanding, yes, but a view of heaven as life; not heaven as post-life.

She would not want to leave her young visitors with the impression that language should be forced to stay alive merely to be. The vitality of language lies in its ability to limn the actual, imagined, and possible lives of its speakers, readers, writers. Although its poise is sometimes in displacing experience, it is not a substitute for it. It arcs toward the place where meaning may lie. When a president of the United States thought about the graveyard his country had become, and said, "The world will little note nor long remember what we say here. But it will never forget what they did here," his simple words were exhilarating in their life-sustaining properties because they refused to encapsulate the reality of 600,000 dead men in a cataclysmic race war. Refusing to monumentalize, disdaining the "final word," the precise "summing up," acknowledging their "poor power to add or detract," his words signal deference to the uncapturability of the life it mourns. It is the deference that moves her, that recognition that language can never live up to life once and for all. Nor should it. Language can never "pin down" slavery, genocide, war. Nor should it yearn for the arrogance to be able to do so. Its force, its felicity, is in its reach toward the ineffable.

Be it grand or slender, burrowing, blasting or refusing to sanctify; whether it laughs out loud or is a cry without an alphabet, the choice word or the chosen silence, unmolested language surges toward knowledge, not its destruction. But who does not know of literature banned because it is interrogative; discredited because it is critical; erased because alternate? And how many are outraged by the thought of a self-ravaged tongue?

Word-work is sublime, she thinks, because it is generative; it makes meaning that secures our difference, our human difference — the way in which we are like no other life.

We die. That may be the meaning of life. But we *do* language. That 25 may be the measure of our lives.

"Once upon a time . . ." Visitors ask an old woman a question. Who are they, these children? What did they make of that encounter? What did they hear in those final words: "The bird is in your hands"? A sentence that gestures toward possibility, or one that drops a latch? Perhaps what the children heard was, "It's not my problem. I am old, female, black, blind. What wisdom I have now is in knowing I cannot help you. The future of language is yours."

They stand there. Suppose nothing was in their hands. Suppose the visit was only a ruse, a trick to get to be spoken to, taken seriously as they have not been before. A chance to interrupt, to violate the adult world, its miasma of discourse about them. Urgent questions are at stake, including the one they have asked: "Is the bird we are holding living or dead?" Perhaps the question meant: "Could someone tells us what is life? What is death?" No trick at all; no silliness. A straightforward question worthy of the attention of a wise one. An old one. And if the old and wise who have lived life and faced death cannot describe either, who can?

But she does not; she keeps her secret, her good opinion of herself, her gnomic pronouncements, her art without commitment. She keeps her distance, enforces it and retreats into the singularity of isolation, in sophisticated, privileged space.

Nothing, no word follows her declaration of transfer. That silence is deep, deeper than the meaning available in the words she has spoken. It shivers, this silence, and the children, annoyed, fill it with language invented on the spot.

"Is there no speech," they ask her, "no words you can give us that   30 help us break through your dossier of failures? through the education you have just given us that is no education at all because we are paying close attention to what you have done as well as to what you have said? to the barrier you have erected between generosity and wisdom?

"We have no bird in our hands, living or dead. We have only you and our important question. Is the nothing in our hands something you could not bear to contemplate, to even guess? Don't you remember being young, when language was magic without meaning? When what you could say, could not mean? When the invisible was what imagination strove to see? When questions and demands for answers burned so brightly you trembled with fury at not knowing?

"Do we have to begin consciousness with a battle heroes and heroines like you have already fought and lost, leaving us with nothing in our hands except what you have imagined is there? Your answer is artful, but its artfulness embarrasses us and ought to embarrass you. Your answer is indecent in its self-congratulation. A made-for-television script that makes no sense if there is nothing in our hands.

"Why didn't you reach out, touch us with your soft fingers, delay the sound bite, the lesson, until you knew who we were? Did you so despise our trick, our modus operandi, that you could not see that we were baffled about how to get your attention? We are young. Unripe. We have heard all our short lives that we have to be responsible. What could that possibly mean in the catastrophe this world has become; where, as a poet said, 'nothing needs to be exposed since it is already barefaced'? Our inheritance is an affront. You want us to have your old, blank eyes and see only cruelty and mediocrity. Do you think we are stupid enough to perjure ourselves again and again with the fiction of nationhood? How dare you talk to us of duty when we stand waist deep in the toxin of your past?

"You trivialize us and trivialize the bird that is not in our hands. Is there no context for our lives? No song, no literature, no poem full of vitamins, no history connected to experience that you can pass along to help us start strong? You are an adult. The old one, the wise one. Stop thinking about saving your face. Think of our lives and tell us your particularized world. Make up a story. Narrative is radical, creating us at the very moment it is being created. We will not blame you if your reach exceeds your grasp; if love so ignites your words that they go down in flames and nothing is left but their scald. Or if, with the reticence of a surgeon's hands, your words suture only the places where blood might flow. We know you can never do it properly — once and for all. Passion is never enough; neither is skill. But try. For our sake and yours forget your name in the street; tell us what the world has been to you in the dark places and in the light. Don't tell us what to believe, what to fear. Show us belief's wide skirt and the stitch that unravels fear's caul. You, old woman, blessed with blindness, can speak the language that tells us what only language can: how to see without pictures. Language alone protects us from the scariness of things with no names. Language alone is meditation.

"Tell us what it is to be a woman so that we may know what it is to   35
be a man. What moves at the margin. What it is to have no home in this place. To be set adrift from the one you knew. What it is to live at the edge of towns that cannot bear your company.

"Tell us about ships turned away from shorelines at Easter, placenta in a field. Tell us about a wagonload of slaves, how they sang so softly their breath was indistinguishable from the falling snow. How they knew from the hunch of the nearest shoulder that the next stop would be their last. How, with hands prayered in their sex, they thought of heat, then sun. Lifting their faces as though it was there for the taking. Turning as though there for the taking. They stop at an inn. The driver and his mate go in with the lamp, leaving them humming in the dark. The horse's void steams into the snow beneath its hooves and the hiss and melt are the envy of the freezing slaves.

"The inn door opens: a girl and a boy step away from its light. They climb into the wagon bed. The boy will have a gun in three years, but now he carries a lamp and a jug of warm cider. They pass it from mouth to mouth. The girl offers bread, pieces of meat, and something more: a glance into the eyes of the one she serves. One helping for each man, two for each woman. And a look. They look back. The next stop will be their last. But not this one. This one is warmed."

It's quiet again when the children finish speaking, until the woman breaks into the silence.

"Finally," she says. "I trust you now. I trust you with the bird that is not in your hands because you have truly caught it. Look. How lovely it is, this thing we have done — together."

The Reader's Presence

1. Identify each of the narrative lines Morrison establishes in this essay. Consider carefully not only the first narrative Morrison tells, the one beginning "Once upon a time there was an old

woman" (paragraph 4), but also the other narratives embedded in
the essay. What knowledge might she hope her audience will absorb from each of the narratives (paragraph 2)? Discuss the overall function — and effects — of Morrison's use of narrative.

2. Although Morrison is best known for her novels, she is also a respected literary and cultural critic. Discuss the function of interpretation in this essay. What are the possible interpretations of the
bird in the young visitors' hands? In what specific ways are the
different interpretations mutually exclusive, or do they work together to create a larger meaning? How do you interpret the significance of the final reference to the bird: "I trust you with the
bird that is not in your hands because you have truly caught it"
(paragraph 39)? What has led up to this riddle-like insight? Atten-
tive readers interpret not only the words on the page but also the
spaces. How do you read the space between paragraphs 25 and
26? Compare and contrast what comes before and after that
space.

3. This is a difficult essay because not all the meaning lies readily accessible on the surface. Choose the paragraph that you found
most perplexing, and read it carefully, several times, making a
comment or observation in the margins about every phrase. You
might start by making sure you can identify the basics, such as the
referents to each pronoun. Then move on to matters related to the
writer's presence. What kinds of verbs does she use? What adjectives? What kinds of images? Are there patterns among the words
and phrases you have marked, and do these patterns repeat in
other parts of the essay? With what effect(s)?

78

Richard Rodriguez

Toward an American Language

*Richard Rodriguez (b. 1944) has contributed articles to many magazines and
newspapers, including* Harper's, American Scholar, *the* Los Angeles Times, *and
the* New York Times, *in which "Toward an American Language" (published
under a different title) appeared in 1989. His most sensational literary accomplishment, however, is his autobiography,* Hunger of Memory: The Education of
Richard Rodriguez *(1987). In it, Rodriguez outlines his positions on issues such
as bilingualism, affirmative action, and assimilation, and concludes that current
policies in these areas are misguided and only serve to reinforce current social in-*

equalities. Currently, he works as an education consultant, lecturer, and freelance writer. His most recent book is Days of Obligations: An Argument with My Mexican Father *(1992).*

About the experience of writing his autobiography, Rodriguez comments, "By finding public words to describe one's feelings, one can describe oneself to oneself. . . . I have come to think of myself as engaged in writing graffiti."

For a hundred years Americans have resorted to Huckleberry Finn's American summer for refreshment. As much as Huck, Americans resist the coming of fall, the chill in the woods, the starched shirt, the inimical expectation of the schoolmarm. All city ways. Individualism is the source of America, the source of our greatness. But America is a city now and individualism has become our national dilemma.

America's individualism derives from low-church Protestantism. They taught us well, those old Puritans. Distrust the tyranny of the plural. Seek God with a singular pronoun. They didn't stop there. Puritans advised fences. Build a fence around what you hold dear and respect other fences.

TO SUIT ANY TASTE

The antisocial inclination of eighteenth-century Puritans paradoxically allowed for the immigrant America of the nineteenth century. Lacking a communal sense of itself — there was no "we" here — how could America resist the coming of strangers? America became a multiracial, multireligious society because a small band of Puritans didn't want the world.

The outsider is not the exception to America, rather the outsider is the archetypal citizen. In him, and only in him, in her — suitcase in hand, foreign-speaking, bewildered by the crowd — can Americans recognize ourselves. We recognize the stranger in us. For we are a nation of immigrants, we are accustomed to remind ourselves. We see ourselves as strangers to one another, all of us bewildered by the city.

Immigrants may be appalled by the individualism they find when   5
they get here — skateboards; slang; disrespect; Daisy Miller; Deadheads — it's all the same. But this same individualism allows the immigrant to purchase a new life. Each new immigrant has a stake in the perpetuation of American individualism. Here the immigrant is freed from the collective fate of his village. Once here, the immigrant has already eluded the destiny of his father.

The limits of American generosity are the limits of Puritan individualism. We accept the stranger, sure we do, but we are suspicious of any assimilationist insinuation such as that the stranger might eventually change us: Two in their meeting are changed.

With the exception of the army, the classroom is the most subversive

institution of America. The classroom works against our historical inclination by chipping away at any tangible distance between us. In the classroom, children are taught that they belong to a group. Children are
taught that there is a national culture, a public language, a plural pronoun implied by the singular assertion of the Pledge of Allegiance.

About fifteen years ago, I got involved in the national debate over
bilingual education. Proponents of bilingual classrooms argued that non-
English-speaking children would have an easier time of it in school if they
could keep a hold on heritage as a kind of trainer-wheel; if they would be
allowed to use their "family language" in classrooms.

What I knew from my own education was that such a scheme would
betray public education. There is no way for a child to use her family language in a classroom unless we diminish the notion of public school, unless we confuse the child utterly about what is expected of her. Bilingual
classrooms imply we are going to expect less.

BECAUSE IT'S GOOD FOR YOU

Family language distinguishes one child from all others. Classroom   10
language, on the other hand, is unyielding, impersonal, blind, public —
there are rules, there are limits, there are inevitable embarrassments, but
there are no exceptions. The child is expected to speak up, to make himself understood to an audience of boys and girls. It is an unsentimental
business.

At the time — in the mid-1970s — I took bilingual enthusiasts to be a
romantic lot, a fringe of the Ethnic Left. Fifteen years have passed and
bilingual education has become a bureaucracy. I still believe that bilingualism is a confused ideology. But I now believe the confusion is willful
and characteristically American. Americans have always been at war with
the idea of school. We shrink from the idea of uniformity — as our Puritan fathers would shrink — as from the image of the melting pot. We say
we want the advantages of public life, but we do not want to relinquish
our separateness for it. We want to coexist, not change.

In my mind, bilingual education belongs to those sentimental and violent American years, the sixties, when my generation imagined we had
discovered individualism. There was a conveniently dishonorable war to
protest. But Americans went to war against the idea of America. We went
to war against anyone over thirty, against our parents, against memory.
We marched in the name of "the people," exclusive of at least half the
population.

The radical sixties were not such an isolated time. In the nineteenth
century there were nativist riots against an expanding notion of America,
against any idea of a plural pronoun. Should we now, in retrospect, be
surprised that the black civil rights movement (the heroic march toward
integration) was undermined, finally, by subsequent cries for black separatism? Another example of American ambivalence.

We think we are united only by a clean consent, and yet the rest of the world can spot us a mile off. America exists. Americans end up behaving more like each other alive, even in disagreement, than we resemble dead ancestors. There is a discernible culture about us, tangible in the spaces between us, that connects Thomas Jefferson with Martin Luther King, Jr. Trouble is, the lesson of that culture, the indoctrination of that culture in schools, implies that we form a "we." Our professors have lost the conviction of it. A unifying canon — an intellectual line which might implicate us all by virtue of our arrival here — seems an impossibility. Our professors have begun to fish in other streams, seeking alternatives to Western Civ.

In 1989 the majority of immigrants do not come from Europe. Now   15
Americans describe the distance we maintain from one another as "diversity." The problem of our national diversity becomes, with a little choke on logic, the solution to itself. "We should celebrate diversity," teachers, bureaucrats, join to tell us — that is what America means, they say. And they are right.

FAVORITE FLAVORS

Traditionally it has been <u>pragmatism</u> that forced Americans to yield to the fiction of a nation indivisible. War, for example. The U.S. Army took your darling boy, with his allergies and his moles and his favorite flavor and reduced him to a uniform. The workplace is very nearly as unsentimental.

In the nineteenth century, America compromised Puritanism with pragmatism. In order to work, to continue existing as a country, America required some uniform sense of itself.

In the nineteenth century, even as the American city was building, Samuel Clemens romanced the nation with a celebration of the wildness of the American river. But in the redbrick cities, and on streets without trees, the river became an idea, a learned idea, a civilizing idea, taking all to itself. Women, usually women, tireless, overworked women, stood in front of rooms filled with the children of immigrants, teaching those children a common language. For language is not just another classroom skill, as today's bilingualists would have it. Language is the lesson of *grammar* school. And from the schoolmarm's achievement came the possibility of a shared history and a shared future. To my mind, this achievement of the nineteenth century classroom was an honorable one, comparable to the opening of the plains, the building of bridges. Grammar school teachers forged a nation.

My own first attempts to read *Huckleberry Finn* ended in defeat. I entered the classroom as a Spanish-speaking boy. I learned English with difficulty, but rightly enough. Huck spoke a dialect English, not the English I learned. ("You don't know about me without you have read. . . .") Eventually, but this was long after, I was able to discern in Huck's dilemma — how he chafed so at school! — a version of my own. And, later still, to discern in him a version of the life of our nation: Huck as the archetypal bilingual child!

My fear is that today Huck Finn would emerge as the simple winner.   20
The schoolmarm would be shown up as a tyrannical supremacist. I tell you the schoolmarm is the hero of America. My suspicion is that many of our children — dropouts and graduates alike — are learning the lesson of communality remedially, from the workplace. At the bank or behind the counter at McDonald's, or in the switch room of the telephone company, people from different parts of town and different parts of the country, and different countries of the world learn that they have one thing or another in common. Initially, a punch clock. A supervisor. A paycheck. A shared irony. A takeout lunch. Some nachos, some bagels, a pizza. And here's a fortune cookie for you: Two in their meeting are changed.

All the while the professors speak limply of diversity, which is truly our strength. But diversity which is not shared is no virtue. Diversity which is not shared is a parody nation.

The river owes its flux and its swell and its entire strength to its tributaries. But America was created in autumn by the schoolmarm, mistress of all she surveyed.

The Reader's Presence

1. The leverage point in Rodriguez's case against bilingualism is his claim: "With the exception of the army, the classroom is the most subversive institution of America" (paragraph 7). What does he see as the principal contributions of the classroom — and of what he calls "the schoolmarm" — to the development of a shared American language? In what respect is the notion of a *public* school central to his argument? Draw on your own experience as a basis for agreeing (or disagreeing) with his assertion that "public school" minimizes diversity and that the nineteenth-century "schoolmarm is the hero of America."

2. Identify the point of view from which Rodriguez speaks. What do you make of his repetition of *our* in the opening paragraph? Explain why you do (or do not) feel comfortable identifying with this use of *our* — and his subsequent use of *us*. What are the principal sources of his diction, metaphors, and allusions? How do you respond to the image of those who view bilingual education as "a kind of trainer-wheel" (paragraph 8)? Consider also what Rodriguez gains (and loses) by opening his argument by alluding to Mark Twain's *Huckleberry Finn*. In what ways is this moment similar to — and different from — his assertion near the beginning of paragraph 2: "They taught us well, those old Puritans"?

3. Discuss the extent to which you agree with Rodriguez's claim that Puritan values and ethics lie at the center of American society. How does Rodriguez reconcile this notion with his subsequent statement: "The outsider is not the exception to America, rather the outsider is the archetypal citizen" (paragraph 4)? Is Rodriguez's own view of this issue articulated from the vantage point of an outsider? Point to specific words and phrases — as well as to compositional strategies — to validate your response.

79

Randy Shilts

Talking AIDS to Death

Author and journalist Randy Shilts (1951–1994) was the leading American reporter on the AIDS epidemic from the early 1980s, when he wrote his first article on the disease, until his death from AIDS-related complications in 1994. A staff reporter for the San Francisco Chronicle, *he was one of the first openly gay journalists to work for a major city newspaper. Shilts's familiarity with covering the AIDS epidemic resulted in his highly acclaimed best-seller,* And the Band Played On: Politics, People, and the AIDS Epidemic *(1987), which has been translated into six languages and released in fourteen nations. He also wrote* The Mayor of Castro Street: The Life and Times of Harvey Milk *(1982) and more recently* Conduct Unbecoming: Gays and Lesbians in the U.S. Military *(1993).* "Talking AIDS to Death" *originally appeared in* Esquire.

When Shilts worked at public television station KQED in San Francisco in the late 1970s, he was assigned to cover only gay issues. "It was a real fight to cover that first non-gay story at KQED," Shilts later remembered. Unlike his editor, Shilts refused to believe that our personal identities artificially limit our capacity to write on a range of topics. "I think you can be fair and tell both sides of the story, no matter who you are or what you are writing about. . . . If you just stick to the facts, you are doing the right thing."

I'm talking to my friend Kit Herman when I notice a barely perceptible spot on the left side of his face. Slowly, it grows up his cheekbone, down to his chin, and forward to his mouth. He talks on cheerfully, as if nothing is wrong, and I'm amazed that I'm able to smile and chat on, too, as if nothing were there. His eyes become sunken; his hair turns gray; his ear is turning purple now, swelling into a carcinomatous cauliflower, and still we talk on. He's dying in front of me. He'll be dead soon, if nothing is done.

Dead soon, if nothing is done.

"Excuse me, Mr. Shilts, I asked if you are absolutely sure, if you can categorically state that you definitely can*not* get AIDS from a mosquito."

I forget the early-morning nightmare and shift into my canned response. All my responses are canned now. I'm an AIDS talk-show jukebox. Press the button, any button on the AIDS question list, and I have my canned answer ready. Is this Chicago or Detroit?

"Of course you can get AIDS from a mosquito," I begin.   5

Here, I pause for dramatic effect. In that brief moment, I can almost hear the caller murmur, "I *knew* it."

"If you have unprotected anal intercourse with an infected mosquito, you'll get AIDS," I continue. "Anything short of that and you won't."

The talk-show host likes the answer. All the talk-show hosts like my answers because they're short, punchy, and to the point. Not like those boring doctors with long recitations of scientific studies so overwritten with maybes and qualifiers that they frighten more than they reassure an AIDS-hysteric public. I give good interview, talk-show producers agree. It's amazing, they say, how I always stay so cool and never lose my temper.

"Mr. Shilts, has there ever been a case of anyone getting AIDS from a gay waiter?"

"In San Francisco, I don't think they allow heterosexuals to be wait-   10
ers. This fact proves absolutely that if you could get AIDS from a gay waiter, all northern California would be dead by now."

I gave that same answer once on a Bay Area talk show, and my caller, by the sound of her a little old lady, quickly rejoined: "What if that gay waiter took my salad back into the kitchen and ejaculated into my salad dressing? Couldn't I get AIDS then?"

I didn't have a pat answer for that one, and I still wonder at what this elderly caller thought went on in the kitchens of San Francisco restaurants. Fortunately, this morning's phone-in — in Chicago, it turned out — is not as imaginative.

"You know, your question reminds me of a joke we had in California a couple of years back," I told the caller. "How many heterosexual waiters in San Francisco does it take to screw in a light bulb? The answer is both of them."

The host laughs, the caller is silent. Next comes the obligatory question about whether AIDS can be spread through coughing.

I had written a book to change the world, and here I was on talk   15
shows throughout America, answering questions about mosquitoes and gay waiters.

This wasn't exactly what I had envisioned when I began writing *And the Band Played On*. I had hoped to effect some fundamental changes. I really believed I could alter the performance of the institutions that had allowed AIDS to sweep through America unchecked.

AIDS had spread, my book attested, because politicians, particularly those in charge of federal-level response, had viewed the disease as a political issue, not an issue of public health — they deprived researchers of anything near the resources that were needed to fight it. AIDS had spread because government health officials consistently lied to the American people about the need for more funds, being more concerned with satisfying their political bosses and protecting their own jobs than with telling the truth and protecting the public health. And AIDS had spread because indolent news organizations shunned their responsibility to provide tough, adversarial reportage, instead basing stories largely on the Official Truth of government press releases. The response to AIDS was never even remotely commensurate with the scope of the problem.

I figured the federal government, finally exposed, would stumble over itself to accelerate the pace of AIDS research and put AIDS-prevention programs on an emergency footing. Once publicly embarrassed by the revelations of its years of shameful neglect, the media would launch serious investigative reporting on the epidemic. Health officials would step forward and finally lay bare the truth about how official disregard had cost this country hundreds of thousands of lives. And it would never happen again.

I was stunned by the "success" of my book. I quickly acquired all the trappings of bestsellerdom: *60 Minutes* coverage of my "startling" revelations, a Book-of-the-Month Club contract, a miniseries deal with NBC, translation into six languages, book tours on three continents, featured roles in movie-star-studded AIDS fund-raisers, regular appearances on network news shows, and hefty fees on the college lecture circuit. A central figure in my book became one of *People* magazine's "25 Most Intriguing People of 1987," even though he had been dead for nearly four years, and the *Los Angeles Herald Examiner* pronounced me one of the "in" authors of 1988. The mayor of San Francisco even proclaimed my birthday last year "Randy Shilts Day."

And one warm summer day as I was sunning at a gay resort in the   20 redwoods north of San Francisco, a well-toned, perfectly tanned young man slid into a chaise next to me and offered the ultimate testimony to my fifteen minutes of fame. His dark eyelashes rising and falling shyly, he whispered, "When I saw you on *Good Morning America* a couple weeks ago, I wondered what it would be like to go to bed with you."

"You're the world's first AIDS celebrity," enthused a friend at the World Health Organization, after hearing one of WHO's most eminent AIDS authorities say he would grant me an interview on one condition — that I autograph his copy of my book. "It must be great," he said.

It's not so great.

The bitter irony is, my role as an AIDS celebrity just gives me a more elevated promontory from which to watch the world make the same mistakes in the handling of the AIDS epidemic that I had hoped my work would help to change. When I return from network tapings and celebrity glad-handing, I come back to my home in San Francisco's gay community and see friends dying. The lesions spread from their cheeks to cover their faces, their hair falls out, they die slowly, horribly, and sometimes, suddenly, before anybody has a chance to know they're sick. They die in my arms and in my dreams, and nothing at all has changed.

Never before have I succeeded so well; never before have I failed so miserably.

I gave my first speech on the college lecture circuit at the University   25
of California [at] Los Angeles in January 1988. I told the audience that there were fifty thousand diagnosed AIDS cases in the United States as of that week and that within a few months there would be more people suffering from this deadly disease in the United States than there were Americans killed during the Vietnam War. There were audible gasps. During the question-and-answer session, several students explained that they had heard that the number of AIDS cases in America was leveling off.

In the next speech, at the University of Tennessee, I decided to correct such misapprehension by adding the federal government's projections — the 270,000 expected to be dead or dying from AIDS in 1991, when the disease would kill more people than any single form of cancer, more than car accidents. When I spoke at St. Cloud State University in Minnesota three months later, I noted that the number of American AIDS cases had that week surpassed the Vietnam benchmark. The reaction was more a troubled murmur than a gasp.

By the time I spoke at New York City's New School for Social Research in June and there were sixty-five thousand AIDS cases nationally, the numbers were changing so fast that the constant editing made my notes difficult to read. By then as many as one thousand Americans a week were learning that they, too, had AIDS, or on the average, about one every fourteen minutes. There were new government projections to report, too: by 1993, some 450,000 Americans would be diagnosed with AIDS. In that year, one American will be diagnosed with the disease every thirty-six seconds. Again, I heard the gasps.

For my talk at a hospital administrators' conference in Washington in August, I started using little yellow stick-ons to update the numbers on my outline. That made it easier to read; there were now seventy-two thousand AIDS cases. Probably this month, or next, I'll tell another college audience that the nation's AIDS case load has topped one hundred thousand and there will be gasps again.

The gasps always amaze me. Why are they surprised? In epidemics, people get sick and die. That's what epidemics do to people and that's why epidemics are bad.

When Kit Herman was diagnosed with AIDS on May 13, 1986, his   30
doctor leaned over his hospital bed, took his hand, and assured him, "Don't worry, you're in time for AZT." The drug worked so well that all Kit's friends let themselves think he might make it. And we were bolstered by the National Institutes of Health's assurance that AZT was only

the first generation of AIDS drugs, and that the hundreds of millions of federal dollars going into AIDS treatment research meant there would soon be a second and third generation of treatments to sustain life beyond AZT's effectiveness. Surely nothing was more important, considering the federal government's own estimates that between 1 and 1.5 million Americans were infected with the Human Immunodeficiency Virus (HIV), and virtually all would die within the next decade if nothing was done. The new drugs, the NIH assured everyone, were "in the pipeline," and government scientists were working as fast as they possibly could.

Despite my nagging, not one of dozens of public-affairs-show producers chose to look seriously into the development of those long-sought second and third generations of AIDS drugs. In fact, clinical trials of AIDS drugs were hopelessly stalled in the morass of bureaucracy at the NIH, but this story tip never seemed to cut it with producers. Clinical trials were not sexy. Clinical trials were boring.

I made my third *Nightline* appearance in January 1988 because new estimates had been released revealing that one in sixty-one babies born in New York City carried antibodies to the AIDS virus. And the link between those babies and the disease was intravenous drug use by one or both parents. Suddenly, junkies had become the group most likely to catch and spread AIDS through the heterosexual community. Free needles to junkies — now there was a sizzling television topic. I told the show's producers I'd talk about that, but that I was much more interested in the issue of AIDS treatments — which seemed most relevant to the night's program, since Ted Koppel's other guest was Dr. Anthony Fauci, associate NIH director for AIDS, and the Reagan administration's most visible AIDS official.

After fifteen minutes of talk on the ins and outs and pros and cons of free needles for intravenous drug users, I raised the subject of the pressing need for AIDS treatments. Koppel asked Fauci what was happening. The doctor launched into a discussion of treatments "in the pipeline" and how government scientists were working as fast as they possibly could.

I'd heard the same words from NIH officials for three years: Drugs were in the pipeline. Maybe it was true, but when were they going to come out of their goddamn pipeline? Before I could formulate a polite retort to Fauci's stall, however, the segment was over, Ted was thanking us, and the red light on the camera had blipped off. Everyone seemed satisfied that the government was doing everything it possibly could to develop AIDS treatments.

Three months later, I was reading a week-old *New York Times* in Kit's room in the AIDS ward at San Francisco General Hospital. It was April, nearly two years after my friend's AIDS diagnosis. AZT had given him two years of nearly perfect health, but now its effect was wearing off, and Kit had suffered his first major AIDS-related infection since his original bout with pneumonia — cryptococcal meningitis. The meningitis could be treated, we all knew, but the discovery of this insidious brain

35

infection meant more diseases were likely to follow. And the long-promised second and third generations of AIDS drugs were still nowhere on the horizon.

While perusing the worn copy of the *Times*, I saw a story about Dr. Fauci's testimony at a congressional hearing. After making Fauci swear an oath to tell the truth, a subcommittee headed by Representative Ted Weiss of New York City asked why it was taking so long to get new AIDS treatments into testing at a time when Congress was putting hundreds of millions of dollars into NIH budgets for just such purposes. At first Fauci talked about unavoidable delays. He claimed government scientists were working as fast as they could. Pressed harder, he finally admitted that the problem stemmed "almost exclusively" from the lack of staffing in his agency. Congress had allocated funds, it was true, but the Reagan administration had gotten around spending the money by stingily refusing to let Fauci hire anybody. Fauci had requested 127 positions to speed the development of AIDS treatments; the administration had granted him 11. And for a year, he had not told anyone. For a year, this spokesman for the public health answered reporters that AIDS drugs were in the pipeline and that government scientists had all the money they needed. It seemed that only when faced with the penalty of perjury would one of the administration's top AIDS officials tell the truth. That was the real story, I thought, but for some reason nobody else had picked up on it.

At the international AIDS conference in Stockholm two months later, the other reporters in "the AIDS pack" congratulated me on my success and asked what I was working on now. I admitted that I was too busy promoting the British and German release of my book to do much writing myself, and next month I had the Australian tour. But if I *were* reporting, I added with a vaguely conspiratorial tone, *I'd* look at the *scandal* in the NIH. Nobody had picked up that *New York Times* story from a few months ago about staffing shortages on AIDS clinical trials. The lives of 1.5 million HIV-infected Americans hung in the balance, and the only way you could get a straight answer out of an administration AIDS official was to put him under oath and make him face the charge of perjury. Where I went to journalism school, *that* was a news story.

One reporter responded to my tip with the question: "But who's going to play *you* in the miniseries?"

A few minutes later, when Dr. Fauci came into the press room, the world's leading AIDS journalists got back to the serious business of transcribing his remarks. Nobody asked him if he was actually telling the truth, or whether they should put him under oath to ensure a candid response to questions about when we'd get AIDS treatments. Most of the subsequent news accounts of Dr. Fauci's comments faithfully reported that many AIDS treatments were in the pipeline. Government scientists, he said once more, were doing all they possibly could.

The producer assured my publisher that Morton Downey, Jr., would   40
be "serious" about AIDS. "He's not going to play games on this issue,"

the producer said, adding solemnly: "His brother has AIDS. He understands the need for compassion." The abundance of Mr. Downey's compassion was implicit in the night's call-in poll question: "Should all people with AIDS be quarantined?"

Downey's first question to me was, "You *are* a homosexual, aren't
you?"

He wasn't ready for my canned answer: "Why do you ask? Do you
want a date or something?"

The show shifted into an earnest discussion of quarantine. In his television studio, Clearasil-addled high school students from suburban New
Jersey held up MORTON DOWNEY FAN CLUB signs and cheered aggressively
when the truculent, chain-smoking host appeared to favor a kind of
homespun AIDS Auschwitz. The youths shouted down any audience
member who stepped forward to defend the rights of AIDS sufferers, their
howls growing particularly vitriolic if the speakers were gay. These kids
were the ilk from which Hitler drew his Nazi youth. In the first commercial break, the other guest, an AIDS activist, and I told Downey we would
walk off the show if he didn't tone down his gay-baiting rhetoric. Smiling
amiably, Downey took a long drag on his cigarette and assured us,
"Don't worry, I have a fallback position."

That comment provided one of the most lucid moments in my year as
an AIDS celebrity. Downey's "fallback position," it was clear, was the
opposite of what he was promoting on the air. Of course, he didn't *really*
believe that people with AIDS, people like his brother, should all be
locked up. This was merely a deliciously provocative posture to exploit
the working-class resentments of people who needed someone to hate.
AIDS sufferers and gays would do for this week. Next week, if viewership
dropped and Downey needed a new whipping boy, maybe he'd move on
to Arabs, maybe Jews. It didn't seem to matter much to him, since he
didn't believe what he was saying anyway. For Morton Downey, Jr., talking about AIDS was not an act of conscience; it was a ratings ploy. He
knew it, he let his guests know it, his producers certainly knew it, and his
television station knew it. The only people left out of the joke were his
audience.

The organizers of the Desert AIDS Project had enlisted actor Kirk   45
Douglas and CBS morning anchor Kathleen Sullivan to be honorary
cochairs of the Palm Springs fundraiser. The main events would include a
celebrity tennis match pitting Douglas against Mayor Sonny Bono, and a
fifteen-hundred-dollar-a-head dinner at which I would receive a Lucite
plaque for my contributions to the fight against AIDS. The next morning
I would fly to L.A. to speak at still another event, this one with Shirley
MacLaine, Valerie Harper, and Susan Dey of *L.A. Law.*

The desert night was exquisite. There were 130 dinner guests, the
personification of elegance and confidence, who gathered on a magnificent patio of chocolate-brown Arizona flagstone at the home of one of
Palm Springs's most celebrated interior designers. A lot of people had

come simply to see what was regarded as one of the most sumptuous dwellings in this sumptuous town.

When I was called to accept my reward, I began with the same lineup of jokes I use on talk shows and on the college lecture circuit. They work every time.

I told the crowd about how you get AIDS from a mosquito.

Kirk Douglas laughed; everybody laughed.

Next, I did the how-many-gay-waiters joke.   50

Kirk Douglas laughed; everybody laughed.

Then I mentioned the woman who asked whether she could get AIDS from a waiter ejaculating in her salad dressing.

That one always has my college audiences rolling in the aisles, so I paused for the expected hilarity.

But in the utter stillness of the desert night air, all that could be heard was the sound of Kirk Douglas's steel jaw dropping to the magnificent patio of chocolate-brown Arizona flagstone. The rest was silence.

"You've got to remember that most of these people came because   55
they're my clients," the host confided later. "You said that, and all I could think was how I'd have to go back to stitching slipcovers when this was done."

It turned out that there was more to my lead-balloon remark than a misjudged audience. Local AIDS organizers told me that a year earlier, a rumor that one of Palm Springs's most popular restaurants was owned by a homosexual, and that most of its waiters were gay, had terrified the elite community. Patronage at the eatery quickly plummeted, and it had nearly gone out of business. Fears that I dismissed as laughable were the genuine concerns of my audience, I realized. My San Francisco joke was a Palm Springs fable.

As I watched the busboys clear the tables later that night, I made a mental note not to tell that joke before dinner again. Never had I seen so many uneaten salads, so much wasted iceberg lettuce.

A friend had just tested antibody positive, and I was doing my best to cheer him up as we ambled down the sidewalk toward a Castro Street restaurant a few blocks from where I live in San Francisco. It seems most of my conversations now have to do with who has tested positive or lucked out and turned up negative, or who is too afraid to be tested. We had parked our car near Coming Home, the local hospice for AIDS patients and others suffering from terminal illnesses, and as we stepped around a nondescript, powder-blue van that blocked our path, two men in white uniforms emerged from the hospice's side door. They carried a stretcher, and on the stretcher was a corpse, neatly wrapped in a royal-blue blanket and secured with navy-blue straps. My friend and I stopped walking. The men quickly guided the stretcher into the back of the van, climbed in the front doors, and drove away. We continued our walk but didn't say anything.

I wondered if the corpse was someone I had known. I'd find out Thursday when the weekly gay paper came out. Every week there are at least two pages filled with obituaries of the previous week's departed. Each week, when I turn to those pages, I hold my breath, wondering whose picture I'll see. It's the only way to keep track, what with so many people dying.

Sometimes I wonder if an aberrant mother or two going to mass at   60
the Most Holy Redeemer Church across the street from Coming Home Hospice has ever warned a child, "That's where you'll end up if you don't obey God's law." Or whether some youngster, feeling that first awareness of a different sexuality, has looked at the doorway of this modern charnel house with an awesome, gnawing dread of annihilation.

"Is the limousine here? Where are the dancers?"

The room fell silent. Blake Rothaus had sounded coherent until that moment, but he was near death now and his brain was going. We were gathered around his bed in a small frame house on a dusty street in Oklahoma City. The twenty-four-year-old was frail and connected to life through a web of clear plastic tubing. He stared up at us and seemed to recognize from our looks that he had lapsed into dementia. A friend broke the uncomfortable silence.

"Of course, we all brought our dancing shoes," he said. "Nice fashionable pumps at that. I wouldn't go out without them."

Everyone laughed and Blake Rothaus was lucid again.

Blake had gone to high school in a San Francisco suburb. When he   65
was a sophomore, he told us, he and his best friend sometimes skipped school, sneaking to the city to spend their afternoons in the gay neighborhood around Castro Street.

It's a common sight, suburban teenagers playing hooky on Castro Street. I could easily imagine him standing on a corner not far from my house. But back in 1982, when he was eighteen, I was already writing about a mysterious, unnamed disease that had claimed 330 victims in the United States.

Blake moved back to Oklahoma City with his family after he graduated from high school. When he fell ill with AIDS, he didn't mope. Instead, he started pestering Oklahoma health officials with demands to educate people about this disease and to provide services for the sick. The state health department didn't recoil. At the age of twenty-two, Blake Rothaus had become the one-man nucleus for Oklahoma's first AIDS-patient services. He was the hero of the Sooner State's AIDS movement and something of a local legend.

Though the state had reported only 250 AIDS cases, Oklahoma City had a well-coordinated network of religious leaders, social workers, healthcare providers, gay-rights advocates, state legislators, and businessmen, all committed to providing a sane and humane response to this frightening new disease.

"I think it's the old Dust Bowl mentality," suggested one AIDS organizer. "When the hard times come, people pull together."

My past year's travels to twenty-nine states and talks with literally   70 thousands of people have convinced me of one thing about this country and AIDS: Most Americans want to do the right thing about this epidemic. Some might worry about mosquitoes and a few may be suspicious of their salad dressing. But beyond these fears is a reservoir of compassion and concern that goes vastly underreported by a media that needs conflict and heartlessness to fashion a good news hook.

In Kalamazoo, Michigan, when I visited my stepmother, I was buttonholed by a dozen middle-aged women who wondered anxiously whether we were any closer to a vaccine or a long-term treatment. One mentioned a hemophiliac nephew. Another had a gay brother in Chicago. A third went to a gay hairdresser who, she quickly added, was one of the finest people you'd ever meet. When I returned to my conservative hometown of Aurora, Illinois, nestled among endless fields of corn and soy, the local health department told me they receive more calls than they know what to do with from women's groups, parishes, and community organizations that want to do something to help. In New Orleans, the archconservative, pronuke, antigay bishop had taken up the founding of an AIDS hospice as a personal mission because, he said, when people are sick, you've got to help them out.

Scientists, reporters, and politicians privately tell me that of course *they* want to do more about AIDS, but they have to think about the Morton Downeys of the world, who argue that too much research or too much news space or too much official sympathy is being meted out to a bunch of miscreants. They do as much as they can, they insist; more would rile the resentments of the masses. So the institutions fumble along, convinced they must pander to the lowest common denominator, while the women and men of America's heartland pull me aside to fret about a dying cousin or co-worker and to plead, "When will there be a cure? When will this be over?"

"I think I'll make it through this time," Kit said to me, "but I don't have it in me to go through it again."

We were in room 3 in San Francisco General Hospital's ward 5A, the AIDS ward. The poplar trees outside Kit's window were losing their leaves, and the first winter's chill was settling over the city. I was preparing to leave for my fourth and, I hoped, final media tour, this time for release of the book in paperback and on audiocassette; Kit was preparing to die.

The seizures had started a week earlier, indicating he was suffering either from toxoplasmosis, caused by a gluttonous protozoa that sets up housekeeping in the brain; or perhaps it was a relapse of cryptococcal meningitis; or, another specialist guessed, it could be one of those other nasty brain infections that nobody had seen much of until the past year. Now that AIDS patients were living longer, they fell victim to even more exotic infections than in the early days. But the seizures were only part of it. Kit had slowly been losing the sight in his left eye to a herpes infection.

75

And the Kaposi's sarcoma lesions that had scarred his face were beginning to coat the inside of his lungs. When Kit mentioned he'd like to live
until Christmas, the doctors said he might want to consider having an
early celebration this year, because he wasn't going to be alive in
December.

"I can't take another infection," Kit said.

"What does that mean?"

"Morphine," Kit answered, adding mischievously, "lots of it."

We talked briefly about the mechanics of suicide. We both knew people who'd made a mess of it, and people who had done it right. It was
hardly the first time the subject had come up in conversation for either of
us. Gay men facing AIDS now exchange formulas for suicide as casually
as housewives swap recipes for chocolate-chip cookies.

Kit was released from the hospital a few days later. He had decided   80
to take his life on a Tuesday morning. I had to give my first round of interviews in Los Angeles that day, so I stopped on the way to the airport to
say good-bye on Monday. All day Tuesday, while I gave my perfectly
formed sound bites in a round of network radio appearances, I wondered:
Is this the moment he's slipping out of consciousness and into that perfect
darkness? When I called that night, it turned out he'd delayed his suicide
until Thursday to talk to a few more relatives. I had to give a speech in
Portland that day, so on the way to the airport I stopped again. He
showed me the amber-brown bottle with the bubble-gum-pink morphine
syrup, and we said another good-bye.

The next morning, Kit drank his morphine and fell into a deep sleep.
That afternoon, he awoke and drowsily asked what time it was. When
told it was five hours later, he murmured, "That's amazing. I should have
been dead hours ago."

And then he went back to sleep.

That night, Kit woke up again.

"You know what they say about near-death experiences?" he asked.
"Going toward the light?"

Shaking his head, he sighed, "No light. Nothing."   85

His suicide attempt a failure, Kit decided the timing of his death
would now be up to God. I kept up on the bizarre sequence of events by
phone and called as soon as I got back to San Francisco. I was going to
tell Kit that his theme song should be "Never Can Say Good-by," but
then the person on the other end of the phone told me that Kit had lapsed
into a coma.

The next morning, he died.

Kit's death was like everything about AIDS — anticlimactic. By the
time he actually did die, I was almost beyond feeling.

The next day, I flew to Boston for the start of the paperback tour, my
heart torn between rage and sorrow. All week, as I was chauffeured to
my appearances on *Good Morning America, Larry King Live,* and various CNN shows, I kept thinking, it's all going to break. I'm going to be

on a TV show with some officious government health spokesman lying to protect his job, and I'm going to start shouting, "You lying son of a bitch. Don't you know there are people, real people, people I love out there dying?" Or I'll be on a call-in show and another mother will phone about her thirty-seven-year-old son who just died and it will hit me all at once, and I'll start weeping.

But day after day as the tour went on, no matter how many official   90
lies I heard and how many grieving mothers I talked to, the crackup never occurred. All my answers came out rationally in tight little sound bites about institutional barriers to AIDS treatments and projections about 1993 case loads.

By the last day of the tour, when a limousine picked me up at my Beverly Hills hotel for my last round of satellite TV interviews, I knew I had to stop. In a few weeks I'd return to being national correspondent for the *Chronicle*, and it was time to get off the AIDS celebrity circuit, end the interviews and decline the invitations to the star-studded fund-raisers, and get back to work as a newspaper reporter. That afternoon, there was just one last radio interview to a call-in show in the San Fernando Valley, and then it would be over.

The first caller asked why his tax money should go toward funding an AIDS cure when people got the disease through their own misdeeds.

I used my standard jukebox answer about how most cancer cases are linked to people's behavior but that nobody ever suggested we stop trying to find a cure for cancer.

A second caller phoned to ask why her tax money should go to funding an AIDS cure when these people clearly deserved what they got.

I calmly put a new spin on the same answer, saying in America you   95
usually don't sentence people to die for having a different lifestyle from yours.

Then a third caller phoned in to say that he didn't care if all those queers and junkies died, as did a fourth and fifth and sixth caller. By then I was shouting, "You stupid bigot. You just want to kill off everybody you don't like. You goddamn Nazi."

The talk-show host sat in stunned silence. She'd heard I was so *reasonable*. My anger baited the audience further, and the seventh and eighth callers began talking about "you guys," as if only a faggot like myself could give a shit about whether AIDS patients all dropped dead tomorrow.

In their voices, I heard the reporters asking polite questions of NIH officials. Of course, they had to be polite to the government doctors; dying queers weren't anything to lose your temper over. I heard the dissembling NIH researchers go home to their wives at night, complain about the lack of personnel, and shrug; this was just how it was going to have to be for a while. They'd excuse their inaction by telling themselves that if they went public and lost their jobs, worse people would replace them. It was best to go along. But how would they feel if *their* friends, *their* daughters were dying of this disease? Would they be silent — or would they shout? Maybe they'll forgive me for suspecting they believed that ultimately a bunch of fags weren't worth losing a job over. And when I got home, I was going to have to watch my friends get shoved into powder-blue vans, and it wasn't going to change.

The history of the AIDS epidemic, of yesterday and of today, was echoing in the voices of those callers. And I was screaming at them, and the show host just sat there stunned, and I realized I had rendered myself utterly and completely inarticulate.

I stopped, took a deep breath, and returned to compound-complex   100 sentences about the American tradition of compassion and the overriding need to overcome institutional barriers to AIDS treatments.

When I got home to San Francisco that night, I looked over some notes I had taken from a conversation I'd had with Kit during his last stay in the hospital. I was carping about how frustrated I was at the prospect of returning to my reporting job. If an internationally acclaimed best seller hadn't done shit to change the world, what good would mere newspaper stories do?

"The limits of information," Kit said. "There's been a lot written on it."

"Oh," I said.

Kit closed his eyes briefly and faded into sleep while plastic tubes fed him a cornucopia of antibiotics. After five minutes, he stirred, looked up, and added, as if we had never stopped talking, "But you don't really have a choice. You've got to keep on doing it. What else are you going to do?"

The Reader's Presence

1. Consider the presence Shilts establishes for himself in the essay. How does he blend both professional expertise and private experience? How are these reflected in the structure of the essay itself?

2. Of what importance are television and radio talk shows to the essay? Why do you think Shilts included as much information as he did about them? What role do the callers play in the essay? What does the reader learn through them? How do the callers help Shilts structure his argument?

3. In what sense is this an essay about arguments? What happens to Shilts during the course of his arguments? Why is talking such a key part of the essay? Reread the section on the Palm Springs fund-raiser carefully (paragraphs 45–57). Why was Shilts surprised by the audience's reaction? How does his anecdote of that audience's response affect *your* response as an audience of the essay?

80

Jonathan Swift
A Modest Proposal

Jonathan Swift (1667–1745) was born and raised in Ireland, son of English parents. He was ordained an Anglican priest, and although as a young man he lived a literary life in London, he was appointed against his wishes to be dean of St. Patrick's Cathedral in Dublin. Swift wrote excellent poetry, but is remembered principally for his essays and political pamphlets, most of which were published under pseudonyms. Swift received payment for only one work in his entire life, Gulliver's Travels *(1726), for which he earned £200. Swift's political pamphlets were very influential in his day; among other issues, he spoke out against English exploitation of the Irish. Some of Swift's more important publications include* A Tale of a Tub *(1704),* The Importance of the Guardian Considered *(1713),* The Public Spirit of the Whigs *(1714), and* A Modest Proposal *(1729).*

Writing to his friend Alexander Pope, Swift commented that "the chief end I propose to my self in all my labors is to vex the world rather than divert it, and if I could compass that designe without hurting my own person or Fortune I would be the most Indefatigable writer you have ever seen."

For Preventing the Children of Poor People in Ireland
from Being a Burden to Their Parents or Country,
and for Making Them Beneficial to the Public

It is a melancholy object to those who walk through this great town[1] or travel in the country, when they see the streets, the roads, and cabin doors, crowded with beggars of the female sex, followed by three, four, or six children, all in rags and importuning every passenger for an alms. These mothers, instead of being able to work for their honest livelihood, are forced to employ all their time in strolling to beg sustenance for their helpless infants: who as they grow up either turn thieves for want of work, or leave their dear native country to fight for the pretender in Spain,[2] or sell themselves to the Barbadoes.[3]

---

[1]*this great town:* Dublin. — EDS.
[2]*pretender in Spain:* James Stuart (1688–1766); exiled in Spain, he laid claim to the English crown and had the support of many Irishmen who had joined an army hoping to restore him to the throne. — EDS.
[3]*the Barbadoes:* Inhabitants of the British colony in the Caribbean where Irishmen emigrated to work as indentured servants in exchange for their passage. — EDS.

I think it is agreed by all parties that this prodigious number of children in the arms, or on the backs, or at the heels of their mothers, and frequently of their fathers, is in the present deplorable state of the kingdom a very great additional grievance; and, therefore, whoever could find out a fair, cheap, and easy method of making these children sound, useful members of the commonwealth, would deserve so well of the public as to have his statute set up for a preserver of the nation.

But my intention is very far from being confined to provide only for the children of professed beggars; it is of a much greater extent, and shall take in the whole number of infants at a certain age who are born of parents in effect as little able to support them as those who demand our charity in the streets.

As to my own part, having turned my thoughts for many years upon this important subject, and maturely weighed the several schemes of our projectors,[4] I have always found them grossly mistaken in their computation. It is true, a child just dropped from its dam may be supported by her milk for a solar year, with little other nourishment; at most not above the value of 2s.,[5] which the mother may certainly get, or the value in scraps, by her lawful occupation of begging; and it is exactly at one year old that I propose to provide for them in such a manner as instead of being a charge upon their parents or the parish, or wanting food and raiment for the rest of their lives, they shall on the contrary contribute to the feeding, and partly to the clothing, of many thousands.

There is likewise another great advantage in my scheme, that it will prevent those voluntary abortions, and that horrid practice of women murdering their bastard children, alas! too frequent among us! sacrificing the poor innocent babes I doubt more to avoid the expense than the shame, which would move tears and pity in the most savage and inhuman breast.

The number of souls in this kingdom being usually reckoned one million and a half, of these I calculate there may be about 200,000 couple whose wives are breeders; from which number I subtract 30,000 couple who are able to maintain their own children (although I apprehend there cannot be so many, under the present distress of the kingdom); but this being granted, there will remain 170,000 breeders. I again subtract 50,000 for those women who miscarry, or whose children die by accident or disease within the year. There only remain 120,000 children of poor parents annually born. The question therefore is, how this number shall be reared and provided for? which, as I have already said, under the present situation of affairs, is utterly impossible by all the methods hitherto

5

---

[4]*projectors:* Planners. — EDS.
[5]*2s.:* Two shillings; in Swift's time one shilling was worth less than twenty-five cents. Other monetary references in the essay are to pounds sterling ("£."), pence ("d."), a crown, and a groat. A pound consisted of twenty shillings; a shilling of twelve pence; a crown was five shillings; a groat was worth a few cents. — EDS.

proposed. For we can neither employ them in handicraft of agriculture; we neither build houses (I mean in the country) nor cultivate land; they can very seldom pick up a livelihood by stealing, till they arrive at six years old, except where they are of towardly parts;[6] although I confess they learn the rudiments much earlier; during which time they can, however, be properly looked upon only as probationers; as I have been informed by a principal gentleman in the county of Cavan, who protested to me that he never knew above one or two instances under the age of six, even in a part of the kingdom so renowned for the quickest proficiency in that art.

I am assured by our merchants, that a boy or a girl before twelve years old is no salable commodity; and even when they come to this age they will not yield above 3£. or 3£. 2s. 6d. at most on the exchange; which cannot turn to account either to the parents or kingdom, the charge of nutriment and rags having been at least four times that value.

I shall now therefore humbly propose my own thoughts, which I hope will not be liable to the least objection.

I have been assured by a very knowing American of my acquaintance in London, that a young healthy child well nursed is at a year old a most delicious, nourishing, and wholesome food, whether stewed, roasted, baked, or broiled; and I make no doubt that it will equally serve in a fricassee or a ragout.[7]

I do therefore humbly offer it to public consideration that of the 120,000 children already computed, 20,000 may be reserved for breed, whereof only one-fourth part to be males; which is more than we allow to sheep, black cattle, or swine; and my reason is, that these children are seldom the fruits of marriage, a circumstance not much regarded by our savages; therefore one male will be sufficient to serve four females. That the remaining 100,000 may, at a year old, be offered in sale to the persons of quality and fortune through the kingdom; always advising the mother to let them suck plentifully in the last month, so as to render them plump and fat for a good table. A child will make two dishes at an entertainment for friends; and when the family dines alone, the fore and hind quarter will make a reasonable dish, and seasoned with a little pepper or salt will be very good boiled on the fourth day, especially in winter.

I have reckoned upon a medium that a child just born will weigh 12 pounds, and in a solar year, if tolerably nursed, will increase to 28 pounds.

I grant this food will be somewhat dear, and therefore very proper for landlords, who, as they have already devoured most of the parents, seem to have the best title to the children.

Infants' flesh will be in season throughout the year, but more plentiful in March, and a little before and after: for we are told by a grave au-

10

---

[6]*towardly parts:* Natural abilities. — EDS.
[7]*ragout:* A stew. — EDS.

thor, an eminent French physician,[8] that fish being a prolific diet, there are more children born in Roman Catholic countries about nine months after Lent than at any other season; therefore, reckoning a year after Lent, the markets will be more glutted than usual, because the number of popish infants is at least three to one in this kingdom: and therefore it will have one other collateral advantage, by lessening the number of papists among us.

I have already computed the charge of nursing a beggar's child (in which list I reckon all cottagers, laborers, and four-fifths of the farmers) to be about 2s. per annum, rags included; and I believe no gentleman would repine to give 10s. for the carcass of a good fat child, which, as I have said, will make four dishes of excellent nutritive meat, when he has only some particular friend or his own family to dine with him. Thus the squire will learn to be a good landlord, and grow popular among the tenants; the mother will have 8s. net profit, and be fit for work till she produces another child.

Those who are more thrifty (as I must confess the times require) may flay the carcass; the skin of which artificially[9] dressed will make admirable gloves for ladies, and summer boots for fine gentlemen.

As to our city of Dublin, shambles[10] may be appointed for this purpose in the most convenient parts of it, and butchers we may be assured will not be wanting: although I rather recommend buying the children alive, and dressing them hot from the knife as we do roasting pigs.

A very worthy person, a true lover of his country, and whose virtues I highly esteem, was lately pleased in discoursing on this matter to offer a refinement upon my scheme. He said that many gentlemen of this kingdom, having of late destroyed their deer, he conceived that the want of venison might be well supplied by the bodies of young lads and maidens, not exceeding fourteen years of age nor under twelve; so great a number of both sexes in every country being now ready to starve for want of work and service; and these to be disposed of by their parents, if alive, or otherwise by their nearest relations. But with due deference to so excellent a friend and so deserving a patriot, I cannot be altogether in his sentiments; for as to the males, my American acquaintance assured me from frequent experience that their flesh was generally tough and lean, like that of our schoolboys by continual exercise, and their taste disagreeable; and to fatten them would not answer the charge. Then as to the females, it would, I think, with humble submission be a loss to the public, because they soon would become breeders themselves: and besides, it is not improbable that some scrupulous people might be apt to censure such a

15

[8]*French physician:* François Rabelais (c. 1494–1553), the great Renaissance humanist and author of the comic masterpiece *Gargantua and Pantagruel.* Swift is being ironic in calling Rabelais "grave." — EDS.
[9]*artificially:* Artfully. — EDS.
[10]*shambles:* Slaughterhouses. — EDS.

1

practice (although indeed very unjustly), as a little bordering upon cruelty; which, I confess, has always been with me the strongest objection against any project, how well soever intended.

But in order to justify my friend, he confessed that this expedient was put into his head by the famous Psalmanazar[11] a native of the island Formosa, who came from thence to London about twenty years ago: and in conversation told my friend, that in his country when any young person happened to be put to death, the executioner sold the carcass to persons of quality as a prime dainty; and that in his time the body of a plump girl of fifteen, who was crucified for an attempt to poison the emperor, was sold to his imperial majesty's prime minister of state, and other great mandarins of the court, in joints from the gibbet, at 400 crowns. Neither indeed can I deny, that if the same use were made of several plump young girls in this town, who without one single groat to their fortunes cannot stir abroad without a chair,[12] and appear at the playhouse and assemblies in foreign fineries which they never will pay for, the kingdom would not be the worse.

Some persons of a desponding spirit are in great concern about the vast number of poor people, who are aged, diseased, or maimed, and I have been desired to employ my thoughts what course may be taken to ease the nation of so grievous an encumbrance. But I am not in the least pain upon that matter, because it is very well known that they are every day dying and rotting by cold and famine, and filth and vermin, as fast as can be reasonably expected. And as to the young laborers, they are now in as hopeful a condition: They cannot get work, and consequently pine away for want of nourishment, to a degree that if at any time they are accidentally hired to common labor, they have not strength to perform it; and thus the country and themselves are happily delivered from the evils to come.

I have too long digressed, and therefore shall return to my subject. I think the advantages by the proposal which I have made are obvious and many, as well as of the highest importance.

For first, as I have already observed, it would greatly lessen the number of papists, with whom we are yearly overrun, being the principal breeders of the nation as well as our most dangerous enemies; and who stay at home on purpose to deliver the kingdom to the Pretender, hoping to take their advantage by the absence of so many good Protestants, who have chosen rather to leave their country than stay at home and pay tithes against their conscience to an Episcopal curate.

Secondly, The poor tenants will have something valuable of their own, which by law may be made liable to distress[13] and help to pay their

20

---

[11]*Psalmanazar:* George Psalmanazar (c. 1679–1763) was a Frenchman who tricked London society into believing he was a native of Formosa (now Taiwan). — EDS.

[12]*a chair:* A sedan chair in which one is carried about. — EDS.

[13]*distress:* Seizure for payment of debt. — EDS.

landlord's rent, their corn and cattle being already seized, and money a thing unknown.

Thirdly, Whereas the maintenance of 100,000 children from two years old and upward, cannot be computed at less than 10s. a-piece per annum, the nation's stock will be thereby increased £50,000 per annum, beside the profit of a new dish introduced to the tables of all gentlemen of fortune in the kingdom who have any refinement in taste. And the money will circulate among ourselves, the goods being entirely of our own growth and manufacture.

Fourthly, The constant breeders beside the gain of 8s. sterling per annum by the sale of their children, will be rid of the charge of maintaining them after the first year.

Fifthly, This food would likewise bring great custom to taverns, where the vintners will certainly be so prudent as to procure the best receipts[14] for dressing it to perfection, and consequently have their houses frequented by all the fine gentlemen, who justly value themselves upon their knowledge in good eating; and a skilful cook who understands how to oblige his guests, will contrive to make it as expensive as they please.

Sixthly, This would be a great inducement to marriage, which all wise nations have either encouraged by rewards or enforced by laws and penalties. It would increase the care and tenderness of mothers toward their children, when they were sure of a settlement for life to the poor babes, provided in some sort by the public, to their annual profit instead of expense. We should see an honest emulation among the married women, which of them would bring the fattest child to the market. Men would become as fond of their wives during the time of their pregnancy as they are now of their mares in foal, their cows in calf, their sows when they are ready to farrow; nor offer to beat or kick them (as is too frequent a practice) for fear of a miscarriage.

Many other advantages might be enumerated. For instance, the addition of some thousand carcasses in our exportation of barreled beef, the propagation of swine's flesh, and improvement in the art of making good bacon, so much wanted among us by the great destruction of pigs, too frequent at our table; which are no way comparable in taste or magnificence to a well-grown, fat, yearling child, which roasted whole will make a considerable figure at a lord mayor's feast or any other public entertainment. But this and many others I omit, being studious of brevity.

Supposing that 1,000 families in this city would be constant customers for infants' flesh, besides others who might have it at merry-meetings, particularly at weddings and christenings, I compute that Dublin would take off annually about 20,000 carcasses; and the rest of the kingdom (where probably they will be sold somewhat cheaper) the remaining 80,000.

25

[14]*receipts:* Recipes. — EDS.

I can think of no one objection that will possibly be raised against this proposal unless it should be urged that the number of people will be thereby much lessened in the kingdom. This I freely own, and it was indeed one principal design in offering it to the world. I desire the reader will observe, that I calculate my remedy for this one individual kingdom of Ireland and for no other that ever was, is, or I think ever can be upon earth. Therefore let no man talk to me of other expedients: of taxing our absentees at 5s. a pound: of using neither clothes nor household furniture except what is of our own growth and manufacture: of utterly rejecting the materials and instruments that promote foreign luxury: of curing the expensiveness of pride, vanity, idleness, and gaming in our women: of introducing a vein of parsimony, prudence, and temperance: of learning to love our country, in the want of which we differ even from Laplanders and the inhabitants of Topinamboo:[15] of quitting our animosities and factions, nor acting any longer like the Jews, who were murdering one another at the very moment their city was taken:[16] of being a little cautious not to sell our country and conscience for nothing: of teaching landlords to have at least one degree of mercy toward their tenants: lastly, of putting a spirit of honesty, industry, and skill into our shopkeepers; who, if a resolution could now be taken to buy only our native goods, would immediately unite to cheat and exact upon us in the price the measure, and the goodness, nor could ever yet be brought to make one fair proposal of just dealing, though often and earnestly invited to it.

Therefore I repeat, let no man talk to me of these and the like expedients, till he has at least some glimpse of hope that there will be ever some hearty and sincere attempt to put them in practice.   30

But as to myself, having been wearied out for many years with offering vain, idle, visionary thoughts, and at length utterly despairing of success, I fortunately fell upon this proposal; which, as it is wholly new, so it has something solid and real, of no expense and little trouble, full in our own power, and whereby we can incur no danger in disobliging England. For this kind of commodity will not bear exportation, the flesh being of too tender a consistence to admit a long continuance in salt, although perhaps I could name a country which would be glad to eat up our whole nation without it.

After all, I am not so violently bent upon my own opinion as to reject any offer proposed by wise men, which shall be found equally innocent, cheap, easy, and effectual. But before something of that kind shall be advanced in contradiction to my scheme, and offering a better, I desire the author or authors will be pleased maturely to consider two points. First, as things now stand, how they will be able to find food and raiment for

---

[15]*Laplanders and the inhabitants of Topinamboo:* Lapland is the area of Scandinavia above the Arctic Circle; Topinamboo, in Brazil, was known in Swift's time for the savagery of its tribes. — EDS.

[16]*was taken:* A reference to the Roman seizure of Jerusalem (A.D. 70). — EDS.

100,000 useless mouths and backs. And secondly, there being a round million of creatures in human figure throughout this kingdom, whose subsistence put into a common stock would leave them in debt 2,000,000£. sterling, adding those who are beggars by profession to the bulk of farmers, cottagers, and laborers, with the wives and children who are beggars in effect; I desire those politicians who dislike my overture, and may perhaps be so bold as to attempt an answer, that they will first ask the parents of these mortals, whether they would not at this day think it a great happiness to have been sold for food at a year old in the manner I prescribe, and thereby have avoided such a perpetual scene of misfortunes as they have since gone through by the oppression of landlords, the impossibility of paying rent without money or trade, the want of common sustenance, with neither house nor clothes to cover them from the inclemencies of the weather, and the most inevitable prospect of entailing the like or greater miseries upon their breed for ever.

I profess, in the sincerity of my heart, that I have not the least personal interest in endeavoring to promote this necessary work, having no other motive than the public good of my country, by advancing our trade, providing for infants, relieving the poor, and giving some pleasure to the rich. I have no children by which I can propose to get a single penny; the youngest being nine years old, and my wife past childbearing.

The Reader's Presence

1. Consider Swift's title. In what sense is the proposal "modest"? What is modest about it? What synonyms would you use for *modest* that appear in the essay? In what sense is the essay a "proposal"? Does it follow any format that resembles a proposal? What aspects of its language seem to resemble proposal writing?
2. For this essay Swift invents a speaker, an unnamed, fictional individual who "humbly" proposes a plan to relieve poverty in Ireland. What attitudes and beliefs in the essay do you attribute to the speaker? Which do you attribute to Swift, the author?
3. Having considered two authors (the speaker of the proposal and Swift), now consider two readers — the reader the speaker imagines and the reader Swift imagines. How do these two readers differ? Reread the final paragraph of the essay from the perspective of each of these readers. How do you think each reader is expected to respond?

81

Henry David Thoreau
Civil Disobedience

Regarded today as one of the central literary figures of the nineteenth century, in his lifetime Henry David Thoreau (1817–1862) was for the most part viewed as a talented but largely unsuccessful disciple of Ralph Waldo Emerson. In fact, although the two men held many beliefs in common, Thoreau possessed a fiercely independent intellect together with political convictions that sometimes alienated Emerson. Thoreau articulates his thoughts on political activism in the essay "Civil Disobedience" (1849), which influenced the nonviolent strategies of both Mahatma Gandhi and Martin Luther King, Jr. Despite the considerable impact of his writing on contemporary thought, it was not until the 1930s that Thoreau's masterpiece, Walden *(1845), began to be studied widely, and only more recently that the value of his other writings has been recognized.*

In his journal Thoreau once commented, "We cannot write well or truly but what we write with gusto. The body, the senses, must conspire with the mind. . . . Often I feel that my head stands out too dry, when it should be immersed. . . . Whatever things I perceive with my entire man, those let me record, and it will be poetry. The sounds which I hear with the consent and coincidence of all my senses, these are significant and musical; at least, they only are heard."

I heartily accept the motto, — "That government is best which governs least"; and I should like to see it acted up to more rapidly and systematically. Carried out, it finally amounts to this, which also I believe, — "That government is best which governs not at all"; and when men are prepared for it, that will be the kind of government which they will have. Government is at best but an expedient; but most governments are usually, and all governments are sometimes, inexpedient. The objections which have been brought against a standing army, and they are many and weighty, and deserve to prevail, may also at last be brought against a standing government. The standing army is only an arm of the standing government. The government itself, which is only the mode which the people have chosen to execute their will, is equally liable to be abused and perverted before the people can act through it. Witness the present Mexican war, the work of comparatively a few individuals using the standing government as their tool; for, in the outset, the people would not have consented to this measure.

This American Government, — what is it but a tradition, though a recent one, endeavoring to transmit itself unimpaired to posterity, but each instant losing some of its integrity? It has not the vitality and force of a single living man; for a single man can bend it to his will. It is a sort of wooden gun to the people themselves. But it is not the less necessary for this; for the people must have some complicated machinery or other, and hear its din, to satisfy that idea of government which they have. Governments show thus how successfully men can be imposed on, even impose on themselves, for their own advantage. It is excellent, we must all allow. Yet this government never of itself furthered any enterprise, but by the alacrity with which it got out of its way. *It* does not keep the country free. *It* does not settle the West. *It* does not educate. The character inherent in the American people has done all that has been accomplished; and it would have done somewhat more, if the government had not sometimes got in its way. For government is an expedient by which men would fain succeed in letting one another alone; and, as has been said, when it is most expedient, the governed are most let alone by it. Trade and commerce, if they were not made of India-rubber, would never manage to bounce over the obstacles which legislators are continually putting in their way; and, if one were to judge these men wholly by the effects of their actions and not partly by their intentions, they would deserve to be classed and punished with those mischievous persons who put obstructions on the railroads.

But, to speak practically and as a citizen, unlike those who call themselves no-government men, I ask for, not at once no government, but *at once* a better government. Let every man make known what kind of government would command his respect, and that will be one step toward obtaining it.

After all, the practical reason why, when the power is once in the hands of the people, a majority are permitted, and for a long period continue, to rule is not because they are most likely to be in the right, nor because this seems fairest to the minority, but because they are physically the strongest. But a government in which the majority rule in all cases cannot be based on justice, even as far as men understand it. Can there not be a government in which majorities do not virtually decide right and wrong, but conscience? — in which majorities decide only those questions to which the rule of expediency is applicable? Must the citizen ever for a moment, or in the least degree, resign his conscience to the legislator? Why has every man a conscience, then? I think that we should be men first, and subjects afterward. It is not desirable to cultivate a respect for the law, so much as for the right. The only obligation which I have a right to assume is to do at any time what I think right. It is truly enough said, that a corporation has no conscience; but a corporation of conscientious men is a corporation *with* a conscience. Law never made men a whit more just; and, by means of their respect for it, even the well-disposed are daily made the agents of injustice. A common and natural result of any undue respect for law is, that you may see a file of soldiers, colonel, captain, corporal, privates, powder-monkeys, and all, marching in admirable order over hill and dale to the wars, against their wills, ay, against their common sense and consciences, which makes it very steep marching indeed, and produces a palpitation of the heart. They have no doubt that it is a damnable business in which they are concerned; they are all peaceably inclined. Now, what are they? Men at all? or small movable forts and magazines, at the service of some unscrupulous man in power? Visit the Navy-Yard, and behold a marine, such a man as an American government can make, or such as it can make a man with its black arts, — a mere shadow and reminiscence of humanity, a man laid out alive and standing, and already, as one may say, buried under arms with funeral accompaniments, it may be, —

> "Not a drum was heard, not a funeral note,
>   As his corse to the rampart we hurried;
> Not a soldier discharged his farewell shot
>   O'er the grave where our hero we buried."[1]

The mass of men serve the state thus, not as men mainly, but as machines, with their bodies. They are the standing army, and the militia, jailers, constables, posse comitatus, etc. In most cases there is no free exercise whatever of the judgment or of the moral sense; but they put themselves on a level with wood and earth and stones; and wooden men can perhaps be manufactured that will serve the purpose as well. Such command no more respect than men of straw or a lump of dirt. They have the same sort of worth only as horses and dogs. Yet such as these even are commonly esteemed good citizens. Others — as most legislators, politicians, lawyers, ministers, and office-holders — serve the state chiefly with their heads; and, as they rarely make any moral distinctions, they are as likely to serve the Devil, without *intending* it, as God. A very few, as heroes, patriots, martyrs, reformers in the great sense, and *men*, serve the state with their consciences also, and so necessarily resist it for the most part; and they are commonly treated as enemies by it. A wise man will only be useful as a man, and will not submit to be "clay," and "stop a hole to keep the wind away,"[2] but leave that office to his dust at least: —

> "I am too high-born to be propertied,
> To be a secondary at control,
> Or useful serving-man and instrument
> To any sovereign state throughout the world."[3]

5

---

[1] *"Not a drum was heard. . . .":* Lines from the Irish poet Charles Wolfe's "The Burial of Sir John Moore of Corunna." — EDS.

[2] *"clay"* and *"stop a hole . . .":* From William Shakespeare's *Hamlet* (Act V, scene i). — EDS.

[3] *"I am too high-born. . . .":* From William Shakespeare's *Hamlet* (Act V, scene ii). — EDS.

He who gives himself entirely to his fellow-men appears to them useless and selfish; but he who gives himself partially to them is pronounced a benefactor and philanthropist.

How does it become a man to behave toward this American government to-day? I answer, that he cannot without disgrace be associated with it. I cannot for an instant recognize that political organization as *my* government which is the *slave's* government also.

All men recognize the right of revolution; that is, the right to refuse allegiance to, and to resist, the government, when its tyranny or its inefficiency are great and unendurable. But almost all say that such is not the case now. But such was the case, they think, in the Revolution of '75. If one were to tell me that this was a bad government because it taxed certain foreign commodities brought to its ports, it is most probable that I should not make an ado about it, for I can do without them. All machines have their friction; and possibly this does enough good to counterbalance the evil. At any rate, it is a great evil to make a stir about it. But when the friction comes to have its machine, and oppression and robbery are organized, I say, let us not have such a machine any longer. In other words, when a sixth of the population of a nation which has undertaken to be the refuge of liberty are slaves, and a whole country is unjustly overrun and conquered by a foreign army, and subjected to military law, I think that it is not too soon for honest men to rebel and revolutionize. What makes this duty the more urgent is the fact that the country so overrun is not our own, but ours is the invading army.

Paley,[4] a common authority with many on moral questions, in his chapter on the "Duty of Submission to Civil Government," resolves all civil obligation into expediency; and he proceeds to say, "that so long as the interest of the whole society requires it, that is, so long as the established government cannot be resisted or changed without public inconveniency, it is the will of God that the established government be obeyed, and no longer. . . . This principle being admitted, the justice of every particular case of resistance is reduced to a computation of the quantity of the danger and grievance on the one side, and of the probability and expense of redressing it on the other." Of this, he says, every man shall judge for himself. But Paley appears never to have contemplated those cases to which the rule of expediency does not apply, in which a people, as well as an individual, must do justice, cost what it may. If I have unjustly wrested a plank from a drowning man, I must restore it to him though I drown myself. This, according to Paley, would be inconvenient. But he that would save his life, in such a case, shall lose it. This people must cease to hold slaves, and to make war on Mexico, though it cost them their existence as a people.

---

[4]*Paley:* William Paley (1743–1805), English philosopher and clergyman and the author of *Principles of Moral and Political Philosophy* (1785). — EDS.

In their practice, nations agree with Paley; but does any one think   10
that Massachusetts does exactly what is right at the present crisis?

> "A drab of state, a cloth-o'-silver slut,
> To have her train borne up, and her soul trail in the dirt."[5]

Practically speaking, the opponents to a reform in Massachusetts are not
a hundred thousand politicians at the South, but a hundred thousand
merchants and farmers here, who are more interested in commerce and
agriculture than they are in humanity, and are not prepared to do justice
to the slave and to Mexico, *cost what it may.* I quarrel not with far-off
foes, but with those who, near at home, coöperate with, and do the bid-
ding of, those far away, and without whom the latter would be harmless.
We are accustomed to say, that the mass of men are unprepared; but improvement is slow, because the few are not materially wiser or better than
the many. It is not so important that many should be as good as you, as
that there be some absolute goodness somewhere; for that will leaven the
whole lump. There are thousands who are *in opinion* opposed to slavery
and to the war, who yet in effect do nothing to put an end to them; who,
esteeming themselves children of Washington and Franklin, sit down with
their hands in their pockets, and say that they know not what to do, and
do nothing; who even postpone the question of freedom to the question
of free-trade, and quietly read the prices-current along with the latest ad-
vices from Mexico, after dinner, and, it may be, fall asleep over them
both. What is the price-current of an honest man and patriot to-day?
They hesitate, and they regret, and sometimes they petition; but they do
nothing in earnest and with effect. They will wait, well disposed, for others to remedy the evil, that they may no longer have it to regret. At most,
they give only a cheap vote, and a feeble countenance and Godspeed, to
the right, as it goes by them. There are nine hundred and ninety-nine patrons of virtue to one virtuous man. But it is easier to deal with the real
possessor of a thing than with the temporary guardian of it.

All voting is a sort of gaming, like checkers or backgammon, with a
slight moral tinge to it, a playing with right and wrong, with moral questions; and betting naturally accompanies it. The character of the voters is
not staked. I cast my vote, perchance, as I think right; but I am not vitally
concerned that that right should prevail. I am willing to leave it to the
majority. Its obligation, therefore, never exceeds that of expediency. Even
voting *for the right* is *doing* nothing for it. It is only expressing to men
feebly your desire that it should prevail. A wise man will not leave the
right to the mercy of chance, nor wish it to prevail through the power of
the majority. There is but little virtue in the action of masses of men.
When the majority shall at length vote for the abolition of slavery, it will
be because they are indifferent to slavery, or because there is but little

[5]*"A drab of state. . . .":* See Cyril Tourneur's *The Revenger's Tragedy* (1607), (Act IV,
scene iv). — EDS.

slavery left to be abolished by their vote. *They* will then be the only slaves. Only *his* vote can hasten the abolition of slavery who asserts his own freedom by his vote.

I hear of a convention to be held at Baltimore, or elsewhere, for the selection of a candidate for the Presidency, made up chiefly of editors, and men who are politicians by profession; but I think, what is it to any independent, intelligent, and respectable man what decision they may come to? Shall we not have the advantage of his wisdom and honesty, nevertheless? Can we not count upon some independent votes? Are there not many individuals in the country who do not attend conventions? But no: I find that the respectable man, so called, has immediately drifted from his position, and despairs of his country, when his country has more reason to despair of him. He forthwith adopts one of the candidates thus selected as the only *available* one, thus proving that he is himself *available* for any purposes of the demagogue. His vote is of no more worth than that of any unprincipled foreigner or hireling native, who may have been bought. O for a man who is a *man,* and, as my neighbor says, has a bone in his back which you cannot pass your hand through! Our statistics are at fault: The population has been returned too large. How many *men* are there to a square thousand miles in this country? Hardly one. Does not America offer any inducement for men to settle here? The American has dwindled into an Odd Fellow, — one who may be known by the development of his organ of gregariousness, and a manifest lack of intellect and cheerful self-reliance; whose first and chief concern, on coming into the world, is to see that the Almshouses are in good repair; and, before yet he has lawfully donned the virile garb, to collect a fund for the support of the widows and orphans that may be; who, in short, ventures to live only by the aid of the Mutual Insurance company, which has promised to bury him decently.

It is not a man's duty, as a matter of course, to devote himself to the eradication of any, even the most enormous wrong; he may still properly have other concerns to engage him; but it is his duty, at least, to wash his hands of it, and, if he gives it no thought longer, not to give it practically his support. If I devote myself to other pursuits and contemplations, I must first see, at least, that I do not pursue them sitting upon another man's shoulders. I must get off him first, that he may pursue his contemplations too. See what gross inconsistency is tolerated. I have heard some of my townsmen say, "I should like to have them order me out to help put down an insurrection of the slaves, or to march to Mexico; — see if I would go"; and yet these very men have each, directly by their allegiance, and so indirectly, at least, by their money, furnished a substitute. The soldier is applauded who refuses to serve in an unjust war by those who do not refuse to sustain the unjust government which makes the war; is applauded by those whose own act and authority he disregards and sets at naught; as if the state were penitent to that degree that it hired one to scourge it while it sinned, but not to that degree that it left off sinning for a moment. Thus, under the name of Order and Civil Government, we are all made at last to pay homage to and support our own meanness. After the first blush of sin comes its indifference; and from immoral it becomes, as it were, *un*moral, and not quite unnecessary to that life which we have made.

The broadest and most prevalent error requires the most disinterested virtue to sustain it. The slight reproach to which the virtue of patriotism is commonly liable, the noble are most likely to incur. Those who, while they disapprove of the character and measures of a government, yield to it their allegiance and support are undoubtedly its most conscientious supporters, and so frequently the most serious obstacles to reform. Some are petitioning the state to dissolve the Union, to disregard the requisitions of the President. Why do they not dissolve it themselves, — the union between themselves and the state, — and refuse to pay their quota into its treasury? Do not they stand in the same relation to the state that the state does to the Union? And have not the same reasons prevented the state from resisting the Union which have prevented them from resisting the state?

How can a man be satisfied to entertain an opinion merely, and enjoy   15
it? Is there any enjoyment in it, if his opinion is that he is aggrieved? If you are cheated out of a single dollar by your neighbor, you do not rest satisfied with knowing that you are cheated, or with saying that you are cheated, or even with petitioning him to pay you your due; but you take effectual steps at once to obtain the full amount, and see that you are never cheated again. Action from principle, the perception and the performance of right, changes things and relations; it is essentially revolutionary, and does not consist wholly with anything which was. It not only divides states and churches, it divides families; ay, it divides the *individual,* separating the diabolical in him from the divine.

Unjust laws exist: Shall we be content to obey them, or shall we endeavor to amend them, and obey them until we have succeeded, or shall we transgress them at once? Men generally, under such a government as this, think that they ought to wait until they have persuaded the majority to alter them. They think that, if they should resist, the remedy would be worse than the evil. But it is the fault of the government itself that the remedy *is* worse than the evil. *It* makes it worse. Why is it not more apt to anticipate and provide for reform? Why does it not cherish its wise minority? Why does it cry and resist before it is hurt? Why does it not encourage its citizens to be on the alert to point out its fault, and *do* better than it would have them? Why does it always crucify Christ, and excommunicate Copernicus and Luther, and pronounce Washington and Franklin rebels?

One would think, that a deliberate and practical denial of its authority was the only offense never contemplated by government; else, why has it not assigned its definite, its suitable and proportionate penalty? If a man who has no property refuses but once to earn nine shillings for the state, he is put in prison for a period unlimited by any law that I know, and determined only by the discretion of those who placed him there; but if he should steal ninety times nine shillings from the state, he is soon permitted to go at large again.

If the injustice is part of the necessary friction of the machine of government, let it go, let it go: perchance it will wear smooth, — certainly the machine will wear out. If the injustice has a spring, or a pulley, or a rope, or a crank, exclusively for itself, then perhaps you may consider whether the remedy will not be worse than the evil; but if it is of such a nature that it requires you to be the agent of injustice to another, then, I say, break the law. Let your life be a counter friction to stop the machine. What I have to do is to see, at any rate, that I do not lend myself to the wrong which I condemn.

As for adopting the ways which the state has provided for remedying the evil, I know not of such ways. They take too much time, and a man's life will be gone. I have other affairs to attend to. I came into this world, not chiefly to make this a good place to live in, but to live in it, be it good or bad. A man has not everything to do, but something; and because he cannot do *everything*, it is not necessary that he should do *something* wrong. It is not my business to be petitioning the Governor or the Legislature any more than it is theirs to petition me; and if they should not hear my petition, what should I do then? But in this case the state has provided no way: its very Constitution is the evil. This may seem to be harsh and stubborn and unconciliatory; but it is to treat with the utmost kindness and consideration the only spirit that can appreciate or deserve it. So is all change for the better, like birth and death, which convulse the body.

I do not hesitate to say, that those who call themselves Abolitionists   20 should at once effectually withdraw their support, both in person and property, from the government of Massachusetts, and not wait till they constitute a majority of one, before they suffer the right to prevail through them. I think that it is enough if they have God on their side, without waiting for that other one. Moreover, any man more right than his neighbors constitutes a majority of one already.

I meet this American government, or its representative, the state government, directly, and face to face, once a year — no more — in the person of its tax-gatherer; this is the only mode in which a man situated as I am necessarily meets it; and it then says distinctly, Recognize me; and the simplest, the most effectual, and, in the present posture of affairs, the indispensablest mode of treating with it on this head, of expressing your little satisfaction with and love for it, is to deny it then. My civil neighbor, the tax-gatherer, is the very man I have to deal with, — for it is, after all, with men and not with parchment that I quarrel, — and he has voluntarily chosen to be an agent of the government. How shall he ever know well what he is and does as an officer of the government, or as a man, until he is obliged to consider whether he shall treat me, his neighbor, for whom he has respect, as a neighbor and well-disposed man, or as a maniac and disturber of the peace, and see if he can get over this obstruction to his neighborliness without a ruder and more impetuous thought or speech corresponding with his action. I know this well, that if one thousand, if one hundred, if ten men whom I could name, — if ten *honest* men only, — say if *one* HONEST man, in this State of Massachusetts, *ceasing to hold slaves,* were actually to withdraw from this copartnership, and be locked up in the county jail therefor, it would be the abolition of slavery in America. For it matters not how small the beginning may seem to be: What is once well done is done forever. But we love better to talk about it: That we say is our mission. Reform keeps many scores of newspapers in its service, but not one man. If my esteemed neighbor, the State's ambassador, who will devote his days to the settlement of the question of human rights in the Council Chamber, instead of being threatened with the prisons of Carolina, were to sit down the prisoner of Massachusetts, that State which is so anxious to foist the sin of slavery upon her sister, — though at present she can discover only an act of inhospitality to be the ground of a quarrel with her, — the Legislature would not wholly waive the subject the following winter.

Under a government which imprisons any unjustly, the true place for a just man is also a prison. The proper place to-day, the only place which Massachusetts has provided for her freer and less desponding spirits, is in her prisons, to be put out and locked out of the State by her own act, as they have already put themselves out by their principles. It is there that the fugitive slave, and the Mexican prisoner on parole, and the Indian come to plead the wrongs of his race should find them; on that separate, but more free and honorable ground, where the State places those who are not *with* her, but *against* her, — the only house in a slave State in which a free man can abide with honor. If any think that their influence would be lost there, and their voices no longer afflict the ear of the State, that they would not be as an enemy within its walls, they do not know by how much truth is stronger than error, nor how much more eloquently and effectively he can combat injustice who has experienced a little in his own person. Cast your whole vote, not a strip of paper merely, but your whole influence. A minority is powerless while it conforms to the majority; it is not even a minority then; but it is irresistible when it clogs by its whole weight. If the alternative is to keep all just men in prison, or give up war and slavery, the State will not hesitate which to choose. If a thousand men were not to pay their tax-bills this year, that would not be a violent and bloody measure, as it would be to pay them, and enable the State to commit violence and shed innocent blood. This is, in fact, the definition of a peaceable revolution, if any such is possible. If the tax-gatherer, or any other public officer, asks me, as one has done, "But what shall I do?" my answer is, "If you really wish to do anything, resign your office." When the subject has refused allegiance, and the officer has resigned his office, then the revolution is accomplished. But even suppose blood should flow. Is there not a sort of blood shed when the conscience is wounded? Through this wound a man's real manhood and immortality flow out, and he bleeds to an everlasting death. I see this blood flowing now.

I have contemplated the imprisonment of the offender, rather than the seizure of his goods, — though both will serve the same purpose, — because they who assert the purest right, and consequently are most dangerous to a corrupt State, commonly have not spent much time in accumulating property. To such the State renders comparatively small service, and a slight tax is wont to appear exorbitant, particularly if they are obliged to earn it by special labor with their hands. If there were one who lived wholly without the use of money, the State itself would hesitate to demand it of him. But the rich man — not to make any invidious comparison — is always sold to the institution which makes him rich. Absolutely speaking, the more money, the less virtue; for money comes between a man and his objects, and obtains them for him; and it was certainly no great virtue to obtain it. It puts to rest many questions which he would otherwise be taxed to answer; while the only new question which it puts is the hard but superfluous one, how to spend it. Thus his moral ground is taken from under his feet. The opportunities of living are diminished in proportion as what are called the "means" are increased. The best thing a man can do for his culture when he is rich is to endeavor to carry out those schemes which he entertained when he was poor. Christ answered the Herodians according to their condition. "Show me the tribute-money," said he; — and one took a penny out of his pocket; — if you use money which has the image of Caesar on it, which he has made current and valuable, that is, *if you are men of the State,* and gladly enjoy the advantages of Caesar's government, then pay him back some of his own when he demands it. "Render therefore to Caesar that which is Caesar's, and to God those things which are God's," — leaving them no wiser than before as to which was which; for they did not wish to know.

When I converse with the freest of my neighbors, I perceive that, whatever they may say about the magnitude and seriousness of the question, and their regard for the public tranquillity, the long and the short of the matter is, that they cannot spare the protection of the existing government, and they dread the consequences to their property and families of disobedience to it. For my own part, I should not like to think that I ever rely on the protection of the State. But, if I deny the authority of the State when it presents its tax-bill, it will soon take and waste all my property, and so harass me and my children without end. This is hard. This makes it impossible for a man to live honestly, and at the same time comfortably, in outward respects. It will not be worth the while to accumulate property; that would be sure to go again. You must hire or squat somewhere, and raise but a small crop, and eat that soon. You must live within yourself, and depend upon yourself always tucked up and ready for a start, and not have many affairs. A man may grow rich in Turkey even, if he will be in all respects a good subject of the Turkish government. Confucius said: "If a state is governed by the principles of reason, poverty and misery are subjects of shame; if a state is not governed by the principles of reason, riches and honors are the subjects of shame." No: Until I want the protection of Massachusetts to be extended to me in some distant Southern port, where my liberty is endangered, or until I am bent solely on building up an estate at home by peaceful enterprise, I can afford to refuse allegiance to Massachusetts, and her right to my property and life. It costs me less in every sense to incur the penalty of disobedience to the State than it would to obey. I should feel as if I were worth less in that case.

Some years ago, the State met me in behalf of the Church, and commanded me to pay a certain sum toward the support of a clergyman whose preaching my father attended, but never I myself. "Pay," it said, "or be locked up in the jail." I declined to pay. But, unfortunately, another man saw fit to pay it. I did not see why the schoolmaster should be taxed to support the priest, and not the priest the schoolmaster; for I was not the State's schoolmaster, but I supported myself by voluntary subscription. I did not see why the lyceum should not present its tax-bill, and have the State to back its demand, as well as the Church. However, at the request of the selectmen, I condescended to make some such statement as this in writing: — "Know all men by these presents, that I, Henry Thoreau, do not wish to be regarded as a member of any incorporated society which I have not joined." This I gave to the town clerk; and he has it. The State, having thus learned that I did not wish to be regarded as a member of that church, has never made a like demand on me since; though it said that it must adhere to its original presumption that time. If I had known how to name them, I should then have signed off in detail from all the societies which I never signed on to; but I did not know where to find a complete list.

I have paid no poll-tax for six years. I was put into a jail once on this account, for one night; and, as I stood considering the walls of solid stone, two or three feet thick, the door of wood and iron, a foot thick, and the iron grating which strained the light, I could not help being struck with the foolishness of that institution which treated me as if I were mere flesh and blood and bones, to be locked up. I wondered that it should have concluded at length that this was the best use it could put me to, and had never thought to avail itself of my services in some way. I saw that, if there was a wall of stone between me and my townsmen, there was a still more difficult one to climb or break through before they could get to be as free as I was. I did not for a moment feel confined, and the walls seemed a great waste of stone and mortar. I felt as if I alone of all my townsmen had paid my tax. They plainly did not know how to treat me, but behaved like persons who are underbred. In every threat and in every compliment there was a blunder; for they thought that my chief desire was to stand the other side of that stone wall. I could not but smile to see how industriously they locked the door on my meditations, which fol-

25

lowed them out again without let or hindrance, and *they* were really all that was dangerous. As they could not reach me, they had resolved to punish my body; just as boys, if they cannot come at some person against whom they have a spite, will abuse his dog. I saw that the State was half-witted, that it was timid as a lone woman with her silver spoons, and that it did not know its friends from its foes, and I lost all my remaining respect for it, and pitied it.

Thus the State never intentionally confronts a man's sense, intellectual or moral, but only his body, his senses. It is not armed with superior wit or honesty, but with superior physical strength. I was not born to be forced. I will breathe after my own fashion. Let us see who is the strongest. What force has a multitude? They only can force me who obey a higher law than I. They force me to become like themselves. I do not hear of *men* being *forced* to live this way or that by masses of men. What sort of life were that to live? When I meet a government which says to me, "Your money or your life," why should I be in haste to give it my money? It may be in a great strait, and not know what to do: I cannot help that. It must help itself; do as I do. It is not worth the while to snivel about it. I am not responsible for the successful working of the machinery of society. I am not the son of the engineer. I perceive that, when an acorn and a chestnut fall side by side, the one does not remain inert to make way for the other, but both obey their own laws, and spring and grow and flourish as best they can, till one, perchance, overshadows and destroys the other. If a plant cannot live according to its nature, it dies; and so a man.

The night in prison was novel and interesting enough. The prisoners in their shirt-sleeves were enjoying a chat and the evening air in the doorway, when I entered. But the jailer said, "Come, boys, it is time to lock up;" and so they dispersed, and I heard the sound of their steps returning into the hollow apartments. My room-mate was introduced to me by the jailer as "a first-rate fellow and a clever man." When the door was locked, he showed me where to hang my hat, and how he managed matters there. The rooms were whitewashed once a month; and this one, at least, was the whitest, most simply furnished, and probably the neatest apartment in the town. He naturally wanted to know where I came from, and what brought me there; and, when I had told him, I asked him in my turn how he came there, presuming him to be an honest man, of course; and, as the world goes, I believe he was. "Why," said he, "they accuse me of burning a barn; but I never did it." As near as I could discover, he had probably gone to bed in a barn when drunk, and smoked his pipe there; and so a barn was burnt. He had the reputation of being a clever man, had been there some three months waiting for his trail to come on, and would have to wait as much longer, but he was quite domesticated and contented, since he got his board for nothing, and thought that he was well treated.

He occupied one window, and I the other; and I saw that if one stayed there long, his principal business would be to look out the window. I had soon read all the tracts that were left there, and examined where former prisoners had broken out, and where a grate had been sawed off, and heard the history of the various occupants of that room; for I found that even here there was a history and a gossip which never circulated beyond the walls of the jail. Probably this is the only house in the town where verses are composed, which are afterward printed in a circular form, but not published. I was shown quite a long list of verses which were composed by some young men who had been detected in an attempt to escape, who avenged themselves by signing them.

I pumped my fellow-prisoner as dry as I could, for fear I should never   30
see him again; but at length he showed me which was my bed, and left me to blow out the lamp.

It was like traveling into a far country, such as I had never expected to behold, to lie there for one night. It seemed to me that I never had heard the town-clock strike before, nor the evening sounds of the village; for we slept with the windows open, which were inside the grating. It was to see my native village in the light of the Middle Ages, and our Concord was turned into a Rhine stream, and visions of knights and castles passed before me. They were the voices of old burghers that I heard in the streets. I was an involuntary spectator and auditor of whatever was done and said in the kitchen of the adjacent village-inn, — a wholly new and rare experience to me. It was a closer view of my native town. I was fairly inside of it. I never had seen its institutions before. This is one of its peculiar institutions; for it is a shire town. I began to comprehend what its inhabitants were about.

In the morning, our breakfasts were put through the hole in the door, in small oblong-square tin pans, made to fit, and holding a pint of chocolate, with brown bread, and an iron spoon. When they called for the vessels again, I was green enough to return what bread I had left; but my comrade seized it, and said that I should lay that up for lunch or dinner. Soon after he was let out to work at haying in a neighboring field, whither he went every day, and would not be back till noon; so he bade me good-day, saying that he doubted if he should see me again.

When I came out of prison, — for some one interfered, and paid that tax, — I did not perceive that great changes had taken place on the common, such as he observed who went in a youth and emerged a tottering and gray-headed man; and yet a change had to my eyes come over the scene, — the town, and State, and country, — greater than any that mere time could effect. I saw yet more distinctly the State in which I lived. I saw to what extent the people among whom I lived could be trusted as good neighbors and friends; that their friendship was for summer weather only; that they did not greatly propose to do right; that they were a distinct race from me by their prejudices and superstitions, as the Chinamen and Malays are; that in their sacrifices to humanity they ran no risks, not even to their property; that after all they were not so noble but they treated the thief as he had treated them, and hoped, by a certain outward observance and a few prayers, and by walking in a particular straight though useless path from time to time, to save their souls. This may be to judge my neighbors harshly; for I believe that many of them are not aware that they have such an institution as the jail in their village.

It was formerly the custom in our village, when a poor debtor came out of jail, for his acquaintances to salute him, looking through their fingers, which were crossed to represent the grating of a jail window, "How do ye do?" My neighbors did not thus salute me, but first looked at me, and then at one another, as if I had returned from a long journey. I was put into jail as I was going to the shoemaker's to get a shoe which was mended. When I was let out the next morning, I proceeded to finish my errand, and, having put on my mended shoe, joined a huckleberry party, who were impatient to put themselves under my conduct; and in half an hour, — for the horse was soon tackled, — was in the midst of a huckleberry field, on one of our highest hills, two miles off, and then the State was nowhere to be seen.

This is the whole history of "My Prisons."   35

I have never declined paying the highway tax, because I am as desirous of being a good neighbor as I am of being a bad subject; and as for supporting schools, I am doing my part to educate my fellow-countrymen now. It is for no particular item in the tax-bill that I refuse to pay it. I simply wish to refuse allegiance to the State, to withdraw and stand aloof from it effectually. I do not care to trace the course of my dollar, if I could, till it buys a man or a musket to shoot one with, — the dollar is innocent, — but I am concerned to trace the effects of my allegiance. In fact, I quietly declare war with the State, after my fashion, though I will still make what use and get what advantage of her I can, as is usual in such cases.

If others pay the tax which is demanded of me, from a sympathy with the State, they do but what they have already done in their own case, or rather they abet injustice to a greater extent than the State requires. If they pay the tax from a mistaken interest in the individual taxed, to save his property, or prevent his going to jail, it is because they have not considered wisely how far they let their private feelings interfere with the public good.

This, then, is my position at present. But one cannot be too much on his guard in such a case, lest his action be biased by obstinacy or an undue regard for the opinions of men. Let him see that he does only what belongs to himself and to the hour.

I think sometimes, Why, this people mean well, they are only ignorant; they would do better if they knew how: why give your neighbors this pain to treat you as they are not inclined to? But I think again, This is no reason why I should do as they do, or permit others to suffer much greater pain of a different kind. Again, I sometimes say to myself, When many millions of men, without heat, without ill will, without personal feeling of any kind, demand of you a few shillings only, without the possibility, such is their constitution, of retracting or altering their present demand, and without the possibility, on your side, of appeal to any other millions, why expose yourself to this overwhelming brute force? You do not resist cold and hunger, the winds and the waves, thus obstinately; you quietly submit to a thousand similar necessities. You do not put your head into the fire. But just in proportion as I regard this as not wholly a brute force, but partly a human force, and consider that I have relations to those millions as to so many millions of men, and not of mere brute or inanimate things, I see that appeal is possible, first and instantaneously, from them to the Maker of them, and, secondly, from them to them-selves. But if I put my head deliberately into the fire, there is no appeal to fire or to the Maker of fire, and I have only myself to blame. If I could convince myself that I have any right to be satisfied with men as they are, and to treat them accordingly, and not accordingly, in some respects, to my requisitions and expectations of what they and I ought to be, then, like a good Mussulman and fatalist, I should endeavor to be satisfied with things as they are, and say it is the will of God. And, above all, there is this difference between resisting this and a purely brute or natural force that I can resist this with some effect; but I cannot expect, like Orpheus,[6] to change the nature of the rocks and trees and beasts.

I do not wish to quarrel with any man or nation. I do not wish to   40
split hairs, to make fine distinctions, or set myself up as better than my neighbors. I seek rather, I may say, even an excuse for conforming to the laws of the land. I am but too ready to conform to them. Indeed, I have reason to suspect myself on this head; and each year, as the tax-gatherer comes round, I find myself disposed to review the acts and position of the general and State governments, and the spirit of the people, to discover a pretext for conformity.

> "We must affect our county as our parents,
> And if at any time we alienate
> Our love or industry from doing it honor,
> We must respect effects and teach the soul
> Matter of conscience and religion,
> And not desire of rule or benefit."[7]

I believe that the State will soon be able to take all my work of this sort out of my hands, and then I shall be no better a patriot than my fellow-countrymen. Seen from a lower point of view, the Constitution, with all its faults, is very good; the law and the courts are very respectable; even this State and this American government are, in many respects, very ad-

---

[6]*Orpheus:* A legendary Greek poet and musician whose music had the power to move inanimate objects and tame wild animals. — EDS.
    [7]**"We must affect. . . .":** See *The Battle of Alcazar,* a play by George Peele (c. 1558–1598). — EDS.

mirable, and rare things, to be thankful for, such as a great many have described them; but seen from a point of view a little higher, they are what I have described them; seen from a higher still, and the highest, who shall say what they are, or that they are worth looking at or thinking of at all?

However, the government does not concern me much, and I shall bestow the fewest possible thoughts on it. It is not many moments that I live under a government, even in this world. If a man is thought-free, fancy-free, imagination-free, that which *is not* never for a long time appearing *to be* to him, unwise rulers or reformers cannot fatally interrupt him.

I know that most men think differently from myself; but those whose lives are by profession devoted to the study of these or kindred subjects content me as little as any. Statesmen and legislators, standing so completely within the institution, never distinctly and nakedly behold it. They speak of moving society, but have no resting-place without it. They may be men of a certain experience and discrimination, and have no doubt invented ingenious and even useful systems, for which we sincerely thank them; but all their wit and usefulness lie within certain not very wide limits. They are wont to forget that the world is not governed by policy and expediency. Webster[8] never goes behind government, and so cannot speak with authority about it. His words are wisdom to those legislators who contemplate no essential reform in the existing government; but for thinkers, and those who legislate for all time, he never once glances at the subject. I know of those whose serene and wise speculations on this theme would soon reveal the limits of his mind's range and hospitality. Yet, compared with the cheap professions of most reformers, and the still cheaper wisdom and eloquence of politicians in general, his are almost the only sensible and valuable words, and we thank Heaven for him. Comparatively, he is always strong, original, and, above all, practical. Still, his quality is not wisdom, but prudence. The lawyer's truth is not Truth, but consistency or a consistent expediency. Truth is always in harmony with herself, and is not concerned chiefly to reveal the justice that may consist with wrong-doing. He well deserves to be called, as he has been called, the Defender of the Constitution. There are really no blows to be given by him but defensive ones. He is not a leader, but a follower. His leaders are the men of '87. "I have never made an effort," he says, "and never propose to make an effort; I have never countenanced an effort, and never mean to countenance an effort, to disturb the arrangement as originally made, by which the various States came into the Union." Still thinking of the sanction which the Constitution gives to slavery, he says, "Because it was a part of the original compact, — let it stand." Notwithstanding his special acuteness and ability, he is unable to take a fact out of its merely political relations, and behold it as it lies

---

[8]*Daniel Webster:* Daniel Webster (1782–1852), a distinguished American lawyer, politician, and orator. — EDS.

absolutely to be disposed of by the intellect, — what, for instance, it behooves a man to do here in America to-day with regard to slavery, — but ventures, or is driven, to make some such desperate answer as the following, while professing to speak absolutely, and as a private man, — from which what new and singular code of social duties might be inferred? "The manner," says he, "in which the governments of those States where slavery exists are to regulate it is for their own consideration, under their responsibility to their constituents, to the general laws of propriety, humanity, and justice, and to God. Associations formed elsewhere, springing from a feeling of humanity, or any other cause, have nothing whatever to do with it. They have never received any encouragement from me, and they never will."

They who know of no purer sources of truth, who have traced up its stream no higher, stand, and wisely stand, by the Bible and the Constitution, and drink at it there with reverence and humility; but they who behold where it comes trickling into this lake or that pool, gird up their loins once more, and continue their pilgrimage toward its fountain-head.

No man with a genius for legislation has appeared in America. They are rare in the history of the world. There are orators, politicians, and eloquent men, by the thousand; but the speaker has not yet opened his mouth to speak who is capable of settling the much-vexed questions of the day. We love eloquence for its own sake, and not for any truth which it may utter, or any heroism it may inspire. Our legislators have not yet learned the comparative value of free-trade and of freedom, of union, and of rectitude, to a nation. They have no genius or talent for comparatively humble questions of taxation and finance, commerce and manufactures and agriculture. If we were left solely to the wordy wit of legislators in Congress for our guidance, uncorrected by the seasonable experience and the effectual complaints of the people, America would not long retain her rank among the nations. For eighteen hundred years, though perchance I have no right to say it, the New Testament has been written; yet where is the legislator who has wisdom and practical talent enough to avail himself of the light which it sheds on the science of legislation?

The authority of government, even such as I am willing to submit to, — 45 for I will cheerfully obey those who know and can do better than I, and in many things even those who neither know nor can do so well, — is still an impure one: to be strictly just, it must have the sanction and consent of the governed. It can have no pure right over my person and property but what I concede to it. The progress from an absolute to a limited monarchy, from a limited monarchy to a democracy, is a progress toward a true respect for the individual. Even the Chinese philosopher was wise enough to regard the individual as the basis of the empire. Is a democracy, such as we know it, the last improvement possible in government? Is it not possible to take a further step towards recognizing and organizing the rights of man? There will never be a really free and enlightened State until the State comes to recognize the individual as a higher and independent power, from which all its own power and authority are derived, and treats him accordingly. I please myself with imagining a State at last which can afford to be just to all men, and to treat the individual with respect as a neighbor; which even would not think it inconsistent with its own repose if a few were to live aloof from it, not meddling with it, nor embraced by it, who fulfilled all the duties of neighbors and fellow-men. A State which bore this kind of fruit, and suffered it to drop off as fast as it ripened, would prepare the way for a still more perfect and glorious State, which also I have imagined, but not yet anywhere seen.

The Reader's Presence

1. Thoreau originally delivered these remarks as a lecture entitled "The Relation of the Individual to the State," and first printed them under the title "Resistance to Civil Government." (The title "Civil Disobedience" first appeared in posthumous printings.) Compare and contrast these titles. Which do you think best expresses the overall purpose of his essay? Why? Where in the text does Thoreau most directly state his purpose? To whom are his remarks addressed? Point to specific words and phrases to verify your response.

2. Thoreau builds his argument on two assertions: "That government is best which governs not at all" and that "Government is at best but an expedient." Prepare a list of the examples he presents to clarify and support these assertions. Comment on the effectiveness of these examples. What does he establish as the moral arbiter of his actions? Summarize his argument against paying taxes. What does he mean when he says that an "honest man" must "withdraw from this co-partnership"? How would Thoreau respond to the allegation that his remarks are a recipe for anarchy? In this respect, pay special attention to the final few paragraphs. What argument does he mount there to resist such notions?

3. Thoreau's remarks have had a far-reaching impact on twentieth-century political thought and action, and especially on the principles and practices of such prominent voices in the struggle for freedom as Mahatma Gandhi and the Reverend Martin Luther King Jr. What is there about Thoreau's fierce individualism that has influenced so many later social and moral activists?

4. In addition to the substantive points he makes, what features can you identify as the hallmarks of Thoreau's individualistic prose style? What evidence might you point to in "Civil Disobedience" to illustrate Thoreau's definition of the art of writing (articulated in his journal entry for August 22, 1851): "Sentences which suggest far more than they say, which have an atmosphere about them, which do not merely report an old, but make a new impression, sentences which suggest as many things and are as durable as a Roman aqueduct: to frame these, that is the *art* of writing."

82

Mark Twain

The Damned Human Race

Mark Twain, the pseudonym of Samuel Clemens (1835–1910), was a master satirist, journalist, novelist, orator, and steamboat pilot. He grew up in Hannibal, Missouri, a frontier setting which appears in different forms in several of his novels, most notably in his masterpiece Adventures of Huckleberry Finn *(1869). His satirical eye spared very few American political or social institutions including slavery, and for this reason, as well as because it violated conventional standards of taste,* Huckleberry Finn *created a minor scandal when it was published. Nonetheless, with such books as* The Innocents Abroad *(1869),* Roughing It *(1872),* Old Times on the Mississippi *(1875),* The Adventures of Tom Sawyer *(1876), and* The Prince and the Pauper *(1882), Twain secured himself a position as one of the most popular authors in American history. "The Damned Human Race" comes from* Letters from the Earth *(1938). Twain built his career upon his experiences in the western states and his travels in Europe and the Middle East, but he eventually settled in Hartford, Connecticut. His last years were spent as one of the most celebrated public speakers and social figures in the United States.*

Reflecting upon the experience of writing, Twain once wrote in his notebook, "The time to begin writing an article is when you have finished it to your satisfaction. By that time you begin to clearly and logically perceive what it is that you really want to say."

I have been studying the traits and dispositions of the "lower animals" (so-called), and contrasting them with the traits and dispositions of man. I find the result humiliating to me. For it obliges me to renounce my allegiance to the Darwinian[1] theory of the Ascent of Man from the Lower Animals; since it now seems plain to me that that theory ought to be vacated in favor of a new and truer one, this new and truer one to be named the *Descent* of Man from the Higher Animals.

In proceeding toward this unpleasant conclusion I have not guessed

---

[1]Charles Darwin (1809–1882) published *The Descent of Man* in 1871, a highly controversial book in which he argued that humankind had descended from "lower" forms of life. — EDS.

or speculated or conjectured, but have used what is commonly called the scientific method. That is to say, I have subjected every postulate that presented itself to the crucial test of actual experiment, and have adopted it or rejected it according to the result. Thus I verified and established each step of my course in its turn before advancing to the next. These experiments were made in the London Zoological Gardens, and covered many months of painstaking and fatiguing work.

Before particularizing any of the experiments, I wish to state one or two things which seem to more properly belong in this place than further along. This in the interest of clearness. The massed experiments established to my satisfaction certain generalizations, to wit:

1. That the human race is of one distinct species. It exhibits slight variations — in color, stature, mental caliber, and so on — due to climate, environment, and so forth; but it is a species by itself, and not to be confounded with any other.

2. That the quadrupeds are a distinct family, also. This family exhibits variations — in color, size, food preferences and so on; but it is a family by itself.

3. That the other families — the birds, the fishes, the insects, the reptiles, etc. — are more or less distinct, also. They are in the procession. They are links in the chain which stretches down from the higher animals to man at the bottom.

Some of my experiments were quite curious. In the course of my reading I had come across a case where, many years ago, some hunters on our Great Plains organized a buffalo hunt for the entertainment of an English earl — that, and to provide some fresh meat for his larder. They had charming sport. They killed seventy-two of those great animals; and ate part of one of them and left the seventy-one to rot. In order to determine the difference between an anaconda and an earl — if any — I caused seven young calves to be turned into the anaconda's cage. The grateful reptile immediately crushed one of them and swallowed it, then lay back satisfied. It showed no further interest in the calves, and no disposition to harm them. I tried this experiment with other anacondas; always with the same result. The fact stood proven that the difference between an earl and an anaconda is that the earl is cruel and the anaconda isn't; and that the earl wantonly destroys what he has no use for, but the anaconda doesn't. This seemed to suggest that the anaconda was not descended from the earl. It also seemed to suggest that the earl was descended from the anaconda, and had lost a good deal in the transition.

I was aware that many men who have accumulated more millions of money than they can ever use have shown a rabid hunger for more, and have not scrupled to cheat the ignorant and the helpless out of their poor servings in order to partially appease that appetite. I furnished a hundred different kinds of wild and tame animals the opportunity to accumulate vast stores of food, but none of them would do it. The squirrels and bees and certain birds made accumulations, but stopped when they had gathered a winter's supply, and could not be persuaded to add to it either honestly or by chicane. In order to bolster up a tottering reputation the ant pretended to store up supplies, but I was not deceived. I know the ant. These experiments convinced me that there is this difference between man and the higher animals: He is avaricious and miserly, they are not.

In the course of my experiments I convinced myself that among the animals man is the only one that harbors insults and injuries, broods over them, waits till a chance offers, then takes revenge. The passion of revenge is unknown to the higher animals.

Roosters keep harems, but it is by consent of their concubines; therefore no wrong is done. Men keep harems, but it is by brute force, privileged by atrocious laws which the other sex were allowed no hand in making. In this matter man occupies a far lower place than the rooster. 10

Cats are loose in their morals, but not consciously so. Man, in his descent from the cat, has brought the cat's looseness with him but has left the unconsciousness behind — the saving grace which excuses the cat. The cat is innocent, man is not.

Indecency, vulgarity, obscenity — these are strictly confined to man; he invented them. Among the higher animals there is no trace of them. They hide nothing; they are not ashamed. Man, with his soiled mind, covers himself. He will not even enter a drawing room with his breast and back naked, so alive are he and his mates to indecent suggestion. Man is "The Animal that Laughs." But so does the monkey, as Mr. Darwin pointed out; and so does the Australian bird that is called the laughing jackass. No — Man is the Animal that Blushes. He is the only one that does it — or has occasion to.

At the head of this article[2] we see how "three monks were burnt to death" a few days ago, and a prior "put to death with atrocious cruelty." Do we inquire into the details? No; or we should find out that the prior was subjected to unprintable mutilations. Man — when he is a North American Indian — gouges out his prisoner's eyes; when he is King John, with a nephew to render untroublesome, he uses a red-hot iron; when he is a religious zealot dealing with heretics in the Middle Ages, he skins his captive alive and scatters salt on his back; in the first Richard's time he shuts up a multitude of Jew families in a tower and sets fire to it; in Columbus's time he captures a family of Spanish Jews and — but *that* is not printable; in our day in England a man is fined ten shillings for beating his mother nearly to death with a chair, and another man is fined forty shillings for having four pheasant eggs in his possession without being able to satisfactorily explain how he got them. Of all the animals, man is the only one that is cruel. He is the only one that inflicts pain for the pleasure of doing it. It is a trait that is not known to the higher ani-

[2]In his nonfiction Twain often introduced newsclippings as evidence of human atrocity. In this instance the article has been lost, but Twain is most likely referring to the religious persecutions that followed the 1897 Cretan revolt. — EDS.

mals. The cat plays with the frightened mouse; but she has this excuse, that she does not know that the mouse is suffering. The cat is moderate — unhumanly moderate: She only scares the mouse, she does not hurt it; she doesn't dig out its eyes, or tear off its skin, or drive splinters under its nails — manfashion; when she is done playing with it she makes a sudden meal of it and puts it out of its trouble. Man is the Cruel Animal. He is alone in that distinction.

The higher animals engage in individual fights, but never in organized masses. Man is the only animal that deals in that atrocity of atrocities, War. He is the only one that gathers his brethren about him and goes forth in cold blood and with calm pulse to exterminate his kind. He is the only animal that for sordid wages will march out, as the Hessians did in our Revolution,[3] and as the boyish Prince Napoleon did in the Zulu war,[4] and help to slaughter strangers of his own species who have done him no harm and with whom he has no quarrel.

Man is the only animal that robs his helpless fellow of his country —   15
takes possession of it and drives him out of it or destroys him. Man has done this in all the ages. There is not an acre of ground on the globe that is in possession of its rightful owner, or that has not been taken away from owner after owner, cycle after cycle, by force and bloodshed.

Man is the only Slave. And he is the only animal who enslaves. He has always been a slave in one form or another, and has always held other slaves in bondage under him in one way or another. In our day he is always some man's slave for wages, and does that man's work; and this slave has other slaves under him for minor wages, and they do *his* work. The higher animals are the only ones who exclusively do their own work and provide their own living.

Man is the only Patriot. He sets himself apart in his own country, under his own flag, and sneers at the other nations, and keeps multitudinous uniformed assassins on hand at heavy expense to grab slices of other people's countries, and keep *them* from grabbing slices of *his*. And in the intervals between campaigns he washes the blood off his hands and works for "the universal brotherhood of man" — with his mouth.

Man is the Religious Animal. He is the only Religious Animal. He is the only animal that has the True Religion — several of them. He is the only animal that loves his neighbor as himself, and cuts his throat if his theology isn't straight. He has made a graveyard of the globe in trying his honest best to smooth his brother's path to happiness and heaven. He was at it in the time of the Caesars, he was at it in Mahomet's time, he was at it in the time of the Inquisition, he was at it in France a couple of

---

[3]*Revolution:* Approximately 17,000 mercenaries from Hesse, a part of Germany, fought for the British during the American Revolution. — EDS.
[4]*Zulu war:* Napolean III's son died while fighting for the British during the 1879 Zulu rebellion in what is now the Republic of South Africa. Great Britain annexed the Zulu territory shortly after, and that is the context for Twain's remarks in the next paragraph. — EDS.

centuries, he was at it in England in Mary's day,[5] he has been at it ever since he first saw the light, he is at it today in Crete — as per the telegrams quoted above — he will be at it somewhere else tomorrow. The higher animals have no religion. And we are told that they are going to be left out, in the Hereafter. I wonder why? It seems questionable taste.

Man is the Reasoning Animal. Such is the claim. I think it is open to dispute. Indeed, my experiments have proven to me that he is the Unreasoning Animal. Note his history, as sketched above. It seems plain to me that whatever he is he is *not* a reasoning animal. His record is the fantastic record of a maniac. I consider that the strongest count against his intelligence is the fact that with that record back of him he blandly sets himself up as the head animal of the lot: Whereas by his own standards he is the bottom one.

In truth, man is incurably foolish. Simple things which the other ani- 20 mals easily learn, he is incapable of learning. Among my experiments was this. In an hour I taught a cat and a dog to be friends. I put them in a cage. In another hour I taught them to be friends with a rabbit. In the course of two days I was able to add a fox, a goose, a squirrel and some doves. Finally a monkey. They lived together in peace; even affectionately.

Next, in another cage I confined an Irish Catholic from Tipperary, and as soon as he seemed tame I added a Scotch Presbyterian from Aberdeen. Next a Turk from Constantinople; a Greek Christian from Crete; an Armenian; a Methodist from the wilds of Arkansas; a Buddhist from China; a Brahman from Benares. Finally, a Salvation Army Colonel from Wapping. Then I stayed away two whole days. When I came back to note results, the cage of Higher Animals was all right, but in the other there was but a chaos of gory odds and ends of turbans and fezzes and plaids and bones and flesh — not a specimen left alive. These Reasoning Animals had disagreed on a theological detail and carried the matter to a Higher Court.

One is obliged to concede that in true loftiness of character, Man cannot claim to approach even the meanest of the Higher Animals. It is plain that he is constitutionally incapable of approaching that altitude; that he is constitutionally afflicted with a Defect which must make such approach forever impossible, for it is manifest that this defect is permanent in him, indestructible, ineradicable.

I find this Defect to be *the Moral Sense.* He is the only animal that has it. It is the secret of his degradation. It is the quality *which enables him to do wrong.* It has no other office. It is incapable of performing any other function. It could never have been intended to perform any other. Without it, man could do no wrong. He would rise at once to the level of the Higher Animals.

---

[5]*Mary's day:* In the time of Mary I, who reigned as Queen of England between 1553 and 1558; her vigorous persecution of Protestants earned her the nickname "Bloody Mary." — EDS.

Since the Moral Sense has but the one office, the one capacity — to enable man to do wrong — it is plainly without value to him. It is as valueless to him as is disease. In fact, it manifestly *is* a disease. *Rabies* is bad, but it is not so bad as this disease. Rabies enables a man to do a thing which he could not do when in a healthy state: kill his neighbor with a poisonous bite. No one is the better man for having rabies. The Moral Sense enables a man to do wrong. It enables him to do wrong in a thousand ways. Rabies is an innocent disease, compared to the Moral Sense. No one, then, can be the better man for having the Moral Sense. What, now, do we find the Primal Curse to have been? Plainly what it was in the beginning: the infliction upon man of the Moral Sense; the ability to distinguish good from evil; and with it, necessarily, the ability to *do* evil; for there can be no evil act without the presence of consciousness of it in the doer of it.

And so I find that we have descended and degenerated, from some far   25
ancestor — some microscopic atom wandering at its pleasure between the mighty horizons of a drop of water perchance — insect by insect, animal by animal, reptile by reptile, down the long highway of smirchless innocence, till we have reached the bottom stage of development — namable as the Human Being. Below us — nothing. Nothing but the Frenchman.

There is only one possible stage below the Moral Sense; that is the Immoral Sense. The Frenchman has it. Man is but little lower than the angels. This definitely locates him. He is between the angels and the French.

Man seems to be a rickety poor sort of a thing, any way you take him; a kind of British Museum of infirmities and inferiorities. He is always undergoing repairs. A machine that was as unreliable as he is would have no market. On top of his specialty — the Moral Sense — are piled a multitude of minor infirmities; such a multitude, indeed, that one may broadly call them countless. The higher animals get their teeth without pain or inconvenience. Man gets his through months and months of cruel torture; and at a time of life when he is but ill able to bear it. As soon as he has got them they must all be pulled out again, for they were of no value in the first place, not worth the loss of a night's rest. The second set will answer for a while, by being reinforced occasionally with rubber or plugged up with gold; but he will never get a set which can really be depended on till a dentist makes him one. This set will be called "false" teeth — as if he had ever worn any other kind.

In a wild state — a natural state — the Higher Animals have a few diseases; diseases of little consequence; the main one is old age. But man starts in as a child and lives on diseases till the end, as a regular diet. He has mumps, measles, whooping cough, croup, tonsillitis, diphtheria, scarlet fever, almost as a matter of course. Afterward, as he goes along, his life continues to be threatened at every turn: by colds, coughs, asthma, bronchitis, itch, cholera, cancer, consumption, yellow fever, bilious fever, typhus fevers, hay fever; ague, chilblains, piles, inflammation of the entrails, indigestion, toothache, earache, deafness, dumbness, blindness, influenza, chicken pox, cowpox, smallpox, liver complaint, constipation, bloody flux, warts, pimples, boils, carbuncles, abscesses, bunions, corns, tumors, fistulas, pneumonia, softening of the brain, melancholia and fifteen other kinds of insanity; dysentery, jaundice, diseases of the heart, the bones, the skin, the scalp, the spleen, the kidneys, the nerves, the brain, the blood; scrofula, paralysis, leprosy, neuralgia, palsy, fits, headache, thirteen kinds of rheumatism, forty-six of gout, and a formidable supply of gross and unprintable disorders of one sort and another. Also — but why continue the list? The mere names of the agents appointed to keep this shackly machine out of repair would hide him from sight if printed on his body in the smallest type known to the founder's art. He is but a basket of pestilent corruption provided for the support and entertainment of swarming armies of bacilli — armies commissioned to rot him and destroy him, and each army equipped with a special detail of the work. The process of waylaying him, persecuting him, rotting him, killing him, begins with his first breath, and there is no mercy, no pity, no truce till he draws his last one.

Look at the workmanship of him, in certain of its particulars. What are his tonsils for? They perform no useful function; they have no value. They have no business there. They are but a trap. They have but the one office, the one industry: to provide tonsillitis and quinsy and such things for the possessor of them. And what is the vermiform appendix for? It has no value; it cannot perform any useful service. It is but an ambuscaded enemy whose sole interest in life is to lie in wait for stray grape-seeds and employ them to breed strangulated hernia. And what are the male's mammals for? For business, they are out of the question; as an ornament, they are a mistake. What is his beard for? It performs no useful function; it is a nuisance and a discomfort; all nations hate it; all nations persecute it with a razor. And because it is a nuisance and a discomfort, Nature never allows the supply of it to fall short, in any man's case, between puberty and the grave. You never see a man bald-headed on his chin. But his hair! It is a graceful ornament, it is a comfort, it is the best of all protections against certain perilous ailments, man prizes it above emeralds and rubies. And because of these things Nature puts it on, half the time, so that it won't stay. Man's sight, smell, hearing, sense of locality — how inferior they are. The condor sees a corpse at five miles; man has no telescope that can do it. The bloodhound follows a scent that is two days old. The robin hears the earthworm burrowing his course under the ground. The cat, deported in a closed basket, finds its way home again through twenty miles of country which it has never seen.

Certain functions lodged in the other sex perform in a lamentably inferior way as compared with the performance of the same functions in the Higher Animals. In the human being, menstruation, gestation and parturition are terms which stand for horrors. In the Higher Animals these things are hardly even inconveniences.

For style, look at the Bengal tiger — that ideal of grace, beauty, physical perfection, majesty. And then look at Man — that poor thing. He is the Animal of the Wig, the Trepanned Skull, the Ear Trumpet, the Glass Eye, the Pasteboard Nose, the Porcelain Teeth, the Silver Windpipe, the Wooden Leg — a creature that is mended and patched all over, from top to bottom. If he can't get renewals of his bric-a-brac in the next world, what will he look like?

He has just one stupendous superiority. In his intellect he is supreme. The Higher Animals cannot touch him there. It is curious, it is noteworthy, that no heaven has ever been offered him wherein his one sole superiority was provided with a chance to enjoy itself. Even when he himself has imagined a heaven, he has never made provision in it for intellectual joys. It is a striking omission. It seems a tacit confession that heavens are provided for the Higher Animals alone. This is matter for thought; and for serious thought. And it is full of a grim suggestion: that we are not as important, perhaps, as we had all along supposed we were.

The Reader's Presence

1. What conventional attitudes does Twain satirize in this essay? How does he reverse our sense of higher and lower? In what ways is the essay a response to Darwin's theory of evolution? What does Twain expect his readers to know of that theory?

2. How would you specifically identify the target of Twain's satire? What idea or ideas is he making fun of? What groups of people is he making fun of? Who might be shocked by his reasoning? Do you find any parts of the essay intellectually or religiously shocking? Explain why or why not.

3. Why do you think Twain puts his essay into the form of a scientific report of experiments? What effect does that have upon the reader? How "scientific" do you think his experiments are? Do you think Twain is also making fun of scientific reasoning? What evidence would you bring in from the essay to say he is or isn't?

83

John Edgar Wideman
The Night I Was Nobody

John Edgar Wideman was born in 1941 in Washington, D.C., and grew up in Homewood, a Pittsburgh ghetto. Much of his fiction is set in Homewood or neighborhoods like it, and it explores issues facing the black urban poor in America. He has published over a dozen books, including Brothers and Keepers *(1984), a memoir that focuses on his brother Robby; the novel* Philadelphia Fire *(1990); and* The Stories of John Edgar Wideman *(1992). Wideman was a Rhodes scholar at Oxford University (1963) and a Kent fellow at the University of Iowa Writing Workshop (1966). He is also an athlete and a member of the Philadelphia Big Five Basketball Hall of Fame. Recently he published* Fatheralong: A Meditation on Fathers and Sons, Race and Society *(1995). "The Night I Was Nobody" appeared in* Speak My Name: Black Men on Masculinity and the American Dream *(1995).*

When Wideman lived in Cheyenne and taught at the University of Wyoming (1975–1986), an interviewer inquired whether he felt a distance between his life and his fiction. "My particular imagination has always worked well in a kind of exile," *he responded. "It fits the insider-outsider view I've always had. It helps to write away from the center of action." Currently he is affiliated with the University of Massachusetts at Amherst and lectures at colleges all over the United States.*

On July 4th, the fireworks day, the day for picnics and patriotic speeches, I was in Clovis, New Mexico, to watch my daughter, Jamila, and her team, the Central Massachusetts Cougars, compete in the Junior Olympics Basketball national tourney. During our ten-day visit to Clovis the weather had been bizarre. Hailstones as large as golf balls. Torrents of rain flooding streets hubcap deep. Running through the pelting rain from their van to a gym, Jamila and several teammates cramming through a doorway had looked back just in time to see a funnel cloud touch down a few blocks away. Continuous sheet lightning had shattered the horizon, crackling for hours night and day. Spectacular, off-the-charts weather flexing its muscles, reminding people what little control they had over their lives.

Hail rat-tat-tatting against our windshield our first day in town wasn't exactly a warm welcome, but things got better fast. Clovis people

606

were glad to see us and the mini-spike we triggered in the local economy. Hospitable, generous, our hosts lavished upon us the same hands-on affection and attention to detail that had transformed an unpromising place in the middle of nowhere into a very livable community.

On top of all that, the Cougars were kicking butt, so the night of July 3rd I wanted to celebrate with a frozen margarita. I couldn't pry anybody else away from "Bubba's," the movable feast of beer, chips, and chatter the adults traveling with the Cougars improvised nightly in the King's Inn Motel parking lot, so I drove off alone to find one perfect margarita.

Inside the door of Kelley's Bar and Lounge I was flagged by a guy collecting a cover charge and told I couldn't enter wearing my Malcolm X hat. I asked why; the guy hesitated, conferred with a moment with his partner, then declared that Malcolm X hats were against the dress code. For a split second I thought it might be that *no* caps were allowed in Kelley's. But the door crew and two or three others hanging around the entranceway all wore the billed caps ubiquitous in New Mexico, duplicates of mine, except theirs sported the logos of feed stores and truck stops instead of a silver X.

What careened through my mind in the next couple of minutes is essentially unsayable but included scenes from my own half-century of life as a black man, clips from five hundred years of black/white meetings on slave ships, auction blocks, plantations, basketball courts, in the Supreme Court's marble halls, in beds, back alleys and back rooms, kisses and lynch ropes and contracts for millions of dollars so a black face will grace a cereal box. To tease away my anger I tried joking with folks in other places. Hey, Spike Lee. That hat you gave me on the set of the Malcolm movie in Cairo ain't legal in Clovis.

But nothing about these white guys barring my way was really funny. Part of me wanted to get down and dirty. Curse the suckers. Were they prepared to do battle to keep me and my cap out? Another voice said, Be cool. Don't sully your hands. Walk away and call the cops or a lawyer. Forget these chumps. Sue the owner. Or should I win hearts and minds? Look, fellas, I understand why the X on my cap might offend or scare you. You probably don't know much about Malcolm. The incredible metamorphoses of his thinking, his soul. By the time he was assassinated he wasn't a racist, didn't advocate violence. He was trying to make sense of America's impossible history, free himself, free us from the crippling legacy of race hate and oppression.

While all the above occupied my mind, my body, on its own, had assumed a gunfighter's vigilance, hands ready at sides, head cocked, weight poised, eyes tight and hard on the doorkeeper yet alert to anything stirring on the periphery. Many other eyes, all in white faces, were checking out the entranceway, recognizing the ingredients of a racial incident. Hadn't they witnessed Los Angeles going berserk on their TV screens just a couple months ago? That truck driver beaten nearly to death in the street, those packs of black hoodlums burning and looting? Invisible lines

5

were being drawn in the air, in the sand, invisible chips bristled on shoulders.

The weather again. Our American racial weather, turbulent, unchanging in its changeability, its power to rock us and stun us and smack us from our routines and tear us apart as if none of our cities, our pieties, our promises, our dreams, ever stood a chance of holding on. The racial weather. Outside us, then suddenly, unforgettably, unforgivingly inside, reminding us of what we've only pretended to have forgotten. Our limits, our flaws. The lies and compromises we practice to avoid dealing honestly with the contradictions of race. How dependent we are on luck to survive — *when* we survive — the racial weather.

One minute you're a person, the next moment somebody starts treating you as if you're not. Often it happens just that way, just that suddenly. Particularly if you are a black man in America. Race and racism are a force larger than individuals, more powerful than law or education or government or the church, a force able to wipe these institutions away in the charged moments, minuscule or mountainous, when black and white come face to face. In Watts in 1965, or a few less-than-glorious minutes in Clovis, New Mexico, on the eve of the day that commemorates our country's freedom, our inalienable right as a nation, as citizens, to life, liberty, equality, the pursuit of happiness, those precepts and principles that still look good on paper but are often as worthless as a sheet of newspaper to protect you in a storm if you're a black man at the wrong time in the wrong place.

None of this is news, is it? Not July 3rd in Clovis, when a tiny misfire   10 occurred, or yesterday in your town or tomorrow in mine? But haven't we made progress? Aren't things much better than they used to be? Hasn't enough been done?

We ask the wrong questions when we look around and see a handful of fabulously wealthy black people, a few others entering the middle classes. Far more striking than the positive changes are the abiding patterns and assumptions that have not changed. Not all black people are mired in social pathology, but the bottom rung of the ladder of opportunity (and the space *beneath* the bottom rung) is still defined by the color of the people trapped there — and many *are* still trapped there, no doubt about it, because their status was inherited, determined generation after generation by blood, by color. Once, all black people were legally excluded from full participation in the mainstream. Then fewer. Now only some. But the mechanisms of disenfranchisement that originally separated African Americans from other Americans persist, if not legally, then in the apartheid mind-set, convictions and practices of the majority. The seeds sleep but don't die. Ten who suffer from exclusion today can become ten thousand tomorrow. Racial weather can change that quickly.

How would the bouncer have responded if I'd calmly declared, "This is a free country, I can wear any hat I choose"? Would he thank me for standing up for our shared birthright? Or would he have to admit, if pushed, that American rights belong only to *some* Americans, white Americans?

We didn't get that far in our conversation. We usually don't. The girls' faces pulled me from the edge — girls of all colors, sizes, shapes, gritty kids bonding through hard clean competition. Weren't these guys who didn't like my X cap kids too? Who did they think I was? What did they think they were protecting? I backed out, backed down, climbed in my car and drove away from Kelley's. After all, I didn't want Kelley's. I wanted a frozen margarita and a mellow celebration. So I bought plenty of ice and the ingredients for a margarita and rejoined the festivities at Bubba's. Everybody volunteered to go back with me to Kelley's, but I didn't want to spoil the victory party, taint our daughters' accomplishments, erase the high marks Clovis had earned hosting us.

But I haven't forgotten what happened in Kelley's. I write about it now because this is my country, the country where my sons and daughter are growing up, and your daughters and sons, and the crisis, the affliction, the same ole, same ole waste of life continues across the land, the nightmarish weather of racism, starbursts of misery in the dark.

The statistics of inequality don't demonstrate a "black crisis" — that perspective confuses cause and victim, solutions and responsibility. When the rain falls, it falls on us all. The bad news about black men — that they die sooner and more violently than white men, are more ravaged by unemployment and lack of opportunity, are more exposed to drugs, disease, broken families, and police brutality, more likely to go to jail than college, more cheated by the inertia and callousness of a government that represents and protects the most needy the least — this is not a "black problem," but a *national* shame affecting us all. Wrenching ourselves free from the long nightmare of racism will require collective determination, countless individual acts of will, gutsy, informed, unselfish. To imagine the terrible cost of not healing ourselves, we must first imagine how good it would feel to be healed.

15

The Reader's Presence

1. The incident Wideman recounts in this essay takes place on the eve of July Fourth, "the fireworks day, the day for picnics and patriotic speeches" (paragraph 1). Look closely at the modifiers he chooses to describe the Fourth of July. Given the events that took place in Clovis that night, comment on the significance of each phrase. How else might he have described this holiday, and why might he have intentionally discarded those descriptions? Identify — and comment on the effectiveness of — other moments in

the essay when Wideman refers to the Fourth of July in related themes.

2. An extended metaphor to weather runs through this essay. Trace the analogy through the comparisons and contrasts Wideman makes or implies. In what specific ways, for instance, are the townsfolk described in paragraph 2 like or unlike the weather? How does this change as the essay progresses? How does racism resemble and differ from the weather? Given this guiding metaphor, does Wideman leave his reader with much hope for an end to racism?

3. In paragraph 6, Wideman mentions several courses of action he might have taken in reaction to the bouncer at Kelley's bar. What would be the pros and cons of each possible reaction? How would each one measure up to the "individual acts of will, gutsy, informed, unselfish" that he mentions in the last paragraph? What other courses of action might he have considered? What factors made him choose the course he took? In paragraph 12 he recounts the beginning of a hypothetical dialogue with the bouncer, and in paragraph 13 he writes, "We didn't get that far in our conversation. We usually don't." In your judgment, would it be better or worse if we did engage in these dialogues? Might Wideman's essay itself be seen as an attempt to open such a dialogue? To what extent is the essay "as worthless as a sheet of newspaper to protect you in a storm" (paragraph 9)? If "law or education or government or the church" (paragraph 9) can't provide an end to racism, what can?

84

Terry Tempest Williams

The Clan of One-Breasted Women

The environmentalist and writer Terry Tempest Williams (b. 1953) lives in Salt Lake City. She is naturalist-in-residence at the Utah Museum of Natural History and is also active in the movement to expand federally protected wilderness areas in Utah. In Refuge: An Unnatural History of Family and Place (1991), *she documents the epidemic of cancer caused by nuclear weapons tested in Utah during the 1950s and meditates upon the meaning of this tragedy for her family. "The Clan of One-Breasted Women" appears in* Refuge. *Her first book,* Pieces of a White Shell: A Journey to Navajoland (1984), *received a Southwest Book Award. She is also the author of* Coyote's Canyon (1989) *and more recently of* Desert Quartet *(1995) and* An Unspoken Hunger: Stories from the Field *(1994).*

Reflecting upon her motivation for writing about her personal experience with cancer, Williams notes, "Perhaps I am telling this story in an attempt to heal myself, to confront what I do not know, to create a path for myself with the idea that 'memory is the only way home.'"

I belong to a Clan of One-Breasted Women. My mother, my grandmothers, and six aunts have all had mastectomies. Seven are dead. The two who survive have just completed rounds of chemotherapy and radiation.

I've had my own problems: two biopsies for breast cancer and a small tumor between my ribs diagnosed as a "borderline malignancy."

This is my family history.

Most statistics tell us that breast cancer is genetic, hereditary, with rising percentages attached to fatty diets, childlessness, or becoming pregnant after thirty. What they don't say is that living in Utah may be the greatest hazard of all.

We are a Mormon family with roots in Utah since 1847. The "word   5
of wisdom" in my family aligned us with good foods — no coffee, no tea, tobacco, or alcohol. For the most part, our women were finished having their babies by the time they were thirty. And only one faced breast cancer prior to 1960. Traditionally, as a group of people, Mormons have a low rate of cancer.

Is our family a cultural anomaly? The truth is, we didn't think about it. Those who did, usually the men, simply said, "bad genes." The women's attitude was stoic. Cancer was part of life. On February 16, 1971, the eve of my mother's surgery, I accidentally picked up the telephone and overheard her ask my grandmother what she could expect.

"Diane, it is one of the most spiritual experiences you will ever encounter."

I quietly put down the receiver.

Two days later, my father took my brothers and me to the hospital to visit her. She met us in the lobby in a wheelchair. No bandages were visible. I'll never forget her radiance, the way she held herself in a purple velvet robe, and how she gathered us around her.

"Children, I am fine. I want you to know I felt the arms of God   10
around me."

We believed her. My father cried. Our mother, his wife, was thirty-eight years old.

A little over a year after Mother's death, Dad and I were having dinner together. He had just returned from St. George, where the Tempest Company was completing the gas lines that would service southern Utah. He spoke of his love for the country, the sandstoned landscape, bareboned and beautiful. He had just finished hiking the Kolob trail in Zion National Park. We got caught up in reminiscing, recalling with fondness our walk up Angel's Landing on his fiftieth birthday and the years our family had vacationed there.

Over dessert, I shared a recurring dream of mine. I told my father that for years, as long as I could remember, I saw this flash of light in the night in the desert — that this image had so permeated my being that I could not venture south without seeing it again, on the horizon, illuminating buttes and mesas.

"You did see it," he said.

"Saw what?   15

"The bomb. The cloud. We were driving home from Riverside, California. You were sitting on Diane's lap. She was pregnant. In fact, I remember the day, September 7, 1957. We had just gotten out of the Service. We were driving north, past Las Vegas. It was an hour or so before dawn, when this explosion went off. We not only heard it, but felt it. I thought the oil tanker in front of us had blown up. We pulled over and suddenly, rising from the desert floor, we saw it, clearly, this golden-stemmed cloud, the mushroom. The sky seemed to vibrate with an eerie pink glow. Within a few minutes, a light ash was raining on the car."

I stared at my father.

"I thought you knew that," he said. "It was a common occurrence in the fifties."

It was at this moment that I realized the deceit I had been living under. Children growing up in the American Southwest, drinking contaminated milk from contaminated cows, even from the contaminated breasts of their mothers, my mother — members, years later, of the Clan of One-Breasted Women.

It is a well-known story in the Desert West, "The Day We Bombed   20
Utah," or more accurately, the years we bombed Utah: above ground atomic testing in Nevada took place from January 27, 1951 through July 11, 1962. Not only were the winds blowing north covering "low-use segments of the population" with fallout and leaving sheep dead in their tracks, but the climate was right. The United States of the 1950s was red, white, and blue. The Korean War was raging. McCarthyism[1] was rampant. Ike[2] was it, and the cold war was hot. If you were against nuclear testing, you were for a communist regime.

Much has been written about this "American nuclear tragedy." Public health was secondary to national security. The Atomic Energy Commissioner, Thomas Murray, said, "Gentlemen, we must not let anything interfere with this series of tests, nothing."

Again and again, the American public was told by its government, in spite of burns, blisters, and nausea, "It has been found that the tests may be conducted with adequate assurance of safety under conditions prevail-

---

[1]*McCarthyism:* The practice of publicizing accusations of political disloyalty or subversion without sufficient regard to evidence. Associated with Senator Joseph McCarthy (1908–1957). — EDS.

[2]*Ike:* President Dwight D. Eisenhower (1890–1969) was known as "Ike." — EDS.

ing at the bombing reservations." Assuaging public fears was simply a matter of public relations. "Your best action," an Atomic Energy Commission booklet read, "is not to be worried about fallout." A news release typical of the times stated, "We find no basis for concluding that harm to any individual has resulted from radioactive fallout."

On August 30, 1979, during Jimmy Carter's presidency, a suit was filed, *Irene Allen v. The United States of America*. Mrs. Allen's case was the first on an alphabetical list of twenty-four test cases, representative of nearly twelve hundred plaintiffs seeking compensation from the United States government for cancers caused by nuclear testing in Nevada.

Irene Allen lived in Hurricane, Utah. She was the mother of five children and had been widowed twice. Her first husband, with their two oldest boys, had watched the tests from the roof of the local high school. He died of leukemia in 1956. Her second husband died of pancreatic cancer in 1978.

In a town meeting conducted by Utah Senator Orrin Hatch, shortly   25
before the suit was filed, Mrs. Allen said, "I am not blaming the government, I want you to know that, Senator Hatch. But I thought if my testimony could help in any way so this wouldn't happen again to any of the generations coming up after us . . . I am happy to be here this day to bear testimony of this."

God-fearing people. This is just one story in an anthology of thousands.

On May 10, 1984, Judge Bruce S. Jenkins handed down his opinion. Ten of the plaintiffs were awarded damages. It was the first time a federal court had determined that nuclear tests had been the cause of cancers. For the remaining fourteen test cases, the proof of causation was not sufficient. In spite of the split decision, it was considered a landmark ruling. It was not to remain so for long.

In April 1987, the Tenth Circuit Court of Appeals overturned Judge Jenkins's ruling on the ground that the United States was protected from suit by the legal doctrine of sovereign immunity, a centuries-old idea from England in the days of absolute monarchs.

In January 1988, the Supreme Court refused to review the Appeals Court decision. To our court system it does not matter whether the United States government was irresponsible, whether it lied to its citizens, or even that citizens died from the fallout of nuclear testing. What matters is that our government is immune: "The King can do no wrong."

In Mormon culture, authority is respected, obedience is revered, and   30
independent thinking is not. I was taught as a young girl not to "make waves" or "rock the boat."

"Just let it go," Mother would say. "You know how you feel, that's what counts."

For many years, I have done just that — listened, observed, and quietly formed my own opinions, in a culture that rarely asks questions because it has all the answers. But one by one, I have watched the women in my family die common, heroic deaths. We sat in waiting rooms hoping for good news, but always receiving the bad. I cared for them, bathed their scarred bodies, and kept their secrets. I watched beautiful women become bald as Cytoxan, cisplatin, and Adriamycin were injected into their veins. I held their foreheads as they vomited green-black bile, and I shot them with morphine when the pain became inhuman. In the end, I witnessed their last peaceful breaths, becoming a midwife to the rebirth of their souls.

The price of obedience has become too high.

The fear and inability to question authority that ultimately killed rural communities in Utah during atmospheric testing of atomic weapons is the same fear I saw in my mother's body. Sheep. Dead sheep. The evidence is buried.

I cannot prove that my mother, Diane Dixon Tempest, or my grand-mothers, Lettie Romney Dixon and Kathryn Blackett Tempest, along with my aunts developed cancer from nuclear fallout in Utah. But I can't prove they didn't.   35

My father's memory was correct. The September blast we drove through in 1957 was part of Operation Plumbbob, one of the most intensive series of bomb tests to be initiated. The flash of light in the night in the desert, which I had always thought was a dream, developed into a family nightmare. It took fourteen years, from 1957 to 1971, for cancer to manifest in my mother — the same time, Howard L. Andrews, an authority in radioactive fallout at the National Institutes of Health, says radiation cancer requires to become evident. The more I learn about what it means to be a "downwinder," the more questions I drown in.

What I do know, however, is that as a Mormon woman of the fifth generation of Latter-day Saints, I must question everything, even if it means losing my faith, even if it means becoming a member of a border tribe among my own people. Tolerating blind obedience in the name of patriotism or religion ultimately takes our lives.

When the Atomic Energy Commission described the country north of the Nevada Test Site as "virtually uninhabited desert terrain," my family and the birds at Great Salt Lake were some of the "virtual uninhabitants."

One night, I dreamed women from all over the world circled a blazing fire in the desert. They spoke of change, how they hold the moon in their bellies and wax and wane with its phases. They mocked the presumption of even-tempered beings and made promises that they would never fear the witch inside themselves. The women danced wildly as sparks broke away from the flames and entered the night sky as stars.

And they sang a song given to them by Shoshone grandmothers: 40

Ah ne nah, nah	Consider the rabbits
nin nah nah —	How gently they walk on the earth —
ah ne nah, nah	Consider the rabbits
nin nah nah —	How gently they walk on the earth —
Nyaga mutzi	We remember them

oh ne nay —	We can walk gently also —
Nyaga mutzi	We remember them
oh ne nay	We can walk gently also

The women danced and drummed and sang for weeks, preparing themselves for what was to come. They would reclaim the desert for the sake of their children, for the sake of the land.

A few miles downwind from the fire circle, bombs were being tested. Rabbits felt the tremors. Their soft leather pads on paws and feet recognized the shaking sands, while the roots of mesquite and sage were smoldering. Rocks were hot from the inside out and dust devils hummed unnaturally. And each time there was another nuclear test, ravens watched the desert heave. Stretch marks appeared. The land was losing its muscle.

The women couldn't bear it any longer. They were mothers. They had suffered labor pains but always under the promise of birth. The red hot pains beneath the desert promised death only, as each bomb became a stillborn. A contract had been made and broken between human beings and the land. A new contract was being drawn by the women, who understood the fate of the earth as their own.

Under the cover of darkness, ten women slipped under a barbed-wire fence and entered the contaminated country. They were trespassing. They walked toward the town of Mercury, in moonlight, taking their cues from coyote, kit fox, antelope squirrel, and quail. They moved quietly and deliberately through the maze of Joshua trees. When a hint of daylight appeared they rested, drinking tea and sharing their rations of food. The women closed their eyes. The time had come to protest with the heart, that to deny one's genealogy with the earth was to commit treason against one's soul.

At dawn, the women draped themselves in mylar, wrapping long streamers of silver plastic around their arms to blow in the breeze. They wore clear masks, that became the faces of humanity. And when they arrived at the edge of Mercury, they carried all the butterflies of a summer day in their wombs. They paused to allow their courage to settle.

The town that forbids pregnant women and children to enter because of radiation risks was asleep. The women moved through the streets as winged messengers, twirling around each other in slow motion, peeking inside homes and watching the easy sleep of men and women. They were astonished by such stillness and periodically would utter a shrill note or low cry just to verify life.

The residents finally awoke to these strange apparitions. Some simply stared. Others called authorities, and in time, the women were apprehended by wary soldiers dressed in desert fatigues. They were taken to a white, square building on the other edge of Mercury. When asked who they were and why they were there, the women replied, "We are mothers and we have come to reclaim the desert for our children."

45

The soldiers arrested them. As the ten women were blindfolded and handcuffed, they began singing:

> *You can't forbid us everything*
> *You can't forbid us to think —*
> *You can't forbid our tears to flow*
> *And you can't stop the songs that we sing.*

The women continued to sing louder and louder, until they heard the voices of their sisters moving across the mesa:

> *Ah ne nah, nah*
> *nin nah nah —*
> *Ah ne nah, nah*
> *nin nah nah —*
> *Nyaga mutzi*
> *oh ne nay —*
> *Nyaga mutzi*
> *oh ne nay —*

"Call for reinforcements," one soldier said.

"We have," interrupted one woman, "we have — and you have no idea of our numbers."

I crossed the line at the Nevada Test Site and was arrested with nine other Utahns for trespassing on military lands. They are still conducting nuclear tests in the desert. Ours was an act of civil disobedience. But as I walked toward the town of Mercury, it was more than a gesture of peace. It was a gesture on behalf of the Clan of One-Breasted Women.

As one officer cinched the handcuffs around my wrists, another frisked   50
my body. She found a pen and a pad of paper tucked inside my left boot.

"And these?" she asked sternly.

"Weapons," I replied.

Our eyes met. I smiled. She pulled the leg of my trousers back over my boot.

"Step forward, please," she said as she took my arm.

We were booked under an afternoon sun and bused to Tonopah,   55
Nevada. It was a two-hour ride. This was familiar country. The Joshua trees standing their ground had been named by my ancestors, who believed they looked like prophets pointing west to the Promised Land. These were the same trees that bloomed each spring, flowers appearing like white flames in the Mojave. And I recalled a full moon in May, when Mother and I had walked among them, flushing out mourning doves and owls.

The bus stopped short of town. We were released.

The officials thought it was a cruel joke to leave us stranded in the desert with no way to get home. What they didn't realize was that we were home, soul-centered and strong, women who recognized the sweet smell of sage as fuel for our spirits.

The Reader's Presence

1. Paragraph 3 reads, "This is my family history." Which parts of her essay are particular to her family, and what do they add to the larger social history of her time and place? How does her family's religion, Mormonism, play into the family history? What does she gain by drawing on the earlier spiritual tradition of the Shoshones, which is rooted in the same geographical area? What other "families," besides her nuclear and extended family, might Williams belong to?

2. Examine carefully — and discuss in detail — the role of dream and reality in this essay. Characterize the power of each. Consider also the relationship between dream and nightmare. How do you read the "dream" Williams recounts in paragraphs 38 and following? Characterize the relationship between that dream and the "civil disobedience" she recounts in the following section (paragraph 48 ff.).

3. Discuss the role of language in the essay. You might begin by examining instances of what might be termed Orwellian doublespeak. (In this context you might refer to Orwell's "Politics and the English Language" and/or Morrison's "Nobel Lecture, 7 December, 1993," both collected in this volume.) What are the dangers and ironies inherent in this euphemistic, obfuscating prose? Examine carefully Williams's own language and that of the Shoshones, as well as the written doctrines and documents to which Williams alludes or refers. Finally, reread paragraph 51, where she refers to her pen and paper as "weapons." How effective a weapon is this essay itself in the battle for social justice?

Alternate Tables of Contents ─────

THEMATIC TABLE OF CONTENTS

Moments of Insight

Growing Up

Family

Physical Appearance

CONTEMPORARY ISSUES (ESSAYS FROM THE 1990s)

Families

Gender and Sexuality

Ethnic Identity

The Streets

COMPLETE SHORT ESSAY READER (5 PAGES OR FEWER)

CROSS-CURRICULAR TABLE OF CONTENTS

Gay, Lesbian, and Transgender Studies

African American Studies

© 1984 by Stephen Jay Gould, from *The Flamingo's Smile: Reflections in Natural History* by Stephen Jay Gould. Reprinted by permission of W. W. Norton & Company, Inc.

Donald Hall, "On Moving One's Lips, While Reading." From *Principal Products of Portugal* by Donald Hall. Copyright © 1995 by Donald Hall. Reprinted by permission of Beacon Press, Boston.

Pete Hamill, "Crack and the Box." Reprinted by permission of International Creative Management, Inc. Copyright © 1990 by Pete Hamill. First appeared in *Esquire*.

Linda M. Hasselstrom, "Why One Peaceful Woman Carries a Pistol" from *Land Circle: Writings Collected from the Land* by Linda Hasselstrom, © 1991. Reprinted by permission of Fulcrum Publishing, Inc.

Linda Hogan, "Dwellings," from *Dwellings: A Spiritual History of the Living World* by Linda Hogan. Copyright © 1995 by Linda Hogan. Reprinted by permission of W. W. Norton, Inc.

John Hollander, "Mess" from *The Yale Review*, 83:2, April 1995. Reprinted by permission of Blackwell Publishers.

Langston Hughes, "Salvation" from *The Big Sea* by Langston Hughes. Copyright renewed © 1968 by Arna Bontemps and George Houston Bass. Reprinted by permission of Hill and Wang, a division of Farrar, Straus & Giroux, Inc.

Zora Neale Hurston, "How It Feels to Be Colored Me" from *World Tomorrow*, II (May 1928). Reprinted by permission of Clifford J. Hurston.

Edward Iwata, "Race Without Face" from *San Francisco Focus*, May 1991. Reprinted by permission of the author.

Pico Iyer, "In Praise of the Humble Comma." Copyright © 1988 by Time Inc. From *Time* Magazine. Reprinted by permission of Time Inc.

June Jordan, "Nobody Mean More to Me Than You and the Future Life of Willie Jordan" from *On Call: Political Essays* by June Jordan (South End Press, 1985). Reprinted by permission of the author.

Jamaica Kincaid, "Girl" from *At the Bottom of the River* by Jamaica Kincaid. Copyright © 1983 by Jamaica Kincaid. Reprinted by permission of Farrar, Straus & Giroux, Inc.

Jamaica Kincaid, "On Seeing England for the First Time." Copyright © 1991 by Jamaica Kincaid, reprinted by permission of The Wylie Agency, Inc.

Martin Luther King Jr., "Letter from Birmingham Jail." Reprinted by arrangement with The Heirs to the Estate of Martin Luther King Jr., c/o Writer's House, Inc. as agent for the proprietor. Copyright © 1963 by Martin Luther King Jr., copyright renewed 1991 by Coretta Scott King.

Barbara Kingsolver, "Stone Soup" from *High Tide in Tucson* by Barbara Kingsolver. Copyright © 1995 by Barbara Kingsolver. Reprinted by permission of HarperCollins Publishers, Inc.

Maxine Hong Kingston, "No Name Woman." From *The Woman Warrior* by Maxine Hong Kingston. Copyright © 1975, 1976 by Maxine Hong Kingston. Reprinted by permission of Alfred A. Knopf, Inc.

Nancy Mairs, "A Letter to Matthew" from *Plaintext* by Nancy Mairs. Reprinted by permission of the University of Arizona Press. Copyright © 1986 The Arizona Board of Regents.

David Mamet, "The Rake: A Few Scenes from My Childhood." From *The Cabin* by David Mamet. Copyright © 1992 by David Mamet. Reprinted by permission of Random House, Inc.

Marvin Minsky, "Will Robots Inherit the Earth?" from *Scientific American*, October 1994. Reprinted with permission. Copyright © 1994 by Scientific American, Inc. All rights reserved.

N. Scott Momaday, "The Way to Rainy Mountain," copyright © 1967 by N. Scott Momaday, from *The Way to Rainy Mountain*. First published in *The*

Reporter, January 26, 1967. Reprinted by permission of the University of New Mexico Press.

Paul Monette, "Can Gays and Straights Be Friends?" Originally appeared in *Playboy* Magazine, May 1993. Reprinted by permission of the Wendy Weil Literary Agency on behalf of the author's literary estate.

Toni Morrison, Nobel Lecture, 7 December 1993. © The Nobel Foundation, 1993. Reprinted by permission.

Gloria Naylor, "A Question of Language." Reprinted by permission of Sterling Lord Literistic, Inc. Copyright © 1986 by Gloria Naylor.

Joyce Carol Oates, "Christmas Night 1962" from *Will You Always Love Me? and Other Stories* by Joyce Carol Oates (Dutton). © The Ontario Review, Inc., 1996. Reprinted by permission.

Joyce Carol Oates, "They All Just Went Away" from *The New Yorker,* October 16, 1995. © The Ontario Review, Inc. 1995. Reprinted by permission.

Susan Orlean, "The American Man at Age Ten" from *Esquire,* December 1992. Copyright © 1992 by Susan Orlean. Reprinted by permission of Arthur Pine Associates, Inc.

George Orwell, "Politics and the English Language" from *Shooting an Elephant and Other Essays* by George Orwell, copyright 1946 by Sonia Brownell Orwell and renewed 1974 by Sonia Orwell, reprinted by permission of Harcourt Brace & Company, the estate of the late Sonia Brownell Orwell, and Martin Secker and Warburg Ltd.

George Orwell, "Shooting an Elephant" from *Shooting an Elephant and Other Essays* by George Orwell, copyright 1950 by Sonia Brownell Orwell and renewed 1978 by Sonia Pitt-Rivers, reprinted by permission of Harcourt Brace & Company, the estate of the late Sonia Brownell Orwell, and Martin Secker and Warburg Ltd.

Walker Percy, "The Loss of the Creature" from *The Message in the Bottle* by Walker Percy. Copyright © 1975 by Walker Percy. Reprinted by permission of Farrar, Straus & Giroux, Inc.

Noel Perrin, "The Androgynous Man," *The New York Times,* February 5, 1984. Copyright © 1984 by The New York Times Co. Reprinted by permission.

Katha Pollitt, "Why Boys Don't Play with Dolls," *The New York Times,* October 8, 1995. Copyright © 1995 by The New York Times Co. Reprinted by permission.

Adrienne Rich, "Split at the Root: An Essay on Jewish Identity" (abridged), from *Blood, Bread, and Poetry: Selected Prose 1979–1985* by Adrienne Rich. Copyright © 1986 by Adrienne Rich. Reprinted by permission of the author and W. W. Norton & Company, Inc.

Alberto Alvaro Ríos, "Green Cards" from *Indiana Review,* October 1, 1995. Copyright © 1995 Alberto Alvaro Ríos. Reprinted by permission of the author.

Richard Rodriguez, "Toward an American Language." Copyright © 1989 by Richard Rodriguez. Reprinted by permission of Georges Borchardt, Inc., for the author.

Judy Ruiz, "Oranges and Sweet Sister Boy." Copyright © 1988 by Judy Ruiz. Reprinted by permission of the author. First published in *Iowa Woman,* Summer 1988.

Scott Russell Sanders, "The Men We Carry in Our Minds." Copyright © 1984 by Scott Russell Sanders; first appeared in *Milkweed Chronicle;* reprinted by permission of the author and Virginia Kidd, Literary Agent.

Richard Selzer, "The Language of Pain." Copyright © 1994 by Richard Selzer. Reprinted by permission of Georges Borchardt, Inc., for the author. Originally appeared in *The Wilson Quarterly.*

Randy Shilts, "Talking AIDS to Death" from *Esquire,* March 1989. Reprinted by permission of the author.

Leslie Marmon Silko, "Yellow Woman and a Beauty of the Spirit." Reprinted with the permission of Simon & Schuster from *Yellow Woman and a Beauty of the Spirit* by Leslie Marmon Silko. Copyright © 1996 by Leslie Marmon Silko.

Gary Soto, "The Childhood Worries, or Why I Became a Writer." Copyright © 1995 by Gary Soto. First appeared in *The Iowa Review*, Spring/Summer 1995. Reprinted by permission of the author.

Brent Staples, "Just Walk on By: A Black Man Ponders His Power to Alter Public Space." Copyright © 1986 by Brent Staples. Reprinted by permission of the author.

Shelby Steele, "On Being Black and Middle Class." Reprinted from *Commentary*, January 1988, by permission; all rights reserved.

Amy Tan, "Mother Tongue." First published in *The Threepenny Review*. Copyright © 1990 by Amy Tan. Reprinted by permission of the author.

Amy Tan, "Jing-Mei Woo: Two Kinds." From *The Joy Luck Club* by Amy Tan. Copyright © 1989 by Amy Tan. Reprinted by permission of The Putnam Publishing Group.

Deborah Tannen, "Gender Gap in Cyberspace." Copyright © 1994 by Deborah Tannen. Reprinted by permission of the author. First appeared in *Newsweek*.

Lewis Thomas, "The Tucson Zoo," copyright © 1977 by Lewis Thomas, from *The Medusa and the Snail* by Lewis Thomas. Used by permission of Viking Penguin, a division of Penguin Books USA Inc.

Sallie Tisdale, "A Weight That Women Carry." Copyright © 1993 by *Harper's Magazine*. All rights reserved. Reproduced from the March issue by special permission.

Calvin Trillin, "A Traditional Family" from *Too Soon to Tell*. Published by Farrar, Straus & Giroux. Copyright © 1995 by Calvin Trillin. Reprinted by permission of Lescher & Lescher, Ltd.

Mark Twain, "The Damned Human Race" from *Letters from the Earth* by Mark Twain, edited by Bernard DeVoto. Copyright 1938, 1944, 1946, 1959, 1962 by The Mark Twain Company. Copyright renewed. Reprinted by permission of HarperCollins Publishers, Inc.

John Updike, "The Mystery of Mickey Mouse." From *The Art of Mickey Mouse*, ed. by Craig Yoe and Janet Morra-Yoe. Introduction by John Updike. Copyright © 1991 The Walt Disney Company. Introduction copyright © 1991 John Updike. Reprinted with permission by Hyperion.

Alice Walker, "Beauty: When the Other Dancer Is the Self" from *In Search of Our Mothers' Gardens: Womanist Prose*, copyright © 1983 by Alice Walker, reprinted by permission of Harcourt Brace & Company.

Alice Walker, "In Search of Our Mothers' Gardens" from *In Search of Our Mothers' Gardens: Womanist Prose*, copyright © 1974 by Alice Walker, reprinted by permission of Harcourt Brace & Company. "Women" from *Revolutionary Petunias and Other Poems*, copyright © 1970 by Alice Walker, reprinted by permission of Harcourt Brace & Company.

E. B. White, "Once More to the Lake" from *One Man's Meat* by E. B. White. Copyright 1941 by E. B. White. Reprinted by permission of HarperCollins Publishers, Inc.

John Edgar Wideman, "The Night I Was Nobody." Copyright © 1996 by John Edgar Wideman, reprinted by permission of The Wylie Agency, Inc.

George F. Will, "Printed Noise" from *The Pursuit of Happiness and Other Sobering Thoughts*. © 1978, Washington Post Writers Group. Reprinted with permission.

Terry Tempest Williams, "The Clan of One-Breasted Women." From *Refuge: An Unnatural History of Family and Place* by Terry Tempest Williams. Copy-

Index of Authors and Titles ───────